The Theology
of the First Christians

The
Theology
of the
First
Christians

WALTER SCHMITHALS

Translated by O. C. Dean, Jr.

Westminster John Knox Press
Louisville, Kentucky

Translated from *Theologiegeschichte des Urchristentums:*
Eine problemgeschichtliche Darstellung,
© 1994 Verlag W. Kohlhammer GmbH, Stuttgart-Berlin-Cologne.
Chapters 10 and 15 have been added by the author.

Unless otherwise noted, scripture quotations are from the New Revised Standard Version
of the Bible, copyright © 1989 by the Division of Christian Education
of the National Council of the Churches of Christ in the U.S.A.,
and are used by permission.

Book design by Jennifer K. Cox
Cover design by Alec Bartsch

First edition
Published by Westminster John Knox Press
Louisville, Kentucky

This book is printed on acid-free paper that meets the
American National Standards Institute Z39.48 standard. ∞

PRINTED IN THE UNITED STATES OF AMERICA
97 98 99 00 01 02 03 04 05 06 — 10 9 8 7 6 5 4 3 2 1

Library of Congress Cataloging-in-Publication Data

Schmithals, Walter.
   [Theologiegeschichte des Urchristentums. English]
   The theology of the first Christians / Walter Schmithal ;
translated by O.C. Dean, Jr. — 1st ed.
      p.   cm.
   Includes bibliographical references and indexes.
   ISBN 0-664-25615-5 (alk. paper)
   1. Bible. N.T.—Theology.   2. Theology, Doctrinal—History—Early
church, ca. 30–600.   I. Title.
BS2397.S34513   1997
230′. 12—dc21

                                       97-23139

CONTENTS

PREFACE

The fragmentary nature of our tradition does not allow us to write a developmental history of early Christian theology that is in any sense complete (cf. Luz 1983, 143). Ferdinand Christian Baur and his successors in the Tübingen School were able to conceal this state of affairs only because they adapted the available information to an a priori developmental law that in their view was valid for all historical processes. Better grounded was the attempt of the history-of-religions school to observe and describe the basic theological developments in the progression from Palestinian to Hellenistic Jewish Christianity and then to Pauline Gentile Christianity. The transition from Jerusalem to Antioch, however, was as smooth as that from Jewish to Gentile Christianity, for Palestine was broadly hellenized, and numerous God-fearing Gentiles belonged to the Hellenistic synagogues.

It is understandable, therefore, that some scholars have renounced altogether the presentation of a complete progression of early theological history and tried to replace it with the sketching of individual "developmental lines," each with its own supporting groups or schools (Köster and Robinson 1971). It is a bold undertaking, however, to connect individual fragments in our tradition with each other in a developmental line and an even bolder one to construct such a line out of one individual fragment, especially when the traditions come to us mostly without a time or place of origin. How, for example, can one give the miracle stories their own developmental line beside the Passion kerygma when the former are found only with and in relation to the latter? The *Gospel of Thomas* doubtless has some sort of literary relationship with the sayings source (Q) of the Gospels, but a *historical* linking of the two in their own unit of tradition cannot be demonstrated. And a Johannine developmental line can be constructed only if one first sorts the Johannine writings into individual strata and then integrates these strata into the development of a Johannine school, about which nothing is otherwise known.

Moreover, during the construction of largely anonymous developmental lines, the important theologians and individual writers, together with their special intentions, recede inappropriately into the background. By contrast, one can observe in Paul's Christology, soteriology, eschatology, and so forth how quite divergent developmental lines meet and cross in a way that is highly reflective theologically and methodologically. Thus, based on this insight as well, there is not a great deal of cogency in a picture of early Christian theological history that proceeds in lines and schools largely separated from each other. At the same time the letters of Paul show that the basic theological developments had already taken place in the earliest apostolic period and in the triangle formed by Jerusalem, Damascus, and Antioch—that is, in the lively personal encounters between and the mutual awareness of the leading theologians (cf. Gal. 1:15–2:16). For this reason also, the central connections and commitments in the Christian churches, even before the development of the "catholic" church, were always stronger than special linear theological developments, and from the beginning the distinction between orthodoxy and heresy was in principle unproblematic.

In view of the foregoing observations, and because, in any case, the history of early Christian theology does not lend itself to being adequately grasped and offered in its totality, the present contribution toward understanding that history is focused especially on *basic* theological themes and decisions that are *signposts* of future theological development. Renunciation of completeness, concentration on essentials, and presentation of material in individual, problem-oriented investigations are all interrelated. What are some of the most important objectives of this study?

Since Reimarus, scholars have recognized and disputed the problem of how one can explain historically the transition from Jesus to Jesus Christ, from proclaimer to proclaimed, from the message of Jesus to the Christian kerygma. It is obvious that this transition, which gave birth to Christology and thus to Christianity itself, includes elements of both continuity and discontinuity. But how are we to evaluate the two, and how are they to be defined objectively and placed together in an illuminating historical relationship?

Connected with these questions are the problems—encountered initially in the literary history—of the juxtaposition of the sayings tradition and the Markan narrative material. Since there is no reference in the early sayings tradition to the christological kerygma, the two traditions can hardly have dipped into a common "pot" of oral or written tradition, whose contents they then adopted selectively in mutual observation and consideration. To speak of two early Christian "developmental lines," however, also seems problematic when we observe that the two lines already seem to be connected with each other in the sayings source (Q) and in the Gospel of Mark. What theological or historical process effected this uniting of quite different complexes of tradition?

When in 1913 Bousset gave his justly esteemed history of the early faith in Christ the title *Kyrios Christos,* he assumed that the worship of Christ Jesus as exalted Lord was an especially important step in the history of theology. Today the importance of Bousset's statement of the problem and its religious-historical implications has not changed, even if not all of his attempted solutions have survived.

The fact that the Christologies of adoption and preexistence are found together, as we can see as early as Paul, is an important theological problem requiring just as much theological-historical clarification as the juxtaposition of incarnational and Passion soteriologies, especially since the two areas are so closely intertwined. Also in these thematic contexts we will not achieve convincing solutions without considering religious-historical presuppositions.

Paul looks back on and assumes the already mentioned basic decisions. How does he develop his own theology under these conditions? Is his theology determined from the beginning by a constant impetus, or does it experience substantial alterations? To what extent is Paul important as the coordinator of already extant forms of the Christian confession, and to what extent as the creator of his own theological design? What is the origin of his obviously characteristic doctrine of justification, and what significance does it have in the context of his theology?

In general, not enough attention has been given to the fact that until the Pharisaic-rabbinic reorganization of Judaism, which became necessary after the outcome of the Jewish war, the majority of Christians lived in the context of the synagogue, and that their exclusion from the synagogue, which was unavoidable in the wake of this reorganization, had serious consequences for them. Can we discern in the course of the second Christian generation theological-historical developments that are rooted in this *aposynagōgos*?

Most of the problems addressed in this overview are treated in one of the following individual studies, but they are all found in other contexts as well. In Paul's time baptism and the Lord's Supper were already in their present form and as a rule apparently a part of the worship of the churches. Hence the theological-historical view of these two worship activities, undertaken here in independent investigations, recapitulates the essential aspects of the various theological developments with which they were connected. The same is true of the understanding of the church, the theological importance of the Gospels, and the establishment of Christian ethics—three studies that also consider the later experience of exclusion from the synagogue. The fact that the examination of the origin of the New Testament canon closes the series of individual essays does not mean that early Christian theological history extends to the formation of the canon; it indicates, however, that the history of Christian origins and beginnings could not be written if the early church had not intentionally preserved for us as binding Holy Scripture the authoritative testimonies of its early period.

Heresies in the environment of early Christianity do not get their own treatment. That would be conceivable if Gnosticism were treated as a by-product of the formation of Christian theology. In fact, however, Gnosticism is older than Christianity; therefore it comes into play in the following investigations whenever and wherever individual elements of early Christian theology are influenced by or in contradiction with Gnostic thought. The situation is different with Marcionism and its antecedents, for the radical rejection of the Old Testament essentially grows out of experiences within Christianity. Since there were objections to such a rejection from the beginning, however, it is not Marcionism but the disagreement with it—or with the tendencies leading to it—that belongs in the area of early Christian theological history.

Although these individual studies are related and build on each other, each is a complete unit and understandable in itself. Occasional repetitions must therefore be accepted in the bargain and, since they concern essential developmental steps, should be regarded by the reader as aids and not as burdens. Where the present investigations rest on earlier published studies, this is made known in the listed references. In addition to occasional cross references, the subject index will be especially helpful in orienting the reader more completely on individual topics, thematic areas, and developments.

For some readers it will be irritating that in some cases I have not always chosen to subscribe to opinions that have achieved a certain scholarly consensus, whereas in other areas, where I am following well-worn trails, I can generally be assured of the approval of colleagues who see themselves confirmed. A consensus is comfortable because it allows one to forgo individual thinking and independent substantiation. But it is also deceptive, for it can cloud one's vision, silence unanswered questions, and veil problems. Hence nothing requires substantiation as much as a self-substantiating consensus. Bousset (1907, 5*) praises a colleague who considered it worth the effort "to reexamine the foundations, while most are content to keep building." For me, the fact that such a procedure is sometimes felt to be burdensome and irritating is not a reason for misgivings.

1

Jesus, Apocalypticism, and the Origins of Christology

After apocalypticism came to be understood in the nineteenth century as an independent religious phenomenon and Hilgenfeld (1857) discovered in it the "missing link" between Old Testament piety and primitive Christianity, it was above all Johannes Weiss (1892) who placed Jesus in the apocalyptic movement. Albert Schweitzer (1913, 232) gave Weiss's study the same importance as the first "life of Jesus" of D. F. Strauss and attempted with his "logical eschatology" to complete what Weiss had begun. The latter, writes Schweitzer (p. 390), "had Jesus think and speak eschatologically in some central parts of his teaching but on the whole presented his life . . . uneschatologically." The "logical eschatology" solution attempted with much imagination to remedy this relative deficiency. In 1900, when Weiss published a new revision of his study, he was already convinced "that the actual basic idea is essentially recognized today" (1964, xi), and in fact, every theologian to be taken seriously today assumes a positive relationship—however more closely defined—between Jesus, or the Jesus tradition, and apocalypticism (cf. Klein 1982, 271ff.).

From the beginning Weiss was unable to do much with his historic discovery. Although in principle he presented Jesus as an apocalyptist, he held to the liberal idea of the "kingdom of God" as it had been worked out by Ritschl in relation to Kant and Enlightenment theology, because it was best suited "for bringing the Christian religion to our race and, properly understood and expressed, to awakening and cultivating a healthy and vigorous religious life, which we need today" (1964, xi). "We no longer ask that grace might come and the world pass away; rather, we live with the happy confidence that even *this* world will become more and more the showplace of a 'humanity of God'" (1892, 67). Schweitzer was also convinced that we must follow this path, which in his view is already sketched in Paul, through whom the supernatural realm of apocalypticism begins to become the ethical realm and "thereby change from something to be expected into something to be realized" (1967, 204).

In spite of such consolations and over against them, the most influential consequence of the discovery of Jesus' apocalyptic message was the overcoming of ethicizing liberal theology, in whose bosom that discovery had been unwillingly made; this happened at first through parts of the developing history-of-religions school and then definitively through dialectical theology. God was taken seriously as the "wholly other," and his dominion, the kingdom of God, as an entity that could not be realized in earthly history through human effort. In 1939 Bultmann concluded that the work of Weiss and his successors, "by confronting a domesticated understanding of Christianity with the frightening foreignness of the New Testament proclamation . . . helped to bring about a new and genuine understanding of the New Testament proclamation, which in the present influences all areas of theology" (p. 246). Yet this new understanding is not simply the apocalyptic one. The distinction was now made in theology between apocalypticism and eschatology, which made it possible, for example, also to speak of "present eschatology" (cf. Bultmann 1964; Klein 1982, 270–71; Althaus 1987). While apocalypticism is interested at least superficially in what the kingdom of God will be like and when its imminent arrival will take place, eschatology is concerned with the crisis of the world, the either-or of historical decision, the new creation of human beings through the Word of God, the turn of the age through the Christ event, and the inbreaking of the new into the old, which can be comprehended only dialectically. For this distinction between apocalypticism and eschatology, dialectical theology appeals to the New Testament itself. Here Bultmann holds—with doubtful justification, as will be seen—that the eschatological reinterpretation of apocalypticism is "the real work of Paul" (1964, 68), and also that the eschatology of the Gospel of John obviously cannot be described as "apocalyptic."

Through this exegetically sound development, the problem of the relationship of Jesus' proclamation to apocalypticism was linked with the additional problem of the relationship of Jesus' proclamation to early Christianity's eschatological message of Christ, and in this way the first problem became more problematic than it had at first appeared. There seems to be a difference between the apocalyptic "historical Jesus" and the eschatological "biblical Christ," which is not far from what Reimarus thought he perceived at the beginning of his corresponding statement of the problem (cf. Schweitzer 1913, 234–35), and which—in view of a *discontinuity,* however defined, between Jesus and the beginnings of Christian theology—allowed one to assert the apocalyptic orientation of Jesus and at the same time deny an essentially apocalyptic character of early Christian faith. The disinterest of German Protestant theology in the "historical Jesus," which has been observed since the beginnings of dialectical theology, must be seen in this context.

A discontinuity between the "historical Jesus" and the "proclaimed Christ," however, has caused increasing uneasiness. But if one wanted to hold to the constancy of Jesus' message and the proclamation of Christ without apocalypticizing the Christian kerygma, the only option was an attempt to dispute the apocalyptic nature of Jesus' proclamation. In regard to the focus of Jesus' preaching, this happened especially in the "new quest of the historical Jesus" that Käsemann initiated in 1953, and in 1967 Strobel, with appropriate evaluation of the situation, judged the presentation of Jesus' preaching of the kingdom of God as follows: "In the modern theological and exegetical debate, hardly any of its original, strongly apocalyptic character is to be felt anymore. In the view of today's exegetes and New Testament scholars, the proclamation of Jesus and his followers was not actually intended apocalyptically. Its emphasis lay rather on the call to decision in the present, and the actual event of salvation occurred in Jesus' words" (p. 12).

Bultmann, along with his teacher Weiss, had connected Jesus with apocalypticism. "Jesus is distinguished from apocalypticism only in that he gives no description of the salvific future" (1958, 38). Yet in *Jesus* (1926) Bultmann had already *interpreted* Jesus' apocalypticism in an eschatologically existential way; the apocalyptic mythology "ultimately slips away from the great fundamental viewpoint that veils it, from Jesus' conception of humankind as called to decision by God's future action" (1926, 41; cf. 1925, 35–36). And in connection with this he made his well-known assertion that Jesus' (apocalyptic!) "*appearance and his proclamation imply a Christology,* insofar as he requires a decision about his person as the bearer of the Word of God, a decision on which salvation or perdition depend" (1960, 16; cf. 1958, 36). These statements—which were formulated within the context of an eschatologically existential *interpretation* of apocalyptic thought and with which Bultmann claimed, more wrongly than rightly, to have achieved the transition from the message of Jesus to the kerygma of Christ—were historically objectivized by many of his students and then served to dispute the apocalyptic nature of the preaching or appearance of Jesus. With the help of an "implied Christology" such statements put the church's kerygma (of Christ) already in Jesus himself, so that Jesus' "proclamation of the near *basileia* is itself the nearness of this *basileia.* Thus he enters his message as the embodied promise, as it were, and can no longer, like the Baptist, be understood in the category of forerunner but only—if a category must be used—in that of a mediator who brings in the eschatological age by announcing it" (Käsemann 1964c, 118). This view attempts to avoid the inconsistency of achieving the *historical* transition of the message of Jesus into the church's kerygma of Christ through an existential *interpretation* of the former. "Jesus began with the apocalyptically defined message of the Baptist, yet his own preaching was not constitutively shaped by apocalypticism but rather proclaimed the immediacy of the God who is near. One who took this step cannot, in my opinion, have been waiting on the coming Son of Man, the reestablishment of the people of twelve tribes in the messianic kingdom, and the concomitant inbreaking of the Parousia, in order to experience the nearness of God" (Käsemann 1964a, 99).

Whether one speaks in this context of "self-realizing eschatology" (Jeremias 1962b, 29; cf. 1971, 81ff.) or of the "paradoxical message . . . that the future kingdom of God is already at work in the present" (Kümmel 1956, 146), or states that Jesus "brought the kingdom of God with his gospel" (Käsemann 1960b, 211) and calls human beings to daily worship "as if no shadow lay over the world" (1964c, 110), or lets "pardon and conversion in Jesus' word" be the same thing (Bornkamm 1956, 85), or places directly in Jesus a "realized eschatology" (Dodd 1936) or interprets the parables of Jesus by saying that "through his announcement of salvation, it now becomes manifest" (Conzelmann 1974b, 37), or hears Jesus proclaim "what was anxiously awaited as what has *now* appeared" (Linnemann 1989, 262), or is convinced that "Jesus regarded this world as possibly the place of God's salvific dominion" (Merkel 1991, 161), all of these regard Jesus as the conqueror of apocalyptic piety and consider the early Christian kerygma the continuation of Jesus' message thus defined. Yet here the role played by the unambiguously apocalyptic Easter confession becomes a virtually unsolvable problem, for the more one separates the earthly Jesus from apocalypticism, the more incomprehensible becomes the fact that for his disciples Jesus' way ended apocalyptically. What is more, with the presupposition of an objective continuity from the proclamation of Jesus to the kerygma of Christ, how could the message of Jesus ever be transposed into the form of a mythic kerygma of incarnation, cross, resurrection, and exaltation? Is it not true that the less apocalyptic Jesus' message was, the greater was the discontinuity and a corresponding new beginning in the context of the Easter experience that is presupposed by the origin of the kerygma of Christ? The often heard idea that the Easter event had only the function of revalidating Jesus' message after the catastrophe of Good Friday is in any case untenable, for on the one hand, the formulated kerygma of Christ never validated Jesus' message until the Apostles' and Nicene creeds, and on the other, the early Synoptic tradition nowhere indicates that it was not validated until Easter.

In spite of this, Käsemann concludes, not without reason, that "hardly a New Testament scholar will still share A. Schweitzer's answer" (1964c, 107). Yet on the question of the relationship of the earthly Jesus to apocalypticism, we are, on the whole, in the same situation today that Weiss evoked a century ago with his sensational book. The problems and aporias of the question have become clearer, but the question itself is still unanswered. For against the recent distancing of Jesus from apocalypticism, Strobel—and not only he—has protested "out of scholarly concern" that "elementary historical and religious-historical circumstances may be missing or underestimated in the current discussion" (1967, 7). I hold these concerns to be justified and Jesus' proclamation to be a message in the context of apocalypticism, and at the same time, I am convinced that only with this presupposition does the transition from Jesus' message to the church's faith in Christ become understandable.

Jesus as Apocalyptist

The difficulty of determining Jesus' relationship to apocalypticism is only superficially related to the fact that there has not always been agreement on how to define the phenomenon of apocalypticism. For in principle apocalypticism is actually an unambiguous phenomenon that consists in the dualism of two antagonistically joined ages and the conviction that the turn of the age is imminent (Schmithals 1973). Yet the implementation of this basic schema can be quite variable in individual cases, without calling into question apocalypticism itself and its specific understanding of existence.

The real difficulty lies in the state of our tradition (cf. Klein 1982, 271). Understandably, it is above all the more or less authentic extant fragments of Jesus' proclamation that have been examined in regard to their relationship to apocalypticism, but they *substantiate* the present dilemma. On the one hand, those who dispute the apocalyptic shaping of Jesus' message on the basis of our tradition must admit that even in the tradition of the Gospels, there is no lack of sayings of an apocalyptic nature (Bornkamm 1956, 85). Yet on the other hand, those who portray Jesus essentially as an apocalyptist cannot escape the insight that the Synoptic Gospels describe Jesus not only as an eschatological prophet but also as a rabbi and teacher of wisdom, who sets up moral demands for the shaping of life and disputes the interpretation of the law, as if it were a question of stabilizing the present world order. Therefore Schweitzer (1901, 14) observed "in all acuteness" the "juxtaposition of two world views."

In 1926 Bultmann cited the basic possibilities for avoiding this dilemma (84ff.; cf. 1925, 11): either one ignores the wisdom-related, creation-friendly proclamation of Jesus (thus, for example, J. Weiss 1892), or one rejects his apocalyptic message (thus, for example, Volkmar 1870, 530ff.; Käsemann 1964a, 99), or one follows the majority and attempts some kind of synthesis of these two traditions. The corresponding idea that our tradition reflects a revolution in Jesus' own activity from an initially "ethical" to a later "apocalyptic" way of thinking had already been rejected by Schweitzer (1901, 14–15). He himself understood Jesus' moral instruction in the sense of a radical interim ethic as commandments for only the elect, who are preparing themselves for the now dawning kingdom of God (1967, 89ff.). Haupt (1895) held the view that Jesus did not mean the apocalyptic ideas literally but tried to understand them "spiritually." Bultmann traces both strands of tradition back to an existential basic meaning of the necessity of a decision in the present in view of God's future (1925, 35–36; 1926, 90ff.). Kümmel (1956, 81ff.), Bornkamm (1956, 85), Grässer (1977, xiii), Becker (1972, 79ff.), Müller (1977), and many others have the coming kingdom of God in the person of Jesus extend into his presence and consequently understand Jesus' ethic as activity based on the goodness of God already experienced in the present, but his *apocalyptic* teaching is understood as *eschatological* promise in the sense of the early Christian kerygma.

On the whole, such syntheses are not satisfying because ethics and eschatology or apocalypticism "are hardly linked together" in the Jesus tradition that has come down to us (Conzelmann 1974b, 36; cf. Hahn 1974, 47). But they also run into resistance and contradiction in the details. The transposition of apocalyptic statements into kerygmatic eschatology means, in fact, an elimination of the former, not a synthesis, and thus the liberal idea of a development of Jesus from apocalypticism to "Christology" would have a comparatively greater probability. As ingenious as Bultmann's existential analysis is, it does not solve the historical or religious-historical problem, for apocalypticism and the ethical shaping of the world belong on different levels of religion and tradition, and their existential unification is completely ruled out for the consciousness of Jesus' contemporaries. The idea of the interim ethic runs aground both religious-historically and exegetically: apocalypticism is not otherwise connected with an interim ethic, nor does the apocalyptic expectation of the end play any kind of role in the ethical demands of Jesus (cf. Bultmann 1926, 88ff.). With this, however, we must fall back on the alternative first named by Bultmann, without interpreters having seen clear criteria for tracing back to Jesus the one *or* the other strand of tradition, neither of which can reproduce the message of Jesus *as a whole*.

Like the evaluation of the Jesus tradition as a whole, the interpretation of individual sentences is also disputed—apart from any questions of authenticity. What, for example, does Luke 11:20 mean: "But if it is by the finger of God that I cast out the demons, then the kingdom of God has come to you"? In this saying, is the apocalyptic teaching *replaced* by "the conviction of Jesus that the future kingdom of God has begun in his activity" (Kümmel 1956, 101; cf. Klein 1982, 273)? Or is the apocalyptic teaching, on the contrary, taken to that point in time where any calculation of the end becomes meaningless, because the kingdom of God has come near enough to grasp, as Jesus states, according to J. Weiss (1892, 21), with "solemn prophetic enthusiasm," so that in the "sayings of the present" the temporal nearness of the kingdom of God is expressed "as increased imminent expectation" (Grässer 1977, xvii)? Luke 10:18, "I watched Satan fall from heaven like a flash of lightning" (cf. Vollenweider 1988), is subject to the same dispute among interpreters. The idea is doubtless apocalyptic, but does the saying speak apocalyptically of an "event that is already placed in the sphere of God as reality and is on the point of breaking through on earth" (Müller 1977, 420), or is it speaking unapocalyptically of the fact "that God wants to realize eschatological salvation in the world" (ibid., 440)? Other passages, such as Luke 10:23–24 par.; 17:20; Mark 3:27 par.; Matt. 11:2–6 par., are similarly controversial (cf. Becker 1972, 71ff.). And thus even the most penetrating exegetical analyses do not allow one to decide the question of the presence or future of the kingdom of God in Jesus' proclamation on the basis of such individual passages and to assert, for example, that "the statements about the presence of the kingdom of God are unambiguous and are solidly anchored in the ancient Jesus tradition" (Klein 1982, 273; cf. Merkel 1991).

If we want to proceed, we must try to gain a standpoint outside the Synoptic tradition of Jesus' proclamation that makes available a criterion for more closely determining the relationship of Jesus to apocalypticism. Certainly, this standpoint cannot be "the complete public activity" of Jesus (Schweitzer 1913, 390), which Schweitzer reconstructed in a consistently apocalyptic way. The idea that "Jesus, filled with the glow of the near expectation of the end, sent his disciples out to a hasty mission in Palestine and himself proclaimed an interim ethic, and finally, when his hopes deceived him, tried to force divine intervention with his journey to Jerusalem and died in the attempt," as Käsemann (1964c, 107–8) succinctly reproduces Schweitzer's view, is an interpretation of the Gospel accounts that with good reason no scholar is prepared to emulate. We are even less well-informed about the public activity of Jesus, the context of his proclamation, than we are about the proclamation itself. There are, however, some clear individual observations that are relevant for our question:

1. Jesus began with the message of the Baptist, which was apocalyptically determined (Strobel 1967, 108); in large measure Becker's (1972) contradictory statements only seem to assert the opposite, since he uses a narrow conception of apocalypticism. John called people to repentance in view of the imminent judgment of the world. He gathered the elect, who were supposed to survive the last judgment. Käsemann (1964c, 108) judges correctly: "We must not forget that

Jesus' baptism by John is one of the indubitable events of the historical life of Jesus. For this means that Jesus began with the glowing imminent expectation of the Baptist and therefore let himself be 'sealed' against the threatening judgment of wrath and entered into the holy remnant of the people of God." Hence those who dispute the apocalyptic nature of Jesus' preaching must postulate a profound development in Jesus, who first followed the Baptist but soon fell "in deed and word" into clear "contradiction with this beginning" (Käsemann 1964c, 108). We find nothing of this development—which has little probability in itself in view of the brief time of Jesus' activity—in the tradition, which, on the contrary, witnesses very broadly to the thoroughly harmonious relationship of John and Jesus (cf. only Matt. 11:1ff. par.).

2. Jesus' activity flows into the confession of his resurrection. This confession of the resurrection of the dead, however, is a central assertion of apocalypticism, especially since the oldest Easter faith interprets the resurrection of Jesus as the beginning (not the prolepsis, as Schade [1981, 168] says) of the general resurrection of the dead: Jesus is the "first fruits of those who have died" (1 Cor. 15:20; cf. Rom. 1:4; 6:1ff.; 1 Cor. 6:14; Col. 1:18; Rev. 1:5; Matt. 27:52–53; Acts 26:2 *1 Clem.* 24.1). In no way can we speak here of a "christological characterization" (Klein 1982, 274); this concept is not christological at all. It binds imminent expectation and the confession of Jesus' resurrection very closely together and for this reason alone cannot be a late theologoumenon, as Grässer (1977, xxxii), Merklein (1981, 3–4), and Schade (1981, 164), for example, hold. It is an idea so broadly attested, and also found in pre- and extra-Pauline formulas (1 Cor. 15:20; Rom. 1:4; Col. 1:18), that it is impossible that Paul could have been the first to inscribe the resurrection of Jesus "on the apocalyptic horizon of the general resurrection of the dead" (thus Becker 1976, 17).

Rather, just the opposite is true: this idea is found in every case in an already developed, christologically domesticated form; Christians are not resurrected "like" Jesus but as the followers of their *Kyrios,* as members of his body. How else would it have been possible, after Jesus' resurrection was first understood as an exceptional event establishing his majesty, for this event to be leveled into the general resurrection of the dead? The assertion that "interest in the resurrection of dead members of the community" is the presupposition of the idea that Jesus is the "first fruits of those who have died" (Becker 1975, 119) has no support from the tradition. "The category in which the primary and immediate Easter experience is apperceived . . . is the idea of the general . . . resurrection of the dead at the end of the world" (Lohfink 1980, 169; cf. Allison 1987). This corresponds to the likewise not yet christological confession of God as the one "who raised Jesus our Lord from the dead" (Rom. 4:24; cf. 8:11; 2 Cor. 4:14; Gal. 1:1; Col. 2:12). "Access to the oldest Easter kerygma is blocked when one ignores this apocalyptic connection" (Käsemann 1964c, 110).

3. Of special importance in this context is the oldest original text that yields information on the origins of Christology, namely, the pre-Pauline formula in Rom. 1:3–4. Of the earthly Jesus it merely says that he is descended from the family of David and thus brings with him the necessary prerequisite for the call as Messiah;

for the rest, the idea in Rom. 1:3 is the same as in Phil. 2:7b: "in human likeness." His appointment as "Son of God" occurs "according to the Spirit of holiness" and "by resurrection from the dead" (Rom. 1:4). This last formulation speaks of the general resurrection of the dead, which accordingly began with Jesus but has not yet been continued. Rather, the first from the dead was exalted as Son of God through the working of God's Spirit. The development of the idea is clear: the earthly Jesus, predisposed as David's offspring to be Son of God, is resurrected, in the context of the general resurrection of the dead, as the first from the dead and at the same time is adopted as the messianic Son through the Spirit of God. Thus the confession of Christ rests on the central idea of apocalypticism: the dawning turn of the age.

4. Jesus was crucified by the Romans. That has repeatedly provided a reason to classify him with a group of political agitators, but this is contradicted by the completely unfanatical Jesus tradition and the corresponding stance of early Christendom. Yet Jesus really suffered the death of a political criminal at the hands of the Romans. Even if this happened "because of a misunderstanding of his activity as political" (Bultmann 1960, 12), this misunderstanding must, nonetheless, be based on his activity. But what could have provoked this misunderstanding if it was not the expectation of the imminent dawning of the kingdom of God, which meant the end of all earthly kingdoms? The Romans could hardly have drawn a line of distinction between the fanatical hope for the son of David and the apocalyptic expectation of the coming of the kingdom of God, both of which would revolutionize earthly conditions, especially since the boundary between the two was often fluid. The idea that Jesus went to Jerusalem "to confront the people there in the holy city with the message of the kingdom of God and in the final hour to call them to a decision" (Bornkamm 1956, 142–43) may be no more than an attractive assumption at best. In any case, however, the Romans saw their power and the peace of civilization threatened by the subversive preaching of the kingdom of God. Since Jesus was certainly not a zealot, this observation leads to the conclusion that he announced apocalyptically a revolution in earthly conditions.

5. In *all* levels of tradition in the New Testament the Spirit plays an important role. He is also found in the prekerygmatic sayings tradition (Mark 3:28–29 par.; Matt. 10:19–20). Prophets have great importance (Matt. 10:41). Especially the eschatological or apocalyptic sayings, such as Mark 3:28–29 par.; 9:1; Matt. 10:23; 12:28; and Luke 10:18, bear the traits of prophetic-pneumatic insight. The gifts of the Spirit in early Christianity, however, are understood and interpreted entirely in the context of the eschatological promises of the Old Testament (Rom. 5:5; 8:23ff.; Acts 2:17ff.); the Spirit is the first gift and pledge of the completion of salvation and in this way originally a complement of the dawning kingdom of God. One can hardly dispute the apocalyptic origin of this unified part of tradition, which is found in all early traditions and therefore goes back to the history of Jesus, for there is no religious-historical basis for any other origin. Only the apocalyptic prophet is sacrosanct (Mark 3:28–29); only with the beginning of dualistic experiences of the *pneuma* does the testing of the spirits become possible and necessary (1 Cor. 12:1–2; 1 Thess. 5:19ff.; 1 John 4:1ff.).

Thus Jesus' appearance is surrounded as closely as conceivable by apocalyptic motifs. In view of this, it is an exegetical act of desperation to remove Jesus from this otherwise correctly perceived context. Thus Bousset declares: "The person of Jesus and his gospel remain a creative miracle" (1903, 66). "One had to come who was greater than an apocalyptist and rabbinical theologian" (1926, 524). What was methodologically possible under the banner of the liberal concept of personality, however badly it may have been carried out, appears in Käsemann—in whose view Jesus' message contradicts the apocalyptic repentance preaching of the Baptist and the reapocalypticized proclamation of the early church—under the banner of the history of religion as arbitrary despite, or because of, an express appeal to liberalism (1964c, 109; similarly Linnemann 1989). The idea that "the historian in particular must speak of an incomparable mystery of Jesus," which consists in the notion "that we cannot treat him properly with the usual categories" (ibid.), is a hardly tolerable judgment precisely on historical grounds.

As a historian one must decide rather that one is more faithful to the Synoptic tradition when one understands Jesus' message in the context of the apocalyptic piety of Judaism. The apocalyptic concept of time and the accompanying call to repentance cover the greater part of sayings tradition. To trace this whole complex to the early church (Käsemann 1964a, 99–100), which *actually* held to the Baptist and only *nominally* to Jesus and yet at the same time kept itself clearly apart from the disciples of John, is not only historically unlikely but also runs counter of the observation that the apocalyptic logia of the Jesus tradition still show no relationship whatever to the kerygma of Christ.

Thus if the apocalyptic parts of the sayings tradition belong to its core, to which Jesus' proclamation is especially close, then the wisdom parts, the moral instructions for everyday conduct, and the statements of unrestrained joy over creation (cf., for example, Luke 6:31 par.; 12:6–7, 22–34 par.; Matt. 5:45 par.) must belong to a different strand of tradition, which was closely related to the corresponding Jewish piety, as shown by numerous rabbinical parallels. The fact that this wisdom material does not appear in the doublets that the evangelist Mark adopted from the sayings tradition reveals that it was not until relatively late that the material found its way into the traditional sayings of Jesus—presumably not until the final redaction of the sayings source and as a conscious correction of the previous sayings tradition, which was essentially apocalyptic. Cf. also Schmithals 1985, 384ff.

Jesus proclaimed the coming kingdom of God in the spirit of apocalypticism. This perception forms the foundation—already correctly observed by Johannes Weiss—for the proper understanding of early Christian development. The fact that Jesus did not instruct the circle of the elect esoterically about the end, but publicly exhorted all to repentance in view of the end and offered the opportunity of salvation especially to sinners and the underprivileged of the kingdom of God, is a particular expression of apocalypticism, not its suppression. When Jesus forgoes retrospective historical presentations from which the time of the end can be calculated, this is easily explained by the prophetically proclaimed, apocalyptic imminent expectation, which calls attention to the signs of the present end time (Luke

12:54–56 par.; cf. Patsch 1972, 129). If it is correct that "in Jesus' proclamation the future is proleptically present and consequently has broken through the two-age schema" (Klein 1982, 274), such prolepsis—assuming that it can be demonstrated—does not mark a "decisive difference from apocalypticism" (ibid.) any more than the Spirit, who works in the apocalyptic prophets as down payment on the coming age and who announces and reports the imminent turn of the age, makes the turn of the age and the coming of the time of salvation superfluous. "The fact that Jesus saw the dawning eschatological kingdom of God already in his activity," as Luz (1983, 151) among many other scholars assumes, in no way negates the fact (also according to Luz's accurate conviction) "that he is dealing with the real end of the world and with the comprehensive, universal realization of the kingdom of God in the near future." Nor is Jesus' proclamation removed from the environment of an apocalyptic message by Conzelmann's presumably correct judgment: "Grace and judgment are not formally equated in his proclamation. What Jesus proclaims is exclusively gospel and thus grace. And judgment is the shadow that this light casts" (1974b, 40).

Those who might attempt in such ways to soften the apocalyptic conditioning of Jesus' proclamation on the basis that they would like to achieve a transition to the Christ kerygma of the early church are no less deceived than the scholars who comprehend Jesus' message completely apart from apocalypticism; for at the beginning of that kerygma stands a bluntly apocalyptic datum: the resurrection of Jesus from the dead as the first fruits of those who have died. "Thus the fact remains: Jesus proclaims the immediate nearness of the kingdom of God. And he imagined this nearness very much in a *temporal* sense. . . . The view that Jesus had in mind some kind of nontemporal nearness of the kingdom of God strikes me as absurd. It not only postulates an anachronistic state of affairs but also robs Jesus' preaching of its seriousness and its clear contour" (Lohfink 1982b, 49–50).

The Apocalyptic Message of Jesus and the Church's Confession of Christ

How is the apocalyptic message of Jesus related to the early church's proclamation of Christ? First one must observe that the early Christian faith formulas of every provenance only rarely contain apocalyptic concepts, including the idea of the Parousia. This observation not only refutes overwhelmingly Käsemann's assertion that apocalypticism is "the mother of all Christian theology" (1964a, 100), but at the same time it attests a striking discontinuity between the message of Jesus and his church's proclamation of Christ.

This discontinuity apparently rests on a fundamental break. For it is also striking that in the tradition-historically demonstrable environment of the faith formulas, the apocalyptic logia of the sayings tradition are also completely missing. Therefore the pervasive absence of apocalyptic eschatology in the faith formulas cannot itself be sufficiently explained by the information that apocalyptic expectation forms the assumed context and unavoidable presupposition of the kerygmatic formula material, even if, naturally, one may not dispute the idea that future eschatology in the early church could continue to follow apocalyptic conceptions. To the extent, however, that apocalyptic statements are found with the Christ kerygma, as is the case, for example, in Paul, these are not taken from the Jesus tradition but reproduce general apocalyptic topoi; the exception of 1 Thess. 4:15, which would only prove the rule, is a late, post-Pauline text (Schmithals 1988a, 74ff.). We must also note in this context that in the early period the apocalyptic title *Son of Man* can be found neither in the faith formulas nor in their environment, for example, in Paul.

This break with Jesus' apocalyptic proclamation and the corresponding sayings tradition was not, however, a break with Jesus. The discontinuity in the content of the message is accompanied by the constancy of the person of Jesus. The church confesses *christologically* the Jesus whose proclamation was *apocalyptic*. This peculiar relationship of discontinuity and constancy is based on and made possible by the confession of Jesus' resurrection. The kerygma of early Christendom is explicitly or implicitly Easter kerygma. Through the Easter event the message of the earthly Jesus is replaced by his person: in place of the memory and tradition of his sayings comes the confession to Jesus himself as the exalted Christ. In this way the observed discontinuity is covered by the recognized difference between proclaimer and proclaimed. Easter, however, not only substantiates the discontinuity but at the same time also marks the continuity in this discontinuity, for the resurrection from the dead is, of course, an apocalyptically expected event that was announced in Jesus' message! The Easter faith in the exalted Christ, which replaces Jesus' apocalyptic preaching, also connects thereby with his message. In any case, we would misinterpret the Easter confession if we did not understand it as a confession in an apocalyptic context.

The relationship, however, of discontinuity and continuity between Jesus' proclamation, on the one hand, and the church's proclamation of Christ, on the other, presents itself as the relationship of *expectation and fulfillment* of this expectation (cf. Allison 1987, 169ff.). Jesus announced God's imminent eschatological act of salvation apocalyptically. For the present, he expected the crisis of the old age and the dawning of the dominion of God. What Jesus "expected as the manifest deed of God" is "proclaimed and experienced by the early church as the hidden but real deed of God" (Strobel 1967, 191). "If Jesus understood himself as an eschatological figure, then Easter meant the strengthening of the message of the imminent kingdom in the sense that the time of its realization must be regarded as arrived. We must emphasize that the newness of the resurrection certainly has its place in a logical religious-historical development" (ibid., 88). On the basis of Easter, the cross and incarnation receive the status of eschatological events of salvation. Here the crisis of the world announced by Jesus takes place; here the reign of God comes in. If Jesus went to Jerusalem in expectation of the imminent apocalyptic revolution, then the early church proclaimed Jesus himself and his destiny of death and resurrection as this revolution: thus continuity and discontinuity belong together in the same mutually exclusive way in which expectation and fulfillment belong together.

The post-Easter community of disciples understood itself as the community of salvation. It understood the Spirit working in it as the promised Spirit of the new age and the charismata as the gifts of the time of salvation. In this way it is not the earthly Jesus who is the sufficient requirement for the existence of the church, but the Easter confession. Even God is now defined in a Christian way based on Easter as the one "who raised Jesus our Lord from the dead" (Rom. 4:24; 8:11; 2 Cor. 4:14; Gal. 1:1). New Testament theology and thus Christian theology in general are to be sketched on the basis of Easter. This formal determination has the theological sense of binding Christian theology and proclamation to the Jesus "who not only, like the historical Jesus, promised salvation but also has already brought it" (Bultmann 1960, 25). Where the Easter event remains the starting point of Christian faith, the faith offers participation in eschatological salvation in the sense of 2 Cor. 5:17: "So if anyone is in Christ, there is a new creation: everything old has passed away; see, everything has become new!"

Thus Käsemann's statement that apocalypticism was the mother of Christian theology (1964a, 100) must be turned around: the overcoming of apocalypticism in the fulfillment of the apocalyptic expectation of God's imminent activity is the mother of all Christian theology. The reversion to pure apocalyptic expectation itself amounts to a falling away from the theological foundations of the Christian confession, for it denies the once-and-for-all nature of the Christ event. At the same time, keeping open the difference between the historical Jesus and the biblical Christ observed in the Enlightenment proves to be theologically necessary, because wherever the message of Jesus is regarded historically correctly as apocalyptic expectation and at the same time lifted up dogmatically as a criterion of what is Christian, then Christian proclamation threatens to become salvationless.

From Apocalyptic Intermezzo to "Faith"

Only if we begin with the essentially apocalyptic nature of Jesus' activity can we convincingly reconstruct the transition from his apocalyptic message to the christological kerygma, a transition regulated by the Easter event. Yet this leaves open many questions of detail. Whether Jesus himself ascribed to his work or his person a special role in the coming turn of the age remains uncertain. Our sources lead us most easily to the assumption that Jesus expected the coming of the Son of Man, with whom he is not identical, or, if Vielhauer (1957) should be right, the immediate coming of the kingdom of God or God himself. Whether Jesus planned for his own death, whether he gave it a significance in the end event, whether he set a time interval between his death and the dawning of the turn of the age, we do not know. Whatever is said on this does not exceed the bounds of more or less probable religious-historical reconstruction or psychological assumption. Also on the immediate attitude of the disciples toward Jesus' death and their reaction to the events of Good Friday, there is no historically reliable tradition. Terms such as "flight of the disciples," "failure of the disciples," and "despair" are not historically verifiable. Our passion story presupposes the christological kerygma but does not recapitulate its origin and development. And the idea, found in various versions, that the confession that God raised Jesus from the dead marks "the new way out of the crisis in the idea of God brought on by the death of Jesus" (Klumbies 1992, 164) cannot be derived from the early forms of this confession, which knows nothing of such a crisis and can be understood completely in continuity with Jesus' apocalyptic message.

Yet with this confession of Jesus' resurrection as the first fruits of those who have died, we are on sound historical ground. This apocalyptic view handed down in the context of the christological kerygma asserts, in agreement with Jesus' proclamation, the now occurring turn of the age and the dawning of the age of salvation and is thus close to such sayings of the Jesus tradition as Luke 10:18; 11:20, but it does not imply a Christology and in this sense does not yet contain the early Christian kergyma. Therefore one has to begin with an "apocalyptic intermezzo," a term apparently coined by Klein (1982, 275). There is also no adequate religious-historical foundation for a *direct* translation of a (real or alleged) claim of majesty by the earthly Jesus into the christological confession by means of the Easter experience; Jewish messianism and the apocalyptic expectation of a resurrection are in no way related to each other. The Jewish idea of the "elevation" of a righteous one, to which one often refers in this connection (Eduard Schweizer), has no connection with the apocalyptic idea of resurrection, and the thesis that Judaism is familiar with the eschatological resurrection of individual prophets (Klaus Berger) has no adequate basis in the texts. In view of this, those who cannot recognize "a purely apocalyptic intermezzo as the prehistory of early Christian eschatology" and who derive "the eschatological new orientation directly from the Easter events" (Klein 1982, 275) must abandon the historical question and withdraw to "the uncertainty of the factors establishing the eschatology" (ibid., 277). The traditions let us know with sufficient clarity, however, that with the Messiah confession and the corresponding idea of exaltation we have an eschatologically new interpretation of the formerly purely apocalyptic statement of resurrection, and at the same time they tell us which driving forces led to this development.

In this connection our attention is first given to Simon Peter and his prominent role in the sudden change from expectation to fulfillment, or from the apocalyptic message of Jesus to the eschatological faith in Christ. That Peter was the first Easter witness is beyond all doubt (cf. 1 Cor. 15:5; Luke 24:34; John 20:1ff.; Mark 16:7). The first confession of the Messiah is likewise firmly linked with the person of Peter.

The problem of the relationship of these two events to each other is mostly ignored. It also remains superficially concealed by the fact that already in the Gospel of Mark, Peter's Messiah confession is anchored in the life of Jesus, and many scholars still follow this chronology today (cf. Cullmann 1960, 196ff.). But this pre-Easter dating is decisively contradicted by the Markan messianic secret theory, into which Mark 8:27–30 is placed through Jesus' commandment of silence (8:30) and which presupposes that before Easter Jesus' Messiahship was not known even in the circle of his followers (Wrede 1901; Bultmann 1967c). Moreover, Bultmann (1931, 277) correctly judges that without doubt the resurrected One is speaking in Matt. 16:17–19. The pre-Pauline traditions of Rom. 1:3–4 and Phil. 2:6ff. still speak of the nonmessianic activity of the earthly Jesus, and also the basic text of the Gospel of Mark still applies no messianic title to Jesus during his public activity (Schmithals 1985, 418). Peter's Messiah confession comes after Easter, and it is the evangelist Mark who transfers it into the pre-Easter situation. But does it follow "that Peter's Easter experience was the hour of birth of the church's faith in the Messiah" (Bultmann 1931, 277)? Contradicting this is not only the insight that initially the Easter confession concerned the general resurrection of the dead and did not refer especially to Jesus and the importance of his person. But also, in the traditions of the first Easter testimony by Peter and of the Messiah confession by Peter, we have clearly separate traditions that do not describe the same event, as shown by the fact that the evangelist could move the Messiah confession into the pre-Easter situation. And Schweitzer (1913, 383) correctly doubts that the pure "fact of the resurrection" could lead the disciples to the idea that "the crucified One was the Messiah." "In certain circles . . . there was even a belief in the resurrection of the Baptist. But he was in no way the Messiah on this account." If Schweitzer concludes from this observation that Jesus himself had already given his disciples indications of his (the Messiah's!) resurrection, the tradition provides a different answer.

In the so-called transfiguration story, originally an Easter report (Wellhausen 1909, 71; Schmithals 1986, 399ff., 721ff.) that is presupposed as such in 2 Peter 1:16–18; *Apocalypse of Peter* 15–17, the Easter testimony and Messiah confession of Peter are connected, but they are at the same time characteristically separated from each other in such a way that this story still clearly reflects the historical development. What is theologically relevant is not the subjective Easter testimony of Peter but the appearance of the resurrected One, and not Peter's Messiah confession but the proclamation of the Son of God by the heavenly voice; both are historically appropriate (1 Cor. 15:5; Luke 24:34; Mark 8:29) in the original version of the story exclusively before the eyes and ears of Peter (Schmithals 1986, 401). Between the two events a curious episode is inserted: Peter wants to build dwellings for Jesus, Moses, and Elijah (Mark 9:5); this undertaking is characterized as irrational (9:6). What does that mean? Dibelius gave the right answer to this question: "What Peter says in Mark 9:5 gives information about what is not meant. The sense is not that a blessed state has dawned, in which it would be worthwhile to set up tents for the holy men" (1959, 276). The tent dwellings are the dwellings of the end time or the age of salvation (Zech. 2:14; 14:16ff.; Rev. 7:15; 21:3). Thus in an apocalyptic frame of reference, Simon sees the end of time and history already dawning. His offer to erect dwellings reflects the original apocalyptic interpretation of the resurrection of Jesus as the dawning of the general resurrection of the dead. This interpretation of the Easter event is rejected as false by the narrator of the transfiguration story. In his view, Peter, in his initial dismay, was overpowered by the event and not able to grasp its meaning correctly. By contrast, the events are correctly comprehended by those who understand that Jesus' resurrection and transformation are prerequisite to his presentation as "Son of God." Thus understood, the resurrection of Jesus is taken out of the apocalyptic context of the general resurrection of the dead and becomes *the* eschatological event in a new sense that "abolishes" apocalypticism.

When the resurrected One is installed as Lord of the world, the present time of the old age is transformed dialectically into the eschatological age. The end of history and the dawn of the kingdom of God happen on and on in the middle of history, wherever believers live not out of the immanent possibilities of this world but place themselves in the world under the kingdom of the Son of God, which is not of this world. The end of this age, expected by apocalypticism, and the dawn of the kingdom of God, the dualistically regarded turn of the age, is "historicized": though the Christ event clearly separates the "once" of the old age from the "now" of the new, this "now" is not an objective reality but a historical possibility that must be grasped and continually actualized by believers. Thus Simon's words and the criticism of them reflect a fundamental theological development within the early post-Easter period, namely, the overcoming of the apocalyptic intermezzo by the confession of Jesus as the Messiah and Son of God.

Beginning with Peter's Messiah confession, the early church, with growing clarity (Bultmann 1960, 25), replaced the apocalypticism still retained in the original Easter confession with a dialectically understood eschatology. The extent to which initially the *Christ* Jesus was primarily seen still apocalyptically as the "one who is coming again" can hardly be decided with sufficient certainty on the basis of our sources. Hahn's judgment that Jesus' Messiahship "first became known precisely not in the light of his resurrection and exaltation . . . but in regard to his powerful action in the Parousia" (1963, 180) can hardly be verified by critical examination (Vielhauer 1965, 176ff.; Conzelmann 1967, 87), and the oldest formulaic material shows, in any case, that the Christ title had "its original home not in eschatology but in soteriology" (Vielhauer 1965, 184). Yet this judgment does not mean much for the beginnings of the Jewish Christian church in Palestine, especially since eschatology and soteriology are not alternatives. In the meantime it allows the determination that in principle Peter's Messiah confession gives the primacy of soteriology over apocalypticism, or exaltation over the Parousia. In any case, Peter's Messiah confession means the actual turn from apocalypticism to soteriology or to the possibility of eschatological existence. To this extent the founding date of the church is not *Easter* but a certain *interpretation* of the Easter event—which at least tends to eliminate its apocalyptic character—namely, the Messiah confession of Peter. Accordingly the designation of Simon as the "rock" of the church (Mark 3:16 par.) rests only indirectly on his Easter confession but directly on his Messiah confession, and thus in this regard also, Matt. 16:16ff. rests on old tradition.

The described process can be further clarified with the help of Luke 22:31–32:

"Simon, Simon, listen! Satan has demanded to sift all of you like wheat,
   but I have prayed for you that your own faith may not fail; and you, when
   once you have turned back, strengthen your brothers."

This logion from Luke's special material is now found within the announcement of Peter's denial. In this passage it is apparently connected with the evangelist Luke's constant effort to trivialize the weaknesses of Jesus' disciples and apostles, especially those of Peter. The testing of Peter, which is to be expected as a result of the logion, lies in the future, after his imminent denial, but it is not described in more detail; Luke is apparently thinking of Peter's Easter testimony (cf. Luke 24:34). Apart from the clause, "when once you have turned back," the logion has no connection with the denial story or, indeed, with the passion story in general. Rather, this clause is in clear tension with the idea that Peter's faith will not fail, and Luke's attempt to soften the denial by announcing it through this tension-filled logion is forced and hardly convincing.

The conclusion is that "when once you have turned back" is an addition by Luke, as is generally accepted today (cf. already Bultmann 1931, 287–88). Then, however, we are dealing with a tradition competing with the denial story, which cannot have originally belonged in the passion situation, since a connection with the passion story is not indicated and a historical background within the passion event cannot be produced in the context of our tradition (Dibelius 1959, 201; Linnemann 1970, 72ff.); therefore, in its *original* historical place, this tradition need not have contradicted the denial tradition. In comparison with this, the assumption that an honorable addressing of Peter in the passion story was displaced at a later time by a secondary denial tradition, but taken up again even later by Luke in a makeshift way, is extremely unlikely.

The vivid picture of the "sifting" in no way presupposes "compellingly a general falling away of the disciples with the sole exception of Peter." This impression is suggested only by the secondary passion situation that speaks of the failure of *all* disciples. The picture itself, by contrast, speaks of a profound *crisis* within the circle of disciples, which leads to a separation of reliable and false disciples; the latter are sifted out (Linnemann 1970, 74). Linnemann (p. 76) holds the view that in Luke 22:31–32 we are dealing with an early Christian prophetic saying that the church should prepare for a special assault, presumably a persecution. Yet a persecution situation is not indicated; the precise description of behavior and the successful effectiveness of Peter leads more to a *vaticinium ex eventu* than to an old prophetic saying, and the name *Simon* instead of *Peter* would be an anachronism in the post-Easter situation presupposed by Linnemann, as Klein (1961, 94–95) has correctly shown.

These observations lead to a definite, clearly datable event that is reflected in the tradition that underlies Luke 22:31–32. The still purely apocalyptic understanding of Easter by Peter and the circle of twelve (1 Cor. 15:5) inevitably had to lead to a crisis when the first fruits Jesus was not followed by the other dead and the course of this world continued. The ghost of the delay of the Parousia, which has often been conjured up in modern scholarship, was alive in this early situation of the church and was *theologically decisive only* in this situation. This crisis is reported in Luke 22:31–32. It leads to the end of the close circle of twelve, which in the old tradition is linked only with the Easter appearances (1 Cor. 15:5), not with the Messiah confession, and which forms the council of elders of the still apocalyptic community of salvation (cf. Luke 22:29–30). The "fall" of Judas Iscariot, one of the twelve, as a spectacular "falling away" belongs in this crisis situation (Schmithals 1986, 597ff.). We know nothing about the behavior and fate of most of the other members of the circle of twelve. But Simon withstood and overcame this crisis for the benefit of the developing church with the "Messiah confession," the eschatological reinterpretation of the apocalyptic understanding of Easter, and since then he has consequently been called the "rock."

In addition to Luke 22:31–32, Matt. 16:17 also speaks of this (cf. also Matt. 14:28–32; John 21:15ff.): "Blessed are you, Simon son of Jonah! For flesh and blood has not revealed this to you, but my Father in heaven." With this confession the delay of the Parousia was overcome *in principle,* and the theological foundation was laid upon which the disappointing imminent expectation could be overcome whenever it became a problem again. Thus *historically* the logion of Luke 22:31–32 in its original version—that is, together with Simon's Messiah confession—belongs to the corresponding origin of the church, and to Christian theology, as well as to the distinction of Simon with the title *rock* (Matt. 16:18). *Literarily* Luke 22:31–32, as an *announcement* of these events, belongs in an earlier situation, presumably in the pre-Markan report on the Easter calling of Peter and the twelve and thus to Mark 3:16 in the original Easter anchoring of this calling narrative (cf. Schmithals 1986, 729ff.).

It is not by accident that we find in the logion of Luke 22:31–32 the concept of faith, which stands very close to the resurrection and Messiah confessions of Peter in terms not only of content but also of time. For while the term *faith* is still lacking in the prechristological sayings tradition, it is found already early in the whole breadth of early Christian theological developments. Thus it must have been coined already in Palestinian Jewish Christianity. The pre-Pauline formulaic material already speaks of faith in *God,* who raised Jesus from the dead (Rom. 4:24; 10:9; cf. 6:8), and then of the faith "that Jesus died and rose again" (1 Thess. 4:14). "To become Christian" traditionally means "to come to believe" (cf. Rom. 10:14; 1 Cor. 3:5; 15:2, 11; 2 Cor. 4:13), that is, to come to faith "in Jesus Christ" (Gal. 2:16; Rom. 3:22, 26; 10:14; Phil. 1:29), and Paul can also saddle Peter with this expression (Gal. 2:16). The apostle is also sent to awaken faith in the gospel (Rom. 10:14ff.; 1 Cor. 15:11; 1 Thess. 2:13; Phil. 1:27; Mark 1:15). On this theological basis Paul uses the term *faith* as a noun or as a verb, absolutely or with attributes and in many variations refined to a designation of Christian existence (Rom. 1:8, 12; 15:13; 1 Cor. 1:21; 13:2, 13; 14:22; 16:13; Phil. 1:25–29; Col. 1:4; 1 Thess. 1:7; 2:10), and this generalized usage of the term soon became the usual. Nevertheless, it is specific and characteristic of Paul and his "conversion theology" to speak of faith as the universal way of salvation that is open to all people and replaces the work of the law (Rom. 1:5, 16–17; 3:21–4:22; 9:30–33; Gal. 2:16; 3:1ff.). The prototype of the Gospel of Mark also uses the concept of faith in a both reflective and central way and thereby shows the way in which it was used in certain areas of early Hellenistic Jewish Christianity (Mark 1:15; 2:5; 5:34, 36; 9:23–24; 10:52; 16:16–17).

Already in the Old Testament *believing* God served as the expression for the relationship with God that encompasses one's entire existence, is made possible by God himself, and includes trust, reverence, hope, obedience, and faithfulness (Gen. 15:6; Isa. 7:9; 28:16; Hab. 2:4). Yet the number of these passages is small, and the Jewish writings of the New Testament period seldom refer to the Old

Testament conception of faith. Thus the new faith experience of the community gifted with eschatological salvation seems to have led to a reaching back to the previous biblical concept, which apparently occurred already in the context of the apocalyptic intermezzo (belief that God raised Jesus from the dead: Rom. 4:24; 10:9), though we still cannot bring to light the spontaneity or the theological consideration of this momentous process.

On the Tradition-historical
Problem of the Jesus Tradition

With Peter's Messiah confession began the formation of the christological confession that proclaims, through ways that were originally separated but in Paul already flow together, the *Christ* Jesus as the crucified and resurrected One (1 Cor. 15:3ff.) or as the self-humbling and exalted One (Phil. 2:6–11). This confession tradition not only largely dispensed with apocalyptic elements in its eschatological statements but also, and above all, passed over the proclamation and activity of Jesus as reported in the Gospels; in the early Christian baptismal formulas and in the early church confessions, in which the *theologia crucis* and the *theologia incarnationis* are united, the statements of passion theology connect directly with statements that speak of the miraculous birth or the preexistence and the incarnation or true humanity of the Son of God. This observation agrees with the still more striking fact that the corresponding Jesus tradition is missing in the theological realm of influence of the christological, soteriological confessions; in the entire early Christian tradition, apart from the Gospels, one finds virtually no material from the Synoptic tradition until well into the second century. Thus only in the Gospels have even the potentially authentic Jesus traditions survived, that is, the apocalyptic logia and parables from the state of expectation that was "suspended" at Easter, yet they are no longer in this state but are now in a broad narrative tradition that is already shaped christologically and kerygmatically.

How is one to explain this double state of affairs, the lack of Jesus tradition of whatever provenance both in the formulated confessions and in the theological developments of, for example, the letters of Paul? The situation as such and the necessity of an appropriate explanation were felt more acutely in the early period of historical Bible scholarship than was the case later. At that time the favorite notion was that the Gospel literature originally contained private sketches for personal remembrance, which only later received general significance in the church, an idea that also lay behind the two-sources theory: Mark did not want the memories of Peter to be lost, nor Matthew the sayings of Jesus that remained in his memory. Where this idea was recognized as untenable in the face of the kerygmatic, community-related character of the Jesus tradition, that tradition was often relegated to a position outside the central apostolic proclamation; Herder, for example, established for it a special order of "storytellers," and analogous explanations are still found today.

In consideration of the kerygmatic character of the Jesus tradition, however, the idea prevailed toward the end of the last century that a broad stream of oral traditions was gathered in our Gospels, appearing first in the Gospel of Mark and the sayings source; Martin Dibelius and Rudolf Bultmann, following the procedure of Johannes Weiss, attempted within the framework of "form history" (*Formgeschichte*) to uncover the history of these oral traditions. Yet the total victory of form history allowed the problem of the "Synoptic deficiency," of the "apocryphal" character of this oral tradition, to fall into oblivion: wherever, as a result of the methodological premises of form history, one should have encountered the kerygmatically coined oral Jesus tradition—for example, in the Pauline letters—it was not found. Therefore the proposals of form history increasingly lost cogency. It is not by chance that Käsemann returns to the older ways of explanation when he responds to the question How could things have moved again from the doxology of the proclaimed One to the story of the proclaimer, and within the context of the kerygma? with the statement that the "appeal to the form of the Gospel report, to the story of the Palestinian proclaimer," served to ward off fanaticism (1964b, 66). Incidentally, this statement cannot be right: the Gospels of Mark, Matthew, and Luke do not interact with fanaticism, while Paul and John take the position of fighting fanaticism with the help of the "truly incarnate One" and the "truly crucified One," that is, with the confessional formulations that had not yet appeared in connection with the Jesus traditions.

Yet Käsemann had correctly seen that the connection of the "Synoptic tradition" with the christological kerygma was a relatively late process and that only in view of this fact can the "Synoptic deficiency" be explained at all. Indeed, we can also easily see that the early church could not formulate its christological, soteriological kerygma in *direct* recourse to the proclamation and activity of Jesus, which belonged to the state of *expectation*. A confession that was based on the *fulfillment* of this expectation preserved in itself this superseded state, but in the manner of its "suspension." This means, however, that it is not the *absence* of the traditions from and about the earthly Jesus in the post-Easter kerygma that needs explaining, but their presence!

If one were able to assume a broad stream of oral tradition vis-à-vis the exegetical results, the premises of form history would be in a position to make the *kerygmatization* of the pre-Easter tradition understandable, but they offer no explanation for this traditional material as such. Therefore the starting point for a solution to the tradition-historical problem of the Jesus traditions cannot be the hypothesis, worked out by form history, of a widespread oral reproduction of Jesus' sayings and stories, which cannot be demonstrated as such anywhere but in the Gospel literature itself, and then only with the presupposition of the two-source theory. In fact, this illuminates not only the further history of the writing of the Gospels but is also helpful in revealing the older tradition history of the Gospel traditions. Yet here we must distance ourselves from the curious view that the material of the sayings source (Q) and the Gospel of Mark originally belonged to a common stream of tradition, was then divided into the two Synoptic sources, but was later brought together again by the evangelists. Apart from its internal improbability, this view also founders on the fact that the narratives of the Gospel of Mark are thoroughly shaped by Christology and kerygma, but the logia of the sayings source appear in an essentially prekerygmatic, apocalyptic form. It is true that in some passages there is a small overlap in form and content between the Gospel of Mark and the sayings source (Q), which is resolved by redaction-critical analysis (Schmithals 1985, 404ff.): the oldest stratum of the sayings tradition (Q[1]) has no narrative material, and the basic text of the Gospel of Mark does not yet contain any sayings tradition in the form of doublets of Q logia. Thus the basic text of Mark was shaped from the beginning by the kerygma and contained no apocalyptic material. The old sayings tradition, however, remained on the level of apocalyptic expectation. It has not only no passion and Easter story but also no Christology. It sees John the Baptist on the same level as Jesus (Matt. 11:11a, 12, 18), understands Jesus' death as the fate of a prophet (Luke 13:34ff.), and takes no notice of Easter or of Peter and the twelve, the first Easter witnesses.

Thus if we want to solve the tradition-historical problem of the Jesus tradition, we must analyze the oldest material of the sayings source (Q) and that of the Gospel of Mark independently of each other, determining in each case its origin and the various groups who have handed it down. In the following chapter we will attempt this, using the Son of Man sayings, and we will confirm that Jesus expected and announced the coming of the kingdom of God, and that on the basis of Easter, his followers regarded this expectation as having been fulfilled in Jesus himself. We can no longer determine whether and to what extent in the carrying out of this process the Christology rests on the impression that the *person* of Jesus made on Peter and the first disciples, and the soteriology is rooted in the *proclamation* with which Jesus announced the *salvation* of the kingdom of God.

2

Jesus and the Son of Man:
A Key to Early Christianity's
History of Theology and Tradition

Although the following study will not delve into the religious-historical question of the origin of the title *Son of Man,* it presupposes that this messianic title refers to a heavenly figure connected with Dan. 7:13–14, who is found in the context of the apocalyptic conceptual world and at the turn of the age will carry out the judgment of the world (4 Ezra 13:1–13; *1 Enoch* 38.2; 39.6–7; 46.1ff.; 48.4ff.; 55.4; 62.13ff.; 69.27ff.; cf. Kümmel 1984, 159ff.). In this way the Son of Man belongs intrinsically to apocalypticism, which has no place for a political Messiah descended from David, yet without the apocalyptic expectation that the turn of the age and the coming kingdom of God are necessarily dependent on this figure of the judge. In view of Son of Man's roots in apocalypticism, the observation that this figure is found almost exclusively in the sayings of Jesus indicates the apocalyptic character of Jesus' proclamation and its environment.

At the same time it is noteworthy, on the one hand, that the title *Son of Man* is found in all the Gospels alongside *Christ, Son of God, Lord,* and so forth as a messianic title for Jesus—where it is striking that Jesus always speaks of himself as the Son of Man in the third person. On the other hand, however, this title is completely absent from the whole kerygmatic teaching and confessional tradition and in all the traditions dependent on it outside of the Gospels—in Paul, for example—for in our tradition the idea that Jesus' resurrection was "interpreted as the exaltation and enthronement of the Son of Man" (Hengel 1972, 65) is simply excluded in connection with the term *Son of Man.* This curious way in which the title *Son of Man* does or does not appear has brought forth in the last one hundred years a scarcely surveyable wealth of literature, mostly in relation to the question of Jesus' messianic self-consciousness, yet this scholarly activity has not resulted in a common solution to the many layers of Son of Man problems (cf. the recent report of the literature in Kümmel 1991, 391ff.; Hare 1970). This literature—however one might judge its individual conclusions—shows that the history of early Christianity cannot be understood without considering the Son of Man problem, and at the same time the notable and relatively comprehensive store of relevant tradition promises enlightening insights into important processes in the theological history of early Christianity, which without this tradition would remain hidden from us. These insights, not the question of Jesus' self-consciousness, are the topic of the following study, which is based on the now common classification of the Son of Man sayings into three groups: the sayings of (1) the suffering and resurrected One, (2) the presently acting Son of Man, and (3) the coming Son of Man.

The Three Explicit
Passion Announcements of Mark

It is advisable to begin with the passion announcements of the Gospel of Mark because these announcements in particular contain stereotypically the title *Son of Man*, which is invariably missing in the corresponding teaching and confessional formulas of the Pauline and pre-Pauline tradition. This raises doubts as to whether we are dealing with early tradition in these passion announcements, which are adopted by the later evangelists. There are indeed vexing questions concerning the quite frequently and controversially treated question of a foundation in tradition for the three Markan announcements (Mark 8:31; 9:31; 10:32–34) and a related priority within this trio (Haufe 1966, 130ff.; Hoffmann 1973), for all three passion announcements are redactional formulations of the evangelist Mark (cf. Dibelius 1959, 227ff.; Schmidt 1919, 218). The motif of the passion announcement as such was already available to the oldest evangelist through his traditions (cf. Mark 10:38–39; 12:6ff.; 14:22ff., 27). The material he used comes essentially from the passion and Easter narrative available to him, as well as from familiar teaching and confessional formulations of the early church. By contrast, the following charac- teristic words, in which Jesus announces the coming passion and resurrection of the *Son of Man*, are Mark's own work:

> Then he began to teach them that the Son of Man must undergo great suf- fering, and be rejected by the elders, the chief priests, and the scribes, and be killed, and after three days rise again. (8:31)

There can be no doubt about the redactional origin of the introduction to this first of the three passion announcements (cf. Mark 6:2; 9:31). (On the christolog- ical term *suffering* [as in Mark 9:12] cf. Heb. 2:18; 5:8; 9:26; 1 Peter 2:21, 23.) *Great suffering* is also a traditional phrase (*Assumption of Moses* 3.11; Jos. *Ant.* 13.268, 403) that is also found in Mark 5:26; 9:12 (cf. Matt. 27:19; *Barn.* 7.11). The modifier *great* (literally, "many things") is generally a favorite expression of the evangelist Mark. "Be rejected" goes back to the early Christian scriptural proof (Ps. 118:22 LXX), which was known to Mark from his source (Mark 12:10; cf. Acts 4:11; 1 Peter 2:4ff.; *Barn.* 6.4). The phrase "elders, chief priests, and the scribes," which is always redactional in this arrangement, refers to the triad of Jewish op- ponents in Jerusalem (Wendling 1908, 177ff.; Schulz 1967, 131–32; Schmithals 1986, 506–7), that is, the members of the Sanhedrin (Mark 11:27; 14:1, 43, 53, 55; 15:1, 31). (On the broadly traditional character of "be killed" [as in 9:31; 10:34] cf. Mark 12:7–8; 14:1; 1 Thess. 2:15; on "rise" [as in Mark 9:31; 10:34] cf. Mark 9:9–10; Rom. 14:9; 1 Thess. 4:14.) The assertion that Mark himself prefers *cru- cify* to *kill* (Strecker 1967, 25) is incorrect; *crucify* occurs only in Mark's source (Mark 15:15, 24, 27; 16:6) and in the direct adoption of this source (15:14, 20b,

25), whereas *kill* is also redactional in 14:1. Also, in view of Mark 9:9–10, the reference to 14:28; 16:6, where Mark employs the conceptuality of the confessional formulas (cf. 1 Cor. 15:4; Rom. 4:25), cannot support the thesis that in redactional expressions Mark prefers *be raised* to *rise* (Strecker 1967, 24–25).

"After three days" (as in Mark 9:31; 10:34) is often considered proof of a pre-Markan stratum of the tradition of the passion announcements. Strecker, for example, explains that "after three days" is "in contradiction with Mark 14:58; 15:29 ('in three days') and—presupposing a 'Greek counting'—also with the presentation of the Markan passion story" (1967, 24–25). But one must not presuppose for Mark the Greek way of counting, which in "after three days" does not count the starting day, for in the passion announcements—in a perhaps intentionally archaic way, as in the likewise redactional information in 14:1 (Dibelius 1959, 180)—he follows the Jewish way of counting, which includes the first day in the three days and which he found already present, for example, in 9:2 (cf. Luke 2:46; Acts 25:1; 28:17; Güttgemanns 1970, 222; Schenke 1971, 24). The contradiction of the other way of speaking in Mark 14:58; 15:29 is diminished by that fact that it is found on the lips of Jesus' opponents. The *must* that determines Jesus' passion and resurrection is the *divine must,* which already defines the pre-Markan passion story (10:32a; 14:49b; 15:5; etc.): people only *seem* to affect Jesus' way of suffering, which in truth proceeds according to God's will as announced in the scripture (1 Cor. 15:3–4). Also in Mark 9:11; 13:10 there is a corresponding *must* from the pen of the evangelist, whereas in 13:7, 14; 14:31 it comes directly from the tradition.

> . . . for he was teaching his disciples, saying to them, "The Son of Man is
> to be betrayed into human hands, and they will kill him, and three days
> after being killed, he will rise again." (9:31)

In terms of tradition-historical material, the second of the passion announcements contains, beyond Mark 8:31, only the announcement that Jesus will "be betrayed into human hands." As in Mark 10:33, the evangelist adopts this information directly from the passion story before him (14:41), which for its part utilizes the oldest confessional and teaching tradition (Rom. 4:25; 8:32; 1 Cor. 11:23; Gal. 2:20; Eph. 5:2; cf. Mark 14:21, 42, 44; 15:1, 15). Instead of "into the hands of sinners" (Mark 14:41), in the present case the evangelist chooses the synonymous (cf. 8:33; Luke 24:7) "into human hands" (literally, "into the hands of men") in order, as in Mark 2:27–28; 14:21 (cf. Matt. 9:6, 8) to make the pun on "Son of Man"/ "men," which is apparently important to him and indicates in a way yet to be clarified the redactional significance of the *Son of Man* title in general and especially in the context of the passion announcements.

> He took the twelve aside again and began to tell them what was to happen
> to him, saying, "See, we are going up to Jerusalem, and the Son of Man
> will be handed over to the chief priests and the scribes, and they will con-
> demn him to death; then they will hand him over to the Gentiles; they will
> mock him, and spit upon him, and flog him, and kill him; and after three
> days he will rise again." (10:32b–34)

In the third passion announcement are four motifs that do not occur in the same form in the two previous announcements but are all found in the passion story itself. The first is a combination of two motifs from Mark 8:31 and 9:31, namely, the deliverance of Jesus by God into the hands of the chief priests and scribes, which is described in 14:10–11, 18, 21, 41ff. The evangelist mentions further the condemnation to death pronounced by the members of the Sanhedrin according to 14:64 and then their deliverance of Jesus to the Gentiles, which the passion story reports in 15:1, 10. The fourth of the new motifs is the mocking of Jesus, it is described in 15:15ff. (cf. 14:65). In view of its close relationship to the passion story, which is to be observed in any case, the assumption of a special tradition for the third Markan passion announcement is unnecessary. If Tödt (1959, 159ff.) asserts that the *intention* of Mark 10:33–34 does not agree with the *intention* of the passion story and therefore the third passion announcement is older than the passion narrative, this argument must be turned around: since the passion story is essentially pre-Markan, the special intention of 10:33–34 betrays the hand of the evangelist. Also contrary to Tödt (ibid.), the observation that the term *flog* does not appear in the passion narrative cannot substantiate an independent tradition for 10:33–34, for Mark is simply reducing the various terms for *strike* that occur in 14:65 and 15:15ff. to *one* term.

Since the context of the three passion announcements is doubtless redactional, and since the stereotypical title *Son of Man*—which is never connected with the passion tradition outside of the Gospel of Mark and the tradition flowing from it— cannot be an indication of a tradition already present before the evangelist, everything suggests that Mark himself formed the three passion announcements as such from material already available to him. This statement is supported by the striking fact of *three* announcements, a number that doubtless goes back to the evangelist. For this triad as such points in any case to the evangelist's great interest in these parallel passages and the *Son of Man* title anchored *in them;* in form they may be compared to the threefold prayer in Gethsemane and the threefold denial by Peter. This "intensity of the Markan redactional work" (Strecker 1967, 31) fits well with the redactional origin of the three passages, especially since Tödt (1959, 134) correctly shows that the three passion announcements have "a great significance in the *composition* of the oldest Gospel."

To these observations we must add form-historical considerations. If one holds, namely, to the assumption of an originally independent tradition of at least one of the passion announcements, one would have to demonstrate for it, based on form-historical premises, a characteristic *form* and *Sitz im Leben* ("situation in life"). That neither of these is possessed by the basis in tradition of the three passages, however reconstructed, has been convincingly shown by Güttgemanns (1970, 214ff.), who has found in the passion announcements a rewarding object for an attack against those exegetes who in their analysis of the passion announcements have gone to work with less caution than the fathers of the form-historical school. That is, under the form-critical aspect, the Markan passion announcements are formless, for they exist only as they are and only here, and analogies are also unknown. Their "form" apparently came into being ad hoc out of the evangelist's redactional interests and on account of the passion story, as well as in loose connection with corresponding short teaching and confessional formulas. This lack of "form" corresponds to the absence of a *Sitz im Leben*. Dinkler (1967, 297) determined that the aim (*skopos*) of the source was "to overcome the scandal of the cross through a prediction of the Son of God and to legitimate the event of the cross as willed by God." Now, an aim does not demonstrate a *Sitz im Leben,* and, moreover, the Markan passion announcements totally lack the *soteriological* accent, rightly considered by Dinkler to be indispensable, which from the beginning bears the *must* of Jesus' death on the cross (cf. 1 Cor. 15:3–4; Rom. 4:25). Tödt (1959, 147, 185–86, 197–98), who correctly recognizes this, makes a virtue of necessity: the lack of any soteriological interpretation in the Markan passion announcements points to their great age.

There is no indication, however, that the Christian church in the early period understood the "must" of Jesus' death in any way other than christologically and soteriologically. The reference to Lukan passages such as Luke 17:25; 24:7, 20, 26, 46; Acts 1:3; 3:13, 18; 17:3; 26:23, which, to be sure, formulate a nonsoteriological passion kerygma (Wilckens 1961, 108ff., 136ff.), provides no support here, since these passages are redactional (Conzelmann 1964, 187–88) and the *elimination* of soteriological aspects of the *theologia crucis* by the third evangelist is obvious (cf., for example, Luke 22:27 with Mark 10:45) and also well grounded in the reason for his writing (Schmithals 1980, 11ff.). And in the three Markan passion announcements, who wanted to find the *skopos* alleged by Tödt (1959, 185): "If the rejection and suffering give the appearance that the Son of Man lost his authority, then the resurrection proves its validity and power"? The "must" reveals without distinction Jesus' passion and resurrection; an *opposition* of passion and resurrection is not indicated even inchoately. But even if one concedes Tödt the named *skopos* and a great age for the tradition of the passion announcements, this still does not gain them a *Sitz im Leben.*

Therefore it is not coincidental that in regard to the passion proclamations Dibelius (1959, 232) concludes that "certainly they come from the evangelist." Curiously ignoring the form-*historical* task, Bultmann only states: "I will not spend time with the passion and resurrection predictions, which have long been recognized as secondary formations of the church" (1931, 163); yet we may presume that a judgment similar to that of Dibelius lies behind this noteworthy renunciation of the eliciting of the *form* and *Sitz im Leben* of the present formations of the church, especially since Bultmann also points to the "purely esoteric instruction" in Mark 8:31; 9:30–32; 10:32–34 (1931, 357), that is, to a clearly redactional motif (even in his opinion: 1931, 371) of the oldest synoptist. Therefore Strecker (1967, 29) also judges with reason that "the existence of this kind of formulated, isolated passion prediction is hard to verify." But since he traces Mark 8:31 back to a pre-Markan tradition, he holds this passion announcement to be a fragment of a larger unit of tradition, which is composed of 8:27–29, 31, 32b–33. Thus he shifts the form-historical question to this larger tradition and in this way makes it definitively unanswerable, for this alleged piece of tradition is all the more formless and consequently also has no *Sitz im Leben* in the sense of form history.

Thus the form-historical consideration of the Markan passion announcements also suggests regarding them on the whole as redactional formations. Even for those who do not share this view, however, the question arises regarding the redactional intention and purpose of the evangelist Mark, toward which he emphatically directs the reader's attention with the well-considered choice of *three* statements. Nowhere else does Mark give his redactionally important assertions such strong support.

There are other redaction-critical observations to be made. First, all three announcements occur in the context of a special *instruction of the disciples*. In Mark 10:32 Jesus gathers "the twelve" around him expressly for this purpose; in 9:31 he "was teaching his disciples," and likewise in 8:31 Jesus is found (since 8:27) in conversation with his disciples. The observation that in Mark the teaching of the disciples is always christological teaching—at least in effect—points again to the significance of the already striking stereotypical title *Son of Man* in the three announcements. Yet there can be no question of a narrowly esoteric or secret teaching about the suffering Son of Man. It does not appear in connection with any announcement of the commandment of silence, and the remark in 8:32a that Jesus announced the suffering and resurrection of the Son of Man "quite openly" can be understood as merely an express indication that one does not need to shy away from making such announcements in public. We may also note that a significant role seems to be played by the place where Jesus gives the instruction. The first and third announcements occur outside of Galilee; the second takes place in Galilee, but in this case the evangelist states expressly that when Jesus traveled through his homeland, *he did not want anyone to know it* (9:30; cf. 9:32). Apparently with the passion announcements, in contrast to the Messiah confession, it was not a question of a secret teaching, but in *Galilee* there was no audience. Finally in all three cases the misunderstanding of the disciples regarding the announcement that the Son of Man must suffer and be resurrected is ascertained, yet with varying clarity. In Mark 8:32–33 the reaction of Peter shows that he did not understand Jesus; in 9:32—in Galilee!—the evangelist introduces the misunderstanding motif in "classical" form; in 10:32, finally, the disciples' fear serves as proof of their misunderstanding; this shows that they now know what threatens to happen, since Jesus is setting out for Jerusalem, but do not understand *why* what they fear will happen must happen (cf. Wrede 1901, 97).

It is true that these various features cannot be directly interpreted, especially since they do not in themselves allow us to perceive a connection between them. Each in its own way, however, and above all in concert, helps to fit the announcements intensively into the redactional structure of the Gospel.

The Son of Man in the
Passion Announcements of Mark

The key to understanding the passion announcements lies primarily in these passages themselves. For in addition to a short description of Jesus' destiny—as also described in the traditional teaching and confessional formulas and in the passion and Easter narratives, to which we have already given our attention—they also each begin with the term *Son of Man,* which is foreign to those formulas themselves and to the corresponding narrative in its original version.

It is notable how precariously the scholars who posit a model for the Markan passion announcements decide the question of whether or not the *Son of Man* title is a part of this model and the models of the evangelist. This is due to the fact that on the one hand sayings about the suffering and rising Son of Man are absent from the pre- and extra-Markan tradition, and on the other hand a specifically redactional sense of this term does not seem to be recognizable. In this regard Strecker (1967, 27; cf. Tödt 1959, 134) assumes "that the tradition directly before Mark, the tradition thriving within and immediately outside the Markan community, created this idea." Yet this only transposes the problem from the redaction-historical light into the tradition-historical darkness, where it can no longer be solved, for Strecker prudently does not ask what in that pre-Markan tradition could have given rise to such an abstract idea, yet at the same time he ignores Mark's unmistakable interest in the sayings of the suffering *Son of Man.* Nevertheless, he claims to find Son of Man sayings from this pre-Markan community tradition also in Mark 10:45 and 14:21. These two Son of Man sayings, however, do not come as such from the community tradition (see below); rather, they add to the number of *redactional* sayings about the suffering Son of Man.

Even more out of the question is the idea of anchoring the sayings about the suffering Son of Man in an old Palestinian tradition, as Tödt attempts. For *in the time after Mark* there is actually no talk of the suffering *Son of Man* either *before* or *alongside* or outside the tradition coming from Mark himself. In the whole breadth of the instructionally and confessionally formulated, theologically considered, narrative *theologia crucis* of the early Christian period, the *Son of Man* title does not occur, even outside the Markan strand of tradition. The old sayings tradition, which underlies the sayings source Q, has Son of Man sayings but does not contain the kerygma of Jesus' suffering and resurrection. That leads to the conclusion that Mark was probably the first to speak of the suffering *Son of Man,* and this conclusion is compelling if a redaction-historical reason can be demonstrated for his use of this term.

Why does he choose this new and striking way of speaking? In Wrede's epochal book on the messianic secret, the author curiously does not consider the problem presented by the christological title *Son of Man.* Actually, he does not include the passion announcements in the problems of the Markan messianic secret but evaluates them, without regard to the title *Son of Man,* solely under the viewpoint of "real life of Jesus" or "view of the church." He sees the announcements as "the naked expression of the church's view" and states: "They are the most precise formulation of the idea that Jesus knew the passion story accurately in advance, as it really happened. They belong, accordingly, in the chapter on early Christian apologetics" (1901, 90). This is a tradition-historical, not a redaction-historical explanation. It is unconvincing, for no apologetic tendency is to be found in the passion announcements, and the *Son of Man* title that is prominent in them remains unexplained. Therefore it is also not possible to transform Wrede's explanation into a redaction-historical one, especially since the apologetic tendency described by Wrede is totally foreign to the Gospel of Mark.

Among other things, Wrede has missed an observation that Dinkler (1967, 296) aptly reproduces and which classifies all the passion announcements and with them the term *Son of Man* among the christological themes of the Markan redaction: in Mark 8:31 we find "the first passion announcement and the striking jump from the *Christ* title in Peter's confess to the *Son of Man* title on the lips of Jesus. As we find the text in Mark today, the identification of the two titles is presupposed . . ." But since the text as it appears today goes back to the evangelist himself, he apparently identifies the suffering Christ with the Son of Man in a carefully considered way; for Mark it is a question of the unity of the christological tradition and the Son of Man tradition, in which Jesus always speaks in third person of the Son of Man, as if of another person.

In fact, the passion announcements themselves also point in this direction. On the one hand, they recite in a very formal and schematic way striking information about the passion story, without interpreting it in any way; thus when this information occurs in the context of the passion announcements, Mark connects with it no specific soteriological interest in order, for example, to give the reader of the following narrative a *theological* way of reading in advance. With the exact reproduction of the detailed information, however, it becomes clear to each *reader* of the Gospel — who, in contrast to the still uncomprehending listeners, has the following passion story already in view — that the Son of Man who will suffer the described fate is Jesus himself, who announces the passion and resurrection of the Son of Man. For the reader of the Gospel the sayings about the suffering Son of Man can only refer to the one whom the Christian church confesses as the Christ, who for them was crucified, died, was buried, and rose. On the other hand, however, he is never referred to with the titles *Christ* or *Son of God,* which are already familiar to the reader, and Jesus does not simply speak of himself in first person but speaks rather of the "Son of Man" in third person. This way of speaking reveals (and yet still conceals) Mark's redactional intention.

Before this intention can be discovered, we must first examine the other sayings of the suffering Son of Man as to whether they confirm the insights gained thus far and perhaps carry them further. At this point we can ignore Mark 9:12b. This interruptive parenthetical remark is probably "a post-Markan but pre-Matthean interpolation" (Strecker 1967, 29), apparently a marginal comment on verse 13 that comes from a copyist who wanted to note the striking parallel between the fates of the Baptist and Jesus, and which landed in an unfortunate place in the text (cf. Lohmeyer 1953, 183).

> As they were coming down the mountain, he ordered them to tell no one
> about what they had seen, until after the Son of Man had risen from the
> dead. (9:9)

With this remark the evangelist Mark is not attempting — as Wrede (1901, 66ff.) states with the approval of many interpreters — to give the time at which the messianic secret can be revealed, for according to 14:61ff. Jesus himself announces his majesty publicly before his sentencing (cf. Sjöberg 1955, 106). Rather, the determination "until after the Son of Man had risen from the dead" refers only to the preceding commandment of silence, which for its part is related to the transfiguration story and apparently seeks to explain how an event that, according to Mark, happened *before* Easter could be told as an Easter story; for Mark had the transfiguration story before him still in its original version as an Easter narrative (see p. 14 above). In any case, the redactional origin of Mark 9:9b is beyond question. The evangelist carries out the giving of the time following the model of the passion announcements, and naturally he mentions only the resurrection of the Son of Man. Since this can mean only the resurrection of Christ Jesus (8:29) or the Son of God (9:7), who, however, is mentioned only in third person as the Son of Man, Mark again achieves in unmistakable form the identification of the speaking Christ Jesus with the Son of Man of whom he is speaking.

"For the Son of Man came not to be served but to serve, and to give his life a ransom for many." (10:45)

The interminably often treated problems of Mark 10:45 solve themselves if one is ready also in regard to this saying to assume a redaction of the evangelist that is guided by his special interest (cf. Wendling 1908, 133). Mark composed 10:45 from four traditional motifs. (1) The basic content is formed by an old, originally Jewish Christian doctrinal statement, which understands Jesus' death as a ransom paid for "many" (that is, for all; cf. Friedrich 1982, 82ff.), and here we should compare especially 1 Tim. 2:6 and Titus 2:14. The pre-Markan passion narrative does not use the motif of the ransom, nor is its interpretation of the passion event based on this concept (cf. Schmithals 1986, 685ff.). (2) The word *came* is one of the stereotypical christological, soteriological formulations with which the church regarded retrospectively the salvific work of Jesus (cf. Bultmann 1931, 167): Mark 1:38; 2:17b; 12:6; 1 Tim. 1:15; Luke 19:10; John 18:37. Perhaps this motif came to the evangelist in direct connection with the first one named: "Jesus Christ came to give his life a ransom for many" (cf. 1 Tim. 1:15 with Mark 2:17b), if he did not get it directly from the source underlying 2:17b. Supporting the latter assumption is the observation that the evangelist composed 10:45 in the form of an alternative statement ("not . . . but . . .") corresponding to 2:17, which has little significance in the present case. The two possibilities, incidentally, do not need to be mutually exclusive. (3) The image of *serving* (cf. Pol. *Phil.* 5.2) comes from Mark 10:43–44 and makes it possible to add the saying in 10:45 as a theologically profound substantiation of the "church order" in 10:42–44, which brings Paul to mind (Rom. 15:3; 2 Cor. 8:9; Phil. 2:5ff.). Yet the transition is abrupt and also problematic, as already observed by Wellhausen (1909, 85; cf. Kertelge 1975). (4) Above all, Mark shapes the traditional and to some extent appropriately accommodated atonement saying as a *Son of Man* statement in analogy with the traditional Son of Man sayings—a singular ad hoc composition. "Thus at work here is the same hand that inserted the passion predictions" (Wendling 1908, 133). Jesus identifies himself—albeit still in third person but at the same time unmistakably—with the *Son of Man* in a powerful christological, soteriological doctrinal and confessional statement of his coming and giving his life as a ransom, which every reader who is at all familiar with early Christian tradition can relate only to the Christ Jesus. In this way Mark 10:45 *in itself* makes a statement that is apparently especially important for the evangelist Mark and which causes him to form a redactional saying of Jesus based on the already mentioned tradition.

> "For the Son of Man goes as it is written of him, but woe to that [man] by whom the Son of Man is betrayed! It would have been better for that [man] not to have been born." (14:21)

Mark 14:21 is based on a logion from the sayings tradition, as shown by the doublet in Matt. 18:6–7/Luke 17:1–2 (cf. *1 Clem.* 46.9), which comes from the sayings source Q. Luke has probably best preserved the original saying. Mark had already used parts of this saying in 9:42. In 14:21 he reshapes the original general warning against causing offense for the church or in the church by relating it especially to the offense that the "betrayer" Judas will give. With this reshaping Mark introduces the concept of "betrayal," through which the singular expression "the Son of Man goes" is provoked, and with which, on the one hand, reference is made directly to the "betrayal" of Judas (14:10, 18, 41–42) but, on the other hand, the expression indirectly takes up the older confessional tradition according to which God is the one who hands Jesus over (Rom. 4:25; 8:32; 1 Cor. 11:23; 2 Cor. 4:11; Gal. 2:20; Eph. 5:2, 25; cf. Isa. 53:6, 12 and see p. 255 below). The recurring Greek verb *paradidonai* means "to hand over," but it can also have the special meaning "to betray." The choice and use of this term make unmistakable the identity of the one who is said to be handed over or betrayed: Jesus Christ, as he appears from the beginning in the confession of the church and then also in the betrayal story. "As it is written" is one of the stereotypes of the old doctrinal formulas (1 Cor. 15:3–4; Mark 9:12–13; cf. Mark 8:31) and in the present case probably refers to Isa. 53:6, 12. But by twice calling the Christ Jesus the "Son of Man," Mark creates — this time on the basis of the sayings tradition! — one of the typical redactional sayings in which Jesus speaks of himself in third person as the *suffering* Son of Man. The evangelist's intention here is the same as the earlier identification of the Son of Man with the Christ Jesus or that of the traditional sayings of the Son of Man with the christological, kerygmatic tradition, which confesses Jesus as the one crucified and raised for the salvation of humankind. How important this idea is to the evangelist is shown in the present case by the careful stylization of the redactional passage with the help of the repeated play on words: "Son of Man"/ "man."

> "The hour has come; the Son of Man is betrayed into the hands of sinners. Get up, let us be going. See, my betrayer is at hand." (14:41b–42)

Many interpreters agree with Bultmann's judgment (1931, 288) that "as the impressive climax, 'the hour has come' must have originally closed the scene." Then the evangelist himself would have formulated the words that follow and in this way created a parallel to the Son of Man saying in Mark 14:21: the Jesus who is betrayed into the hands of sinners, the Christ of the church's confession, is identical with the Son of Man, of whom Jesus himself had spoken as if of another person. In this saying Jesus refers twice to his betrayal or being handed over, using the verb *hand over/betray* in different ways: first, in the sense of the old confessional tradition that rests on Isa. 53:6, 12, which uses the *passivum divinum* (*God hands over*), but then with reference to the *betrayal* by Judas; thus we seem to have a secondary doublet. Moreover, this suggests that the original storyteller whose report Mark uses characterized the "hour" that has come more precisely than the hour announced in Isa. 53:6, in which "the Lord has laid on him the iniquity of us all" (Kuhn 1952/53, 273; Tödt 1959, 184). Thus there is reason to think that Mark's source closed with the words, "The hour has come; I am betrayed (handed over, delivered) into the hands of sinners." Mark moves the "I" into the doublet formed by him ("my betrayer"), while replacing the "I" in the source with the more important *Son of Man*. But however one evaluates the tradition-historical problem of Mark 14:41b–42 in detail, we have before us again a characteristic saying of the suffering Son of Man, in which the evangelist has accomplished in the most direct way possible the identification of the Christ now betrayed onto his way of suffering and of the Son of Man mentioned in third person by Jesus himself in his logion (cf. Wendling 1908, 206).

In summary, we may make several observations. As was true of the three explicit passion announcements in the Gospel of Mark and is now also the case in the analogous Son of Man sayings that concern the passion and resurrection of Jesus, it is always a question of *instruction to the disciples* and never involves an express commandment of silence. With the exception of Mark 9:9, all the sayings are spoken outside of Galilee, but like the second passion announcement in 9:31, which takes place in Galilee, 9:9 contains the motif of the disciples lack of understanding. In all Markan sayings about the suffering Son of Man there is a unified basic schema; the introductory Son of Man concept is always connected with a central christological confessional statement: in 8:31; 9:9; 9:31, and 10:32ff. with the basic time information in the kerygma, in 10:45 with the soteriological interpretation of this information, and in 14:21, 41b–42 with the term *hand over/betray,* so that we can also observe a clear continuation of the instruction of the reader. The formation of all sayings of the suffering and resurrected Son of Man, which is uniform in principle, identifies these sayings as redactional and at the same time forcefully places their (as yet uninterpreted) assertion before the eyes of the reader. The striking observation that all sayings of the suffering Son of Man occur only *after* Peter's Messiah confession in 8:29, and thus presuppose this for their understanding, underlines the *christological* content of each instruction and at the same time explains provisionally why this instruction is shared without exception with the disciples, who are the only listeners of Jesus who have heard Peter's Messiah confession.

The Sayings on the
Present Work of the Son of Man

The well considered placement of all the redactional sayings about the suffering and resurrected Son of Man after Peter's Messiah confession also allows us to presume that the two sayings "on the Son of Man at work in the present"

(Bultmann 1965, 31) are understandable only from the redaction-critical viewpoint, for they occupy "an unusual position in that they are a whole six chapters (over one third of the Gospel) away from the remaining twelve, which are spread over the second half of the Gospel" (Wendling 1908, 204). Moveover, the two passages are similar to each other; they go "far beyond the formalism of the others. . . . Everything otherworldly, everything in the future is swept away; here the 'Son of Man' is simply equivalent to the living, present Jesus" (Wendling 1908, 207).

> "But so that you may know that the Son of Man has authority on earth to forgive sins"—he said to the paralytic . . . (2:10)

Syntactically and logically, this Son of Man saying breaks the unity of the story of the healing of the paralytic, in which it is therefore a secondary insertion. Notable, first, is the awkward transition from the direct address in the purpose clause to the narrative "he said to the paralytic," which originally may have simply continued the previous narrative: "Then he said to the paralytic . . ." The purpose clause also confuses the train of thought. Jesus' preceding question in 2:9 "is a vexing question; the opponents must have had no reply" (Dibelius 1959, 63; cf. Wendling 1908, 210): "Which is easier, to say to the paralytic, 'Your sins are forgiven,' or to say, 'Stand up and take your mat and walk'?" Both are equally difficult and impossible for human beings. Thus Jesus expects no answer to the alternatives in his question. The purpose clause in the present text, by contrast, points Jesus' question toward a particular answer, so that the promise of the forgiveness of sins is validated by the difficult healing. This not only nullified the theological point of the story, which in no way attempted to validate an easier happening through a more difficult one; now it is also disturbing that the scribes, who are offended by Jesus' granting of the forgiveness of sins, have no answer to his question, although in his purpose clause Jesus already presupposes an answer: healing is more difficult.

Many scholars trace the purpose clause back to an originally independent logion (Wendling 1908, 210; cf. Boobyer 1954). But a logion with the content that the Son of Man forgives sins would be without analogy, and if we replace the title *Son of Man* with *Christ* (Lohmeyer 1953, 54), we get a saying of strange banality. Shifting the insertion into "the stage of the dispute collection" (Kertelge 1973, 211) would also remain arbitrary, if such a collection could be demonstrated. We can demonstrate, however, the evangelist's interest in the christological title *Son of Man,* and he himself actually formulated the present Son of Man saying ad hoc in regard to the power to forgive sins (Mark 2:7), accepting the unfortunate syntax and logic in the bargain (cf. Hay 1970).

> "So the Son of Man is lord even of the sabbath." (2:28)

What is true of Mark 2:10 is also true of 2:28 (Wendling 1908, 211); here also we have a redactional expansion of the story adopted by Mark. Though the syntactic connection between 2:28 and the preceding Jesus saying in 2:27 causes no problem, in terms of content the two logia make different statements. The saying, "The sabbath was made for humankind, and not humankind for the sabbath"

(2:27), with which Jesus justifies the plucking of grain on the sabbath, places *humankind* above the sabbath, but in the following saying it is the *Son of Man*. There is no indication that we should relate the two sayings in a meaningful theological way, for example: the Son of Man brings humankind freedom vis-à-vis the sabbath. On the contrary, "so" at the beginning of 2:28 creates a very unclear logical sequence (versus, for example, 10:8). It is not coincidental that Matthew and Luke omit 2:27 and thus avoid the tension between the two closing logia of the Markan narrative. Apparently Mark is as little concerned in 2:28 as in 2:10 about a clear theological relationship to the context; rather, in both places his concern is the Son of Man saying itself. Yet its connection with the preceding logion must not be left out of consideration, for through this connection arises the characteristic pun "man"/ "Son of Man," which the evangelist repeats in 9:31 and 14:21 (where it is doubled), and which he introduced indirectly (cf. Wendling 1908, 211–12) already in 2:10 (in connection with 2:7). "This playing with the two terms cannot be mere coincidence" (ibid., 211). Moreover, it is notable that through the striking "even" in 2:28, which refers "directly back to 2:10" (ibid., 210–11), Mark has joined together the two sayings about the presently active Son of Man: as the Son of Man can forgive sins, so *also* is he lord of the sabbath.

What is the redactional function of the two sayings about the present activity of the Son of Man, which are expressly related to each other in such a way? It is notable that both sayings are spoken *publicly* and therefore naturally do not fall under the commandment of silence to which the related cries of the demons (Mark 1:24–25, 34b) are subjected before the same public in Capernaum. This observation corresponds to a second one, namely, that the various instructions to the disciples about the suffering and resurrected Son of Man do not need to be kept secret either. Yet a public violation of Jesus' messianic secret at such an early point in the context of the Gospel of Mark would be quite incredible. Consequently, in the Son of Man sayings of Mark 2:10, 28 Jesus speaks publicly, though not openly but in veiled fashion, of his messianic status. In fact, the term *Son of Man* is itself a veiled expression. It *can* be understood as a title of messianic sovereignty, but it *can* also mean simply "man" or "human being." Naturally, *the reader* of the Gospel has long known—for example, through the messianic announcement of the Baptist (Mark 1:7–8), the voice from heaven at Jesus' baptism (1:11), and the confessions of the demons—that Jesus is the "Son of God"; therefore *the reader* gathers from 2:10 and 2:28 that when Jesus spoke in third person about the Son of Man, he spoke of himself and appropriated for himself the ambiguous term *Son of Man* as sovereign messianic title. At the same time, however, the reader learns that the *contemporaries* of Jesus did not have, and were not supposed to have, the same understanding, for contemporaries who do not know anything about Jesus' secret can understand 2:10 and 2:28 only in the sense that Jesus is speaking of *humankind in general*. In the context of this interpretation the redactional "so" at the beginning of 2:28 also becomes immediately clear: it is supposed to provoke from those who are outside the misunderstanding that Jesus is speaking of *humankind,* and thus it preserves his messianic secret. And similarly, the scribes, who according to 2:7 attribute the forgiveness of sins only to *God* in his eschatological judgment, learn that *human beings* also possesses such authority, as Matthew 9:8 expressly formulates, making manifest the misunderstanding intentionally provoked by Mark (cf. Wellhausen 1909, 16).

If modern scholars since Grotius have resolved the conscious, veiling ambiguity of the first two Markan sayings about the presently active Son of Man in a tradition-historical way by explaining that a saying of Jesus that originally spoke of *humankind,* or perhaps of himself as a humble human being, was later misunderstood or reinterpreted christologically in the church (Wellhausen 1909, 16; Bultmann 1965, 31; Polag 1977, 111ff.; Higgins 1980; Leivestad 1982; Müller 1984), Mark could not have foreseen the possibility of such a historical-critical interpretation of his redactional creations. For the evangelist it was a matter of *the hidden identification of Jesus and the majestic Son of Man,* as in the sayings about the suffering and resurrected Son of Man (cf. Theobald 1988, 42ff.). This interest also explains the repeated play on words, "man"/ "Son of Man." The *hiddenness* was for Jesus' contemporaries. They heard Jesus talk of "humankind," without comprehending the christological sense of this talk. This corresponds to the motif of the misunderstanding of the disciples in the context of the sayings about the suffering and resurrected Son of Man. Thus from the beginning of his activity, Jesus left no doubt even publicly that he is the Messiah/Son of Man. At the same time, however, he did not express this fact openly and understandably for his contemporaries but kept his messianic secret from them. The *identification* is made for the readers. They know from the beginning that Jesus is the Son of God and also know that as the Messiah/Son of Man he forgives sins and is lord of the sabbath. In order to make this messianic sovereignty of his known to readers, he also spoke of himself as the Son of Man. Regarding information obviously so important for the readers, the evangelist Mark, at the beginning of his Gospel in 2:10, 28, introduces the *Son of Man* title into his sources in two significant theological contexts (the forgiveness of sins, freedom from the Jewish law) and at the same time connects it with the christological passages 1:7–8, 11, 24–25, 34b, which have already explained to his readers the sovereignty of Jesus. *Son of Man* is thus a "secret" title of sovereignty encompassing the whole messianic activity of Jesus.

The Revelation of the
Secret Epiphany of the Son of Man

The Son of Man saying in Mark 14:62, with which Jesus answers the high priest's question as to whether he is the Christ, is an initial key to the interpretation of the previous observations.

> Jesus said, "I am; and 'you will see the Son of Man seated at the right hand
> of the Power,' and 'coming with the clouds of heaven.'" (14:62)

This verse is part of the redactional report on the proceedings of the Sanhedrin (14:55–65), which Mark inserted into his source (Wendling 1908, 177ff.; Winter 1962; Braumann 1961; Schmithals 1986, 650ff.). But even those who do not trace this entire report back to the evangelist himself still consider at least Mark

14:61b–62, the high point of the presentation, to be a heavily edited insertion by Mark (cf. Vielhauer 1965, 203–4). For in 14:61b–62 we undoubtedly have the second highest *redactional* peak (after 8:27ff.) of the Gospel of Mark: the sovereign titles *Christ* and *Son of God,* already known *to the reader* from Jesus' secret epiphany (in the high priest's question) and *Son of Man* (in Jesus' answer) now come together in an open epiphany that reveals the previous secret. The redactional intention of this scene is complex. We learn, among other things, why in the evangelist's opinion Jesus had to conceal his Messiahship during his public activity and could reveal it only within the small circle of his disciples under the seal of silence: otherwise he would not have been able to act, for the public confession of his sovereignty, which results in the present scene, is regarded by the Sanhedrin as blasphemy deserving death, and it is promptly answered with the sentence of death. At the same time the death sentence and its execution confirm for readers that Jesus really had publicly claimed to be the Messiah/Son of Man.

For our present context, however, it is especially interesting that with Mark 14:62 the veil is removed from all previous Son of Man sayings. If earlier Jesus always spoke in third person of the Son of Man as if of another being, in effect provoking occasionally the understanding that Son of Man = man/human being (2:10, 28), announced a suffering and resurrection of the "Son of Man" that was incomprehensible even to the disciples, and otherwise spoke in traditional apocalyptic fashion about the coming Son of Man (8:38; 13:26), now he proclaims, while consciously retaining the third person form of speech, his identity with the Son of Man as Christ and Son of God (cf. Vielhauer 1965, 72). "If in 8:38 the *ochlos* [crowd] could at best understand the third person literally, then 14:62 would be downright meaningless without the equation Jesus = Son of Man. The artificial construction is perfectly obvious" (Wendling 1908, 205). The veiling of his self-testimony, which was necessary until the end of his work for the very sake of this work, is lifted by Jesus himself at the end of his earthly activity. Wherever he spoke of the Son of Man, he used this apocalyptic title to speak of himself as the Messiah and Son of God, who forgives sins (2:10) and is lord of the sabbath (2:28), who is betrayed into the hands of sinners (14:21, 41–42), must undergo great suffering and be killed and rise again (8:31; 9:9, 31; 10:33), and gives his life as a ransom for many (10:45)—and who will come again in judgment (8:38; 13:26). The revelation of the *secret* epiphany confirms the secret *epiphany.* Our passage is the key carefully crafted by the evangelist for all the Son of Man sayings in his Gospel, and for this reason no more such sayings come after 14:62.

In all this we must observe that in Mark 14:62 not only is the "messianic secret" revealed and in this connection the ambiguous term *Son of Man* unambiguously defined as a title of messianic sovereignty, but beyond this the two sayings about the *coming* Son of Man that are handed down by Mark (8:38; 13:26)—the only Son of Man sayings in the Gospel of Mark that are not of redactional origin—are especially related to the exalted Christ. If in this way Mark focuses attention in 14:62 on the apocalyptic sayings *handed down within the Jesus tradition,* then in his redactional introduction and presentation of the Son of Man who in the sense of the Christian confession acts and suffers, is resurrected and exalted, he is apparently guided throughout by his interest *in identifying Jesus as he is found in the church's christological confession with the Son of Man of traditional teaching.*

In order to determine what occasioned this interest, we must analyze the two pre-Markan sayings about the coming Son of Man, for the two sayings about the coming Son of Man passed on by the evangelist form the basis of the redactional sayings about the Son of Man who is active on earth, suffers, and is exalted (cf. Wendling 1908, 204ff.).

The Reason for the Son of Man
Redaction of the Evangelist Mark

"Those who are ashamed of me and of my words in this adulterous and sinful generation, of them the Son of Man will also be ashamed when he comes in the glory of his Father with the holy angels." (Mark 8:38)

"Then they will see 'the Son of Man coming in clouds' with great power and glory." (13:26)

The provenance from the old sayings tradition attests Mark 8:38 (par. Matt. 16:27; Luke 9:26) as a doublet from the sayings source Q in Matt. 10:32–33/Luke 12:8–9, which Luke on the whole passes on better than Matthew and which at least in the first member contains the title *Son of Man* (Schulz 1972, 66ff.; Kümmel 1975b, 215–16; Vielhauer 1965, 101ff.). There is no doublet of Mark 13:26, but there can be no doubt that the evangelist Mark found this saying as part of a comprehensive apocalyptic model, which reaches its high point in Mark 13:24–27; at least 13:24–27 contains no specifically Christian elements. If one does not want to assume an isolated strand of tradition, the "little apocalypse" in Mark 13, which reaches its high point and end in 13:24–27, still belongs—with whatever boundaries—in the stratum of tradition excerpted by Mark from the sayings tradition (for details cf. Schmithals 1986, 555ff.).

In Mark 13:26 in its pre-Markan apocalyptic context there is by no means any assumption that the speaker, be it Jesus or someone else, is identical with the Son of Man, and for the readers "this equation results only when they place 13:26 with the other passages in which Jesus brings the term *Son of Man* more or less into close proximity with an *I*." "Here the evangelist is following closely a source in which the expression *Son of Man* is used with clear reference to the vision in Daniel (7:13), in which 'one like a son of man' comes with the clouds of heaven" (Wendling 1908, 204). But Mark 8:38 does not at all indicate that "not two persons but two *statuses* of the same person" are distinguished (Vielhauer 1965, 101ff.). Thus like Vielhauer, one can judge only when one *presupposes* the identification of the speaker with the Son of Man. Against this, however, is the clear wording of the (independent) saying, as well as the observation that in the early Christian confessional tradition the exalted Christ never bears the *Son of Man* title. That "at the last judgment Jesus will appear as guarantor or witness for the prosecution, that is, that he announces his future Son of Man function"

(Horstmann 1969, 40) is a sentence whose two (different!) assertions have no support in the logion that they seek to clarify. Also in Mark 8:38 the speaker and the Son of Man are to be distinguished. "Only with the presupposition of this distinction is it meaningful to relate present and future to each other in this parallel" (Jüngel 1962, 242).

Yet Conzelmann (1974a, 47–48) argues that in early Christendom one must strictly distinguish between *faith* in the salvific work of Jesus and the *expectation* of his Parousia, and this relationship of faith and expectation makes understandable "why the Son of Man title is not used in the credo and why it is placed exclusively in Jesus' self-assertions"—and indeed in the striking style of a self-assertion in third person. This information is not helpful, if only because the expectation of the One to come is also a part of the early Christian creedal statements (1 Thess. 1:10; Phil. 3:20–21). Also the precise conceptual and at the same time refined stylistic distinction assumed by Conzelmann could be credited only to a reflective theologian and be expected to be found in his school, but not in this case in the effectively diffuse and broadly diversified church tradition. Furthermore, in the view proposed by Conzelmann, the confessions of faith and the logia of expectation would have to have arisen and been passed on in a close relationship. The tradition-historical results, however, yield a different picture: in the context of the faith formulas asserting the salvific work of Jesus, for example, in Paul, the apocalyptic Son of Man sayings are not found, but in the context of the early Son of Man sayings, for example, in the sayings tradition, the soteriological kerygma is not found. Thus the particular nature of the apocalyptic Son of Man sayings must not be too hastily explained in terms of systematic theology; first it must be analyzed and evaluated in terms of tradition history.

The starting point for such an analysis of the two Markan sayings about the coming or judging Son of Man must be the recognition that the speaker is not identical with the Son of Man and that consequently the two sayings belong to a pre-Christian stratum of tradition. Polag (1977; cf. already Harnack 1907, 162ff.; Tödt 1959; Hoffmann 1972; Schulz 1972), in a study that in this respect is on the whole convincing, has demonstrated that the old sayings tradition was still generally unchristological: Jesus bears no christological title; the confession of the incarnate or the crucified and resurrected One is missing; Jesus dies the death of a prophet rejected by his people (Matt. 23:37ff. par.); nor do we find other fundamental experiences and actions of the early Christian church such as baptism, the Lord's Supper, confession of faith, pneumatology, and so forth. Not until the later redaction of this sayings tradition (Q^1), in the edition of the sayings source used by Matthew and Luke, is an intentional christologization of the traditional material undertaken. This insight can be confirmed by the demonstration that all the "doublets," that is, all the material adopted by the evangelist Mark from the sayings tradition (Q^1), are prechristological and prekerygmatic—that is, Jewish apocalyptic material.

Yet this analysis of the sayings tradition, suggested by exegetical results at least as early as Wrede's study on the messianic secret in the Gospels (1901), has its tradition-historical difficulties. "The conceptual field of the primary tradition of Q in its actual delineation cannot be integrated as such into the history of the early church" (Polag 1977, 187). Indeed! Therefore, based on the above observations Tödt (1959; cf. Bornkamm 1958, 758; Hoffmann 1972) concluded that the kerygma of the passion and Easter were consequently not the original and fundamental message of the church; rather, on the basis of the Easter experience, the early church validated Jesus' message anew, despite his failure on the cross. This was correctly contradicted by Vielhauer (1975, 325ff.), among others, on chronological grounds: Paul was converted to a christological kerygma of the passion and Easter. Yet Vielhauer's own explanation that the kerygma was always *presupposed* can therefore be no more correct than Polag's related attempt to explain the situation, which he correctly observed, through an early Christian "historicism," under the guidance of which the church conserved and passed on, without any relationship to its acute faith, memories of Jesus' proclamation as such (1977, 131). Polag also assumes a "strong power of application on the part of readers" (1977, 143), who understood unchristological things nonetheless christologically, and for this he wrongly appeals to the presentation in the Old Testament (present in written form and christological!). The assumption of such a "historicism" involves a unique anachronism, and the whole early Christian history of tradition actually shows how much the present confession of faith has always permeated the traditional material from the beginning.

In fact, if one does not replace the tradition-historical with an inadequate psychologizing explanation, the kerygmatically christological church cannot have been the bearer of the unkerygmatic and unchristological sayings tradition. This essentially apocalyptic, prophetic tradition, in which Jesus' own proclamation is apparently taken up, must have constituted a different association of communities and have been used by it. "Accordingly the objective examination of Q must accept the momentous knowledge that behind Q stands *one* particular community as bearer of the tradition" (Schulz 1972, 42; cf. Lührmann 1972, 101; Hoffmann 1972). Yet it is out of the question that this community was defined by the Easter experience, as assumed by the above named scholars (Bornkamm, Tödt, Lührmann, Schulz, and Polag), for the still unchristological and prekerygmatic sayings tradition contains not the slightest hint of the Easter event, but rather continues without interruption the message of Jesus in *expectation* of the turn of the age. To the extent that there was a post-Easter, prechristological "intermezzo" (see pp. 12ff. above), this comes precisely under the explicit impression that Jesus was resurrected as "the first fruits of those who have died" (1 Cor. 15:20; Rom. 1:4; Col. 1:18; Matt. 27:52ff.; Acts 26:23) and in the sign of the stereotypical confession to "God, who raised Jesus from the dead" (cf. Gal. 1:1; Rom. 4:24; 8:11; 2 Cor. 4:14; Col. 2:12), that is, on the level of the *fulfillment* of the expectation awakened by Jesus, on which Jesus' proclamation is "suspended"—and also for this reason the pre-Easter sayings tradition is no longer found in the vicinity of this Easter message.

Moreover, it is unlikely or impossible that *all* of Jesus' followers were affected by the exceptional Easter experience of Peter and the twelve (1 Cor. 15:5). A more or less large circle of hearers and followers of Jesus must have continued to consider Jesus, along with John and like him (cf. Matt. 11:11a, 12–13, 18–19 par.), to be a prophet who announced the coming turn of the age and died the martyr's death of a messenger of God (Luke 13:34 par.). These followers took note of Jesus' public death, yet not of his hidden resurrection, or they did not "believe" that God had raised Jesus from the dead (see p. 18 above). They are the earliest bearers of the sayings tradition (Q^1) and, according to this tradition, at that point did not confess Jesus as the Christ nor identify him with the coming Son of Man. For the prechristological sayings tradition contains the mass of sayings about the coming or judging Son of Man, which—whether they are authentic or not—speak of the Son of Man without exception in third person, distinguishing the Son of Man from the speaker: Luke 6:22; 11:30 par. (Jesus' preaching of repentance is confirmed by the judgment of the Son of Man announced in it); 12:10 par.; 12:40 par.; 17:23–24 par. (the coming of the Son of Man is not a limited, local event but immediately reaches the whole world); 17:26, 30 par.; Matt. 10:23; 19:28.

When the assumption of a "Jesus church that had taken no notice of the Easter kerygma" is called "fantastic" by Kümmel (1975a, 305), thereby avoiding a discussion of the issue, he does not consider that it would be truly a "fantastic" idea to assume that in a very short time the esoteric Easter experience had reached and convinced all the followers of Jesus. Rather, the phenomenon of the prekerygmatic and unchristological sayings tradition attests compellingly the existence of such a community of followers persisting in a state of expectation, which probably encompassed the hearers of the Baptist as well as followers of Jesus (cf. Luke 7:24–35 par.). This viewpoint is involuntarily conceded by the statement that "this problem seems not yet to have been sufficiently clarified in recent discussion" (Kümmel 1975a, 306). The prekerygmatic Jesus church continues to remain within the scope of the tradition. To the extent that the followers of the earthly Jesus or of the Baptist who found themselves in that church did not later join the church confessing the Christ kerygma (Acts 18:24ff.; cf. 19:1ff.; Schmithals 1982, 171ff.), they were considered by the church fathers to be Judaizing sectarians (cf. Iren. 1.26.2; 3.21.1; 4.33.4; 5.1.3; Hipp. *Haer.* 7.34; Tert. *Haer.* 33; Origen *Contra Celsum* 5.61; Euseb. *Hist. Eccl.* 2.27; Epiph. *Haer.* 28.6.1; Hilgenfeld 1884, 421ff.; Klijn-Reinink 1973). The fact that this theologically deficient church and its tradition nevertheless became significant for the theological history of early Christianity is related to a historical development that is seen above all in the complex theory of the messianic secret in the Gospel of Mark.

The Messianic Secret
and Its Revelation

Wrede, in his impressive book *Das Messiasgeheimnis in den Evangelien* [The Messianic Secret in the Gospels] (1901), understood the theory of the messianic secret in the Gospel of Mark as an auxiliary hypothesis with which the early church attempted to establish a balance between the nonmessianic memories or traditions of Jesus' life and message, on the one hand, and the christological confession that rested on the Easter experience, on the other. For Mark, writes Wrede, the motifs of the messianic secret theory came together with his traditions, but they had to be older than the mass of Jesus narratives passed down in these traditions, which were open and by origin christological. Thus the evangelist Mark is by no means the creator of this theory, as Wrede was often misunderstood later. Rather, the oldest evangelist was, according to Wrede, a writer of limited ability, who "awkwardly sought to form history out of ideas" and "actually did not think from one point in his presentation to the next" (1901, 132, 135); he found the individual motifs of the messianic secret theory already in his sources and imposed them on all his material. "Historically, the idea cannot be understood at all directly from Mark. It was already there; Mark stood under its power, and thus one must not even speak of a 'tendency'" (1901, 145). "It would indeed be very highly desirable if such a Gospel were not the oldest" (1901, 148).

Later research has not supported this critical evaluation of the writer Mark. Moreover, studies in form and redaction criticism have come to the now generally accepted conclusion that the messianic secret theory involves a redactional tendency of the evangelist himself. This, however, negates the explanation with which Wrede had interpreted this complex of motifs. For it is impossible to accept the idea presupposed by Wrede that *one* Christian community passed on unchristological traditions *as such, until the time of Mark,* and that it was the evangelist himself who amalgamated them with christological traditions, using a secret theory that he himself had developed. The situation is different, however, if one has recognized that there was an independent strand of nonmessianic sayings tradition reaching into Mark's time, which was preserved and passed on by its own circle of bearers. For with this presupposition, the interpretation of the messianic secret complex proposed by Wrede can be combined with the insights of later redaction criticism, and the result is that the theory of the messianic secret goes back to the evangelist Mark and serves to make understandable the existence of the nonmessianic Jesus tradition in a situation in which the Christian church had long looked back on a messianic or messianized life, work, and teaching of Jesus. At the same time it also serves to demonstrate the deficient character of the unchristological tradition and win its bearers to the *Christian* church.

With this presupposition the early history of the Son of Man sayings proves to be the key to an essential development within early Christian theological history. The Christian church of all theological persuasions, which was guided by the kerygma of the passion and Easter, never applied to Jesus the title *Son of Man,* which is found exclusively in the old sayings tradition (Q^1) and the traditions coming from it. This is especially easily explained if Vielhauer (1965, 55ff., 92ff.; cf. Schürmann 1975; Teeple 1965) is correct and Jesus himself announced only the imminent kingdom of God and not the coming Son of Man. It would indeed have been unusual if the early church that confessed Jesus as the Christ had ignored the only messianic title that is found in Jesus' own proclamation. Thus we must assume that the apocalyptic Son of Man sayings in the sayings tradition were not passed down originally by the followers of Jesus but belonged instead to another area of tradition in the environment of the movement around the Baptist and Jesus. Yet it would also have been understandable if in the context of the *fulfillment* event of Easter, the confession of Jesus as the *Christ* and *Son of God* had, from the beginning, displaced the title *Son of Man,* which belongs on the level of salvific *expectation.* In any case, the figure of the Son of Man belongs only to the early sayings tradition (Q^1), which goes back to Jesus' proclamation, yet was also fed by other apocalyptic traditions. This tradition takes no notice of Easter and the Christology connected with Easter, or of the kerygma of incarnation and the passion of Jesus. Thus the bearers of this tradition are to be sought outside the *Christian* church. They probably lived in Galilee.

Mark, who wrote some time between 75 and 90, encountered these traditions and their bearers, who presumably left Palestine as a result of the Jewish war. He asked himself how there could be a nonmessianic Jesus tradition, whose authenticity he did not dispute, and solved this puzzle with the help of the messianic secret theory, which he extrapolated as well as he could from the complex motifs in the traditions he had before him. Apparently he was guided in his enterprise not least of all by the missionary interest of winning the followers of the earthly Jesus to the *Christian* church.

In this context an especially important role was played by the *Son of Man* title, in addition to the commandment of silence, the disciples' lack of understanding, the esoteric instruction of the disciples, and the parable theory. Mark is convinced that in the nonmessianic sayings tradition Jesus used—always in third person— the title *Son of Man* as a *veiling self-designation,* in order not only to assert his sovereignty but also to be able to continue working. The Galilean followers of Jesus, however, who passed on Jesus' Son of Man sayings, *consistently* misunderstood Jesus' words, according to Mark, because he did not reveal his secret until Jerusalem; for only before the Sanhedrin (Mark 14:62) does Jesus identify himself expressly as the Son of Man (who is coming *again;* cf. 13:26). In order to clarify this misunderstanding, Mark chooses as examples from the prechristological sayings tradition two logia about the coming Son of Man (8:38 and 13:26), which he comments on accordingly and makes the basis of the Son of Man sayings that he himself forms. Mark 13:26 receives its commentary in 14:62, but 8:38 is immediately explained by two expansions added by the evangelist. For Mark writes, on the one hand, going beyond his source: "Those who are ashamed of me *and of my words* . . ." (cf. 8:34). Through this addition he joins the proclamation and person of Jesus together in such a way that in keeping with the church's Christology, Jesus himself becomes the content of his proclamation, including his announcement of the Son of Man. A corresponding intention also determines the other expansion, namely, the words "his Father," which are related to the Son of Man only in this passage. If God is the "Father" of the Son of Man, then the Son of Man is no longer only the eschatological judge but also and above all the "Son" of the Father, that is, the "Son of God" (Mark 1:11; 9:7; 13:32). Hence the equating of Jesus, Christ, Son of God, and Son of Man publicly and directly before the Sanhedrin in Mark 14:61–62 is already a hidden part of the proclamation of Jesus in Galilee, according to 8:38.

The two Son of Man sayings about the coming judge, which were adopted from the sayings tradition and are possibly authentic, were reinterpreted by Mark to refer to the coming Christ and are the basis of the sayings formed by the evangelist himself about the suffering and resurrected, as well as presently active, Son of Man. In these sayings the identification of the coming Son of Man of Jesus' proclamation with Jesus himself as the Christ of the church's confession becomes clearer than in the original sayings. For in the redactional sayings of these two categories the Son of Man is given functions or destinies, which, especially when regarded from the Easter viewpoint, can only be related to Jesus himself: the Son of Man forgives sins; he abolishes the law; he is condemned by the Sanhedrin and handed over to the Gentiles, by whom he is mocked, spat upon, flogged, and killed; he gives his life as a ransom for many and is raised from the dead on the third day. When Mark makes a logion of the sayings tradition the basis of his redactional formation in 14:21, his interest becomes especially clear, as it did in 8:38 and 14:62 in his going back to prechristological tradition: for the bearers of this tradition, which they only inadequately understand, he wants to emphasize the real meaning. According to the evangelist's intention, the outwardly unconnected *juxtaposition* of the sayings of the coming Son of Man and those of the suffering and resurrected Son of Man, which becomes especially clear in the relationship of 8:31 and 8:38 (Bultmann 1967d, 276), is supposed to instill in the consciousness of readers an insight into the *unity* of all Son of Man sayings, that is, the identification of the expected judge with the coming Christ. In all his new formations Mark must naturally maintain speech in third person, because only in this way of speaking can the Messiah/Son of Man *secret* be expressed. This gives rise to the stereotypical third person manner of speaking, which is always maintained in the later Gospels and abandoned only by Luke in Acts 7:56.

If Mark has the sayings of the betrayed, suffering, and resurrected Son of Man spoken only during the teaching of the disciples and outside of Galilee (or during an incognito stay in Galilee: Mark 9:31), then this state of affairs agrees with the observation, which Mark must have also made, that the Son of Man sayings from the prekerygmatic sayings tradition are silent about the passion and Easter; thus in Galilee Jesus cannot have spoken publicly about the suffering, death, and resurrection of the Son of Man. At the same time, this state of affairs also tells once again that the bearers of the old sayings tradition had their home in Galilee and probably did not leave Jesus' homeland until the confusion of the Jewish war.

Thus what was already seen essentially correctly by Wendling (1908, 204ff.; cf. Brandt 1893, 566) is confirmed by the analysis of the Son of Man sayings of the Gospel of Mark: before Mark there was no Son of Man title for Jesus in the tradition of the church; it was Mark who introduced it into the Synoptic tradition by adopting it from the prechristological Jesus tradition; he did this at first in a veiled way and then in 14:62 in the openly christological sovereign title of the usual confession of Christ, which had not previously occurred as such. Consequently there was never a special Son of Man Christology. Besides the two mentioned and possibly authentic Son of Man sayings of apocalyptic provenance, Mark adopted into his Gospel some other sayings from the prekerygmatic tradition, which are also found as "doublets" in the sayings source Q (Laufen 1980), in order to demonstrate the identification of the Christ Jesus of the church's confession with the teacher and prophet of the sayings tradition.

After the Gospel of Mark (Wellhausen 1905, 73ff.; Jülicher and Fascher 1931, 344ff.; Bultmann 1908, 127) the sayings material was edited completely, or at least more completely, in the form of the sayings source, especially with christological revision and expansion (Polag 1977). Also going back to this redaction is the present form of Luke 7:34 par. and 9:58 par., two logia in which Jesus refers to his own earthly activity in third person as the work of the Son of Man, and which, like the analogous Markan sayings, have the function of placing under the sign of Christology the numerous sayings about the coming Son of Man from the sayings tradition. It is quite conceivable that the author or redactor of the sayings source Q and the evangelist Mark are identical; Luke 10:22–24 par., a part of the sayings source Q, contains the *Markan* secret theory (Schmithals 1980, 125–26), and the Baptist narratives that we find in Mark 1 underlie the Baptist stories in the sayings source Q.

Apparently the Gospel of Mark and the sayings source were passed down together and in this way reached both Matthew and Luke in the same form. In any case, the sayings source Q was composed as an expansion of the Gospel of Mark, which it presupposes. Therefore we must not inquire about an independent position of the sayings source Q in the life of the church. It served the ecclesiastical approbation of the traditional material of the bearers of the prechristological sayings tradition and eased its entrance into the Christian church; presumably this was also its real purpose. In any case, the traditions of the sayings source Q in themselves never formed the doctrinal foundation of the early Christian church. Therefore it is logical that this early Christian writing was not considered in the formation of the canon. Yet through the Gospels of Matthew and Luke, its material was conveyed to the church and consequently has become theologically influential in various ways since the second century (see pp. 322ff. below).

3

Kingdom of God and Kingdom of Christ: A Pre-Pauline Tradition in 1 Cor. 15:20–28

In 1 Cor. 15:1–58 and 16:13–24 we have an independent letter of Paul to Corinth, which lacks only the epistolary opening, that is, the preface and thanksgiving. The body of the letter opens with 15:1 and in form resembles Gal. 1:11 (cf. 2 Cor. 1:8; Phil. 1:12; Rom. 1:13; etc.). The closing of the letter is fully preserved in 16:15–23.

The relatively early time of this letter's composition within the Pauline correspondence with Corinth is indicated above all by the fact that Paul concludes from the denial of the resurrection by the Corinthian heretics (15:12, 29) that they rejected any expectation of the hereafter (15:19, 29–30); at this point he has not yet recognized the dualism and ecstasy of the heretics who teach the immortality of the *pneuma* after liberation from the body. In 15:8–9 we also learn that Paul still does not have to defend himself against attacks on his apostolic authority, as he will in his later correspondence (cf. Schenk 1969, 223ff.).

Even if one wants to allow this dating and its underlying literary analysis only as a possibility, it is advisable for methodological reasons to interpret 1 Corinthians 15, both as a whole and in detail, on its own terms and on the basis of the state of Paul's knowledge as perceived in this part of the correspondence (cf. Doughty 1975, 76) and to give only limited consideration to the remaining correspondence. The significance of this methodological suggestion will be seen above all in the interpretation of the especially controversial passage 1 Cor. 15:20–28, in which already traditional material is sometimes presumed.

The Train of Thought in 1 Corinthians 15

In 15:1–11, without naming an immediate stimulus, Paul gives the reason for his comments: *Christ has risen*. As is widely recognized today, he employs in support of this statement a set formula of instruction or confession that he himself had already received and passed on to the church in Corinth. The general view is that this formula comprises 15:3b–5. With the remembrance of this tradition, which was generally recognized in the churches, and with the enumeration of further eyewitnesses of the resurrected One in 15:6–8 (10), Paul's purpose was not to deliver a historical proof for the resurrection of Jesus; rather, his intention, which is expressly named in 15:11, is to stress, in opposition to the heretics, the *consensus* of Christendom regarding the proclamation that "Christ has been raised" (Barth 1970, 517–18).

In the following section, 15:12–19, Paul places over against his repeated consensus ("Christ is proclaimed as raised from the dead") the assertion of "some" in Corinth that "there is no resurrection of the dead." The proclamation of the resurrection of Christ from the dead refutes the assertion that there is no general resurrection of the dead, for as Paul argues in 15:13 and repeats in 15:15b and 15:16, if there is no resurrection of the dead, then Christ cannot have been raised either. In 15:14 and 15:17–19 he lists the devastating consequences of this false assertion. Paul does not specifically formulate the argumentation presupposed in 15:12–19, namely, that the resurrection of the dead and the resurrection of Christ as a special case of the general resurrection of the dead are inseparably bound together, and that therefore the one stands or falls with the other and in this sense the resurrection of Jesus assures the resurrection of Christians. This observation has led some scholars to the view that the heretics in Corinth disputed the general resurrection of the dead but not the resurrection of Jesus (Conzelmann 1969, 303–4). But apart from the fact that such a divided view is hard to relate to the history of religion, and also apart from the fact that Paul in no way holds the heretics to be inconsistent at this point, but rather *confronts* them with the proclamation of the resurrection of Jesus from the dead, the apostle expressly adds the presupposition of his argumentation in 15:20–23: Christ is the "first fruits" (*aparchē*) of those who are resurrected from the dead. In this sense, already in 15:13–19 everything points "to the inseparable connection between the resurrection of Christ and of Christians" (Sellin 1986, 264).

The third section, 15:20–28, like the two previous ones, is also introduced by Paul with the signal, "Christ has been raised from the dead" (15:20a). With the explanation given in 15:20 and repeated in 15:23, that the resurrected Christ, as such, is the "first fruits of those who have died," Paul describes, in the interest of his argumentation, the resurrection of Jesus as the first act of the general resurrection from the dead. With this explanation the apostle reaches the goal of his previous comments: the proclamation of the resurrection of Christ from the dead implies the confession of the general resurrection of the dead. And with this explanation Paul returns to the earliest, prechristological interpretation of the Easter experience in the circle of disciples, an interpretation that still operates entirely on the apocalyptic level of the preaching of the earthly Jesus and is also visible in Rom. 1:4; 1 Cor. 6:14; Col. 1:18; Rev. 1:5; Matt. 27:52–53; Acts 26:23; *1 Clem.* 24.1. Käsemann completely misses the main point of the Pauline argumentation when he has Paul say that Christ's resurrection is "for the time being still the great exception in which we participate in no way other than in hope" (1964c, 128). However right this may be in itself, it does not express Paul's idea. Rather, like the apocalyptic interpretation of the Easter event already adopted by him, Paul understands the resurrection of Jesus as the beginning of the general resurrection of the dead, and thus what interests him is not the time interval between the two but their essential unity. "The term *aparchē* implies that the rest will follow" (Weiss 1910, 356; cf. Barrett 1968, 350–51; Baumgarten 1975, 100–101; Hill 1988, 299).

In this sense the hardly transparent argumentation in 15:21–22 is also to be understood as a reduction of Jesus' resurrection to the status of a precedent for the general resurrection of the dead. The core of this argument is traditional, as shown by the parallel in Rom. 5:18–19. The original sense of the independent tradition becomes evident in the Romans passage: human beings, as sinners and as righteous people, are of primary importance, not their separation into Jews and Gentiles (cf. Schmithals 1988b, 170ff.). Thus the tradition itself confronts the Jewish particularistic consciousness of election with Christian universalism: all people, without distinction, are justified through Christ, just as all, without distinction, sinned in Adam.

Yet this traditional and original idea no longer defines 15:21–22. Although the traditional *all* is still found in 15:22, it is no longer emphasized in the sense of universalism. Already in 15:21 the stress is entirely on "through a *human being.*" Paul points to the *human nature* of Jesus with the intention of understanding Jesus as "first fruits" of the remaining dead; in this way he is able to underline his argument that the proclamation of Jesus' resurrection excludes any denial of the general resurrection. But 15:22 explains more precisely the sentence thus understood in 15:21 (cf. Barrett 1968, 351). The "all" in 15:22b includes only Christians, as 15:23 shows. Paul's intention once again is to establish the inseparable connection between the resurrection of Christ and that of *all* Christians ("all will be made alive in Christ") and therefore "the certainty of the resurrection of Christians" (Doughty 1975, 80–81; cf. Hill 1988, 305; Wilcke 1967, 72ff.). As the believer is inseparably bound in death to Adam, so also in life to the Christ who died and rose (cf. 1 Thess. 4:13–14; 2 Cor. 4:14). The difference consists only in the *tagma,* the place in the order of events, and in this sense Paul can summarize his argumentation concisely: "Christ the first fruits, then at his coming those who belong to Christ" (15:23a). Here again it is not at all a question of the order of events but, as the antistrophe "Christ . . . those who belong to Christ" indicates, of Christ and Christians belonging together (cf. Sellin 1968, 263; Doughty 1975, 80–81).

Yet the different *tagma* of Christ and the Christians includes a qualitative — namely, christological — difference, which is likewise indicated in 15:22, and this christological difference is also implied in the announcement following in 15:24 that Christ will ultimately hand over his *kingdom* to God. The understanding of the following idea, however, is difficult; the train of thought does not seem to proceed smoothly. Therefore Barrett (1968, 353–54) connects 15:20–22 with 15:12–19 but holds that 15:23–28 is a relatively independent course of argumentation. Consequently 15:24–28 requires a separate discussion, and the emphasis of the present study will be on the analysis of this passage, which contains a pre-Pauline tradition that is instructive in terms of theological history.

In 15:29–34 Paul expands the theological argumentation carefully built up in three steps in 15:1–28, first through an argument *ad hominem:* the deniers of the resurrection are inconsistent when they have themselves baptized on behalf of the dead (15:29). Then the apostle refers to his willingness to sacrifice himself, which would be meaningless without the expectation of the resurrection from the dead (15:30–32a; without this expectation everyone could live from day to day). Finally, he closes with the admonition not to be disturbed by false teachers.

The next section (15:35–55), in contrast to the previous comments, was not conceived as a letter. Here we have, in the form of a diatribe, an instructional text whose ideas come, without exception, from the Hellenistic synagogue. The objection in 15:35 comes from a "Hellenist," for whom the restoration of the material body at the resurrection of the dead would seem to be absurd. In 15:36–44 Paul, who as a Jew cannot imagine a bodiless existence, offers the ontic possibility of a resurrection body. In 15:45–49 he adds to this a scriptural proof (yet v. 46 is probably a post-Pauline marginal gloss; cf. Weiss 1910, 376). The instructional statement in 15:50 rejects the objection of 15:35 and the preceding argumentation in final and summary fashion. Then follow in 15:51–52 an additional apocalyptic instruction and in 15:53–57 a climax that becomes hymnlike and returns to epistolary style — in 15:56 we no doubt have, as in 15:46, a secondary marginal gloss (cf. J. Weiss 1910, 380). With the christologically shaped doxology of 15:57 (cf. 2 Cor. 8:16; 9:15) Paul takes up the epistolary style again. The preceding teaching text in 15:35–55 is only loosely connected with the concrete situation in Corinth and therefore may be neither explained in detail based on this situation nor directly considered in the interpretation of 15:1–34. The closing admonition in 15:58 and 16:13–14 is already a part of the close of the letter, which extends to 16:23.

The Literary Problem of 15:20–28

The problem of 15:24–28 consists, first, in the lack of clarity in the thought process (cf., e.g., Hill 1988 with Lambrecht 1990), but above all in the problem of fitting these verses into Paul's train of thought. Their subject is neither the resurrection in general nor specifically the connection between Jesus' resurrection and the resurrection of Christians; it is instead "the end," that is, the "end of the age" (Matt. 28:20; 1 Cor. 1:8; 10:11; etc.), which will be completed in the handing over of the "kingdom" to the Father (15:24a, 28). In the context of this theme, the kingdom of Christ is described first in regard to its task of subjugating or annihilating the enemies of God and then in regard to its limitation. It is only in this connection that we find in 15:26 the one direct reference to the main thought in 1 Corinthians 15: death is the last enemy (cf. Lindemann 1987, 89).

> [20] But in fact Christ has been raised from the dead, the first fruits of those who have died. [21] For since death came through a human being, the resurrection of the dead has also come through a human being; [22] for as all die in Adam, so all will be made alive in Christ. [23] But each in his own order: Christ the first fruits, then at his coming those who belong to Christ. [24a] Then comes the end, [24b] when he hands over the kingdom to God the Father, [24c] after he has destroyed every ruler and every authority and power. [25a] For he must reign [25b] until he has put all his enemies under his feet. [26] The last enemy to be destroyed is death. [27a] For "God has put all

things in subjection under his feet" [cf. Ps. 8:6]. [27b] But when it says, "All things are put in subjection," it is plain that this does not include the one who put all things in subjection under him. [28a] When all things are subjected to him, [28b] then the Son himself will also be subjected to the one who put all things in subjection under him, [28c] so that God may be all in all.

The transition to the theme of the "end" is accomplished in 15:23 with a clear break in the thought. All three "orders" (*tagmata*) named in 15:23 are related to the "all" who will be made alive, yet this relationship is not relevant for the words "then comes the end." Attempts have been made to meet this difficulty by translating the Greek word *telos* as "remnant" (= those remaining) instead of as "end" (J. Weiss 1910, 357–58; Lietzmann 1949, 80; Wallis 1975) and identifying this remnant with the unbelievers, who would consequently be raised in the third order after Christ and Christians. At the same time, one was able with this interpretation to achieve a balance with the presentation of a double resurrection in Revelation 20 (thus Kreitzer 1987, 131ff.). Yet *telos* does not mean "remnant" but "end" or "goal." In addition, the idea that the resurrection of unbelievers will follow when Christ hands the kingdom over to God the Father hardly makes sense, since Paul leaves absolutely no time interval between the Parousia and the consummation (Kümmel in Lietzmann 1949, 193). Moreover, Paul speaks elsewhere only of the resurrection of believers, and since according to 15:22b all are made alive "in Christ," unbelievers can hardly be in the picture. Finally, in 15:24 Paul describes the "end" expressly as the handing over of the kingdom of the Son to the Father, not as a third act of the resurrection (cf. also Wilcke 1967, 85ff.).

Thus, as is generally recognized today, beside the first two "orders" Paul places "a disparate element" (Kümmel in Lietzmann 1949, 193), and he changes the theme with the phrase "then comes the end." The entire statement in 15:23, which essentially is only a variation of 15:20, probably serves especially to introduce this change of topic: after the resurrection of Jesus, which is already completed, come his Parousia and the resurrection of Christians, and then the handing over of his power and kingdom to the Father. Before 15:23 Paul relates the resurrection of Christ, in accordance with the context, only to the resurrection of Christians—that is, in its original, apocalyptic sense. In 15:24–28, however, it is interpreted christologically as "exaltation": the resurrected One sits at the right hand of God, exercises his lordship, and prevails against the enemies of God (cf. Matt. 28:18ff.; Phil. 3:21; Eph. 1:20ff.; 2:5–6; 1 Peter 3:22; Col. 2:12ff.; Heb. 1:3–4; Mark 16:15ff.), in order finally to hand his kingdom over to God. This raises the question of what 15:24–28 means in the context of the present letter.

Paul's Intention in 15:23–28

Only with reluctance does one follow the view of Lietzmann and others (cf. Lindemann 1987, 105ff.) that "the end" is described by Paul "in a brief apocalyptic excursus in verses 25–28 without any close connection with the main topic" (Lietzmann 1949, 81); it is "an apparently irrelevant digression" (Freeborn 1964, 558). The texts of 1 Cor. 15:1–58; 16:13–24 are too carefully thought out for such an unmotivated digression to seem probable. Furthermore, the theme of this little letter, the annihilation of death, is found in 15:(24–)26 and is therefore sufficiently clear even in this alleged digression.

One kind of interpretation of 15:24–28, which is found in many variations, sees Paul involved in a disagreement with enthusiasts in Corinth. Schniewind has Paul telling the Corinthians, who feel superior to the demonic powers, that the annihilation of these powers is yet to come, and that the last two of the three eschatological acts (15:23–24) "have *not yet* occurred" (1952, 123). Schniewind's view is followed by Güttgemanns (1966, 70ff.)—Jesus is only the "first fruits"; the cosmic powers are *not yet* subjugated—and from this understanding of 15:24–28 he concludes that the Corinthian heretics assert in the sense of 2 Tim. 2:18 that they are already "raised," namely, as pneumatics who in essence are identical with Christ. Similarly, Käsemann (1964c, 127ff.) holds that for Paul it was a question of anchoring the "present eschatology of the enthusiasts" apocalyptically and thereby keeping it within bounds; for the time being Christ's resurrection is still the great exception, and the perfection of the kingdom of Christ is yet to come. Wolff especially emphasizes extensively the alleged "strictly temporal orientation of statements" in 15:23–28, with which Paul "corrects an enthusiastic anticipation of the resurrection" (1982, 177ff.). Moreover, he sees the humanity of Jesus (15:21) stressed against spiritualism and perceives even in the emphasis on the sole sovereignty of God (15:24, 28) a protest against the pneumatics' claim of sovereignty. Cf. further Brandenburger 1962, 71–72; Freeborn 1964, 557ff.; Barth 1970, 515ff.; Robinson and Köster 1971, 31–32; Schweizer 1975, 303; Becker 1976, 80ff.; Lindemann 1987, 106–7.

Such scholars as Sellin (1986) and Doughty (1975) have correctly objected to this interpretive model. At no point in 15:20–28 does Paul seek to emphasize a temporal separation, but rather "the fact that Christ and Christians belong together" (Sellin 1986, 263), as is appropriate in the context, in which the topic is the *certainty* of the resurrection, not the fact that it has not yet come (cf. Luz 1968, 337; Doughty 1975, 77–78). The "first fruits" (15:20, 23) announces the fulfillment; it does not refer to something yet to come; the future—"all will be made alive" (15:22)—is required by the context and as such is unstressed. The reference to the Parousia (15:23) contains a *not yet* no more than the mention of death as the *last* enemy (15:26), and the enumeration of the orders (15:23–24) names in apocalyptic fashion what must necessarily follow, but not what is still distant. The emphasis is on the victorious kingdom of Christ, not on the overcoming of the enemy that is yet to come. And in the hymnlike praise of God's sole sovereignty in the climax in 15:28, no one can derive a protest against the Corinthian opponents' claim of a present fulfillment, which is criticized in 1 Cor. 4:8. To this we must add the fundamental consideration that 1 Corinthians 15 is to be explained *on its own terms* and in the context of the information that Paul possessed at the time when he composed this section of the Corinthian correspondence.

At this time, however, he still regarded the Corinthian heretics, rightly or wrongly, as deniers of the resurrection who had no hope in death (15:29–34), not as dualistic enthusiasts. Methodologically, it is unreliable to understand Paul's argumentation in 15:23–28 in the light of the later correspondence.

Therefore a different view, represented, for example, by Luz (1968), Doughty (1975) and in essence also by Sellin (1986), correctly interprets 15:23–28 out of the immediate context of 1 Corinthians 15. "For Paul apocalypticism here is not a brake on an enthusiasm that anticipates God's activity but the means of bearing witness in the face of a lack of faith that abandons the future" (Luz 1968, 350), and in such a way that Paul "develops the certainty of the resurrection of the dead out of its necessity in the whole historical, apocalyptic scheme of things" (J. Weiss 1910, 362). Under these circumstances and in this sense, 15:26 is the central assertion: between the resurrection and the Parousia (15:23) the kingdom of Christ serves the purpose of destroying all demonic powers (15:24c) and subduing the enemies of God (15:25, 27a), the last of which is death (cf. Luz 1968, 348; Sellin 1986, 273). The "all" that is repeated no fewer than eight times (15:24c, 25, 27, 28ab), which Paul himself inserts into the passages he cites from Psalm 110 (15:25), forms the basis of the argumentation (cf. Barth 1970, 523; Baumgarten 1975, 104; Hill 1988, 302; Sellin 1986, 272ff.). If Christ must destroy *all* enemies, then this must also include the last and greatest: death. The repeated *emphasis* on the idea that *all things* are subject to Christ leads to a notable tension with the traditionally formulated climax in 15:28c, "so that God may be all in all," and it also gives rise to the exegetical explanation in 15:27b. Consequently that emphasis probably goes back to Paul not only in 15:25 but also elsewhere in 15:24–28.

The victory over the last enemy (cf. 15:57) is followed by the Parousia of Christ and the resurrection of Christians (15:23), as well as the "end," when Christ hands his kingdom over to God (15:24b, 28). If we understand 15:24–28 in this way, this part of the argumentation, which at first seems like a digression, fits well into the train of thought. Here 15:(22–)23 forms a connecting link with 15:20–21 (22): already addressed in 15:22 and going beyond 15:20–21, the christological difference between Christ on the one hand—who has not only arisen as first fruits but has also been exalted and installed in the heavenly kingdom—and dead Christians on the other is explained by Paul, along with the corresponding temporal difference within the basically unified process of the resurrection of the "first fruits" and all others who have fallen asleep. Paul's explanation is that the exalted Christ must first conquer death, which continues to hold Christians prisoner. Both the designation of Christ as the "first fruits" of those who have fallen asleep and the conception of the sovereignty of Christ over death unite to convey in 15:20–28 the certainty, which was shaken in Corinth, that Christians will also rise. The statement in 15:26 that death will be conquered as the last enemy forms the clear culmination in this argumentational context. Therefore to consider this very verse 15:26 (together with 15:24c) to be an "element of tradition" (Becker 1976, 85) is a gross exegetical error in judgment. Rather, 15:26 clearly incorporates into the epistolary context a tradition adopted by Paul.

The Pre-Pauline Tradition Used
in 15:20–28: Exaltation as *Kyrios*

Yet the insight into Paul's intention in 15:20–28 now also brings to light the "excess" that can be observed in 15:24–28, for it does not serve Paul's intention. The main topic here is the idea found in 15:24ab, 27b–28 that Christ will hand over his kingdom to the Father. This idea, which is placed thematically at the beginning in 15:24ab and is foreign to the context, encompasses the whole passage (15:24–28), whereas the motif of the victory of Christ over death, which fits the context, has been simply inserted into this main idea and could be removed from it with no difficulty. This observation is underlined by J. Weiss's reflection (1910, 360) on whether the sentence in 15:26, which is entirely related to the context, might be a secondary marginal gloss, even though the words *all his enemies* in 15:25 and *destroyed* in 15:24c, which clearly lead up to 15:26 ("The last enemy to be destroyed is death"), warn us decisively against the temptation to remove 15:26 from its context. Such a procedure would also essentially remove the link connecting 15:24–28 with the context, which must have been important to Paul himself.

Luz (1968, 346) assumes that for the presentation of the handing over of the kingdom of the Son to the Father, Paul adopted "a Christian apocalyptic tradition," although, according to Luz, this tradition cannot be further defined in scope, form, and *Sitz im Leben*. Supporting this assumption—in addition to the tensions with the immediate context, which must be examined more closely—is first the observation that otherwise the motif of the handing over of the kingdom to the Father plays no role in the present writing. Furthermore, a corresponding conception occurs nowhere else in Paul's letters; for him the confession *Kyrios Christos* is universal and not limited by time (cf. Phil. 2:9–11), the love of God remains connected with the person and work of Christ (Rom. 8:38–39), and the life of one who dies with Christ is an ongoing life with him (Rom. 6:8–11; 14:7ff.; 1 Thess. 5:10; 2 Cor. 5:14). Also, Paul speaks nowhere else of the *kingdom* (15:24b) or the *reigning* (15:25a) of Christ, and the absolute term *the Son* (15:28b), emphasized by *himself,* is unique in Paul. Finally, the abrupt transition from the hymnlike climax in 15:28 ("Here the chapter might end"—Barrett 1968, 361) to the sober continuation of the letter's train of thought in 15:29–34 ("The rhetorical questions begin extremely abruptly"—J. Weiss 1910, 362; cf. Luz 1968, 341) is understandable only if Paul is not composing freely in 15:28.

To the extent that these observations are convincing, however, Paul's use of such a tradition becomes a puzzle, for in speaking of the handing over of the kingdom of the Son to the Father, that tradition does not illuminate the Pauline argumentation in 1 Corinthians 15 but rather on the whole darkens it, particularly in regard to the idea also included in 15:24–28 that the exalted Christ will defeat death as the last enemy. Concerning this problem Luz attempts to help with the edifying statement that Paul spoke of the resurrection of Jesus "ultimately for the sake of God's divinity" (1968, 351)—an idea that is far from the context and is simply not to be conveyed by the continuation of the train of thought in 15:29–34. Nor does it become more enlightening when Sellin understands it "as a reaction to an implicit dualism of the Corinthian pneumatics" and with the idea that through the resurrection of the dead God validates his claim on the whole creation (1986, 276; cf. Wolff 1982, 184–85). This interpretation, which is also foreign to the context, cannot be derived from the originally Hellenistic, pantheistic expression, "God is all in all." The fact that Sellin himself (cf. Lindemann 1987, 106–7), who otherwise disputes, with good reason, the antienthusiast references in 15:20–28, nevertheless asserts such a thing for 15:24b, 27b–28 is less an explanation of the text than an expression of embarrassment. Even less helpful is the view of Baumgarten (1975, 105) that in 15:28 God is praised in a hymnlike way as the one who resurrects the dead.

A methodological observation can lead us out of this dilemma: as a rule Paul hands down set traditional formulations in toto, without shortening the passages that he quotes from his sources, even when he needs or can use only a single traditional idea or concept in his argumentation. Examples of such a procedure include Rom. 3:25; Phil. 2:6–11; Gal. 3:27–28; and also, of course, 1 Cor. 15:3–5. In these and other cases the "excess" beyond the context of the letter aids in the determination and reconstruction of the tradition. It is therefore to be assumed, in contrast to Luz's view, that the context-foreign statements in 15:24b, 27b–28, concerning the handing over of the kingdom of Christ to God, do not belong to an independent, self-sufficient tradition but are part of a greater piece of tradition that Paul was, for the most part, able to integrate appropriately into the context (cf. Becker 1976, 85–86). Also supporting this idea is the fact that one can hardly imagine a form-determined tradition that has as its subject only the *return* of the kingdom of Christ to God but not the earlier *handing over* to Christ by God; the clause, "he must reign until . . ." (15:25) presupposes a statement about Jesus' accession to sovereignty, that is, about his resurrection and exaltation.

We have already often noted that in the use of Ps. 110:1 in connection with the idea of the exalted Christ battling and defeating the powers hostile to God, which is present in 15:24–27, we are dealing with a fixed topos of tradition that is also found in Eph. 1:20ff.; 1 Peter 3:21–22; and Pol. *Phil.* 2.1 (cf. Loader 1978, 217). Thus there is no apparent reason for the assumption that in 15:20–28 Paul was the first to combine this tradition "with the tradition of the handing over of the kingdom of the Son to God" (Luz 1968, 346), when the latter could hardly have ever existed in isolation. The three mentioned passages speak in a fixed pattern of the resurrection of Jesus Christ, of his exaltation to God's right hand, and of the subjection of demonic powers. The hymn of Philippians also follows this schema in Phil. 2:9–11, even if it uses Isa. 45:23 instead of Ps. 110:1. It is the basis of Rom. 8:34 (resurrection and exaltation) in connection with Rom. 8:38–39 (impotence of temporal powers) and also radiates from Phil. 3:20–21; Col. 1:13; 2:12–15; 3:1; Heb. 1:3–4, 13; 2:6–8; 8:1; 10:12–13; 12:2; 1 Tim. 3:16; Acts 2:32–33, 34–35; and so forth. In addition, this schema is the basis of the second part of the pre-Pauline doctrinal formula in Rom. 1:3–4, when Rom. 1:4 asserts the resurrection of the dead, the resulting designation of Jesus as Son of God, and his powerful role as ruler.

In particular cases this pattern is variable and capable of different emphases as well as various expansions. In 1 Peter 3:18; Phil. 2:6–8; Rom. 8:32, 34; Col. 1:13; 2:12–15; 1 Tim. 3:16; Heb. 1:3–4; 10:12–13; 12:2, we find, in addition to resurrection and exaltation, the salvific *death* of Jesus or his *humbling*, and in 1 Peter 3:19–20 also Christ's *descent into hell* and his preaching among the dead. In Eph. 1:22–23 the idea of the victorious kingdom of Christ is specified in regard to him as the *head of the church*, in Acts 2:32–33 regarding the *sending of the Spirit*, in Acts 2:34–35; 5:30–31 regarding the *repentance of Israel*, in 1 Tim. 3:16 and Mark 16:19 regarding the *mission to the world*, in Pol. *Phil.* 2.1 regarding the *judgment* of the living and the dead, in Phil 2:10–11 regarding *adoration* by the whole universe, in Rom. 14:9 regarding *those who have died* in Christ, who are still under his kingdom. Rom. 8:34 speaks of the intercession of the exalted One in judgment; Phil. 3:20–21 and Mark 14:61 par., as well as 1 Cor. 15:23, speak of his Parousia. This breadth of variation and the capability of expansion of the traditional motif hinders attempts, undertaken above all in regard to Eph. 1:20ff. and 1 Peter 3:18ff., to reconstruct a definite source, for example, a hymn that sings of Jesus' resurrection, exaltation, and victory over powers; therefore such attempts (cf. Schille 1962, 103; Sanders 1965, 220ff.) are as a rule rather restrained. Deichgräber reconstructs from Eph. 1:20 a small "fragment" of a "hymn," yet with the proviso "that this reconstruction is burdened with many uncertainties" (1967, 164–65); he regards 1 Peter 3:18–22, however, as a passage in which the author assembles various traditional material "from kerygmatic formulas or hymnic material" (1967, 173). Luz speaks, without detailed analysis, of an "ancient liturgical piece" (1968, 344) that underlies Eph. 1:20ff.; Dibelius of a "kind of hymn" (1953, 64) as the traditional foundation of this passage. Bultmann (1967b, 293) regards a piece of tradition reconstructed by him from 1 Peter 3:18–22 as a confession or a fragment of a hymn; Wengst (1972, 163), who attempts a different, "naturally hypothetical" reconstruction, regards it as a hymn.

Thus the attempts to establish a firm tradition from Eph. 1:20ff. and 1 Peter 3:18–22, as well as Pol. *Phil.* 2.1 and 1 Cor. 15:23ff., and so forth, remain unsatisfactory. Nor are we enlightened by the information that each statement "depends on already present formulations but has not yet jelled into a set form" (Gnilka 1971, 94; cf. Deichgräber 1967, 173; Goppelt 1978, 241–42). In Paul's time formulas that were fixed, even if not invariable, were already normal and necessary, as shown, for example, by 1 Cor. 15:3–5; by contrast the individual formulations presupposed by Gnilka and others remain formless and without a *Sitz im Leben*. Also, the agreement in the overall conception of 1 Peter 3:21–22; Eph. 1:22ff.; Pol. *Phil.* 2.1; and 1 Cor. 15:23ff. (cf. Rom. 1:4; 8:34, 38–39) can hardly be coincidental, especially since it is in no way determined by the context. Therefore with Loader—who, however, also integrates the martyrological formula of the death of Christ into the original tradition—we must speak of "a catechetical chain or loose confessional affirmation" (1978, 212). Yet if it is not possible to gain a fixed formulation that underlies all these related texts, then this may be due to the fact that already at an early stage the logic of the original formulation was no longer meaningful enough or strong enough and therefore was richly varied, modified, and expanded in the ways described.

Whatever the situation may have been in the individual case, however, the "ideal" basic model of the original tradition can still be clearly recognized. *First there is an older and originally independent confession that God raised Jesus from the dead* (cf. Rom. 4:24; 8:11; 1 Cor. 6:14; 1 Thess. 1:10), which was probably still apocalyptic and prechristological (see pp. 6–7, 12ff. above); *then, on the basis of Ps. 110:1* (Ps. 68:18 in Eph. 4:8) *came the statement that the resurrected One was exalted as Kyrios to the right hand of God. Finally, as a detailed carrying out of this exaltation motif, also in connection with Ps. 110:1* (or Ps. 68:18), *we have the statement that the exalted One must defeat or has already defeated the powers hostile to God.* This *Kyrios* tradition is exclusively oriented toward Christology. It represents a possibly already hellenistic counterpart of the primitive christological confession that Jesus is the Messiah, and it must be as old as this confession. It is a self-contained, self-sufficient confessional or instructional formulation. "Ps CX 1 was used at a very early stage in the development of christological thought to interpret the meaning of the resurrection" (Loader 1978, 216).

As shown by 1 Cor. 15:23–24; Phil. 3:20–21; Pol. *Phil.* 2.1, for example, this tradition is linked in various ways with apocalyptic eschatology, out of which it grew as a continuing, christological interpretation of the simple assertion of the resurrection (Jesus has risen as the first fruits of those who have died); a relationship with the "imminent expectation" (of the end), however, can no longer be discerned (versus Loader 1978, 216). But tradition was open to the eschatological idea that the exalted one as the *Kyrios* is the heavenly ruler of the world and the Lord of his church (Eph. 1:22–23; 4:7–9; Phil. 2:10–11). This openness to various eschatological ideas apparently characterized the tradition from the beginning—and presumably by intention. Soteriological perspectives, by contrast, to the extent that they are not implicit in the eschatological defeat of the powers, were not originally found and probably did not yet exist at the time of origin of the described tradition. After they arose, however, they became connected with the older tradition as motifs of both the *theologia incarnationis* (Phil. 2:6–11) and the *theologia passionis* or *crucis* (1 Peter 3:18–22; Rom. 8:34; Heb. 10:12–13). And the pre-Pauline "faith formula" (Käsemann 1973, 356), "For to this end Christ died and lived again, so that he might be Lord of both the dead and the living" (Rom. 14:9), substantiates with the fact that the exalted Lord suffered death the comforting certainty that Christians who have died will also not be removed from his kingdom (cf. Heb. 2:14–15; 2 Tim. 1:10), an idea that one could later easily connect with the "descent into the kingdom of the dead," whether in order to fight against the powers of Hades (Rev. 1:18; Barth 1992, 85ff.) or to preach among the dead (1 Peter 3:19–20).

Thus in 15:20–28 Paul uses a characteristic and well-defined expansion of the described older confessional and instructional formulation.

Tradition and Pauline
Interpretation in 15:24–28

Pointing to the essentially pre-Pauline character of 15:24–28 are not only the observations already made that (1) the motif of the handing over of the kingdom of the Son to the Father in 15:24ab, 27b–28 is foreign to the context and non-Pauline both as a whole and in particular concepts, and (2) in early Christian lit-

erature there are clear substantive and formal parallels to the information in
15:24c–25 on the subjugation of powers hostile to God. Also striking are the many
often noted tensions and doublets in 15:24–28, which indicate the coming together
of tradition and Pauline interpretation. Worthy of note in this regard are four observations that are in part intertwined.

(1) First of all, we must mention the doubling of "when" (*hotan*), which occurs
both in 15:24bc and in 15:27–28. In 15:24 the second "when" clause is clearly subordinated to the first, which with the description of the "end" anticipates 15:28b
("then"); thus the second "when" clause introduces the discussion in 15:25–27 of
the events that precede the "end," namely, the handing over of the "kingdom" of
the Son to the Father. "The juxtaposition of the two temporal clauses could be explained by saying that Paul interprets in his sense an unfamiliar traditional statement in a second dependent clause" (Luz 1968, 343; cf. Koch 1986, 20, 244). In
the second doubling it is notable that the "when" in 15:27b is not used temporally
but conditionally; the "when" in 15:28a, however, is temporal. This difference can
be avoided if one follows an old recommendation that is linguistically possible and
translates 15:27b as follows: "But when he (Christ!) says, 'All things are put in
subjection,' then . . ." (Wilcke 1967, 106; Senft 1979, 200; Wolff 1982, 183; Lambrecht 1982, 502ff.). J. Weiss correctly objects: "This interpretation is very artificial; above all, the scene in which Christ makes a report to the Father on the
accomplished subjection is very theatrical" (1910, 360).

(2) In 15:27a we no doubt have a quotation from Ps. 8:7 (LXX; 8:6 in NRSV), as
shown by the following exegetical gloss with the quotation formula "when it says."
The change from second person in the text of the Septuagint ("you have put all things
under his feet") to the present third person is conditioned by the context, and *hypo
tous podas* instead of *hypokatō tōn podōn* (LXX) is a stylistic assimilation to the quotation in 15:25b (cf. Lindemann 1987, 100). If this assimilation occurs ad hoc, 15:25
cannot have been formulated by Paul but rather represents tradition. In harmony with
this observation is the fact that in 15:27a we do not have a quotation (versus Lindemann 1987, 96–97) but merely an allusion (Lambrecht 1982, 509–10) that follows
very freely the text of the Septuagint (Conzelmann 1969, 322ff.; Lambrecht 1982,
506–7; Koch 1986, 19–20). The possibility that the same author cited one of the two
related passages freely but quoted the other exactly is very unlikely.

(3) Verse 25b, like the quotation in 27a, speaks of the *subjection* of hostile powers. The aim is not the *destruction* of the enemies but the *weakening* and *submis-
sion* of the powers, as shown by the broad tradition in Phil. 2:10–11; 3:21; Eph.
1:20–21; 1 Peter 3:22; Col. 2:10, 15; Pol. *Phil.* 2.1; Heb. 2:5ff. and by the fact that
in the end the Son subjects himself to God as the powers do (15:28). By contrast,
15:26, the context-consistent key sentence of the intention pursued by Paul in
15:24–28, and the second "when" clause in 15:24c speak of "destroying" demonic
powers and death, an interpretation of the traditional motif that is required and
determined only by Paul's guiding interest in 1 Corinthians 15, namely, the
substantiation of the hope for resurrection of the dead (Becker 1976, 84). This
gives rise to the singular idea that Christ defeats the hostile powers and (then?) de-
stroys them, as well as to tension with 15:28, where the destruction of the universe

is plainly excluded. Furthermore, the connection of "defeat of the powers" (tradition) and "destruction of death" (Pauline redaction) produces the idea that the resurrected Christ also has power over death, a notion that is not previously attested (Becker 1976, 84).

(4) Finally, the striking change of subject in 15:24–28 is unusual, unclear, and controversial among scholars. Christ is without doubt the subject who hands the kingdom over to the Father in the "when" clause of 15:24b, as well as in 15:25a, which speaks of Christ's own sovereignty (versus Heil 1993). The subject of the intervening "when" clause in 15:24c, however, is God, according to Aono (1979, 26), who argues that here tradition (15:24b) and Pauline redaction (15:24c) meet, but this view is rightly contradicted by, for example, Barrett (1968, 357), Lambrecht (1982, 508–9), and Lindemann (1987, 93–94). Whether or not the subject changes between 15:25a and 15:25b and consequently whether Christ himself (thus the majority; cf. Wilcke 1967, 105; Luz 1968, 340; Conzelmann 1969, 334; Lambrecht 1982, 507; Wolff 1982, 182) or God puts his enemies under his feet (thus, for example, Barrett 1968, 258; Lindemann 1987, 95ff.; Heil 1993) is the topic of vigorous discussion. A change of subject within 15:25, however, would be difficult and could not be assumed at all unless "Paul actually consciously quoted Ps. 109:1 (LXX) and expected, moreover, the reader to recognize the quotation and know that the Psalms verse speaks of God" (Lindemann 1987, 96)—an extremely unlikely assumption. Baumgarten (1975, 104) believes a conscious ambiguity is possible. In the undoubtedly Pauline statement in 15:26, which is completely in harmony with the context, the acting subject is unnamed; a *passivum divinum* can be assumed only if we, like Aono (1979, 26–27), make God also the subject of "destroyed" in 15:24c. Those who see God already acting in 15:25b will also regard him as the acting subject in 15:27a, who subjects everything to Christ, especially since God is also the subject in the quoted Ps. 8:6 and he is expressly named as subject of the subjecting in 15:27b–28 (Lindemann 1987, 100). Those, however, who with most interpreters hold Christ to be the subject of 15:25b, who himself puts all enemies under his feet, face the question whether they see Christ also acting in 15:27a (Wilcke 1967, 105; Conzelmann 1969, 336; Baumgarten 1975, 104; Wolff 1982, 183; Lambrecht 1982, 510–11) or God, who subjects everything to Christ (J. Weiss 1910, 360; Luz 1968, 340). The change of subjects remains equally unsatisfactory whether it comes early in 15:25b, later in 15:27a, or not until 15:27b.

Therefore it is understandable that the judgments of interpreters are often ambivalent and uncertain (cf., for example, Luz 1968, 340; Barrett 1968, 358; Baumgarten 1975, 104). More convincing, by contrast, is Lietzmann's concise substantiation of his judgment that Christ must still be the subject in 15:27a: "This is clearly shown by 27b, for the correction would be meaningless if God is regarded as already the subject in 27a" (1949, 81; cf. Wilcke 1967, 105; Conzelmann 1969, 326); but the idea that 15:27b only "contains the—admittedly decisively emphasized—reference to an obvious state of affairs" (Lindemann 1987, 101) is not very helpful. In any case, the ambiguities of the change of subjects in 15:24–28 also suggest a solution that analyzes the coming together of pre-Pauline tradition and Pauline redaction.

The Pre-Pauline Tradition

On the basis of the foregoing observations we can reconstruct the tradition adopted by Paul with varying degrees of certainty. The beginning of the tradition with the confession of Jesus' resurrection is deduced from Eph. 1:20; 1 Peter 3:21; Col. 2:12; Pol. *Phil.* 2.1, and the confession speaks of *God* raising Jesus from the dead, as Eph. 1:20; Col. 2:12; and Pol. *Phil.* 2.1 say, along with the older formulas to be found in Rom. 4:24; 8:11; 1 Cor. 6:14; 2 Cor. 4:14; Gal. 1:1; 1 Thess. 1:10; 1 Peter 1:21; Heb. 13:20. The wording of Pol. *Phil.* 2.1 or Rom. 4:24 offers a possible formulation—first because of the formal introduction of the essentially identical confessions in these two passages:

> We believe in him who raised Jesus from the dead . . .

The simple "Jesus" instead of "Jesus Christ" in Pol. *Phil.* 2.1 is suggested because of the relevant parallels (Rom. 4:24; 1 Thess. 1:10; etc.) and because of the title *Son* found later in the tradition. Paul replaced this beginning of the tradition with the more comprehensive christological formula quoted in 1 Cor. 15:3–5, which he had received because of the listing of the oldest Easter witnesses, and with the repetition of its resurrection statement in 15:12, 15, 17, 20. Also in 15:15 we find that God is the express subject of the statement, whereas in the other passages the *passivum divinum* of 15:4 is continued.

Following the statement of the resurrection in the tradition is the announcement of Jesus' exaltation with reference to Ps. 110:1. On the basis of Eph. 1:20; Pol. *Phil.* 2.1; and Rom. 8:34, we may presume the following wording:

> . . . and seated him at his right hand . . .

In any case, God is still the subject (cf. Acts 5:31), not Jesus himself as later in Mark 16:19; Heb. 8:1; 10:12; 12:2. Paul did not quote this line either, yet he applies the idea of the exaltation to the right hand of God indirectly in the "christological distinction" of 15:20–23 and directly in the statements on the "kingdom" (15:24b) and on the reigning (15:25a) of the exalted One.

Verse 24ab forms the transition to the part of the tradition that is directly received and related by Paul, in accordance with his context, to the destruction of death; it speaks of the reigning activity of the exalted Jesus. With "then comes the end" (15:24a) Paul introduces somewhat abruptly (see above) the motif of the *kingdom* of Christ, thus anticipating the main idea of the following tradition: the handing over of the kingdom to the Father (cf. Hill 1988, 318). Under the given circumstances, this procedure is not awkward but results in the appearance of a non-Pauline formulation in 15:24b (cf. Luz 1968, 343). The motif of the transfer of the kingdom as such, however, comes from the tradition in 15:28; "kingdom" takes up the traditional "reigning" from 15:25, and the absolute "to the Father" reflects the corresponding phrase "the Son" in 15:28b. Thus the first "when" clause in 15:24b comes from Paul himself.

The second "when" clause in 15:24c, referring back to the time before 15:24ab, describes the nature and manner of the Son's reign. The already mentioned parallels identify this clause as primarily traditional. Yet the introduction, "after he has destroyed," comes from Paul. From the beginning he places his tradition, which spoke of Christ's *reign* over hostile powers, under the contextual viewpoint of the *destruction* of all powers and thus also of death. In this spirit he could also have introduced the double "every" with "ruler" and "authority and power" (see above). Yet the emphasis on the comprehensive reign of the Son was probably already in the tradition (cf. Phil. 2:10; 3:21; Rom. 8:38; Eph. 1:21; Pol. *Phil.* 2.1; etc.), and perhaps only the *second* "every" goes back to Paul. Therefore there is no reason not to regard the wording of 15:24c (cf. Eph. 1:21) as essentially from the tradition:

> . . . over every ruler and authority and power.

Thus the doublet of the two "when" clauses as found in 15:24 goes back to Paul, who with his second "when" clause has to move back before the time of the handing over of the kingdom already reached in the first "when" clause. Hence, as in 15:27–28, it is evoked by the joining of tradition and Pauline argumentation.

Verse 25 comes entirely from tradition. Originating with Paul, presumably, are only the "all," with which he enriched, for reasons already mentioned, the citation of Ps. 110:1 (cf. Sellin 1986, 273), and the substantiating "for" with which Paul announces 15:25 as an explanation of 15:24c and, in connection with 15:24c, defines more precisely the *subjection* of the temporal powers, of which tradition speaks, in terms of their destruction. In the pre-Pauline tradition, by contrast, 15:25 begins anew with the idea that the reign of the Son at the right hand of God serves the fulfillment of a particular task and as such is temporally limited:

> He must reign
> until he has put all his enemies under his feet.

The obvious change from *God* as subject in the preceding part of the tradition to *Jesus,* who is the subject in both parts of the sentence in 15:25, underlines the form and content of the new beginning.

Verse 26 comes from Paul and constitutes the aim and focus of his own argumentation in 15:24–28. Verse 27a underlines the context-consistent statement of 15:26. "The substantiating function of the . . . quotation in verse 27a lies . . . in *panta,* which shows that death cannot be excepted" (Sellin 1986, 273; cf. Wilcke 1967, 105). Thus 27a also comes from Paul's hand, as we already learned in earlier discussions. In 15:28a, which belongs to Paul's source, we find a mere *reference* to Ps. 9:6, which corresponds formally to the likewise traditional *reference* to Ps. 110:1 in 15:25; it does not emphasize "all," but rather the *subjection* of all powers. Paul doubles the reference by quoting Ps. 9:6 expressly in 27a, and since the "all" in this quotation is placed emphatically at the beginning, he has in this way—analogous to his procedure in 15:25—again underlined the tradition as he understands it.

In view of the fact that Paul's tradition was interested in the limitation of the power of Christ by the power of God, and because of the "all" thus emphasized in 15:27a, it seemed advisable for Paul to expressly exclude God from this "all" in

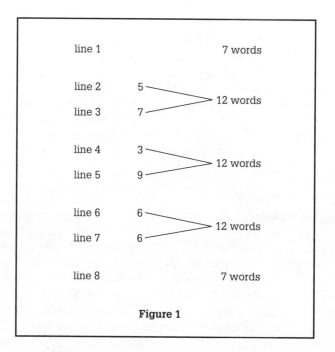

Figure 1

his exegetical explanation of 15:27b. In this way he also gained a smooth transition to the climax of his source in 15:28. Thus 15:27b likewise comes from Paul's pen. By contrast, 15:28 is part of and the end of the pre-Pauline tradition, with the exception of the expansion that belongs substantively to 15:27b: ". . . the one who put all things in subjection under him." These words, which allude to the "last enemy," again emphasizes "all" in accordance with the context.

Thus this tradition has the following overall form:

> We believe in him who raised Jesus from the dead
> and seated him at his right hand
> over every ruler and authority and power.
>
> He must reign
> until he has put all his enemies under his feet.
>
> But when all things are subjected to him,
> then the Son himself will also be subjected,
> so that God may be all in all.

Uncertainties, above all in the first three lines, must be taken into account. Yet the correctness of the reconstruction in principle is also supported by the symmetry of the word count in the eight lines and three sentences of the Greek text, as shown in Figure 1.

There is no disturbing change of subject here. In the first sentence the Father is the one who acts; in the second sentence the Son acts; in the third sentence, a sort of synthesis of the two previous sentences, the Son subjects himself to the Father so that God may be all in all. In this sense the idea is circular, and when the first and last lines are actually emphasized by each having seven words, this circular phenomenon is also made formally visible. In the reconstructed text neither Ps. 110:1 nor Ps. 9:6 is quoted, but the two related texts are alluded to, as is similarly the case in Pol. *Phil.* 2.1; Eph. 1:20–22; and 1 Peter 3:22 (cf. Phil. 3:20–21).

The *Sitz im Leben* and the Theological-historical Significance of the Tradition

To answer the question of the *Sitz im Leben* of a fixed formulation of tradition like the present one in the life of the church, we have the usual categories of creed, song, hymn, liturgy, and so forth. As a rule, the satisfactory classification into one of these categories has proved unsuccessful for the many formulations of set pieces of tradition identified or reconstructed by scholars. With the majority of the relevant texts it is probably a question of *teaching texts* that serve the instruction of either the congregation or primarily church leaders and teachers. Naturally, this origin does not exclude the liturgical or confessional use of appropriate instructional texts, for the baptismal confession evidently grew out of central teaching formulas. Be that as it may, in the present case we are without doubt dealing with a teaching text.

Yet the teaching in this instructional text is unusual. The New Testament does not otherwise speak of a temporal limitation of the kingdom of Christ, and the later development of christological dogma clearly excluded the subordinationism underlying this limitation. It is no accident that the thought of 15:24b, 28 caused the church fathers some embarrassment (cf. Schendel 1971; Lienhard 1983), and Dembowski (1969, 348) still concludes that "sharp content criticism is advised" in regard to this presentation. By contrast, Marcellus of Ancyra, who was ultimately judged a heretic, liked to refer to 1 Cor. 15:23–28 in his theology, which emphasized the unity of God. Yet already in the New Testament period the unconditional connection of the salvation of God with the salvific work of Christ, as well as the *Kyrios* Christology of Hellenistic thought and the *Logos* Christology of the Gospel of John, excludes the idea of distinguishing the sovereignty of Christ from the sovereignty of God on the basis that the former is provisional and incomplete.

Yet if this distinction occurs in the instructional text used by Paul in 15:20–28—even without a direct devaluation of the kingdom of Christ—there was probably a guiding apologetic interest. The announcement of the kingdom of Christ and the development of the *Kyrios* Christology, which underlies the present tradition, must have come into conflict with the strict monotheism of the Hellenistic synagogue. In the present teaching text this conflict is smoothed over in a thoroughly nontrinitarian way. The tradition used by Paul "teaches pure monotheism" (Wilcke 1967, 108). The christological confession itself remains intact, but theologically it is constrained in a monotheistic way. It is true that God raised and exalted Jesus to a sovereign position at his right hand, in keeping with Ps. 110:1, but he will get back the authority transferred to the Son as soon as the latter has fulfilled the eschatological, soteriological assignment given him by the Father and has forced the powers hostile to God into obedience.

Therefore it is no accident that the teaching text selects the "subordinationist" designation *Son of God* as christological title, although the biblical foundation of the presupposed exaltation Christology, Ps. 110:1, contains the title *Kyrios,* which was familiar to every Hellenistic Jew from the daily acclamation *of God.* Apparently this instructional text is immediately concerned with countering a ditheistic understanding of the spreading *Kyrios* Christology, a concern that is understandable in its particular *Sitz im Leben,* the apologetic effort of the Christian community within the synagogue, and was appropriately realized in this context. The statement as such, however, could not and cannot be established dogmatically. Even Paul, the missionary to the Gentiles, no longer shared the ideas underlying the teaching text; it is all the more understandable that in the postapostolic period the idea that the kingdom of Christ was limited temporally did not reappear. The tradition that was still familiar to Paul was forgotten, and its concern was taken up in the controversies leading up to trinitarian dogma and finally realized by the doctrine of the Trinity in the categories of Greek substance thought.

Paul himself is interested only in the assertion that the resurrected Son who is exalted to the right hand of the Father subjects all enemies; otherwise he quotes the apologetic teaching text without comment and without personal interest in its direct assertion. How much he reflected on it, we cannot say. Yet to the climax of the related hymn of Phil. 2:6–11, the confession that Jesus Christ is Lord, Paul himself adds the expansion "to the glory of God the Father." This is a clear reminiscence of the teaching text underlying 1 Cor. 15:20–28 (cf. especially 15:24b), which reveals how Paul probably understood the assertion that even Christ subjected himself to the Father: the salvific work of Christ and the confession of his kingdom happen for the glory of God (cf. Luz 1968, 351ff.; Schendel 1971, 24)! Thus he seems to have comprehended his source essentially doxologically and understood it in analogy to Rom. 11:36 and 1 Cor. 8:6.

We can now summarize the results of the present analysis for early Christian theological history. *At the beginning* stands the confession that God raised Jesus from the dead. This confession is directly connected with Jesus' preaching of the kingdom of God; it still moves completely within the context of apocalyptic expectation and understands Jesus' resurrection from the dead as the onset of the kingdom of God and as the beginning of the general resurrection of the dead. *Then* already at an early time, this confession is interpreted christologically ("Jesus is the Messiah"), with the help of Ps. 110:1 and, possibly under Hellenistic influence, also with the idea that as *Kyrios* he was exalted to the right hand of God and has the soteriological task of defeating powers hostile to God. Thus Jesus' preaching of the coming kingdom of God is related to Jesus' own heavenly kingdom. *Continuing* this history, early Christendom develops its fundamental christological confession through a wealth of borrowed and adapted christological (adoption Christology, preexistence Christology, etc.), soteriological (became human "for us," suffered, and so forth), and eschatological ideas, the last of which can also be directly connected with the still prechristological Easter confession (dying with Jesus in order also to be resurrected with him; see pp. 99ff. below). The other possibility is to validate its confession apologetically, which is the case in our present text.

4

Paul's Conversion Theology

The theology of the apostle Paul, as revealed by his extant letters, contains strata of different origin that can be distinguished with varying degrees of clarity. Paul's theological accomplishment consists not only in what he himself thought and formulated but also in the power with which he was able to adopt various directions and developments in early Christianity and combine them into what we call "Pauline theology." If we succeed in recognizing the stratifications in Paul's theology and separating the individual layers, we will gain insights into early Christian theological history that are conveyed to us only with difficulty by later traditions. Paul is both the oldest immediate witness of this history and by far the most valuable; with his help we can then illuminate the early roots of later testimonies in the history of Christian theology.

Of special interest in this connection is the theology of those early churches to whose confession Paul was converted—churches that he had vigorously persecuted according to his own testimony (Gal. 1:13–14, 23; 1 Cor. 15:9; Phil. 3:6) and the legendary report of the Acts of the Apostles (Acts 7:58; 8:1ff.; 9:1ff.). For there can be no doubt that Paul's "conversion theology" contains the theology that he himself had emphatically fought and which was connected with the person of Stephen according to the report in Acts; in any case, it cannot be identical with the theology of the original church in Jerusalem, since at the same time this church was apparently able to exist relatively unmolested by persecutors. As will be confirmed in detail in the course of the following investigation, the dualistic and Gnostic elements of Paul's theological language are characteristic of this conversion theology of his, and their specific provenance reveals that in Paul's letters they are by no means spread evenly over the entire writing and over all theological topics. Some discussions are defined by them; others are completely free of them. It is also significant that the Synoptic tradition contains none of these dualistic or Gnostic elements, whereas the Gospel of John is considerably influenced by them. In view of this Bultmann (1967a, 102) has indicated, not without reason, that one must "accept the fact that Johannine Christianity represents an older type than the Synoptic." In any case, in the realm of Paul's conversion theology we have an *early Christian* theological development in the real sense of this phrase.

Gnostic Language and Ideas in Paul

In Pauline theology Gnostic and dualistic ideas and terms are found primarily in two large areas: anthropology and ecclesiology. In regard to anthropology we must mention above all the dualism of "flesh" (or "body") and "Spirit," with whose help—for example, in Rom. 8:2–11 and in Gal. 4:21–31—Paul makes vivid the either-or of sin and grace or of law and gospel (cf. Rom. 7:5–6, 18, 25b; Gal. 3:3; 5:16–24; 6:8); this dualism is expressed especially bluntly in John 3:6 (cf. 1:13): "What is born of the flesh is flesh, and what is born of the Spirit is spirit." In the same sense in 1 Cor. 2:10–3:4 we have the "natural" people (*psychikoi*) or "people of the flesh" (*sarkinoi, sarkikoi*), for whom the divine is foolishness, and the "spiritual" people (*pneumatikoi*), who have the "mind of Christ" (cf. Rom. 7:14; see pp. 127ff. below). Also dualistic is the talk of the transitory outward self and the immortal inner self, which is found in 2 Cor. 4:6 and similarly in Rom. 7:22–25a (cf. Eph. 3:16) and is related to the image of the "treasure in clay jars" (2 Cor. 4:7–12) and the expectation of being able to take off the "earthly tent," in which we "groan," and of gaining a heavenly dwelling (2 Cor. 4:7ff.; 5:1ff.; Rom. 8:23–25). In the context of Paul's historical thinking, in the idea found in Rom. 7:14–25 that human beings are sold into sin and can no longer even recognize themselves in their fallen state, we find a reflection of the dualistic idea that the heavenly self of human beings is banished into the "body of death" (Rom. 7:24) and is robbed of its knowledge of its heavenly home (cf. Jonas 1954, 96, 113ff.).

The ecclesiological complex of dualistic, Gnostic language includes above all a characteristic linguistic field that is often summed up by representatives of the history-of-religions school with the catch phrase "mystical doctrine of redemption" or "mysticism of Christ." Central here is the idea of the assembly of Christians, or "spiritual" people, who are a part of the "body of Christ" (cf. Schmithals 1969, 32ff.). One is "baptized into" this body (1 Cor. 12:13; Gal. 3:27; see pp. 216ff. below), and the ritual formula of the meal celebration interprets the unity and the breaking of the bread for the many in the "body of Christ": "The bread that we break, is it not a sharing in the body of Christ? Because there is one bread, we who are many are one body, for we all partake of the one bread" (1 Cor. 10:16b–17). "Christ" or the "body of Christ" is identified with the fullness of the "Spirit" (Rom. 8:9–10; 1 Cor. 12:12–13), and thus believers share in the spiritual body of Christ (2 Cor. 13:13; Phil. 2:1) and the church or "Christ" is equated with the totality of the redeemed (1 Cor. 1:13; 12:12–13; Gal. 3:16; 3:27–29). This corresponds to the idea that we are in Christ and Christ is in us (Gal. 1:22; 2:20; 3:27–28; 4:19; Rom. 16:7; 2 Cor. 13:5; Col. 1:26–27), as well as the terse idea of being "of Christ," that is, a part of the body of Christ (1 Cor. 3:23; 15:23; Gal. 3:29; 5:24). The same idea occurs graphically in the image of the one body that is composed of various members, the spiritual people (1 Cor. 6:15; 12:13, 27; Rom. 12:5), and this image is immediately followed by Paul's teaching about ministries and gifts, both with regard to its fundamental enthusiastic structure (1 Cor. 2:10–16; 12:4ff.; Rom. 12:5) and in many individual traits (1 Cor. 12:8, 10, 28ff.; 14:18; 2 Cor. 5:11ff.; Gal. 1:1, 11–12; etc.): individual members have various gifts, but all gifts come from one and the same Spirit. Also noteworthy in this connection is the announcement of the spiritual universalism that transcends natural and social differences—"There is no longer Jew or Greek, there is no longer slave or free, there is no longer male and female; for all of you are one in Christ Jesus" (Gal. 3:28; cf. 1 Cor. 12:13; Col. 3:10–11)—which is linked with the devaluation of the particularistic Jewish law (Gal. 3:19–20). The opposition of "spirit" and "letter" has an enthusiastic origin (2 Cor. 3:6; Rom. 2:29; 7:6; cf. Rom. 10:5ff.), even if Paul frees this juxtaposition from its dualistic roots. Finally, let us also refer to the formulas of a present eschatology—according to which "being in Christ" already means the turn of the age (2 Cor. 5:17; Rom. 6:23; cf. Rom. 6:4, 11, 13; 8:1), even if the definitive redemption "out of the body" is yet to come (2 Cor. 4:16–18)—and to the corresponding instructions for life "in the Spirit" instead of "in the flesh" (Rom. 8:2ff.; Gal. 5:16–6:1).

In the background of the cited terms and ideas stands the mythic process in which a heavenly spiritual being falls into the power of demonic forces and is divided by them into many parts and enclosed in the prison of many material bodies, from which it frees itself through the newly awakened knowledge of its unlosable divine substance. Thus this terminology reflects a self-contained and complete dualistic system of fall and redemption. This system does not have a personal redeemer figure. The "body of Christ" itself, which is newly constituted by the liberation of the "spirit" from the "flesh," draws its scattered members to itself. That in this dualistic system we are dealing with a system of *Jewish* Gnosticism can be inferred from the fact that we can observe it in the background of the theology of the Jewish Christian Paul. This is demonstrated by the fact that the heavenly, earthly, both protological and eschatological, fallen and self-redeeming central figure, the "redeemed Redeemer" of the system, bears the name *Christ*. And it is confirmed by the observation that a *theo*logical or cosmic dualism of two equally original powers is foreign to the cited terms and ideas preserved in Paul's language; the system indirectly attested by his conversion theology was monistic (cf. Jonas 1954, 332–33), without any revelation of how to explain the origin of the demonic power or matter contrary to God out of the unity of God. Within this monistic structure the statement offered by Paul incidentally in Gal. 3:19–20—that God did not give the law himself but through the mediation of angels (cf. Schlier 1962, 157–58)—also remains a motif critical of the law, with whose help a Gnostic Judaism is opened up universally.

Preexistence Christology

In Jewish Gnosticism, which forms part of the background of Paul's conversion theology, *Christ* was the title of the mythic central figure, that is, the "proto-human being" imprisoned in bodies who reconstitutes himself out of his scattered members. In the Christianity that Paul persecuted and to which he was converted, *Jesus* must have been Christ in person, as already shown by the fact that this Jesus encounters Paul at his conversion as the resurrected and exalted Christ (1 Cor. 15:8). Yet these two Christologies cannot be combined. The language adopted from the mythos, "Christ in us" and "we in Christ," must therefore have been understood as *Christian* language, as we can sufficiently study in Paul, in the sense of a historical (*geschichtlich*) determination of human beings through the Jesus Christ of the church's confession. This observation addresses an essential aspect of the process that was carried out in the Christian adaptation of Jewish Gnostic language.

This process can be discerned and described more precisely. Paul reveals throughout that he is familiar with the ideas of preexistence Christology. This Christology is also found in formulaic material (cf. 2 Cor. 8:9; 1 Tim. 1:15; John 3:16; 5:24; Ign. *Eph.* 19.2):

> God [sent] his own Son in the likeness of sinful flesh, and to deal with sin, he condemned sin in the flesh. (Rom. 8:3)

> But when the fullness of time had come, God sent his Son, born of a woman . . . so that we might receive adoption as children. (Gal. 4:4–5)

These formulas speak of the *sending* of the Son. They presuppose his subsequent exaltation and return to the Father, but they do not represent an abbreviation of the formulas comprising humbling *and* exaltation. Rather, the latter (Phil. 2:6–11; 1 Tim. 3:16; Col. 1:15–20; John 3:13, 31; Heb. 1:1–4; etc.) are regarded as secondary combinations of the sending formulas with the likewise originally independent exaltation formulas (Rom. 1:4; 10:9; 1 Cor. 15:23–25; Mark 16:19; etc.). This formal observation by itself excludes the possibility that the humbling statements grew out of the concept of exaltation, as Hengel (1975, 106) and Hofius (1976, 73), for example, explain. And the notion that this "introduction of the preexistence idea into Christology" occurred "out of internal necessity" already in pre-Pauline times in the Palestinian primitive church without religious-historical influences from the outside (Hengel 1975, 105ff., 111–12) runs aground on the simple observation that for a long time preexistence Christology ocurred in only a relatively narrow strand of tradition. Hellenistic Jewish Christianity knows only adoption Christology (Rom. 1:3–4; Mark 1:9–11) and later developed the view of the virgin birth as it is found in the prehistories of the Gospels of Matthew and Luke. Not only did preexistence Christology remain foreign to the whole Synoptic tradition in all its strata, but also the "apostolic" baptismal creed has still not adopted it even today.

The origin of preexistence Christology can be illuminated only in religion-historical ways. "The human being Jesus became . . . actually only the bearer of all the powerful predicates that were already established" (Wrede 1905, 86). The corresponding derivation of the idea from the heavenly Son of Man, which has often been suggested, fails on the point that the Son of Man tradition and the preexistence idea are nowhere connected. Better substantiated is the favorite derivation of preexistence Christology from Jewish concepts of the preexistent wisdom that God sends to earth (Merklein 1979, 48ff.; Müller 1990, 14ff.). But the basic motifs of christological preexistence and the sending formulas, namely, *humbling* and sending for the *salvation* of humankind, do not come from the wisdom tradition, which consequently must have exercised only a secondary influence. More likely, therefore, is the derivation of preexistence Christology from the Gnostic myth of redemption, as widely advocated in the history-of-religions school (cf. Bultmann 1952, 10–11). It requires a notable correction, however, vis-à-vis the proposals of the history-of-religions school. For when Bultmann, for example, assumes that the idea of the incarnation of the Redeemer was "originally Gnostic," one must respond: "As far as we can know, none of the pre-Christian redeemer figures is a concrete figure" (Fischer 1973, 262). Nor do any of the Gnostic systems to be inferred from the New Testament scriptures presuppose a redeemer figure who is sent from heaven and at the same time is concrete and human. Jewish Gnosticism, which underlies the Pauline language, even clearly excludes such a figure, for it designates the *sum of the sparks of the Spirit* as the "Christ." In the early period of Gnosticism, redemption occurs through an original revelation, through a heavenly call, through the ecstatic prophet who acquires his information in an ascent to heaven, and above all through the redeemed themselves, who become active as redeemers: the already awakened spiritual people (*pneumatikoi*) raise those who are still sleeping (cf. Bultmann 1967e, 244ff.; Schmithals 1961, 103ff.). The earthly, human redeemer of the later Gnostic systems, who is completely the Christ of the church's proclamation, was probably of Christian origin (cf. Schenke 1973, 218).

Nevertheless, "the rise of preexistence Christology is causally related" to the Gnostic concepts of redemption and redeemer (Schenke 1973, 205; Rudolph 1975, 546ff.). It is true that preexistence Christology originated within Christianity, not before the meeting between one branch of early Christianity and Jewish Gnosticism but rather through this meeting, in that the figure of Christ Jesus was assimilated to the Gnostic idea of redemption and redeemer: Jesus is no longer the human being exalted as Son of God (Rom. 1:3–4; Mark 1:9–11) but the heavenly Son of God who humbles himself in the form of a human being, whom God sent to human beings for their redemption, "so that we might receive adoption as children" (Gal. 4:5; cf. Colpe 1961; Yamauchi 1973, 163ff.). In Gnosticism the lost state of human beings is conceived in such a radical way that their redemption cannot come from the world. Redemption means redemption *from* the world; however and through whomever it comes, it must come from outside the world (cf. Jonas 1954, 106ff., 120ff.). If this concept of redemption is connected with the church's Savior figure, the earthly and exalted Christ Jesus, the result is almost necessarily preexistence Christology. That this happened as a "logical consequence of christological thinking" in order to announce "the *whole revelation of God* and the *whole salvation* in his Christ Jesus" (Hengel 1975, 139) is a belated theological judgment. The actual process is initially religious-historical and therefore to be interpreted in a more reserved fashion in regard to its theological implications. For the Antiochene christological formulas and the corresponding Synoptic tradition show that up until the Apostles' Creed preexistence Christology was not needed to proclaim the "whole revelation of God."

It is correct to say, however, that the church's preexistence Christology did not assimilate Christianity to Gnosticism but, on the contrary, sought to use a Gnostic category to assert Christianity against Gnosticism itself. Therefore the church's preexistence Christology speaks in a decidedly anti-Gnostic way of Christ's becoming *flesh* (Phil. 2:6ff.; Rom. 8:3; John 1:14) and of the redemption of the *world* (John 3:16). At the same time it overcomes the mythic identity Christology of Jewish Gnosticism, the "I am Christ" of the spiritual people (1 Cor. 1:12); for *Jesus,* as the Christ, is the one sent by God and the *opposite* of human beings. Retained mystical formulas such as "in Christ" or "Christ in us" can be understood in the context of the church's Christology only as an expression of the historical (*geschichtlich*) status of human beings as children of God, which is based on faith in Christ; this is undoubtedly the case in Paul. We should also observe that preexistence Christology was connected early on or even from the beginning with the idea of the mediator role of the preexistent Son of God in creation (1 Cor. 8:6; Col. 1:16–17; John 1:3; Heb. 1:2)—an idea whose antidualistic aim in the context of the church's Christology cannot be doubted. Thus the formation of preexistence Christology was an *ecclesiastical* process that related the Gnostic idea of heavenly redemption and heavenly redeemers to the Christ Jesus of its own confession and in this way made possible an extensive adoption of Gnostic terms and ideas, while eliminating the Gnostic understanding of existence (cf. Baird 1979). That this preexistence Christology was an integral component of Paul's conversion theology is seen in the fact that it forms a natural foundation of his faith in Christ in general, whereas he cited the Antiochene adoption Christology only in a formulaic manner (Rom. 1:3–4).

Stratifications in Paul's Theology

In addition to the passages in the Pauline letters that are greatly shaped by Gnostic and dualistic structure and terms, such as Rom. 7:14–8:30; 1 Cor. 2:6–3:4; and so forth—which are strictly anthropologically oriented and in which the preexistence and mission Christologies is found (Rom. 8:3) but the death of Jesus originally played no role—there are other passages and statements in which the corresponding influences are completely or almost completely lacking. I have arranged them into three complexes, which produce a total of four strata of Pauline theology. Here I omit consideration of the essentially paraenetic material adopted from the Hellenistic synagogue, since it is not characteristic of Pauline thought and as a rule was brought from the synagogue by members of his church who were mostly former "God-fearers" (see p. 339 below).

First there is the category of apocalyptic motifs and ideas. They are found above all in 1 Corinthians 15; the comparable section of 1 Thess. 4:13–18 is probably only partially from Paul (Schmithals 1988a, 74ff.), and 2 Thess. 2:1–12 cannot be attributed to Paul himself. In addition, however, the Pauline literature is permeated with ideas, terms, and formulations of apocalyptic origin (cf., for example, Rom. 8:18ff; 11:25; 16:20a; 1 Cor. 1:8–9; 2:6–9; 6:2, 10; 7:29ff.; 2 Cor. 5:10; Phil. 3:20–21; 1 Thess. 5:1–3). The eschatological, ecclesiological idea of the "people of God" or the "saints" and the "called" (for example, in Rom. 1:6–7; 8:28ff.; 9:24) also comes from the apocalyptic soil of early Christianity and is therefore clearly distinguished from the spatial conception of the church as the "body of Christ." Apocalyptic ideas form a strong element in Pauline theology, though it is not defined by apocalypticism, and we must not call Paul an apocalyptist (Baumgarten 1975). The relatively broad scattering of apocalyptic motifs over wide areas of the Pauline literature and the insertion of apocalyptic motifs into variously formed Pauline trains of thought, as well as the fact that Paul held to the near expectation—however little he may have emphasized it—show that from the standpoint of theological history we must regard apocalypticism as a basic element of Pauline theology. It is no doubt true that much of the apostle's Jewish heritage lies concealed behind his apocalyptic ideas, yet his apocalyptic material is thoroughly shaped by Christology and essentially adopts a basic motif of early Palestinian Christianity, namely, the expectation that the Jesus who was exalted as Christ will come as the eschatological Savior and Judge, as well as the apocalyptically conceived turn of the age and general resurrection of the dead. Gnostic and dualistic elements are generally not found in the expressly apocalyptic sections of Pauline theology, but apocalyptic terms do occur in connection with the already described Gnostic stratum of Pauline theology (see below).

The second complex is formed of christological, soteriological formulas that proclaim the salvific death of Jesus and his victorious resurrection and exaltation to the right hand of God (e.g., Rom. 1:3–4; 3:25–26a; 4:25; 8:32; 1 Cor. 15:3ff.; 2 Cor. 4:14; 5:19), together with the statements of *Kyrios* Christology that build on this (1 Cor. 8:5–6; 10:21–22; 11:3–4; 12:3; 14:9; 15:23ff.; Phil. 1:23; 2:9–11; cf. pp. 57ff. above) and especially the teaching on redemption (e.g., Rom. 3:21ff.; 5:18–19; 6:1ff.; 8:31ff.; 14:7–9, 15; 1 Cor. 1:18ff.; 15:20–22, 57; 2 Cor. 4:6; 13:4; Gal. 2:15–16; 6:14). The extent to which this conceptual world goes back to the Palestinian primitive church is disputed and, in view of the rapid transition to Hellenistic Jewish Christianity, can hardly be stated for certain. The tradition evident in the letters of Paul is, in any case, already shaped by the Hellenistic churches, whose early center we must seek in the Syrian-Cilician area and its capital Antioch (cf. Gal. 1:21). Whether at all and to what extent Paul was perhaps already familiar with the conceptual world of this *theologia passionis* during the early period before and after his conversion must remain open. In any case, he probably did not take up these ideas, which were themselves still developing, and connect them with his conversion theology until his long years of activity in Syria and Cilicia. Yet a thorough mixing of the two theological "language games" cannot be observed; in spite of similar intentions, the two retain their relative independence in Paul.

The third complex, finally, is formed by Paul's original theological ideas. Here we are concerned above all with the form of the "doctrine of justification" that resulted from interaction with the synagogue, especially as it is developed in Romans 1–11 and in the Letter to the Galatians. With its help Paul can offer to the God-fearing Gentiles attached to the synagogue full salvation *as Gentiles* outside the Jewish ethnic and social unit. Therefore the corresponding development of the doctrine of justification probably did not occur until the time when Paul initiated the formation of independent Gentile Christian churches outside the synagogue. The doctrine of justification eliminates Israel's priority in salvation: as in Adam *all* people without distinction have sinned, so will they *all* be saved through faith in Jesus Christ; "For God has imprisoned all in disobedience so that he may be merciful to all" (Rom. 11:32). Unavoidably this involves the abolition of the law: "For Christ is the end of the law" (Rom. 10:4). Yet Christian universalism and the corresponding insight into freedom from the law already form an essential part of Paul's conversion theology (cf. Gal. 1:16; 2:15–16). The theological basis for the critique of the law, however, which Paul gives in connection with his presentation of the universalist doctrine of justification (Rom. 3:5–6, 19–20, 31; 5:13–14, 20–21; 7:1–16; Galatians 3–4) and which attempts to lay out the salvific significance of the law that is surpassed by faith, belongs entirely to the apostle himself. This observation is not equally true of the new foundation of ethics after the abolition of the law (Rom. 3:7–8; 6:1ff.; Gal. 5:13–6:10), because for this purpose Paul can also turn to the circumstances surrounding the establishment of the liberal Hellenistic synagogue (cf. esp. Rom. 12:1–2, 9ff.; 13:8–10; see pp. 339ff. below), yet his own christologically directed thinking is clearly and characteristically recognizable. Also the comments on the destiny of unbelieving Israel in Romans 9–11 essentially offer authentic Pauline reflections. Terminologically, the original Pauline doctrine of justification is related above all to the Antiochene *theologia passionis* and its formulated christological teaching material, as shown not least of all by the concept of the "righteousness" (of God) (cf. Rom. 3:25–26; Strecker 1976; Schnelle 1983). Thus in the Pauline doctrine of justification we find a universalist working out of the theology of the Hellenistic Jewish Christianity of Antioch, carried out above all by Paul himself and resting on the foundation of his conversion theology. To what extent this Jewish Christianity itself was already also under Paul's influence can be determined only with difficulty, yet it is notable that Paul feels he is also in agreement with Peter "that a person is justified not by the works of the law but through faith in Jesus Christ" (Gal. 2:16). The fact that Paul creates the synthesis of his conversion theology with the theology of Hellenistic Jewish Christianity, using especially the conceptual framework of the latter, supports the observation that he carried out his law-free Gentile mission in amicable communion with the intrasynagogal mission of Hellenistic Jewish Christians, as had been decided at the so-called Apostolic Council (Gal. 2:1ff; see pp. 113ff. below).

From what has been said thus far we can see that the overall structure of Pauline theology as it now stands was fed by various sources in early Christian theological history, and that Paul's "Damascene" conversion theology and the theology of "Antiochene" Jewish Christianity must have each attained their self-contained consistency independently. The two legacies stand within the context of Pauline theology, complementing each other yet clearly separate. This is consonant with the observation that the narrative material of the Gospel of Mark, doubtless the clearest and at the same time a rather diverse outpouring of early Hellenistic Jewish Christian theology, remained completely free from the Gnostic elements that can be observed in Paul. Since, however, the Hellenistically formed Antiochene components of Pauline theology grew, on the one hand, out of Palestinian early Christianity and provide, on the other hand, a basis for the Pauline doctrine of justification, this confirms that the complex of dualistic and Gnostic ideas in Paul's letters reflects the apostle's conversion theology, which he had at first fought vigorously. This explains why some formulaic expressions from this early complex, such as "in Christ," as well as Damascene preexistence Christology are found in *all* strata of Pauline theology. Also, we cannot know how and where Paul could have adopted only in a later period a consistent complex that is fundamental and indispensable in his anthropology and ecclesiology. Thus this complex must represent the conversion theology of the apostle, especially since one cannot assume that it was Paul himself who took up the dualistic elements of his theological language and thought in his encounter with a Jewish Gnosticism. In this case it would have been Paul's own original achievement to adapt certain Gnostic concepts and structures to Christianity and transpose the dualism of substance into historical (*geschichtlich*) thinking, and he would have become in his early years the creator of the "Johannine" theology that he himself later suppressed. There is nothing, however, that could make this construction seem probable, and when later in his Gentile Christian mission territory Paul encounters a competing Gnostic mission, he shows that he was not previously familiar with the original thinking of Gnosticism. Thus Paul must have encountered the Gnostic elements of his anthropology, Christology, and ecclesiology when they were already in an ecclesiastical context. He adopted them in the context of an already "orthodox" Christian system.

Observations on Paul's Conversion

There are indeed clear indications that at his conversion Paul gave himself to an ecclesiastical Christianity filled with enthusiasm, which grew out of dualistic ground or arose in a fruitful encounter with a dualistic enthusiasm. It is true that he gives only laconic information about that crucial process in his life, but even his brief remarks are instructive. Paul describes the conversion and calling process in the "mystical" language of Gnosticism: it pleased God to reveal his Son "in me" (Gal. 1:16, literal). This unusual "in me" could have been understood by Paul in the sense of the pure dative case: God revealed his Son *to me* (NRSV). For the foregoing comment in Gal. 1:15 puts his calling experience into traditional Old Testament conceptual language (Jer. 1:5; Isa. 49:1), which is linked with the central reference to God's grace (cf. 1 Cor. 15:10): God chose me in my mother's womb and called me through his grace. By contrast, the phrase "in me" simply does not belong to the formal terminology of the calling narratives of Old Testament–Jewish provenance, but to the originally mythically understood figure of speech "Christ in us." In the context of the Gnostic awakening process, "in me" means that the inner *pneuma*-Christ speaks ecstatically and lets anyone thus awakened know: "I am (a part) of Christ."

There can be no doubting the "enthusiastic" character of Paul's calling experience in view of his own statements (Gal. 1:15–16; 1 Cor. 15:9–10; cf. 2 Cor. 4:6). A corresponding basic feature is maintained even in the legendary reports of the Acts of the Apostles (9:1ff.; 22:3ff.; 26:9ff.). If this enthusiastic character in itself could also have been determined by an apocalyptic prophetism and was actually perhaps also influenced by it (see below), the other observations on the conversion of Paul place him, with regard to his religious-historical classification, in a pneumatology of dualistic origin.

The "mysteries" occasionally communicated by Paul in the form of a saying (Rom. 11:25–26; 1 Cor. 15:51–52; cf. 1 Cor. 2:6–10a) without doubt belong in an apocalyptic context, yet in the named passages Paul passes on apocalyptic tradition but not direct and personally received enthusiastic teaching. It is different with his assertions that he too is an ecstatic, even if he makes use of this gift only in his personal communication with God (2 Cor. 5:13); he speaks in tongues more than anyone else, even if in church he would rather speak five understandable words than ten thousand in tongues (1 Cor. 14:18–19); he can boast of the visions and revelations of the Lord and report on ecstatic heavenly journeys, whether in the body or outside the body, even if he would prefer to distance himself from *this* "person in Christ" (2 Cor. 12:1–10); he is also capable of mighty works of the Spirit, even if he wants to speak of this only in the role of a fool (2 Cor. 12:11–12; cf. Rom. 1:19; Heb. 2:4). It is clear that these practices are not the expression of an apocalyptic prophecy but the utterances of a dualistic enthusiasm. Moreover, the apologetic and polemical context of all these utterances shows that these experiences and practices were not part of Paul's missionary praxis, but that Paul was forced by his opponents against his will to document that he can also match their enthusiastic claims. In this way, suppressed and theologically sublimated (2 Cor. 12:6ff.) experiences, which must have already been experiences of the *Christian* Paul, suddenly reappear in the form of a fool's speech. They are structurally related to the enthusiastic conversion experience and therefore no doubt belong to Paul's Damascene conversion theology, which suggests again that one of its origins is to be found in a dualistic, Gnostic current of early Christianity.

Paul says that God revealed his Son to him so that he might proclaim him among the Gentiles. This formulation is connected with the claim of the apostle, expressly made in Gal. 1:11–12 (cf. 1:1; 1 Cor. 11:23), that he received his gospel directly from Christ in the process of his calling. According to this statement the gospel was not shared with him in the form of a tradition acquired through teaching (Schlier 1962, 48). This surprising assertion stands in stark contrast to the naturalness with which Paul uses numerous traditions of various provenance as the foundation of his proclamation, and all the more in contradiction with the fact that he, for example, in 1 Cor. 15:1–11, expressly communicates his gospel to the church as one that he also received from ecclesiastical tradition (cf. Sanders 1966). Thus in Gal. 1:11–12 we have an older theological structure from the time of his conversion and calling that he had suppressed in the interest of presenting the agreement of his gospel with the other apostles, but which he can resort to again as a weapon against the reproach that his gospel is of human origin and not from God. The enthusiastic character of this theological motif is apparent, and if one considers that the content of the gospel directly communicated to the apostle, according to his statement in Gal. 1:11–12, is the Christ himself, whom God revealed "in him," that is, the "Christ in us," then one again runs into a clear, albeit Christianized, reflex of the Gnostic identity Christology, in which the knowledge of the *pneuma*-self identical with the "Christ," that is, enthusiastic self-knowledge, com-

prises the entire content of the message. *To this extent* one may say that Paul "is—
cum grano salis—a Gnostic" (Heitmüller 1912, 324). This temporal meeting of
conversion and direct communication of the gospel formulated in this religious-
historical context confirms anew that the dualistic, Gnostic motifs must have belonged to Paul's conversion theology.

At his conversion Paul received "grace and apostleship" (Rom. 1:5), for in Gal.
1:1, where the topic is his apostolate, in Gal. 1:11–12, where he speaks of his reception of his gospel, and in Gal. 1:15–16, where the subject is his call to the Gentile mission, he mentions in each case the same "revelation of Jesus Christ," and
also in 1 Cor. 9:1–2; 15:9–10, conversion, communication of the gospel, and calling as apostle come directly together. A great deal of research and writing has been
done on the origin of the apostolate in early Christianity, without any unanimous
result being achieved. My own studies (1961) have led to the conclusion that the
title *apostle* and the structure of the apostolic office could have come from neither
Palestinian nor Hellenistic Jewish Christianity but, in the context of the triad of
apostles, prophets, and teachers (1 Cor. 12:27–29), was adopted from a Jewish
Gnosticism by the pre-Pauline Christianity whose earliest testimony is the conversion theology of Paul. The ongoing discussion has not made me doubt this derivation, and thus the result of this observation is also that Paul must have received
the Gnostic motifs of his theology in connection with his calling as apostle and
consequently at the time of his conversion.

Finally, we must consider that Paul was converted to a law-free, universalist
Christianity, which had already organized itself outside the synagogal unit (Gal.
1:16). Regarding this insight, "a consensus has arisen in the meantime in the more
recent research to the effect that it was not the confession of Jesus as the Messiah
that moved the Pharisees to take action against the church but the freedom from
the law practiced by the Christians persecuted by Paul" (Suhl 1975, 30). This problem must be put into sharp focus. At his conversion Paul, *as a Jew,* gave up obedience to the law, which he had previously vigorously defended against the
Christians whom he persecuted. Thus the freedom from the law fought by him was
of a fundamental kind and also affected the adherents of the synagogue. It was not
a question of a practical or theoretical softening of the legal system, as was possible also in Judaism in the sense of the principle adopted by Paul from a Hellenist
synagogue that circumcision is nothing but what is important is obeying the moral
commandments (1 Cor. 7:19; Gal. 5:6; 6:15; cf. Rom. 2:26). It was, rather, a question of an antinomianism that generally disputed the priority of the Jews.

The universalism in principle of this Christianity also conditioned the freedom from the law, but the church did not open itself to the Gentiles as a consequence of a more or less lax practice of the law. Because there was no longer a
difference between Jews and Gentiles, the differentiating law also had to fall.
Palestinian Jewish Christianity, which never gave up the law (Gal. 2:1–10) and
therefore never suffered persecution for it, cannot have been the origin of this
universalism. Nor does the Hellenistic Jewish Christianity of Syria come into
question as the place of origin of fundamental freedom from the law, for it understood itself, whenever it opened itself to God-fearing Gentiles, still as an

intrasynagogal movement, even if its understanding of the law was not strictly Judaistic. Accordingly, the Antiochene traditions, which are familiar to us from Paul and the Gospel of Mark, do not, in distinction to Paul, advocate a fundamental universalism; their relatively late texts must still expressly justify the acceptance of the uncircumcised into the church (Mark 7:24–30). Therefore it is no coincidence that we also have no information indicating that Paul persecuted *Jewish Christianity* in Palestine or Syria. In fact, the Christian universalism fought by him at first but then recognized after his conversion can be explained only against the religious-historical background of his conversion theology.

Paul himself passed on to us the corresponding universalist formulas, according to which there is "no longer Jew or Greek" (Gal. 3:28; 1 Cor. 12:13; Col. 3:10–11; cf. Rom. 10:12), and the abolition of these traditional differences is valid "in Christ" (Gal. 3:28) or "in the one Spirit," which forms the "body of Christ" or "Christ" himself (1 Cor. 12:12ff.; Col. 3:11; Eph. 2:18–19). In the mentioned formulas the two terms *Jew* and *Greek* are always mentioned and always at the beginning; thus in the universalism that abolishes ethnic differences, it is a question of an emphasized assertion. Only in 1 Cor. 7:1–24, where Paul is not quoting the formula but presenting it as a principle of division, is this order modified for the sake of the context: man-woman (7:1–17); Jew-Greek (7:18–20); slave-free (7:21–24). We must also point to Rom 7:4 in this connection: "You have died to the law through the body of Christ." Käsemann (1973, 179) may be right when he does not see this "very enigmatic" formulation as related either to the body of the crucified One or especially to the body of Christ of the church, but understands it "formulaically," in that Paul simply wants to say that *Christians* have died to the law. Hidden behind such a traditional formulation, however, is the original mythic idea that the shift into the spiritual and thus universal body of Christ involves the surrender of the particularist Torah, of Jewish particularity and exclusivity.

The dualistic background of the present formulaic language is thus unmistakable: earthly distinctions lie only in the body and the flesh; the supernatural *pneuma,* the "Christ in us," knows neither the difference of man and woman nor that of free and slave nor that between peoples and cultures. Since Gnostic dualism concerns liberation from the shackles of the body and the gathering of the *pneuma,* pneumatic universalism is an essential basic feature of its thought. This basic feature was possessed by early Christianity, whose spread into the area around Damascus we can observe. And Paul also adopted this feature and this Christianity at his conversion—reshaped, naturally, into the historical (*geschichtlich*) thinking of the faith, for Paul did not need to declare the natural and social difference unreal in a dualistic sense, when he no longer granted any significance to them for membership in the body of Christ.

The Origins of Paul's Conversion Theology

We can no longer answer with certainty the question of the concrete reason for that early and fruitful meeting between certain circles of early Christianity and a Jewish Gnosticism, a meeting that resulted in the universalist and law-free Christendom that was persecuted by Paul and to which he was converted. Was the Christian theology formulated in Gnostic terms and ideas supposed to facilitate missionary activities among the Gnostics? Or are we dealing with a theology of Jewish Gnostic converts who even with their devotion to Christianity remained close to the heart of Old Testament–Jewish thinking, without giving up universalism and freedom from the law? Or did certain internal theological signs, such as the delay of the Parousia, lead one branch of early Christianity to a theological development that succeeded with the help of Gnostic categories? Or was it primarily a question of the theological achievement or written work of an important and influential Jewish Christian theologian who was fascinated with Gnostic universalism?

Even if this question must remain open, we can still say that it was an *apocalyptically* oriented Christianity that in its encounter with a Jewish Gnosticism was transformed theologically in the way described. For the Gnostic elements in Paul's language are largely unrelated to his "Antiochene" traditions and his universalist doctrine of justification worked out in interaction with the synagogue, but they are relatively closely connected with apocalyptic motifs. Let us look at some examples.

In 2 Cor. 5:17 the mystical Gnostic language of "being in Christ" is connected with the apocalyptic schema of the ages: "So if anyone is in Christ, there is a new creation: everything old has passed away; see, everything has become new!" The connection of the two components, which are quite different in terms of the history of religion, is the closest conceivable and is inseparable; thus it is original.

An analogous observation can be made in regard to Gal. 4:4–5: "But when the fullness of time had come, God sent his Son . . . so that we might receive adoption." The preexistence and mission Christology, which Paul adopted with his conversion, is joined in this pre-Pauline formulation (cf. Müller 1990, 15), which Paul expanded according to the context in the spirit of his doctrine of justification (". . . born under the law, in order to redeem those who were under the law . . ."), with the apocalyptic topos of the "fullness" of time, that is, the idea that God has given the old age a period of time, and at its "fulfillment" the turn of the age will occur.

In 1 Cor. 2:10–16 Paul passes on in a hardly broken fashion essential structures of the dualistic identity pneumatology: natural people are *unable* to understand God's word; spiritual people are *unable* to close God out. This is by far the most Gnostic section in Paul's letters (see pp. 127ff. below). With the help of this idea Paul clarifies his preceding statements in 1 Cor. 2:6–9, according to which mysteries were revealed to him that remain hidden from the rulers of this age and which he can share only with "spiritual people" (cf. 1 Cor. 3:1–4). The comments in 1 Cor. 2:6–9 are completely apocalyptically oriented, but they are connected inseparably and virtually without transition with the dualistic terminology and conceptual world in 1 Cor. 2:10–3:4.

Similarly, in the revelation schema present in Col. 1:24–29 the structure of the apocalyptic revelation process and the corresponding content of this revelation are connected with the language of the "mystical" Christology (see pp. 64ff. above). Paul makes known a mystery that remained hidden from the people in the old age but was revealed to the "Gentiles," namely, that the Gentiles will also share in the coming glory. The revelatory saying itself, however, through which "God chose to make known how great among the Gentiles are the riches of the glory of this mystery," speaks the language of mysticism: "Christ in you" (Col. 1:27), that is, the Christ-*pneuma* is also in you Gentiles.

The relatively self-contained dogmatic section Rom. 7:14–8:30, which bears no relationship to the main theme of the Letter to the Romans and no doubt was not first conceived for it (cf. Schmithals 1988b), speaks of the total sinfulness of humankind and of redemption essentially in Gnostic conceptual structures, ideas, and terms. After the corresponding beginnings of present eschatology in Rom. 8:12–16, however, Paul shifts in 8:17 to a presentation of future eschatology, which works essentially with apocalyptic material, even though in a sublimated form. The "Spirit," which in dualistic thinking is the human self awakened from sleep and liberated from the prison of the body, as Rom. 8:3ff. shows, is consequently found in 8:23–27 as a gift of God, namely, as a down payment on the salvation of the coming age.

The ideological presuppositions of the substantial, spatial thinking of Gnosticism and the historical, temporal conceptual world of apocalypticism are completely different, but the existential experience of reality connects the two dualistic movements with each other (Winter 1975, 56ff.; Schmithals 1973, 67ff.). Gnosticism and apocalypticism are marked by a radical pessimism in regard to the present world. The sinful fall of Adam, which spoiled the creation, corresponds completely with the fall of the primal human being into the demonic creation. Gnosticism and apocalypticism hold that a development of the present world for the better is not possible, and they strive for a revolutionary turning point: for the former, the liberation of the spirit from everything material; for the latter, the end of the old and the onset of the new age. For Gnosticism and apocalypticism it is not natural communities but *individual people* who will survive from the old age into the new, the righteous and the spiritual people, who have this one distinguishing trait in common and are found among *all* peoples. In both religious currents the expected turning point is unique and irreversible: the old age will not come again, and matter will be definitively annihilated when the spirit has left it. Also, the prophetic-eschatological enthusiasm of apocalypticism and the pneumatic-dualistic enthusiasm of Gnosticism form one basis on which both movements can agree.

Thus a branch of evangelistically active Palestinian Jewish Christianity, which was essentially characterized by apocalypticism, apparently encountered a Jewish Gnosticism at a very early time. The result of this encounter was the theology that we have come to know as the conversion theology of Paul. Imprisonment under the power of sin, from which human beings cannot free themselves, was conceived as radically as in Gnosticism and apocalypticism (Rom. 7:18ff.). Christ is no longer primarily the one to come, as in apocalypticism, but the one who has come, as in Gnosticism; the salvation event is proclaimed primarily not as expected but as having already happened in the sending, humbling, and incarnation of the Son, and believers are promised adoption as children (Gal. 4:4–5). The Spirit is no longer conceived dualistically, as in Gnosticism, but is understood in the early Christian, apocalyptic sense as eschatological gift, as the down payment of salvation (Rom. 5:5; 8:23; 2 Cor. 5:5). The gospel does not proclaim redemption from the world but rather offers redemption in the Old Testament–Jewish sense to the world. Nevertheless, Jewish particularism and the corresponding conception of the law are abandoned. In the dialectic of the "already now" and the "not yet" of salvation, the problem of the delay of the Parousia is overcome. The extent to which the Palestinian confession of Jesus—not only as the one who is coming again but also as the Christ and *Kyrios* exalted to the right hand of God—connected the simply apocalyptic expectation with the "already now" of salvation is disputed and hardly still to be determined with any certainty. If this was already supposed to have been more or less the case, then the described process that generated Paul's conversion theology did not create the "already now" and the "not yet" of eschatological salvation but only promoted the development and made adequate means of expression available to progressive theological thinking.

This interpretative process was in no way accidental, unintentional, or coincidental. It betrays a substantial and responsible capability of theological interpretation and a specific theological and missionary interest. If in this connection we want to mention a name or a school at all, only Stephen and his group are possible. There is agreement in critical research that the presentation in Acts 6–7 is largely the product of Luke's redactional intentions; it shows that he is interested above all in emphasizing the unity and unanimity of the early church and in making differences and tensions as invisible as possible. Therefore it is only with difficulty that we can get a picture of the historical Stephen and his church. It is certain, however, that Stephen and his circle of seven headed an independent Christian community and that theologically it was considerably different from the Jewish Christianity grouped around the "twelve apostles." It is no coincidence that the "Hebrews" apparently remained essentially unmolested when the "Hellenists" were persecuted. The most important special theological opinion of the group around Stephen—which is played down by Luke but still perceivable, and which also led to their persecution—concerns the fundamental freedom from the law and Christian universalism (Acts 6:13–14) that we also find in Paul's conversion theology. Therefore, if one wants to name Stephen and the leadership group of seven in the present context (cf. Cullmann 1975, 41ff.), the connection of the persecutor Paul with Stephen (Acts 7:57; 8:1) would have some historical support. There are, however, other observations supporting the connection between the church of Stephen and the conversion theology of Paul.

Concerning the conversion of the Ethiopian eunuch (Acts 8:26–40), Haenchen (1961, 265) states with reason: "It was the first Gentile conversion in the tradition of Hellenistic Christians." In any case, it may rest on good tradition that Philip, one of the seven, was an important missionary in Stephen's circle (cf. Acts 8:5ff.; 21:8). The fact that Luke has the first conversion of Gentiles occur through Peter (Acts 10:1–11:18), corresponds to his tendency to have all developments stem from the circle of the twelve apostles. In reality, however, the beginnings of planned mission work among the Gentiles are found in the circle around Stephen.

The report on Philip's activity in Samaria (Acts 8:5ff.) and his encounter with the "magician" Simon is strongly determined by the redactional tendencies of Luke, who again gives the Jerusalem twelve an essential role in the solution of the problems in Samaria. We must assume that Simon was an outstanding representative of Jewish-Samaritan Gnosticism, who was claimed by the Gnostics as one of their fathers but was fought by early Christendom as a Gnostic heretic (Just. *Apol.* 1.26), and that in the Lukan report on the meeting between Philip and Simon we have a testimony of the earliest relationship between Christianity and Gnosticism. What historical information Luke could have utilized here can no longer be determined with any probability. But in any case, his account is probably based on the early connection of Jewish Gnosticism and Christianity that produced Paul's conversion theology, which Damascene Christianity at the same time clearly used to set itself apart from Gnosticism.

The Acts of the Apostles preserves some traditional traces of the Gnostic enthusiasm of the early church and especially of glossolalia (2:3–4, 13; 10:44ff.; 11:15; 19:6). Luke attempts to include these traces in the activity of the "twelve apostles," in accordance with his general tendency; he probably passed them on only for this reason. In fact, however, dualistically rooted glossolalia, speaking in the heavenly language of the *pneuma* (cf. 1 Cor. 12:10, 30; 14:26–27), seen from the standpoint of the history of religion, has a completely different origin and, regarded from the standpoint of religious phenomenology, a totally different appearance from the prophetic-apocalyptic enthusiasm that was alive in the Jerusalem church. It is quite conceivable that the mentioned motifs come from traditions about the community of Stephen and are thus related to Paul's assurance that he is better able than anyone else to speak in tongues (1 Cor. 14:18–19; cf. 2 Cor. 5:13).

There is much to be said for the often substantiated thesis that the Philip of the twelve (Acts 1:13; John 1:43ff.) and the Philip of the circle of the seven (Acts 6:5) are identical (cf. Euseb. *Hist. Eccl.* 3.39.9; 5.24.2). Not only does Philip then form a personal link between the Jerusalem Jewish Christians, on the one hand, and the "Hellenists" (Acts 6:1) and Paul, on the other, but with this presupposition such an identification also points objectively to the connection of Paul's conversion theology with the circle around Stephen, since Philip is to be classified with an enthusiastic Christianity, however sublimated it might be (Acts 8:9ff.; 21:8–9).

Furthermore, in the present context the question arises as to whether the origin of the circle of the seven and the center of law-free Hellenism, as well as the place of Stephen's martyrdom, are really to be sought in Jerusalem, as the Lukan presentation claims. All observations up to this point speak against this location. According to all appearances, Jewish Gnosticism had its home in Samaria; Paul, as Gal. 1:22 indicates, was not active as a persecutor in Judea (Heitmüller 1912, 327; Strecker 1976, 482–83) but in Damascus, where he was converted; and according to Acts 21:8, the Philip of the circle of Stephen had his home in Caesarea. Stephen's strange statement about the land promised to Abraham "in which *you* are now living" (Acts 7:4) is easily explained if Luke still knew that Stephen and his circle were not from Judea. In general, it is only with difficulty that we can imagine that Jerusalem could have been the place of origin of a law-critical universalism fought by Jewish Christians, which had to be persecuted outside of Jerusalem. The circle of seven around Stephen (Acts 6:5) was not in touch with the leadership of the Jewish Christian church of Antioch, which likewise seems to have comprised seven persons (Acts 13:1; 15:27, 32), although according to the Lukan presentation the Antiochene church is supposed to have arisen on account of the persecution that came upon Stephen and his Hellenists (Acts 11:19ff.). This inconsistency also suggests that Stephen was only secondarily transposed to Jerusalem. For Luke, however, no place of origin other than Jerusalem comes into the picture, for according to his purpose the whole of Hellenistic Christianity is an integrated part of the one Jewish Christian church, from which all developments come directly, and not a special independent Christian group.

Even if in many respects we cannot get beyond hypotheses, possibilities, and at best probabilities, we can still say with certainty that the Christianity to which Paul was converted was also the native soil of characteristic Johannine theology. The latter, however, followed a developmental course of its own, which was quite independent of Paul.

Conclusion

In summary, from what has been said we may draw the following conclusions for the development of theological history in early Christianity. The Palestinian Jewish Christianity of Jerusalem and the twelve grew out of the apocalyptic message of Jesus and an acute expectation of the inbreaking of the kingdom of God, and as a result of Peter's Messiah confession and the exaltation soteriology (the exalted *Kyrios* defeats the powers hostile to God; see p. 54 above), it had possibly already more or less outgrown them. It developed perhaps simultaneously in two clearly distinct directions during its movement into the Hellenistic area.

On the one hand, the encounter with Jewish Gnosticism led to a universalist and Torah-critical, strongly anthropologically shaped theology with preexistence Christology and a soteriology oriented toward the incarnation of the Redeemer and the nullification of the power of sin; the representatives of this theology organized themselves outside the synagogue in independent churches (*ekklēsiai*). Damascus, where Paul persecuted the Christian community, was probably one—or the—center of this church. Within the New Testament we observe the result of this development in the conversion theology of Paul and in one basis of "Johannine" theology.

On the other hand, the spread of Christianity within the Hellenistic synagogues led to a Christianity with a Christology of adoption, which was oriented soteriologically toward the event of the cross and resurrection and toward the concept of the "forgiveness of sins." This Christianity had also largely freed itself from its apocalyptic origins. Syrian Antioch was one early center of this Hellenistic Christianity, whose understanding of the law was not substantially different from that of the liberal synagogue and which also opened its arms early on to the numerous God-fearing Gentiles within the synagogue. In the context of the New Testament we see this Christianity above all in the broad stream of formulaic teaching material that is found in the letters of Paul, as well as in the narrative material of the Gospel of Mark. Yet the later theological development generally rests to a great degree on this Hellenistic Christianity that developed considerable strength in the protection of the synagogue and only after the catastrophe of the Jewish war and the following Pharisaic-rabbinical reorganization of Judaism had to depart from the institution of the synagogue (see pp. 263ff. below).

Paul was converted to the "Damascene"—or, speaking anachronistically, "Johannine"—type of Christianity, which he had previously persecuted. "Paul was initiated into a Gnostic interpretation of Christianity, which almost from the very beginning . . . served as an alternative for the primitive eschatology of Jerusalem and the liberal interpretation of Antioch" (Quispel 1980, 13). He then entered the "Antiochene" traditions and later, on this double basis and with the retention of some apocalyptic elements from the roots of primitive Christianity in interaction above all with Hellenistic Judaism, he worked out his Gentile Christian theology and above all his specific doctrine of justification.

5

Christology and Soteriology
in Hellenistic Churches before Paul

In his *Vorlesungen über die neutestamentliche Theologie* Ferdinand Christian Baur goes directly from his presentation of the teachings of Jesus, which are "not theology at all but religion" (1864, 45), to Paul as the first Christian theologian and to Paul's "doctrinal conception." In his lectures Baur wants to trace the course of the theological development of early Christianity as far as the Johannine doctrinal conception, in which "New Testament theology [reaches] its highest stage and its most complete form" (1864, 351). By contrast, according to Baur the Judaic teachings of the older apostles marks a step backward behind the Christian principle that "was already contained *implicitly* in the teachings of Jesus" (1864, 128) and first made explicit by Paul. Yet Baur does not discuss how those moronic older apostles, under "the whole impression that the life of Jesus and his ultimate destiny had made on them" (1864, 126), realized that such a witness of divine truth could not stay dead. It was enough that with their confession of the resurrection of Jesus they laid down the objective basis on which Paul, who understood how to interpret the death of the resurrected Christ, was able to find his characteristic Christian standpoint in a both sudden and profound revolution in his religious consciousness at Damascus. Only at this point does the history of early Christian theology begin.

The advocates of the life-of-Jesus theology, who took a position against Baur's Tübingen school and included especially Baur's former student Albrecht Ritschl and the leading New Testament scholar Heinrich Julius Holtzmann, could not allow Christian theology to begin with the Pauline doctrinal conception. In their opinion Jesus' proclamation already *explicitly* contained the essential content of the Christian gospel, and thus Jesus' personal disciples, who passed on his message, could not be excluded from the theological history of early Christianity as ignoramuses. Holtzmann, who in his *Neutestamentliche Theologie* is still strongly bound by the Tübingen historical picture, ascertains in the older apostles, as compared with Jesus' gospel, an "undeniable loss in religious and moral values"(1897, 1:352) but at the same time a retention of the "unconditional personal worth" of Jesus (ibid., 354). "The impression of his person in its spiritual power proved to be decisive" (ibid.), and through the resulting confession to the resurrection of the crucified One, to his exaltation to the role of messianic king, to the expectation of his coming again, one "compensates" for the loss of essential basic ideas of Jesus' gospel (ibid., 352). The tension between the two contrary effects of Jesus on his circle of disciples, the loss of religious values, and the exaltation of Jesus to Son of God also remain undiscussed by Holtzmann, but the "positive" reaction of the disciples to the impression of Jesus' personality, which Holtzmann observes, allowed and required the first formation of Christology, the dogmatic interpretation of Jesus' death, and the organization of the church, including baptism, the Lord's Supper, and the diaconate, to be presented as developments in the period *before* the formation of the Pauline doctrinal conception. Thus Paul began with christological, soteriological, and ecclesiological statements of doctrine that were rooted in the ongoing influence of the personality and teachings of Jesus and formed with the help of the Holy Scripture of the Old Testament, which were read and searched with eyes enlightened by faith in Christ.

At the turn of the last century the history-of-religions school as a rule classified the kingdom-of-God preaching of *Jesus* with the mental and conceptual world of apocalypticism, which had in the meantime become foreign—even where this school felt that for its present proclamation it was necessary to proclaim the kingdom of God as the highest moral ideal, as in the life-of-Jesus theology (J. Weiss 1892; cf. Schweitzer 1901). In this way the history-of-religions scholars, in contrast to members of the Tübingen and Ritschlian schools, succeeded in describing a relatively smooth transition from the proclamation of Jesus to the Easter experience and the theology of the Palestinian primitive church. This made it necessary, however, to postulate a differentiation or development within pre-Pauline Christianity, since one could not have Paul directly follow the apocalyptic Christianity of Palestine, as the presentation in Acts and numerous religious-historical observations on the letters of Paul demonstrate. "Between Paul and the Palestinian primitive church stand the Hellenistic churches in Antioch, Damascus, and Tarsus" (Bousset 1921, 75). For the history-of-religions school these Hellenistic churches constitute the most important factor and the driving force in the course and development of early Christian theological history—a view that has rightly found broad agreement.

Yet the rather rough distinction between Palestinian and Hellenistic early churches, which is regularly found among the representatives of the history-of-religions school and is also still influential in Bultmann's *Theologie des Neuen Testaments* (1953), needed and needs some correction. Thus when Bousset calls the Hellenistic churches before Paul a "Gentile Christian early church" (1921, 75), he fails to recognize that as a rule these churches—as we can observe, for example, in the especially influential church in Antioch—were organized *within* the synagogue and therefore must be called "Hellenistic Jewish Christian," even if they probably drew increasingly more God-fearing Gentiles than born Jews. To designate them for this reason as "mixed churches" (Conzelmann 1959, 129), however, is unfortunate, since we are not in the habit of designating the Hellenistic synagogues with their many God-fearers as "mixed synagogues," but we cannot simply set "Palestinian" over against "Hellenistic" either, as was observed relatively early by O. Holtzmann (1906, 70ff.). Since the time of Alexander, Palestine was increasingly permeated with Hellenistic culture and language, and the transition from Palestinian Judaism to the synagogues in the worldwide Diaspora, especially in nearby Syria, was smooth. The difficulties that Bousset, for example, faces when he must assign baptism, the Eucharist, the sacrificial death of Jesus, and so forth either to Palestinian or Hellenistic early Christianity are therefore essentially resolved with an objective insight into the situation of Judaism in the early Christian period.

Yet for Bousset the terms *Palestinian* and *Hellenistic* signalize not only a geographical difference but above all a specifically religious-historical or theological development in early Christianity. For the Palestinian primitive church, Jesus is "the coming Messiah who is to come in glory, and the basic mood of the disciples [is] the fervent expectation of his coming. The *Kyrios* of the Hellenistic early church, however, is an *entity present* in worship. With his presence he surrounds and encloses his church in the worship service and fills it with his wonderful powers from heaven. Only now can we say: 'Where two or three are gathered in my name, I am there in their midst'" (1921, 103). With these words Bousset describes the change from apocalyptic *hope* of salvation to the hopeful *experience* of salvation, a change that even in the pre-Pauline period had already overcome in principle the problem of the so-called delay of the Parousia. Here the experience of already present salvation rests on the knowledge that Jesus, who as "Lord" sits at God's right hand, has defeated or is defeating the powers hostile to God (Phil. 2:10; 1 Cor. 15:23–28; cf. Rom. 8:38; Col. 2:10, 15; Eph. 1:20ff.; 1 Peter 3:21–22; Pol. *Phil.* 2.1; see p. 54 above). It must remain an open question whether and to what extent this change may be described as the "hellenization" of beginning Christianity, or whether it was, rather, basic religious experiences, like those also found in Old Testament Jewish piety, that dissolved the apocalyptic high tension.

In any case, the majestic title *Kyrios* for Jesus, which in Bousset's view supports a "hellenization," does not serve to answer the alternative question of how and on what basis—still a controversial question (cf. Kramer 1963)—one can explain the emergence of this title in early Christianity, for the petition, "Our Lord, come!" (*Marana tha,* 1 Cor. 16:22; Rev. 22:20; cf. Phil. 3:20–21) still belongs entirely in the realm of apocalyptic expectation, whereas the confession, "Jesus Christ is Lord" (Phil. 2:11; Rom. 10:9; 1 Cor. 12:3; 2 Cor. 4:5) reflects a present state of salvation. Thus the transition from the longing hope for the coming of the "Lord" to the praise of his present kingdom is smooth, and the two experiences can occur not only beside each other but also with each other. The latter is clearly the case, for example, in Paul, who can easily fall back on "Palestinian" formulas of apocalyptic expectation:

> But our citizenship is in heaven, and it is from there that we are expecting a Savior, the *Lord* Jesus Christ. He will transform the body of our humiliation that it may be conformed to the body of his glory, by the power that also enables him to make all things subject to himself. (Phil. 3:20–21)

> ". . . and to wait for his Son from heaven, whom he raised from the dead—Jesus, who rescues us from the wrath that is coming." (1 Thess. 1:10)

At the same time Paul lives entirely in the "Hellenistic" certainty of present salvation:

> See, now is the acceptable time; see, now is the day of salvation! (2 Cor. 6:2b)

> The grace of the *Lord* Jesus Christ, the love of God, and the communion of the Holy Spirit be with all of you. (2 Cor. 13:13)

On the one hand, the community of the *Didache* also baptized its members in the name of the Father, the Son, and the Holy Spirit, enjoyed food and drink at the Lord's Supper, understood itself as the church, followed the ecclesiastical division of week days and days of fasting, elected bishops and deacons, used the Synoptic tradition, and in short lived completely in the manner of the mainstream church. On the other hand, however, it persisted until into the second century not only in its Christology based on the standpoint of the Palestinian primitive church but was also resistant to "Hellenistic" soteriology; it knew neither incarnation nor passion as salvific events but expected salvation entirely from the coming of the Lord "on the clouds of heaven to repay each person according to his [or her] actions" (*Did.* 16.8).

Thus if the sharp distinctions of the history-of-religions school between "Palestinian" and "Hellenistic" have to give way to a more adaptable picture of early Christian theological history, so must we make greater distinctions within the Christianity entering the realm of the Hellenistic world than Bousset, for example, does when he names in one breath "the Hellenistic churches in Antioch, Damascus, Tarsus" (1921, 75). Naturally, Tarsus should be left totally out of consideration, for to put the birthplace of Paul beside Damascus and Antioch presupposes not only a unified entity, "pre-Pauline Hellenistic Christianity," but also the notion that in Tarsus there was already a Christian church before the conversion or mission of Paul, which can hardly be derived from Acts 9:30; 11:25–26. By contrast, there were undoubtedly pre-Pauline communities of Christians in Antioch and Damascus, yet communities with such diverse Christology, soteriology, and ecclesiology that one may not speak of pre-Pauline Hellenistic Christianity as a single entity, as is still generally done even today in the wake of the history-of-religions school (cf., for example, Hengel 1972).

The godfather of this leveling view is the historical picture in Acts, which sketches a straight line development, always directed by the apostles, from the church's formation in Jerusalem through the persecution of Stephen to the spread of the gospel in Judea and Samaria, then on to Antioch and finally to Rome (cf. Acts 1:8). The picture in Acts reveals no internal tensions or theological development at all within Christianity, but this harmonious view of history contradicts itself. For example, Luke has persecution descend on Stephen and his circle but not on other Christians; he sees the church in Damascus as the object of persecution and the place of Paul's conversion but gives it no other significance in the history of early Christianity; and he lets the leadership circle of seven around Stephen (Acts 6:5) stand unrelated to the authorities of the Antiochene church (13:1; 15:22, 27).

"Damascene" Christianity

In chapter 4 we reported in detail on Paul's conversion theology, which was presumably based on the activity of Stephen (Schmithals 1982, 65–66). We cannot say with certainty whether and to what extent Damascus itself—whose inhabitants, according to Josephus (*Bell.* 1.422; 2.561), included a considerable number of Jews and God-fearers—became the headquarters and center of a church association or the theological school that is clearly discernible in Paul's conversion theology. The fact that he persecuted the Damascene church, was converted in Damascus, and also worked there a long time (Acts 9:1ff.; Gal. 1:13–17; 2 Cor. 11:32–33) does not necessarily lead to that assumption, although it is difficult to see how a different place could have played a corresponding role. Therefore Damascus may have been just as representative of early Hellenistic Christianity as Antioch. In this sense we can speak of both "Antiochene" and "Damascene" Christianity and thereby designate two characteristically different theological schools, which, however, should not at the same time be restricted geographically by such a designation.

Since Paul was converted in Damascus to the theological form of early Christianity that he had earlier persecuted, we can learn from the basic stratum of his own theology that Damascene Christianity advocated a law-critical universalism, which revealed the power of sin that encompasses all humankind and which offered every individual the freedom that comes from God to escape this power of sin. The concept of sin here is based not on sinful acts but on the motif of the "alienation" of human beings from the truth of their existence. The preexistence Christology developed in Damascene theology corresponds to the unconditional *extra nos* of the idea of redemption. The idea of preexistence—to which, according to Wisd. Sol. 9:1 (1 Cor. 8:6; cf. Col. 1:16–17; John 1:3; Heb. 1:2), the motif of the mediator of creation was already attached at an early time—was a necessary part of the christological schema of the "humbling and exaltation" of the Son of God (Phil. 2:6–11; 2 Cor. 8:9). It is noteworthy that God himself, and not the Son of God, is always the subject of the salvation event (2 Cor. 5:19, 21; Gal. 4:4). Soteriology, to the extent that it was not limited to the traditional confession of the cosmic reign of the Lord Christ, had to develop in the context of this incarnational Christology. This development occurred in various ways, and often the separation from the apocalyptic roots of the kerygma is still considered. In Gal. 4:4–5 Paul turns to a formula according to which the incarnation of the Son of God at the end of the old age means the acceptance of human children as children of God:

> But when the fullness of time had come,
> God sent his Son,
> born of a woman . . .
> so that we might receive adoption as children.

The formula in 2 Cor. 5:21 uses similar categories:

> For our sake he made him to be sin
> who knew no sin,
> so that in him we might become the righteousness of God.

It is the preexistent One who as such knew no sin and who humbled himself to sinners in order to put them right with God ("righteousness of God"), an idea that also underlies Rom. 8:3, apparently formulaically (Schmithals 1988b, 261ff.):

> [God sent] his own Son in the likeness of sinful flesh, and . . . condemned sin in the flesh . . .

The motif of "reconciliation," taken from social and political life (Friedrich 1982, 95ff.; Breytenbach 1989) is found in the formula expressly quoted by Paul in 2 Cor. 5:19 (cf. Rom. 5:10; 2 Cor. 11:21; Col. 1:20, 22; 2 Thess. 2:2):

> . . . in Christ God
> was reconciling the world to himself,
> not counting their trespasses against them . . .

The formulation "reconciling the *world*" gives strong emphasis to the universalism that marks Damascene theology.

In addition, in some variation we find the "mystical" soteriology of "being in Christ," which does not describe the redemption process as such but names its consequences. In 2 Cor. 5:17, a pre-Pauline formulation carefully stylized with twelve Greek words, the break with apocalypticism can be seen especially well:

> If anyone is in Christ,
> there is a new creation:
> everything old has passed away;
> see, everything has become new!

Universalism is emphasized in the teaching text Gal. 3:26–28 (cf. 1 Cor. 12:12–13; Col. 3:11), a seven line passage with thirty-six (three times twelve) Greek words that is only slightly reworked by Paul:

> For in Christ Jesus you are all children of God through faith.
> As many of you as were baptized into Christ
> have clothed yourselves with Christ.
> There is no longer Jew or Greek,
> there is no longer slave or free,
> there is no longer male and female;
> for all of you are one in Christ Jesus.

As the cited formulaic material shows, the profound theological thinker of Damascene Christianity also shows a talent for artful formulation, which in some cases approaches poetic art. This is especially to be noted in the comprehensive texts that are divided into verses and called "hymns," although we do not know whether they were used earlier in catechesis or worship. Especially well known is the pre-Pauline Christ hymn of the Letter to the Philippians (2:6–7, 9–11). It consists of two verses, each of which forms a single sentence or seven lines, and it is expanded characteristically by Paul at the end of each verse. The original text has the following wording:

He was of divine nature
but did not regard it as an indispensable possession,
to be like God,
but emptied himself,
took on the nature of a slave,
took on human form,
and was regarded as a human being among human beings.

Therefore God also exalted him
and gave him the name
that is above every name,
so that at the name of Jesus every knee should bend,
in heaven and on earth and under the earth,
and every tongue should confess
that Jesus Christ is Lord

These two verses follow strictly the schema of the "humbling and exaltation." The preexistent One does not regard his divine being as a "free lunch" but gives it up for reasons not stated and humbles himself, assuming human nature. For this he receives the highest honor that God can give: he becomes the LORD (*Kyrios*). Paul quotes the impressive text with paraenetic purpose: "Let the same mind be in you that was in Christ Jesus" (Phil. 2:5); that is, be humble and thoughtful of the needs of others. The text of the hymn itself does not indicate such a paraenetic intention, nor does it contain any recognizable soteriological aspect, which is inserted by Paul with reference to his *theologia crucis:* "He humbled himself and became obedient to the point of death—even death on a cross" (Phil. 2:8). This makes it difficult to grasp the concrete intention of the theological writer to whom we owe this Christ hymn. If we consider that under the influence of the oriental cult of the ruler the Roman emperors in early Christian times equated themselves with the gods and let themselves be venerated cultically as *kyrios,* it was probably the intention of our song to place the true *Kyrios,* whom God raised because he humbled himself, over against this self-elevation of the human *kyrios* of a political worship service. Included in such a statement is a soteriological concept ("My grace is sufficient for you"—2 Cor. 12:9), which at the same time justifies a corresponding paraenetic usage of the song (cf. 2 Cor. 8:9). This juxtaposition is indirect, but for contemporary Christian readers it was unmistakable.

The hymn that underlies the prologue to the Gospel of John, by contrast, develops a comprehensive theological conception. If the following reconstruction is correct (cf. Schmithals 1992, 260ff.), the prologue consists of three verses of six lines each, with the stress in each case clearly on the last line. Each line forms a complete clause, and each verse consists of thirty-five Greek words:

In the beginning was the *Logos,*
and the *Logos* was with God,
and the *Logos* was God.
He was in the beginning with God.

All things came into being through him,
and without him not one thing came into being.

What has come into being in him was life,
and the life was the light of all people.
The light shines in the darkness,
and the darkness did not overcome it.
To all who received him
he gave power to become children of God.

And the *Logos* became flesh
and [he] lived among us,
and we have seen his glory,
[and he was] full of grace and truth.
The law indeed was given through Moses;
grace and truth came through Jesus Christ.

The first verse speaks of God himself, his unity with the *Logos,* and creation; the second verse of the original revelation, human sin, and the children of God in pre-Christian time. The third verse mentions the incarnation of the *Logos* and speaks of the Christian church, which as the truth of God celebrates the grace that is given to all people through Jesus Christ as a replacement for the law.

Comparable hymns, which can sometimes be reconstructed better, sometimes not as well, are found in, for example, Col. 1:15–20; Eph. 1:3–10; 1 Tim. 3:16; Heb. 1:3ff. They all represent Damascene preexistence Christology, an incarnational soteriology, and the corresponding universalism, and they thereby confirm that in Paul's conversion theology, deep theological reflection is balanced with poetic art.

"Antiochene" Adoption Christology

On the whole, "simple" Hellenistic Jewish Christianity of the Antiochene variety, which seemingly developed relatively smoothly out of Palestine and spread into the synagogues of the nearby Syrian region and soon into the whole inhabited earth, initially influenced the thought and faith of the early church more strongly than the Damascene Christianity outside the synagogue, which was able, nonetheless, to prevail against Antioch later in the trinitarian and christological controversies of the imperial church. The great and special importance of the Antiochene church in early Christian times can also be gleaned from Acts 11:19–26 (cf. Gal. 1:21) if we take away the schematism of the writer Luke, which defines this section. In Antioch on the Orontes, the third largest city in the empire after Rome and Alexandria, there lived a large Jewish community with numerous synagogues and many God-fearing Gentiles. Here the Christian mission among Jews and Gentiles found its most fertile field. There is no historical basis for Luke's making the banishment of the Jerusalem Hellenists and the martyrdom of Stephen responsible for this spread of the gospel to Antioch (Acts 11:19), for those who were not tolerated in Jerusalem would hardly have found a right of domicile in the Antiochene synagogue either. The lively connections from Jerusalem and Judea via the Phoenician coast to Syria and Antioch and back again conveyed the Christian message from one place to the other without further cause. Acts 13:1 reports the leadership of five Antiochene prophets and teachers, apparently headed by Barnabas, of whom at least three, according to Luke, are supposed to have come from Jerusalem (11:20ff.). Since this special information involves an expression of Luke's tendency to derive all developments from the primitive church in Jerusalem, one can argue that the prophets Judas and Silas (15:25ff.), the later companions of Paul (15:40), who according to Luke are likewise supposed to be from Jerusalem, were from Antioch and with the five aforementioned prophets and teachers formed an Antiochene leadership group with seven members, analogous to the circle of seven "deacons" around Stephen. To the extent that the Antiochene church is to be regarded as the mother church of the Hellenistic Christianity that organized itself within the synagogue association until banishment from the synagogue in the wake of the rabbinic reorganization after 70, Hellenistic Jewish Christianity, by far the largest part of early Christianity, can generally be called "Antiochene."

In distinction to Paul's Damascene conversion theology, the church in Antioch taught the adoption Christology inherited from the Palestinian church, which was expanded or replaced by the ideas of conception by the Spirit and of the virgin birth, according to the testimony of the Gospels of Matthew and Luke written some two generations later. The oldest and classical testimony to adoption Christology is found in Rom. 1:3–4, where Paul recalls a traditional formula, whose curious character was already pointed out by Strauss (1836, 692–93) and whose traditional nature is granted and convincingly substantiated by all recent commentators:

> ... who was descended / from [the seed of] David / according to the flesh
> and was declared / to be Son of God with power / according to the spirit
> of holiness / by resurrection from the dead ...

This traditional passage is formulated with its members in parallel, yet with a clear emphasis. The first line comprises three parts with seven Greek words; the second, four parts with twelve words; thus the whole formula has seven parts. This careful stylization indicates that Paul did not modify the traditional text, a fact that is connected with the function of the formula in the Letter to the Romans. Paul inserts this formula already in the opening of his letter—a singular procedure—and as a closer definition of the "gospel of God" that he proclaims. The formula, however, does not contain the Damascene preexistence Christology usually advocated by Paul but the Antiochene adoption Christology that was widespread in the rest of Hellenistic Christianity. Thus, when introducing himself to the Roman Christians unknown to him, Paul intentionally chooses an idea that was, as a rule, familiar to Christians from the East who had migrated to the capital of the empire and a doctrinal formulation that was probably not unfamiliar to them. In this way he hopes to find an open ear among his readers in Rome, where he would like to gather a church. Thus he shows his familiarity with both the

Damascene preexistence Christology and the Antiochene adoption Christology, and he apparently does not believe that the two views are mutually exclusive.

The formulaic contents of *both* christological conceptions presuppose that the life, teachings, and works of the earthly Jesus do not reveal his christological majesty. For the preexistence Christology in the hymn of Phil. 2:6–7, 9–11, this observation is plainly the key to interpreting the humbling and exaltation of Jesus: because the preexistent Son willingly empties himself of his majesty, assumes the form of a slave, and lives as a human being among human beings, God grants him the highest status of *Kyrios*. By contrast, the formula found in Rom. 1:3–4 does not presuppose a humbling of Jesus, since his majesty begins only with his resurrection and exaltation. With this presupposition, the formula in Rom. 1:3–4 merely states in its first part Jesus' predisposition for his coming status, for according to the usual idea, the Messiah is a descendant of David, as asserted by Nathan's prediction in 2 Sam. 7:12–16 (cf. Pss. 89:4–5; 132:11), which after the loss of the political independence of the state of Judah was related to the messianic bringer of salvation of the end time (Isa. 11:1ff.; Jer. 23:5; Ezek. 34:23–24). Yet the title *son of David,* attested since *Psalms of Solomon* 17.21 for the Messiah, is not found in Rom. 1:3–4, and we must not read it into "from the seed of David." In Rom. 1:3–4 Jesus is presented only as one of many descendants of David, and such a lineage is a necessary presupposition for his adoption and exaltation as the messianic Son of God (cf. 2 Tim. 2:8; John 7:42). Furthermore, on the life of the one born "from the seed of David according to the flesh," there is nothing christologically significant to say, for this life does not yet stand in the light of the exalted One, in which it is placed only later by the evangelists, who shift the adoption from the act of resurrection to the event of baptism or into the process of the miraculous conception and thus before the beginning of Jesus activity.

Adoptionist Christology as such comes into play at the moment in which the Easter experience is comprehended and interpreted as the exaltation of the resurrected Jesus as the Christ, Son of God, or *Kyrios*—all these majestic titles are intentionally put together by Paul in Rom. 1:3–4; that is, adoptionist Christology is brought to bear with the Messiah confession of Peter. Consequently, it is of Palestinian origin and is more "archaic" than the already developed preexistence Christology of Paul's conversion theology. By presenting Jesus emphatically as a descendant of David, the first line of the formula points decidedly to the Jewish Christian origin of the pre-Pauline tradition. Nothing certain about the age or place of origin of the text can be determined on the basis of linguistic observations, especially since the choice between Palestinian and Hellenistic is problematic for reasons mentioned at the beginning. Yet one can ask whether the reference to the lineage of Jesus from David involves a *conscious* rejection of the majestic title *son of David,* so that the statement of the whole tradition would be: Jesus is descended from David, as is fitting for the Messiah, but he is not the "son of David" but the "Son of God." In this case the formula would already work against a political misinterpretation of Jesus' messianic majesty, as happened later, for example, in Mark 12:35–37a and *Barn.* 12.10–11, and one would not be allowed to place the text too early. This special apologetic interpretation, however, is not suggested by the wording of the formula, as is already seen in the fact that modern interpreters as a rule read the majestic title *son of David* into "from [the seed of] David" without thinking; and it is also not otherwise required, especially since a corresponding delimitation is not attested before the outbreak of the Jewish war. Therefore we are probably dealing with a doctrinal formula of fundamental dogmatic character, the object of which is to substantiate or confess the messianic majesty of Jesus with a reference to his Davidic descent and his exaltation after the resurrection from the dead.

The "Antiochene" Soteriology
Based on Jesus' Passion

When the church confesses that God raised the crucified Jesus from the dead, called him as Messiah, adopted him as God's Son, and placed him at God's right hand in the position of heavenly ruler, this unavoidably draws attention to Jesus' death and raises the question: Why should Jesus acquire his majesty, according to God's will, through death? Where the followers of Jesus were not receptive to the Easter experience, they could easily—as happened in the old sayings tradition—interpret Jesus' death as a prophet's fate, with which he authenticated his ministry and the truth of his message (Luke 13:34 par.; see p. 20 above). And even for Damascene preexistence Christology and its schema of humbling and exaltation, Jesus' death was not particularly a problem. It is part of the "true humanity" with which Jesus humbled himself, and it is the gate for returning to the Father; Paul added Phil. 2:8 to the traditional hymn.

In Hellenistic Christianity of the Antiochene variety, however, Jesus' death was interpreted in a thoroughly soteriological way (on this problem cf. Bieringer 1992). The relevant formulas and formulations, which Paul hands down in his letters, reveal no original formula, and the various soteriological ideas suggest no basic or initial idea. By contrast, there are formulas and stereotypical formulations from which one can conclude that the interpretation of Jesus' death as a salvific event originally made use of the text of Isaiah 53 and thus is *directly related to scripture*. In Isa. 53:4 is the "for us" of the suffering and dying of God's servant, as in Rom. 8:32; 1 Cor. 1:13; 11:24; 2 Cor. 5:14, 21; Gal. 2:20; 1 Thess. 5:10. In Isa. 53:5, 6, 10, 12 we find the "for our transgressions . . . for our iniquities" of his suffering, as in Rom. 4:25a; 1 Cor. 15:3; Gal. 1:4. Isa. 53:6, 12 speaks of the dedication of the obedient servant, as does Rom. 4:25a; 8:32; 1 Cor. 11:23; Gal. 1:4; 2:20. Isa. 53:11 says that the servant brings God's righteousness to "many" and is comparable to Rom. 3:25; 4:25b; 2 Cor. 5:21. Since in none of the mentioned cases can one as a rule detect a specific influence of the text of the Septuagint, we should assume that the Palestinian early church had already interpreted Jesus' death soteriologically with the help of Isaiah 53, and thus in the smooth transition of the Christian message into the Greek language area, an "open" conceptuality not directly based on the text of the Septuagint took shape and was assumed into the formulaic material, which seems to have been first fixed as such in the Greek language. Especially notable in this connection is the fact that the "*for* us" of Isaiah 53 is rendered in the Septuagint with the Greek *peri* or *dia,* but in early Christianity, as a rule, the preposition is *hyper*. From this we may conclude that the Greek formulation was fixed already in the Palestinian period.

In any case, it is no coincidence that "for us" or "for our sins" and the reference to the "righteousness of God" are also found in the Damascene formula in 2 Cor. 5:21, which grasps the work of salvation in the schema of humbling and exaltation without special reference to Jesus' death. The same background is also betrayed by the formula quoted by Paul in 2 Cor. 5:19, which already praises God's worldwide work of salvation: "In Christ God was reconciling the world to himself, not counting their trespasses against them," which likewise does not give special regard—if any—to Jesus' suffering death. In this connection, perhaps one may also point to the earlier formation adopted in 1 Cor. 1:30, whose expansion, undertaken by Paul in accordance with the context, is easily removed, and which in its pre-Pauline version develops more precisely the "for us" in the three steps of (1) the justification that has occurred, (2) the present sanctification, and (3) the coming redemption: Christ Jesus "became for us . . . righteousness and sanctification and redemption" (see pp. 126–27 below). Yet we cannot tell whether the soteriology of this formula is oriented in a Damascene way toward the incarnation or in an Antiochene way toward Jesus' death.

As a soteriological statement, "for us" or "for our sins" is sufficient in itself and does not necessarily need additional substantiation with the help of cultic or juristic categories (Rom. 5:6–8; 8:32; 1 Cor. 1:13; 11:24; Gal. 1:4; 2:20; 1 Thess. 5:10; Titus 2:14; 1 Peter 2:21, 24). Naturally, these can be added on a case by case basis without their taking the form of independent doctrinal statements, as happened in part in later theology, for example, in the satisfaction theory of Anselm of Canterbury. We find the category of substitution, which already governs Isaiah 53 (2 Cor. 5:14; Gal. 3:13), the motif of the covenantal sacrifice (1 Cor. 11:25; 1 Peter 1:2; Heb. 13:20), the concept of a sacrifice of atonement (Rom. 3:25; Eph. 5:2; 1 Peter 1:19; John 1:29, 36; Heb. 7:27; 9:14), the idea of redemption from the power of evil (Gal. 3:13; 4:5; 1 Tim. 2:6; Titus 2:14; 1 Peter 1:18; 2 Peter 2:1; Mark 10:45; Rev. 5:9; 1 John 4:10), and so forth (cf. Friedrich 1982, Barth 1992, and p. 99 below). We must remember, however, that as a rule these views were not clearly distinguished from each other in the religious experience of people in antiquity. Thus it is even less appropriate to make the cultic theory of atonement—which was in any case not familiar to the Hellenistic synagogue, which had no cultic sacrifice—the presupposition of all statements that speak of Jesus Christ's work of salvation, which happened "for us," as do, for example, Hofius (1989, 1ff.) and Stuhlmacher (1983; 1989).

The death of Jesus appears as the divine act of salvation only in the light that falls on it from Jesus' resurrection and exaltation. For this reason, the double formulas that put death and resurrection together—and also are reflected stereotypically in the early stages of tradition (Rom. 4:25; 6:1ff.; 8:34; 14:9; 1 Cor. 15:3b–5; 2 Cor. 5:15; 1 Thess. 4:14; 5:10)—are an especially appropriate expression of Antiochene soteriology.

Rom. 4:24b–25

The combined formula in Rom. 4:24b–25, with which Paul closes the second main section of his letter dealing with universal justification by faith, deserves attention appropriate to its prominent position:

24b [We] believe in him who raised Jesus our Lord from the dead,
25a who was handed over to death for our trespasses
25b and was raised for our justification.

Here we have a confession of faith whose use in teaching or in worship or perhaps in baptism can no longer be defined. The formula already contains the first two articles of the later triadic confession: the first line speaks of God the Father, the second of God the Son.

The first line, which speaks christologically of God as the one who raised Jesus from the dead, was originally independent and contains the not yet christologically or soteriologically developed early Easter confession, as it is found in Rom. 8:11; 10:9b; 2 Cor. 4:14; Gal. 1:1; 1 Thess. 1:10; Col. 2:12. The christological apposition "our Lord" is a later expansion, which was possibly inserted by Paul, for without this expansion, each of the three lines contains six Greek words; and thus the christological title in the first line, which disturbs this formal structure, must in any case have been added to the already completed three-part formula. Therefore one will not be able to demonstrate directly in terms of the history of tradition or literature the three steps in historical theology from the still apocalyptic confession of the resurrection through the christological *Kyrios* acclamation to the soteriological "for our sakes" in the formula of Rom. 4:24b–25.

The two christological, soteriological lines in 4:25 without doubt represent a secondary expansion of the older piece of theological tradition in 2:24b, and in this expansion we can also observe in a direct literary way the general process of theological history. The change of subject from "God" in the main clause of the first line to "Jesus" in the relative clause of the two following lines, as well as the double reference to the resurrection in the first and third lines, excludes the possibility that 4:24b–25 was originally conceived as a unit. It is unlikely, however, that in composing the Letter to the Romans, Paul joined two originally independent traditions, for the form of this confession—three lines of six words each—could hardly have originated accidentally from independent traditions. Yet in view of the un-Pauline and at the same time traditional conceptuality of the last two lines, their pre-Pauline character is also certain (cf. Schmithals 1988b, 148), and therefore we may assume that the present formula of faith reveals the origins of a pre-Pauline development toward an Antiochene passion soteriology. In light of the new experience that the resurrected One was exalted as Christ or Son of God, the originally apocalyptic confession to *God,* who raised Jesus from the dead, was already expanded before Paul through an interpretation oriented toward Isaiah 53 (cf. 1 Cor. 8:6), which expresses the knowledge of a present experience of salvation. This salvation is described with the language of being handed over "for our trespasses" (cf. Isa. 53:5, 12) and raised "for our justification" (cf. Isa. 53:11). In accordance with the parallelism of its members, both expressions make the same statement with different words, and one must accordingly also regard the "handing over" (Isa. 53:12) to death and the "raising" (53:10–12) of Jesus as one coherent act, as one salvation event. Analogous to the pre-Pauline formula in Rom. 3:25 (cf. 2 Cor. 5:21), "justification" consists in the forgiveness of trespasses.

It would be mistaken to assume in early Christianity a developed theory of atonement, reconciliation, or substitution behind this formula of faith as its foundation beyond the stimuli coming from Isaiah 53. The knowledge that the eschatological forgiveness of sins already announced by John the Baptist and grasped as promise in his baptism became an event in Jesus' passion was not primarily conveyed theoretically but acquired existentially, and the light that fell from Isaiah 53 on Jesus' death and resurrection was fully sufficient as the foundation of this knowledge. More precise dogmatic categories of interpretation are part of the ongoing development.

Rom. 3:25

One such *ongoing* development can be observed in the formula that Paul adopted in Rom. 3:24–26 and expanded interpretively. Yet the scope of the pre-Pauline tradition is disputed; it must be determined above all on the basis of the Pauline expansions, that is, with the help of observations on specific Pauline theology. The result of a corresponding analysis (cf. Schmithals 1988b, 120ff.) produces the following form of Paul's model:

> . . . whom God put forward as a sacrifice of atonement
> by his blood
> to show his righteousness,
> through the forgiveness of sins

This formula consists of two parts of two lines each in continuous sentence construction; each first line comprises five Greek words, each second line four, so that each part contains nine words.

The beginning of the formula with a relative pronoun referring to Jesus is characteristic of this kind of traditional material (Rom. 4:25; 1 Cor. 1:30b; Phil. 2:6; and elsewhere). We can no longer determine to which preceding statement the relative clause was attached, yet there is no reason not to assume as the main clause, analogous to Rom. 4:25b–26, a formulation such as, "We believe in God, who raised Jesus from the dead . . ." Also supporting such a *theological* main clause is the observation that as in Rom. 4:25; 1 Cor. 1:30b; 2 Cor. 5:19, 21, God is the one who acts with and through the death of Jesus for the salvation of humankind: the God who raised Jesus from the dead had previously handed him over to death. It is possible that the theological main clause and the christological dependent clause were spoken responsively, and that we may assume teaching as the primary role of the formula in the life of the church, namely, in the baptismal instruction, and thus we probably have here a dialogue between teacher and student. Naturally, we cannot exclude a corresponding use in worship, but the formula does not reveal a specific reference to the baptismal liturgy or to the celebration of the Lord's Supper.

The soteriological interpretation of Jesus' death is made with the help of the

Greek term *hilastērion,* which in the contemporary Hellenistic world meant in the general sense something that "atones": a means of atonement, an atoning sacrifice, an atoning gift, a time of atonement, or a place of atonement. In the Septuagint the mercy seat of the ark of the covenant is especially designated as a *hilastērion,* which on the great day of atonement is to be sprinkled with the blood of the sacrificial animal (Exod. 25:17–22; Lev. 16:11–17), even if this special day belongs in the postexilic period in which the ark was no longer present. The word *hilastērion* in the present formula has often been related particularly to the great day of atonement. Jesus would then be the means of atonement or sacrifice of atonement and at the same time the locus of atonement that replaces the Old Testament cult. In the formula, however, there is no indication of a relationship to the day of atonement and to the sacrifice still practiced in the Jerusalem temple, and a polemical relationship of Hellenistic Christianity to the Jerusalem cult, from which Judaism in the Diaspora was also separated, is quite unlikely. There is no way that the average Hellenistic Jewish Christian could derive from the formula a specific reference to the Jewish festal and cultic calendar. Therefore with *hilastērion* one must normally think of atonement in general (Friedrich 1982, 60ff.).

The "atonement" that Jesus makes occurs "by his blood" (cf. Rom. 5:9; 1 Cor. 11:25), since in the context of the idea of atonement, the formula appropriately circumscribes Jesus' death. Here as elsewhere, we should not turn to a particular theory of atonement, least of all to the juridical construction of Anselm's doctrine of atonement, according to which Jesus, through his death, must satisfy the justice or righteousness of God. The formula is based rather on the widespread familiar idea that guilt must be expiated if it is to be removed and the guilty person to be set free. God himself has accomplished this act of atonement through Jesus' death and thereby given sinners the assurance that they have been relieved of their guilt. God not only expresses his *will* to forgive but also turns forgiveness into a real event.

God does this publicly, and thus the sacrifice of atonement also becomes a memorial to atonement, for the term used in the formula, *put forward,* which is used in the Septuagint for the public setting out of the show bread (Exod. 40:23; Lev. 24:9), makes Jesus' atoning death evident to all. When "put forward as a sacrifice of atonement" is read aloud, the hearer or confessor is apparently supposed to imagine the execution of Jesus on the cross, which occurred in public. In this way the Hellenistic church turns Jesus' shameful, offensive death on an instrument of torture intended for a criminal into the victory symbol of its faith. With this the formula's statement also comes close to the universalism of the Damascene church, as found, for example, in 2 Cor. 5:19 ("reconciling the world to himself"), yet without expressly reaching it, for while Hellenist Jewish Christianity gladly opened itself to God-fearing Gentiles, it did this only within the prescribed boundaries of the synagogue. Not until Paul was the formula interpreted in a decidedly universalistic way, with respect to his Gentile Christian churches, when he inserted "through faith" (3:25) and appended "out of faith" (3:26). For in the context of the Letter to the Romans, "faith," as opposed to the "works of the law," designates the access to salvation that is open to all people without distinction.

With the atoning event of Jesus' death God proves "his righteousness," that is, his "faithfulness" to his chosen people (cf. Pss. 31:1ff.; 36:6ff.). The term *right-eousness* is also found in the pre-Pauline traditions in Rom. 4:25; 8:30; 1 Cor. 1:30b; 6:11; 2 Cor. 5:21, yet in these passages with a view toward *human beings* justified by God and led back to faithfulness to God. The talk of the "righteous-ness of God" (cf. Rom. 1:17; 3:21–22; etc.) always implies the justification of sin-ful human beings, so that even when in the term *righteousness of God* the genitive is supposed to be understood grammatically as *genitivus subjectivus* (righteous-ness appropriate to God), one cannot exclude the *genitivus objectivus* or *genitivus auctoris* (the righteousness given by God). The Damascene formula in 2 Cor. 5:21 ("... so that in him we might become the righteousness of God") shows especially well the transition from "righteousness of God" to "righteousness through God," and in Rom. 3:26 Paul, not without an objective basis, interprets the phrase "right-eousness of God" in the formula with the statement that God "is righteous [or just—*dikaion*] and that he justifies [*dikaiounta*]."

As in Rom. 4:25; 1 Cor. 15:3, and in general in pre-Pauline Antiochene soteri-ology, the object of the "righteousness of God" shown to humankind in the pres-ent formula is also the "forgiveness of sins." Thus, between God and human beings there are sinful deeds, the individual trespasses that God in his "righteousness" for-gives. This soteriology, which remains connected with the contemporary thinking of the synagogue, largely prevailed in the following Christian generations and sup-pressed or swallowed the more fundamental, more comprehensive understanding of sin and redemption that is already found in Damascene theology and then in Paul, as shown, for example, by the formulation: "[God] *sent* his Son to be the *atoning sacrifice* for our sins" (1 John 4:10). This development also could not hin-der Paul's attempt to interpret the formulations and concepts of Antiochene sote-riology in the spirit of his conversion theology. This attempt is especially easy to observe in the Pauline context of the present formula. Paul affirms that God shows his "righteousness" in the forgiveness of sins but relates this statement to the hu-man "sins previously committed" and thus to the past in the time of God's "for-bearance," as the apostle himself expands the traditional formula (3:25b–26a). Then, however, in 3:26b he adopts literally the phrase "to prove . . . that he him-self is righteous" again from the tradition and interprets it to the effect that in the eschatological now, God's righteousness "justifies the one who has faith" and transports the believer completely back into that original relationship with God in which the believer forgoes all glory and lets God's grace suffice. Thus God not only forgives sins but also, and above all, frees one from the power of sin, as Paul shows in detail in Romans 7–8.

1 Cor. 15:3–5

For a long time the Christ formula in 1 Cor. 15:3–5, which Paul expressly quotes as traditional material that he himself also received, has been considered especially characteristic of Hellenistic Jewish Christianity. As a rule it is assumed that this for-mula expresses in a fundamental way the soteriology of the Antiochene churches, but as closer analysis shows, this could hardly be accurate, even if the double for-mula were unquestionably oriented toward the central proclamation of salvation.

The exact form of the tradition is disputed, yet the possible differences do not affect the substance of the text. The fourfold "that," which makes the formula a construction of four parallel statements dependent on "I handed on . . . received" and is found nowhere else in comparable texts, probably comes from Paul. In his reshaping the apostle probably also assimilated an original title *the Christ* to his own linguistic usage by omitting the article, if the formula did not open, as in comparable cases, with a relative pronoun ("who"). If one assumes an independent sentence, the pre-Pauline tradition must have read:

> The Christ died / for our sins / in accordance with the scriptures /
> and was buried,
> and was raised / on the third day / in accordance with the scriptures /
> and appeared to Cephas (then to the twelve).

The phrase, "then to the twelve," like the further Easter witnesses added in the following verses 6–8, seems to be a secondary addendum inserted already in development of the pre-Pauline tradition. For without this addition the two members of the double formula each contain twelve Greek words, a stylization that is probably more original than the now present emphasis in the last line.

Even in the details the formula is constructed in parallel fashion. "Buried" belongs with "died," and "appeared" with "raised." In each case the second statement confirms the first. One who was buried has really died; one who has died but appears alive has been raised from the dead. We do not get the impression, however, that the formula is used apologetically against the questioning of Jesus' real death and his actual resurrection, and there is nothing from such an early time about a theory of apparent death. Rather, the formula attempts to convince the church that Jesus really died our death "for us" and at the same time overcame it as the resurrected One.

A specific tendency is betrayed, however, by his striking repetition of "in accordance with the scripture," especially since it is connected with "for our sins" and "on the third day." These two pieces of information are totally incongruous with each other. "For our sins," which is related to Isaiah 53, is traditional and also of highest theological importance. "On the third day" completely lacks such theological weight and probably does not come from an already fixed tradition, for the time of the resurrection is not otherwise mentioned by tradition. The dating of the finding of the empty grave and of the first appearances on the third day, which we find in the later narrative tradition of the Gospels, goes back to the present formula. It is likely that the phrase "on the third day" is an exegetical discovery that was inserted only because of "in accordance with the scripture" and that it refers to Hos. 6:2 — the only possibility. Thus the weight of the formula rests on the repeated "in accordance with the scripture." For this tradition formula it was important to demonstrate the Christian confession of the death and resurrection of Jesus as *in agreement with scripture*. Yet there is no actual scriptural *proof,* nor is one intended. The formula gives only limited consideration to the wording of Isaiah 53 and Hos. 6:2, although a corresponding concrete scriptural reference is no doubt presupposed. The formula is not guided by biblical scholarship but by the all-encompassing interest in basing the confession "Christ died and rose for our sins" on the traditions of the people of God. This specific interest identifies the formula as missionary teaching material and locates it in Jewish Christianity or in the evangelization and instruction of Gentiles attached to the synagogue as God-fearers, who recognized the authority of the scripture and did not want to give it up. The view that the formula was translated from an original Semitic text (Jeremias 1966) cannot be adequately substantiated (Conzelmann 1969, 298ff.); the formula probably originated in Greek-speaking Jewish Christianity.

1 Cor. 11:23–25

The words of institution of the Lord's Supper recalled by Paul for the Corinthians are doubtless from older tradition, even if the comment that Paul received this tradition "from the Lord" suggests that he independently reshaped the tradition according to his theological insight. The repeated instruction "Do this in remembrance of me" places these words in a Hellenistic church, for valid arguments cannot be made against the convincing view of Lietzmann (1949, 58; cf. Conzelmann 1969, 233–34) that this interpretation of the celebration is analogous to Greek meals for remembrance of the dead. In terms of content the statement is related to the information that the meal was arranged by Jesus himself "on the night when he was betrayed [handed over; delivered]"; the two statements may even have come into being together with this marginal note. In any case, the Hellenistic church made the custom of the common meal of remembrance of Jesus' death understandable to its members with the help of a custom familiar to them, and in 11:26 Paul himself interprets this information to the effect that with the celebratory meal the church *proclaims* the death of the Lord; thus the idea is not remembrance but proclamation. This interpretation probably already agrees with the pre-Pauline tradition, which contributed to the saying over the bread the "for you" that is still missing in the Markan parallel tradition (Mark 14:22) and which in this inclusive way defines Jesus' death as a salvific death.

Another determination is added to the saying over the cup, which, however—unlike the "for you" of the bread saying and the "betrayed [handed over; delivered]" of the context—does not go back to Isaiah 53 but to Jer. 31:31 (38:31 LXX), where God promises his people a new covenant, which according to Jer. 32:40 (39:40 LXX) will be an "everlasting" covenant, that is, the eschatological covenant. According to the word over the cup, this new covenant is established by Jesus' sacrificial death. That may be meant in the sense of Exod. 24:8 (cf. Zech. 9:11), where the concluding of the covenant on Sinai is sealed with a sacrifice. It can also refer, however, to Jer. 31:34 (38:34 LXX), according to which in the new covenant God will "remember their sin no more," and thus the new covenant rests on the fact that Jesus "was handed over to death for our trespasses" (Rom. 4:25). The two ideas may merge with each other, yet this does not mean that the interpretation of the cup as the "blood of the covenant" is based on the idea of atonement or substitution. In any case, the Hellenistic Jewish Christian church does not, in its Lord's Supper sayings, place any value on developing a special theory regarding the salvific power of Jesus' death; rather, it wants to establish and strengthen its members in the communion of the new covenant and the presence of the Lord Jesus. Sufficient for this are the key sayings "This is my body" and "This cup is the new covenant in my blood" or "This is my blood of the covenant" (Mark 14:24), which even without a more elaborate doctrinal conception turn the stumbling block of Jesus' death into the certain basis of eschatological salvation. (See pp. 251ff. below.)

Dying and Rising with Christ

The "mystical" idea of dying and rising with Christ (Rom. 6:1–11; Phil. 3:10–11; 2 Cor. 4:10; 5:14–15; Gal. 2:19; 6:14, 17; Col. 2:20) or of suffering with and being glorified with Christ (Rom. 8:17) is difficult to place in terms of theological history and therefore requires special consideration. It originally had nothing to do with the spatial idea, rooted in the mythos of dualism, of "being in Christ," which is loosely connected with the idea of suffering, dying, and rising with Christ in Gal. 2:19–20; Col. 2:11–12; and Phil. 3:9–10. Rather, in the history-of-religions school it was determined indisputably, despite many objections, that this early Christian motif was shaped under the influence of contemporary mystery piety (Friedrich 1982, 87ff.), and thus its origin in a Hellenistically influenced Christianity is assured. It does not, however, necessarily presuppose the soteriological confession based on Isaiah 53 that Christ died and rose "for us," and actually in its original form it was probably meant entirely eschatologically: those who die as Christians may be certain of the resurrection in discipleship to Jesus, the "first fruits of those who have died" (1 Cor. 15:20; Rom. 1:4; Col. 1:18; Rev. 1:5; Matt. 27:52–53; Acts 26:23). In 2 Tim. 2:11 we find a corresponding "saying" expressly quoted: "If we have died with him, we will also live with him."

We should also observe that life with Christ (1 Cor. 15:20ff.) is understood in a purely future way in Rom. 6:5, 8, whereas for Paul himself in Rom. 6:1ff. it is a question of new life with Christ in the present. Without going any further into the difficult question of which tradition-historical problems are revealed in Rom. 6:1ff, we can state that the motif as such is older and has different emphases from its ethical application in this passage, and that in its original significance it was probably closer to the still apocalyptically defined early church and its conception that Jesus was resurrected as the "first fruits": "If we have died with Christ, we believe that we will also live with him" (Rom. 6:8). In this way the mode of expression offered by mystery piety enabled certain early Christian circles, which can hardly be more precisely located, to overcome the problem of the death of individual Christians before the Parousia. In a corresponding sense that *predates* the soteriological "for us" of Jesus' suffering and dying, Paul himself uses the present motif also in Phil. 3:10–11 and Rom. 8:17, yet in both passages already with the additional reference to the *suffering* with or for the sake of Christ: the power of Jesus' resurrection is understood properly by those who enter into the communion of his suffering and become like him in his death, in the expectation that they themselves will thereby also attain the resurrection of the dead and be glorified with Jesus (cf. also 2 Tim. 2:12). A new stage in theological history is reached with this idea of dying and living with Christ in the two-part pre-Pauline formula in Rom. 14:9:

> For to this end Christ died and lived again,
> so that he might be Lord of both the dead and the living.

The "for us" of Jesus' death and resurrection is still lacking, yet the resurrection is interpreted henceforth as exaltation into the heavenly kingdom, and consequently the hopeful idea of living with Christ becomes eschatological and is expressed in the idea that the dominion of the *Kyrios* Christ extends to Christians who have died.

The extent to which the further carrying out of the idea of dying with and being resurrected with, which soteriologically goes beyond the future sense and context, is attributable to Paul himself, and to what extent it came about before and apart from Paul, can be precisely determined only with difficulty, especially since we lack fixed formulaic material connected with this idea. It is notable that the Gospel of Mark, without being influenced here by Paul, works with this soteriologically expanded motif and adopts it into the passion story (Schmithals 1986, 421ff., 684ff.; see p. 320 below). Also the breadth of variation with which it is found in Paul attests that this idea that is linked with him was essentially already available before him. He had perhaps already adopted it in part in his conversion theology. In any case, this is suggested by the apparently already traditional connection of the baptismal act (as the drowning of the old self) with the theologoumenon of "dying with Christ," to which he returns in Rom. 6:3, 8 (cf. pp. 126–28 below):

> . . . all of us who have been baptized into Christ Jesus
> were baptized into his death . . .
> But if we have died with Christ,
> we believe that we will also live with him.

For Paul himself, however, in Rom. 6:1ff. it is a question of refuting the synagogal reproach that the person justified by faith instead of the law is a potential sinner: those who with Christ have died to sin can no longer live in it! But in the presentation of this idea, which seems to have been originally Paul's own, the apostle holds entirely to Antiochene Christology when he develops his view with the help of the terms "crucified with" (6:6), "died with" (6:8), "buried with" (6:4), and "live with" (6:8), which he recalls for the Christians in Rome, who were unknown to him, with a threefold "we know" (Rom. 6:3, 6, 9). A similar phenomenon is found in 2 Cor. 5:14, where Paul first quotes a formulaic expression of older provenance, "one has died for all," in order immediately to interpret it "mystically": "Therefore all have died." Also, the theological intention of this passage, with its use of the "mystical" motif, corresponds to the ethicizing idea of Rom. 6:1ff.: those who have died with Christ no longer live for themselves but for the one who died "for them," that is, by serving one's neighbor.

In Gal. 2:19–20, in an obviously typical Pauline passage, the idea of "I have been crucified with Christ, so that I might live to God" is connected with both

Damascene ("Christ lives in me") and Antiochene ("who gave himself for me") conceptuality and, moreover, with the genuine Pauline teaching of justification ("through the law I died to the law"). Consequently, with the "I" who dies with Christ, it is a question of the "old" self, which seeks to achieve its righteousness in the works of the law, whereas the new self does "not nullify the grace of God" (Gal. 2:21).

In Gal. 6:14 Paul refers, in a way that is characteristic of his own theology, to the cross of Christ, "by which the world has been crucified to me, and I to the world." Thus in this passage, as in Gal. 2:19–21, he relates dying with Christ in a fundamental sense to the death of the old self, which boasts its own righteousness. The following reference in 6:17 to the fact that he bears the stigmata of Jesus on his body probably belongs on the same conceptual level, yet the "mystical" motif is clearly narrowed to Paul's apostolic existence. This is also the case in the related passage 2 Cor. 4:10–12: "We are . . . always carrying in the body the death of Christ, so that the life of Jesus may also be made visible in our bodies," namely, when for its salvation the church recognizes in the fate of the apostle that the power of the new life comes from God and not from human beings. Finally, in Col. 2:20 (cf. 2:12; 3:1ff.) the ethical aspect again predominates, as in Rom. 6:1ff.; Gal. 2:19–20; and 2 Cor. 5:14–15, yet in such a way that the new self, which has died with Christ, is free from the "regulations" of the Torah: "If with Christ you died to the elemental spirits of the universe, why do you live as if you still belonged to the world? Why do you submit to regulations . . . ?"

The idea that the old self dies with Christ but the new lives with him, through him, and for him, essentially corresponds to the idea of the individual person being "born again," which is connected above all with baptism (Titus 3:5; John 3:3–7; cf. 2 Cor. 4:16; Col. 3:10), and both ideas are likewise rooted in mystery piety. Yet the rare and late appearance in early Christianity of the concept of being "born again" does not allow, in terms of theological *history,* an analysis of the corresponding motif, which as an interpretation of the baptismal event was probably adopted into a Hellenistic Christianity from its environment—possibly from Jewish Christianity, for Philo also knew and used the corresponding term.

6

Paul's Theological Development
as a Mirror of the Theological History
of Early Christianity

The question of a development in Pauline theology was first actively discussed in the wake of the Tübingen School and in the context of the general idea of progress in the middle of the last century (cf. Schweitzer 1911, 22ff.). The issue is also getting a relatively large amount of attention again in the present (Buck and Taylor 1969). On the one hand, such theological development is sought and found in regard to the *doctrine of justification,* which Paul is not supposed to have worked out until his later battles with Judaizing opponents (Sabatier 1870; Strecker 1976, 479ff.; Schade 1981, 115ff.; Schnelle 1981, 100–101; Schulz 1985, 234), and also in regard to his changing *understanding of the law* (Holtz 1971; Hübner 1978; Wilckens 1982; Schulz 1985, 234; 1987, 301ff.; Räisänen 1986; and Schnelle 1989, 49ff.). Development is found in *eschatology* (Hunzinger 1968; Marxsen 1969; Wiefel 1974; Storck 1980; Lüdemann 1980, 213ff.; Klein 1986; Becker 1987; Schnelle 1989, 37ff.), in *ethics* (Schulz 1987, 290ff.), and in Paul's *relationship with Israel,* which is said to have changed in the course of the apostle's activity (Penna 1986; Schnelle 1989, 77ff.). On the other hand, the problems of a double anthropology (Jewish or Hellenistic) and a corresponding double soteriology (juridical or mystical), which attracted a great deal of interest within the history-of-religions school after the study by Lüdemann (1872), as well as developments in Paul's Christology, are given relatively little attention today (cf., however, Strecker 1976; Schnelle 1986).

In contrast to the various attempts of contemporaries and fellow disputants of the Tübingen School to demonstrate developments in Paul on the basis of the extant letters, Pfleiderer (1973, 29–30) points to the essential unity of Pauline theology and calls attention to the local situations that occasioned the theological peculiarities of individual letters: "If we find nothing about the doctrine of justification in the First Letter to the Thessalonians, we also find very little about this concept in the Corinthian letters, and in both cases for the same obvious reason: in a purely Gentile Christian community there was no reason for an exposition of the doctrine of justification in its particular form, which was conditioned by the categories of Jewish thought" (cf. Lowe 1941; Kümmel 1971/72). Based on corresponding methodological considerations, other scholars conclude that also in regard to eschatology the "construction of a gradual development" proves to be impossible (Hoffmann 1966, 327) and that "there is no room for a development in Paul's statements about the next world" (Gnilka 1968, 88; cf. Erlemann 1992); the various eschatological conceptions are given "from the beginning" and are "determined and accentuated by various situations of a personal and communal nature" (Grundmann 1961/62, 17; Luz 1968, 356ff.; Lindemann 1991; Erlemann 1992, 223).

In fact, the methodological procedure used in the attempted reconstruction of developments in Pauline theology is in many respects highly questionable. In the past scholars often worked with a development especially of eschatological ideas from the first to the second Corinthian letter or from the main letters to the later letters from prison, including the Letter to the Philippians, or from the early Letter to the Galatians to the main letters of the third missionary journey, in which, as a rule, certain experiences with heretics or persecutors, which were examined psychologically, are supposed to have effected a theological transformation in Paul. In most cases today, however, the temporal difference between 1 Thessalonians, which is dated in the second missionary journey and "as the only testimony of early Pauline theology and ethics" should occupy "the key position" (Schulz 1985, 235), and the main letters of the third missionary journey forms the starting point of the investigation: the experiences that Paul had in the eastern part of the Roman Empire in battles with his opponents in Galatia, Corinth, and Philippi are supposed to have caused the reshaping of his theological ideas. Yet profound theological developments have also been observed even from Galatians to Romans (Hübner 1978), between the letters to Corinth and those to Galatia and Philippi and also to Rome (Wilckens 1982; Schnelle 1989), from 1 Corinthians through Philippians to 2 Corinthians (Storck 1980), and so forth.

As a rule, not only did one feel relieved of the effort (typical is Schade 1981, 173ff.) to advance the considerable arguments for the dating of the correspondence with Thessalonica also in the time of the third missionary journey (Michaelis 1954, 221ff.; Hyldahl 1986, 107ff.), but there was also a failure to note that the time between the second and third missionary journeys was relatively short and therefore, in view of the total time of Paul's activity, was insignificant in terms of possible Pauline developments. Thus we must we exclude the idea that Paul changed his theological orientation in a significant way during the one year in which the letters were written that definitely belong to the third missionary journey. In general, there is little likelihood that important theological developments in Paul occurred in the late period of his independent missionary work, after the establishment of his educational activity and in the forum of his already founded and theologically established European churches. How did Paul inform his scattered students and his churches about modifications in his views? The letters whose comparison allegedly leads to the discernment of changes in his thinking do not reveal such information; rather, they leave it up to the churches to draw the necessary conclusions and reorient themselves theologically.

Finally, no notice has been taken of how meager, how temporally limited, and how arbitrarily selected, in view of Paul's total work, is the legacy of the Pauline letters available to us for the reconstruction of a theological development. The dogmatic determination of the Pauline canon offers no adequate basis for such historical analyses. Though the context-related nature of Paul's assertions is, as a rule, generally conceded, it is, in fact, pushed aside in favor of a comparison of individual assertions and corresponding developments that has not been thought out historically and hermeneutically. As a rule, furthermore, literary-critical problems remain unconsidered, although they are of decisive importance precisely in regard to the First Letter to the Thessalonians, the star witness in all theories. In 1 Thess. 2:14–16 (position on Israel) or 4:15–18 (eschatology), for example, is it even a question of texts from the hand of Paul (see pp. 275–76 below; Schmithals 1988a, 74ff.)? When such critical questions—each important in itself—are added together, they make it clear that the numerous attempts to demonstrate theological developments in Paul during his few years of activity in the European mission field do not, as a rule, get beyond the level of arbitrary constructions.

The foregoing does not call into question theological developments in Paul and the possibility of their reconstruction, but the methodological point of departure for the determination of such developments cannot be the temporal difference—which is relatively small at best—between individual Pauline letters that are by chance available to us and are always situation-related. Rather, the earlier phases of Paul's thinking are to be discerned only in the *stratification* of his theological ideas, which are in principle to be examined uniformly and tradition-critically in the *entirety* of the available theological legacy of the apostle. For in his letters Paul uses not only numerous more or less fixed traditions, which do not come from his own theological reflection, but also, and above all, fixed teaching texts from his theological educational activity. These texts, which occur in abundance in his teaching letter to Rome, are also very much in evidence in the remaining letters and must be regarded as both the presupposition and foundation of all examinations of Pauline theological development (see chapter 7). The essential theological developments of Paul can be discerned and their causes inferred not from attempts to distinguish theological statements through a comparison of individual letters with each other and against each other—as carried out, for example, by Schnelle (1989) in a way that is especially consistent yet uncritical in regard to his own methodological assumptions—but through the objective and temporal *differentiation,* in terms of form and tradition criticism, of theological ideas *within* the essentially *unified* theological conception achieved by Paul in the extant letters.

In this way these theological developments are integrated into the theological history of early Christianity and shed light upon that history. Those who believe they can infer theological developments in Paul from the temporal differentiation of his letters see only acute experiences and their personal processing by the apostle, whereas the numerous pre- and extra-Pauline traditions in the letters of Paul show that the apostle, in spite of his theological competence, did not understand himself as a solitary, sovereign theologian but as a member of the general Christian teaching and confessional community, who until the end placed great worth on the agreement of his missionary work among the Gentiles with the leadership of the Christian mission within the synagogues (Rom. 15:25ff.). The authentic theological development of Paul, which becomes more observable in the later writings, reveals much of the general theological history of early Christianity.

On Paul's Universalist "Conversion Theology"

Any discussion of Paul's Christian beginnings must start with the fact that he was converted to the Christianity that he had persecuted. Since, however, he did not persecute Christianity in general but a particular variety of Christianity, his conversion experience reveals a theological differentiation in early Christianity that is not entirely concealed by the intentionally harmonized presentation of the author of Acts, who nonetheless still distinguishes between the "Hebrews" under the leadership of Peter, John, and the twelve, and the "Hellenists" under Stephen and the "seven." According to everything that we know, the Christianity organized within the association of the synagogue remained relatively unmolested in the persecution in which Paul took part (Acts 8:1; Gal. 1:17–19; but cf. Acts 12:1ff.). Paul persecuted instead "the church of God" (Gal. 1:13; 1 Cor. 15:9), or simply "the church" (Phil. 3:6; cf. Gal. 1:22–24), an independently organized Christian group according to the account in Acts (6:1ff.), which he probably also had in mind in Gal. 1:22, for Paul never uses the designation *church* (*ekklēsia*) for the Christians in Jerusalem or for other Jewish Christian groups. It was chosen rather by the "Hellenists" under the leadership of Stephen in order to express the "consciousness of a discontinuity with regard to a past characterized by the law" (Schrage 1963, 199–200). Paul himself pursued his activity as persecutor outside the land of the Jews (Gal. 1:17; Acts 9:1ff.), in accordance with his roots in the Greek-speaking Diaspora, but Gal. 1:22 attests that there were also "churches" in Palestine that were once persecuted, yet not by Paul himself, who otherwise could not have said that he was unknown to the "churches" (*ekklēsiai*) in Judea and that they had only heard of his conversion (cf. Suhl 1975, 30ff.). We know nothing about the process of persecution; it probably consisted essentially in the tracking down and denunciation of Christians before the appropriate Gentile authorities, who could not allow citizens who no longer belonged to the synagogue to escape the imperial sacrifice. Paul does not speak of a *bloody* persecution; the martyrdom of Stephen (Acts 7:54ff.), the leader of the "churches," was probably an exception. Paul clearly states, however, the aim of the persecution, namely, the destruction of the "church" (Gal. 1:13, 23; cf. Acts 9:21).

In view of the fact that before the Jewish war those who paid the temple tax — even Jewish Christians and God-fearing Gentiles or Gentile Christians (Jos. *Ant.* 14.7.2; *Bell.* 2.197, 409–10; Tacitus *Historiae* 5.5; Matt. 17:24ff.) — were tolerated and as a rule even welcomed as members of the synagogue association, regardless of their convictions, the persecution of the "church" could have affected only the Christians who had rejected the right of the synagogue to exist as a social organization, or Judaism as an independent religion. Thus the criticism of the law by these Christians, which Paul presupposes in Gal. 1:13–14; Phil. 3:4ff., which is also mentioned in Acts 6:13–14, and the context of which Paul at his conversion felt called as a *missionary to the Gentiles* (Gal. 2:16), cannot be a question of an intra-Jewish conflict over the understanding of the law provoked by the lax interpretation of the law by many adherents of the Hellenistic synagogue. Rather, it must have been of a more fundamental nature and the result of a radical universalism that in principle breaks the bounds of the synagogue. Paul passes on — more than once and with variations — the central teaching formula of this universalism, which was apparently part of a baptismal paraenesis:

> There is no longer Jew or Greek,
> there is no longer slave or free,
> there is no longer male and female;
> for all of you are one in Christ Jesus.
> (Gal. 3:28; cf. 1 Cor. 12:13;
> Col. 3:10–11; 1 Cor. 7:18–20)

The pre-Pauline Adam-Christ typology in Rom. 5:11–19 (cf. 1 Cor. 15:21–22) also serves on the basis of its origin to express and demonstrate this universalism. In that *all* people are included in Christ, as in Adam, the difference between Jews and Gentiles is abolished as secondary and superseded, and the particularism of "Abraham's children" (Rom. 9:6–7) or the Torah of Moses proves to be overcome eschatologically.

The terminology *in Christ* (Gal. 3:26, 28; 1 Cor. 15:22), *into Christ* (Gal. 3:27) or *into one body* (1 Cor. 12:12–13), *putting on Christ* (Gal. 3:27; cf. Col. 3:10), *belonging to Christ* (Gal. 3:29), *all and in all* (Col. 3:11), and *one Spirit* (1 Cor. 12:13) points to the theological context in which this universalism is found. Here we encounter the early Christian theology that has been designated from various points of view as "physical," "ontic," "mystical," "dualistic," "Hellenistic," "realistic," "ontological," and so forth, and which is characterized by, among other things, preexistence Christology (Phil. 2:6ff.), a universalist anthropology with a radical conception of sin (Rom. 7:17ff.), an incarnational soteriology (Gal. 4:4; Rom. 8:3–4; Col. 1:19–20), dualistic language (Rom. 7:18; 8:2ff.), aspects of a present eschatology (2 Cor. 5:17), body-of-Christ ecclesiology (1 Cor. 10:16b–17; 12:4ff.), and an ethic guided not by prayer but by the Spirit (Gal. 5:16ff.) (see chapter 4). Here we encounter at the same time the native soil of Johannine Christianity, which, as Bultmann saw, "represents an older type than the Synoptic" (1967a, 102). Expressly Old Testament traits are not found in this theological system; the law is not given by God himself but by "angels" (Gal. 3:19–20). The dominant universalism does not allow a particular election and revelation, and therefore a special discussion of the meaning of the Torah, as found later in Paul as the integrating part of his doctrine of justification, is also superfluous.

This doctrine of justification is rooted in the universalist conversion theology of Paul, even if the apostle did not develop it in his characteristic way until later, in his disagreement with the synagogue. After his conversion, however, Paul held the law to be unsuitable for bringing salvation to people and proclaiming faith in the God "who justifies the *ungodly*" (Rom. 4:5), because all people without distinction have sinned in Adam, and God has imprisoned all people as unbelievers in order to show mercy to all (Rom. 11:32). Thus the term *righteousness* is already found in an early formula of Damascene provenance, which speaks of the humbling of the one who descended from the heavenly world into the reality of sin:

> For our sake he made him to be sin who knew no sin,
> so that in him we might become the righteousness of God.
>
> (2 Cor. 5:21)

Now as earlier, there are various attempts to escape the insight that Paul was converted to a Christianity whose Jewish confessors "declared the law to be fundamentally abolished and thereby contested any religious priority of Israel" (Klein 1984, 62). Thus Strecker (1976, 484ff.), who is followed by his student Schnelle (1989, 15ff.), holds the confession of Jesus as the Christ to be the essential reason for the early persecution of Christians, although this intra-Jewish confession could never have been such a reason, and although this reason would also have had to lead to the persecution of the "Hebrews" in Jerusalem. By contrast, Wilckens (1982, 155), like Räisänen (1986, 21–22, 242ff.), limits the criticism of the Torah by the "Hellenists," who were persecuted by Paul, to a criticism of the temple cult, which was put forth because Jesus' atoning sacrifice made the temple cult superfluous. But any form of the *theologia crucis* is foreign to the conversion theology of Paul, and temple and cult criticisms were in vogue everywhere in Judaism and even in its holy scriptures (cf. Klein 1984, 62). Also entirely incomprehensible is the view of Becker (1987, 108) that the baptism of God-fearers *in* the synagogue could have initiated the persecution. Two motifs seem to be behind such attempted explanations. First, one cannot explain how at such an early time in primitive Christianity there could have been such a basic abrogation of the law. Second, the later activity of Paul does not seem to correspond to these origins and beginnings of his conversion theology.

The first of these concerns could be allowed if the development from Peter and the twelve to Stephen and the seven, or from Jerusalem to Damascus, had to be explained by purely internal Christian events, as the author of the book of Acts attempts to do, with varying degrees of success. Yet the observed development from the early church kerygma encompassed in the framework of apocalyptic dualism to the "Johannine" type of Pauline conversion theology can be understood without difficulty as a more comprehensive religious-historical process (see pp. 74ff. above). It apparently takes place in the early intra-Palestinian transition of Judaean Jewish Christianity in the realm of an enthusiast-dualist direction of contemporary Judaism (Simon Magus), in which the corporeal, particular, and national gives way to the universal and pneumatic. Stephen and the "Hellenists" (Acts 6:1) transposed the dualism of substance of this dualistic Judaism into Old Testament, historical (*geschichtlich*) thinking and in this framework redeveloped Christology, soteriology, ecclesiology, and eschatology; in so doing they retained the originally pneumatic-dualistically based universalism, which in its Christian version the synagogue must have rightly felt as an attack threatening its existence.

Paul's Early Gentile Mission
within the Synagogue

The second concern that Paul saw as a missionary to the Gentiles requires a more thorough examination. In Gal. 1:17 Paul says that after his conversion he went to Arabia and after a time returned from there to Damascus. His commitment to the Christianity he had fought necessarily resulted in his being subject to persecution himself. This is enough to explain why he did not remain in Damascus after his conversion but escaped from the persecutors into the kingdom of the Nabataeans bordering on Syria, which had been connected in a usually friendly way with the Maccabeans and Herodians (cf. Acts 2:11) and which promoted Greek as the language of culture. We learn nothing about the length of his stay there or his possible activities. According to 2 Cor. 11:32–33 (cf. Acts 9:24–25), however, Paul finally came into conflict with the Nabataean authorities. This suggests undesirable missionary activity on the part of Paul. Between 30 and 32 Herod Antipas had, for Herodias's sake, cast out the daughter of the Nabataean king Aretas, to whom he was married (Mark 6:17–18), which led to war between Aretas and Herod. Under these circumstances, Aretas may have persecuted Paul, the Jew and Christian missionary to the Gentiles, as an active representative of Jewish interests.

But what made Paul's return to Damascus possible? And what is more, how could Paul, in the third year after his conversion, go to Jerusalem unhindered and make contact with the leaders of the primitive church there (Gal. 1:18–20)? Even if the persecution of the universalist "church of God" was not organized by the Jerusalem Sanhedrin, whom the author of Acts makes responsible for these activities (Acts 6:12; 9:1–2), Paul cannot in any case have gone to Jerusalem unmolested under the circumstances mentioned in Gal. 1:13ff. and spent fourteen days there with Peter and James, the brother of Jesus. Nothing indicates that Paul, as a member of a persecuted segment of early Christendom, stayed unrecognized in Jerusalem and was supported by the primitive church. What could have motivated him to travel to Jerusalem under such circumstances? If the Jewish Christians there had secretly housed Paul in their midst under the conditions of a persecution situation and made contact with him (about what?), this would have been a mortal danger for them also, a risk for which there could have been no justification whatever, either for them or for Paul.

To this we must add a further observation. In Gal. 1:22–24 Paul reports that he was personally unknown "to the churches of Judea" that he had "formerly" persecuted, and he underlines this statement with the doxological indication that they had only "heard" (literally, "were constantly hearing"—*conjugatio periphrastica*) of his preaching of the gospel and "glorified God because of me." What intention is Paul pursuing with this comment? This remark *follows* the information that after his first visit in Jerusalem he went to Syria and Cilicia (Gal. 1:21). Hence this striking notice is given from the viewpoint of the activity between his first and second visits in Jerusalem, and in the context of the intention pursued by Paul in Gal. 1:1–2:10 it is supposed to make especially clear that in the meantime he had not stepped on Judaean soil and thus had no further direct contact with the older apostles (Gal. 1:17). Consequently, in Gal. 1:22–24 we find an indirect assertion by Paul that he did not receive his gospel from human authorities, and at the same time, in a way that corresponds to 1 Cor. 15:9–10 and follows the foregoing account of his previous life, he bursts into praise of the grace of God given to him. Now the phrase "churches of Judea" in Gal. 1:22–24 naturally does not refer to the "Hebrews" of Jerusalem, who for the most part apparently escaped the persecution—and thus "who formerly was persecuting us" in Gal. 1:23 does not apply to them—and to whom Paul, moreover, was personally known; nor does it refer to other Jewish Christian communities that may have arisen in Palestine. Rather, in accordance with Paul's use of language, it concerns assemblies of circumcised and uncircumcised Christians whom Paul, according to Gal. 1:13–14, 23, once tried to annihilate and who apparently can now exist unmolested even in Palestine. Hence the double occurrence of *pote* ("then, formerly, once") in 1:23 refers not only to Paul's former activity as persecutor and destroyer but also to these "churches in Judea" themselves, who were once persecuted and now enjoy a right to exist.

Finally, in this context we must look at Paul's missionary work in Syria and Cilicia, of which he speaks in Gal. 1:21a and which followed his first visit in Jerusalem. In spite of Acts 11:19ff., we do not have any reliable information on the origins and beginnings of Christian missions in Antioch and vicinity. Without doubt, Paul joined a work that had already been started and was theologically distinctive, as shown by the formulaic material handed down by Paul himself. Characteristically different from the formulas of his conversion theology, this material attests for Antiochene Christianity (see 88ff. above) an adoptionist Christology (Rom. 1:3–4) and an ethical understanding of sin with a corresponding soteriology (Rom. 3:25; 4:25; 1 Cor. 15:3–4), as well as a traditional eschatology (Rom. 5:21; 6:8, 23; 1 Thess. 1:10). The idea that in the beginning Paul worked in the shadow of Barnabas is probable (cf. Acts 4:36; 11:25–26, 30; 13:2; 1 Cor. 9:6) but cannot be demonstrated and is to be excluded at the latest for the period after Gal. 2:1. Without doubt, Paul, in accordance with his commission (Gal. 1:16; Rom. 15:16ff.), was active with Barnabas as *missionary to the Gentiles*. It may be coincidental that Acts is silent about persecutions to which the missionaries were subjected during the time of Paul's Syrian and Cilician missionary activity. Yet one should not entirely ignore this observation in view of the fact that even Paul himself gives no information about contemporary events that one could date with certainty in this period, even if Paul's activity might have led to tensions within the synagogue and 2 Cor. 11:24 could refer to this period. In any case, however, it is noteworthy that apart from the short notice in Gal. 1:21a, Paul never speaks in his letters in a clear way about his activity in Syria and Cilicia, although it lasted longer than ten years (Gal. 2:1) and thus encompassed a considerable part of his life's work. In this mission area Paul apparently had no churches with which he remained in lasting contact. Nowhere, apart from the coincidental notice in Gal. 1:21a, do his letters betray that east of Galatia there was also a place of extended Pauline activity. When he gathered a collection in *his* churches, none were in Syria and Cilicia, where there were indeed Christian, but not Pauline, churches.

In any case, this remarkable state of affairs cannot be explained with the initially attractive proposal of Lüdemann (1980) that in Gal. 1:21 Paul is naming Syria and Cilicia only as a first destination of his journey, but not as a place of long-term activity, and that his missionary work from Galatia to Greece actually falls in the thirteen years (Gal. 2:1) between the first two trips to Jerusalem. This arbitrary view has no basis. Rather, in my opinion it precludes any appropriate understanding of Paul's itinerary and of the Apostolic Council. It is based on an excess of auxiliary hypotheses, premises, and free constructions, and it also unnecessarily disrupts the accounts in Acts. There is no reason, much less necessity, to give up the extensive coincidence of the chronologies offered us by Paul's letters and the Acts of the Apostles in order to benefit an artificial reconstruction and at the same time throw tradition into confusion.

By way of example, let us point out two things. On the one hand, since in Gal. 1:10ff. Paul is attempting—even in Lüdemann's view—to demonstrate through a historical account his independence from Jerusalem, in Gal. 1:21 he could not have kept silent about a lengthy stay in Europe. Indeed, he has to make an effort to clarify to some extent the fact that he worked for years in Syria and Cilicia without ever visiting nearby Palestine. On the other hand, for the view that even the incident reported in 2:11ff. occurred *before* the Apostolic Council, Lüdemann appeals to the possibility of a revision of the temporal sequence, for which ancient rhetoric provides within a *narratio*. But even if we accept the questionable analogy of a letter to rhetoric, he overlooks the fact that the passage from Quintilian (4.2.83), quoted by him (1980, 78) as proof of such a possibility, states that for such a revision, which is allowed only in exceptional cases for the sake of the clarity of the argumentation, the speaker must give good reasons. In Gal. 2:11ff., however, this is by no means the case, and we cannot, furthermore, recognize a good reason why Paul should have added without transition the immediate reason for the Apostolic Council, which Lüdemann judges to be the Antiochene incident. Rather, Paul would have completely confused his argumentation; he would have failed to give the necessary reasons for his behavior and would also have consciously deceived his readers about the temporal sequence of the events, for he clearly sets the temporal sequence of his account: "when" (Gal. 1:15) . . . "then" (1:18) . . . "then" (1:21) . . . "then" (2:1) . . . "when" (2:11).

In my view, the striking fact that Paul's long-term and apparently largely trouble-free activity in Syria and Cilicia no longer comes up in connection with his later involvement in founding and leading churches can be explained only by the idea that the Apostolic Council separating the two phases of his work meant a fundamental break in the missionary activity of the apostle to the Gentiles. Only in connection with this event does he establish independent Gentile Christian churches, whereas earlier he was active like and with Barnabas among the God-fearing Gentiles *in the context of the institution of the synagogue*. In 1 Cor. 9:20–21 he looks back on this aspect of his work:

> To the Jews I became as a Jew, in order to win Jews. To those under the
> law I became as one under the law . . . so that I might win those under the

> law. To those outside the law I became as one outside the law . . . so that
> I might win those outside the law.

And his opponents may have this effectiveness in mind in Gal. 5:11. The vacillating attitude of Barnabas (Gal. 2:13; cf. Acts 15:36ff.) is also easily explained with this presupposition.

At the same time, however, that means that at the time of the Apostolic Council, in a way still to be determined, Paul returned to the beginnings of his activity as a Christian and apostle to the Gentiles, while previously he had had to go his way as apostle to the Gentiles, to which he was called (Gal. 1:16), under the restrictive conditions of synagogal life. In fact, the observations noted in the preceding section all become understandable only when one assumes that the persecution of universalist Damascene Christianity by the synagogue, in which Paul had actively participated before his conversion, was successful for the synagogue to the extent that Jewish Christians who had traveled this radical path as a rule rejoined the synagogue with their Gentile mission and thus followed the Antiochene way of otherwise Hellenistic Christianity. The apparent triumph of the Jewish authorities, which nonetheless assured the existence of Gentile Christian communities within the synagogal institution, probably rested on a formal agreement between Jewish authorities and representatives of early Christendom. The fact that the Lord's brother James took over the leadership of the primitive church in Jerusalem was possibly the presupposition or consequence of this agreement (Gal. 1:19; 2:9, 12). Had the "Hebrews" in Jerusalem condoned the persecutions? Hardly! But they probably worked out the compromise and in this way brought about peace. After this compromise Paul was able to travel to Jerusalem, and the visit with Peter and James attested in Gal. 1:19 probably led to the agreement on the manner of Paul's future missionary work.

Not all Damascene churches had to join in this agreement in order to escape the pressure of persecution. Yet we can note that the churches with unquestionably Damascene theology within whose sphere the basic text of the Gospel of John came into being were excluded from the synagogal association during the period of the Pharisaic-rabbinic restoration of the synagogue in the generation after the Jewish war (John 9:22; 12:42; 15:18–16:4). Thus they must have bowed to pressure and surrendered their radical universalism. In Rome, however, Paul finds "strong" Christians who, without being heretics, want to accept into the Gentile Christian church only members who make a break in principle with Jewish customs (Rom. 14:1ff.), which goes beyond the Pauline viewpoint. In Rom. 11:11–24(31) Paul speaks especially clearly against Christians who regard Israel as rejected and consider (Gentile) Christians to be elected *in place of* Israel. The causes of the disturbances in the environs of the Roman synagogues that are attested by Suetonius (*Claudius* 25.4; cf. Acts 18:2) probably correspond to the conflicts that led to the early persecutions of Christians on the part of the synagogue, in which Paul himself participated because he saw Jewish particularism threatened. Also the hyperpaulinism with which the author of the two-part Lukan work had to deal (Schmithals 1982), like Marcion later on, made a fundamental break with Judaism. Such observations indicate more or less compellingly that the ideas and perhaps also the organization of the radically universalist or anti-synagogal Damascene Christianity of the early period survived into a later time. On the whole, however, the founding of Gentile Christian churches in Palestine, Syria, and Cilicia seems to have occurred within the context of the synagogal association; thus Gentile Christians remained in the status of God-fearers, and the self-understanding of the synagogue—the exclusive election of Israel and the basic distinction between Jew and Gentile—was not called into question. In these churches, consequently, the "Noachian commandments" (cf. Leviticus 17–18) and the rules of the "Apostolic decree" (Acts 15:29; 21:25) continued to be observed.

This in no way means that when Paul participated in this kind of Gentile mission, he surrendered the theological convictions acquired at his conversion. Rather, in the period of his intrasynagogal Gentile mission in Syria and Cilicia, he continued to adapt Antiochene Hellenistic Jewish Christianity's view of the salvific *death* of Jesus (see pp. 91ff. above) to his characteristic soteriology of the *cross* of Jesus (1 Cor. 1:18ff.; Gal. 3:1; 6:14), which bound salvation to faith alone and therefore did not recognize a priority of salvation for Israel (cf. Gal. 5:6; 6:15; 1 Cor. 7:19). Yet his specific doctrine of justification and the corresponding conception of the meaning and function of the Jewish law was probably not yet developed in this phase of his missionary activity, for there was no reason for such development as long as the Gentile mission was carried out in the context of the Hellenistic synagogue and the God-fearers qualified observance of the law. The soteriological formulas of this period actually do not yet presuppose the specific doctrine of justification (1 Cor. 1:30; 7:19; 15:3ff.; Gal. 5:6; 6:15; Rom. 4:25; 5:21); at this point Paul still uses the term *righteousness* unspecifically (Schnelle 1983, 44ff.). His specific teaching of justification and the law, by contrast, is directed toward the unconditional freedom from the law of Gentile Christians and the universalism of the proclamation of faith. According to the testimony of Galatians and Romans, Paul develops it in his debate with the synagogue, and thus it apparently belongs to the period after the Apostolic Council during which Paul was in transition to a new phase of his missionary activity, in which he led God-fearing Christians out of the synagogue and founded independent Gentile Christian churches "in the world." This teaching states the *universality* of sin and of righteousness based on faith and defines the salvation-historical function of the Jewish law, which is now nullified by faith. It does not alter the Pauline gospel but puts it into a form that was suited to offering Gentile Christians—against the resistance of the synagogue, which did not want to lose its God-fearing members—the assembly of a "church" (*ekklēsia*) organized outside the synagogal association. In this regard, Wrede (1907, 72) had good reason to call the specific doctrine of justification, which occurs only "where it is a question of strife with Judaism," a "battle doctrine" with which Paul fights against the synagogue for its God-fearing members and for the benefit of an independent Gentile Christian church.

Paul's Independent Gentile Mission
outside the Synagogue

The successful persecution of radical universalist Christianity limited its mission to the Gentiles to the realm of life within the synagogue. As time passed, this must have been increasingly felt by Paul as a restriction of his commission to evangelize among the Gentiles, for the "full number" (Rom. 11:12, 25) of Gentile Christians could hardly be attained in the context of the Jewish institution of the synagogue. Paul achieved the liberation of his missionary work from the restraining bonds of the synagogue, without thereby reestablishing the earlier persecution situation, through the agreements of the Apostolic Council. At this point, the multiple problems of Gal. 2:1–10 can be discussed only by concentrating on the limited theme of the present investigation and not dealing with the still growing literature.

> [1] Then after fourteen years I went up again to Jerusalem with Barnabas, taking Titus along with me. [2] I went up in response to a revelation. Then I laid before them (though only in a private meeting with the acknowledged leaders) the gospel that I proclaim among the Gentiles, in order to make sure that I was not running, or had not run, in vain. [3] But even Titus, who was with me, was not compelled to be circumcised, though he was a Greek. [4] But because of false believers secretly brought in, who slipped in to spy on the freedom we have in Christ Jesus, so that they might enslave us — [5] we did not submit to them even for a moment, so that the truth of the gospel might always remain with you. [6] And from those who were supposed to be acknowledged leaders (what they actually were makes do difference to me; God shows no partiality) — those leaders contributed nothing to me. [7] On the contrary, when they saw that I had been entrusted with the gospel for the uncircumcised, just as Peter had been entrusted with the gospel for the circumcised [8] (for he who worked through Peter making him an apostle to the circumcised also worked through me in sending me to the Gentiles), [9] and when James and Cephas and John, who were acknowledged pillars, recognized the grace that had been given to me, they gave to Barnabas and me the right hand of fellowship, agreeing that we should go to the Gentiles and they to the circumcised. [10] They asked only one thing, that we remember the poor, which was actually what I was eager to do. (Gal. 2:1–10)

Thus Paul travels to Jerusalem "in response to a revelation" (2:1). This statement corresponds to Gal. 1:12, 16, according to which the conversion and calling of Paul occur not from a human source but through a "revelation of Jesus Christ." Accordingly, the events of the Apostolic Council have an importance for Paul that is comparable to the consequences of his calling as the missionary to the Gentiles.

Paul lays before the Jerusalem primitive church, especially "the acknowledged leaders" (2:2, 6–7), the gospel that he is proclaiming among the Gentiles (2:2), namely, "the gospel for the uncircumcised" (2:7). This cannot mean a special gospel (cf. 1:6ff.), nor can Paul have presented the one gospel to the Jerusalem authorities for evaluation. Rather, Paul is thinking of the special nature of his successful missionary work among the Gentiles, as also shown by the clarification, "in order to make sure that I was not running, or had not run, in vain" (2:2), and above all by 2:3, in which Paul graphically reports the positive reaction of the "pillars" to his commission: the Gentile Christian Titus was not required to be circumcised. We are not to infer from this information that the requirement of circumcision was nevertheless raised—much less that Paul had traveled to Jerusalem because of such a requirement. Rather, in 2:3, with a clear reference to the demand of circumcision made in *Galatia,* Paul is describing a characteristic of his Gentile mission that was accepted as a matter of course by those in Jerusalem, a mission whose success he reported to them and which passed on to the uncircumcised Gentiles full participation in the gifts of the gospel. Whereas the God-fearers in the synagogue were still denied full participation in the people of God of the old covenant, the gospel that Paul preached to uncircumcised Gentiles granted them unrestricted membership in the communion of saints. This was a fundamental theological decision that Paul owed to the universalism of his conversion theology and which he had not surrendered in the long time during which he carried out his Gentile mission in the context of the synagogal institution. According to Gal. 2:7–9, 15ff. the Jewish Christian primitive church shared this decision with full theological conviction.

In Gal. 2:4–5 Paul speaks of difficulties he had in successfully completing the negotiations in Jerusalem. The "false believers [Greek *brothers*] secretly brought in, who slipped in . . ." are usually understood to be brusque Jewish Christians. Yet this brings viewpoints from Luke's literary work in Acts 15 into Gal. 2:1–10. The idea that there was a special Jewish group in Jerusalem that was so little integrated into the primitive church that it had to (and could!) slip into the negotiations has no support and is extremely unlikely. It is a question, rather, of representatives of the Jewish authorities, with whom the earlier agreement had already been made and led to the end of the persecutions by integrating the Gentile mission into the synagogue. They saw to it that Christians did not go beyond the bounds of the synagogal brotherhood, but the Christian Paul does not concede to them the designation of *brother* that was usual in the synagogue and possibly claimed by them. Paul says nothing of the possibility of their demanding the circumcision of Titus, which, in view of the numerous uncircumcised God-fearers who were welcome in the synagogue at that time, would be unthinkable. In 2:4–5 Paul addresses instead the difficulties he has overcome in connection with the agreements on which he reports in the following verses and in which the question of the circumcision of Gentile Christians plays no role at all. Apparently, however, the Jewish authorities attempted to place certain conditions on Paul's planned establishment of independent Gentile Christian churches. General considerations, as well as 2:10, suggest that one condition was that these churches should pay the temple tax (cf. Matt. 17:24ff.). In view of the loose, diverse synagogal association before the Jewish rebellion, a "Gentile Christian synagogue" would not have been unusual. Yet

Paul rejected such a requirement for the sake of "the freedom we have in Christ" (2:4; cf. Matt. 17:26!) and "the truth of the gospel" (2:5), for a binding of Gentile Christians to the synagogue would have meant at least tendentially a further binding to the law, which found its goal and end in Christ. Under such circumstances it is understandable that Paul, following the report in 2:6 on the rejected demands of the false believers who had slipped in, states that the "acknowledged leaders"—apparently in contrast to the representatives of the Jewish authorities—had made no demands on him. Thus Paul prevailed against Jewish ideas, and the "pillars" at least did not object at this point, which, if the payment of the temple tax was demanded, is already understandable in view of 2:10.

What distinguishes the agreements reached according to 2:7–9 from the previous missionary practice that Paul reports in Jerusalem according to 2:2? The answer to this question comes from the wording of the agreement, if one understands it in connection with the effectiveness of Paul after the Apostolic Council, which is made known to us in his letters. After the Jerusalem conference Paul begins in Cyprus(?) and Galatia, that is, in new and virgin missionary territory where the name of Christ was still unknown (cf. Rom. 15:20), with the founding of Gentile Christian churches *outside* the synagogue. To suggest that in Jerusalem it was for Paul only a question of a rearrangement of the Antiochene situation and that during the Apostolic Council "no one had even an inkling that Paul would soon leave Antioch and do missions on a global scale" (Becker 1993b, 92) is to fail to appreciate the fact that in Jerusalem Paul was striving for this global new beginning of his work, and it fails to explain the fact that Paul had no churches of his own in Syria. As long as he carried out his Gentile mission within the synagogue, a basic separation between the Jewish and Gentile missions was not necessary, as 1 Cor. 9:20–21 shows. This had to change with the advent of independent Gentile Christian churches without a connection with the synagogue and the law. The experience of the early persecution period had shown that the synagogue could not allow the Christian mission to contest the special position of Israel and to let Jews and Gentiles be *one* "in Christ" and without the law (3:28). Therefore, in connection with the founding of independent Gentile Christian churches outside the synagogue, Paul now forwent evangelization among the Jews, for whom he earlier "became as one under the law" (1 Cor. 9:20), yet this happened with the assumption that the evangelization of the Jews would be pursued especially by Peter under the direction of the Jerusalem "pillars." This Jewish mission was vitally important not only for Jewish Christianity and Paul, for whom the exclusion of his own people from the gospel was unthinkable (Rom. 11:11ff.), but to some extent also for the Jews themselves, who did not want to lose the Gentile Christian members of the synagogue to the Gentile Christian churches. Thus there was a convergence of the interests of the Jerusalem negotiation partners, including those whom Paul disparagingly called "false believers secretly brought in." The agreements enabled Paul to found law-free Gentile Christian churches outside the synagogal association and at the same time assured the existence of intrasynagogal Palestinian and Hellenistic Jewish Christianity. "Paul could agree to the retention of the custom of circumcision by the Jerusalem Jewish Christians, because by giving up circumcision in a Jewish environment, they would have destroyed their own basis of existence. At the same time, however, this retained custom could no longer be understood by the Jerusalemites themselves as necessary for salvation. If that had been the case, there would have been no agreement with Paul" (Marxsen 1978, 69). In fact, Paul can hold Peter to the common conviction "that a person is justified not by the works of the law but through faith in Jesus Christ" (Gal. 2:16).

If Jewish and Gentile Christianity were in this way united in an amicable agreement, a particular bone of contention between Paul and the synagogue remained in the form of the dispute over the God-fearers, whom the synagogue did not want to give up but Paul wanted to win for his churches. Paul's specific teaching about justification and the law has its *Sitz im Leben* in this disagreement, in which Paul, in appealing to God-fearing Gentiles and in discussion of the counterarguments of the synagogue, must demonstrate that and why the law fulfilled its function with Christ. With the agreements of the Apostolic Council, Paul returns to the original ecclesiological intentions of the universalist gospel of his Damascene conversion theology, in the sense that now he can pursue a mission to the Gentiles that is not restricted by its connection with the synagogue, yet with the presupposition that he must, for well-considered reasons, forgo a Jewish mission carried out by himself and accept the organizational separation of Jewish and Gentile Christian churches. Thus he had to give up the vision of an actual abolition of the distinction between Jews and Gentiles, which probably formed the basis of his conversion theology, even if for him there continued to be neither Jew nor Greek "in Christ." From Romans 1–11 above all, we can deduce that Paul emphasizes the *universalist tendency* of the doctrine of justification and how he wants to validate it in order to win for his law-free churches the God-fearing Gentiles of the synagogue and the Gentile Christians living in his mission territory.

Contrary to widespread opinion, the agreements of the Apostolic Council remained in effect until Paul's death or until the end of the Jewish war, which created new conditions. Peter actually did evangelize in the synagogues, in parallel to Paul's Gentile mission, as can be learned from Gal. 2:11; 1 Cor. 1:12; 9:5. The purpose of the last and even the next to last journey of Paul to Jerusalem named in Acts 18:22 was probably to hold further discussions in the context of the agreement of Gal. 2:1–10 regarding Paul's planned missions in Italy and Spain. It is not coincidental that on his last journey Paul delivers a large collection to Jerusalem, in accordance with the statement in Gal. 2:10, and since he apparently also expected his Roman church in the future to share in the support of Jerusalem (cf. Rom. 15:27), it is also clear how accommodating he was in urging the Jewish Christians of Jerusalem toward ongoing cooperation with his Gentile Christian churches. That this cooperation was not without problems for the Jerusalem church is shown by Paul's fear that the gift he was delivering might not be acceptable to the Jewish Christians, because the "unbelievers"—namely, the Jewish authorities—might be more critical of cooperation with Paul and his law-free Gentile mission than they were at the time of the Apostolic Council (Rom. 15:30–32). Such fears, however, were apparently unfounded. In contrast to the tendentious account in Acts, Paul was able to leave Palestine as a free man (Schmithals 1982, 219–20); and if both Peter and Paul died as martyrs in Rome, which can hardly be doubted, then both apostles evangelized to the end of their lives in the spirit of the agreements of the Apostolic Council.

Thus the historical picture that was developed in the middle of the last century in the Tübingen School under the leadership of F. C. Baur, and is still influential today, does not correspond to the actual situation. That picture started with a rough opposition of Jewish and Gentile Christians, of the Jerusalem authorities James and Peter on the one hand and Paul the missionary to the Gentiles on the other, an opposition that was not resolved until the postapostolic period in "early catholicism." Yet the opponents with whom Paul had to deal in his churches at the time of his third missionary journey were neither envoys of the first apostles in Jerusalem nor legalistic Judaizers in general, but representatives of the virulent enthusiastic dualism in contemporary Judaism. Thus in the sometimes strong disagreements that we can observe in Paul's letters, it is not a question of rearguard actions against a form of Jewish Christianity that is already obsolete in terms of theological history, but of the beginning of the battle against Gnosticism, in which the church would be involved into the third century. And so-called early catholicism is not a synthesis of Jewish Christianity and Paulinism but the relative straightforward continuation of Antiochene Christianity after its expulsion from the synagogue. Its connection with the far less important Pauline churches was probably not initiated until the formation of the canon, which made the Pauline heritage available to the church at large.

Naturally, the relationship between Jewish authorities and the Jewish Christian church in Jerusalem remained in flux and also affected relations between Jewish Christian and Pauline churches, as shown in an instructive way by the Antiochene conflict (Gal. 2:11ff.). This incident occurred in the context of the valid presuppositions of the agreements made at the Apostolic Council. It did not result solely from Peter's behavior in Antioch, for Peter had already put himself in the wrong when he came to Antioch (Gal. 2:11), where Paul confronted him. Peter—on a missionary journey that, in accordance with the Jerusalem agreement, probably led him, like Paul, into the still unevangelized eastern part of Asia Minor (Galatia)—had apparently practiced table fellowship with Gentile Christians living free of the law, which in the eyes of the Jewish authorities could have appeared to be a violation of the Jerusalem agreement; this brought the thereby threatened Jerusalem church into the picture (Gal. 2:12), and it reprimanded Peter. It must have been evident that closer interaction between synagogal Jewish and Gentile Christians on the one hand and the churches of Paul living free from the law on the other could not be arranged in Jerusalem, for even in the different synagogues a variety of behavior could be observed in relation to the Gentiles. Jewish Christianity, however, from which the radical universalism of the Damascene churches had sprung, was subject to special controls, restrictions, and threats in Jerusalem—and not just since the end of the time of persecution. "The Jewish Christians in Jerusalem were suspect anyway because of their critical attitude toward the law. If one of their leaders was in close fellowship with Gentiles (or Gentile Christians) and this became known in Jerusalem, Christians in the capital city would be in danger. Thus Peter was in a genuine dilemma" (Marxsen 1978, 69). In this situation he and the other Jewish Christians pulled back (Gal. 2:12–13; cf. Acts. 13:13), and Paul cannot criticize this as such. He was struck, however, by the fact that not only did his coworker Barnabas anxiously withdraw and return to the synagogal association (Gal. 2:13; Acts 15:36ff.) but also that in the wake of this conflict Gentile Christians from the newly founded, law-free churches also seem to have turned (again) to the synagogue (Gal. 2:14). And thus through the Jewish Christians' understandable and justified consideration of the interests of the Jerusalem primitive church, the agreements of the Apostolic Council were affected to the detriment of the law-free Pauline mission to the Gentiles. Nevertheless, the Antiochene incident in no way caused an abrogation of the accords of the Apostolic Council or a lasting disturbance of the established cooperative work; rather, one learned by one's mistakes, and more prudence was exercised in contacts between the two groups of churches.

After the catastrophe of the Jewish war, when the synagogue reorganized itself under the leadership of the Pharisaic rabbinate, there was also a new situation for the Christian communities within the synagogue. Now not only God-fearing Gentiles but also (Jewish) Christians, along with all other groups who could not accept the Pharisaic understanding of the law, had to leave the synagogue, and the agreements of the Apostolic Council became pointless. In the decades to the turn of the century and beyond, Christian communities concerned themselves with the problems of this *aposynagōgos* and with the task of reorganizing themselves outside the synagogue and under the pressure of the newly instituted persecution and also bringing together in individual places the previously separated Christian communities, which naturally was not simple in view of differing theological developments (see pp. 263ff. below). On the whole, the "early catholic" literature preserved in and outside the New Testament shows that the influence of synagogal Christianity in the developing "catholic" church was stronger than that of independent Gentile Christianity, especially since more than a few parts of the Gentile Christian heritage drifted away into the Gnostic and Marcionite heresies (cf. 2 Tim. 2:14–18; Acts 20:29–30; 1 John 1:18–19; Bauer 1934).

Summary

In short we can say that Paul was converted to Damascene Christianity, which had already completely removed the distinction between Jews and Gentiles and in principle had nullified the Torah for Jewish Christians. Paul always held to the basic structure of his conversion theology: preexistence Christology, incarnation soteriology, a radical understanding of sin, universalism, aspects of present eschatology; for Jews and Gentiles he recognized only the one way of salvation through faith in Jesus Christ. The treatise in Rom. 7:14–8:30 preserves this early theology more or less intact.

The persecution of this radical universalist Christianity by the synagogue made it immediately necessary for Paul to carry out his Gentile mission henceforth within the institution of the synagogue. During this period of his activity in Syria and Cilicia he adopted important theological ideas from Hellenistic Jewish Christianity, above all the conception of the salvific significance of Jesus' death, and on this foundation he built his characteristic theology of the cross. Also in this phase of his activity the universality of the gospel for Jews and Gentiles without distinction and the salvation of all through faith in Jesus Christ formed the unalterable foundation of his preaching. Yet he no longer expected that Jews should surrender their identity; rather, he could become a Jew to the Jews, in order to win Jews to Christ.

He held fast to such tolerance (cf. 1 Corinthians 8; Rom. 14:1–15:7) when at the Apostolic Council, in agreement with the Jewish Christian primitive church, he succeeded in implementing a compromise with the Jewish authorities, which enabled him to form independent, law-free, Gentile Christian churches outside the synagogue, with the proviso that he renounce involvement in the Jewish mission, which Peter committed himself to carrying out in the Diaspora. For the purpose of the goal of the separation of Gentile Christians from the synagogue during the transition to or at the beginning of his activity as an independent missionary to the Gentiles, Paul worked out as a "battle doctrine" his specific doctrine of justification, including a corresponding interpretation of the law surpassed by the coming of Christ, which we know above all from Galatians and Romans. The universalist formulas of his conversion theology and the genuine Pauline *theologia crucis* assert nothing different from his later doctrine of justification, but unlike it, the universalist soteriology was not developed especially in disagreement with the synagogue and with an eye to the attempt to win God-fearing Gentiles for the independent, law-free churches. Important theological developments in Paul are no longer to be observed during his independent missionary work after the Apostolic Council.

7

Traditional Teaching Texts in Paul's Letters, with the Example of 1 Cor. 1:10–3:23

The task of determining the character of Paul's original letters is complicated by the seldom disputed fact that we have those letters not in their original form but in redactional writings, on whose shape and composition it would naturally be difficult to achieve full agreement in detail. As a result, there is disagreement in particular over whether the letters of the apostle, or certain ones of them, are special writings that are to be interpreted entirely in terms of the immediate occasion, or whether in some cases we have an apostolic teaching text that, even if written for a specific reason, attempts to elevate the addressees' basic level of knowledge. In the first case it is possible, and in the second to be expected, that Paul is turning to fixed teaching material, whether from traditions that he himself had already received or from teaching texts written by the apostle for instructing his coworkers or church members. The discovery of such teaching material not only aids a better understanding of the letter into which it is integrated. The more scholars are able to isolate pre-Pauline traditions in the apostle's letters through form-critical and content analyses, the better early Christian theological history can be reconstructed. And the more clearly instructional and school texts from Paul's own pen can be separated from their epistolary context, the better Paul's own theological development can be reconstructed. For even if such teaching texts are adapted in a letter to a particular situation, they belong to a certain state of knowledge and perhaps reach back into a phase of the apostle's activity that precedes the composition of the letter by years or even decades.

In this context, if we want to achieve satisfying results, we must enter the circle of literary criticism and of form criticism, and this circle is, in fact, also occupied by those who assume the integrity of an individual letter or of all the letters available to us in the Pauline corpus. Yet the literary integrity of *all* of Paul's letters can be assumed only by force, even if one grants that he was able to ignore the usual rules of epistolary communication. For even in this case one must concede (1) that the train of thought of his letters is conclusive, (2) that in each case they grow out of *one* situation of the author and his readers and consequently exhibit a unified level of communication, and (3) that the fundamental rules of the epistolary form are observed. Since this is not true at least in individual cases (2 Corinthians; Philippians; Romans 16) in the extant *corpus Paulinum,* it seems methodologically inadequate when many scholars are satisfied with the minimum of obviously essential literary-critical operations. We must assume instead that as a letter writer Paul basically operated within the context of the usual norms familiar to his readers, and therefore, with this assumption in mind, we are faced with the task of the literary-critical reconstruction of his extant correspondence.

With this presupposition I have considered 1 Cor. 1:1–3:23; 4:14–21 to be an independent writing by Paul (1984, 48ff.). The fact that for reasons of both form and content, 4:14–21 is part of the conclusion of a letter (Schenk 1969, 235–36), whose situation, moreover, is not in harmony with 16:8–9 (J. Weiss 1910, xli–xlii), cannot be disputed on convincing grounds, even if this conclusion has largely been ignored by recent commentaries (Merklein 1992, 318ff.). Yet against my earlier view, I would like to ascribe the opening of the letter in 1:1–9 to a different writing, for the praise of the church in 1:4–9 does not fit well with the following body of the letter in 1:10–3:23. In particular, Paul cannot very well credit the church with the full measure of the gifts of grace in 1:4–9, if in 3:1–4 he must reproach them as incapable of receiving "spiritual" talk. The opening of the letter in 1:1–2a, 3–9 belongs better to the earlier "answering letter," to which the section on gifts of the Spirit (ch. 12–14) also belongs.

The following analysis is limited to the corpus of the letter in 1:10–3:23, whose unity is not disputed. It is occasioned by the reproach directed against Paul that in Corinth he neglected the proclamation of "wisdom." It is the first time in his correspondence with the church in Corinth that Paul feels called upon to make a *personal apologia* (Schmithals 1984, 21ff.). In view of this, it is understandable that he does not directly mention the reproach of his opponents, but the reason can be clearly recognized. Following the principle that a good attack is the best defense, Paul first faults the Corinthians for their divisions (1:10–17a). To infer from the four Corinthian slogans in 1:12 four parties in Corinth that are in contention with each other is no more permissible than the idea that Paul is not addressing any differences in teaching. The main object of criticism is the idea of making an appeal to *people;* those who, for example, make an appeal to Paul do not necessarily do so against the doctrinal opinions of Apollos. At the beginning of the body of the letter Paul is mainly concerned with taking the initiative and on his part making reproaches with which he later connects his defense (3:1–23). Serving this purpose is the reference to the quarrels in Corinth, which — whatever they may have been — lead to the church members' appealing to human authorities instead of to Christ.

In 1:17 Paul gains the object of the following comments and thus of the actual theme of the letter "in a rather backward way"; the "suddenly and unexpectedly" (J. Weiss 1910, 23) introduced negation "not with eloquent wisdom" (1:17) marks this theme and his reason. The wisdom talk that is missing in Paul is, in his belief, correctly missing, and for good reason. The apologetic based on this principle determines the letter through 3:8 and again in 3:18–20. It is offered instructively and at times polemically, yet Paul does not give the impression, as in later correspondence, that he feels driven into a corner and seriously threatened in his apostolic authority as far as the Corinthians are concerned. Just as unexpectedly as he introduced the apologetic theme of his letter, in 3:4 Paul returns to the introductory polemic against the party slogans and in 3:5–23 again attacks the appeal to people; after the preparation in 3:10–15, in 3:16–20 (cf. also 3:21 with 1:29, 31), he combines apologetic and polemic when he abruptly attacks the wisdom teachers who found fault with him for failing to preach wisdom.

In 4:14, immediately following 3:23, Paul moves to the closing of the letter. According to 4:17 he assumes the presence of Timothy in Corinth and recommends him, as cofounder of the church (2 Cor. 1:19), for the task of reminding the Christians in Corinth "of my ways in Christ Jesus, as I teach them everywhere in every church." The "ways" taught by Paul cannot refer to the apostle's personal walk. Rather, in connection with a widespread Old Testament idiom (Michaelis, *TWNT* 5:50ff.), the expression designates the fixed rules and principles of Pauline teaching, which are known to the church (cf. 1 Cor. 11:23ff.) and must be called to mind when they are inadequately observed. There is no special focus here on ethical principles; rather, the term *way* corresponds to the linguistic usage in Acts 9:2; 19:9, 23; 22:4; 24:14, 22, where the author designates Christian teaching as a certain "way" within Judaism. Accordingly, "my ways in Christ Jesus," which Paul proclaims in all the churches, are the fundamental teachings of Gentile Christian Pauline theology, and when Paul similarly makes these "ways" the foundation of his teaching in all the churches, and thus Timothy can recall them in Corinth, he is obviously using this term to refer to fixed teaching material.

This insight agrees with the observation that in the corpus of the letter, especially in its thematic main section 1:18–3:4, Paul is appealing in an unusually intensive way to such traditional teaching material. What he is calling to mind here is apparently less a question of general missionary and baptismal proclamation than of special teaching material for school instruction.

The Foolishness of the Cross and
the Wisdom of Philosophy in 1 Cor. 1:18–25

The first of these teaching texts, which is analyzed in detail elsewhere (see pp. 146ff. below), comprises 1:18–25; it contains no epistolary elements apart from the disturbing "to us" in 1:18, which many manuscripts rightly omit and which Paul made have inserted ad hoc. We have here "a basic discussion on the relationship of the gospel of the cross to philosophy" (J. Weiss 1910, 24), specifically, to Greek popular philosophy as it was found in Paul's time. The addressee of this teaching text is the church, which, in the face of the influential religious propaganda of popular philosophy, is supposed to be strengthened in its Christian self-understanding, which rests on the message of the cross of Christ. No direct references of any kind to the Corinthian situation are to be derived from this passage, and however one wants to describe the Corinthian heresy or the various errors in Corinth, an incursion of contemporary Greek philosophy into the church is actually out of the question. Therefore one must also ask whether the situation-related key word *wisdom* in 1:17 came to the apostle from Corinth at all, or whether in regard to the fixed teaching text, he himself connected the term *wisdom* with the reproach that he had withheld the message for the "perfect" from the church (cf. Conzelmann 1969, 74). For outside of the present writing, "wisdom" is the topic in an analogous situation at most in 2 Cor. 1:12, whereas according to 1 Cor. 8:1, 7, 10–11; 13:2, 8, the term common in Corinth for the higher knowledge missed in Paul is *gnosis*. In this connection one must also note that Paul does not directly introduce the reproach of his opponents as such, and the abrupt way in which he moves in 1:17b to the corresponding theme is best explained by the fact that he wants to introduce the conceptuality of the following teaching text.

In any case, this teaching text in 1:18–25 judges the Greek understanding of existence under the key word *wisdom*. God-given wisdom opened for the Greeks the way to life, as the divine law had for the Jews (1:22–23), and as the Jews failed because of the law, so also the Greeks because of wisdom, in Paul's view (1:21), and thus the cross becomes in the same way for both the judging or saving power of God. The central *theologia crucis* of the text reveals its origin in the *Pauline* educational operation and at the same time attributes to it an advanced phase in the apostle's activity, in which the Damascene incarnation Christology and soteriology were already expanded through the Antiochene passion soteriology. The fact that the concepts of the doctrine of justification are not found probably indicates that Paul had not yet worked them out when he formulated the present teaching text, which consequently came into being at a time when Paul was pursuing his missionary activity among the God-fearing Gentiles in Syria and Cilicia in the context of the institution of the synagogue (Gal. 1:21ff.; see pp. 108ff. above).

The Chosen Church
according to 1 Cor. 1:26–31

[26a] Consider your own call, brothers and sisters: [26b] not many of you were wise by human standards, not many were powerful, not many were of noble birth. [27a] But God chose what is foolish in the world to shame the wise; [27b] God chose what is weak in the world to shame the strong; [28] God chose what is low and despised in the world, things that are not, to reduce to nothing things that are, [29] so that no one might boast in the presence of God. [30] He is the source of your life in Christ Jesus, who became for us wisdom from God, and righteousness and sanctification and redemption, [31] in order that, as it is written, "Let the one who boasts, boast in the Lord." (cf. Jer. 9:23–24)

In 1:26a Paul begins in the style of a letter. Yet the anaphoric form and the ellipsis in 1:26b raise the question whether in 1:26 we are not already dealing with fixed material. The form of 1:27–28 reveals that it is indeed such material through the epistolary expansion of the formally recognizable source and through the fact that we have here a fundamental discussion that is not especially related to the

Corinthian circumstances. The following text probably represents the older tradition on which 1:27–28 is based:

> God chose what is foolish in the world
> to shame the wise (27a);
> God chose what is weak in the world
> to shame the strong (27b);
> God chose what is low and despised in the world
> [to shame the high and mighty] (28).

This triad consists of three parallel double lines, each of eight plus four (= twelve) Greek words. In itself, the expansion present in the last member of the Pauline text in 1:28 represents the emphasis of a rhetorical recommendation and in this respect could belong to the source (J. Weiss 1910, 37), yet in the present case it proves, for reasons of both form and content, to be an epistolary expansion. The phrase "what is low" (*agenē*) in 1:28 requires as antithesis "of noble birth" (*eugeneis*) in 1:26b, and the intensification from "low" to "despised" to "things that are not" transposes the vivid reality of the original triad into the philosophical milieu of the preceding teaching text. Here Paul ignored the fact that, as he still presupposes in 1:26b, there are also in the Christian church individuals, who are wise, strong, and of noble birth, who as such are "shamed" by the cross but who in no way belong to the "things that are" that will be reduced "to nothing." Thus 1:28 has been expanded in epistolary style, and the emphasis of this expansion lies on the philosophical terms already given in the context. The addition of the "despised" apparently serves the transition from the traditional "what is low" to "things that are not" in order to moderate the tension between the two.

For the Greek philosophers there is nothing higher than *being,* and "nothing more belittling or disparaging can be said in Greek and especially Platonic thought" than when one classifies something with what is not (J. Weiss 1910, 37). Thus in connection with the preceding teaching text in 1:18–25, Paul intentionally introduces philosophical ideas into his source in order to intensify it with regard to the worldly wise, who count themselves among the "being": God chooses "things that are not" in order "reduce to nothing things that are." As in Rom. 4:17 vis-à-vis the Jews, in 1:28–29 vis-à-vis the Gentiles the motif of *creatio ex nihilo* serves as an expression of the divine work of salvation (Schrage 1991, 210ff.). The choice of "reduce to nothing" instead of "shame" corresponds to the intensification from "what is low" to "things that are not." In the context of such epistolary intensification of his source, apparently already in 1:27b, in anticipation of and in transition to the neuter expansions in 1:28, which correspond to philosophical ways of speaking, Paul substituted the neuter phrase "the strong" for the masculine "powerful," which is also required by 1:26b.

The immediate continuation and closing of this piece of tradition is formed by 1:29, 31, whereas in 1:30 we have an independent formula, introduced in epistolary style, which belongs to the preceding teaching text in terms of neither form nor content. By contrast, 1:31 resumes, "after the detailed outpouring of 1:30, the thought of vv. 26–29" (J. Weiss 1910, 43), and in such a way that 1:29 summarizes the statement of Jer. 9:23, and 1:31 corresponds to Jer. 9:24, whereas 1:30 interrupts this coherent scriptural reference. With "as it is written" verse 31 also connects formally with 1:29, while the preceding "in order that" inserted secondarily by Paul creates a transition that is possible in terms of content but so harsh and incorrect linguistically that this alone suggests the preformulated character of 1:31. If in 1:29 we read with a portion of the text sources "in the presence of him" instead of "in the presence of God," 1:29 and 1:31 each have seven and thus a total of fourteen Greek words, so that the whole teaching text underlying 1:26–31, constructed according to gematrial rules, seems to be:

> . . . so that no one might boast in the presence of [him] (29)
> . . . as it is written, "Let the one who boasts, boast in the Lord" (31)

It is true that "in the presence of him" is not as well attested as "in the presence of God," but the change from the pronoun to the noun is more easily imaginable than the reverse direction, since the isolated sentence, "Let no one boast in the presence of God," requires the noun, which in such a way could easily have gone from the oral saying into the literary text.

The beginning of this fixed teaching text cannot be reconstructed with as much certainty. The anaphoric triad in 1:26b, however, which recalls 1:20, was probably traditional, as suggested by the observation that in the "powerful" and those "of noble birth" we apparently have designations that were originally also found in the following triad and were replaced by other terms ("the strong," "things that are") in the epistolary modifications in 1:27b–28. In the originally epistolary formulation in 1:26b one also expects to find, in reference to the preceding discussion, the "wise of the world" instead of the "wise according to human standards." With the assumption that 1:26b is tradition, it is easy to assume that with reference to the epistolary introduction in 1:26a (cf. 1:24), Paul moved the verb now missing in 1:26b forward (cf. J. Weiss 1910, 35). The sentence introducing the teaching text now contains twelve Greek words, and the whole tradition reads:

> Not many of the wise according to human standards, not many of the
>   powerful, not many of noble birth were called,
> but God chose what is foolish in the world to shame the wise,
> and God chose what is weak in the world to shame the strong,
> and God chose what is low to shame those of noble birth,
> so that no one might boast in the presence of him; as it is written: "Let the one
>   who boasts, boast in the Lord."

Thus this teaching text comprises four members with twelve and one, the last member, with fourteen Greek words. In this way and with the striking closing with a scripture quotation, a final emphasis is clearly given. The teaching text lacks any direct reference to the Corinthian situation. It belongs, rather, to the "ways" that Paul teaches in all the churches (4:17). He speaks of God's activity exclusively from an ecclesiological viewpoint. The underlying christological and soteriological ideas are not indicated. In this respect, this teaching text cannot be easily placed in the development of Pauline theology. Even the term and idea of "boasting" do not make a placement possible, for this term is used by Paul in so many ways and without a specific connection with a certain theological stratum that it is not suited to "dating" in terms of historical theology. Yet the idea of the present teaching text, as well as its conceptuality, is so closely connected with the tradition adopted in 1:18–25 as to suggest that the two texts are roughly contemporary. An original connection between them is suggested even more by the fact that the tradition underlying 1:26–31 develops what is already asserted in a different way in 1:18–20. But whereas in 1:18–25 the ecclesiological aspect only gives the context for a fundamental interaction with Greek philosophy, in the prototype of 1:26–31 it defines the idea itself. If in 1:18–25 Paul is strengthening the church by demonstrating the foolishness of worldly wisdom as such, in the text underlying 1:26–31 he does so by interpreting the social makeup of the church as an expression of the divine way of salvation and the divine will to salvation. If the one teaching text came into being during Paul's Syrian activity, then this is therefore also true of the other, which represents an Antiochene pendant to the Damascene body-of-Christ ecclesiology, expanding the spatial way of thinking with a historical (*geschichtlich*) one.

A Pre-Pauline
Teaching Formula in 1 Cor. 1:30

Paul's reason for inserting 1:30 into the traditional context is difficult to ascertain. Various considerations may have come together in his mind. In any case, the beginning of the verse ("He is the source of your life in Christ Jesus . . .") takes up again the motif of free election from 1:24, 27–28 and relates this general statement from his source to the addressees in Corinth; in this sense it connects directly with 1:29, the rejection of boasting in oneself (cf. 1:31; 2:5). The relative clause in 1:30b expands the teaching text with a comprehensive christological, soteriological statement. In this clause "wisdom" is given first-position emphasis and in the sense of "he is our wisdom" connects the prototype underlying 1:26–31 with the preceding christologically shaped teaching text in 1:18–25.

In all this it is noteworthy that for this insertion Paul uses a pre-Pauline tradition in the relative clause:

> ". . . who for us from God was made to be righteousness and sanctification and redemption"

Supporting the traditional origin of this formulation is, first, its participial style, as in, for example, Rom. 1:3–4; 3:25; 4:25; Phil. 2:6. In response to a main clause such as "We believe in the Lord Jesus Christ" (cf. Rom. 4:24–25), possibly spoken by the teacher in the catechism, the pupils answer with educational relative clauses that describe the work of Christ, and these are what Paul likes to bring to his readers' minds as known material of the faith. We should also observe and note (1) the triadic form of the confession or teaching statement (righteousness, sanctification, redemption), (2) its secondary expansion through the context-related, but at the same time stylistically infelicitous and substantively disturbing, "wisdom," (3) the transition from the epistolary second person (1:30a) to the instructional third person (1:30b), which is to be compared with that in Rom. 4:25, and (4) the pre-Pauline usage of the terms *righteousness, sanctification,* and *redemption.* The added fourth term *wisdom* leads interpreters who are unaware of the traditional background of 1:30 to assume that the other terms also designate, each in itself, the whole salvation event, which would in fact hardly be appropriate for a traditional teaching statement. But there can be no question of this in view of the systematic arrangement of these three terms, especially since *righteousness* must not be burdened with the whole weight of the Pauline doctrine of justification (Schnelle 1983, 45). *Righteousness* without doubt means the gift of salvation. By contrast, *sanctification* is, as in Rom. 6:19, 22; 1 Thess. 4:3, 4, 7; 1 Tim. 2:15; Heb. 12:14, the fruit of justification, the new life whose aim is eternal life (Rom. 6:22). Then *redemption* must refer, as in Rom. 8:23; Luke 21:28, for example, to this eschatological aim of righteousness and sanctification. Thus the triadic teaching statement gives a sequence of steps that lead from entrance into the church through justification and righteousness to the Christian life in sanctification and finally to eschatological redemption.

Whether "from God" is traditional or was added by Paul and thus in the pre-Pauline formula a *passivum divinum* pointed to God's activity (cf. Rom. 4:25) can hardly be decided. The instructional, systematic structure of the sentence makes it unlikely that it is of liturgical origin, as Käsemann (1964b, 50), for example, assumes, and points rather to the catechism and presumably baptismal instruction, as a comparison with 1 Cor. 6:11 suggests. The origin of the statement in Syrian, Antiochene (Jewish) Christianity can be assumed with certainty on the basis of its conceptuality.

The Wisdom of Spiritual People
according to 1 Cor. 2:6–3:4

In 2:1–5 we have a purely epistolary text in which Paul continues the theme in 1:17. The introductory "and I" (cf. 2:3) means that Paul also expressed himself in his preaching in Corinth in accordance with God's salvific action, as it was presented in the first of the preceding teaching texts and verified ecclesiologically in the second. While Paul had introduced this apologetical theme of his letter, the justified renunciation of the teaching of wisdom, in 1:17 without special reference to the Corinthian situation, he now refers the addressees to the corresponding experience that they have had with his missionary preaching. With this the reproach that moved Paul to write his letter comes more clearly into view: other teachers are agitating against him with the assertion that he had kept from the church "wisdom" or the "gnosis" and thus concealed the true gospel from them (cf. 2 Cor. 4:3). This presupposition gives the epistolary section 2:1–5 its particular shape. Paul explains that he has indeed with good reason proclaimed to the Corinthians, without "lofty words or wisdom" (2:1) and without "plausible words of wisdom" (2:4), exclusively the testimony of God (2:1), namely, the crucified Christ, "so that your faith might rest not on human wisdom but on the power of God" (2:5). When in 2:3, in the middle of his train of thought, Paul points out that even his personal, unself-confident appearance in Corinth was appropriate to his modest message (cf. Phil. 2:12–13), an indirect reproach against the triumphantly appearing new teachers (cf. 2 Cor. 4:5; 10:12; 12:11; etc.) is unmistakable.

In 2:1–5 Paul seems to treat the theme conclusively, and the apologia appears successful. Paul did not dispute the reproach of a missing wisdom teaching but accepted it; at the same time, however, he rejected it with a reference to the heart of the divine work of salvation and the central content of the apostolic message. Wisdom empties the word of the cross (1:17) and flatters human boasting (1:29–31; 2:5). In this sense 2:1–5 is a closing statement, and Paul can return to his introductory counterreproach, the appeal to human beings that was virulent in Corinth. The appropriate catchphrase, which he takes up and treats in 3:3–4 and afterwards, has already been given in 2:5: "Not on human wisdom but on the power of God."

In the meantime, Paul holds to his apologia. Even if this is not surprising in itself, we are surprised by the manner in which in 2:6–3:4 he reacts to the now even more clearly recognizable reproach that he kept "wisdom" from the Corinthians: "Yet among the mature we do speak wisdom" (2:6), and since the Corinthians are as yet still not mature (3:1–4), he could not proclaim wisdom to them. After he had explained since 1:17 that the proclamation of wisdom was not his concern because faith must not rest on human work, this new explanation has the effect of "a sharp contrast" (J. Weiss 1910, 52), "an emphatic antithesis" (Conzelmann 1969, 77). The contradiction can be resolved if one determines that Paul was previously speaking of missionary preaching and the ground of faith, but now he is speaking about the message to those who stand firmly on this ground, and this is indeed probably what Paul meant. The present expansion, however, which "retroactively unsettles" the previous section (Conzelmann 1964, 74), then becomes surprising. Yet its assertion is in itself clear and unmistakable.

Paul also claims to be able to speak on "wisdom," but he does this only for the "mature." Thus his talk about wisdom does not belong to the faith-awakening and church-founding preaching of the gospel; it occurs, rather, in the realm of a post-baptismal instruction of those who are advanced. The fact that he has previously withheld wisdom from the Corinthians shows how little importance it has for his understanding of the building up of the church. If, nevertheless, in spite of the brusque criticism of all talk about wisdom in 1:17b–2:5, he now places value on the declaration that he is basically and completely capable of the missing talk about wisdom, then there can be only apologetic reasons for this. Paul apparently believes it possible that the reproach that he is not able to speak of wisdom has made an impression in Corinth, and he fears that his focusing on the fundamental preaching of the crucified Christ is not sufficient to destroy this impression. Therefore, although the Corinthians cannot (yet) verify his claim from their own experience, he asserts that he is capable of speaking "words of wisdom" but does so only among the "mature," which does not include the Corinthians. His opponents in Corinth were easily able to dismiss this argumentation as cheap talk. When Paul, after his aggressive and theologically fundamental defense in 1:17b–2:5, engages nonetheless in a comparatively weak apologetic, this shows that he sees himself still seriously threatened in his apostolic authority, even if not driven into a corner. This impression is not moderated by the fact that the apostle turns his defense into an attack on the "immaturity" of the Corinthians, a reproach that he skillfully connects with the introductory polemic against the appeal to human beings (1:10ff.).

More than once in the Pauline correspondence we find a similarly structured apologia in response to similar reproaches by Paul's opponents. If they find the praxis of glossolalia missing in his activity, the apostle counters that he can "speak in tongues" more than anyone else, but in church he would rather say five normal words for the members' edification than ten thousand words in a tongue (1 Cor. 14:18–19). If some opponents play their own ecstasies off against Paul's sober preaching, he also claims ecstatic experience for himself but attributes it to his personal contacts with God, because the "love of Christ" requires the upbuilding of the church with intelligible speech (2 Cor. 5:11–15). And if his opponents boast of their "visions and revelations," he too can be of service with such things, yet only in the context of a fool's speech, for he regards the fact that he was once transported into paradise as an unusual distinction but not as proof of his apostolic status (2 Cor. 12:1–10). The information that he speaks "wisdom" but only among the "mature" fits entirely into this apologetic schema.

When the exegete does not look at the particular situation that moves Paul in this way to the unusual comments in 2:6–3:4, the present passage, the "proud word," is often explained with reference to the "religious elation of the apostle" (J. Weiss 1910, 67), which in the history-of-religions school is customarily derived from contacts with Hellenistic mysticism. This psychologizing explanation, however, leaves us with the unsolvable puzzle of how in such a way Paul can paralyze the praise of the cross and the humility of apostolic existence, which he began to sing in 1:17b–2:5. Therefore other interpreters maintain that the "wisdom" of 2:6, which Paul proclaims among the "mature" can be no other wisdom than the "wisdom of God" of 1:24, namely the crucified Christ (Merklein 1992, 224), that the "mature" are consequently "all Christians" (Schrage 1991, 249), and that "God's wisdom, secret and hidden" (2:7) refers to the "salvific decree of God" revealed on the cross (ibid., 250). The fact that one is constantly running into such a harmonizing interpretation even in 2:6–16 makes clear the concession that is always ready in corresponding explanations, namely, that Paul's "fundamental position" is "filled with other tendencies" (Schrage 1991, 264). Especially the explanation of the apostle in 3:1–4 that he was not able to impart "wisdom" to the Corinthians, who are immature and "of the flesh," shows "compellingly" that the "wisdom" of 2:6–16 "does not concern the preaching of the cross, for Paul has *not* withheld this from the Corinthians despite their immaturity" (J. Weiss 1910, 53).

Yet the particular occasion for Paul's comments in 2:6–3:4 does not explain the style of his argumentation. All interpreters are struck by the total change in conceptuality vis-à-vis the preceding comments, which becomes unmistakable by 2:10 at the latest and remains inexplicable especially to those who assert a consistency of thought in 1:17b–3:4. The terminology of the *theologia crucis* is replaced by a multilayered, at times crudely dualistic and mysterious language, which in part is in itself quite unusual in Paul. Today it is popular to trace this surprising conceptuality back to borrowings from Paul's opponents in Corinth. There is nothing, however, that would indicate such a connection. On the contrary, Conzelmann (1969, 76) rightly objects to such a view "that the passage in itself is unpolemical. It is precisely the very different context that is polemical." It may not be very happily observed that the whole thing is "borne by a solemn mood" (J. Weiss 1910, 52), but it is correct that in 2:6–16, and largely in the present passage as a whole, the epistolary tone, which is not clearly evident again until 3:1–4, retreats entirely in favor of the instructional.

If we take a closer look, however, we see that the present passage does not form a unit in terms of tradition and the history of religion, and thus not in terms of conceptuality either. Apocalyptic ways of thinking and speaking dominate in 2:6–10a, but Gnostic-dualistic ways in 2:10b–16.

> [6] Yet among the mature we do speak wisdom, though it is not a wisdom of this age or of the rulers of this age, who are doomed to perish. [7a] But we speak God's wisdom, secret and hidden, [7b] which God decreed before the ages for our glory. [8a] None of the rulers of this age understood this; [8b] for if they had, they would not have crucified the Lord of glory. [9a] But, as it is written,
> "What no eye has seen, nor ear heard,
> nor the human heart conceived,
> [9b] what God has prepared for those who love him"—
> [10a] these things God has revealed to us through the Spirit"

In 2:6–10a there is apparently no fixed underlying model, but we can observe a traditional schema of argumentation, which occurs in various implementations; it appears in Paul himself also in Rom. 11:25; 1 Cor. 15:51; Col. 1:24–29, after Paul in Eph. 3:1–13; Rom. 16:25–26; 2 Tim. 1:9–10; Titus 1:2–3; 1 Peter 1:20, and in the modern period it has become established with the concept of the "schema of revelation" (Dahl 1957; Lührmann 1965, 124ff.; Wolter 1987). The specific form of this schema in 2:6–10a is determined by the context in which it is found. This is shown first of all by the concept *wisdom,* whose usage is suggested by the rooting of the revelation schema in Jewish wisdom thinking (Wisd. Sol. 9:13–17; Bar. 3:9–4:4; Rom. 11:33ff.), but which is not characteristic of the apocalyptic expression of the schema and in the present case was taken out of the context. The dependence on the context is shown further in the delimitation "not a wisdom of this age" (2:6b), a variation of the traditionally formulated "wisdom of the world" in 1:20 adapted to the present apocalyptic style. Also, the fact that through the *crucifixion* of Jesus by the "rulers of this age" (2:8) Paul demonstrates their ignorance of the hidden secrets of God's wisdom is explained by the *theologia crucis* presented in 1:17a–25; 2:2.

Incorporated in this way into the context of the letter and in this respect freely formed, the previously given schema of revelation permeates 2:6–10a in a circular argumentation and determines the character of this verse. At the beginning (6a) and the end (10a) we read that God's secret has been "revealed to us" and proclaimed to the "mature." This secret concerns a gift of salvation that God established "before the ages" (7b) but hid from the "rulers of *this* age" (8a), and thus it also remained hidden from the people of this age (9a), for God has prepared this secret gift of salvation for the people of the new age "who love him" (9b). All of this is conceived and said in the framework of the two-age schema: knowing about the Fall, in the creation of this world God had already planned and prepared the next world, which is intended for the righteous and will never pass away. This and the further determination that God established the mystery "for our glory" (7b) demonstrate that the present schema belongs to apocalypticism in terms of both form and content: the hidden wisdom asserted in the schema of revelation is "essentially eschatological" and refers to "what God planned 'for the glorification' of his elect" (J. Weiss 1910, 55) and what is based on the crucifixion of the "Lord of Glory" (8b).

Paul did not believe it necessary—and because of 3:1–4 also not possible—to reveal the mystery itself or to give an example of the hidden eschatological wisdom. Nonetheless, we are not left totally in the dark, because Paul gives such examples elsewhere:

> Listen, I will tell you a *mystery!*
> **We will not all die,**
> **but we will all be changed**
> (1 Cor. 15:51)

> So that you may not claim to be wiser than you are, brothers and sisters, I want you to understand this *mystery:* a hardening has come upon part of Israel, until the number of the Gentiles has come in. And so **all Israel will be saved**. (Rom. 11:25–26a)

> . . . according to God's commission that was given to me for you, to make the word of God fully known, the *mystery* that has been *hidden* throughout the *ages* and generations but has now been *revealed to his saints*. To them God chose to make known how great among the Gentiles are the riches of the *glory* of this *mystery,* which is **Christ in you,** the hope of *glory*. It is he whom we proclaim, warning everyone and teaching everyone in all wisdom, so that we may present everyone mature in Christ. (Col. 1:25–28; cf. Eph. 3:1–13)

In the last passage from Colossians, which is also especially close terminologically to 1 Cor. 2:6–10a, Paul *expands and completes* (Col. 1:25) the preaching of his coworker Epaphras, who had founded the church on faith, love, and hope (Col. 1:4–7), through a "mystery" that leads them to perfect knowledge, a viewpoint that is lacking in the post-Pauline parallel Eph. 3:1–13. The mystery concerned "the universalist spread of the message of salvation and the winning also of Gentiles for the gospel" (Wolter 1987, 307). Thus with Christian universalism and the law-free Gentile mission it was a question of a *donum superadditum* that was not already given with the Christian message itself but rested on a revelation that "fulfilled" the word of God, that is, brought it to its eschatological fullness (Col. 3:25; cf. Rom. 11:12, 25). This revelation is issued, in keeping with its eschatological content, on the one hand in an apocalyptic manner when it places the once of the old age over against the now of the turn of the age, but on the other hand it is brought into a "mystical" formulation: "Christ is [also] in you [Gentiles]." Thus the present tradition comes from Paul's Damascene conversion theology, which grew out of a meeting of the essentially apocalyptically rooted Palestinian primitive Christianity with a dualistic, universalistic Judaism and also reveals something of the enthusiastic process of this fruitful meeting (see pp. 74ff. above).

The actual mystery is, in any case, stated in three Greek words, or in 1 Cor. 15:51 antithetically in twice three words, presumably the didactically rooted style of such revelations (cf. Jos. *Bell*. 6.301). The content of the revealed mystery always refers to the mysteries of the end time or the turn of the age, which is in line with the observation that talk of "mysteries" and their revelations generally belongs to the fixed repertoire of apocalyptic literature (cf. Lührmann 1965, 98ff.). The apocalyptic rooting of the named revelations is also shown in the fact that they belong not to individual bearers of the Spirit but are the tradition of the community of salvation; not even Paul is the receiver of revelatory sayings: he is their proclaimer.

Other passages also show that Paul has in mind for "mature" Christians a continuing instruction, which, similar to 2:6–10a, is separate and not essential for salvation:

> Let those of us then who are *mature* be of the same mind; and if you think
> differently about anything, this too God will reveal to you. (Phil. 3:15)

This apparently ironically formulated polemical passage is not easy to decipher in detail, but it is in any case to be understood in the light of Paul's earlier emphasis on his own imperfection: it is enough to be seized by Christ, even if God still has special revelations prepared.

> Brothers and sisters, do not be children in your thinking; rather, be infants
> in evil, but in thinking be adults. (1 Cor. 14:20)

This is an admonition to which Paul attaches a specific instruction on "maturity."

First Corinthians 2:6–10a (in connection with 3:1–4) must also be understood in the context of such tradition, even if the dualistic language in 3:1–4, provoked by 2:10b–16 or its application to the Corinthians, is supportable only with difficulty in view of the fact that Paul is addressing baptized Christians. The thought of the epistolarily written, intertwined polemic and apologia, however, is clear: the Corinthian church has not been sufficiently able to rid itself of the "works of the flesh" (Gal. 5:19–20); the immature "people of the flesh" in Corinth, who are "behaving according to human inclinations" (1 Cor. 3:1–4), lacked and still lack the measure of "maturity" that would enable Paul to reveal to them the mysteries of "wisdom." In terms of the history of theology, especially noteworthy in this connection is the way in which Paul deals with the apocalyptic mysteries. For the apocalyptist it is a matter of essential truths that are directly connected with his expectation of the imminent turn of the age, and we can probably also understand in this way the corresponding mysteries in the proclamation of Jesus and in Palestinian Jewish Christianity. "Being in Christ" and the "word of the cross," which has already brought the turn of the age for believers (cf. 2 Cor. 5:17), move these mysteries as a rule to the periphery of theological thinking and proclamation. The believer does not need to know them; the "mature" can learn them, even if in general they satisfy curiosity more than they build up the church.

If in 1 Cor. 2:6–10a Paul was in principle formulating in epistolary fashion and relatively freely in connection with a traditional schema, in the following section we find an originally independent tradition.

> [10a]. . . these things God has revealed to us through the Spirit; [10b]*for the Spirit searches everything, even the depths of God.* [11]*For what human being knows what is truly human except the human spirit that is within? So also no one comprehends what is truly God's except the Spirit of God.* [12]*Now we have received not the spirit of the world, but the Spirit that is from God, so that we may understand the gifts bestowed on us by God.* [13]And we speak of these things in words not taught by human wisdom but taught by the Spirit, interpreting spiritual things to those who are spiritual. [14]*Those who are unspiritual do not receive the gifts of God's Spirit, for they are foolishness to them, and they are unable to understand them because they are spiritually discerned.* [15]*Those who are spiritual discern all things, and they are themselves subject to no one else's scrutiny.* [16]"For who has known the mind of the Lord so as to instruct him?" [Isa. 40:13] But we have the mind of Christ. (1 Cor. 2:10–16)

The independence of this passage is demonstrated first on the basis of the prevailing dualistic gnostic language and world of ideas. We have here the clearest proof that Paul's theological language contains a level that presupposes a Jewish Gnosticism. Above all, the opposition of unspiritual (natural) and spiritual (pneumatic) people can be explained only by a dualism of substance (see pp. 64ff. above). Moreover, the "we" in 2:10b–16 is the "we" of the community of spiritual people, the pneumatics; it is not the apostolic "we" as in 2:6–7; this is seen especially clearly in 2:12. Verse 10a, by contrast, connects the apostolic "we" with the "we" of the "mature" (cf. 2:9b). In this way, as well as through the anticipatory introduction of the term *Spirit,* Paul provides in 10a a transition to the tradition in 2:10b–16.

Yet in this tradition 2:13 has clearly been added secondarily by Paul, for in 2:13 the apostolic "we" is again speaking, and also in terms of content, in 2:13 Paul carefully connects the thought of 1:17b; 2:1, 4, 6 with the language and ideas of the received tradition that he makes the basis of 2:10b–16; the negation in 2:13a takes up the *epistolary context;* the position takes up the motif of *tradition.* Here 2:13b reveals Paul's current interest in this piece of tradition, for this identifies Paul as a pneumatic and shows that he is absolutely equal to the—correctly understood!—criteria of the opponents, who miss his "spiritual" talk.

Verse 16 probably also comes from Paul. Verse 15 is a better, more appropriate close of the tradition than v. 16; the change from "Spirit" (*pneuma*) to "mind" (*nous*) is better comprehended as an expansion of the tradition understood with conceptual strictness than as tradition itself; likewise, the transition from the Spirit of God to the explicit Christology of the "mind of Christ" is best explained when accomplished by Paul himself; Paul also uses the quotation from Isa. 40:13 (LXX) in Rom. 11:34; the "we" in 2:16 is at least on the boundary between the community "we" and the apostolic "we," and with 2:16 Paul is indeed following his apparent intention to move on to 3:1 and thus to his own apostolic behavior.

Consequently, the traditional section is comprised of 2:10b–12, 14–15. The statement in 2:10b forms the basis that introduces the topic. On the foundation of the Platonic statement that like is known only to like, 2:10b makes the assertion that the "Spirit" searches everything, even the depths of the divinity. The theme is then explicated above all through the negative statement that the natural human being cannot comprehend God, and this is summarized in closing in 2:15. In the sequence *basic sentence, explication, résumé,* we can recognize a fixed schema of argumentation that is often found in Paul (see pp. 141–42 below). The basic sentence makes a comprehensive statement ("everything"), which is solidified by the explication or discussion and repeated in the résumé, usually in reinforced form, as in the present case through the expansion "and they are themselves subject to no one else's scrutiny."

Above all 2:12 shows that and how the dualistic schema that underlies the tradition had already been adapted in a Christian sense in the tradition. The church has *"received"* the Spirit coming from God, which alienates it from the "spirit[!] of the world"—thus the latter is not essential for the "spiritual" person; rather, God first gives the Spirit and thereby the condition for knowledge of God, and the church is now able to comprehend what it has been *given* by God. The indirect christological reference is unmistakable, for the "gift" (*charis*) that the "spiritual" person as such "comprehends," or perceives and accepts, is the event of salvation, the grace (*charis*) shown to human beings "in Christ." Also the talk of the "spirit of the world" abolishes the ontic dualism that provided the foundation for the present tradition. Thus with few strokes ("spirit of the world," "gift of God") the presupposed dualistic conception is made historical. Apparently the present teaching text especially pursues this intention. It maintains the elation of the pneumatics and their rough distinction from the unspiritual people, but it replaces the divine self-confidence that rests on material thinking with the self-understanding of the "blessed sinner." The present teaching text understands dualistic thinking better than that thinking understands itself, in that it interprets its ideas in a Christian way, an act of considered theological reflection apparently undertaking with missionary intention. In this way both "teaching" and "teaching tradition" came into being, for while every dualistically minded pneumatic searches the Divine directly, those who *receive* the Spirit as unavailable gift learn with his help to understand what is handed down in tradition about the salvific action of God.

This fascinating hermeneutical or religious-historical process of interpretation yields considerable insight into the theological history of early Christianity. As the apparently pre-Pauline tradition in 2:10b–12, 14–15 shows, Paul adopted a Gnostic language that was already adapted to Christianity, rather than Christianizing this language and world of ideas himself. This language must have been that of Damascene theology, shaped by preexistence Christology and incarnational soteriology, a theology he pursued because of its law-critical universalism and to which he was converted (see chapter 4). The meeting between the apocalyptic Jewish Christianity of Palestine (cf. 2:6–10a) and a universalist Jewish gnosis, from which Paul's conversion theology was generated, is among the fundamental and, as the genuine "Johannine" theology also shows, most consequential experiences of early Christian theological history. Both the Antiochene theology of Hellenistic Jewish Christianity with its adoption Christology and passion soteriology—in which the teaching texts 1:18–25 and 1:26–29, 31, as well as the saying in 1:30, are rooted—and the Pauline doctrine of justification that builds on them are secondary to Paul's conversion theology in the overall structure of Pauline theology.

8

Paul and Greek Philosophy

In contrast to the situation in the later histories of dogma, the encounter between early Christianity and contemporary philosophy did not decisively shape the theological history of early Christianity, which essentially fed on Jewish sources, including Jewish Gnosticism and Jewish Hellenism. Nonetheless, such an encounter did take place; it left behind clear traces in early Christian theology and is of no small hermeneutical importance for early Christian theological history. Early Christendom was aware that its proclamation inside and outside the synagogue was in competition not only with the political and mythical theology of the time but also with the views of existence that were offered especially by the representatives of popular philosophy. In both cases the question of the reality and truth of human existence was lively, and the more a missionary movement like Christianity penetrated into the Hellenistic world, the less it could avoid dealing—both in connection and in contradiction—with the answers to this question that were to be found in the environment of its listeners. Hence it was only following the example of the Hellenistic synagogue, which, as Philo of Alexandria shows, was able to amalgamate the Jewish heritage to a greater or lesser degree with the insights of Greek philosophy.

The use of the letters of Paul in this chapter to present the encounter of early Christianity with the philosophy of its time requires no special rationale. Here we will not consider the obvious points of contact between the Pauline paraenesis and the particular attitudes of contemporaries in popular philosophy, even when they occasionally come into view. These contacts are explained by the secular nature of the ethics of Paul, who recommends to his churches: "Whatever is true, whatever is honorable, whatever is just, whatever is pure, whatever is pleasing, whatever is commendable, if there is any excellence and if there is anything worthy of praise, think about these things" (Phil. 4:8). The early Christian churches, who must withdraw from public worship and thus also for the most part from public responsibility, consciously adapt their personal behavior and lifestyle to the best norms of contemporary morality and claim for themselves no special insights in the realm of ethics, to say nothing of having revolutionary aims in mind (see chapter 17).

Connection and Contradiction

Since the time of the early church, the apparent closeness of the ideas of Seneca, Epictetus, and other popular philosophers to much of what we read in the letters of Paul constitutes an often treated problem. If in antiquity there was no timidity about making secret Christians out of the Stoics, who were beloved because of their high-minded ethics, around the last turn of the century highly regarded scholars such as Th. Zahn and K. Kuiper advocated the more apologetic view that the pagan Epictetus knew and used the letters of Paul. Today, in the wake of the history-of-religions school and through studies by G. Heinrici, P. Wendland, E. Norden, J. Weiss, R. Bultmann, and other scholars, the conviction has prevailed that the meager remnants of what the modern period has called the "Cynic-Stoic diatribe" of the imperial age are connected by form and content with a broad, diverse tradition, with which the corresponding passages in Paul's letter also had contact. There are differences of opinion only in the way in which this contact occurred. Since the studies of Heinrici (1900, 441ff.), Bonhoeffer (1911), Pohlenz (1949), Clemen (1924), and others, the view has become more and more established that the ideal of the Stoic wise man and the Pauline understanding of existence are fundamentally different from each other, despite many analogous features. Yet the idea that the multiple formal and conceptual contacts between Paul and the Cynic-Stoic diatribe can be sufficiently explained with reference to the shared material of the Hellenistic everyday language, as especially Bonhoeffer and Heinrici hold, was and is rightly doubted. There is, however, still no agreement over the way in which Paul became acquainted with the diatribe's ideas and ways of expression, how extensive his directly or indirectly gained knowledge was, and with what degree of his own reflection he inserted this knowledge in the context of his theology. Did Paul read or even study the corresponding religious literature of Hellenism, as Reitzenstein (1919, 66) assumes, or had he personally investigated a nonliterary teaching or school activity of popular philosophy?

We can say with certainty that many kinds of diatribe-like material came to Paul through the medium of the synagogue, in which he grew up. This is true of some stylistic elements (cf. Thyen 1955) but also of some of the ideas and especially, as has already often been shown, of the statements that the invisible divinity can be perceived through the eyes of reason (Rom. 1:20–21) and that Gentiles observe moral laws "instinctively," as their conscience bears witness to them (Rom. 2:14). The first of these two statements is found in a synagogal judicial sermon on the Gentiles *quoted* by Paul, in which their rational knowledge of God was related to the revelation of the Creator-God in his creation, as found already in Wisdom of Solomon 13–15. The other statement belongs to an argumentation of the Hellenistic synagogue likewise merely *quoted* by Paul, with which the unity of the Mosaic Torah and natural moral law is presented. But even a glorification of God like that in Rom. 11:36a (cf. 1 Cor. 8:6; Acts 17:28), "From him and through him and to him are all things"—whose most concise Hellenistic parallel is found in Marcus Aurelius 4.23, "O nature, from you are all things, in you are all things, to you are all things"—comes from the synagogue, which had already put this Stoic formula into the service of the creation faith.

Other adoptions of Stoic ideas by Paul were originally Christian, even if not necessarily originally Pauline. Gal. 3:26–28 contains a *pre-Pauline* teaching formula often used by Paul elsewhere (1 Cor. 7:17–24; 12:13; Col. 3:11), as shown by its form, by the Pauline expansion "through faith" (Betz 1974, 81; 1988, 320ff.) and by the content that goes beyond the epistolary context (see p. 86 above). This teaching formula, which comes from Paul's Damascene conversion theology and follows an argumentation model often found in Epictetus, also comes close to Stoic ideas in terms of content:

> For in Christ Jesus you are all children of God through faith.
> As many of you as were baptized into Christ have clothed yourselves with Christ.
> There is no longer Jew or Greek,
> there is no longer slave or free,
> there is no longer male and female;
> for all of you are one in Christ Jesus.

Both the cosmopolitanism found in this formula and the relativization of the differences between free and slave, as well as the equality of women, belong from the beginning to Stoic principles. Natural law or nature in general and the Logos that governs everything do not permit social barriers to be erected between people; by nature all people have the same worth; all are to share the same recognition and the same moral formation and education. Naturally, the Christian teaching formula in Gal. 3:26–28 does not argue in the context of Stoic intellectualism and in the name of human autonomy. It is not irrationality that erects barriers between people; they are, rather, the consequence of human sin, and thus it is not rational insight but only faith and redemption through Christ that lead to adoption by God—Epictetus also calls the wise man "child of God" (1.9.6)—which, consequently, can be concretely realized only in the life of a particular Christian community. But even with such disagreement in content, the formula is without question related to Stoic ideas.

This example of a pre-Pauline Christian tradition shows that, and how, early Christian theology considered Stoic ideas in the Hellenistic world and with hermeneutic reflection adopted them to express its own ideas. Paul himself proceeds in the same way. In 1 Cor. 7:1–24 he takes up in his own epistolary form the traditional idea cited in Gal. 3:26–28. Based on an inquiry from the church in Corinth, in 1 Cor. 7:1–17 he deals with the relationship of man and woman, presupposing their equality. He pursues his argumentation with a saying of the Lord, with his apostolic instruction, and with general experience, and regarding the question of marriage and divorce he concludes that where possible all Christians should remain in the status in which they find themselves. In the following section Paul expands this basic statement into a general principle. According to 7:18–20 Jews and Greeks, circumcised and uncircumcised should also remain as they are, and this advice is substantiated with a principle from the liberal Hellenistic synagogue: "Circumcision is nothing, and uncircumcision is nothing; but obeying the commandments of God is everything" (7:19). In 7:21–24 Paul recommends to slaves that they not seek their freedom: "For whoever was called in the Lord as a slave is a freed person belonging to the Lord, just as whoever was free when called is a slave of Christ" (7:22). J. Weiss (1910, 189) correctly ascertains that the explanation of this paradox must be "drawn from the Stoic concept of freedom." The Stoics teach a freedom that rests on the distinction between the inner life, which is at a person's disposal, and the outer circumstances of life, over which one has little control. Truly "free is the one for whom nothing happens against one's will and whom no one can hinder" (Epictetus 1.11.9), and such freedom comes when one has learned "to want everything as it happens" (1.11.15). It is obvious that by linking freedom to liberation through Christ, Paul understands the lack of freedom more radically than the Stoics, for whom freedom is unavoidable with rational self-reflection.

This example from 1 Cor. 7:1–24, in which a specific inquiry from Corinth is raised to the level of general principle, involves a great deal of pre-Pauline Christian tradition. In 1 Cor. 9:19–22, however, it is without question Paul himself who is writing, as the pervasive autobiographical tone reveals:

> *For though I am free with respect to all, I have made myself a slave to all, so that I might win more of them.*
> To the Jews I became as a Jew, in order to win Jews.
> *To those under the law I became as one under the law* (though I myself am not under the law) *so that I might win those under the law.*
> *To those outside the law I became as one outside the law* (though I am not free from God's law but am under Christ's law) *so that I might win those outside the law.*
> To the weak I became weak, so that I might win the weak.
> *I have become all things to all people, that I might by all means save some.*

Within the correspondence to Corinth, this passage, which has been expanded in the spirit of the underlying source and in which Paul also employed the already observed circular argumentation schema of the diatribe, belonged originally to the discussion of the question of eating meat offered to idols in 1 Cor. 8:1–13; 10:23–33 and follows either 8:13 (Schmithals 1984, 39) or, more likely, 10:33. Thus in connection with the *freedom* of Christians asserted by Paul, it is a question here, as in 10:29, of the authority (8:9; cf. 6:12; 10:23) to be freely permitted to eat meat slaughtered by Gentiles, which is forbidden to the Jews because of impurity. Here Paul feels "like a Stoic wise man" (J. Weiss 1910, 243), yet as one liberated by Christ and thus, in a typical, paradoxical Pauline expression similar to 7:22 (cf. Rom. 6:18), as one called to serve the principle of love of neighbor.

In regard to the relationship to popular philosophy established by Paul himself, we must point especially to Rom. 12:1, where with *logikē latreia* ("reasonable service"; NRSV: "spiritual worship") Paul without question takes up a favorite expression of the Stoics, and with the reference to a worship service (*latreia*) that is appropriate to the Logos, he also adopts Stoic thought. For the phrase *logikē latreia* in Rom. 12:1 is found beside the references to the ancient cult of sacrifice ("a living sacrifice, holy and acceptable to God"), apocalyptic piety ("do not be conformed to this world"), and the religiosity of the mysteries ("be transformed by the renewing of your minds"). Hence it represents the special piety of popular philosophy in a thoroughly *epistolary* context shaped by Paul himself, and thus in this case one can hardly speak of "Jewish transmission" (Lietzmann 1933, 108). Through the considered joining of four conceptual fields from Paul's religious environment—which also in many other ways determine his theological language and in Rom. 12:1–2 unite to express the central Pauline idea that human beings find the truth of their existence solely in the grace of God—Paul reveals that the connection with the language and conceptual world of popular philosophy not only serves him in the superficial sense of reaching a semantic understanding with readers and hearers, but also that he is at the same time aware that his message answers definitively and "in truth" the questions that have found a provisional, inadequate, or false answer in the cult of sacrifice and philosophy, in apocalypticism and mystery worship.

We are also to understand in this sense especially the paradoxical descriptions of the apostolic office and of Christian existence in general that are found in 2 Cor. 4:8–11 and 6:9–10 (cf. 2 Cor. 12:10; Phil. 4:12–13), whose Stoic parallels have often been pointed out (Bultmann 1910, 27, 80–81; Windisch 1924, 207ff.):

> We are afflicted in every way, but not crushed;
> perplexed, but not driven to despair;
> persecuted, but not forsaken;
> struck down, but not destroyed (2 Cor. 4:8–9)
>
> as unknown, and yet are well known; as dying, and see—we are alive;
> as punished, and yet not killed;
> as sorrowful, yet always rejoicing;
> as poor, yet making many rich;
> as having nothing, and yet possessing everything. (2 Cor. 6:9–10)

"The rhetoric is entirely that of the diatribe" (Windisch 1924, 209). The two passages, even if not purely epistolary, are nonetheless originally Pauline and are testimonies of the apostle's independent hermeneutical reflection, through which certain insights and experiences of popular philosophy are adopted, radicalized, and "lifted up" under the direction of the witness to Christ. This is also true of the catalogs in 1 Cor. 4:11–12; 2 Cor. 11:23–29 (cf. Ebner 1991).

An Argumentation Schema
of the Diatribe

After Bultmann's dissertation of 1910 the "style" of the Cynic-Stoic diatribe in the narrower sense was not examined again in a monograph until more recently by Stowers (1981) and Schmeller (1987). The diatribe-based dialogic style occurs in numerous Pauline passages, above all in the Letter to the Romans, in which Paul develops his ideas in a dialogue with the objections of his opponents or hearers (Rom. 2:1; 3:2, 8–9; 4:1; 6:1, 15; 7:7, 13; 9:14; 11:1, 11; etc.). In regard to this style, Bultmann held that Paul, without having a concrete dialogue partner before him, used such objections in this way in a purely external dependence on the form of the diatribe, in order to bring into stark expression the paradox of his statements. Other scholars were convinced that the letter to Rome is a lively reflection of the dialogue that Paul had carried on here and there with the Jews in the synagogues. Still other interpreters held that the dialogue partners mentioned by Paul in a diatribelike manner are the direct addressees and readers of his writing in Rome. In contrast to this, the more recent studies have shown that the diatribe of the imperial era in no way directly reflected the popular Cynic-Stoic preaching, as Bultmann (1910) also presupposed, but that it probably came from the philosophical *education system*. With corresponding traditions, for example, the *Dissertations* of Epictetus, we are dealing with didactically developed *teaching texts* that only *imitated* the dialogue, with *typical* questioners and opponents, even where they were presented orally or, as was probably the rule, were dictated to the students. This is also true of the teaching texts of the Letter to the Romans, which follow the models of popular philosophy. We cannot say whether Paul knew such teaching texts or whether the diatribe's dialogic way of teaching was conveyed to him by way of its adaptation in the synagogue, against which he argued above all in Romans, especially since the one possibility does not exclude the other.

In any case, Paul probably acquired, without the synagogal connection, an argumentation schema of the diatribe that can already be found in an analysis of Gal. 3:26–28 and 1 Cor. 9:19–22. In Paul this schema is also found in Rom. 3:9b–19; 8:31–39; 11:33–36; 1 Cor. 3:21–23; 8:4–6; 12:4–11; Phil. 4:11–13, whereas it does not occur in the deutero-Pauline letters. In Epictetus it is found, for example, in *Diss.* 1.18.21–23; 3.20.4–6; 4.3.1–3. In Paul we find in most cases a connection not only formally with the style but also in the content of the ideas of the diatribe, for example, in 1 Cor. 3:21–23:

> So let no one boast about human leaders. For all things are
>   yours,
> whether Paul of Apollos or Cephas
> or the world or life or death
> or the present or the future—
> all belong to you, and you belong to Christ, and Christ belongs to God.

The course of the argumentation in this schema is circular. First, the teacher sets up a thesis, the *basic statement* (a), which is taken, as a rule, from tradition and which in the present case is linked with the epistolary context through "So let no one boast about human leaders." Then in the often expanded middle part of the argumentation, the *explication* (b), this basic statement is discussed, developed in the sense of the context, explained, tempered in the fire of objections, or supported by general experiences and recognized statements. Finally comes the *résumé* (c); it repeats with clear final emphasis the now substantiated and assured basis statement, which is often taken as an absolute assertion ("all things," "all," "nothing").

In the present example we have in the basic statement, "all things are yours," the Stoic commonplace that the wise person stands above all things and experiences and in his or her inner freedom is superior to the judgment of other people. At the same time, the execution and christological anchoring of the argumentation in 1 Cor. 3:21–23 (cf. Rom. 8:38–39) points to the completely unstoic substantiation and fulfillment of the independence pathos: the freedom from all external things and judgments is rooted not in an autonomous act of the will guided by rational insight but in the liberation of oneself from such self-conscious lostness in oneself through one's divine reason and the enduring connection with the "Lord Christ," which gives eternal freedom.

The mentioned Pauline texts that follow the described schema are, apart from individual features, not shaped by the synagogal educational institution but are originally Christian even where they adopt synagogal motifs. In terms of the ideas contained in the diatribe, we find the concept of freedom (1 Cor. 9:19–22) and, correspondingly, the motif of the superiority of the wise over all experiences and human judgments (3:21–23), the principle of equality (Gal. 3:26–28; cf. Rom. 3:9b–19), and the related idea of organism (1 Cor. 12:4–11), as well as the idea of autarkical contentedness (Phil. 4:11–13). Also, 1 Cor. 8:4–6 and Rom. 11:33–36 touch on the motif of the one, all-prevailing and wisely shaping Divinity, even if in a Jewish-Christian metamorphosis.

All the mentioned texts, with the exception of the teaching text in Rom. 8:31–39, are incorporated in epistolary fashion and are thus situation-related, but at the same time in every case it is a question of developed teaching material. It probably came from the early Christian teaching and schooling operation, in which widespread ideas of the diatribe were intentionally prepared for Christian missions and the upbuilding of the church and then dictated to students. Such a connection could not have happened without a thorough knowledge of the world of ideas and the style of popular philosophy, as well as the nature and manner of its influence. The extent to which Paul was actively involved or merely receptive to such educational work is difficult to evaluate in detail. Nevertheless, it is noteworthy that in the last described schema in Paul there are no original Pauline ideas from, for example, the doctrine of justification. Universalism (Gal. 3:26–28) and the concept of the organism of the "body of Christ" (1 Cor. 12:4–11) belong to Paul's Damascene conversion theology, and consequently he was probably already familiar with the corresponding argumentation schema. The behavior described in 1 Cor. 9:19–22, becoming "all things to all people," was practiced by Paul in his Antiochene period during his lengthy intrasynagogal (see pp. 108ff. above) missionary work in Syria and Cilicia (Gal. 1:21).

As the analysis of Rom. 12:1–2 shows, however, Paul did not use the described material without reflecting on his religious-historical heritage. For this judgment we do not require a reference to the often cited statement in which Strabo (14.673) characterized Tarsus, Paul's native city according to Acts 22:3: "The zeal that the people of Tarsus apply to philosophy and to general education is so great that even Athens and Alexandria are surpassed." Even without problematic inferences based on this statement, it is out of the question that the heritage, meaning, and function of the ideas and styles of popular philosophy so richly used by Paul could have remained unknown to such an educated, well-traveled, evangelistically active Hellenist as Paul. As a missionary to the Gentiles, he competes with itinerant Cynic-Stoic teachers, and in the face of this competition he intentionally takes up the traditions of the diatribe and employs them in a hermeneutically reflective manner. Therefore also in regard to Paul and the Christian school tradition adopted and further developed by him, one must in fact conclude that in addition to the Hellenistic synagogue "the propaganda of popular philosophy created in broad circles a spiritual atmosphere that will have to be considered in explaining the rapid progress of Christianity and its relationship with philosophy" (Wendland 1907, 53, cf. 118–19). The reasons for the ultimate victory of Christianity over intellectual Stoicism can be derived from the marked purpose with which Paul himself and the traditions adopted by him interpreted and critically reshaped popular philosophical material.

"I Do Not Do the Good I Want": Rom. 7:18–20

An especially instructive text for the relationship between Pauline theology and popular philosophy is found in Rom. 7:18–20:

> For I know that nothing good dwells within me, that is, in my flesh. I can will what is right, but I cannot do it. For I do not do the good I want, but the evil I do not want is what I do. Now if I do what I do not want, it is no longer I that do it, but sin that dwells within me.

This passage introduces an instructional treatise that deals first with sin (Rom. 7:18–25), then redemption (8:1–11) and the new obedience (8:12–17), and finally the eschatological perfection (8:18–30); it closes with a doxologically shaped climax (8:31–39), which was presumably appended secondarily. Paul inserted the treatise, which at its core belongs to an earlier phase of his theological education, into his teaching letter to the Christians in Rome, who were unknown to him. The form of this treatise is best described by Wendland, who gives the following characterization to the "new type of the popular treatise that, despite all dependence on the older development, is stylistically quite different from the old diatribe": "Lucid disposition, systematic arrangement of ideas, broad and doctrinaire presentation, balanced structure . . . diminution of the dialogic element . . ." (1907, 43).

At the beginning of the treatise Paul describes being in sin as alienation of a person from him- or herself. Sinful people totally fail to find themselves. Although even sinners remain human (ontologically), from the ontic standpoint they truly lose themselves: they lose their true selves. In this sense we must speak of an unconscious dichotomy in the self when human beings fall victim to sin: as willing selves, they still reach for what is good, for life, but they seize death without being aware of it. Human beings want life, but they do not find it.

> The other self, which in itself is the same but is in the hands of sin, finds death through the evil that it does. This self is the historical person, the creature, as historical people have appeared since Adam and from Adam.

> In their doing and not knowing *what* they are doing—namely, finding
> death—they question their creatureliness, and as historical people (under
> the power of sin) they disavow their creaturely will to live. One can say
> in short: I want life; I do not want death. Those who want life are human
> beings as creatures; those who find death are historical people as they ap-
> pear in the hands of sin. (Schlier 1977, 232)

Thus in Rom. 7:18–20 "sin" is a transmoral category; the "sinner" simply wants
the good. According to an often expressed view, the apostle is trying to say that
while human beings intend to do what is morally good, they do not succeed in
translating this intention into reality; human beings are too weak to realize their
good will, and therefore, in spite of best intentions, they are guilty again and again.
In this case Paul would be describing a psychological conflict that is familiar to
every human being. In this sense Plato had already spoken of two contending
halves of the soul and compared them with horses that are trying to go in opposite
directions (*Phaedrus* 246 A ff.), and Xenophon had Araspes say, "Without doubt
he must have two souls, for one soul could not be evil and good and at the same
time want something and not want it" (*Cyropaedia* 6.1.41). In Ovid we read:
"Video meliora proboque, deteriora sequor" ("I see and attempt better things, [but]
worse things follow": *Metamorphoses* 7.19–20). Further ancient sources of this
idea are found in Hommel 1961/62.

This understanding of Rom. 7:18–20, which was advocated by Luther along
with the later Augustine, has been correctly challenged by more recent scholarship. What Paul really meant can be clarified, again with the help of Epictetus. On
the man who is alienated from himself in the Stoic sense Epictetus writes: "What
he wants he does not do, and what he does not want he does" (*Diss*. 2.26.4). This
parallel to Rom. 7:18–20 is not only striking in its form but also enlightening in
its content. In the Stoic view, human beings basically want only what is appropriate and useful, and reason tells them what this is. Therefore every "sin" contains
a human self-contradiction: "Every sin involves a conflict" (*Diss*. 2.26.1). When
people fail, it is not because they want to, but by mistake. They deviate from their
rational insight and must be brought back to reason. Then they will do what they
want and they alone can want.

> Every sin contains within it a contradiction. For since sinners want
> not to sin but to act rightly, it is obvious that they do not do what they
> want.
>   What then does the thief want to do? What is useful for him! If steal-
> ing is not useful for him, then he is not doing what he wants. But by na-
> ture every rational soul turns against contradiction. Yet nothing keeps it
> from doing what is contradictory, as long as it does not comprehend that
> it is living in contradiction. Once this is understood, however, it will of
> absolute necessity reject the contradiction and flee from it, just as one
> who has experienced what deception is will of cold necessity reject de-
> ception, while agreeing with it as the truth as long as it is not unmasked."
> (*Diss*. 2.26.1ff.)

Thus Epictetus is no more making a moral judgment about people than Paul is. Human beings are not at all aware of their error. They do not understand themselves; they do not control themselves and do not even know this. They live in an objective contradiction that they do not feel subjectively. The conceptual propinquity of Paul and Epictetus is obvious, and Paul probably intentionally expressed his ideas with the help of the conceptual methods of popular philosophy.

The state of affairs that underlies both cases has been described by Jonas (1964, 561) in the following way:

> Thus understood, the will is not some kind of individual psychic act among others, classifiable among wishes, desires, endeavors, drives, and the like; it is also not something like an express decision. And it is absolutely not something that can appear and disappear again, sometimes present and sometimes absent: rather it is a priori always there and produces all individual acts. . . . Thus the "will" is nothing other than the basic mode of being of existence in general, and the word designates only the existential state of affairs, namely, that the being of existence is such that something is always at stake in its existence, and this again is ultimately itself as what is actually to be pursued in its own being.

Paul designates what is desired by the will in Rom. 7:18–19 with the pair of terms *kalos*/*agathos*—already introduced in 7:12–13, 16, retained in 7:21, and central to Greek philosophy since Socrates—and he does this in the likewise traditional opposition with *kakos*, "evil." The highest good (*agathos*—however comprehended in detail in the various versions of the Greek ideal of existence) that is equated with the Divine appears in what is good (*kalos*). The *kalokagathia* is as *summum bonum* that for which every human being strives by nature, and the wise, free human being who has found him- or herself is the *kalos kai agathos*, the *bonus et optimus* (Apuleius *Met.* 8.9), the good and true human.

Yet Paul understands human alienation more profoundly than Epictetus. Those who are sold to sin cannot be led through their allegedly merely foolish behavior back to themselves through the enlightenment of reason. For those who live in contradiction with themselves, enlightenment about themselves is not enough. Sinners need redemption from themselves as sinners, for their will is held captive, not their reason. They *can*not do what is good. For according to Paul's consistent conviction, those who strive for life, as what is actually to be pursued in their existence, attempt as sinners to gain this life on their own, and thus by grasping for life, they lose it, for life can be expected only from God, "who gives life to the dead and calls into existence the things that do not exist" (Rom. 4:17). Life is a gift that is not at our disposal. Therefore those who want to live in truth must be satisfied with God's grace (2 Cor. 12:9). To want to live on some other basis means to let sin reside in oneself, and trust in the fundamental rationality of all existence is a specific expression of sin.

In such a thoughtful and stylized teaching text as the present treatise, the basic connection with a central terminology of contemporary popular philosophy is not accidental or incidental; it happens with great hermeneutical reflection. With his message Paul wants to bring to bear what his contemporaries in the most noble formulations of their religious thought suggest to their fellow human beings, the "good and true," and for him the really "good and true" are those redeemed from this existence subject to death, who call out, "Thanks be to God through Jesus Christ our Lord!" (Rom. 7:24–25). Since also for Epictetus the wise ones, who overcome the contradiction of sin, orient themselves in their inner freedom completely toward the will of the Divinity, and thus gain the highest good, are the *kalos kai agathos* (*Diss.* 12.7; 2.10.5; 14.10; 2.3.1–2; 24.18, 50, 95, 100; etc.), one does not need to conclude that Paul was familiar with classical Greek philosophy. The basic ideas and terms of the popular philosophy of his time were at his disposal.

The Foolishness of Philosophy and the Wisdom of God

Up to this point we have not observed an express, well considered adoption of popular philosophical terms and styles, but in one text from his correspondence with the church in Corinth, 1 Cor. 1:18–25, Paul deals expressly, and at the same time critically, with the philosophical world view of his Hellenistic contemporaries.

> [18]For the message about the cross is foolishness to those who are perishing, but to us who are being saved it is the power of God. [19]For it is written [cf. Isa. 29:14],
>
>> "I will destroy the wisdom of the wise,
>> and the discernment of the discerning I will thwart."
>
> [20]Where is the one who is wise? Where is the scribe? Where is the debater of this age? Has not God made foolish the wisdom of the world? [21]For since, in the wisdom of God, the world did not know God through wisdom, God decided, through the foolishness of our proclamation, to save those who believe. [22]For Jews demand signs and Greeks desire wisdom, [23]But we proclaim Christ crucified, a stumbling block to Jews and foolishness to Gentiles, [24]but to those who are the called, both Jews and Greeks, Christ the power of God and the wisdom of God. [25]For God's foolishness is wiser than human wisdom, and God's weakness is stronger than human strength.

In this self-contained passage we are dealing not with an epistolary text but with a traditional teaching and school text from the hand of the apostle, which Paul inserts into his letter to Corinth (cf. Peterson 1959, 43; Schrage 1991, 40, 166; see pp. 122–23 above). While before and after the present text the epistolary form is much in evidence, here the only direct hint of a letter is the disturbing "to us" in 1:18, which is omitted by many manuscripts and was apparently added ad hoc by Paul. The "we" in 1:23, by contrast, is not the *we* of the church but of its teachers; the church is always referred to in the third person (those being saved, those who believe, those who are the called).

The connection of 1:10–17, the opening of the body of the letter, with the present section is not immediately apparent. What idea relates the criticism of the division of the church into individual parties, which according to 1:10–17 forms the occasion for the letter, with the theme "Greek wisdom versus the foolishness of the cross"? Not until 2:1ff. does it gradually become evident that one of the parties named in 1:10–17 had faulted Paul for not teaching about wisdom, and from 2:6 on, in clear contradiction to the present piece of tradition, Paul expressly asserts his ability to carry out such a teaching of wisdom and gives reasons for not doing so that are completely different from those in 1:18–25 (see pp. 127ff. above). Thus 1:18–25 contains a teaching that prepares in a basic way for the epistolary discussion, and only with this piece of school teaching is the concept *wisdom* (*sophia*) introduced into the epistolary section; for the corresponding term used in Corinth, as evidenced in 8:1, 10–11; 13:2; and elsewhere, is not *sophia* but *gnosis*. Above all, the observation that in 1:18–25 Paul is dealing not with the idea of the eastern gnosis that had penetrated the Corinthian church but with Greek philosophy identifies this section as a prior tradition. The usual misunderstanding that one must understand this passage directly from the epistolary situation (cf., e.g., Wilckens 1959) causes interpreters to miss essential aspects of Paul's statement.

It is obvious that the present teaching text comes from the *Pauline* educational operation, for it was Paul himself who on the basis of the traditional early Christian talk of Jesus' giving of himself, dying, death, blood, and so forth developed a specific theology of the *cross,* the very "message of the cross" (1:18). This teaching text, which was naturally explained in an instructional fashion, presents the difference between the Christian kerygma and Greek wisdom, and it does so primarily to reassure the church in the face of the influential propaganda of Hellenistic popular philosophy. There is no recruiting address to the philosophers or a discussion with them, with "those who are perishing" (1:18). Verse 18 contains the fundamental thesis that through the foolishness of the cross God saves those who are called; v. 19 substantiates the thesis with an Old Testament quotation, which in the following verses is developed above all in opposition to Greek philosophy and finally underlined with the paradoxical sentence in 1:25.

An interesting marginal exegetical problem is suggested by the question, Why does Paul include the Jews in the consideration at all and why in this way, although the section clearly was conceived around the antithesis of philosophical wisdom and divine foolishness? The "scribe" (*grammateus*) in 1:20 is not the Jewish scribe but one of the Hellenistic wise men who are the topic throughout 1:18–21 and who in 1:22–24 are also clearly distinguished from the Jews. In the imperial age *grammateus* no longer designated the simple scribe but highly placed people with a variety of functions, including even the town mayor and the scribal cult official (cf. Acts 19:35; Apuleius *Met.* 11.17; Lucian *De sacer* 14, in addition to "sophist" and "prophet"; Clemen 1914, 35–36; *RAC* 7/2:1747ff.; Lampe 1992, 61–62). As such the *grammateus* in 1:20 stands beside the "one who is wise" and the "debater" (*syzētētēs*), the "scholastically educated Hellenistic professional philosophers" (Lautenschläger 1992, 283). In 1:22–24, by contrast, the Jews are actually found beside the Greeks, or Gentiles; "stumbling block" and "foolishness" in 1:23 are quite comparable.

In this expansion of the scope Paul is apparently not concerned only with making visible the *universality* of the Christian message and the Christian church, which corresponds to the cosmopolitanism of the popular philosophers observed in Gal. 3:26ff. In that the Christian kerygma seems equally distant from Judaism and the Greek world, Paul is also saying to his church that the Christian criticism of Greek wisdom does not repeat the corresponding Jewish criticism, and with the Greeks the teaching text also guards in this way against the easy misunderstanding that Christianity is a variation of Judaism. Consequently, the Judaism in 1:22 also appears through a rather *pagan* lens with a characteristic unique in Paul, for whereas he usually defines Judaism critically in terms of the Torah and pride in exclusive election, according to 1:22 the seeking of miraculous signs is also characteristic of Judaism, as the "stumbling block" in 1:24 (cf. Gal. 5:11) still indicates. Yet on this singular statement the commentaries point as a rule to Mark 8:11ff. par., the sign-seeking of the Pharisees, who demand of Jesus a verification of his claim. But apart from the fact that such a reference to Synoptic narrative material would be unique in Paul and is naturally entirely excluded in the pagan vision, the Jewish demand for a sign can be understood only in analogy to the Greek desire for wisdom. Therefore it cannot be directed toward the *verification* of a message but must describe the message itself, corresponding to the Greeks' *proclaiming* wisdom.

Thus the philosophy of the Greeks corresponds to the thaumaturgy of the Jews. With the latter we may need to think of the "magic" that penetrated massively toward the west in the imperial age, and whose eastern representatives are usually called "Chaldeans." The comprehensive influence of Judaism and the Septuagint far into pagan sorcery is well attested (Dieterich 1891; Deissmann 1895, 23ff.; Blau 1898; Wendland 1907, 108; Cumont 1930, 59, 173). Acts 13:6ff. and 19:13ff. are the most obvious testimonies of the typical connection of Judaism and magic (cf. also Apuleius *Met.* 90; Jos. *Ant.* 8.45ff.; Pliny *Naturalis Historia* 30.11). In any case, the reference to the Jews in 1:22–24 is only a secondary motif that is supposed to make the antithesis between preaching the cross and Greek wisdom all the more unmistakable.

With the formulation "Greeks desire wisdom" (1:22), Paul, who was probably directly oriented toward the popular philosophy of his time, strikes in a terse, concise way at the heart of Greek thought in general. Whether he is thinking here of the Socratic sense of the *striving* for wisdom, literally the *philo*sophia, or of the wisdom fully attainable by the wise, at which the diatribe of his contemporaries was aimed and which Paul also probably had in mind, must remain open in view of what was for Paul the certain impossibility of knowing God at all through wisdom. In any case, with "wisdom" it was a question of theoretical and practical access to the whole cosmos, which is possible for those using their reason, and a question of access to the "whole of humankind and God" (Epict. *Diss.* 1.9.4) or to the "experience of divine and human things" (*Stoicorum veterum fragmenta*, Arnim, 2 [1924], no. 35).

With "Greeks desire wisdom" Paul summarizes what he has already discussed more precisely in 1:21a. The subject of the knowing, according to 1:21a, is the "world" (*kosmos*). Paul does not select this important philosophical term by chance. According to a famous passage in Plato (*Gorgias* 507e–508a), the wise call the whole of existence *kosmos* (literally, "adornment"), because "heaven and earth and gods and human beings and friendship and harmony and prudence and righteousness" are held together in the fellowship of the "cosmos," so that in the rational view of the cosmos, the divinely true is recognized, and orientation toward the truth, being tied into the harmony of the cosmos, and education in the "good and true" are made possible for human beings. The divine *Logos* or *nous*—which governs the cosmos and gives it its harmonious form, so that it can itself also be called "God" or "divine"—at the same time governs the knowing subject, which is itself of divine nature, and thus for the Greeks the term *kosmos* corresponds to the principle, demonstrable since Democrites, that like is known (only) through like. Yet through 1:20 ("Where is the debater of this age? Has not God made foolish the wisdom of the world?"), Paul puts this originally Greek concept of the cosmos under the negative sign of the world that "did not know." The statement that "the cosmos" did not know God "through wisdom," however, is to be understood in the context of the Greek concept of the cosmos. Paul chooses the term *wisdom* (*sophia*) not only as the opposite of the "foolishness" (*mōria*) of the cross, but also because he can characterize the uncomprehending "cosmos" as the "cosmos" of Greek *philosophia*. Otherwise he could just as well have spoken of *Logos* or *nous* or even *pneuma* (cf. 2:11ff.).

Paul's idea in 1:21a is essentially clear. He disputes the idea that Greek philosophy, with its available means of attaining a rational world view has succeeded in knowledge of the divine and thus of its own truth. There are difficulties with this understanding, and the meaning of "in the wisdom of God" is disputed (cf. Wedderburn 1973). As a rule, for the clarification of this usage reference is made to Rom. 1:19ff., where Paul quotes a synagogal judgment sermon about the Gentiles, who have been guilty of failing to recognize God's majesty *through the works of creation* (von Lips 1990, 329ff.). Verse 1:21a, however, brings in the idea of the creation in concept and content; moreover, with 1:21a as a whole one must understand "in the wisdom of God" primarily in the context of the philosophical thinking of the Greeks themselves, not on the basis of the natural theology of the synagogue, which does not come into the picture anywhere in the present text, and for this reason the Jewish Hellenistic wisdom speculation, which is sometimes brought in to interpret 1:21a, must also remain beyond consideration. In the context of Greek thought, however, "in the wisdom of God," together with "through wisdom," reproduces in a highly considered way what determines the knowledge process of Greek philosophy in general: the "cosmos" knows the divine on the strength of the divine *Logos* living within it. Based on the wisdom of God, the wise grasp through their wisdom the nature of what is and their own place in the harmonious cosmic unity of divine and human. Thus in 1:21a Paul concisely describes the autonomy of the wise, who assume the identity of their logos with the world Logos and find the divine world order in themselves and themselves in the divine world order, like knowing through like; and at the same time he places this way of knowledge under the verdict of "they did not know God."

Accordingly, juxtaposed with the phrases "in the wisdom of God" and "through wisdom" in 1:21a, which belong together not only conceptually but also in terms of content, we find in 1:21b the corresponding double phrase "through the foolishness of our proclamation." "Foolishness" stands over against "wisdom," and "proclamation," as the message coming from outside, stands over against "in the wisdom of God," just as also in 1:21b it is no longer the cosmos but God who is the subject of the salvific event, and *know* is appropriately replaced by *save*.

It is not clear from 1:18–25 whether Paul regards as foolishness the conviction of the Greek wise ones that they are "in the wisdom of God" and therefore can know God, or whether he regards the Greek way of knowledge as feasible in principle and only wants to establish the de facto failure of this way. His interest in 1:18–25 lies without doubt in the fact that all attempts to know God in and through wisdom have failed, not in an ontological reflection. In 1:21 as well as in 1:24, however, Paul is hardly speaking of the "wisdom of God" outside of his own concept of God, and thus it is the God of the Jewish and Christian confession who gave the Greeks the wisdom to know God.

In this connection, however, one must also observe that the Pauline analysis and critique of the Hellenistic knowledge of God stands unmistakably in parallel with the corresponding analysis and critique of the Jewish understanding of salvation, which leads to the conclusion that in regard to the basic human situation Paul makes no distinction between Jews and Greeks (cf. Schottroff 1970, 198). What for the Greeks is "wisdom," is for the Jews the "Torah," the law of Moses. In view of this state of affairs, in 1:23 the "stumbling block" that the proclamation of the cross presents to the Jews who are proud of the law is placed by Paul in parallel with the "foolishness" that this proclamation appears to be to the wise Greeks. "Reduce to nothing" and "that no one might boast," emphasized in 1:28–29 in regard to "wisdom," are also found elsewhere in Paul in his polemic against the law. "Thus it is no wonder that the nullifying of *sophia,* like the abolishing of the *nomos,* is not a way of salvation that affects the Greeks, or the Jews, alone, but an event of salvation that concerns humankind" (Braun 1948/49, 28). It was the intention of the Torah given by God to the people Israel to lead people into life and sustain them in life (Rom. 7:10). But this intention was in fact not realized because of human inability or guilt (Rom. 7:14, 22–23; 8:3–4). Since such a failure of the Jews with the law corresponds to the failure of the Greeks with wisdom, on the basis of this observation one must also assume that in analogy to this Paul regards Hellenistic "wisdom" likewise as a way to life given to the Greeks by the *one* God, corresponding to the Jewish view that the Greeks can know God "naturally" through the creation (Rom. 1:19–20) and that the moral law is also "written on their hearts" (Rom. 2:15). Thus in like fashion, with both the Jews and the Greeks, Paul sees in principle the possibility of life being made available and at the same time radically squandered, so that for both Jews and Greeks even the proclamation of the crucified Christ appears as "foolishness" or "a stumbling block" (1 Cor. 1:23).

Accordingly, in reference to the Jews, Rom. 8:3 forms a rather exact parallel to the judgment about the Greeks and to the proclamation of the salvific activity of God in 1:21:

For God has done what the law, weakened by the flesh, could not do: by sending his own Son in the likeness of sinful flesh . . .

"Wisdom" corresponds to the "law" in 1:21; the inability of "wisdom" to know God corresponds to the inability of the "flesh"; in 1:21 as in Rom. 8:3, God's activity is juxtaposed with human failure; the "sending" in the "flesh" corresponds to the (proclamation of the) foolishness of the cross in 1:21. Thus Paul very intentionally places "Torah" and "wisdom," Jews and Greeks, in parallel, and this fact presupposes a thorough, considered familiarity not only with his Jewish heritage but also with the Greek popular philosophy of his time.

The widespread view that we cannot infer from Paul's letters that he "was educated in one of the Greek school philosophies" (Wilckens, *TWNT* 7:523.48–49) rests, in relation to 1:18–25, on the misunderstanding that this passage is an original epistolary text and receives its contours directly from Paul's opponents, namely, the wisdom teachers in Corinth. Such a view is untenable, even if one may argue about the degree of Paul's philosophical "education." Paul knows what he is talking about when he objects to the philosophical world view of the Greeks; he shows that he is thoroughly familiar with the religious position of his rivals in popular philosophy, and he incorporates his instructional discussion of their position into his theological educational operation. This recognition confirms the insight gained earlier that both consciously and with hermeneutical reflection, Paul connected his writing with the style of the diatribe and with Stoic ideas.

Such a connection does not diminish his objection to the wisdom of the Greeks; rather, when Paul clothes his ideas in a language familiar to his hearers, he is attempting to make both his concern and his objection *understandable*. Paul respects the religious interests of his Jewish and Greek rivals. He knows and says that they too are concerned with the knowledge of God and with human truth, but the Jews' concern "is not enlightened" (Rom. 10:2), and the Greeks do "not yet have the necessary knowledge" (1 Cor. 8:2). Paul takes both questions seriously when he opposes their "knowledge of God" with the central idea of his own theology, being known by God (1 Cor. 8:3), "in order that, as it is written, 'Let the one who boasts, boast in the Lord'" (1 Cor. 1:31).

9

The Church

To speak of the "church" and of church "offices" in the context of early Christian theological history is in a certain sense an anachronism. In regard to the term *church,* earliest Christianity neither possessed its own unified designation for its widely diverging congregational formations, nor was it perceived from the outside as an integrated social entity and given a corresponding designation. The information in Acts 11:26 that the name *Christians* was first used in Antioch—where presumably a Christian group within the synagogue was first given the name because it put the Christ Jesus at the center of its confession—spotlights its special Christian identity, which was only gradually perceived. The Greek term *ekklēsia,* which was borrowed by Latin and survives in the Romance languages (*église, iglesia, chiesa*), was originally common only within a limited congregational union (see below) and only gained ground after the *aposynagōgos* (expulsion from the synagogue: see pp. 263ff. below). The formation and development of a characteristic term like *church* presupposes the existence of a corresponding awareness, which was implicit in the early formation of a confession but took shape in steps: first with the formation of Gentile Christian groups outside the synagogue, then through the expulsion of the Christian communions living within the synagogue in the course of the rabbinic reorganization of the synagogue, and finally in the controversies between orthodoxy and heresy in early Christianity. Even more stratified and variable than the term *church* itself was the *structure* of the Christian churches, whose manifold charismata, ministries, and official functions were slowly and variously formed, arranged, and ranked, until an organization of ecclesiastical *offices* finally emerged.

All the developments of the concept *church* and the understanding of *office* occurred, however, in the context of the broad lines of development along which early Christian theological history was generally moving, and for some time such developments have attracted the attention of historians. Did Jesus found the church? (Did he even want it to exist?) Or is Easter the founding date of the church? How did the early Jewish Christian church understand itself, and what structure did it give itself? The transition from Palestinian Christianity into the universalism of the Damascene conversion theology of Paul, on the one hand, and into the hardly unified Gentile Christianity of the Hellenistic synagogues, on the other, led to the formation of characteristically different conceptions of the church. Their individual natures become even more clearly visible in the letters of Paul, who joined them together in his own "ecclesiology" and in the structure and leadership of his churches. The expulsion of Christian groups from the synagogue and disputes within the church over right doctrine then led in the second and third Christian generations to characteristic developments in ecclesiastical organization and in the structuring of offices. The doctrinal disputes, furthermore, as well as the consequences of the persecution period, made it necessary to focus attention on the problem of church discipline. Yet the breadth of the topic suggests that in the following presentation we should not concentrate primarily on the course of theological history but on its themes and problems and on organizing these in their respective contexts in the history of theology.

The Concept of Church

The Church as the People of God

Without doubt, all developments of the concept of the church rest on the conception of the *people of God,* as early Christianity initially and originally understood itself, for all further developments were accompanied by the idea and the motifs of this conception. It goes back to the Old Testament, yet it is found in early Christianity in the modified form that it had already received through Jewish apocalypticism: the true people of God are no longer identical with the legal and ethnic entity of Israel; they include, rather, the communion of pious Israelites and chosen individuals who in the view of many can also be found among God-fearing Gentiles. Paul expresses this state of affairs with the words: "This means that it is not the children of the flesh who are the children of God, but the children of the promise are counted as descendants" (Rom. 9:8).

The apocalyptic ground in which the early Christian conception of the church as the people of God is rooted makes it difficult to decide to what degree individual motifs of this conception are already to be found in the proclamation of Jesus. The most likely authentic sayings tradition is dominated by the repentance and judgment preaching that is addressed to those who remain excluded from the coming kingdom of God (Luke 3:7–9, 17 par.; 10:10–15; 11:31–32, 37–42 par.); it is preaching on the promise to the elect (Luke 22:28–30 par.). The *future* aspect of Jesus' apocalyptic proclamation (Luke 6:20b–26 par.; 13:28–29 par.) shifts attention from the host of his followers, who already know themselves as earthly members of the eschatological people of God, to the coming kingdom of God as such. This view changes within the Easter church, which increasingly understands itself no longer as only the expectant bearers of the promise but as the multitude of the redeemed, as the wandering people of God. In this sense Loisy's pointed and, because of its terseness, often quoted formulation is apt: Jesus announced the kingdom of God, and what came was the church. Earliest Christendom, however, which, in terms of Christology and soteriology, saw the Easter event as the inbreaking of the new, had rather the experience of continuity in regard to ecclesiology, when it developed the conception of the people of God more fully after Easter.

This experience of continuity was based on the fact that before and after Easter the church knew itself—even if in characteristically varying ways—as the vessel of the eschatological Spirit of God. The warning from the prechristological sayings tradition that a blasphemy against the Holy Spirit will not be forgiven (Mark 3:28–29) shows what a strong position apocalyptic prophecy had in the Jesus movement. In Joel 2:28ff. (3:1ff. in the Hebrew) the gift of God's Spirit is announced for the last time before the turn of the age. Consequently, the Spirit as such was received and experienced as a sure indication of the imminent cosmic turning point, and his individual utterances referred above all to the corresponding temporal dimension: "Truly I tell you, this generation will not pass away until all these things have taken place" (Mark 13:30; cf. 9:1). Such an experience of the Spirit was able to move without a break to the Easter faith and, going beyond the apocalyptic context, to the subsequent formation of a christological confession, which involved, however, a characteristic change in the understanding of the Spirit. For already in Paul the Spirit is no longer the promise-filled gift of the end of the old age but the down payment and first fruits of the new age (Rom. 5:5; 8:23–24; 2 Cor. 1:21–22; 5:1–5; Gal. 4:6–7) and consequently the source of the worshipful life (1 Corinthians 12; 14; Rom. 15:19) and the power of the new obedience in sanctification (Rom. 5:5; 1 Cor. 6:19; 13:1ff.; Gal. 5:16ff.). In this sense there are valid reasons for clearly distinguishing the "water baptism" of John from the Christian "baptism of the Spirit" (Mark 1:7–8) and for designating the Pentecostal outpouring of the Holy Spirit as the founding date of the church (cf. Acts 2:16ff.). Nevertheless, from the point of view of historical theology, the Christian experience of the Spirit—which according to the Pentecost story suddenly and stormily broke into the life of the Easter community of disciples—represents a continuous experience rooted in the pre-Easter period.

Such a continuity can also be observed in the earliest self-designation of Christians. In connection with the gathering of the collection, the "ministry to the saints," Paul calls the Christians in Jerusalem "the saints" in Rom. 15:25, 26, 31; 1 Cor. 16:1; 2 Cor. 8:4; 9:1, 12. And when in 1 Cor. 16:15 he recommends to the Corinthians the house of Stephanas, which they know, because it has devoted itself "to the service of the saints," he is probably likewise thinking of the gathering of the collection, and thus the Jerusalem Christians appear simply as the "saints." In any case, with *saints* Paul is probably adopting the self-designation of the Jerusalem church (H.-F. Weiss 1977, 413). Even the Christians in Rome, who were unknown to Paul and as a rule had come from the East, are addressed by him as "saints" (Rom. 1:7a). Thus the first Christian churches understood themselves as communities of the "saints" (cf. Acts 9:13, 32, 41; 26:10).

This designation goes indirectly back to the Old Testament, which calls Israel a "holy people" (Deut. 7:6; 14:2, 21; 26:19), but directly back to the development of the concept after the Old Testament. For there are now *individuals* who as "saints" form the people of God or his "holy remnant," while others or even the majority of the people are godless (1 Macc. 1:46; *Enoch* 41.8–9). The members of the Essene community of Qumran also called themselves "the holy ones of his people" (1QM 6:5), the "men of holiness" (1QS 5:13; 8:17). But whereas, for example, in the writings of Qumran and also in the Old Testament, *cultic* purity bears the concept of holiness, this aspect was completely lacking in the corresponding early Christian self-designation—apparently from the beginning. In this situation, which was naturally not corrected by Hellenistic Christianity, we can see the underlying apocalyptic native soil of early Christianity.

In accordance with this native soil, the "saints" are also referred to as those "called to be saints" (Rom. 1:7a; 1 Cor. 1:2a), "God's beloved" (= elect; Rom. 1:7a), "those who are sanctified in Christ Jesus" (1 Cor. 1:2a), "God's chosen ones, holy and beloved" (Col. 3:12). Thus the earliest church understood itself as the multitude of the saved chosen by God for the coming kingdom of God; they see themselves as the holy remnant of the people of God separated in the end time from a world devoid of salvation. It is no accident that in the churches of the Revelation to John, which hark back strongly to the apocalyptic roots of Palestinian primitive Christianity, the designation *saints* for Christians (Rev. 5:8; 8:3–4; 22:11; etc.) is still maintained, as is their designation as those who are "called and chosen" (17:14).

This fundamental concept of church, however, also continues to form the basis of the further, expanding development of the understanding of the church; in 1 Thess. 3:13 (cf. 2 Thess. 1:10), for example, when the "saints" are mentioned, the original eschatological aspect is still prominent. In other respects, however, the more the church has to settle down for an indefinite stay in the world, the more the motif of the active sanctification of the saints is emphasized. In the openings of his letters Paul also addresses his own church members as "saints" (1 Cor. 1:1; 2 Cor. 1:1; Phil. 1:1; Col. 1:2), and in the closings of the letters he sends greetings from the saints (2 Cor. 13:12; Phil. 4:21–22). This linguistic usage, which is still not shaped christologically, is already quite formulaic, especially since the designation *saints* is otherwise used simply for the not yet available term *Christians* (Rom. 8:27; 12:13; 16:2, 15; 1 Cor. 6:1–2; Col. 1:4, 12; Philemon 5, 7) and Pauline variations ("the churches of the saints"—1 Cor. 14:33b; "God's chosen ones, holy and beloved"—Col. 3:12) are of questionable authenticity. But it is not *only* formulaic, as is shown, for example, when in 1 Cor. 1:2 Paul precedes the traditional "called to be saints" with the variation "sanctified in Christ Jesus." Thus he intentionally creates a christological reference that gives to the apocalyptically conditioned idea of being called a soteriological enrichment, as the corresponding baptismal reference in 1 Cor. 6:11 shows: "But you were washed, you were *sanctified,* you were justified in the name of the Lord Jesus Christ . . ." (cf. 7:14).

The corresponding formulaic traditional motif of *calling* (1 Cor. 1:2; Rom. 8:30) still has a significant apocalyptic aspect in 1 Cor. 7:17ff.: "Let each of you remain in the condition in which you were called," for "the time is short." And in 1 Thess. 2:12 Paul says in an analogous way that God has called the church "into his kingdom and glory." In general, however, Paul links the idea of calling with viewpoints that go beyond the original apocalyptic horizon. The saints are "called to belong to Jesus Christ" (Rom. 1:6), "called into the fellowship of his Son, Jesus

Christ" (1 Cor. 1:9), in or through the grace of Christ (Gal. 1:6, 15). Above all, the adopted ecclesiological terms *calling, election,* and the like serve Paul as an expression of his doctrine of justification, which excludes all human boasting by those who are chosen (Rom. 4:17; 8:28–30, 33; 11:28–32; 1 Cor. 1:24). Christians are also called, however, to freedom from the law (Gal. 5:8, 13) and into the universal church of Jews and Gentiles without distinction (Rom. 9:7b, 11, 12a, 24; 1 Cor. 1:24). Their calling leads to sanctification (1 Thess. 4:7; 1 Cor. 7:15).

The First Letter of Peter is a characteristic example of how the early Christian idea of the holy remnant and the eschatological people of God was maintained and further developed in Hellenistic Jewish Christianity in its Antiochene form. The epistle is addressed

> To the exiles of the Dispersion . . . who have been chosen and destined by God the Father and sanctified by the Spirit to be obedient to Jesus Christ and to be sprinkled with his blood. (1:1–2)

> Instead, as he who called you is holy, be holy yourselves in all your conduct. (1:15)

> But you are a chosen race, a royal priesthood, a holy nation, God's own people. . . . Once you were not a people, but now you are God's people. (2:9–10)

> Beloved, I urge you as aliens and exiles to abstain from the desires of the flesh that wage war against the soul. (2:11)

> But if you endure when you do right and suffer for it, you have God's approval. For to this you have been called, because Christ also suffered for you . . . (2:20–21; cf. 3:9)

> God . . . has called you to his eternal glory in Christ. (5:10)

Here the christological integration of the idea of God's people has become a matter of course. Only in the doxological closing section of the letter do we find the eschatological viewpoint that in large part originally defined the motif of the chosen people of God. Now, however, they are no longer set apart by this point of view and by a comprehensive apocalyptic criticism of the old age, but by the experience of suffering that results from persecutions for the sake of their confession. Forced out of the synagogue, the Jewish Christian church, vis-à-vis the synagogue and in fellowship with Gentile Christians, sees itself as the chosen race and as God's own people. And since this holy people must live for the time being in the unholy world, the exhortation to sanctification is strongly emphasized. The author no longer dares to call Christians "saints": God is holy, and his people on earth are supposed to be holy.

More powerful than the First Letter of Peter is the imagery of the Letter to the Hebrews, which was written in the same situation of extreme distress and gives a corresponding shape to the idea of the holy people of God. Here we find the way of the "wandering people of God" (Käsemann 1957) toward their heavenly destination (Heb. 13:14), a way that was opened naturally by the "mediator of a new covenant" (12:22–24). The author addresses readers as "brothers and sisters, holy partners in a heavenly calling" (3:1; cf. 6:10; 13:24), and the way of the church in the midst of the temptation to go astray is symbolized by the wandering of the ancient people of God in the wilderness (3:7–11 and elsewhere). The saints "have been sanctified through the offering of the body of Jesus Christ once for all" (10:10 and elsewhere) and thus called to the sanctification without which no one will reach the goal of her or his wandering.

In a different way and for a different reason, the "salvation-historical" design of Luke-Acts is oriented toward the traditional idea of the people of God. Against the Marcionite attempt to separate the Christian church and its message from its Old Testament–Jewish roots, Luke portrays a seamless continuity in which the people of God, unaffected by Israel's rejection of the Christian message, are led on their way from Abraham, Moses, and the prophets through John the Baptist and Jesus, the twelve apostles and Paul, to the worldwide church of Luke's time. Here the eschatological apocalyptic aspect of the early Christian idea of the holy people of God in the end time has clearly receded; this is clearly shown by the fact that Luke writes the second part of his double work as the first church history. In the Revelation to John, by contrast, this very aspect that is neglected by Luke comes to the fore in Revelation 7, for example, when in the face of the tribulations of a persecuted Christendom the number of the elect is "sealed" as God's eternal property, and this multitude is seen standing worshipfully before the throne of the lamb.

Closely connected with the ecclesiological idea of the chosen people of God of the end time are the concept of the "new covenant" and the related idea of the eschatological people of the *covenant,* which refers back to Jer. 31:31. For the "newness" of the "new covenant" is the newness of the new age in accordance with the promise, "See, I am making all things new" (Rev. 21:5). In a way similar to the way the community at Qumran (CD 6:19 and elsewhere) understands itself as the "new covenant" of the "saints" who in the end time are separated from the mass of the people Israel, the early church sees in itself the promise of Jer. 31:31 fulfilled. Yet the idea and the term *new covenant* did not become an ecclesiological commonplace; they are found rather in the context of specific theological reflection. This is already true of the first attestation of this motif. In the words of the Lord's Supper, following the older saying over the bread, we find in analogous formation: "This is my blood of the covenant" (Mark 14:24). Though this developed form of the eucharistic words was already a part of pre–Pauline Christianity, it is hardly of Palestinian origin (see p. 252 below). And since the word over the cup does not refer expressly to Jer. 31:31, but rather to Exod. 24:8 and Zech. 9:11, the motif of the (new) covenant in early Christianity in general probably owed more to scribal reflection than to widespread apocalyptic language and ideas. Especially in the context of the words of institution, the idea of the covenant expresses the church's character of being already established, which it received from the Old Testament. The church of the "new covenant" came into being not on its own authority but as the multitude of those who are *called* into the covenantal relationship created in sovereign fashion by God.

Paul himself reflects on the concept of "covenant" in his disagreement with the synagogue over the role of the law, as shown by both his version of the word over the cup (1 Cor. 11:25; cf. Luke 22:20) and his opposition of the old and new covenants in 2 Cor. 3:4–18 and Gal. 3:15ff.; 4:21ff. (cf. Rom. 7:6; 9:4). The church of the new covenant assembles Jews and Gentiles without distinction, as long as they believe, whereas the old covenant of the law from Sinai made with Israel is abolished in the church of the new covenant. In a new situation and different form, the Letter to the Hebrews repeats this argumentation. For a community that is in danger of abandoning the Christian way and perhaps returning to the synagogue, the author envisions the exceeding glory of the new covenant versus the old, which represents only a foreshadowing of the eschatological community of salvation and whose end is near (Heb. 7:22; 8:8ff.; 9:4, 15ff.; and elsewhere).

The Church as the Body of Christ

The conception of the church as the body of Christ is found in a relatively narrow strain of early Christian theological history, namely, in Paul and in the literature dependent on him and his letters. This observation has occasionally led to the view that Paul himself created this conception. This view is not tenable, however, for the image of the church as the body of Christ and the corresponding "mystical" way of thinking ("we in Christ," "Christ in us," and the like) is already found in pre-Pauline formulaic material (1 Cor. 10:16b–17; Gal. 3:26–28; 1 Cor. 12:13). Paul also works with this complex of ideas and terms secondarily in the context of his own theological ideas. Thus he adopted it as a part of his conversion theology (see chapter 4).

The idea of the "body of Christ" is to be understood spatially, yet the body is regarded as a *pneumatic* (spiritual) body (cf. Rom. 8:9–10). Thus *originally* the phrase meant that the individual pneumatics (that is, people in the Spirit) are parts ("members") of a cosmic form that bears the Jewish name *Christ* (cf. 1 Cor. 12:12). The individual person or the individual church as *pneuma* is "in Christ," and Christ as *pneuma* is "in" the individual pneumatics (cf. Gal. 1:22; 2:20; Col. 3:11; etc.). The religious-historical origin of this concept in the realm of Jewish Gnosticism has already been discussed on pp. 65ff. The adoption of this "spatial" conception by a branch of early Christianity whose understanding of the church was shaped from the beginning by the "salvation-historical" motif of the holy people of God of the end time is understandable when we consider that both Gnostic and apocalyptic dualism lead the multitude of the redeemed out of a world devoid of salvation. In both cases only a *remnant* of humankind is saved; in both cases only *individuals* are rescued from the lost mass of humanity; in both cases such individuals find themselves outside the communion of the Jewish people; in both cases the *Spirit* marks the dawning *eschaton;* in both cases the world, the old age, or matter is dissolved into nothing with the dawn of the kingdom of God or the return into the light.

Naturally, with the transition of the idea of the body of Christ into Paul's conversion theology, the ontic identification of Christ with Christians is abolished. "Christ" is no longer the sum of the members of his body but something different as *Kyrios Christos*. Yet this christological difference, which Paul took for granted, is not clearly established until the deutero-Pauline epistles. The authors of the corresponding passages of Colossians and Ephesians modified the image of the body so that Christ is exalted as the head of the body over the multitude of its members, who are subject to him (Col. 1:18; 2:19; Eph. 1:22–23; 4:15–16; 5:23, 30–31; cf. Col. 1:24). There is no substantial change compared with the conception of the body of Christ in Paul himself, even if we are impressed or amazed by the naturalness with which Paul can formulate in an "ontically identical" fashion and can say "Christ" when he means "church" (1 Cor. 12:12!), although for him Christ is the *Lord* of the church. Nevertheless, a phrase such as "one body *in* Christ" (Rom. 12:5; cf. Col. 1:24) shows that Paul always has in mind the difference between Christ and the church.

The original ecclesiological concept of the "holy people of God" is eschatologically oriented, and the view of the goal of the church's earthly wandering is maintained with varying degrees of intensity even when Christology, soteriology, and ethics are combined with this concept. The concept of the body of Christ, by contrast, contained from the beginning an element of present eschatology: "So if anyone is in Christ, there is a new creation: everything old has passed away; see, everything has become new!" (2 Cor. 5:17). The eschatological goal is the community of the pneumatics or return to the unity of the Spirit. Therefore, based on its origin, the idea of the body of Christ involves a strong "social" component, and it is this *community reference* that enriches Pauline ecclesiology directly, as well as through Paul's development of the corresponding complex of motifs.

It is theologically significant first that the idea of the body of Christ assures the primacy of the church above individual Christians. The church is not an "association"; it is not an open organization of religious persons but a divine establishment that precedes all human endeavor. One is "baptized into one body," "baptized into Christ" (1 Cor. 12:13; Gal. 3:27). In this sense the concept of the body of Christ corresponds to the motif of the "new covenant," which similarly does not represent a union of partners but rather has its origin in a divine arrangement. The primacy of the body above individual members means that when members are received into the church, they must recognize the priority of the community over individual interests and gifts even in a social sense. They are "called into *one* body," says Col. 3:15 in a characteristic joining of the concepts of the people of God and the body of Christ. The church's celebration of the Eucharist always introduces its members anew into this communal relationship:

> The bread that we break, is it not a sharing in [= communion with] the body of Christ? Because there is one bread, we who are many are one body, for we all partake of the one bread. (1 Cor. 10:16b–17)

This withdrawal of the individual behind the community of the children of God is expressed concretely, for example, in the idea that in the church differences of station and status no longer matter. Men and women are equally regarded, and boundaries between people are universally abolished:

> As many of you as were baptized into Christ have clothed yourselves with
> Christ. There is no longer Jew or Greek, there is no longer slave or free,
> there is no longer male and female; for all of you are one in Christ Jesus.
> (Gal. 3:27–28; cf. 1 Cor. 12:13; Col. 3:11; Eph. 2:16; 4:4)

Both the eucharistic formula of 1 Cor. 10:16b–17 and the universalistic formulas
still reveal the dualistic basis of this unified view. Its presupposition consists in the
idea that "*in the Spirit* we were all baptized into one body" (1 Cor. 12:13) and
therefore have put aside corporeal differences. This dualism was already surrendered in the pre-Pauline adaptation of the corresponding ideas. In the abolishing
of natural and social distinctions Paul is thinking entirely of a *historical* act: "For
whoever was called in the Lord as a slave is a freed person belonging to the Lord,
just as whoever was free when called is a slave of Christ" (1 Cor. 7:22).

Above all, the way in which Paul connects the organism idea with the concept of
the body of Christ shows that being inducted into the body of Christ does not mean
a loss of individuality but the enrollment of each person for service to the community of believers. For in the church as organism, various tasks are given to individuals. The idea of the body as an organism was popular in itself; it was employed by
the Stoics as a favorite image for the social order. Whether Paul himself connected
this Stoic motif with the concept of the body of Christ, or whether this connection
was already made before him, can hardly be decided. The pneumatics were concerned only with demonstrating the Spirit as such and therefore were able to appreciate only the ecstatic charismata such as speaking in tongues. By contrast, Paul, with
the help of the image of the body and its members (1 Cor. 12:12ff.), held that all members were given their gifts of the Spirit for the benefit of the whole body (12:7), because "all these are activated by one and the same Spirit, who allots to each one
individually just as the Spirit chooses" (12:11). This asserts not the equality of the
gifts but the equal worth of all members of the church as "children of God," and it
defends against the dualistic disparagement of those who "only" believe. What Paul
develops in this way in 1 Corinthians 12 as the result of an immediate situation is presented instructionally in Rom. 12:4–5 (cf. Eph. 4:11–12) as a fundamental principle:

> For as in one body we have many members, and not all the members have
> the same function, so we, who are many, are one body in Christ, and in-
> dividually we are members one of another.

Paul's consistent use of "ontic-identity" language to describe the church as the
body of Christ was subject to the misunderstanding that Christians constituted
Christ and were primary vis-à-vis him. This led to the emphatic differentiation of
Christ as the head and the church as the members in Col. 1:18; 2:19; Eph. 1:22–23;
4:15–16; 5:23–24, 30–31, yet the ecclesiological assertion was maintained beside
the more prominent christological aspect (cf. also Col. 3:15; Eph. 4:11–12). Moreover, this was probably also the reason why the body-of-Christ ecclesiology was
not taken up and further developed in early Christian history. It is characteristic
that, for example, in *1 Clem.* 37–38 we find the organism idea related to the church
and the image of the church as body, but not the concept of the body of Christ.

The Church as a
Building and as a Planting

The designation of the people of God as the "house" (of Israel, of Jacob, etc.) in the sense of a family or people is quite common in the Old Testament (Ex. 16:31; 2 Sam. 1:12; Jer. 31:31), but the image of a building, as well as building up and tearing down, is also applied to the people of God (Jer. 1:10; 24:6). Early Christendom could use this image when it transposed the older ecclesiological motif of the holy people of God into the image of the holy household of God. The transition is smooth. If judgment begins with the "household of God" (1 Peter 4:17), the focus is more on the family, the people of God, than on the building. Also in 1 Tim. 3:15 the two concepts can hardly be separated: ". . . so that . . . you may know how one ought to behave in the household of God, which is the church of the living God, the pillar and bulwark of the truth." On the whole, the vivid use of the metaphors of house, temple, foundation, cornerstone, building, tearing down, and the like are prominent in early Christendom.

The conception of the community of God as a planting, as well as the images of "planting" and "plucking up," is already found in Jewish tradition (Isa. 5:1ff.; Jer. 24:6; Ezek. 17:1ff.). And in Jer. 1:10; 24:6; Isa. 5:2; 1QS 8:5; and elsewhere (cf. Conzelmann 1969, 94), the images of building and planting are already connected, as is the case especially clearly in 1 Cor. 3:5ff. (cf. Ign. *Eph.* 9): "You are God's field, God's building" (1 Cor. 3:9). The parallelism of the two worlds of images, provided by everyday work in antiquity, makes their application seem like a double parable and makes possible a corresponding parallel presentation.

In the Jewish tradition the two images are essentially *static*. The people *are* a building or a plant, and the question arises whether they have permanence or are torn down and terminated. Therefore the primary context is the idea of judgment and expectation of the community of salvation (1QS 8:5–6), as is seen in the closing parables from the sayings source in the sermon on the plain and the Sermon on the Mount in Luke 6:47–49; Matt. 7:24–27 and in the parable of the wicked tenants in Mark 12:1ff. This world of images is also found in analogous usages in Hellenism (Conzelmann 1969, 93). Early Christendom, by contrast, used these images *dynamically,* as shown, for example, by the frequently encountered term *building up (oikodomē)*; it is used with reference not to the individual but to the church, which is built up from individual "stones" (1 Cor. 8:1; 10:23; 14:12, 17, 26; Rom. 14:19; 15:2; 1 Thess. 5:11). The focus is especially on the building up, expansion, and growth of the church. This observation points to the corresponding idea of the ongoing passage of time for early Christendom, as the expectation of the imminent turn of the age abated and the church began to establish itself in the world. At the same time, it had to be shaped into a church that could develop in relative peace and safety. Therefore, on the basis of its origin, it probably found its home in Hellenistic Jewish Christianity, which was able to survive and flourish in the synagogue until the Jewish war. This location is confirmed when one considers the widespread use of the metaphorical language of the church as building and as planting.

We find active use of both motifs already in Paul. For him they are clearly used *in addition to* the idea of the body of Christ in his conversion theology and are not combined until Eph. 4:12: ". . . for the upbuilding of the body of Christ." Thus he probably acquired them during his activity in Syria and Cilicia. Later we find the two complexes of motifs in various modifications in the deutero-Pauline literature, in 1 Peter, in Hebrews, in the Gospel of Mark (and correspondingly in Matthew, Luke, and Acts), and in the apostolic fathers—that is, in a realm that could have been influenced to such an extent only by Hellenistic Jewish Christianity. The material is extensive and widely scattered. Only examples can be presented here.

> [6]I planted, Apollos watered, but God gave the growth. [7]So neither the one who plants nor the one who waters is anything, but only God who gives the growth. [8]The one who plants and the one who waters have a common purpose, and each will receive wages according to the labor of each. [9]For we are God's servants, working together; you are God's field, God's building.
>
> [10]According to the grace of God given to me, like a skilled master builder I laid a foundation, and someone else is building on it. Each builder must choose with care how to build on it. [11]For no one can lay any foundation other than the one that has been laid; that foundation is Jesus Christ. [12]Now if anyone builds on the foundation with gold, silver, precious stones, wood, hay, straw—[13]the work of each builder will become visible, for the Day will disclose it, because it will be revealed with fire, and the fire will test what sort of work each has done. [14]If what has been built on the foundation survives, the builder will receive a reward. [15]If the work is burned up, the builder will suffer loss; the builder will be saved, but only as through fire.
>
> [16]Do you not know that you are God's temple and that God's Spirit dwells in you? [17]If anyone destroys God's temple, God will destroy that person. For God's temple is holy, and you are that temple. (1 Cor. 3:6–17)

The metaphorical speech of the church as a plant, of the sowing as its founding, of its care, and of its growth is already so familiar that in vv. 6–9 Paul can use it without introduction in his comments about coworkers, to whose efforts the church owes its existence through God's will, and who are obligated not only to preserve the church but also to let it grow and multiply. Within this image there is a limitation of "church" and "office" in the sense that it is God who reconciles the world and institutes the ministry of reconciliation (2 Cor. 5:18).

The sudden transition to the metaphor of the building in v. 9, whose abruptness Paul probably did not even feel, also shows how naturally the church as "building" came to his mind and that he actually understood the vivid language more as a parable. Yet the tone also changes with the image. The workers continue to stand in the foreground, but the focus is now less on the "coworkers" and more on the anonymous botchers or even destroyers. For their sakes Paul presents himself as the skilled master builder who has laid the only possible foundation: Jesus Christ (vv. 10–11; cf. Eph. 2:20; 2 Tim. 2:19). Then in a way that goes beyond the image but is metaphorically instructive, he describes various building materials (v.

12), and finally in a traditional way he connects the image with the idea of judgment (vv. 13–15), yet not of the building but of the builder.

This mild shift in the original content of the image is corrected by Paul in vv. 16–17 when he addresses the *church* and expressly identifies it with the building. This building is a *temple,* a metaphor that the godly of Qumran also used to characterize their holy community (1QS 8:5–9; 9:3–5) and that is found later, for example, in Eph. 2:21–22; 1 Peter 2:5; Ign. *Eph.* 9:1. We can no longer determine whether Paul is thinking not only of the *holiness* of the church but also—like the community by the Dead Sea, for example—of the temple of the *end time* (cf. Ezek. 40ff.; Mark 14:58) and thus connects the primitive community's concept of the church with the Antiochene. It is clear, however, that despite 1 Cor. 6:19 he regards the gathered church, not its individual members, as the dwelling place of the Holy Spirit.

In two post-Pauline texts, Eph. 2:19–22 and 1 Peter 2:4ff., the ecclesiological models of the people of God and of the holy building are combined in a striking and skillfully formed way:

> [19]So then you are no longer strangers and aliens, but you are citizens with the saints and also members of the household of God, [20]built upon the foundation of the apostles and prophets, with Christ Jesus himself as the cornerstone. [21]In him the whole structure is joined together and grows into a holy temple in the Lord; [22]in whom you also are built together spiritually into a dwelling place for God. (Eph. 2:19–22)

> [4]Come to him, a living stone, though rejected by mortals yet chosen and precious in God's sight, and [5]like living stones, let yourselves be built into a spiritual house, to be a holy priesthood, to offer spiritual sacrifices acceptable to God through Jesus Christ . . .
> [9]But you are a chosen race, a royal priesthood, a holy nation, God's own people, in order that you may proclaim the mighty acts of him who called you out of darkness into his marvelous light. (1 Peter 2:4–5, 9)

The connection of the idea of the people of God with the image of the building graphically reflects the development of the concept of the church from the chosen people of the end time to the "church in the world." The church no longer sees itself confronted only with the dawning day but believes that it has moved from death to life. It is no longer waiting only for the coming of its Lord but knows that he is in their midst and they are called to his service. By proclaiming the great deeds of God, it is assisting in the upbuilding of the church. Accordingly, the motif of sanctification also receives its own emphasis. The metaphors of the holy household and the holy priesthood are easily associated with the ideas of the holy sacrifice and the holy people, which allow the church, apart from all legalism, to remember that it must always become what it is.

Even more vividly than by Paul in 1 Cor. 3:11, Christ is inserted here as the cornerstone in the building that is the church. The comparison of Christ with a stumbling block to faith or unfaith goes back to Ps. 118:22; Isa. 8:14–15; 28:16

and originally had a purely christological sense, as shown by Mark 12:10 par.; Acts 4:11; Rom. 9:32–33; etc. The transference of this comparison into the image of the church as a building meant a considerable theological enrichment of the image of the building, especially where it is found in connection with the idea of the people of God. For in the beginning this latter idea had no more of a christological reference than the image of the house or temple. Such a reference is convincingly established when Christ as the cornerstone supports the entire house. In this way Antiochene ecclesiology attained the level of reflection that was reached earlier in the Damascene conversion theology of Paul through the image of the church as the body of Christ or through its variation, which imagined Christ as the head and Christians as his members. When the author of Ephesians inserts Christ as the cornerstone in the house of the church and thereby makes possible the idea that the apostles and prophets (of the new covenant) are the foundation of this church, it is admittedly a daring idea (cf. Matt. 16:18; Rev. 21:14), but it is completely legitimate as a clear contradiction of an enthusiastic understanding of the church that is not linked with the original apostolic message.

Whereas in the epistolary literature we find primarily the image of a building, in the Gospel tradition the image of a planting stands out. The state of affairs is probably related to the fact that already in the Old Testament and early Judaism the image of planting is used in a parabolic way (Isa. 5:1ff.; Ezek. 17:1ff.; 4 Ezra 4:30; 8:41; 9:31) that is characteristic of its occurrences in the Gospel tradition. Yet in Paul we can point to the olive tree parable in Rom. 11:16–24, which goes back to Jewish roots (Jer. 11:16; *1 Enoch* 93.2ff.) and presumably comes from the synagogal paraenesis, where proselytes are regarded as substitutes for Jews who have fallen away. Paul uses it to warn Gentile Christians against feeling superior to the Jews.

The parables of the growing seed and the mustard seed (Mark 4:26–32) come from the prechristological sayings tradition; they speak not of the people of God but of the kingdom of God, which against all appearances will miraculously break forth in great glory. The evangelist Mark, by contrast, relates both parables to the Christian church, which, like the grain that brings forth "first the stalk, then the head, then the full grain in the head" (4:28), grows from small beginnings into a large tree and has the promise of eschatological fulfillment and perfection. Matthew 13:31–32 and Luke 13:18–19 follow this interpretation.

The parable of the sower (Mark 4:3–8, 13–20) is not directed especially toward the Christian church but is intended for *all hearers* of the word; in this sense it reflects the mission situation and on the whole assumes the success of the mission. It is addressed, however, to *church members,* who are compared with the earth or with the plants that sprout from it. The paraenetic character of this allegorizing parable is seen in the fact that it distinguishes within the circle of church members between the rash enthusiasts who do not take root, the serious members who in the long run are not equal to the demands of the word, and the tried and true Christians who as "good soil" bear fruit. In a time that is presumably to be placed after end of the Jewish war, converts are asked above all whether they have considered the costs of discipleship. Luke (8:4ff.) and Matthew (13:3ff.) saw no reason to substantially shift the parable's paraenetic assertion.

Originally in the context of familiar metaphorical material is the allegory of the weeds among the wheat (Matt. 13:24–30), which with its interpretation (13:36–43) belongs to Matthew's special material. Even more clearly than the parable of the sower, it reflects a time and situation in which the church had evidently become a *corpus permixtum,* and the attempt to create or reestablish a communion of the saints had to be resisted. At the same time it shows how the image of planting is adaptable to changed church circumstances. A corresponding variability of this image is also seen in the allegorizing parable of the wicked tenants, which is based on Isa. 5:1ff. and, justifying Jesus' cleansing of the temple, apparently reflects the situation after the destruction of the temple. The sending of the "slaves" and of the "son" and their rejection introduces both "salvation-historical" features and a strong christological aspect into the image of the vineyard, which also changes. For the vineyard is no longer, as in Isa. 5:1ff., the people of God but a metaphor for faithful service to God, which will be taken away from the Jewish leaders and entrusted to the Christian church composed of Jews and Gentiles.

The Church as the Bride of Christ
and as the Flock of the Good Shepherd

Only with difficulty can the images of the church as flock and as bride be classified more precisely in terms of theological history, for they do not occur characteristically in a particular strain of early Christian theology. Both are rooted, however, in the Old Testament and in early Judaism. Since both images are found only in the form of comparisons or metaphors, it is sufficient to assume a more or less direct and in each case independent reference to living Jewish tradition.

As a flock, the old people of God are found, for example, in Ps. 100:3; the new, in Luke 15:3–7. We find strayed, lost, or misled sheep in, for example, Ps. 119:176; Isa. 53:6; Zech 13:7, and then in Mark 6:34; Matt. 10:6; 15:24; 26:31 (quotation of Zech 13:7); 1 Peter 2:25. And there is also the metaphor of the "little flock" in Luke 12:32. We find God as the good shepherd in, for example, Psalm 23; Pss. 78:52; 80:2; Isa. 40:11, and Christ in this role in 1 Peter 2:25; Heb. 13:20. People appear as shepherds in, for example, Num. 27:17; Jer. 23:1ff.; Ezek. 34:2ff.; Zech. 11:15ff.; Ps. 74:21 and correspondingly in Acts 20:28; 1 Peter 5:2–3; John 21:15–17.

This metaphorical world of images is discussed in more detail in New Testament times only in John 10:1–30, but it is not just this talk of a shepherd that produced a broad stream of images in the following centuries, which encompassed especially the written and graphic arts. It is no coincidence that in this detailed metaphorical language we meet for the first time influences that cannot be traced directly back to Old Testament traditions. For the heart of this speech — "I am the good shepherd. I know my own and my own know me, just as the Father knows me and I know the Father" (John 10:14–15a) — with its mutual knowledge of the human and the divine, shows the clear influence of Hellenistic mysticism (cf. 1 Cor. 13:12; Bultmann 1952, 289ff.). The theme of the speech is more christologically than ecclesiologically oriented, but it is discussed not only christologically but also ecclesiologically: "No one will snatch them out of my hand" (10:28); "So there will be one flock, one shepherd" (John 10:16). Even with all of this, however, neither the image of the flock and the shepherd nor its "mystical" elaboration can be recognized as part of a specifically Johannine line of development.

The idea of the church as "bride of Christ" also has many Old Testament roots. In Hosea 1–3 the unfaithfulness of Israel, on the one hand, and God's judgment and enduring faithfulness, on the other, are demonstrated through the example of marriage, and a corresponding metaphor is also found in, for example, Isa. 50:1; 54:1ff.; 62:4–5; Jer. 2:2, as well as in detail in Ezekiel 16. Already at an early time the Song of Songs was related allegorically to the relationship between God as bridegroom and Israel as bride (cf. *TWNT* 4:1094–95). Here we must take into consideration the fact that in the ancient world the union of God and humankind was in many ways understood and described—as well as practiced cultically—in analogy with the relationship between husband and wife. Against this broad religious-historical background, passages such as Mark 2:19–20; Matt. 25:1ff.; and Rev. 19:7, 9; 21:2, 9; 22:17, in which Christ is always clearly found in the image of the groom and the church less clearly in that of the bride, do not necessarily require a special explanation in terms of historical theology.

Noteworthy in the New Testament, moreover, are the discussions in 2 Cor. 11:1–3 and Eph. 5:21–32, which are expanded above all by *2 Clem.* 14. Paul fears that the church in Corinth has been led away from the simple Christian truth by false teachers, as Eve was deceived by the serpent. He bases the corresponding vigorous exhortations, which characterize his "letter of tears" (2 Corinthians 10–13), on the fact that he has promised the church "in marriage *to one husband, to present you as a chaste virgin to Christ*" (2 Cor. 11:2). Paul is pursuing a paraenetic interest, and he combines the concept of the chaste people of God with the seemingly familiar image of Christ as bridegroom and the church as bride, skillfully inserting himself into the picture as matchmaker. Here the image of holy marriage, as in the Revelation to John, is oriented entirely toward the eschatological culmination. It is possible that Paul and the seer John are making use of a Jewish Christian apocalyptic idea, which would naturally be difficult to identify.

Yet it is also possible that Paul abbreviated the material that is found in more detail in the household rules of Eph. 5:21–33, where the relationship of husband and wife is treated. The corresponding passage in Col. 3:18–19 contains only a brief admonition to wives to be subject to their husbands, and to husbands to act lovingly toward their wives, "as is fitting in the Lord." The Letter to the Ephesians provides both admonitions with a broad christological foundation, which in both cases makes use of the idea of the body of Christ. The basis for the subordination of the wife is provided by an analogy: as Christ is the head of the church, so the husband is the head of the wife (5:21–24; cf. 1 Cor. 11:3). The argumentation falls within the framework of the differentiation of the body of Christ into head and members, which is also found elsewhere in Ephesians. The exhortation to men to love their wives also makes use of the motif of holy marriage (Eph. 5:25–27). First, in the context of the Antiochene tradition, the writer states that "Christ loved the church and gave himself up for her" (see pp. 91ff. above) and through baptism cleansed and sanctified her, in order to present her to himself (cf. 2 Cor. 11:2) as a pure, spotless, and holy bride—yet the erotic word itself is avoided. Then in Eph. 5:28–29a the conclusion is drawn for the corresponding behavior of men, yet in such a way that now the term *body* is introduced with respect to Gen. 2:24: husband and wife are one body, and no one hates one's own body, but rather loves it. This prepares the way for the following argumentation, in which the motifs of the body of Christ and holy marriage are connected: "[One cares for the body] just as Christ does for the church, because we are members of his body" (Eph. 5:29b–30). The account of the creation story of the bodily union of husband and wife in Gen. 2:24, which the author of Ephesians quotes in its entirety, is, in his view, speaking of the marriage—again the term itself is avoided—between Christ and the church.

The religious-historical background of this view, which the author of Ephesians uses paraenetically and restricts to one of the household rules, is apparent (cf. Schlier 1958, 264ff.; Theobald 1990): redemption is accomplished as the union of the heavenly Christ with his earthly members. This view apparently comes from a Jewish Gnosticism that was modified under the influence of Christianity. The original idea of the body of Christ did not involve a redeemer figure, but only the image of the members of the "body" that has sunk into matter, which redeems itself and is restored as the "perfect man." This idea is transformed into the "Christian" view that Christ as the head reunites in holy marriage with his lost members.

The mistaken view that the author of Ephesians created this idea himself for the present application is excluded by the independent parallel in *2 Clem.* 14. Clement also follows a paraenetic interest, namely, the ascetic sanctification of the flesh; much of the lack of clarity in his argumentation can be traced back to the fact that the dualistic mythos, which he adopts from an unknown source, is not appropriate to his concern. Clement also refers to the creation story: "The husband is Christ; the wife the church" (*2 Clem.* 14.2). The church is the body of Christ and, like him, preexistent (ibid.); as the earthly church it is the "flesh" of Christ, who himself is "Spirit" (14.3) and wants to give the church a share in the Spirit, who "is the Christ" (14.4).

The mythos adopted in Ephesians 5 and *2 Clem.* 14—and possibly also in 2 Cor. 11:1–3—comes without question from the same place where the Gnostic elements of Paul's conversion theology are also rooted. Yet the meager testimony does not allow us to draw clear historical-theological conclusions from this religious-historical observation. In the present connection this caution is all the more appropriate in view of the fact that based on the texts discussed, the motifs of holy marriage and the union of bride and bridegroom in the context of early Christianity were adopted more for the purpose of paraenetic and eschatological assertions than for specifically ecclesiological statements.

Ekklēsia

In terms of theological history, it has always been especially difficult to classify the term *ekklēsia*, which became the usual designation for the Christian church around the turn of the first century. Apparently it was originally connected neither with the motif of the people of God nor with the idea of the body of Christ nor with the metaphors of building and planting. Such combinations are rare and insignificant (cf. 1 Cor. 14:5, 12; 1 Tim. 3:15; "churches of the saints" in 1 Cor. 14:33 is part of the post-Pauline addition 1 Cor. 14:33b–36). Rarely, the *ekklēsia* of Paul is expressly called the church "in Christ" or "of Christ" (Gal. 1:22; Rom. 16:16; 1 Thess. 1:1; cf. 2:14), yet this happens rather incidentally and not in opposition to another *ekklēsia*. By contrast, the more exact designation *church of God (ekklēsia tou theou)* is stereotypical and without doubt characteristic of the origin of the term: 1 Cor. 1:2; 10:32; 11:16, 22; 15:9; 2 Cor. 1:1; Gal. 1:13; 2 Thess. 1:4; 1 Tim. 3:5, 15; Acts 20:28; cf. 1 Thess. 1:1; 2:14; 1 Cor. 12:28; Phil. 3:6. This observation identifies the term *ekklēsia* as pre-Pauline and could suggest an early Palestinian and possibly even prechristological origin of the designation. Consequently, Roloff (1993, 83, 96), for example, holds *ekklēsia tou theou* to be an "old Jerusalem self-designation." Yet this judgment is contradicted decisively by the attestation of *ekklēsia* in the early Christian period.

The isolated and late occurrences of this designation in Matt. 16:18; 18:17; James 5:14; 3 John 6, 9, 10; and Heb. 2:12; 12:23 contribute nothing to answering the question about its origin. This is especially true since Heb. 2:12 is a quotation from Ps. 21:23 (LXX); in Heb. 12:23; Matt. 18:17; and James 5:14, we hardly have the technical usage; and Matt. 16:18 is probably a gloss from the period of the canon formation. By contrast, *ekklēsia* appears abundantly in Paul and in the deutero-Paulines (62 times), in Acts (23 times), and in Revelation (20 times). This finding simply excludes the idea that the term *ekklēsia* came from Palestinian Christianity or the Hellenistic Jewish Christianity of the synagogue and points without doubt to a Gentile Christian milieu as its place of origin. This milieu can be defined even more precisely, for Paul himself never uses *ekklēsia* for Jewish Christian churches, but always for churches living without the Jewish law, whether for churches of Damascene provenance, which he once persecuted (1 Cor. 15:9; Gal. 1:13; Phil. 3:6; cf. 1 Thess. 2:14), or, as was usually the case, for his own churches. Consequently it is no accident that the designation *ekklēsia* is missing in the opening and main body of the Letter to the Romans, which is not addressed to Pauline church members. Also Paul does not address the broader church as *ekklēsia;* when he subsumes several churches under this term, it is always a question of his own churches or ones that he once persecuted (1 Cor. 6:4; 10:32; 12:28; Gal. 1:13). The "churches of the Gentiles," who are indebted to Prisca and Aquila (Rom. 16:4), are not found beside the "churches of the Jews" but are the *ekklēsiai* outside Palestine. The conclusion is unavoidable: *ekklēsia* was originally a self-designation of Damascene Christendom that Paul adopted and retained for the law-free churches that he himself founded.

This recognition then raises the question, *Where* did the early church obtain the designation *ekklēsia*? There are two possibilities. In the Septuagint *ekklēsia* occurs about 70 times, and always as a designation for the *gathering of the people* and essentially synonymous with the term *synagogue,* which occurs around 200 times. In secular Greek usage the term is also applied as a rule to a gathering of the people (cf. Acts 19:32, 39–40). Thus it is common to both Jews and Jewish Christians, on the one hand, and Gentiles and Gentile Christians, on the other. The observation that at a pre-Pauline time in a Gentile Christian milieu, where there was naturally familiarity with the Septuagint, the term *ekklēsia* was chosen as a self-designation for the Christian church casts doubt on an *alternative* derivation from the biblical or political sphere. It may also be accurate to say that the Christian church that called itself the *ekklēsia tou theou* was thereby *also* claiming to be the true Israel (Roloff 1993, 83). But such an insight still does not offer an adequate explanation for the choice of this designation by a Gentile Christian group. For on the one hand, for such purposes a more obvious term that is both biblical and familiar to Jewish contemporaries would be *synagogue*—for example, "the synagogue of Jesus Christ." On the other hand, the expression *ekklēsia tou theou,* which never occurs in the Septuagint, remains unexplained (cf. Schrage 1963, 186ff.). Therefore Schrage is correct when he sees the choice of *ekklēsia* as essentially guided "by the awareness of a discontinuity vis-à-vis a past characterized by the law" (1963, 199–200), and when in terms of theological history he locates the concept in the circle of "Hellenists" around Stephen, that is, in the realm of Paul's conversion theology.

Yet this explanation still does not suffice. If its correctness is presupposed, then we must ask why the concept *ekklēsia tou theou* occurs in relative independence *alongside* the ecclesiology of the body of Christ, which is likewise a part of Paul's conversion theology. In Gal. 1:22 (cf. 1 Thess. 2:14) Paul refers to the churches persecuted by him as the "churches *in Christ,*" but this phrase does not necessarily point to an original theological-historical connection. Why did he forgo a *christological* predicate and speak "secularly" of the "church *of* God"? On the basis of the previous observations, the answer to this question can only be that *ekklēsia tou theou* is the self-designation of the "body of Christ" for *outsiders.* Hence it is no accident that when Paul says that he persecuted the church, he typically uses *ekklēsia.* The choice of the term *ekklēsia* did not mean a conscious departure from Jewish salvation history, but rather a public, demonstrative, and perhaps also evangelically oriented distancing of the law-free Christian church from the Jewish synagogue. And the term chosen for this purpose was also easily understood by the Gentiles, for both parts of the phrase *ekklēsia tou theou* were within the context of what was familiar to Gentiles in their everyday lives. The fact that this name for a community that understood itself as the "body of Christ," which was coined for outsiders, soon also became the self-designation for those on the inside is understandable, since no other name was available, and those who joined the community had come to know it as an *ekklēsia.* Paul had also joined the community that he had earlier persecuted as the "church of God" (Gal. 1:13; 1 Cor. 15:9). Thus *church of God* was probably the self-designation of Gentile Christian churches from the beginning. Therefore the spread of this designation to the whole of Christendom, which came with the triumphal entry of Gentile Christianity and is to be observed after the expulsion of Jewish Christians from the synagogue (cf. James 5:14), was as well anticipated in terms of theological history as the transition from *church of God* to *church of Jesus Christ,* which is already evident in Paul.

Church Order:
Offices and Ministries

The structure of early Christian churches can be comprehended in only a limited way from the standpoint of *theological* history, for the idea that *divine* law prescribes for the church its order was basically still foreign to early Christendom. Therefore a church could adapt its own order from case to case to meet changing circumstances and necessities. As a rule, questions of order and office did not become controversial, even if doctrinal disputes largely initiated and defined the implementation of order.

Nonetheless, it was not only extratheological factors that determined order in the church. This is shown, for example, in modern times in the often vigorously debated disagreement over the question of how the true church and the visible church are related to each other. The view of Sohm (1909) that in its earthly form early Christianity identified itself completely with the true church is not even true in the first Christian generation, just as, conversely, the idealistic thesis that the true church is entirely invisible is untenable. For early Christendom there was no question that the true church is manifested in the gathered church on earth and also in the new obedience (Matt. 5:13ff.). It was equally obvious to it that weeds were intermingled with the wheat (Matt. 13:24–30). The resultant problem of church discipline, however, was not uniformly resolved in the early Christian period. Gross sinners and heretics were excluded from the community (1 Cor. 5:1–13; Matt. 18:15ff.), yet always with an allowance for the possibility of repentance and forgiveness (2 Cor. 2:5ff.; Matt. 18:21ff.). Achieving complete sanctification of the church through church discipline was neither achievable nor desirable (Matt. 13:36–43). In the time of acute tribulation, the author of the Letter to the Hebrews wants to prevent manifest apostasy with the argument that a renewed penance is out of the question (Heb. 6:4ff.), yet Luke gives a friendly invitation to repentance and return to those who have fallen away in time of persecution (Luke 15). Penance as an *institution,* however, is not discernible in the early Christian period.

Also often discussed is the question of how charismatic guidance and properly ordered direction of the church are related to—and can be coordinated with—each other. Early Christendom does not answer this question but finds instead that the Spirit himself institutes the structures of order. "Anyone who claims to be a prophet, or to have spiritual powers, must acknowledge that what I am writing to you is a command of the Lord," for "God is a God not of disorder but of peace" (1 Cor. 14:37, 33a). In the early Christian period there was no unified understanding of "office," and the transition from free charismata to ordered ministries was therefore accomplished without discernible conflict. The danger that order would become the norm and suppress the Spirit did not become visible until the end of the New Testament period. Yet the problems of the relationship of Spirit and office, of charisma and law, of event and institution have remained topical, for they are imbedded in the essence of the church as earthly manifestation of the true people of God and continue to form the central theological problem of ecclesiastical offices and ministries, which was already visible in the early Christian period. In all early Christian developments, however, there was a concern to understand every office as service and to evaluate every order in terms to its serving function.

"Order" had to be given primarily to the worship of God, but it is indicative that no orders of worship have been handed down to us from the early Christian period. Those that existed must have been variable and also shaped differently from place to place. Naturally we can recognize that the most important "official" duties to be fulfilled in the church concerned the leading of public worship and the shaping of the celebration of the Lord's Supper. Therefore the corresponding functions form the foundation of the later structure of offices.

The Palestinian Primitive Church

Without doubt the Jesus movement was inspired by apocalyptic prophecy. Therefore the prophet was protected from criticism (Mark 3:28–29 par.; *Did.* 11.7), and the one who receives a prophet is promised a prophet's reward (Matt. 10:41). The basic corpus of the Jesus tradition consists of prophetic utterances. Also the circle of the twelve disciples as representatives of the twelve tribes of the true people of God — whether it goes back to a pre-Easter calling or came into being under the influence of the Easter experience — grew out of a prophetically aroused expectation and would be misunderstood as a leadership committee. It was dissolved early on (see p. 16 above), without leaving a vacuum, for the prophetic spirit was not extinguished.

When Paul is in Jerusalem for the first time after his conversion, he visits especially with Peter, who after his fundamental "prophetic" (cf. Matt. 16:17) confession of the Messiah was the outstanding spiritual authority of Christendom (Gal. 1:18). On his second visit, at the so-called Apostolic Council, he met with a committee of three authorities, consisting of James, Peter, and John, whom he calls "leaders," employing a stereotypical expression (*dokountes*) four times (Gal. 2:2, 6, 9) and using the Jewish honorific title *pillars* in Gal. 2:9. All three saw the resurrected Jesus (1 Cor. 15:5, 7) and are thereby identified as charismatics. On the one hand, Paul presents his gospel first to the whole church (Gal. 2:1–2) and only then to the three who "seemed" to be leaders, but on the other hand, he went into the negotiations, in which representatives of the Jewish authorities also took part (Gal. 2:4–5), in a group of three with Barnabas and Titus. In light of these facts, the three "pillars" seem to be less an internal committee of leaders than perhaps a committee formed ad hoc as a negotiating commission of the Jewish Christian church in Jerusalem — an observation that explains why the three "pillars" do not appear elsewhere with this designation. Later James, the brother of the Lord, stands out in Jerusalem (Gal. 2:12; Acts 1:18; Euseb. *Hist. Eccl.* 2.23; Jos. *Ant.* 20.200), which hardly gave Harnack (1910, 26) proper cause to acknowledge "the idea of Chalifat"; James was a charismatic and prophet.

Thus we cannot discern legal structures in the Jerusalem primitive church. The later writings that are most closely connected with the Palestinian church, the Revelation to John and the *Didache,* still give prophecy the most prominent place in the leadership of the church (Rev. 10:11; 11:18; 16:6; 19:10; 22:6, 9; *Did.* 11.13).

Apostles, Prophets, and Teachers

Paul explains in 1 Cor. 12:28 that "God has appointed in the church first apostles, second prophets, third teachers." In the remainder of the verse, after "then," he names further charismata but not persons as charismatics. Therefore J. Weiss (1910, 307) states with some justification that "the combination of these three entities is somewhat formulaic and absolute; the circle is hardly capable of expansion." Yet in Eph. 2:20; 3:5 apostles and prophets are considered the foundation of the church, and teachers follow only at some distance. This corresponds to the situation in *Didache* 11, where only itinerant apostles and prophets are named, but not local teachers, who are mentioned, however, in *Did.* 13.2—which says nothing about apostles—alongside prophets, who are always active in the local church. In 2 Tim. 1:11, by contrast, in the disagreement with Gnostic enthusiasm, the prophet is omitted, or rather replaced by the "herald" (*kēryx*). Also, other "officeholders" can be added to this triad. In Eph. 4:11, for example, after the apostles and the prophets and before the teachers come "evangelists" and "pastors." And in Rom. 12:6–7 Paul himself inserts *diakonia* between prophecy and teaching.

In the triad "apostles, prophets, and teachers," the apostles, as their name suggests, are the itinerant missionaries. In 1 Cor. 15:7ff. we see that they belong to the early period of the church and according to Paul are all Easter witnesses. In this passage Paul calls himself the last of the apostles, yet this could be a subjective judgment. If the strict definition in *Did.* 11.3–6, according to which an apostle could spend only one or at most two days in a church, was still currently important in the time of the *Didache,* the circle of the apostles seems to have been expanded even later than Paul. Their duty is the founding of churches (1 Cor. 3:6, 10), and their means are prophecy (14:6ff.) and teaching (4:17). When they have founded a church, they leave prophets and teachers behind, so that the departure of the apostle does not cause a crisis in the church. In 1 Cor. 12:14 the image of more than one prophet is clearly suggested, but Paul has to put a dualistic, ecstatic prophetism in its place. Nonetheless, in Rom. 12:6 prophecy also stands at the top of the list of charismatic ministries in the local church. Prophets are authoritative and often spontaneous (1 Cor. 14:29ff.) proclaimers of the Christian message (1 Cor. 11:4–5; 1 Thess. 5:20). If they are found in the circle of apostles and teachers, they no longer appear, as did the Palestinian apocalyptists, especially as prophets of the end time; rather, they spread "upbuilding and encouragement and consolation" (1 Cor. 14:3). Their medium, in contrast to the speakers in tongues, is in any case understandable speech (1 Cor. 14:23ff.). Unlike the apostles, they remain, as a rule, in one place, yet there are also itinerant prophets in addition to apostles and teachers (*Did.* 11.7–12; 13.1; cf. Matt. 10:41; Acts 21:10ff.). *Teachers* fulfill their function *also* in corporate worship, as 1 Cor. 14:26 shows. They are not suited for the charisma of spontaneous proclamation but for instruction with the help of traditional, more or less formulaic teaching. Their position *after* prophets, who appear in worship, and deacons, who are presumably involved in the celebration of the Lord's Supper (Rom. 12:6–7; cf. Eph. 4:11), suggests that their duty consists in large part in the instruction of catechumens who are preparing for baptism. The assumption is confirmed by Gal. 6:6: "Those who are taught the word must share in all good things with their teacher."

The triad "apostles, prophets, and teachers" apparently comes from Damascene Christianity. This is indicated already by Paul's note that God has appointed these ministries "in the church," that is, in the *ekklēsia*. Also, the triad is found in neither Palestinian nor Hellenistic Jewish Christianity, whereas it is the foundation of Pauline church order. Furthermore, the missionary office of the apostle—which, in distinction to the offices of prophet and teacher, is character-istic of the present triad—belongs, according to its origin, in the universalist church that Paul once persecuted. For the worldwide mission is rooted in this church, and a Jewish Christian origin of the apostolate is excluded: only Luke forms anachronistically the institution of the "twelve apostles" (Klein 1961), while the Synoptic tradition did not know the concept earlier (in Mark 3:14; Matt. 10:2 "apostle" does not belong to the original text, and in Mark 6:30 it is a purely functional designation). And when in Gal. 1:17–19 (cf. 2:8) Paul counts Peter and—with reservation—James among the apostles, he does this on the basis of his understanding of the apostolate, not based on a corresponding self-under-standing of these two Jewish missionaries. Also in terms of the history of reli-gion, the term *apostle* comes not from Judaism but from Gnosticism (Schmithals 1961). If, however, in the Hellenistic churches persecuted by Paul the standard ministries of apostles, prophets, and teachers were utilized for the upbuilding of the church, the function of the "seven"—who, with Stephen as their head, had au-thority in this church, according to Luke's reliable report (Acts 6:5)—cannot be described as "church leadership." Rather, it was probably a question of repre-sentatives who spoke for their church or community to outsiders, which was nec-essary above all in relation to the synagogue. They were appointed as such representatives because they were active as apostles, prophets, or teachers and possessed authority (cf. Acts 6:6; 21:10).

Paul

Called himself as an apostle in the realm of Damascene Gentile Christianity, Paul made the charismatic triad "apostles, prophets, and teachers" the foundation of the organization of his own churches. Especially instructive in this connection is Rom. 12:6–8, because here Paul communicates to his newly founded church in Rome rules for the regulation of church affairs:

> [6]We have gifts that differ according to the grace given to us:
> prophecy, in proportion to faith;
> [7]ministry, in ministering;
> the teacher, in teaching;
> [8]the exhorter, in exhortation;
> the giver, in generosity;
> the leader, in diligence;
> the compassionate, in cheerfulness.

The symbolic naming of seven functions in itself shows that Paul does not intend a complete enumeration of the charismata that are possible or necessary for church life; he is instead indicating some of the gifts of the Spirit that may be activated. Therefore one can juxtapose this list with many other texts from the apostle's cor-respondence:

> And God has appointed in the church first apostles, second prophets, third teachers; then deeds of power, then gifts of healing, forms of assistance, forms of leadership, various kinds of tongues. (1 Cor. 12:28)

> When you come together, each one has a hymn, a lesson, a revelation, a tongue, or an interpretation [of a speaking in tongues]. Let all things be done for building up. (1 Cor. 14:26; cf. Col. 3:16)

> But we appeal to you, brothers and sisters, to respect those who labor among you, and have charge of you in the Lord and admonish you. (1 Thess. 5:12)

In all charismata the church itself acts: it is not the object of actions undertaken for its sake.

Apart from the openings of letters, Paul invokes his own apostolic office only when he must defend himself against attacks, as in large parts of the Second Letter to the Corinthians. Otherwise "prophecy" and "teaching" are the most important ministries in the churches founded by the apostle, without which a church obviously cannot exist; without a fixed norm, these are also accompanied by other charismatic activities. Paul has no coworkers in high office, nor are there elected church functionaries; the additional mention of "bishops and deacons" in the opening of Philippians is unique in the letters of Paul and comes from a later editor of the Pauline correspondence, who would like to have the circumstances of his own time legitimated apostolically (Schenk 1984, 76ff.). It is significant that in the extensive Corinthian correspondence, which goes into the details of church relationships, no local officeholders are addressed. The exact content of the individual functions named by Paul is never revealed, and this is probably connected with the idea that the apostle does not want to place any limits on the Spirit and wants to allow for variation in church order according to individual gifts and local circumstances. Nevertheless, the emphasis is on the activities of the church gathered for worship: the various duties of proclamation and preparation of the eucharistic celebration by deacons (cf. Just. *Apol.* 1.65), a service that the church in Cenchreae apparently gives to Phoebe (Rom. 16:1). The care of the poor and the sick and the duties of administration, are known in every church. The task of exhortation and encouragement, mentioned as a special charisma in Rom. 12:8, is given to the whole church in 1 Thess. 5:11, 14.

The *service character* of the various duties is always presupposed and sometimes stressed. Although different gifts may have varying importance for the up-building of the church (1 Cor. 12:31), all are activated by one and the same Spirit, so that no member is allowed or able to feel superior to others (12:11ff.). Since the household of Stephanas has devoted itself to the ministry to the saints, one should listen to them and to all who similarly apply themselves and work (16:15–16). Paul himself is the model (cf. Phil. 4:9): "I do not mean to imply that we lord it over your faith; rather, we are workers with you for your joy" (2 Cor. 1:24). "What then is Apollos? What is Paul? Servants through whom you came to believe" (1 Cor. 3:5).

The Letter to the Ephesians, the only extant document that is attributed with certainty to the Pauline school, places apostles and prophets in the beginning period of the church (Eph. 2:20; 3:5). Thus in the second generation, not only have apostles died out, but also prophetic enthusiasm has been crippled. The church, however, is still built up charismatically, not properly organized; the offices of elders and bishops are still unknown. The current ministries are those of "evangelists," "pastors," and, as earlier, "teachers" (Eph. 4:11–12). The first-mentioned evangelists seem to continue the missionary activity of the apostles (cf. 2 Tim. 4:5; Acts 21:8). The pastors exercise (worship?) leadership functions (cf. Acts 20:28–29; 1 Peter 5:2–3; John 21:16), which in Paul himself were fulfilled by "leaders" (Rom. 12:8; 1 Thess. 5:12; 1 Cor. 12:28). As in the earlier period, the activities of teachers were probably—according to individual gifts—instruction, interpretation of scripture, theological education, and so forth; they were probably practiced both in the church and among catechumens. In any case, teachers focused on extant writings and traditional creeds.

Hellenistic Jewish Christianity

We know very little about the organizational shape of Hellenistic synagogues in the first Christian century and even less about what status the fellowship of Jewish Christians and their God-fearing Gentiles had within the synagogal structure. Nevertheless, based on Acts 11:27ff.; 13:1ff.; 15:22, 27, 32; 21:10ff., we may infer, in spite of the many peculiarities of the stamp that Luke left on his traditions, that the prophetic spirit spread out from Palestine to the Christian communities in the Hellenistic synagogues. Naturally, that spirit participated in and may have stimulated the transformation from apocalyptic announcement to Hellenistic Christology and soteriology. The fact that in Acts 13:1 teachers are found alongside prophets requires no special explanation.

In Acts 13:1 five prophets and teachers are mentioned by name. Presumably the original list, which Luke doubtless took from a source, also named the prophets Judas Barsabbas and Silas, the companion of Paul (Acts 15:22, 27, 32), whom Luke uses in his presentation of the Apostolic Council; with them it can hardly be a question of Jerusalemites, as Luke often assumes in the case of other Hellenistic Christians (Schmithals 1982, 141–42). Then in Antioch we also meet a circle of seven authorities, who were selected from the larger number of active charismatics to assume special responsibility. As with the seven "deacons" of Acts 6:6, this responsibility consisted in representing Antiochene Christendom vis-à-vis outsiders and thus the synagogue. They cannot be regarded as elected church leadership.

Whether such leadership existed at all in Hellenistic Jewish Christian churches is doubtful and in any case not demonstrable. Paul, who worked more than a decade in the vicinity of Antioch, reveals nothing of the kind. The synagogues themselves were probably directed by a council of elders, and for this reason alone, a corresponding structure of the Christian communities within the synagogue is unlikely. But for other reasons as well, the Christians organized in the synagogue seem to have formed no community structure of their own. Written toward the end of the first century, the Revelation to John speaks only of an order of prophets, to which the author himself belongs, and even Matthew, whose communities were driven out of the synagogue, speaks of no authorities that stand out above the prophetic ministry (Matt. 10:41). For even Christian scribes—among whom Matthew counts himself and who, like the master of the household, bring out of their treasure what is new and what is old (13:52)—are possessors of a particular charisma. No one among Christians is to be called "rabbi" or "father" or "instructor," as the scribes of the Pharisees do and as might be suggested in the newly independent Christian communities, for in them, all are brothers and sisters, and the greatest among them will be their servant (Matt. 23:8–12). Accordingly, even the exercise of church discipline involves only individual members, or possibly the gathered church (Matt. 18:15ff.); particular offices and ministries are even less evident than in the Pauline churches, which had already been independently organized for some time.

If this was still the situation in the Matthean churches, one cannot expect anything different in Mark and his traditions. James and John, the sons of Zebedee, are deterred from a place of honor in the kingdom of God on Jesus' right and left (Mark 10:35); how then can an ordinary church member lay claim to a prominent position: "Whoever wishes to become great among you must be your servant, and whoever wishes to be first among you must be slave of all" (Mark 10:43–44). This is not said against the performance of certain functions in the church, but it presupposes the necessary ministries of individuals. These, however, apparently require no particular regulation; it is sufficient, rather, to warn against the presumption that an exercised charisma justifies exalted claims. The silence of the evangelist Mark about any kind of concrete formation of church order is all the more eloquent when he treats ethical questions of all kinds in detail; thus offices and ministries have not yet become a problem in the Hellenistic Jewish Christian church.

Like the Gospel of Matthew, the Letter to the Hebrews, which is addressed to the Jewish Christians forced out of the synagogue, is to be dated toward the end of the first century. It has "leaders . . . who spoke the word of God to you" (13:7) and "are keeping watch over your souls" (13:17). They correspond to the coworkers whom Paul calls "those who . . . have charge of you" (1 Thess. 5:12), using a similar expression (cf. *1 Clem.* 1.3; 21.6), and who apparently performed charismatic ministries, as he describes in Rom. 12:6–8, for example. Beyond this, the Letter to the Hebrews does not reveal a church order.

The First Letter of Peter was probably written around the same time. It admonishes the addressees to "serve one another with whatever gift each of you has received. Whoever speaks must do so as one speaking the very words of God" (4:10–11). No different from a half century earlier in Paul, all church members have their own special charisma through which they contribute to the upbuilding of the church. The author names the two gifts of grace that are fundamental for worship: the proclamation of the word, which is supposed to correspond to the traditional confession (cf. Rom. 12:6b), and "service," which, as in Rom. 12:7a and Just. *Apol.* 2:65, was probably a matter of preparing for and leading the celebration of the Lord's Supper. In addition, in 1 Peter 5:1ff. there are "elders" who are supposed to tend the flock eagerly with exemplary willingness to serve, without desire for gain or claim to power; those who are younger are to submit themselves to the authority of the elders. Consequently, older proven and experienced church members assume certain leadership tasks, above all in regard to the administration of money. Here we observe the transition to an office of elder, which has apparently not yet received official shape and, in any case, has not yet become a part of the central worship of the church.

Elders and Deacons

In addition to the singular passage in James 5:14, a developed *office* of elder is known in the New Testament period in the pastoral letters and in the Acts of the Apostles. When besides "elders" (*presbyteroi*), a "bishop" (*episkopos*) is mentioned in 1 Tim. 3:1–2; Titus 1:7; Acts 20:28, it is not a question of a different office; rather, a presbyter is designated as "bishop" when this reflects the duties of his office and ministry (Schmithals 1991, 316ff.). Thus monepiscopacy is still foreign to the pastoral letters.

The pastorals presuppose the existence of elders in the church, yet their "office" seems not to be regulated by anything more than what we were able to learn from 1 Peter 5:1ff. For the rules by which the office of elder is governed in 1 Tim. 1:3–7; 4:14; 5:17; 2 Tim. 1:6; 2:2; Titus 1:5–9 probably go back to the author of the pastoral letters himself. The reason and necessity for such a characteristic development is fully revealed in the pastorals: the invasion of the Gnostic heresy forces the churches to a regulated defense against the spreading errors. Therefore the elders are appointed as guardians of apostolic tradition and as such assume the function of proclaiming the word, which was formerly the task of prophets. Consequently, the triad apostles, prophets, and teachers is found in the characteristic revision, "a herald and an apostle and a teacher" (2 Tim. 1:11). The elder is supposed "to preach with sound doctrine and to refute those who contradict it" (Titus 1:9; cf. 1 Tim. 4:13ff.; 2 Tim. 2:2). For the sake of this task elders must fulfill moral conditions that are not expected of every church member in the same measure, must have belonged to the church a long time, and must be "an apt teacher" (1 Tim. 3:1–7); therefore their selection requires thorough testing (1 Tim. 5:22). In return, the especially capable among the elders deserve double compensation, above all those who labor in preaching and teaching (1 Tim. 5:17). With regard to the ministry of the "deacons," who should likewise be carefully chosen (1 Tim. 3:8–13) and were probably responsible for the Lord's Supper, there was no change in the earlier regulations (Rom. 12:7a; 1 Peter 4:10; cf. Phil. 1:1; Just. *Apol.* 1.65). The order of elders, however, who are responsible for correct preaching and teaching, meant a far-reaching renewal.

Yet we must not overlook the fact that this renewal did not mean a break with charismatic church order, or at least was not felt as a break. The elders are called to their office in order to prevent penetration by false teachers (Titus 1:9) and are installed by the laying on of hands (1 Tim. 4:14; 5:22). This occurs, however, after their selection by the Holy Spirit, that is, by prophetic designation and appointment in the church assembly (1 Tim. 1:18; 4:14), just as the trespasses of elders are to be judged by the gathered church (1 Tim. 5:20). And the talent of the elder for his teaching office rests, as earlier, primarily not on legal authorization but on the charisma that is given to him (1 Tim. 4:14; 2 Tim. 1:6). It is the Spirit himself who in a new time establishes an appropriate order. The newly ordered and newly defined office of elder is supposed to defend against the doctrinal anarchy of the pneumatics. And this defense occurs along the lines of charismatic church leadership, since the pastoral letters have still not reached the point of considering an orderly establishment of the teaching tradition. In this sense the designation of the pastoral epistles as "early catholic" is not appropriate.

All the essential elements of the new order of elders are also found in Paul's farewell speech before the elders of the church of Ephesus in Miletus, which Luke reports in Acts 20:17–34. In my view, the core of this speech and its corresponding passages were adopted by Luke from a source related to the pastoral letters, and thus it is not an independent testimony of the new development (Schmithals 1991). Regarding the danger to the new teachers that also threatened from their own midst, Paul reminds the elders that he proclaimed to them the whole will of God, and he admonished them: "Keep watch over yourselves and over all the flock, of which the Holy Spirit has made you overseers, to shepherd the church of God that he obtained with the blood of his own Son" (Acts 20:28; cf. 14:23). Luke himself is not particularly interested in the order of elders, whether because this was already taken for granted in his churches or because the order of the church was no problem for him and for the church. But he anchored this "Pauline" order, in accordance with his "salvation-historical" interest, in the primitive church tradition (Acts 15:2, 4, 6, 22–23; 16:4; 21:18), yet in such a late phase of the primitive church that we cannot overlook how much he was conscious of the anachronism that he himself had created.

The connection of the apostolic teaching with the institution of the elders proved to be such an effective means in the battle against heretics that it became broadly prevalent in the course of the second century, especially since the charismata were weakening and the congregations of the growing catholic church needed an organizational structure anyway. Yet we cannot set a very early date for the *general* introduction of the office of elder. For with the exception of the already cited passages, the Johannine writings, which lead us far into the second century, also forgo fighting docetic heretics with "official" help. The elder who expresses himself as the author of the Second and Third Letter of John holds no church office but presents himself with his self-designation as an apostolic student from the beginning period of the church. Since the writings of the *corpus johanneum* as genuine "catholic" writings are addressed to the whole of the orthodox church, their author apparently assumes that he cannot yet address the Christendom of his day with the presupposition of a unified order and structure of offices. Therefore he entirely forgoes bringing an "office" into play, no matter what structure he himself would like to consider appropriate.

In *Did.* 15.1–2 the transition to the new structure is especially easy to discern:

Choose for yourselves bishops and deacons, worthy of the Lord, gentle men, not avaricious, truthful, trustworthy. For they too will perform for you the ministry of prophets and teachers.

In Phil. 1:1, in a way that is analogous to the pastoral letters, the editor of the Pauline correspondence anchors the "bishops" and "deacons" of his time in the beginning period of the church. The author of the *First Letter of Clement* (*1 Clem.* 42; 43.1; 44.1–2) proceeds in the same way: as before, he assumes that the calling of the elders is the task of the church (*1 Clem.* 44.3), but he objects to the deposing of elders in Corinth who, in his opinion, were blameless (*1 Clem* 44.3ff.; 47.6; 54.2; 57.1). According to James 5:14, the elders are to be called to pray for the sick. Polycarp of Smyrna is a member of a collegium of elders (Pol. *Phil.*, inscription); in Pol. *Phil.* 6 we find a list of qualifications for elders comparable to 1 Tim. 3:1–7, and in Pol. *Phil.* 5 a list for deacons comparable to 1 Tim. 3:8–13. Justin calls the elder or bishop who leads worship the "president" (*Apol.* 1.67), whereas the Lord's Supper is led by deacons (*Apol.* 1.65).

If all of this still essentially follows the previous line, with the letters of Ignatius we apparently have a theological break. This break is marked less by the monarchical episcopacy as such than by the fact that Ignatius holds that the office of the *one* bishop is an office by divine right; thus at least since Ignatius the apostolic teaching tradition can be connected exclusively with this office. Without the hierarchy that places the *one* bishop above presbyters and deacons—but all office-holders above the church—there can be no talk of the "church," according to Ignatius, and no proper worship can be celebrated (Ign. *Trall.* 3.1; Ign. *Eph.* 5.1; Ign. *Magn.* 6; etc.). Thus with the letters of Ignatius, whenever and by whomever they may have been written, we have left early Christianity, not only temporally but also in terms of theological history, and have entered the period of ancient church history.

10

Worship in Early Christianity

Anyone who wants to offer information about worship in early Christianity is faced with a serious problem: early Christian sources tell us very little about worship. Although there are numerous, sometimes detailed data concerning, for example, the structure of the church and its ministries in Paul, the Gospel of Matthew, the pastoral letters, and other early Christian writings, there are only isolated and rather incidental references to worship. Not until the first half of the second century do the sources begin to flow more freely, and even what we do learn, above all from the *Didache* and from Justin Martyr, leaves many questions unanswered and our thirst for knowledge only partially satisfied. It is symptomatic that the earliest information about the worship of Christians that is to any extent comprehensive comes to us from a non-Christian, namely, from Pliny the Younger, who from ca. 111 to ca. 114 was the legate of the emperor's governor in Bithynia. From there, in the context of the persecution of Christians, Pliny reports in a letter to Trajan (98–117) what the Christians are doing, according to their own accounts.

It is certain that sooner or later baptisms took place, yet our early sources are silent about the details and circumstances of baptismal services. The information is most plentiful concerning the early Christian celebration of the Lord's Supper, which leads one to assume that the Eucharist was at the center of worship and even the essential reason for gathering. It is typical, however, that today there is still no unanimity among scholars even on the important question of whether and in what way independent services of the word existed in early Christendom alongside the eucharistic celebration. Whereas Cullmann (1950, 30) rightly asserts that in the assumption of an original distinction between two separate worship forms we have "one of those scientific dogmas that are repeated in the textbooks so long that they are accepted as facts whose correctness is no longer examined with regard to the sources," Salzmann's 1994 study comes to the conclusion that in the early Christian period a public service of the word took place in the morning and a eucharistic service at night.

In addition to the lack of information about orders of worship and the absence of fixed liturgical pieces that were possibly in use, we are largely ignorant of the time and place of worship services. Did they take place on the sabbath, on Sunday, or on another day? Were they held in the morning, in the evening, or at another hour? Did they occur in a synagogue, in private houses, in meeting houses, or in public places?

The conspicuous disinterest of early Christian tradition in the regulation of worship indicates that the shaping of worship services was a matter of practice and not of creed, and in this respect nothing essential has changed over the course of church history. The structure of worship was largely left to the discretion of the churches, or free rein was given to the Spirit, whom no one was inclined to muffle as long as it was not necessary to defend against contrary spirits; the open manner in which Paul in 1 Corinthians 12–14 deals with pertinent incidents in the worship of the church in Corinth without referring to prescribed regulations also points in this direction. This means, naturally, that the question of worship in early Christianity cannot be initially raised with the expectation that it can be answered in a certain way with an organized presentation or in any detail; one will do well to pose the question differently in regard to individual churches and above all church associations. This conclusion will also guard against the romantic expectation that one can derive from a consideration of early Christian worship solid criteria for the proper structuring of present-day worship and even prescriptions for overcoming crises in worship. In an ongoing relationship with the gospel, continuity and development in the formation of early Christian worship served the tasks faced individually by the churches and were related, in constancy and freedom, to the changing possibilities that were open to different churches at different times.

In view of the somewhat unsatisfying situation regarding historical tradition, scholars like Lietzmann (1926), Bousset (1915), and Wetter (1921, 1922) have attempted to shed light on the darkness of the early period by drawing conclusions about the early evidence and developments based on liturgical traditions a century or two later. This process is open to objection, for it can hardly offer insight into the various problems of early Christendom and has also drawn other kinds of justified criticism; it promises convincing results only if they can be verified by the meager information from early sources. Other scholars, such as Bauer (1930), have turned their attention more to Jewish and Hellenistic cults and assemblies to find models or analogies for early Christian worship services, yet there is no agreement on the extent to which the Christian worship service was patterned after worship in the synagogue. Although from the Talmud we know a great deal about the worship customs of later Judaism, our knowledge of corporate worship in the synagogues of Hellenistic Judaism in New Testament times is at least as limited as our knowledge of early Christian worship services themselves. And the various reports on synagogal services of worship that are found in the Gospel of Luke and in Acts already presuppose the existence of the rabbinical synagogue in the period after the year 70. As a rule, the gathering places of Jewish communities in the Diaspora were called "house of prayer" (*proseuchē*) in the early period, and according to the impression of the Gentiles, Jewish citizens gathered there above all for common prayer. These buildings were often erected by water in order to permit the ritual washings prescribed for the Jews (cf. Acts 16:13, 16). When and in what sense they began in the early period to house worship services in our sense is largely beyond our knowledge (cf. Hengel 1971), and in any case, no baptismal services or meal celebrations were modeled in them.

With such reservations, the following presentation attempts to follow the course of worship in early Christian theological history. We will of necessity give attention to continuities as well as to developments and differences.

The Palestinian Church

We have no direct literary legacy from the Palestinian primitive church. The apostle Paul could have indirectly handed down to us information about Jewish Christian worship in Palestine, for he is the only early Christian author who was in contact with Palestinian Jewish Christians before the Jewish war. From Paul, however, we learn nothing about the worship life of Christians in Jerusalem or Galilee, and it is not easy to judge whether and to what extent what we know about the worship services of his Gentile Christian churches allows us to make inferences back to Jewish Christianity.

Yet we do learn from Paul that at an early time the resurrected Jesus "appeared to more than five hundred brothers and sisters at one time" (1 Cor. 15:6). Whether this appearance took place in Jerusalem or, as is probable, in Galilee, the Jewish Christian church was, in any case, already of considerable size, and it organized its gatherings accordingly. Also at an early time, Peter resided in Jerusalem (Gal. 1:18), where a little later there was a leadership committee of the three "pillars," James, Peter, and John (2:6–9), with whom Paul was able to reach a binding agreement. However the authority of the pillars may have been defined in detail, the committee attests that the Jewish Christian church had an *organization*. Such an organization or representation was necessary primarily in dealing with governmental powers and local authorities; from the year 44 all of Palestine was under imperial governors who, however, intervened very little in the Jews' administration of their own affairs. The organization also served the regulation of the internal affairs of the community, as indicated, for example, by the collection that Paul gathered in various places for the church in Jerusalem (Gal. 2:10 and elsewhere; cf. Schmithals 1994). Yet we have no particular name for this Jewish Christian group. *Ekklēsia,* the term that Paul applies to Gentile Christian churches, is not used by him for the Jerusalem Christians, whom he calls "the saints" (Rom. 15:25–26, 31; 1 Cor. 16:1, 15; 2 Cor. 8:4; 9:1, 12), apparently adopting their own self-designation. Bauer (1930, 9) believes it is possible that "Palestinian Jewish Christians came together in special synagogues," a description that is meaningful if one understands by *synagogue* an assembly or community, but not a building or a legal institution. In fact, however, one might easily assume that hand in hand with public representation and internal organization, the gatherings of the new community were also to a certain degree organized and structured.

Our sources, however, are silent about such matters, for what the Acts of the Apostles reports on the gatherings of the primitive church hardly rests on historical tradition; it reflects, rather, the interests of the author of Acts, whom we call Luke, and the situation in his own community. According to Luke 24:53; Acts

2:46, the temple is the gathering place of the Christian church, and according to Acts 3:1–4:22; 5:12–42, the apostles teach and heal publicly in the temple; thus in analogy with the synagogues, Luke regards the temple, the place of cultic sacrifice and the priesthood, as a house of teaching and worship, which offers an opportunity for missionary preaching. The interest of this presentation consists in portraying Christianity as the authentic Judaism and blaming the break between Christians and Jews on the latter. Yet there is no doubt that the Jewish Christians of Palestine paid the temple tax (see also Matt. 17:24–27), claimed exemption from the cult of the emperor, and in this sense identified themselves as members of the synagogal institution. The extent to which they participated in the temple cult is unknown; they apparently did not fulfill priestly functions, and their apocalyptic, messianic basic position placed them far from the Sadducee branch of Judaism associated with temple service. Naturally, in the context of what was customary, Palestinian Jewish Christians followed the purity laws, the feast times, and the like, yet we cannot say how well the cultic rite described in Acts 21:23–24 contains historically reliable information. Also unknown is whether in Palestine they took part in general gatherings in the synagogues or claimed the local synagogues as houses of worship during fixed times of prayer and at other times. In this sense we may presume that there was probably not a set, generally obligatory custom, and even the use of the synagogue for Christian gatherings, which we may assume, was probably dependent on local conditions. In any case, Jewish Christians, of which there were many, were a special Jewish group, not a splitting-off from Judaism.

As a special group, however, they also needed — perhaps above all — gatherings in which their specifically Christian character was expressed. These must have included baptismal services, if the Jewish Christian church in Palestine was already following the practice of Christian baptism. This, however, is doubtful. More than a few of the members of the Palestinian primitive church had been baptized by John, and a "rebaptism" would hardly have taken place; Apollos, a disciple of John and Jewish Christian, is not given Christian baptism but only further instruction (Acts 19:24–26). After John's death his followers did not continue the custom of baptism in his stead, and opinion is divided on the time, place, and circumstances of the beginnings of baptism "in Christ" or "in the name of Jesus"; all of the evidence suggests that its origin is to be sought in connection with the Gentile mission. In any case, Christian baptism is not the seamless continuation of Johannine baptism seen by Luke in his double volume, where it can be regarded in no other way in view of the practice in his churches, and thus even the first converts in Jerusalem are baptized by the apostles (Acts 2:38, 41). In fact, we have neither historical information about the performance of Christian baptism in the early Jewish Christian churches nor liturgical traditions that point back to such a baptismal service. If there was such a service, we can say nothing about it.

By contrast, we may conclude with almost complete certainty that the specifically Christian gathering of Palestinian Jewish Christians was a meeting centered around a meal. Again, however, we can appeal only with great reservation to the account in Acts 2:41–47, which mentions twice the "breaking of bread" in the

Jerusalem church and raises a number of questions. Apparently, the author of Acts has two forms of worshipful event in mind, a public one that is essentially evangelistic in nature, that serves the "apostles' teaching," and in which the church eagerly participates, and a private one that seems to include above all the meal celebration as well as a regular time of prayer and devotion. This presentation probably reflects the situation during the author's time, and therefore it will be discussed in more detail in the context of the treatment of the "early catholic" churches.

There are, however, sufficient indications to allow us to state that a meal celebration did indeed stand at the center of the worship life of Palestinian Jewish Christendom, a celebratory meal in which its participants on earth anticipated the eschatological banquet in the kingdom of God. We know that pious Jews liked to imagine the coming kingdom of God with the image of a banquet, as vividly revealed, for example, by the New Testament saying in Luke 13:28–29 and par. Matt. 8:11–12 and the parable of the great dinner (Luke 14:16–24 and par. Matt. 22:1–10). In later, theologically further developed times, there are several traditions that in various ways maintain this apocalyptically rooted understanding of the meal. The Gospel of Mark, following the "words of institution" that come from the later Hellenistic church, contains a farewell statement in which Jesus announces that he "will never again drink of the fruit of the vine until that day when I drink it new in the kingdom of God" (Mark 14:25). This statement is often held to be the remnant of an otherwise lost account of a farewell meal of Jesus. In any case, it maintains the remembrance of an apocalyptic, eschatological dimension of the meal celebration that is no longer found in the late words of institution themselves. We can make an analogous observation regarding 1 Cor. 11:26. Following the quotation of the traditional words of institution of the Lord's Supper, Paul interprets the meal activity to the effect that the guests, through their eating and drinking, proclaim the death of the Lord "until he comes." This important eschatological prospect, which is placed at the end of the sentence, is motivated neither by the words of institution themselves nor by the context of 1 Corinthians 11. Thus it is traditional, and with it Paul intentionally integrates the old Palestinian significance of the meal celebration—as he perhaps learned it himself during his visits in Jerusalem—into his own understanding of the Lord's Supper. In the *Didache* (9.1–10.7) in the context of a relatively late *order* of the celebration, there is an understanding of the Lord's Supper that, like the *Didache* in general, is essentially in the Palestinian Jewish Christian tradition and interprets the broken bread in an exclusively eschatological way: as the bread is composed of many kernels of grain, which grew scattered on the mountains, so may God bring his church from the ends of the earth into the kingdom that he has prepared for it. We may also recall passages from the Revelation to John, which is likewise largely filled with the apocalyptic legacy of Palestine: Jesus stands before the door of the gathered church in Laodicea and knocks, in order to eat with it (Rev. 3:20), and 19:9 calls blessed those who are invited to the marriage supper of the Lamb.

In view of the fact that under the influence of Jesus' preaching Palestinian Jewish Christendom lived on the plane of apocalyptic expectation and thus believed that in the near future its resurrected teacher, now exalted as Lord, would appear in a visible initiation of the kingdom of God, we cannot doubt that the mentioned traditions reflect the understanding of the meal shared by these early churches. Lietzmann (1926, 249) expressed the appealing, though unverifiable assumption that with such an understanding the Lord's Supper goes back to a practice that Jesus himself promoted during his lifetime in the circle of the disciples. Then the Easter church would have expanded an already familiar understanding in the sense that they knew their resurrected Lord in their midst and hoped for his coming. This idea may have formed the background for the story of the Emmaus disciples, who know the resurrected Jesus in the breaking of the bread (Luke 24:30–31, 35), and perhaps Palestinian Christendom also already designated the Lord's Supper as "the table of the Lord" (1 Cor. 10:21). As at every meal, bread was always eaten, but the festivity of the meal seems to have been elevated by drinking wine when possible; additional food probably varied according to changing circumstances and individual resources.

This description of the meal customs of Jewish Christendom in Palestine finds vivid confirmation in the fact that in the *Marana tha* of 1 Cor. 16:22b) we have the tradition of a prayerful exclamation in Aramaic; according to 1 Cor. 11:26 (". . . until he comes") and Rev. 22:20 ("Come, Lord Jesus!"), it is to be translated: "Our Lord, come!" It is also found in *Did.* 10.6, where it occurs in the closing part of the Lord's Supper liturgy. Thus in *Marana tha* we have a bit of liturgy from the Palestinian Lord's Supper celebration, which at the same time leaves no doubt that the Palestinian church celebrated its specific Christian worship as an apocalyptic, eschatological meal celebration in expectation of the present and coming Lord Jesus.

As further bits of liturgy from Jewish Christian gatherings we have the Aramaic form of address *abba* (Rom. 8:15; Gal. 4:6), which is often traced back to Jesus himself (cf. Mark 14:36) and is permissible for the children of God, and the Hebrew *amen,* with which the church confirms the speech, the praise, or the petition of one of its members (cf. 1 Cor. 14:16). The fixed elements of synagogal worship that were available to church members—readings from the Old Testament, the proclamation of the law, prayers from the Psalms, and the like—would hardly have been adopted by Jewish Christians in their own gatherings, nor can they be shown to be constituent parts of Christian community gatherings in later times. According to our sources, traditions from the teachings and life of the earthly Jesus also played no role in worship. Jesus was present in the meeting as the exalted Lord himself and spoke through the mouths of the prophets. We must imagine in general that gatherings were ruled by talks and comments, by prayers and hymns, by unarticulated sighs, and by godly discussions of the prophetic Spirit; the still strongly apocalyptically oriented passage Rom. 8:18–27, which comes from Paul's early period, clearly reflects in form and content the freedom of such assemblies, which is connected with the Spirit. In Agabus (Acts 11:27–28; 21:10–14) and Philip, together with his four prophetically gifted daughters (Acts 21:8–9), we learn the names of outstanding prophetic figures in Palestinian Jewish Christianity, who at the same time allow us to conclude that in the gatherings of the church, apocalyptic prophecy definitely had its spokespeople. Yet we learn nothing about the leaders of the worship services.

Without doubt, in Palestinian Jewish Christianity there was no special community "service of the word" in addition to the gatherings already described. Naturally, we cannot exclude special missionary events, but we know nothing about them. Moreover, church assemblies did not have the character of esoteric mystery cults but were probably open to guests and sympathizers; in this way they also helped promotional efforts. What the Spirit had to say concerned all who had ears to hear. Therefore, it is also possible that church gathered not only in private houses but also in synagogues, when this was not prohibited. The times of gathering are not part of the tradition, yet early Christians without question remained with the usual pattern in Judaism and were thus oriented toward a week that was completed with the sabbath; a Sunday celebration by the Jewish Christians of Palestine is not attested.

The Universalist Damascene Churches

Beginning with Palestinian Jewish Christianity, the Christian church developed very early by spreading into the more hellenized world in two characteristically different theological directions. One was rooted immediately in Palestinian Jewish Christianity, which even in the first century was already to a considerable degree hellenized; spatially and spiritually this direction followed the paths through the Hellenistic synagogues that had been created some time earlier by the Jewish synagogue. Such matters and the worship services of the Hellenistic Jewish Christian church that expanded into the environment of the synagogues will be discussed in the next section.

The other direction is seen in the churches that were vigorously fought by the synagogue (Acts 6:11–15; 7:54–8:3) and which Paul, according to his own statements, persecuted and tried to destroy before his conversion (Gal. 1:13–14, 23; 1 Cor. 15:9; Phil. 3:6; cf. Acts 7:58; 8:1; 9:1–2). They had one center of their activity in Damascus, where Paul was converted (Gal. 1:15–17; 2 Cor. 11:32–33; cf. Acts 1:1–25), and the author of Acts traces them back, with good reason, to Stephen and the circle of seven (Acts 6:1–5; 8:1–4). These churches are the topic of the present section. We are relatively well informed about their views, because Paul became acquainted with and persecuted the form of Christianity found in these churches, and because he was also converted to this Christian confession. The teaching concept of these churches forms the basic material of his own theology. By contrast, the presentation in Acts is to be used only with the reservation that its author places historical processes in the light of his own interests and shapes them accordingly. He is also aware, however, that persecution by the Jewish authorities did not affect the Christian church as a whole, which remained unmolested in Palestine (Acts 8:1), but only the special group centered around Stephen. In addition, Luke knows that the group's critical attitude toward the Jewish law and the temple offered the occasion for vigorous persecution even outside the land of the Jews (Acts 6:11–15). Thus he confirms the main information that the letters of Paul tell us about the theology of the Christian community persecuted by him before his conversion.

As in Palestinian Jewish Christianity, in the circle around Stephen it was also the prophetic Spirit that led into all truth. He enriched the christological ideas with the concept of the preexistence of the Jesus who was raised from the dead and exalted as Lord to the right hand of God and, correspondingly, with the important motif of the humbling of the Son of God (Gal. 4:4–5; 2 Cor. 5:21; 8:9; Phil. 2:6–11). Apocalyptic expectation of the coming kingdom of God gave way to the experience of already present salvation and the liberating status of being children of God, for the Spirit working in the church is considered the first fruits of perfection (Rom. 8:23; 2 Cor. 5:5). "For all who are led by the Spirit of God are children of God" (Rom. 8:14), and "if anyone is in Christ, there is a new creation: everything old has passed away; see, everything has become new!" (2 Cor. 5:17).

The cause of the persecution of the church of Stephen, however, was above all its universalism; the church proceeded according to the principle expressed in Gal. 3:26, 28 (cf. 1 Cor. 12:12–13): ". . . in Christ Jesus you are all children of God through faith. . . . There is no longer Jew or Greek, there is no longer slave or free, there is no longer male and female; for all of you are one in Christ Jesus." Thus this church had fundamentally freed itself from Jewish particularism, and it denied the special role of Israel, the special election of Abraham's bodily descendants, and the validity of the Mosaic law. This did not happen for anti-Jewish reasons, for the leaders of the church, like Paul, were themselves Jews and proselytes (Acts 6:5). Nor did it happen in order to dissolve the Jewish people among the Gentile nations; the Jewish nation as a political entity was not directly affected at all by this development. Naturally, the Gentiles were not expected to come to Zion and offer sacrifices there to the God of Israel. The process was rather the opposite: the salvation of Israel, as realized in Christ Jesus, was offered to all nations. It was no longer the particular law of Moses but universal faith in Christ that was the way for all peoples to become children of God. In the context of their own social and national institutions they could become members of the people of God and citizens of the kingdom of God. We do not know how well the holders of these views were aware of the political consequences of this way, which made one Christian church out of Jews and Gentiles and, had it been followed by all, would have taken the cruel Jewish war to its absurd extreme. In any case, Judaism applied bloody persecution against this interpretation of Jewish history and particularity by Damascene Christianity, which understood itself as the true Judaism and at the same time alienated born Jews from traditional Judaism and removed them from the influence of the Jewish authorities; especially from the later life of the apostle Paul we can infer that this first Christian persecution was essentially successful. As will become clear below, even Paul was soon able to carry out his commission for Gentile missions only in the context of the Jewish synagogal institution, until he later found a way to establish Gentile Christian churches outside the synagogue without having to fear Jewish persecution.

The universalist church living outside the synagogue presented itself to *outsiders* in a relatively "neutral" way as the "church [*ekklēsia*] of God," and later Paul kept this designation for his Gentile Christian churches (1 Cor. 1:2; 2 Cor. 1:1; Gal. 1:13; and elsewhere), and thus it ultimately became the general designation for the church. *Insiders* understood and designated themselves as the "body of Christ," and this term preserves an insight into the worship life of this *"ekklēsia* of God."

We have no direct information about the worshipful gatherings of these churches—especially since already at an early time they fell victim to persecutions—but their understanding of the Lord's Supper influenced the words of institution formed in the Hellenistic Jewish Christian church and had a particular effect on Pauline theology. In 1 Cor. 10:16b–17 Paul, who after his conversion joined this church, passes on a formula that gives us a clear insight into the meal celebration of the universalist churches:

> "The bread that we break, is it not a sharing in the body of Christ? Because there is one bread, we who are many are one body, for we all partake of the one bread."

The expression *body of Christ* in this pre-Pauline formula does not refer to the crucified body of Jesus; rather, as a metaphor for describing the church, it is completely independent of the theology of the cross. On the one hand, this image expresses the close connection between the earthly church and the heavenly Christ, who in a later expansion of the image also appears and the "head of the body, the church" (Col. 1:18; 2:19; Eph. 1:22–23; and elsewhere). On the other hand, it presents the image of the relationship of the body and its members, that is, the connection of the individual Christian with the whole church, above all in regard to the universalism of this Christianity, in which not only national and religious but also social differences lose their importance: "There is no longer Jew or Greek, there is no longer slave or free, there is no longer male and female; for all of you are one in Christ Jesus" (Gal. 3:28). The basis of this view is the knowledge that "in the *one* Spirit we were all baptized into *one* body" (1 Cor. 12:13), that is, the experience that the living Spirit of God binds all members of the church to each other and to their Lord. Like the Jewish Christian church of Palestine, the universalist church gathers in the awareness of being children of God and thus being redeemed from the ruin of the sinful world, for "it is the very Spirit bearing witness with our spirit that we are children of God" (Rom. 8:16).

From this information we can infer that the universalist church, continuing the tradition of Palestinian Jewish Christianity, celebrated its services of worship above all in the form of a communion meal. Yet here the act of breaking the bread receives a symbolic meaning, and for this reason the use of the expression *breaking bread* for this meal celebration as a whole (Acts 20:7)—a practice that Luke later uses in connection with the Jerusalem primitive church (Acts 2:42, 46)—probably goes back to this church: the breaking of the one loaf symbolizes the fellowship of the individual church members in the unity of the body of Christ. Thus the original character of the meal as an eschatological banquet oriented toward the future kingdom of God recedes, and the already present newness of the universal fellowship of the children of God—composed of Jews and Gentiles, men and women, free and slave—especially determines the joy of the communion meal.

In other respects the course of corporate worship was probably ordered according to the free rein of the Spirit. The instructions that Paul later gives for the Spirit-inspired gatherings in Corinth were probably brought by him in essence from similar kinds of worship experiences in his early Christian period in Damascus and elsewhere: prophetic speech is to be valued especially highly; it is articulate and understandable and serves the upbuilding, encouragement, and consolation of the congregation (1 Cor. 14:1–4; Rom. 12:6); anyone may prophesy, yet "one by one, so that all may learn and all be encouraged" (1 Cor. 14:31); others give their evaluation of what is said (1 Cor. 14:29); for the rest, one offers a hymn, another a lesson (cf. Rom. 12:7), a third a word of wisdom or knowledge, and so forth, according to the special gift given each one by the Spirit (1 Cor. 12:4–11; 14:26). In his early worship experiences Paul also became familiar with speaking in a tongue and—especially important to him—interpreting this in understandable words, both of which he himself was able to do. The hymn of Christ in Phil. 2:6–7, 9–11—which Paul quotes and expands with verse 8 and which with its schema of the humbling and exaltation of Jesus comes from universalist Christianity—shows that at a relatively early time Christian poets were already at work creating set pieces for worship. There is no tradition that Old Testament scriptures were also read or Old Testament psalms prayed.

In its worship services the church naturally also drew on the Jewish tradition, to which the scriptures of the Old Testament belonged, but it is very unlikely that a Christian church, which consciously held its worship services outside the synagogue and had rejected the law of Moses, at the same time adopted worship customs from the synagogue. In the rest of early Christianity as well, there is no indication that, for example, the formulated confession to the one God in Deut. 6:4ff. (*Shema Israel*), or the Eighteen Benedictions, or the Aaronite blessing (Num. 6:24–26) was used in Christian worship services. There were still no Gospels that could be read, and there are no indications that written or oral precursors of the Gospels existed and were read aloud in worship; in the midst of the gathered church the exalted Christ himself was immediately present through his Spirit. The formulaic triad apostles, prophets, and teachers (1 Cor. 12:28) goes back to universalist Christianity, but unfortunately we cannot define more exactly the duties of teachers in worship (cf. 1 Cor. 14:26).

Regarding the place where worshipful assemblies were held, we can say very little, since the size of the churches is also unknown. The synagogue building was in any case not available, and thus we may assume that worship was held in a Christian home, if a growing number of members did not make other solutions necessary. We must also leave open the question whether and in what way the gathering was led. At the least, table service was required for the celebratory meal. Was the particular head of the household responsible for this? In any case, it is no accident that the "deacon" who was responsible for the celebratory meal was the first fixed ministry in gatherings for worship (Rom. 12:7; Phil. 1:1; 1 Peter 4:10; 1 Tim. 3:8–13; *Did.* 15.1–2; Just. *Apol.* 1.65). In the early period, if a community was already gathering regularly in a set place for the meal celebration, it would also have needed a correspondingly structured ministry.

Since the gathering of the "body of Christ" for the common breaking of bread at the same time served the various described ways of proclamation and teaching, the universalist church may have had special prayer groups but without doubt no special services of the word; and it is doubtful whether there were regular worship events dedicated to missionary purposes. If Paul assumes that in Corinth gatherings for worship were not closed to unbelievers and sympathizers (1 Cor. 14:21–25), the situation was probably no different in the earlier period. In this universalist church Christian baptism was practiced and consequently a baptismal worship service was held; a church that emphatically separated itself from the realm of the synagogue and established its independence needed a rite of initiation. We can observe this phenomenon in some of the traditions that Paul took with him from the universalist church in which he was converted, traditions that he passed on to his Gentile Christian churches. One such text occurs in 1 Cor. 12:13: "For in the *one* Spirit we were all baptized into *one body*—Jews or Greeks, slaves or free." This baptism was "into Christ," as also shown by the related formula in Gal. 3:26–28, for example, and here we are to understand "Christ" as the "body of Christ"; thus baptism placed one in the "church of God," which saw itself connected with Christ as his "body." We may simply presuppose that this baptism took place in a worship context appropriate to its importance for the baptized and for the church. And if it was performed, as is likely, in flowing water or in any case by immersion (cf. Rom. 6:4), there was no place for it in the church's regular worship service. Thus from case to case or at set times, there must have been special baptismal worship services. Unfortunately, we have no information or texts—for example, confessions of faith, prayers, or baptismal admonitions—that would allow us to attribute such services of worship to the universalist church; even the traditions that Paul uses in, for example, 1 Cor. 12:13 and Gal. 3:26–28 have rather more an instructive than a liturgical character. Naturally, we may assume that baptism was not self-baptism but was performed by a baptizer vicariously for the church, and it is easy to assume that a baptismal formula was used, such as, "I baptize you into Christ."

As an innovation fraught with consequences, the *Christian Sunday celebration* probably had its origin in the universalist church. Wherever Christians were part of the institution of the synagogue, there was no reason for them to shift their gatherings from the work-free sabbath day to the first day of the week. By contrast, when a church demonstratively separated itself from the synagogue and its connection with the law of Moses, it could hardly hold to the sabbath, for in the eyes of the Gentiles, the sabbath celebration was the epitome of Judaism and for Jews the alpha and omega of their observance of the law. The shifting of the church gathering to Sunday made it possible to retain the usual Jewish week of seven days and at the same time clearly set Christians apart from the synagogue.

We first encounter Sunday as the day on which Christians gather—soon called the "day of the Lord" (Rev. 1:10; *Did.* 14.1)—in the Gentile Christian churches of Paul (1 Cor. 16:2; Acts 20:7; cf. Rordorf 1962, 190ff.). Yet we cannot show—nor is it very likely—that this custom was first instituted by Paul himself. In the Gospel of Mark, which all later tradition follows, the third day, on which Jesus was resurrected after his crucifixion (1 Cor. 15:4), is placed on the first day in the week (Mark 16:2), a determination that presupposes the Christian Sunday celebration and is not dependent on Pauline tradition. Under these circumstances, however, everything suggests that the Sunday celebration arose in the universalist church and was taken by Paul into his Gentile Christian churches.

Since Sunday was a workday, a Sunday celebration meant a shifting of worship to the marginal times of the day. Whereas in the synagogue one could gather in the morning and afternoon of the sabbath, on Sunday only the time before the beginning and after the end of the day was available. Therefore, with the Sunday celebration the custom prevailed from the beginning of holding the baptismal worship service in the early hours before daybreak, but holding the regular worship celebration, the "Lord's supper" (1 Cor. 11:20)—from which the day soon received its Christian name, "day of the Lord" (cf. Rordorf 1962, 218)—on Sunday evening (cf. German *Abendmahl,* "Holy Communion," literally, "evening meal"). For the universalist church was also probably not inclined to accept the Jewish division of the day, which had the day begin on the evening before the day in question, when in the Jewish Diaspora the usual division (from midnight to midnight) had already gained recognition. In general the establishment of these two times of worship marks the beginning of the Sunday celebration, which consequently can be traced presumably to the universalist church.

The Hellenistic
Jewish Christian Churches

Whereas universalist Christianity achieved a demonstrative break with the synagogue and with life according to the law and was therefore subjected to the pressure of persecution by the synagogue, the Christian faith spread relatively unmolested along the paths cleared by the Hellenistic synagogue in the areas around Palestine and beyond. By their payment of the temple tax, Christians identified themselves as adherents of the synagogue. The transition from Palestine to Syria (and perhaps Egypt) was probably achieved smoothly, since Palestine was also already thoroughly saturated with Greek language and culture (cf. Hengel 1969). The Hellenization of Jewish Christianity on its way from Palestine to Syria and Cilicia before the time of the Jewish war can be relatively well observed, at least in its results. For even if the information in Acts is not very abundant and, moreover, to be evaluated with great care, the apostle Paul, who was active as a missionary in Syria and Cilicia for more than a decade, is an authentic witness to the theological ideas and developments prevalent in the churches there. Furthermore, the traditional material that underlies the Gospel of Mark must also have been basically at home in this region, however one judges it in terms of tradition history. There is no doubt that over the course of time theological development did not take place in the same way in different regions, and in many respects an analysis of Hellenistic Jewish Christian traditions also reveals a quite varied picture. Above all, we must consider the fact that one result of the persecution of universalist Christianity was that it was forced to come to an arrangement with the synagogue, and Paul's activity in Syria and Cilicia in the time before the so-called Apostolic Council is the clearest example. This led, naturally, to a considerable influencing and strong liberalization of Hellenistic Jewish Christianity in general, but in view of our very modest sources, we must guard against the desire to paint a complete picture.

Such insights also make it more difficult to portray the worship life of Hellenistic Jewish Christian churches, for there is no direct information about it in the tradition. In addition, we know almost nothing about life in the synagogues of the Roman provinces around the eastern Mediterranean. Nevertheless, going out from Palestinian Jewish Christianity, the Christian church must have formed a special group within the Hellenistic synagogal institution, and when Acts 11:26 reports that in Syrian Antioch one first spoke of "Christians," this special group is clearly in evidence. Paul confirms the corresponding accounts in Acts, according to which Peter was active as the leading missionary in these churches (Gal. 2:7–8, 11–14; 1 Cor. 9:5). At first, the members of these churches were probably for the most part born Jews, for Paul also expressly states that Peter was entrusted with the apostolic ministry to the Jews or with the gospel for the Jews (Gal. 2:7–9; cf. 2:11–14; 1 Cor. 9:5). But the more the mission moved into Hellenistic territory, the more God-fearing Gentiles were also members of the synagogue, and Paul felt especially sent to the Gentiles (Gal.1:16; 2:7–9; Rom. 1:5–6). We would like very much to know whether in the time before the Apostolic Council Jewish Christians and (God-fearing) Gentile Christians held separate or common worship services, and whether in this sense one can speak of a unified practice. The guideline of the synagogue regarding God-fearing Gentiles, that those who observed a fundamental part of the Torah, the so-called Noachian commandments (Leviticus 17–18), were integrated into their association, also supports the idea of common gatherings of Jewish and Gentile Christians.

Since the worship services of these churches grew out of the meetings of Palestinian Jewish Christians, they must also have been primarily celebratory meals. This assumption is confirmed by the fact that the central cultic text of this worship service is passed on to us in the form of the words of institution of the Lord's Supper, which are communicated to us independently by Paul (1 Cor. 11:23–25) and the Gospel of Mark (14:22–24). By contrast, we have no references to an independent service of the word in addition to the celebratory meal, and it is also unlikely that community members—who as adherents of the synagogue participated in its activities and in this way could best do justice to their missionary commission—also felt it advisable to gather for a separate service of the word. Naturally, this would not exclude prayer fellowships or special missionary events, yet we know nothing definite about such activities (cf. Acts 19:9–10). Perhaps the sequence of Jesus' entry into Jerusalem, the cleansing of the temple, the question of authority, and teachings and discussions with the Jewish authorities in Mark 11–12 reflect an act of missionary proclamation in the realm of the synagogue: the church receives the son of David with an introit according to Psalm 118, presents him as the Lord who in true worship establishes, asserts, and defends his messianic authority again in Israel, and discusses from the Christian viewpoint important doctrinal questions with the members of the synagogue.

In the festive community meal as such, the original significance as an eschato-logical banquet is maintained. In addition, however, in the "words of institution" there is an interpretation of the "elements" of bread and wine. The words of institu-tion of the Lord's Supper tell us less about the course of the meal celebration than about its theological significance and its development. We may deduce that the oldest form of the words is the following:

> This is my body.
> This is my blood of the covenant.

Thus the symbolic interpretation of the bread has been adopted from the univer-salist church and the term *body* also retained in the interpretative saying, which leads to the quite unusual combination of terms, *body and blood,* which is later sometimes transformed into the more familiar *flesh and blood* (John 6:51–56; Just. *Apol.* 1.66.1–2; Ign. *Rom.* 7.3 and elsewhere). The term *body* here, as in 1 Cor. 10:16–17, may at first be taken in two senses and related to both the body of the church and to the crucified body of Jesus. Because of the proximity of the cup say-ing, however, the exclusive interpretation of the bread as the crucified body of Jesus soon prevailed, as the phrase "[given] for you" in 1 Cor. 11:24 definitively shows; the rite of *breaking bread* thereby loses its significance. With the "blood of the covenant" the cup saying recalls the establishment of the covenant and the sacrifice of the covenant (Ex. 24:8; Zech. 9:11) and thus connects with both the hope motif of the Palestinian banquet (cf. Jer. 31:31–34) and the fellowship motif of the bread meal in the universalist church. Corresponding to the general theo-logical development of Hellenistic Jewish Christianity, in the further interpreta-tion of the meal activity the motif of atonement is added to the cup saying (Mark 14:24; Luke 22:20; Matt. 26:28), as well as to the bread saying (1 Cor. 11:24; Luke 22:19): given/poured out for you for the forgiveness of sins. Paul's striking asser-tion that he "received from the Lord" the traditional sayings (1 Cor. 11:23) is best explained if he is trying to say thereby that he owes the *version* of the sayings that he gave the churches to an inspiration of the Lord; on this basis, the emphatic "*new* covenant" and the explanation, "Do this in remembrance of me" (1 Cor. 11:24–25; cf. Luke 22:19–20), probably go back to Paul himself.

Regarding the course of the celebratory meal, 1 Cor. 11:25 (cf. Mark 14:23) in-dicates that wine was not drunk every time; for financial reasons alone, it was probably often missing. In no case, however, was it to be reserved for individual church members (of higher social station?—cf. 1 Cor. 11:21), as shown by the in-struction in Mark 14:23 and Matt. 26:27 that *all* are to drink from the cup. In view of this missing wine, one must not infer from 1 Cor. 11:25 ("after supper") that there was a whole meal every time between the bread and the wine—especially since when Paul is recalling the meal instructions that he had shared with the church in view of its profanation of the Lord's Supper, he asks critically whether the church members do "not have homes to eat and drink in" (1 Cor. 11:22) and tells the hungry to eat at home (1 Cor. 11:34). Thus the Lord's Supper was a cul-tic meal and was not intended to satisfy hunger, even if more bread was probably served than in our modern celebrations (cf. *Did.* 10.1).

As for the rest of the service, we are unable to reconstruct the course of the worship gathering and do not even know whether it opened with the meal, as is probable, or perhaps closed with the meal. In proclamation, singing, and prayer the more or less spontaneously working Spirit continued to set the tone, but there is every reason to believe that increasingly an *ordered* rationale began to prevail in the worship service. Yet the position of a *community preacher* is found nowhere in the early period, and whether the *teachers* already mentioned very early, after apostles and prophets, fulfilled a regular worship function is also unknown in Hellenistic Jewish Christianity. The letters of Paul, however, contain some fixed-formula traditions that definitely go back to Hellenistic Jewish Christianity, for example, Rom. 1:3–4; 3:25–26; 4:25; 10:9; 1 Cor. 8:6; 15:3–5; 2 Cor. 5:19; 1 Tim. 1:15, but only rarely can we attribute such formulas to a certain *Sitz im Leben* in the church. God "raised Jesus our Lord from the dead" (Rom. 4:24; 10:9) and "Jesus is Lord" are obviously confessions that were also called out in worship (1 Cor. 12:3; Rom. 10:9), and it is conceivable that the church gathered for worship also responded to the calls of a prayer leader (for example, "We believe in Jesus Christ . . ." or "Praised by our Lord Jesus Christ . . .") with the formulaic relative clauses that we often find (for example, ". . . who was handed over to death for our trespasses and was raised for our justification"; Rom. 4:25). But do such passages not *primarily* involve teaching material from catechetical education, which as baptismal instruction, for example, was hardly a part of the church's worship service (cf. Gal. 6:6)? Whatever the answer, we may assume that catechesis and worship enjoyed a fruitful mutual relationship (cf. 1 Cor. 14:26). The "hymn of love" in 1 Corinthians 13, as well as some liturgical texts like the heavenly worship service in the Revelation to John, shows the way in which individual apostles, prophets, and teachers were capable of writing hymns and psalms that could enrich the worship service. When Paul writes that in an orderly church gathering one has a hymn, another a lesson, a third a revelation, he is apparently speaking of a hymn and a lesson from prepared material that the speaker brings and not what he or she must create. And when in the heavenly worship service in Revelation doxologies and acclamations and other formulated liturgical material are used, it was probably no different in earthly services of worship.

What was said about the worship of the universalist church regarding the use of Old Testament and Jewish material from synagogal worship is also true of worship in Hellenistic Jewish Christianity. There is no evidence that the worship of Jewish Christians was enriched with familiar material from the synagogal liturgy, and this is unlikely, since the worship services of the synagogue were also open to its constituents who believed in Christ. By contrast, we find in general that the tradition of the Gospels—as it first occurs within Hellenistic Jewish Christianity, namely, in the Gospel of Mark—had its locus in the worship life of the church and therefore was used above all in preaching. Yet this was not true of the early period in which Paul was still active in these churches or of the later Gentile Christian churches of Paul himself, for otherwise his letters could not be as completely free of the corresponding traditions as they in fact are. In the course of time, this doubtless changed, and the first express testimony for the reading of the Gospels in

worship in Justin (*Apol.* 1.67.2) bears witness to this change. When this development took place, however, is a question that is connected with the controversial
history of the Synoptic tradition and is therefore hardly to be answered with unanimity.

It is difficult to determine the place as well as the day and time of the worship
service. We may infer from the accounts in Mark's Gospel, according to which
Jesus taught in the synagogue on the sabbath (Mark 1:21, 39 and elsewhere), that
Christians also spoke in the synagogue. But such accounts tell us nothing about
when and where they celebrated their own worship. Similarly, the tradition of conflicts over the sabbath (Mark 2:23–3:6) shows that in principle Hellenistic Jewish
Christians observed the sabbath, yet here it is only a question of the extent of sabbath holiness, not of matters of worship. Jesus gathered regularly with his own in
a house (Mark 2:15–17; 3:31–35; and elsewhere), and if in connection with the institution of the Lord's Supper a furnished upper room of a house is imagined for
the preparation of the meal (Mark 14:12–16), then the church's celebration of the
meal must have taken place in a similar location; presumably it was no different
in the Palestinian churches. And since both in the Gospel of Mark (7:17) and in
Paul (1 Cor. 11:23) the meal is placed in the time after the end of the day, one can
likewise conclude that the Hellenistic Jewish Christian church also celebrated the
Lord's Supper as an evening worship service. As in the universalist church, this
observation suggests the consideration of a Sunday celebration, especially since
in the Gospel of Mark we find for the first time the first day of the week as the day
of Jesus' resurrection from the dead (Mark 16:1–2). If this is the case, the members of the universalist church, when forced by persecution to join the synagogal
institution, would have held to Sunday for their own service of worship. Yet
whether this day prevailed everywhere in the realm of Hellenistic Jewish Christianity, for which the Sunday celebration was foreign because of its Palestinian
origins, is an open question.

There is also uncertainty about baptism in a worship setting in the Hellenistic
Jewish Christian churches. We have no formulaic material that can be attributed
with any certainty to their baptismal worship services. Nevertheless, there is a stratum of tradition that allows us to infer the understanding of baptism of these
churches. According to this understanding, baptism, which seems to have been
adopted from the universalist churches and performed "in the name of the Lord
Jesus Christ" (1 Cor. 1:13, 15; 6:11; Acts 8:16; and elsewhere), serves, in analogy
to proselyte baptism, the washing away of pagan impurity and the guilt of sin (1
Cor. 6:11; Eph. 5:26; Heb. 10:22; Acts 22:16). This meaning raises doubt that born
Jews who joined the Christian church were also baptized in this form, and when,
as some signs indicate, God-fearing Gentiles were also received into the synagogue through baptism, there may similarly have been a forgoing of a "rebaptism"
when they joined the Christian church. For the rest, however, there can be no doubt
that at least the Gentiles were sooner or later integrated into the Christian community of salvation through baptism (cf. Mark 16:15–16). Since in this context
"washing" is mentioned (1 Cor. 6:11; Acts 22:16), we do not have to presuppose
the ritual of immersion, and thus a washing could also have taken place in the

church's usual service of worship. Whether this was the case or whether an independent service of baptism was always held, whether in individual churches baptism was performed differently, and whether in the course of time there were changes in worship practice—these are all questions whose answers go beyond our knowledge, as does exact information about the places and times of baptismal activity. Nonetheless, we can assume that where the Sunday celebration was usual and independent baptismal services were held, the latter took place in the early hours of the Lord's day.

Pauline Gentile Christianity

For Paul it could not have been satisfactory in the long term to carry out the Gentile mission to which he had been called in the restrictive environment of the synagogue and under the limiting conditions that the Jewish law imposed even on God-fearing Gentiles. After more than ten years of activity in Syria and Cilicia, he succeeded at the so-called Apostolic Council (Gal. 2:10) in reaching an agreement that enabled him to evangelize free of the law among the Gentiles, without the earlier persecution occurring once again. The agreement was relatively simple: with the understanding that the Jerusalem primitive church would evangelize among the Jews in the Diaspora, above all through the apostle Peter, Paul would forgo recruiting members among born Jews and integrating them into his churches that were living free of the law. For the synagogue had no rational reason and also no means to persecute Gentile Christian churches that were organized outside the synagogal institution, even if the mission among the God-fearers of the synagogue (cf. Acts 18:7–8) and the conversion of individual Jews to Gentile Christianity (cf. Acts 18:1–2) provided the latent potential for conflict (cf. Acts 18:12–17). The conflict over table fellowship in Antioch (Gal. 2:11–14) shows that the peaceful coexistence of the Jewish Christian communities living within the realm of the synagogue with the Gentile Christian churches of Paul could give rise to problems. Nonetheless, the agreement of the Jerusalem Apostolic Council promoted worldwide missions and remained in force until the death of Peter and Paul in Rome and until the rabbinic reorganization of the synagogue and the exclusion of Christians from the synagogue in consequence of the destruction of the temple. Until the end of his life, Paul promoted the activities of Jewish Christians through collections from his Gentile Christian churches (Gal. 2:10; Rom. 15:25–32; Schmithals 1994).

We are relatively well informed about Pauline Gentile Christianity through the authentic letters of Paul, and through 1 Corinthians 11 and 12–14 we also gain vivid insights into the worshipful gatherings of the church. Thus it is all the more striking, in view of the errors and confusions in the worship services, that apart from emphasis on the words of institution, Paul does not remind the church in Corinth of established practices and that he also does not assume a fixed leadership and organization in worship. Hence, it is probable that neither of these as yet existed. From 1 Cor. 16:2 and Acts 20:7, however, we learn with certainty that the churches of Paul gathered on Sunday, a custom that they adopted from the universalist churches and which Paul presumably also maintained in his mission in

Syria and Cilicia; for Gentile Christian churches it was advisable to dissolve their cultural ties with Judaism, which were formed by celebration on the sabbath. With the change to Sunday, it follows that the celebratory meal of the church was an evening meal, as can be clearly seen in Acts 20:7–12.

The significance of this celebratory meal for the life of the church can be seen in 1 Cor. 11:17–34 and Acts 20:7–12. Paul calls the meal the "Lord's supper" (1 Cor. 11:20; cf. "cup of the Lord" and "table of the Lord" in 10:21) in contrast to "your own supper" (11:21), to which certain participants degrade the "Lord's supper." It is uncertain whether the expression *Lord's supper* is an ad hoc formation; in Acts 20:7 we find the term *breaking bread,* and later the designation *Eucharist* is found (*Did.* 9.5; Ign. *Eph.* 13.1; Just. *Apol.* 1.66). Thus in Paul's time the meal worship service seems not to have had a set name. In 1 Cor. 11:21 "your own supper" appears to be a regular meal, for Paul confirms that the others remain hungry. Consequently, the "Lord's supper" does not serve as a regular meal, and with his ironic question, "Do you not have homes to eat and drink in?" (11:22), and with the admonition, "If you are hungry, eat at home" (11:34), Paul is by no means introducing new ideas, as he also *recalls* the expressly quoted words of institution in order to restore to the meal its usual character. The limitation contained in the traditional words, "as often as you drink it" (11:25), seems to have been superseded in practice, for in the subsequent comments in 11:26–29 Paul presupposes eating *and* drinking.

Paul's comments on the whole and the words of institution and their explanation in particular reveal a great deal about the theology and the edifying significance of the celebratory meal, but we learn little that is instructive about the course of the event. Above all, it remains unclear whether the gathering for the Lord's Supper also involved speaking during the service, as Paul suggests in 1 Cor. 11:3–16 and chapters 12–14, or whether these passages imply a special service of the word. This question cannot be decided by the fact that the three comments on the worshipful gathering of the church in 11:3–16; 11:17–34; and chapters 12–14 are relatively unconnected and do not refer to each other, because one would otherwise have to assume three kinds of worship. The lack of connection is, in any case, hard to understand and is probably to be explained by the fact that in the First Letter to Corinth, which introduces the oldest collection of Pauline letters, we have a juxtaposition of parts of various letters by Paul to Corinth, assembled according to some educational purpose (Schmithals 1984), and thus the three named passages belong to different epistolary situations.

In all three statements Paul uses the term *ekklēsia* for the gathering of the church, namely, in 1 Cor. 11:16, in 11:18, 22; 12:28, and nine times in chapter 14. In 11:17–18, 20, 33–34 and in 14:23, 26—and only here in Paul—we find for this gathering, in an apparently technical usage, the verb *come together,* in 11:20 and 14:23 with the addition, "in the same place" [not translated in the NRSV; cf. the KJV—Trans.]. The formulation with which Paul introduces the discussion of the disorder at Communion, "When you come together [in the same place], it is not really to eat the Lord's supper" (11:20), gives the impression that such a meeting in one place is *always* a meeting for the ritual meal. Such observations do not suggest that Paul is speaking of different services of worship. Nevertheless, there is no doubt that other elements of worship, such as prophecy, teaching, prayer, singing, and so forth, were added to the meal celebration. Even if we can derive from 11:26 no *command* to proclaim the death of Jesus ("you shall proclaim . . .") but correctly translate with the indicative, "as often as you eat this bread and drink the cup, *you proclaim* the Lord's death . . .," the meal takes place in the context of a proclamation that is not limited to the object of the meal, the "for us" of Jesus' death. Also in the realm of this proclamation are the "divisions" within the gathering, of which Paul speaks in 11:17–19, *before* he addresses the profaning practices that concern the meal itself. This state of affairs is also confirmed by the vivid account of Paul's farewell service of worship in Troas (Acts 20:7–12). Paul preaches until around midnight; then bread is broken, and Paul preaches on until dawn. The narrative has acquired legendary traits, but it apparently goes back to a source that was close to the event. However one may attribute the length of this meeting to the special situation (the founder of the church was making his final departure), the connection between celebration of the meal and proclamation of the word is obvious. Thus there is no evidence that the Gentile Christian church held a separate service of the word apart from the Sunday celebration of the meal—nor can we say why and when this separation is supposed to have taken place.

If this judgment is correct, then both 1 Cor. 11:3–16 and chapters 12–14 give us more details about the expanded meal celebration. In 1 Corinthians 12–14 it is certainly not a question of a special missionary event, a part of the apostolic ministry (cf. Acts 18:7–8; 19:9) to which those in the churches were also invited at given times, for Paul by no means assumes that unbelievers and sympathizers are also present (1 Cor. 14:16, 23–25). Every church member can contribute to the enrichment of the worship service, for example, with a hymn or a lesson (14:6, 26) or with a prayer (11:4–5, 13). Certain functions are apparently assumed by particular church members, who have a corresponding charisma. In Rom. 12:6–8 Paul names first prophets, then deacons, who are responsible for the meal celebration, then teachers (cf. 1 Cor. 4:17; Col. 3:16), who were probably also active outside of worship (cf. Gal. 6:6), and finally the "admonishers" (cf. Col. 3:16), whose function, however, is not clear. Proclamation and prayer occur largely in free "prophetic" speech (cf. also 1 Cor. 12:3; Rom. 8:26–27), with which the church is built up, admonished, and encouraged (1 Cor. 11:4–5; 14:3, 29–33; and elsewhere; 1 Thess. 5:20), by women as well as by men (1 Cor. 11:4–5, 13). The concomitant incomprehensible "speaking in tongues" seems to form a new experience for the church; Paul tries to suppress it. We hear nothing about the reading or interpretation of a text (for example, from the Old Testament); the position of lector is unknown, yet the letters of Paul were read aloud (1 Thess. 5:27; Col. 4:16), and the worship service must have been generally used to promote connections with other churches, who sent letters or traveling guests (cf. *Did.* 11–12). Public church discipline was also a part of the church gathered for worship (1 Cor. 5:1–13; 2 Cor. 2:5–11), which, even when it occurred in an orderly fashion (cf. 1 Cor. 14:33) did not follow an agendalike order. Whatever was presented in terms of fixed instructional material was probably of Christian origin, but we cannot easily say to what extent the educational parts of the letters of Paul were taken up in worship. This can be assumed of the hymns and songs (e.g., Phil. 2:6–11; Col. 1:15–20; cf. Col. 3:16), even if we know nothing of the way in which they were presented. As attractive as it is unprovable is the assumption of Lietzmann (1926, 229) that the meal celebration began with the greeting of the leader: "The grace of the Lord Jesus Christ, the love of God, and the communion of the Holy Spirit be with all of you" (2 Cor. 13:13) and the answer of the congregation: "And with your spirit."

To our knowledge, reception into one of the Gentile Christian churches always took place through baptism, which, according to the information in 1 Cor. 1:13–15, was performed "in the name of Jesus Christ." Paul himself, however, baptized only on exceptional occasions (1:14–16); baptism was the task of the local church. Yet we do not know whether baptism was done by immersion (cf. Rom. 6:3–4) or by washing (cf. 1 Cor. 6:11) or according to the occasion (cf. *Did.* 7.1–3). Nor can we say whether, when, and in what way during Paul's time special baptismal services were held, which naturally had to occur at a given time if the person was to be immersed in flowing water (cf. Acts 8:36–39), in which case a time before dawn on Sunday was available; if need be, a baptism by sprinkling could also take place in the normal service of worship.

The "Early Catholic" Churches

If before the Jewish war there was a peaceful coexistence between Jewish Christian churches living more or less within the Jewish law and law-free Gentile Christian, these two forms of early Christian development were forced into a closer relationship after the Jewish war. This led ultimately to the formation of the unified "early catholic" church, which was a Gentile Christian church, but in it the former Hellenistic Jewish Christianity generally dominated over the Gentile Christianity going back to Paul.

When the temple in Jerusalem was destroyed in 70, synagogal Judaism felt that radical reform was necessary, with the result that the participation of the Jewish Christian community in the synagogal association became impossible. Previously the temple cult and temple tax, administered by the Sadducee caste of priests, loosely joined together numerous different Jewish currents and communions in the association of the synagogue. After the loss of the temple as the binding focal point, the synagogue found a new center in the strict Pharisaic rabbinical understanding of the law, and all groups that could not accept this development were forced out of the synagogue. The details of this process remain hidden from us, because the victorious rabbinate carefully obliterated all traces of the fact that during the time of the temple it had by no means played the dominant role in Judaism. At best we have individual writings of the New Testament from the time around the turn of the first century, which give us information on the process of the exclusion of Jewish Christians from the synagogue, which is given the name *aposynagōgos* in John 9:22; 12:42; 16:2–4; these texts include above all the Gospel of Matthew, Ephesians, Hebrews, and the basic text of the Gospel of John. Yet in these scriptures we learn hardly anything about the praxis of worship in these churches that now had to seek a base outside the synagogal association.

Christendom had more pressing concerns than reforming worship: first, it had to defend itself against Judaizing movements that promoted joining rabbinical Judaism; that is, Christians had to endeavor to unify the church as much as possible in the new situation, and after losing the protection afforded by the special political role that Rome had granted the synagogue, they had to prepare for the now imminent time of persecution. Moreover, the church was soon entangled in serious disputes with Gnostic currents and groups within Christendom, who presumably had had to leave the synagogue and now sought to win the churches for themselves. Yet sooner or later Christians began to integrate elements of the synagogal worship service into their own worship, such as reading scripture and prayers, which we can observe later in early catholic liturgy (cf. *1 Clem.* 59–61; *Did.* 9–10; Bousset 1915), in order to make the departure and transition from the synagogue easier. Sunday seems to have generally prevailed as the day for gathering to worship (Rev. 1:10; *Barn.* 15.9; *Did.* 14.1; Ign. *Magn.* 9.1; etc.); celebration on the sabbath was considered false teaching (Ign. *Magn.* 9.1).

In detail, we can observe that now baptism was required even for born Jews as documentation of membership in the church, as must be concluded from Matt. 3:14–15; John 3:5; Heb. 10:22 (cf. Mark 16:16). A characteristic innovation in this connection is the triadic baptismal formula "in the name of the Father and of the Son and of the Holy Spirit" in Matt. 28:19 (cf. *Did.* 7.1–3), which replaces baptism in the name of Jesus Christ: outside the synagogue, confession to the one God had to be expressly adopted into the Christian baptismal confession. We do not, however, learn anything more about the baptismal service, but with regard to the rite of baptism, what is stipulated in *Did.* 7 must have been generally valid: if possible, baptism was to be in flowing water, in standing water if necessary; if that was also lacking, baptism by sprinkling with three pourings was also allowed. In Heb. 10:23–25 (cf. *Barn.* 4.10) we find the admonition to hold fast to the Christian confessions and not abandon assemblies, but we are not at the same time informed about the course of meetings for worship. The same is true of Matt. 18:17–18, where the assembly is given the function of carrying out exclusion from the community. In Eph. 3:14–21 we are given a congregational prayer with closing doxology, an impressive piece from liturgical praxis that is presumably of Gentile Christian provenance. Whether the Lord's Prayer, as passed on by Matthew with his own additions to the form in the sayings source (Matt. 6:9–13; cf. Luke 11:2–4), is intended as a prayer for a worship service seems quite doubtful; according to *Did.* 8.3 it is to be prayed three times a day, and thus privately.

The Lukan double volume (Luke-Acts) comes from a time when the church had already found its way outside the synagogue. The work describes in detail public teaching in the temple (Luke 19:47; 20:1ff.; 21:37; 24:53; Acts 2:46; 3:1–4:22; 5:12–42) and in brief the home gatherings of the church for teaching, prayer, and the meal, and it also has Paul emphasize that he taught "publicly and from house to house" (Acts 20:20). Thus we see in the author Luke's time above all a church situation that, in the face of the violent persecutions suffered by the church, made it advisable to emphasize that the Christian proclamation does not need to be afraid of the public, to which officials have denied it access. We do not, however, learn more about the worship services for which the oppressed church gathered in houses and about the method of "teaching," apart from the fact that the celebratory meal probably came in the middle of the service (Acts 2:42–47). The hymns in Luke 1:46–55, 68–79, which were written according to the model of Old Testament psalms and presumably came from the evangelist himself, show that and how the Christians were capable of enriching their worship with Christian writings and then also using them to confess their faith as prisoners (Acts 16:25).

Also coming from the persecution situation is the First Letter of Peter, which likewise gives us no immediate insight into the worship of the church. Yet especially in 1:18–21; 2:4–10, 22–25; and 3:18–22, 1 Peter contains formulaic christological tradition, which has been variously analyzed and traced back to hymnic, confessional, or catechetical tradition (cf. Goppelt 1978, 121, 139–40, 204–7, 239–42). No decision that is at all certain can be made about whether and to what extent we have here original liturgical material or material that has been integrated secondarily into the worship service, yet we can ascertain on the whole an increased tendency toward a more fixed arrangement of worship elements.

A corresponding impression of the manner in which one prayed in the Roman worship service presumably in the time around the turn of the first century is conveyed by the impressive prayer in *1 Clem.* 59–61, which very definitely belongs in the tradition of the synagogal praxis of prayer. The laudatory descriptions of the works of God in *1 Clem.* 20 and 33, which in the view of some scholars comes from the Roman liturgy, are rooted in Jewish piety, as is the "Holy, holy, holy is the Lord of hosts" of the angels around God's throne (Isa. 6:3), which the author of *1 Clem.* 34.6 cites directly before the invitation to the church, gathered unanimously "in the same place" (as in 1 Cor. 11:20; 14:23), to make a great effort to call to God "as from one mouth." For the rest, in this long letter from Rome to Corinth we learn nothing about the course of the worship service in either place.

More in the Pauline tradition are the seven letters of Ignatius of Antioch, as well as the possibly later writing of Bishop Polycarp of Smyrna to the church at Philippi. According to today's prevailing opinion, Ignatius wrote his letters around 110 when he was a prisoner on a journey to martyrdom in Rome. What we learn incidentally about worship services in Antioch, as well as in the addressed churches in Asia Minor, follows completely the tendency to separate orthodoxy and heresy and to strengthen the authority of the *one* orthodox bishop, without which no worship should take place. He is the guarantor of orthodoxy in everything that holds the church together (*Magn.* 4; 7), in particular at the celebratory meal (*Smyrn.* 8.1); whether he also held worship services and whether the presbyters always named *after* him fulfilled worship functions cannot be determined; Ignatius put more emphasis on eloquent "silence" (*Eph.* 6.1; *Phld.* 1.1) and the speaker's "bearing" (*Trall.* 3.2) than on the public speeches of the bishop. Yet the latter seems to have led the worship gatherings of the church (*Eph.* 5.2). For the most part, the worship services apparently still ran relatively freely and as moved by the Spirit (cf. *Phld.* 6.1; 7.1). The duties of the deacons clearly go beyond "table service" at the meal celebration, which must have still been put in their hands (*Trall.* 2.3; 3; *Phld.* 10.1; and elsewhere). The holy meal, the Eucharist (*Eph.* 13.1;

Phld. 4; *Smyrn.* 7.1; 8.1; cf. Rom. 7:3) was celebrated on Sunday (*Magn.* 9.1) by breaking the *one* loaf (*Eph.* 20.2), the "medicine of immortality." As is the case in John 6:41–66, Ignatius enrolls the Eucharist in the struggle against the heretics by emphasizing the reference of bread and wine to the flesh and blood of Jesus Christ (*Phld.* 4), for the false teachers dispute the true humanity of the Redeemer and therefore stay away from the meal celebration (*Smyrn.* 7.1). Whether the admonition to come together as often as possible (*Eph.* 13.1; *Pol.* 4.2) because every meeting strengthens the unity of the "general church" (*Eph.* 20.2 and elsewhere; *Smyrn.* 8.2) is also aimed at an increase in meal celebrations or at special meetings for "praise" (*Eph.* 13.1; *Phld.* 10.1) and for "prayer" (*Smyrn.* 7.1) cannot be determined, but the prayer of the gathered church is of great importance for Ignatius (*Eph.* 10.1; 20.1; 21.2; and elsewhere). We also learn that baptisms must not be performed without the presence of the bishop (*Smyrn.* 8.2; cf. *Pol.* 6.2), yet we gain no insight into their performance in worship. Formulaic teaching material is frequently quoted (*Eph.* 7.2; 18.2; *Magn.* 11; and elsewhere), which serves to delineate heresy; whether and how it is used in worship is not apparent.

Like Ignatius, the author of the deutero-Pauline "pastoral letters" to Timothy and Titus also endeavors to resist threatening and expanding heresy, with the help of strict discipline in the church and stringent authorization of the clergy. Bishops and elders are to preserve the church in right belief, above all through intensive teaching (1 Tim. 3:2; 4:13; 5:17; 2 Tim. 4:2; Titus 1:9). Such teaching probably also defined church gatherings to a considerable extent, but the author of the pastoral letters gives us even less insight than Ignatius into the worship of the churches. Nowhere is the meal celebration expressly mentioned or even unambiguously presupposed. Yet in the recalling of hymns (1 Tim. 3:16; 2 Tim. 2:11), prayers (1 Tim. 2:1–6, 8), and doxologies (1 Tim. 1:17) we are probably dealing with liturgical tradition; with the teaching material (1 Tim. 1:15; 2:5; 3:1; 4:8–9; Titus 3:4–7) this is less certain. The "scripture" is placed in the service of right teaching (2 Tim. 3:14–17); it probably also played a role in the worship service (cf. 1 Tim. 1:6–7), and in 1 Tim. 4:13 we may have an early testimony to the reading of scripture in Christian worship. Regarding the performance of baptism (1 Tim. 3:6; Titus 3:4) we learn nothing, and one should not read too much between the lines of the pastoral letters about meetings for worship (versus Holtz 1965). Worth noting and fraught with consequences is the fact that in the face of dualistic false teachers, who along with creation also despised the body and the specifics of reproduction, women were denied active participation in worship services (1 Tim. 2:11–15 and the post-Pauline passage 1 Cor. 14:34–35).

Pliny's Letter to Emperor Trajan

Presumably in the year 112, Pliny the Younger, after he had become the emperor's governor in Bithynia, wrote a letter to the emperor Trajan that not only is one of the most valuable documents about the early persecution of Christians by the Roman state (cf. here Hosaka 1986) but also contains the most important information we have about worship in the postapostolic period (cf. Lietzmann

1962). Yet in both respects the understanding of the letter (Pliny *Ep.* 10.96) is not easy, and in some respects its interpretation is controversial.

Pliny served in northern Asia Minor in a region in which Christianity had already spread broadly in the cities and villages, and temples were beginning to be deserted; sacrificial meat for the temple was hardly still in demand. Before his arrival in Bithynia, Pliny had not been involved in a trial against Christians; therefore, in the letter he asks the emperor for appropriate instruction. He reports to his sovereign that in the case of confessed Christians who were not ready to recant, he simply executed them or, if they were Roman citizens, transferred them to Rome; in any case, he regarded Christians who refused to make the imperial sacrifice as adherents of a hostile and seditious superstition. Those who were denounced as Christians without cause he let go after they cursed Christ, invoked the state gods, and offered incense and wine before a picture of the emperor that Pliny had brought in. He assumes in his letter that the emperor agrees with this double procedure. Problematic for him, however, are the apostates, that is, the accused who are or have been Christians and who maintain either that recently or a long time ago, they gave up their faith in Christ, or that, faced with impending martyrdom, they now deny him. Pliny tests the reliability of their apostasy by having them also curse Christ and revere the images of the gods and the emperor. He is unsure, however, whether he may simply set them free after their apostasy. He would certainly like to, for he is convinced that "a great number of people can be returned to the right way if they are given the possibility of repentance." But is being a Christian in itself not punishable? And does it not require the investigation of crimes such as incest, child murder, and shameful meals of which Christians have been accused? In regard to the last of these, he has thoroughly interrogated Christians regarding what they do in their gatherings, without finding anything punishable. He writes the emperor that he has had two deaconesses flogged in order to learn the truth, but nothing has resulted but "an eccentric and inordinate superstition." In his answer Trajan assures his governor that he has judged appropriately and agrees with Pliny's view that apostates should not be punished.

We are especially interested in the information about worship that Pliny reproduces from the mouths of apostate Christians. When it is evaluated, we must keep in mind that these Christians were not interested in complete information but in their own defense. They were answering particular questions or accusations and not giving a general description of their meetings. Furthermore, we have here secondhand information, and how well the pagan Pliny correctly grasped everything he heard must be clarified in each case. Finally, we must also not forget that the governor is not reporting for the purpose of presenting Christian worship but of pacifying his region and reestablishing the pagan cult, so that instead of emphasizing the widespread accusations, he is at pains to present the harmlessness of what Christians do in their gatherings. The relevant section of Pliny's letter reads as follows:

> They maintained that their whole guilt [*culpa*] or their error consisted only in the fact that they came together on a certain day [*stato die*] before sunrise and with a reciprocal formula [*carmen*] spoke to Christ as if to a god, and also that with an oath [*sacramentum*] they had pledged themselves by

no means to a crime but to commit neither theft nor robbery nor adultery, never to break their word, and never to refuse to return entrusted property when it is demanded back. Afterward all had gone their own way, and later they came together again for a meal, which was held in community and completely innocently [*innoxium*].

This text clearly reveals the questions of the interrogating governor: Have you committed yourself to criminal activity? Were there secret meetings? Did anything unseemly take place at your meals? The former Christians can answer these questions with a clear conscience, and even torture does not produce anything incriminating. But what do we learn about Christian worship at the beginning of the second century? On a set day there is an early worship service. Sunday is the only possibility here; afterward the participants scatter to do their everyday work. This gathering in the early morning is apparently the baptismal service. At its center is the exchange of baptismal questions and baptismal confession. The specifics of the baptismal confession are on the one hand the confession to Jesus Christ and on the other the pledge to a life of moral purity as the equivalent of purification from sins and as the guiding principle for those born again through the water; this corresponds completely with everything that we have learned since Paul about the meaning of baptism. The specific circumstances of the baptismal celebration are not addressed, yet we may assume that it was not held every Sunday, but only as needed, for the later custom of baptizing at Easter the catechumens of a whole year had doubtless not yet developed. The governor did not relate "on a certain day"—that is, on Sunday—only to the evening meeting but also to a *weekly* gathering in the early hours; thus for him it was apparently a question of using a regular meeting time to exclude the suspicion of secret gatherings. In any case, it is obvious that the other celebration was the Sunday celebration of the Lord's Supper. It is mentioned only briefly and in defense against the current virulent accusations that at their meetings Christians did outrageous things and perhaps even ate human flesh. Moreover, the apostates gave assurance that these meetings were suspended after Pliny, on order of the emperor, had prohibited all private gatherings and secret societies (*hetaeria*).

Thus Pliny's letter is easily understandable in the context of what we have already learned about early Christian worship in the meager testimonies up to the time of the turn of the century. Especially noteworthy is the fact that no separate service of the word is attested. Proclamation and prayer are apparently found at baptism and the Lord's Supper, and public missionary events were in any case ill-advised in the time of persecution. Thus this secular document in essence confirms what was previously known.

The *Didache*

A document of a completely different kind is the *Didache,* an early Christian writing whose content was first discovered in 1873 in Constantinople and first published in 1883. It contains a reasonable arrangement of various traditions of Jewish Christian origin that probably come from the first century: a catechism of the two ways, an order for the service of worship, a church discipline, and eschatological apocalyptic teachings. Its collector, frequently called the Didachist, seems to have gathered his material together in the first decades of the second century and brought it up to date. Yet the removal of his additions from the traditions he gathered is possible only with some degree of probability. The information on the order of worship, which we will present and analyze below, is found above all in chapters 7–10. We must note that like the *Didache* as a whole, this information leads into a relatively archaic Jewish Christian milieu that reveals no immediate influence of Damascene or Antiochene, much less Pauline, theology; rather, even more than the Revelation to John, it remains bound to the tradition of Palestinian primitive Christianity. There is, for example, no reference to Jesus' salvific death "for us." We cannot infer, however, from the *Didache*'s role as a theological outsider that the church of the Didachist remained without contact with other Christian movements and developed its worship services only on its own initiative. Even the fact that the Didachist uses the Gospel of Matthew in his instruction shows that he is conscious of his connection with Christendom; in fact, what he reveals of the worship services in his church reflects to a considerable degree the development that had taken place generally in Christendom up until his time.

Baptism is the topic of chapter 7. No day or time is given for the baptismal service, but it must have taken place from case to case on a Sunday (morning?), for the meal celebration occurs regularly on Sunday (*Did.* 14.1). Baptism is performed by an officiant in the presence of the congregation; the officiant, as well as the baptismal candidate and as many church members as possible, are supposed to have fasted before the baptismal ceremony. In any case, the instruction to baptize in flowing water belongs to the old tradition. Also relatively old, apparently, is the concession that when flowing water is lacking, one may use other water, namely, fresh water from a well or in an emergency standing water, perhaps from a cistern. The further concession of baptizing, if need be, with the thrice-performed pouring of water on the head of the candidate probably comes from the Didachist. In any case, the baptism is to take place "in the name of the Father and of the Son and of the Holy Spirit." Thus the baptismal formula literally conforms to the one in Matt. 28:19. Since the Didachist knew the Gospel of Matthew — in *Did.* 8.2 he quotes the Lord's Prayer in the Matthean version — he probably also took the triadic baptismal formula from the baptismal command in Matt. 28:19–20; his tradition may then have still spoken of baptism "in Christ" or "in the name of Jesus" (cf. *Did.* 9.5). The triadic baptismal formula actually presupposes a corresponding baptismal confession in the baptismal service, but on this point the author is silent. Is this an arcane discipline? Or is the archaic theology of the *Didache* still closed to the faith formulas developed elsewhere in Christendom? In any case, the Didachist expressly says only that before the baptism the two-ways catechism quoted in chapters 1–6, that is, the moral instruction that he precedes with the radical commandments of the Matthean Sermon on the Mount, is to be called out and drilled. This instruction adopts the command of Matt. 28:20 that the candidate is to teach "everything that I have commanded you." Both the baptismal confession and the instruction correspond to what Pliny's letter tells us about the baptismal service.

After the Didachist in chapter 8, following the key word *fast* that is found in the foregoing baptismal instructions, also teaches about the private fasting and praying of individual Christians, he returns in chapter 9 to the ordering of the worship service. In *Did.* 9.1–10.7 he passes on a detailed form for the Eucharist, whose archaic character in comparison with other Communion traditions is striking. Although the words of institution were known to the Didachist from the Gospel of Matthew, he makes no attempt to rearrange the order of worship in his church according to this tradition that was widespread in other areas of Hellenistic Christianity. Therefore, some have questioned whether in *Did.* 9–10 we are dealing with a Lord's Supper liturgy at all or perhaps with a "love feast," as attested early on in Jude 12 and Ign. *Smyrn.* 8.2. The theological orientation of the Lord's Supper texts of the *Didache,* however, are not different from the archaic overall picture of strongly eschatological and apocalyptic piety revealed throughout this writing, and the detailed analysis definitely shows that the Didachist communicates fixed parts of the Communion service of his church, and in the order in which they were used.

The author is silent about place and time of day of the meal celebrations, but from *Did.* 14.1 we learn that it took place on Sunday, a workday, and thus without doubt in the evening. If the Didachist introduces the instructions on the baptismal service with "concerning baptism," then the meal service begins with "concerning the Eucharist" (*Did.* 9.1). He presupposes that cup and bread are ready, and he first gives the benedictions that are to be said over the cup and the bread before the meal. Remarkably, the prayer over the cup comes first, presumably an indication of the underlying Jewish meal custom or of the corresponding festal meal of the Palestinian primitive church (cf. Dibelius 1956, 118).

The prayer over the cup (*Did.* 9.2), spoken by the liturgist, reads:

> We thank you, our Father,
> for the holy vine of David, your servant,
> which you have made known to us through Jesus, your servant.

To this the congregation answers:

> To you be glory forever.

The expression *holy vine of David* is unusual, but it can refer only to the promised messianic salvation (cf. Dibelius 1956, 119–20).

Then follows the prayer of the liturgist over the bread, which is parallel to the blessing of the cup (9.3):

> We thank you, our father,
> for life and knowledge,
> which you have made known to us through Jesus, your servant.

And again the congregation responds:

> To you be glory forever.

In the presence of the "bread of life," one is thankful for knowledge of the true, eternal life that comes from Jesus, who is again called by the ancient title *servant* (cf. Isa. 53:11).

Then follows a kind of "interpretive saying" about the bread, which recalls 1 Cor. 10:17 (*Did.* 9.4):

> As this bread was scattered on the mountains and was gathered into one,
> so may your church gather from the ends of the earth into your kingdom.

This time the congregation answers:

> For glory and power are yours through Jesus Christ forever.

Presumably, this interpretive saying is a relatively late piece of liturgy, which possibly was formed by the Didachist in dependence on an interpretation of the bread, as is found in 1 Cor. 10:16b–17, yet placed on the eschatological plane, which determines the overall theology of the *Didache,* and formulated with the help of the widespread Jewish material that is also found in *Did.* 10.5 (cf. Isa. 11:12; Jer. 39:37; Zech. 2:10).

Following these prayers and in view of the now approaching meal, the Didachist adds (*Did.* 9.5): "Let no one eat or drink from your Eucharist except those who have been baptized in the name of the Lord," and he underlines this admonition with a quotation from Matt. 7:6: "Do not give what is holy to dogs." The fact that the meal now follows is also shown by the continuation in *Did.* 10.1: "After satisfaction, you are to give thanks in the following way." The term *satisfaction* in no way refers to an extended meal, but to the fact that in general in antiquity bread was the usual food for satisfying one's hunger, and at the celebration of the Lord's Supper one could eat one's fill of bread.

The prayer of thanksgiving is comprised of three parts. The first part is related to the benedictions over the cup and the bread but does not consider the interpretive saying. The liturgist says (*Did.* 10.2):

> We thank you, holy Father,
> for your holy name,
> which you have caused to reside in our hearts,
> and for knowledge and faith and immortality,
> which you have made known to us through Jesus, your servant.

The congregation makes the usual response:

> To you be glory forever.

The second part of the prayer of thanksgiving draws on the Jewish prayer after a completed meal, but the thanksgiving is related to the special gifts of the Eucharist (*Did.* 10.3–4):

> You, Lord, Ruler of the universe,
> you have created everything for your name's sake;
> you have given human beings food and drink for refreshment, so that they
>   may thank you,

but you have given us spiritual food and drink and eternal life through your
servant.
Above all we thank you because you are mighty [or: we thank you for
everything because you are mighty].

And again the congregation gathered for the meal responds:

To you be glory forever.

The third part of the prayer contains not thanksgiving but a petition for the
church. In content it corresponds in part to the Matthean version of the Lord's
Prayer in *Did.* 8.2, and in part to the interpretive saying in *Did.* 9.4, the third part
of the opening order of the service. Like that order it is probably a later addition
by the same hand (*Did.* 10.5):

Remember, Lord, your church,
to save it from all evil and to perfect it in your love,
and gather it . . . from the four winds into your kingdom, which you have
prepared for it.

As in *Did.* 8.2 (cf. 9.4), the response of the congregation is:

For power and glory are yours forever.

The meal celebration ends with a versicle (*Did.* 10.6):

LITURGIST: May grace come and may the world pass away.

CONGREGATION: Hosanna to the God of David!

LITURGIST: Let those who are holy join in; let those who are not repent.
Maranatha!

CONGREGATION: Amen.

The words "join in" refer not to the meal, which is now past and which was not
celebrated in the form of a transforming Communion, but to the coming of grace:
those who are holy—the meal congregation—may approach the coming kingdom
of God, and for sinners there is still opportunity for repentance (cf. Rev. 22:17;
Nagel 1970, 27). The coming Lord (*Marana tha*) redeems the holy from all evil
and will judge sinners. To this the congregation says its "Amen."

The closing comment of the Didachist is instructive: "But allow the prophets to
give thanks however they want" (*Did.* 10.7). Thus in the worship service there are
still prophets present, who speak from the free inspiration of the Spirit. They probably also helped shape the "word" portion of the worship, about which we otherwise
hear nothing, because it was probably still carried out with great freedom. A special
service of the word is also unknown in the church of the Didachist. By contrast, we
learn in *Did.* 14 that one must confess one's transgressions, and one is not to come to
the gathering at all if one has a quarrel with a neighbor. The Didachist does not pass
on the confessional formula, but in any case, a regular confession of sins preceded the

meal. This seems to be an innovation; one had to learn that even the "saints" do not always live saintly lives. In any case, we observe how even beyond the formulations of the actual meal agenda, the order of the worship service is gradually becoming fixed. This is also indicated by the following instruction in connection with the rules for the worship service: "Select for yourselves bishops [*episcopous*] and deacons . . . for they also serve you in the roles of prophet and teacher" (*Did.* 15.1). Prophets and teachers are charismatics who perform their function according to their charisma in proclamation, prayer, and teaching, apparently without a special commission from the church, yet they have a right to support from the church (*Did.* 13), for also with itinerant charismatics the church unmasks the false prophets but is supposed to support true prophets (*Did.* 11). At one point the Didachist compares the duty of prophets with the ministry of the high priest (*Did.* 13.3). Thus like the teachers in the worship service, they are charismatically active, yet the charisma became weaker, so that in addition to or in place of the prophets, the church had to elect "officeholders" as needed, namely, the mentioned bishops and deacons; the latter were presumably responsible essentially for the preparation and perhaps also the course of the meal celebration; the former possibly for the leading of the worship service in general or also for the proclamation of the word or the reading. The latter is not expressly mentioned, but the fact that the Didachist is at least familiar with the Gospel of Matthew suggests that sooner or later the reading of the Gospel was inserted into his church, as is soon also attested by Justin. We learn nothing about Old Testament readings.

Justin Martyr

With Justin, who was born of pagan ancestry in Palestine in the Greco-Roman city of Flavia Neapolis and ended his course as a Christian martyr in Rome, we move into the middle of the second century and thus already to the very end of the postapostolic age. But that is not the only reason why it is appropriate to close the presentation of early Christian worship with his report. In him we also meet a representative of "normal" Christianity, which had Jewish Christian roots and had long since found its own way outside the synagogue.

Although he was unfamiliar with the letters of Paul and the Gospel of John, Justin endeavored in his own individual way to portray Christianity as the true philosophy. Therefore one must consider whether this intention also influenced his presentation of the Christian worship service. Moreover, this presentation is contained in his *Apology,* which he addresses to the emperor Antonius Pius (138–61) and with which he defends bloodily persecuted Christianity against publicly made accusations, and thus his apologetic interests probably also have colored his presentation. Thus Justin is not shaping an order of worship for the internal use of the church. The course of the church's worship itself, however, is not influenced by a tendentious representation, and since Justin describes this worship service in a thoroughly informative and also relatively detailed way, and thereby reveals that in his time the worship service had assumed a fixed form that remained normative for the following period, his description forms a fitting close for a presentation of the development of early Christian worship.

In *Apol.* 1.61 Justin reports on the order of the baptismal service of worship. Baptism is preceded by instruction in Christian doctrine, but we cannot tell whether a regular instruction of catechumens was already established. The preparation for baptism includes prayer and fasting by both the baptismal candidate and the baptizing church. The candidates promise to live in accordance with the Christian message and ask God for forgiveness of their earlier sins. This apparently involves an act of worship that takes place in an assembly room. "Then they are led by us to a place where there is water." The continuation of the presentation reveals that the whole congregation is not present at the public act of baptism but has gathered in the usual place in order to receive the candidate after baptism; the persecution situation did not allow a public demonstration. Later baptisteries were also built beside the churches, in which the congregation awaited the one who had been baptized in a smaller group. Those to be baptized undergo immersion: the one who has led the candidate, "who has done penance for his sins," into the water pronounces over the one receiving baptism "the name of the Father of the universe and absolute Ruler God and our Savior Jesus Christ and the Holy Spirit." Thus the church uses the triadic baptismal formula, which Justin also knows from the command to baptize in Matt. 28:19 and which he quotes three times in *Apol.* 1.61 with various expansions. In one case the three names are each individually preceded by "in the name of," so that we can conclude that the candidate was immersed three times. For this baptism was without doubt a baptism by immersion, which is also suggested by the fact that Justin repeatedly calls baptism a rebirth and not just a baptism for the forgiveness of sins and for illumination.

It is noteworthy, however, that whereas the candidate's repentance and vow to lead a moral life are mentioned, there is—as in the *Didache*—no reference to a confession of faith, although at the beginning of the chapter faith is expressly named as the presupposition of baptism; from many passages of Justin's extant writings it is clear that there was a corresponding triadic formula of faith in his church, and thus there have even been attempts made to reconstruct a baptismal confession (cf. *Apol.* 1.6, 13, 61; 2.5; *Dial.* 30; 85). The fact that the confession was used only in teaching and not in the act of baptism is not as instructive as the fact that the baptismal vow was emphasized in a defense against accusations of an immoral life, but not the confession of faith, which would have been incomprehensible to the addressees of the *Apology*.

After a long-winded interruption, in which Justin relates baptism to Jewish and pagan water rites, in *Apol.* 1.65 he again picks up the thread of his presentation: "After such a bath we lead the one who has come to faith to the place where those whom we call brethren are gathered." Intercession is made for the church, for the newly baptized, and for Christians and people in all the world, and a special prayer is given that in accordance with the baptismal vow, all may always be found in a state of good works, "so that we may gain eternal salvation." After this prayer a holy kiss (cf. Rom. 16:16; 1 Cor. 16:20; 2 Cor. 13:12) is exchanged as a sign of living together in peace (cf. *Did.* 14.2), and the holy meal, whose course is presented by Justin, is celebrated with the newly baptized.

A problem arises from the fact that Justin repeats this presentation in *Apol.* 1.67

not in connection with baptism but in the context of the church's Sunday service of worship. Is he speaking both times of the same Sunday meal service, so that baptism also takes place on a Sunday and the newly baptized person is taken to a congregation that has already gathered anyway? Nothing in Justin's presentation points in this direction. On the one hand, it is striking that in *Apol.* 1.67 and 1.68 he emphatically stresses that the regular gathering takes place on *Sunday,* the first day of the week of creation and the day of Jesus' resurrection (cf. *Dial.* 24.1; 41.4; 138.1). In the account of baptism, on the other hand, there is no reference to a day. Therefore we must assume that baptism, which was performed only as needed, did not take place at regular times but as the occasion presented itself and in a manner that would draw as little public attention as possible, and thus the church had to have a special gathering if it wanted to receive the newly baptized into its meal fellowship. Naturally, from time to time baptismal Communion and Sunday worship could also have been combined, especially since the meal celebration as such apparently followed the same order, but this seems not to have been the regular practice. In presenting the meal celebration, we will follow the description that Justin gives in *Apol.* 1.67 in connection with the Sunday service, and at the same time we will refer to the description of the baptismal Communion in *Apol.* 1.65, to which Justin himself also makes reference at one point.

In *Apol.* 1.66 Justin expressly states that the participants call the meal the *Eucharist* ("thanksgiving"); thus according to the principle *pars pro toto* the designation for the prayer of thanksgiving has in the meantime become the name for the entire meal activity. Then he explains, in agreement with the *Didache,* that only the baptized may participate in the meal. This does not necessarily exclude the presence of the unbaptized or their participation in worship up to the beginning of the meal celebration. Possibly, these problems were not handled in a uniform way, and Justin seems to know nothing of the later practice of dismissing catechumens after the "word" part of the worship gathering. Finally, in 1.66 Justin refers, in a relatively free quotation, to the words of institution that are familiar to him from the Synoptic tradition. He understands them as an indication that the meal is no ordinary act of eating and drinking but a consecrated meal in which we are fed by the flesh and blood of the Jesus who became flesh. In the meal liturgy, however, the words of institution seem not yet to have been said aloud.

Sunday worship gathers all believers "from towns and villages" in one place. At first there are readings from the Gospels or writings of the prophets, "as long as time allows." Thus for the first time we learn that scripture readings, either from the Gospels or from the prophets, have made their entrance into the Christian worship service. Each church probably possessed one of the Gospel writings; the Old Testament prophets were available only in excerpts. The "law," the most important book read aloud in the rabbinical synagogue, was apparently intentionally ignored.

The position of lector is not mentioned as such, but the reader is not identical with the leader of the worship service. Several times Justin calls the latter the "presider," a relatively neutral term that may conceal a bishop or presbyter, but Justin avoids more specific terms. Were there apologetic reasons for this? Or had no set order taken shape in his churches? In any case, after the reading the presider spoke, admonishing and encouraging hearers to emulate what they had just heard. Thus for the first time we also find an address or sermon with scripture interpretation in the Christian service of worship, and we can observe that the charismatic words and prayers of the prophets and teachers have in the meantime been essentially suppressed by the fixed speech of a presider selected for this purpose; he also continues to lead during the process of the celebration and above all says the prayers. At the same time we find confirmation that a separate service of the word in addition to the meal celebration never existed, but that all forms of proclamation could find their place in the one gathering, at whose center was the meal. For the often encountered view that in Justin's churches the two previously separated forms of the worship service had come together in one celebration has neither a basis in Justin's accounts nor any foundation in the previous history of early Christian worship.

In the actual meal celebration, the entire congregation rises and "sends up prayers," whose form and content are not given. Are they petitions comparable to the prayers that Justin describes at the beginning of the baptismal meal? In *Apol.* 1.17 we learn that even in Justin's time there were regular prayers for the authorities (cf. *1 Clem.* 61; 1 Tim. 2:2). According to *Apol.* 1.13 the gift of life, the work of creation, natural goods, and the expectation of the resurrection are objects of prayer and praise. Such prayers were probably followed, also in the Sunday service, by the holy kiss, which Justin expressly mentions only in *Apol.* 1.65 in connection with the baptismal meal.

Now the bread and the wine, with which water is mixed, are brought before the presider. This was probably the task of the "deacons," whom Justin mentions by this title only when he speaks of the distribution of the bread and wine. The presider takes bread and cup in hand and "sends up praise to the Father of the universe in the name of the Son and the Holy Spirit and gives a long thanksgiving that we have been granted these gifts through him." Here we have the actual "Eucharist," and when the presider prays "to the best of his ability," we may presume that, in contrast to the order of worship in the *Didache,* he is not yet fully bound to a fixed formula. "When he has finished the prayers and the thanksgiving, the whole congregation present agrees with an amen," and "after the thanksgiving of the presider and the agreement of the whole congregation," the deacons distribute bread and wine to those present and also take it to those who are prevented from taking part in the worship service. We do not know whether there was enough bread for worshipers to eat their fill.

Justin mentions this central act of the Eucharist, the thanksgiving that gave its name to the entire celebration, no fewer than three times, presumably because he wants to contradict the rumors of shameful deeds "such as the extinguishing of lights, unbridled excesses, and the eating of human flesh" (*Apol.* 1.26). Probably for the same reason he forgoes making a connection between the Lord's Supper and Jesus' death, although in the dialogue with the Jew Trypho he relates the two to each other in accordance with the words of institution (*Dial.* 41; 70.4; 117.3). Prayers after the meal are no longer mentioned, nor is a closing blessing; Justin is also silent about songs or hymns, although he mentions them elsewhere in his writings along with prayers (*Apol.* 1.13, 17), and fixed responses of several kinds, in addition to "amen," have hardly been lacking in his worship services. He concentrates, however, on what serves his apology of Christianity for pagan readers.

In *Apol.* 1.67 Justin frames his account of the Sunday worship service with a double reference to the loving activity of Christians. From one's own resources and according to one's own estimation, each person contributes toward the support of widows and orphans, the poor, the sick, prisoners, and passing strangers. Gifts are deposited with the presider, who sees to their appropriate distribution. Naturally, this impressive description of the exemplary community life of Christians serves their defense. How such collections and distributions were integrated into the course of the worship service cannot be known, but the Christian labor of love is without doubt connected with the worship event. A love feast (or agape meal: cf. Jude 12; Ign. *Smyrn.* 8.2), however, is not to be found in Justin in the context of the worship service.

11

The Origin and Development of the Early Christian Understanding of Baptism

In his *Grundriss der Theologie des Neuen Testaments,* Conzelmann (1987, 127) begins his treatment of baptism in the following way: "From the beginning baptism is the general rite of induction into the church. Paul presupposes that all Christians are baptized (Rom. 6:3; 1 Cor. 12:13). The church adopted this practice from John the Baptist." Each of these three individual assertions, with which Conzelmann reproduces a seldom questioned consensus of scholars (cf., e.g., Aland 1979), is quite doubtful, and the same is true of the additional assertion "that from the beginning early Christian baptism was performed as baptism *in the name of Jesus Christ*" (Lohfink 1976, 50).

The idea that baptism was practiced "from the beginning" corresponds to the presentation in Acts 2:38–41, yet this presentation does not rest on historical tradition. It reflects, rather, what Luke believes was the case from the beginning, based on the practice of churches in his own time. The commandment of the exalted Christ to baptize in Matt. 28:16–20 (cf. Mark 16:16) reveals only that the tradition available to the evangelist knows nothing about baptismal activity by the earthly Jesus and his disciples; it gives no information about the place, manner, or origin of Christian baptism as it was practiced in Matthew's community. It is noteworthy that this solitary report of an "institution" of baptism comes from the pen of the evangelist himself, who is writing toward the end of the first century, and already contains the relatively late triadic baptismal formula. We have no authentic reports of a practice of baptism by the Jerusalem primitive church. The sayings tradition and sayings source of the Synoptic Gospels know nothing about a Christian baptism, nor do Paul's statements about baptism contain any traditional motifs that can be traced back to Palestinian Jewish Christianity.

In 1 Cor. 12:13 (cf. 1:14–17) Paul does indeed presuppose that the church members in Corinth whom he is addressing have all been baptized. In Rom. 6:3, however, Paul does not seem to make this assumption about the Christians in Rome ("all of us who have been baptized into Christ"). As the date that marks the beginning of Christian existence, Paul typically mentions the time when one "came to believe" (1 Cor. 3:5; 15:2, 11; Gal. 2:16; cf. Rom. 13:11), not "was baptized." We can say with some certainty only that in the Gentile Christian churches of Paul the custom of baptism was generally practiced. Such an observation says nothing about other Christian groups, especially Jewish Christians.

The view that Christian baptism is a continuation and further development of Johannine baptism is also open to considerable questioning. The assertion of the Gospel of John that Jesus himself (John 3:26) and his disciples (4:1–2) were baptizing in addition to John the Baptist has no basis in the older tradition and can be explained by the redactional interests of the fourth evangelist (Schmithals 1992, 333ff.). It is true that Luke, who intentionally reports no commandment of Jesus to baptize, suggests in his two volumes that the primitive church simply continued the baptism of John with the additional reference to the name of Jesus (cf. Luke 3:3 with Acts 2:38), yet this representation is entirely attributable to the redaction of the evangelist and is a characteristic expression of his interest in "salvation history" and its continuity from the old covenant through Jesus to the church. John baptized, but he did not have others baptize, and after the death of the master, his disciples did not continue his baptizing activity (Acts 19:1–7; cf. 18:25). Actually, the baptism of John was a prophetic act completely bound to his *person,* as shown by the exceptional sobriquet "the Baptist," also attested by Josephus (*Ant.* 18.116–19). Christian baptism, by contrast, was performed by the *church* (cf. 1 Cor. 1:12ff.), without mention of the person of the baptizer. In early Christian baptismal tradition there are no echoes of an apocalyptic expectation of the imminent turn of the age, which probably defined John's preaching and baptism for repentance. John baptized penitent Israelites; as far as we can see, Christian baptism, however, was specifically related from the beginning to the mission to the Gentiles (Gal. 3:26–28; Mark 16:15–16; Matt. 28:16–20). Above all, Christian baptism is *transfer baptism;* it transfers the baptized person into the new people of God, and therefore it has a certain affinity with proselyte baptism. This character diverges completely from John's baptism, however one judges it in detail. One must also consider that early Christendom strictly differentiated between its own baptism as "baptism of the Spirit" and the "water baptism" of John (Mark 1:8 par.; Acts 19:1–5); in no way did it observe, or was it thought of as, a continuity. Therefore one cannot avoid the conclusion that "the popular idea that the first Christians after Easter adopted the water baptism of John and Christianized it is more naive than historical" (Barnikol 1956/57, 594).

Finally, in regard to the baptismal formula, the letters of Paul attest that initially baptism was not performed "in the name of Jesus" but "into Christ" (*eis Christon*). And thus this oldest formulation can also serve as a key to knowledge of the origin and development of the early Christian understanding of baptism.

In any case one would do well, if one wants to attain such knowledge, to approach the texts without the judgments cited at the beginning, which owe more to an unthinking consensus than to sober reflection. Actually, our oldest witness, Paul, shows a picture of the early Christian understanding of baptism that is far from that consensus; it is quite differentiated and also not easy to illuminate. We should note here that Paul never makes baptism itself the object of discussion and consequently never develops an adequate theology of baptism. Rather, on various occasions he draws baptism into his argumentation, with the result that the

information needed for a possible Pauline doctrine of baptism occurs only incidentally and accidentally and comes to us more or less in pieces. On the origin and
development of the early Christian understanding of baptism, Paul gives no direct
information, and thus we must gain it indirectly from his traditions.

"Into Christ"

In the formulaic and traditional usages found in Paul, we find an understanding
of baptism as the transference of the one baptized "into Christ" (*eis Christon*), that
is, into the "body of Christ" and thus into the Christian church. Thus we are dealing here with a decidedly ecclesiological view of baptism. In these traditional formulations there is no reference to the salvific event of Christ's incarnation or his
death and resurrection; the transference of the one baptized into the community of
salvation, the body of Christ, is as such a soteriological act. According to the traditional texts this act manifests itself above all in the "spiritual" abolition of religious (Jew/Greek), social (free/slave), and natural (man/woman) differences
between people—a viewpoint that leads one to infer a dualistic background for this
conception linked with the act of baptism. In 1 Cor. 12:12–13 we read:

> [12]For just as the body is one and has many members, and all the members
> of the body, though many, are one body, so it is with Christ. [13]For in the
> one Spirit we were all baptized into one body—Jews or Greeks, slaves or
> free—and we were all made to drink of one Spirit.

In 12:12 Paul introduces the image, widespread especially among the Stoics, of
the body formed as an organism, in order to relate it to the Christian church and
develop it accordingly in the rest of the chapter. This relationship is established
somewhat surprisingly by "so it is with Christ," for both the logic of this comparison and the following sentence show that "Christ" in this usage means the
Christian church, the "body of Christ" (cf. 1 Cor. 12:27). J. Weiss (1910, 303) recognizes here, with reason, "an almost unsolvable problem for us," as to how Christ
"can be thought of" both as the personal Christ and the impersonal church. In
terms of the history of religion, however, this process is explainable. The equating of "Christ" and "church" is found in the "mystical" way of thinking and con-
ceiving that lies *at the foundation* of Paul's conversion theology. In it we find that
"Christ" is not the historical figure of the Redeemer sent by God but the sum of
the pneumatics, the people of the Spirit (see chapter 4). Paul's conversion theology, which confesses Jesus as the Christ, employs that mystical conception and
language above all in ecclesiological relationships. How familiar this language
still is to Paul is shown especially clearly by 1 Cor. 12:12–13: the term *body,* introduced in 12:12 from the standpoint of the organism and with the intention of
the comparison with the Christian church, is associated with the term *body of
Christ,* which in turn evokes *Christ* by itself as a designation for the church.

In the present context 12:13 apparently has the task of making visible the unity
of the body of Christ vis-à-vis the multiplicity and variety of gifts of the Spirit
found in the Christian church, as befits the overall tenor of 1 Corinthians 12.

Accordingly, with "indeed" in 12:14 Paul leads the reader back again to the image of the human body: "Indeed, the body does not consist of one member but of many." In 12:13 the apostle has just pointed twice to the "one Spirit" who activates the various gifts of the many members of the church. Verse 13 fits into the course of the argumentation, but not without tension. For while the image of the organism of the body seeks to establish the "togetherness of *what is different*" with its different functions in the life of the church (Conzelmann 1969, 250), v. 13 speaks of the *abolition* of differences between church members and thus of unity as such. The organism idea of the context is foreign to 12:13. From this it follows that the basic idea of 12:13 is traditional, and in fact a well-formed piece of tradition is recognizable as soon as we remove the doublet "in the one Spirit" that comes from Paul. The result is a four-line statement with the pattern a/b/b/a with 5+4+4+5 Greek words:

> We were all baptized into one body —
> whether Jews or Greeks,
> whether slaves or free
> and we were all made to drink of one Spirit.

The meaning of this independent statement is apparent: "The body of Christ is preexistent with respect to the 'members'" (Conzelmann 1969, 250). Baptism transfers one into the one body of Christ and therefore gives one participation in the Spirit, who is at work in the church—"in Christ" and "in the Spirit" are also used elsewhere interchangeably in Paul (Rom. 8:9–10)—and this Spirit-body abolishes the external differences between people. The intention and the formulaic traditional character of 12:13 are also confirmed by the parallels in Gal. 3:26ff. and Col. 3:9–11 (cf. 1 Cor. 7:[12,] 17–24; Rom. 10:12), even if baptism appears only indirectly in Col. 3:9–11. In Gal. 2:28 and 1 Cor. 7:12–16 we find as a third member "male and female," with which the present formula in 12:13 could also be expanded to a triad, for the Corinthian situation, as it is revealed in 1 Cor. 11:2–6 (cf. 14:33–36), must have prompted Paul to forgo this third member.

A closer analysis of Gal. 3:26–28 also reveals an original baptismal practice in which baptism is performed "into Christ" and understood in such a way that it transfers one into the body of Christ of the church and abolishes natural differences:

> [26]For in Christ Jesus you are all children of God through faith. [27]As many of you as were baptized into Christ have clothed yourselves with Christ.
> [28]There is no longer Jew or Greek, there is no longer slave or free, there is no longer male and female; for all of you are one in Christ Jesus.

The pre-Pauline traditional and at the same time formulaic character of this passage has already been often observed and described (Paulsen 1980, 77–78, n. 16; Betz 1988, 325). This judgment is based first on the change from *we* in 3:25 to *you* in 3:26–28 (and back to *us* and *we* again in 4:3ff.), which suggests a relatively fixed traditional formulation. The already mentioned parallels 1 Cor. 12:12–13; Col. 3:9–11; and 1 Cor. 7:(12,) 17–24 show that at least the dominant motif of 3:26–28, the abolition of natural, social, and ethnic-religious differences "in Christ," is traditional. Especially important is the observation that in the Pauline train of thought this motif is without function. Paul apparently takes up the tradition for the sake of 3:26: believers are no longer minors under a paidagōgos ("disciplinarian," 3:24–25) or under "guardians and trustees" (4:1–2); rather, in Christ they are mature "children of God" (3:26; 4:4ff.) and consequently "heirs" (3:29; 4:1, 7).

In 3:29 Paul connects with the "in Christ Jesus" of 3:26, 28 but otherwise does not consider 3:28; instead, from this tradition he includes only the statement in 3:26 in his train of thought. Also the statement, "There is no longer Jew or Greek," in 3:28 has no reference to the actual train of thought, in which Paul is concerned not with the abolition of the difference between Jews and Greeks but asserts, rather, the replacement of the "law" by "faith" within Judaism (cf. 3:23–25). Paul includes 3:28 only on formal grounds, because he is in the habit of quoting fixed traditional formulations in their entirety, even when he makes reference to only one individual thought in that piece of tradition (cf., e.g., 1 Cor. 15:3ff.; see p. 52 above).

Finally, the elevated style of 3:26–28 points to the tradition adopted in these statements and at the same time allows the form of this tradition to be more exactly determined. In 3:26, in a way similar to Rom. 3:25, Paul has inserted "through faith," which is consistent with the context (cf. Gal. 3:22–25) but competes with "in Christ Jesus" (cf. Betz 1988, 320–21). For there is no way that "in Christ Jesus" can be conceived as a more exact determination of "through faith," nor can the present passage be rendered as "through faith in Jesus Christ"; "faith in . . ." would not be Pauline (cf. Schlier 1949, 127).

Accordingly, the following tradition emerges:

> For you are all children of God in Christ Jesus;
> for as many of you as were baptized into Christ have clothed yourselves with
>   Christ.
> There is not Jew or Greek,
> there is not slave or free,
> there is not male and female;
> For you are all one in Christ Jesus.

Here we have a ring composition of six lines, which follows a frequently found argumentation schema in Paul (see pp. 140ff. above). The first line (*basic statement*) and the last line (*résumé*) are formed in a strikingly parallel fashion. In the middle section, the *explication,* there is a trio of lines with five Greek words each; the three framing sentences each have seven Greek words. Betz (1988, 328) holds that the second line, "as an important clarifying insertion, has a special position." But the form of the tradition supports the idea that the second line was a part of that tradition from the beginning. It introduces the *explication* and is formulated entirely in the language of the "Christ mysticism," which also shapes the remaining lines of the tradition. It is also hard to understand why Paul should have inserted the baptismal reference, which has no function in his train of thought but instead substantiates the following trio. For the formulation "be baptized into Christ," which in 1 Cor. 12:12–13 is connected with the idea of the body of Christ, is linked in the present tradition more closely with the "mystical" idea that those baptized take off the earthly and "put on Christ," so that for them the earthly distinctions of Jew and Greek, free and slave, man and woman are no longer valid.

A third text to consider in this connection is Col. 3:9b–11, even if this passage does not speak directly of baptism. Whether this pericope is Pauline, as I presuppose (Schmithals 1984, 166ff.), or deutero-Pauline can remain unanswered, for the relevant statements in this passage can in no way be explained as a secondary version of 1 Cor. 12:12–13 and Gal. 3:26–28; they rest, rather, on independent tradition. The detailed paraenesis of Col. 3:1–9a is substantiated in the following comments with participles in the aorist, which are best translated with the indicative:

> [9] . . . seeing that you have stripped off the old self with its practices [10]and have clothed yourselves with the new self, which is being renewed in knowledge according to the image of its creator. [11]In that renewal there is no longer Greek and Jew, circumcised and uncircumcised, barbarian, Scythian, slave and free; but Christ is all and in all!

The main idea of this comment follows Paul's characteristic dialectical relationship of indicative and imperative: Be what you are! In this sense 3:9b–10 refers indirectly to baptism (cf. Col. 2:12), in which the transformation of the old self into the new takes place (cf. Lohse 1968, 203); accordingly, Gal. 3:27 (cf. Rom. 13:12b–14) says: "As many of you as were baptized into Christ have clothed yourselves with Christ." But if this formulation in Galatians only presupposes the death of the old self, the Colossians tradition begins with this idea (3:9b). According to 3:10 Christ is the "image" of the "creator," that is, the image of God (cf. Col. 1:15; 2 Cor. 4:4), and in baptism the self is renewed according to this "image" that has been "put on" (Rom. 13:14; Gal. 3:27; cf. Rom. 8:29). For the author of Col. 3:1–11 this means that Christ is the principle of knowledge and the origin of the new life in faith. Yet the older concept that underlies this idea, along with its various images, belongs in the realm of an "identity Christology," as 3:11b still clearly reveals: the new self is identical with Christ and like him the image of its creator. Baptism transfers one "into Christ" or into the "body of Christ" (1 Cor. 12:12–13), and whoever is "in Christ" or has "put on Christ" is a "new creation" (2 Cor. 5:17). For "Christ is all and in all" (3:11b) is only another expression for "all of you are one in Christ" (Gal. 3:28b) or for the simple "Christ" or for the "body of Christ" of 1 Cor. 12:12–13, into whom all have been baptized.

Analogous to Gal. 3:28 and 1 Cor. 12:13, the statement of Col. 3:11 that for the renewed self, earthly distinctions are without substance is unrelated to the train of thought of Colossians and "is doubtless adopted from tradition" (Lohse 1968, 207; cf. Klein 1961, 195). Thus 3:9b–11 essentially forms a traditional unit, and in the present epistolary context 3:11a provides the formal justification for quoting a fixed tradition in its entirety (see p. 52 above). As in 1 Cor. 12:13 and Gal. 3:28a, so also in Col. 3:11 the abolition of the difference between Jew and Greek stands at the top of the list. In the present case this statement is reinforced in two ways. "Greek and Jew" is followed chiastically by "circumcised and uncircumcised," and "uncircumcised" (literally "foreskin" in Greek) is expanded and explained with "barbarian, Scythian," two expressly pejorative examples of the uncircumcised. Thus the emphasis of all three formulas lies on the universalism that has abolished any Jewish priority "in Christ" and made even the most despised Gentiles "children of God" (Gal. 3:27) when through their "baptism into Christ" they clothe themselves "with Christ" (Gal. 3:28) or "with the new self" (Col. 3:10).

The formulaic material we have analyzed comes doubtless from the realm of Paul's conversion theology. This is sufficiently shown by the "mystical" language that completely determines all the formulas, by the emphatic dualism as the central idea of the three traditions, and by the fact that the understanding of baptism is completely within the context of ecclesiology; yet any reference to the event of Jesus' death and resurrection is still missing. It is beyond question, however, that not only Paul himself but also the traditions adopted by him related baptism "into Christ" to the Christ *Jesus* (cf. Gal. 3:26, 28b; Rom. 6:3) and understand by the "body of Christ" those who confess Jesus as the Christ, whatever form this confession may have had. This situation can also be observed in 1 Cor. 10:2, where Paul is speaking to the Gentile Christians of Corinth about the Israelites of Moses' time as "our ancestors"; he explains in traditional fashion that the generation that died in the wilderness because of its disobedience was "baptized into Moses." This expression is formed in analogy to the idea of "baptism into Christ," and since Moses is without doubt regarded not as a collective personality but as an individual person or as the transmitter of the Torah, the same idea also applies to the "Christ" (cf. 1 Cor. 10:4) as the bringer of eschatological salvation.

From the religious-historical point of view, however, we find in the analyzed formulas a "second application" of ideas and language. In the original form of the "Christ mysticism" *Christ* occurs as the sum of the pneumatics, and the "body of Christ" is formed from them as the individual members of the body. The churches that hold to this view constitute themselves through a baptism practiced as a rite of initiation. Through this baptism "into Christ" individuals are inducted into the "body of Christ"; they clothe themselves in "Christ." The "Christ" scattered in his members is restored, in that in this way the "Christ in me" becomes "I in Christ," until finally "Christ is all and in all" and all "are one in Christ." Thus with regard to the religious-historical origin of the previously investigated primitive Christian baptismal understanding, we encounter the pre-Christian "*Christos-anthrōpos* mythos" (Betz 1988, 350–51) of a Jewish Gnosticism (see pp. 64ff. above). This gnosis includes dualism and pneumatic universalism, which lies in the background of 1 Cor. 12:13; Gal. 3:28; Col. 3:11: natural and social distinctions belong to the realm of the flesh and make no difference "in Christ" or "in the Spirit."

In an encounter with that Jewish Christ-gnosis, the Damascene theology presumably of the circle of Stephen, with which Paul became acquainted as its persecutor and to whose convictions he was converted, developed the Palestinian primitive church's confession of Jesus as the Christ into a strongly anthropologically and ecclesiologically shaped theology, using preexistence or incarnation Christology, and thereby also adopted universalism (see pp. 105ff. below). This law-free, universalist church organized itself as an independent community outside the synagogue and also adopted baptism "into Christ" as the rite of initiation required for this community—

now understood as an act that places one into the community that believes in Jesus as the Christ. Likewise, it adopted the community meal of this Jewish group, in which the broken bread symbolized the multiplicity of the members and their coming together into the unity of the body of Christ (cf. 1 Cor. 10:16b–17; see pp. 246ff. below). In this process, which is to be considered religious-historically and is fundamental for the theological history of early Christianity, it was not a question of the transformation of Palestinian primitive Christianity into a Gnostic movement but of the Christian overcoming of Gnostic dualism. Here Damascene early Christianity gave up Jewish particularism and at the same time experienced a theological enrichment, as is attested especially impressively by Romans 7–8.

In this religious-historically demonstrable way, the use of baptism gained entrance into the Christian church, for it can be shown that the later development of the understanding of baptism presupposes the baptism of the Damascene churches. More extensive religious-historical inquiry discovers baptismal ritual and movements of several kinds that were widespread in Palestine at the beginning of the Christian era: John the Baptist, proselyte baptism, Mandaeans, Essenes (Qumran), and so forth (cf. 1 Cor. 15:29; Brandt 1910). In view of this, one can hardly look for a *special* origin of baptism as rite of initiation in the universalist community of Christ-Gnostics who separated from the synagogue, especially since with a dualistic group so strongly connected with Hellenistic syncretism, influences of oriental cult piety cannot be excluded. Mystery cults were also quite familiar with baptismal actions and crossed ethnic and social boundaries. A certain influence of proselyte baptism in a universalist Jewish movement is, to be sure, also possible, whereas the apocalyptically motivated baptism of John cannot have been involved.

Developments in the Early Christian Understanding of Baptism

On the one hand, the spread of the practice of baptism in the rest of Christendom and the diverging development of the understanding of baptism cannot be observed and described as a straight-line process, and such a process probably did not take place. On the other hand, we can detect individual characteristic developments in the course of which the event of baptism is integrated into a variety of soteriological and paraenetic conceptions, without it being always possible to localize or date these developments clearly. The provenance of the Damascene practice of baptism, however, can generally be recognized by the fact that the characteristic expression "into Christ" (*eis Christon*) is also maintained where the ecclesiological aspect, which was originally connected with it, is no longer apparent.

The Understanding of Baptism in the Antiochene Churches

From the previous analysis we have learned that the law-free Christian church, which organized itself outside the synagogal association, was persecuted by Paul in Damascus, and was joined by him after his conversion, constituted itself through baptism "into Christ." At the same time, the correspondingly organized Gentile Christian churches of Paul, which he founded in Asia Minor and Europe after the Apostolic Council, leave no doubt that they also receive their members through the act of baptism. That is seen with special clarity in 1 Cor. 1:13ff. Faced with the divisions among the Christians in Corinth, who attach themselves to different teachers ("I belong to Paul . . . to Apollos . . . to Cephas"), Paul argues: "Was Paul crucified for you? Or were you baptized in [*eis*] the name of Paul?" The apostle places importance on the fact that as he recalls, he baptized only Crispus and Gaius, as well as the house of Stephanas, the "first converts" in the province of Achaia (1 Cor. 16:15, "so that no one can say that you were baptized in [*eis*] my name." Thus baptism is not the task of an outstanding baptizer but of the church into which the baptized are received, for even the apostle is not sent to baptize but to proclaim (1 Cor. 1:17). In this argumentation Paul takes for granted that reception into churches of Pauline, Gentile Christian orientation occurs through baptism.

The original "into Christ" (*eis Christon*), which was presumably already used in the Damascene church in a baptismal *formula* and is still found in "original" form in Gal. 3:27 and Rom. 6:3 (cf. 1 Cor. 10:2; 12:13), became "into the name of Christ" (or "of the Lord Jesus Christ," "of the Lord Jesus," "of the Lord"), while keeping the rather unusual and not easily rendered *eis* (1 Cor. 1:13, 15; Acts 8:16; 19:5; cf. 2:38; 10:48; *Did.* 9.5; *Herm. Sim.* 3.7.3), and was finally expanded to the triadic "in[to] the name of the Father and of the Son and of the Holy Spirit" (Matt. 28:19; *Did.* 7.1, 3). Only in 1 Cor. 6:11; Acts 2:38; 10:48 do we find the usual "in the name," while the old baptismal formula with *eis* is still evident also in John 1:12; 2:23; 3:18; 1 John 5:13, which speaks of faith "in[to] the name"; and Matt. 18:20, which speaks of the gathering of Christians "in[to] my name," that is, Jesus' name. The formulation "into the name" does not come from the Septuagint, to which it is foreign, and therefore can hardly be a Semitism. In the secular Greek world it occurs as a rule when in papyri an entry of a debtor or his payment is made in this way into the account of someone's name, yet this linguistic usage in ancient commerce is too far from the application in the baptismal formula for this to have had an influence on—much less form the original source of—the use in baptism. Since "into" in the physical sense of "into the body of Christ" a part of the oldest baptismal formula, "into the name of" is apparently connected to this fixed formulation and unmistakably establishes the traditional *ecclesiological* formula *christologically*. For through the emphasis on the *name* of Jesus Christ, the christological reference of "into Christ" is made unavoidable, whether the one baptized is transferred to the Lord Jesus Christ (Heitmüller 1903), Christ's gifts of salvation are imparted to the one baptized (Delling 1961), or both viewpoints are connected. This christologically precise expansion of "into Christ," which according to 1 Cor. 1:13, 15 was also adopted by the Gentile Christian churches of Paul, probably took place at the latest when the older baptismal usage was adopted by Antiochene Christianity—a process that, to be sure, can be only partially illuminated.

In any case, however, this Antiochene Christianity had the understanding of baptism that is evident in 1 Cor. 6:11. In 6:9–10 Paul first lists the wrongdoers who will not inherit the kingdom of God: fornicators, idolaters, thieves, drunkards, and so forth; then he continues:

> And this is what some of you used to be. But you were washed, you were sanctified, you were justified in the name of the Lord Jesus Christ and in the Spirit of our God. (1 Cor. 6:11)

Thus baptism "in the name of the Lord Jesus Christ," which Paul unquestionably has in mind here, results in the washing of sins or of pagan impurity; by placing one in the church and giving a share in the Holy Spirit and his gifts, baptism effects active sanctification and righteousness—which Paul misses in some of the Corinthians. The understanding of sin and the soteriology of the present traditional formulations correspond to the theological thinking of Antiochene Christendom: the acts of sin are evident, and redemption consists in the purification of the guilt of sin, symbolized by the water bath of baptism. Though the triad "washed, sanctified, justified" is on the whole traditional, its third member in its pre-Pauline understanding must not therefore be loaded with the entire weight of the Pauline doctrine of justification (Schnelle 1983, 39ff.). The ecclesiological linking of baptism and Spirit, which was suited to the Christian practice of baptism on the basis of its origin, was retained in the soteriological expansion of the understanding of baptism in Antiochene Christianity. The interpretation of baptism as the washing away of pagan impurity or the guilt of sin is also found in Eph. 5:26; Heb. 10:22; Acts 22:16; *Barn.* 11.11 and also for this reason reveals its roots in Hellenistic Jewish Christianity.

This interpretation corresponds to the meaning of proselyte baptism, which was performed for Gentiles who converted to Judaism, after the male converts were first circumcised. The practice of proselyte baptism in the early Christian period is not attested with certainty, yet there can hardly be any doubt that already in the first century the synagogue held it necessary to purify converting Gentiles of their inherent pagan impurity (cf. Jeremias 1958, 29ff.; Schürer 1909, 181ff.). Thus there is every evidence that the Hellenistic Jewish Christian church living within the synagogal association adopted the older Damascene practice of baptism "into Christ" in order, according to the analogy of proselyte baptism, to receive as full members God-fearing Gentiles who joined them through a baptism in the "name of the Lord Jesus," even without circumcision (Brandt 1910, 59). This is suggested even more when in uncertain times God-fearing Gentiles could apparently also be "baptized" without circumcision in the synagogue itself, that is, freed from pagan impurity through a cultic bath, as Schürer (1909, 184) presumes with reference to *Sibylline Oracles* 4.164 and Epictetus *Diss.* 2.9: ". . . where full acceptance into the community of Israel did not take place, at least the water bath was required." The naming of Jesus' name over the one baptized expanded this now Christian baptism beyond the mere achievement of cultic purity to the imparting of eschatological salvation. Therefore it was not a self-baptism but was performed by the Christian church.

Thus Christian baptism does not continue the baptism of John in any apparent way. Nor does it go directly back to Jewish proselyte baptism, by which, however, it was probably influenced under the aegis of Hellenistic Jewish Christianity.

Were Jewish Christians Baptized?

The relatively straight-line development of early Christian baptismal practice and of the understanding of baptism, which the Hellenistic Jewish Christian churches first entered secondarily and in connection with their uncircumcised members, is confirmed by the observation that according to all evidence the baptism of Jewish Christians living in the synagogue was not performed for a long time. If we ignore the historically worthless information in Acts 2:38, 41, we know of no baptism of a Jewish Christian performed in the context of the synagogue, and there is little likelihood that, for example, Peter, the twelve, or the five hundred brothers of 1 Cor. 15:6 received a Christian baptism (cf. Fuller 1979). Christian baptism is unknown to the Jewish Christian Apollos (Acts 18:24–25); as a disciple of John he was not baptized but only taught. Furthermore, there are sufficient indications to assume that the lack of information on the baptism of Jewish Christians is not merely due to a lack of sources.

On the one hand, it is noteworthy that in Mark 16:15–16 and Matt. 28:19 baptism and Gentile mission are still very closely connected, and thus baptism appears to be something specifically for Gentile Christians. On the other hand, we observe that after the completion of the *aposynagōgos,* the exclusion of Christians from the synagogue in consequence of the rabbinic-Pharisaic restoration of the synagogue after A.D. 70, Jewish Christians are called upon to be baptized. Thus in John 3:1–10 (cf. 7:50–52; 9:16b; 12:42) we meet Nicodemus (as in 19:38 we find Joseph of Arimathea), who is a Jewish Christian or a sympathizer of the Christian church. Faced with threatened exclusion from the synagogue and the resulting change to the status of a persecuted Christian, Nicodemus shies away from an open confession and therefore comes to Jesus secretly by night. Jesus challenges him to make an unambiguous decision: "Very truly, I tell you, no one can enter the kingdom of God without being born of water and Spirit" (John 3:5). Thus baptism is the criterion of membership in the Christian church and hence the reason for the *aposynagōgos.* With Jewish Christians, however, it is no longer presupposed but now actually required of them.

The situation in the Gospel of Matthew is similar. One must not give too much importance to the point that Matthew has the only *command* to baptize in the New Testament, although we also must not overlook the fact that *all* nations are to be made disciples *through baptism,* according to Matt. 28:19–20. It is clear, however, that the insertion that Matthew makes in the Markan account of the baptism of Jesus by John points to the present situation:

> [14]John would have prevented him, saying, "I need to be baptized by you, and do you come to me?" [15]But Jesus answered him, "Let it be so now; for it is proper for us in this way to fulfill all righteousness." (Matt. 3:14–15)

With this insertion Matthew directs attention to the church, "which receives its practice from the exemplary actions of Jesus" (Strecker 1962, 180). Supporting this view is, first, the observation that at the beginning of this section (3:13), Matthew, going beyond his source, emphasizes Jesus' determination to be baptized, for Jesus goes to the Jordan with the definite intention of being baptized. Also supporting this view is the "us" in 3:15. The *majestic plural* assumed by some scholars would not be in keeping with the evangelist's language. It seems improbable that the "us" includes only Jesus and John and that the baptism of Jesus is thus an esoteric act, for Jesus is clearly formulating a general principle that is *also* applicable in the present case: "It is proper . . . to fulfill all righteousness." Finally, we have the support of the principle itself. As in Matt. 5:17; 23:32, *fulfill* means "leave out nothing, perform fully." In Matthew (5:6, 10, 20; 6:1, 33; 21:32) *righteousness* always means practiced piety or observance of piety (cf. Strecker 1962, 157–58). Thus the statement in 3:15 means that it is proper for Christians to perform the required practices of piety without omission and consequently above all not to forgo baptism. By his good example Jesus takes the lead; who could fail to follow him (Fridrichsen 1927, 251; Strecker 1962, 179–80)? Matthew writes his whole Gospel in the context of the expulsion of Christians from the synagogue in order to strengthen them in their tribulations and to give them a structure appropriate to their independent organization (Schmithals 1985, 374ff.). For Jewish Christians this now also includes the baptism long familiar to Gentile Christians as an unambiguous sign of confession and membership in the Christian church. This baptism had previously not been practiced within the synagogue—or at least was not obligatory—but now it becomes the criterion of whether one will remain behind as a Jew in the synagogue or go one's way as a Christian under the new conditions.

The same is true for the Letter to the Hebrews, which bears this name with good reason, for this treatise with an epistolary closing is directed toward Christians who are forced out of the synagogue in the carrying out of the *aposynagōgos* and have difficulty finding and asserting their Christian standpoint "in the world." In Heb. 6:1–2 the author summarizes the content of the "basic teaching" for those who are "still an infant," which he does not want to repeat because readers must in the meantime have made progress toward perfection (5:14), and therefore he wants to offer them "perfect" teaching. When he recalls the "foundation," he speaks of "washings" (*baptismoi*), by which he must mean "baptisms" (as the NRSV translates), for the key words of this fundamental catechism are *repentance, faith, washings/baptisms, the laying on of hands, resurrection,* and *last judgment.* Since interpreters without exception presuppose that the addressees of the Letter to the Hebrews were baptized in the usual fashion, they are justifiably puzzled by the reference to washings and the missing reference to baptism; as a rule they are content to report on the many, always unsatisfying attempts at an explanation. If we abandon the presupposition, however, the text becomes understandable. A one-time baptism can be and probably was included in the "washings," but the author does not presuppose that all Jewish Christian readers have received it; rather, he also takes into account other synagogal rites of purification, which were usual in Christian circles.

With this assumption one also does not need to deny any connection between Heb. 6:2 and the other passage in Hebrews that speaks of "washings" (*baptismoi*), as always happens, although the striking conceptual parallel makes such unrelatedness very unlikely. In Heb. 9:9–10 the author, in typological connection with the service of the Jerusalem high priest, speaks of "gifts and sacrifices" that are offered in "the present time," namely, Jewish purity regulations regarding "food and drink and various washings." They are considered temporary and are imposed "until the time comes to set things right," because they "cannot perfect the conscience." Thus the author moves forward to perfect teaching in the sense of 5:11–6:2 and classifies the precepts regarding food, drink, and washings, which had still been observed by the Christians living in the synagogue, as temporary and now surpassed. For Jewish Christians they should be replaced by the one-time purification act of baptism, which in 10:22 the author presents to the readers in Old Testament words (Lev. 8:6, 30; 16:4; etc.): "Let us approach with a true heart in full assurance of faith, with our hearts sprinkled clean from an evil conscience and our bodies washed with pure water." There is no question that the topic here is baptism. When performed externally as a water bath after making a full confession of faith—and thus "into Christ"—it means the purification of one's evil conscience, which the Jewish "washings" fail to accomplish (Heb. 9:9–10); that is, it means the forgiveness of sins. Here readers are not at all "reminded of the fact of their baptism" (H.-F. Weiss 1991, 530–31). Heb. 10:22 contains, rather, a challenge and an indirect invitation to baptism for those who have previously been satisfied with the repeated Jewish washings. Under the assumption that Jewish Christians in the Christian communities within the synagogue had as a rule not been baptized, the "baptismal teaching" of the Letter to the Hebrews is in itself conclusive and at the same time historically illuminating.

Baptized into Christ's Death: Rom. 6:3–4

As a rule, Rom. 6:1ff. is considered *the* Pauline baptismal text. This is true in the sense that in this passage Paul adopts a characteristic understanding of baptism as an important theological statement:

> [3]Do you not know that all of us who have been baptized into Christ Jesus were baptized into his death? [4]Therefore we have been buried with him by baptism into death, so that, just as Christ was raised from the dead by the glory of the Father, so we too might walk in newness of life.

What is important for Paul in this passage, however, is not baptism itself or the development of a—or his—theology of baptism but the refutation of the reproach of the synagogue, cited in Rom. 6:1 (cf. 6:15), that his teaching on grace promotes sin. For the purpose of this refutation Paul returns to the soteriological model of dying and rising with Christ (see pp. 99ff. above). This relatively early model—which can be connected with mystery piety, in spite of many objections to this view—is often used by Paul (2 Cor. 4:10ff.; 5:14–15; Gal. 2:19–20; 6:14, 17; Phil. 3:10–11, 21; Col. 2:20; 3:3ff.), because in the radicality of its conception of sin and redemption it is appropriate to the theology of the apostle. It is also found in the Gospel of Mark, where it interprets the passion event (Mark 9:26–27; 15:21; Schmithals 1986, on this passage), and on the basis of this observation is shown to be pre-Pauline, especially since it has no immediate connection with the specific

Pauline doctrine of justification as such. Since this soteriological model is expressly related to baptism only in Rom. 6:3–4 (Col. 2:12–13 is deutero-Pauline and presupposes Rom. 6:1ff.), this connection is probably not original. Thus the idea of dying and rising with Christ originally interpreted as salvation event not the act of baptism but the "for us" of the confession of Jesus' death and resurrection (see pp. 99ff. above). Yet the inclusion in 6:3–4 of baptism in such an interpretation of the confession probably does not go back only to Paul, for there is much to suggest that in Rom. 6:1ff. Paul is referring to a traditional baptismal saying (cf. Schmithals 1988b, 191) that, in contrast to Paul himself, conceives dying and rising with Christ in a purely future way:

> As many of us as are baptized into Christ Jesus
> are baptized into his death.
> But if we died with Christ,
> so we believe that we will also live with him.

In these four lines, each of which consists of five Greek words, the confession of Jesus' death and resurrection is connected with the act of baptism. Yet the saying does not presuppose an actual passion soteriology; rather, it is eschatologically oriented and is addressed to Christians in view of the fact that they may have to die before the Parousia of Jesus. Its assertion is that those who die as baptized Christians may believe that they will also live with Jesus (cf. 1 Thess. 4:13–14). Thus the saying is relatively ancient and certainly could be of Damascene origin.

Although details may remain in dispute, on the whole Rom. 6:3–4 allows us to follow part of the development of the early Christian understanding of baptism and at the same time the path that Paul took from his conversion theology in Damascus to the Hellenistic Christianity in the synagogue of Antioch. The soteriology of his conversion theology was oriented toward the incarnation, not the passion, and the baptismal formula of Damascene origin already analyzed above also does not consider the death and resurrection of Jesus. Yet in regard to the death of Christians, the reference to Jesus' dying and rising, which the Christian may emulate, could have been meaningful already at an early time. But the actual "for us" of Jesus' death and resurrection and the corresponding "death" of the old self and "resurrection" of the new "with Jesus" belong to Jewish Christianity. And Paul adopted these soteriological ideas as theological gain when he turned to Antiochene Christianity (see pp. 108ff. above). On this path—which after the more or less complete destruction of the universalist and law-critical Christian church of Damascus he naturally did not travel alone—the custom of baptism was taken along and brought up to date in the context of the Gentile mission within the synagogue. The usual description of baptism as a baptism "into Christ" and the corresponding, essentially ecclesiologically refined understanding of baptism were maintained. Yet as demonstrated by 6:3–4, the act of baptism was sooner or later connected with the originally independent soteriological motif of dying and rising with Christ, a connection that is not (yet?) present in the Antiochene understanding of baptism recognizable in 1 Cor. 6:11. This connection could possibly be related to an analogous practice in the context of the mystery cults, which bestow upon the initiate a "rebirth" into divine being (cf. Titus 3:5; John 3:3, 5; Just. *Apol.* 1.61, 66.1; *Dial.* 138.2; cf. 1 Peter 1:3, 23; 2:2; Bauer 1933, 52–53). In any case, the connection was available if one wanted to relate the action of baptism to the traditional confession of the salvific event of death and resurrection, which in this way became the baptismal confession. The baptismal rite here presupposes not the "washing" of 1 Cor. 6:11 but apparently, as in Col. 2:12 (cf. 3:9b–40), the submerging and reemerging that easily lends itself to interpretation as dying and being made alive again.

Anointing, Sealing,
Giving the Spirit: 2 Cor. 1:21–22

Relatively closely connected with the original understanding of baptism are the comments of Paul in 2 Cor. 1:21–22, which do not emphasize the motif of universalism but are still essentially ecclesiologically oriented:

> [21]But it is God who establishes us with you in Christ and has anointed us, [22]by putting his seal on us and giving us his Spirit in our hearts as the first installment.

Although this passage contains many traditional motifs, it is probably not a piece of tradition but was composed by Paul ad hoc as a solemn climax at the close of his argumentation in 1:15–22. He documents the freedom and variety in the understanding of baptism in Gentile Christianity already in the first Christian generation.

God is the producer of the salvation created in Christ (cf. 2 Cor. 4:6; 5:5, 18–19). The "establishment" (presence) in Christ is an ongoing event. It rests on the one-time act of anointing, sealing, and giving the Spirit (in the aorist form). With these words Paul is thinking without doubt of baptism, as signalized already by the words "in [*eis*] Christ." Yet in its details the interpretation is not easy. Does "anointing" designate baptism itself, but "sealing" and "giving the Spirit" the effects of baptism? Or do anointing, sealing, and giving the Spirit stand in parallel and name different significances of baptism? Apart from the fact that an anointing could have been connected with baptism, the idea that anointing and sealing refer to particular actions in addition to the not even mentioned act of baptism is in any case quite unlikely, because the giving of the Spirit is certainly not such an additional act.

From the beginning the *giving of the Spirit* was a part of the Christian understanding of baptism, as 1 Cor. 12:12–13 shows. According to the general early Christian conception, the giving of the Spirit does not occur as the handing over of the Spirit to the individual being baptized; rather, the person receives a share in the Spirit and his gifts when baptism places her or him into the church, which "has" the Spirit. The Spirit is the "first installment" (cf. 2 Cor. 5:5; Eph. 1:14; Rom. 8:23) with respect to the eschatological completion of salvation; the reference to the "first installment" brings to bear the eschatological reservation vis-à-vis an enthusiastic understanding of the Spirit. *Sealing* is an act of taking possession; the seal names the owner and confirms his or her possession. Presumably Paul is alluding to the fact that baptism "into Christ" occurs with the naming of the name *Christ* (cf. 1 Cor. 1:13ff.), by which the one baptized is made the property of the Lord Christ. With this the ecclesiological aspect of baptism is superseded and the personal relationship of the one baptized to Christ is emphasized. With *anointing,* an act of cultic purification, kings, priests, and prophets were consecrated to their service and office in Old Testament times. Does baptism with water as a corresponding act of purification then exalt the one baptized as a "child of God" (cf. Gal. 3:26; 4:4–5; Rom. 8:15; 1 John 2:20, 27)? Or is the idea simply the purifying power of the baptismal water (1 Cor. 6:11; Eph. 5:26; Titus 2:14)?

Conclusion

The practice of Christian baptism was adopted from a Jewish Gnostic baptismal sect in the early universalistic church of Damascene provenance, which was led presumably by Stephen and the circle of "the seven." From the beginning the substantial, mythological understanding of baptism as transference into the restored spiritual body of Christ had a historical (*geschichtlich*), ecclesiological aspect as the eschatological gift of God in the context of the early Christian confession of Christ Jesus and the Holy Spirit. In the course of further development and the expansion of the practice of baptism into the realm of Hellenistic Christianity of Antiochene provenance, there was in various ways a christological and soteriological deepening of the understanding of baptism: dying and rising with Christ, death of the old self and birth of the new, bathing as rebirth, washing away of pagan sins, transfer of the one baptized to the Lord Jesus or transfer of the gifts of Christ to the one baptized, and so forth. The ecclesiological starting point of baptism was always maintained: baptism is conversion baptism and presupposes a public confession of faith; baptism admits one into the new people of God, the Christian church, which performs the baptismal act, and grants one a share in the gifts of the Holy Spirit, whom the individual Christian does not "have" but who is alive in the church. This process explains why for a long time Jewish Christians, who continued to be members of the synagogue and thus made no crossover, by all appearances were not as a rule baptized. In the early Christian period no magical effect of baptism *ex opere operato* can be observed. The triadic expansion of the baptismal formula "into Christ" or "in the name of Jesus" and so forth (Matt. 28:19; *Did.* 7.1; Just. *Apol.* 1.61) does not mean a profound change in the understanding of baptism; it is, rather, only a new expression of the conviction, which existed from the beginning, that Christian baptism conveys the salvation of *God* that is found in *Jesus Christ* and is manifested in the gifts of the *Holy Spirit.*

12

On the Problem of Baptizing Children in Early Christianity

In 1958 J. Jeremias initiated a discussion on the baptism of children in the first four centuries that today has still not come to an end. Jeremias comes to the conclusion that from the beginning, the church also baptized small children. The most thorough disagreement with this thesis came in 1961 from K. Aland. He concludes that the baptism of infants in the New Testament and in the early church was not at all usual. Jeremias and Aland use the same sources and proceed according to the same historical methods, but they come to diametrically opposite conclusions.

These opposite results can also be achieved with less scholarly effort. One side argues with Mark 16:16, which reads: "The one who believes and is baptized will be saved," and reasons that baptism of small children is excluded in the early Christian period because they cannot believe yet. Others, by contrast, point to the fact that in the New Testament all members of the community are considered baptized, and since without question children of all ages also belonged to the community, they were doubtless also baptized. Such contrary conclusions warn against saying that one side or the other is absolutely correct. They suggest, rather, that the basic issue underlying this alternative is either wrongly or too little differentiated and that the solution to the problem is more complicated than this simple either-or makes it seem.

It is no accident that Jeremias began his examination with a differentiated statement of the issue. He distinguishes between, on the one hand, the *conversion baptism* of Jews and Gentiles who after their catechumenate join the Christian church and, on the other, the *baptism of Christians,* that is, of children who were born into Christian families. With *conversion,* according to Jeremias, the children are also baptized without distinction with regard to age. Children who are born into Christian families, by contrast, were not initially baptized. He infers this above all from 1 Cor. 7:14, where Paul first explains that in the marriage of a Christian with a non-Christian the unbelieving partner is "made holy" through the believing one. This principle is apparently adopted from the liberal synagogue, according to which such mixed marriages do not defile the Jewish partner (cf. *1 Clem.* 46.2; *Herm. Vis.* 3.6; *Sim.* 8.8). In 1 Cor. 7:14 Paul then underlines this judgment with an assertion also taken from the Hellenistic synagogue: "Otherwise, your children would be unclean, but as it is, they are holy." J. Weiss (1910, 182) observes that this argumentation "makes sense only if the baptism of children was not yet the custom in the church. For if holiness was not bestowed on the child until baptism, Paul could not prove here what he wants to prove, that the holiness of a Christian is transferred without further ado to those who are close to him [or her] or that the holiness emanating from the Christian is stronger than the 'impurity' emanating from the unbelieving partner." Jeremias agrees with this, yet not in regard to the children who are involved in the *conversion* of an entire family.

If we want to understand this distinction and consider it probable, we must liberate ourselves from the modern idea of the free individual personality and its subjective conviction of faith. Much more than modern people, the ancients were part of a social community and especially part of a "house." The religious connection was also thoroughly communal. In this regard, the children in particular did not possess any independent personal rights vis-à-vis the head of the family.

This means, first, that if a household converted to Christianity, the children were doubtless not left behind. If the house was constituted as a Christian house church through baptism, the children also received their share of the gifts of baptism. Whether and how this baptism was performed in the case of individual children must remain unanswered; here we know nothing. The practice probably varied according to the specific understanding of baptism. In any case, the formal rite of baptism after declaring one's confession of faith was not necessarily performed on children and infants in the same way as adults. Based on a comparison of 1 Cor. 1:16 with Acts 18:8, Aland (1961, 61) concludes that only the head of the family received baptism as the representative of the whole household. This possibility cannot be excluded and would correspond completely with the corporate thinking of antiquity. Hence the concept of child baptism must be understood very broadly and did not necessarily always include an act of baptism performed personally on individual children when a family converted. The father or parents could have represented the whole "house of God."

This also means, however, that if children are born to Christian parents, through their birth and from birth on they share in the gifts of baptism that are present and active in their family. Children born or adopted into this salvific community of God's people share in the gifts that are alive in the community; a member is added to the body of Christ. How could such children be conceived and born and grow up outside the influence of the Holy Spirit that is at work in a Christian house? The necessity of a special baptism for individuals who have newly entered the community through their birth was probably not felt at all when the house itself based its Christian nature on the act of baptism. They stood under the blessing that baptism had bestowed on the house in which they grew up, even if they had not been individually baptized.

Jewish proselyte baptism forms a certain analogy with this double point of view. Gentiles converting to Judaism, along with their children, were purified from pagan impurity through immersion in a bath; children born *after* the conversion naturally remained unbaptized. In any case, in view of ancient cultic solidarity, the idea that with conversion one left a child at first outside of this solidarity until the child was later accepted into the religious fellowship of the family through a "believer's baptism" is just as anachronistic as the assumption that the immature children born of Christian parents had to be admitted into the Christian community through a special act of baptism.

Against the view that the children born to Christian parents were not baptized at all in the early period of Christianity one cannot argue that Paul already presupposes that all members of the church to whom he is writing are baptized Christians. Apart from the fact that this observation was probably valid for the Gentile Christian churches of Paul but not necessarily also for all the Christians in Rome (cf. Rom. 6:3; see p. 214 above), the fact that at the conversion of Gentiles in Paul's church they were baptized does not allow the conclusion that the children born later were also given a supplementary baptism. The children born after conversion were still too small to be addressed by Paul in his letters. Above all, however, Paul is not looking at all at the baptism of each individual when he sees and addresses the Christian church as the multitude of the baptized. Baptism constituted the Christian church and the house church. Even when it was not properly performed on every member of the house church, every member of the house still shared in its gifts. When in 1 Cor. 10:1ff. Paul chooses the passage through the Red Sea as the type of Christian baptism and explains that *all* of the ancestors were baptized in the sea, this "all" does not exclude, on the one hand, the children of all ages also taken through the sea or, on the other hand, the children of the wilderness generation of Israel born *after* the passage through the sea. This "baptism into Moses" was valid for the *community* of the people Israel, which was led by him into freedom and in the wilderness sinned and was punished, not its individual members as such.

Therefore the combination of word, faith, baptism, salvation, which occurs expressly in this way in Eph. 1:13–14 and describes the way of the Christian to salvation, also does not exclude the children of those who have come to salvation, even if the ritual of baptism has not been performed on them at the conversion of the house or after their birth. The same is true of the statement in Col. 2:12 and Eph. 4:4–5 that the *one* church, which lives in the *one* Spirit of the *one* Lord, also knows *one* baptism. Such statements in no way assert that the children born *in* this one church are also baptized themselves. And based on general considerations, it is unlikely that it happened, for what would be the purpose of a special baptism of those who grew up "in the Spirit" as children of the church and members of the body of Christ, when a personal subsequent baptism could not give them more than they had always had? From this state of affairs it is easy to explain why in the New Testament the command to baptize and the command to evangelize are almost exclusively linked with each other (Mark 16:15–16; Matt. 28:19): baptism existed only as conversion baptism; there is no evidence of a baptism of Christians.

For Jeremias the justifiable distinction between the baptism of children at conversion and the forgoing of baptism for children born Christian applies only to the earliest period of the church. He is convinced that the Christian church "at some time between A.D. 60 and 70 moved from the baptism of the children of converts (practiced from the beginning) also to the baptism of children born in the church — and as infants!" (1958, 68). Thus already in the second generation a *unified* practice of baptizing children and infants can be ascertained. Aland rejects Jeremias's distinction and disputes the idea that before the end of the second century there was any form of child baptism in Christendom. Hence the opposing views of the two scholars, which each represent a direction in research, are joined by the common conviction that with regard to baptism, the children who came into the church and those who were born into it were treated *in the same way* from the beginning (Aland) or soon thereafter (Jeremias). Yet this presupposition may be false and may have contributed substantially to the sharp opposition between the views.

Both scholars recognize that from neither the first nor the second century do we have direct testimonies for or against the baptism of children or infants. When we consider that baptism as such is often mentioned and that in such cases in this period it is always a question of conversion baptism, although many Christian generations had been born, then for a long time the question of child baptism must not have been a problem, or the solution to the problem must have been unproblematic. *The simplest explanation of this fact, however, is that the understanding of baptism was still determined by the corporate thinking of antiquity and thus children naturally received their share of the baptismal gift of their own house community, that is, the children of converts through the baptismal act, however carried out in detail, and the children of Christians through their original membership in a baptized house church.* This view of the situation is supported by various observations.

From the second century there are a number of statements by or about leading Christians, especially martyrs, that tell how these church members were Christians from the time they were small. The later martyr Justin, for example, mentions around 155 "many men and women aged sixty or seventy who were instructed from childhood as disciples of Christ" (*Apol.* 1.15.6). From such statements Jeremias concludes that they were baptized as small children. Aland counters that in none of the numerous relevant passages is baptism mentioned; thus these Christians were probably baptized at a later age. Aland is without question correct: there is never a mention of baptism, either child baptism or "believer" baptism. But how can we explain that these Christians, who were born Christian, stereotypically refer to their Christian education as a child but never to their baptism? Yet the latter would have to have been the case if personal baptism had been the decisive act of their becoming Christian, whether it was child baptism, as Jeremias holds, or adult baptism, as Aland maintains. The answer to this question is obvious: these Christians who were already born as Christians were not personally baptized at all. They emphasize that they were already born into the Christian church and even in old age or under the threat of martyrdom did not want to surrender the faith that had always determined their life. Thus from childhood on they shared in the gifts of baptism, which was bestowed on their house by parents or ancestors, but which they still know even in their time as a performed act only at the conversion of non-Christians to the church, not as a baptism that is performed on *Christians* as children or adults.

From the beginning of the third century we have the baptismal instructions of the church order of Hippolytus, according to which children—including infants who cannot make their own confession of faith and for whom the parents must answer the baptismal questions if they are not yet able to talk—are to be baptized *before* the adult men and women, who have already completed a catechumenate of several years. These precepts, however, as Jeremias (1958, 85ff.) has correctly observed, refer to the practice of the conversion baptism of whole houses on Easter morning, not to the baptism of newborn Christians. Yet Jeremias (1962a, 25) believes it probable "that Christian parents also had their newborn children baptized at the Easter baptism." Nevertheless, this is pure speculation. The fact is, however, that the oldest traditional baptismal order, which comes from the time around 215, speaks of the baptism of children only with the conversion of house communities and at the same time presupposes such baptism as normal; on the baptism of children born as Christians, however, it is *still* silent.

In this connection, it is important to observe that the infant baptism of Christians, when we have certain information about it, takes place according to the rite of conversion baptism. This becomes especially clear in the fact that two sponsors must appear, although with infants they cannot in any way fulfill their actual function of accompanying adult baptismal candidates during their usual three years of catechumenate and, after this time of testing and before the baptism, giving their testimony in favor of the candidate. There was, however, never an original service baptism for small children. In my opinion, this necessarily means that the baptism of newborn Christians became established after baptism had otherwise already been established in a fixed and inviolable order with a regulated catechumenate, as was required for conversion baptism.

Around the beginning of the third century Tertullian, in his work *On Baptism,* demanded a postponement of baptism for little children, who should first come to a recognition of the truth of faith for themselves. Jeremias (1958, 95ff.) correctly concludes that this demand presupposes the baptism of infants and small children as the normal practice of the church, which Tertullian, however, regards as problematic. Yet Jeremias also sees that in this work Tertullian has only conversion baptism in mind, in which children belonging to the family are also baptized without consideration of their age. He does not express himself on the baptism of Christian children, and we may assume that he never dealt with their baptism.

Nonetheless, in his later writing *On the Soul* Tertullian reflects in one passage (39.3–40.1) on the children who are born in Christian houses. This passage is not easy to understand and is variously interpreted. He turns his attention first toward the pagan practices that are usual after birth and through which the demons are, as it were, enticed to take possession of the child. Then he says, logically:

> Therefore there is, at least among pagans, in effect no pure birth. For in regard to this the apostle explains [1 Cor. 7:14] that a sanctified mixed marriage produces saints, both because of the Christian descent and because of instruction in Christian teachings; otherwise children are born impure. [Paul] wanted to be understood to the effect that the children of Christians are, so to speak, designated for sanctification and thereby also for salvation. . . . He also had in mind the saying of the Lord [John 3:5]

that only one who is born of water and the Spirit will enter the kingdom of God. Thus every soul is entered under Adam and impure until it has been transcribed into Christ.

Thus Tertullian is warning against regarding being born a Christian and being brought up in a Christian house as a guarantee of Christian salvation. Such a birth and upbringing let one expect salvation, but it is attained only through the personal rebirth that is the topic in John 3:1ff. Since both Aland and Jeremias presuppose that Tertullian related the saying in John 3:5 to baptism, they assume the baptism of Christian children of his time, but Jeremias assumes their baptism right after birth, and Aland understands them to be baptized as adults. It is doubtless more likely that Tertullian demands the postponement of the baptism of children from converted families. It is very doubtful, however, that this presupposition is correct, as even today the connection of John 3:5 with baptism is denied by many interpreters. Therefore, in our passage also, Tertullian is in fact probably not thinking at all of a baptism of children but of rebirth. The children born in Christian houses are by birth and upbringing designated for faith but not therefore also for the baptism that is practiced with conversion to the church.

Around the year 250 Origen refers many times in his writings to the ecclesiastical practice of also baptizing little children. He presupposes this practice as natural and uncontroversial, and with it he substantiates the Christian teaching of the general sinfulness of humankind and the defiling of the newborn by the sinful world. There is no indication, however, that he is thinking of the baptism of Christian children, who naturally were not born "into the sinful world" but into the church, as well as the baptism of converted pagans. Regarding the children of Christians, he may have had the same thoughts as Tertullian. In any case, in his interpretation of Matt. 20:1–16 he relates the workers who worked from the first hour of the day to those who were believers from childhood on and were called from the earliest age to be servants in the kingdom of God; he does not mention a personal baptism.

Christian grave inscriptions from the third century play a large role in the discussion on the baptism of children. Yet in their brevity they say little. With the inscriptions that expressly attest that children of different ages were baptized shortly before their death, it is probably, as Jeremias (1958, 88ff.) assumes, a question of inscriptions placed by the parents of catechumens, who were perhaps also baptized with their sick children. Thus we are again in the realm of conversion baptism. If, however, a deceased two-year-old Zosimos is called "believer from believers" and three twelve-year-old boys are called "believers from birth," then it is without doubt a matter of children of Christian parents, but not necessarily, as both Jeremias and Aland assume, of individually baptized children. The two inscriptions, which are silent about baptism, suggest more probably that the term *believer* is rooted in the children's belonging to a Christian house fellowship, not in a completed baptism. Thus an early Christian child sarcophagus shows two pictures related to the dead child: Jesus as teacher and the raising of Lazarus; Christian upbringing lets one expect the resurrection from the dead. There is no reference to baptism.

In general it is striking how strongly baptism in the early period of the church is always and naturally sought in the case of non-Christians (Matt. 28:16ff.), but for Christian children it is emphatically the proper upbringing "in the Lord" that is required (1 Tim. 3:4; Titus 1:6; *1 Clem.* 21.8; Pol. *Phil.* 4.2; *Barn.* 19.5; *Did.* 4.9), and their baptism is never mentioned. The apologist Aristides explains (15.11) that when a child is born to Christians, they thank God. Felicity, a martyr in the third century, is reported to have given birth in prison to a child, whom she entrusted to a sister's care and upbringing. Such examples could be multiplied. Christian children are mentioned often; their baptism never.

Yet is at least the African bishop Cyprian not a definite witness for the baptism of Christian children? In the spring of 252 he tells his colleague Fidus (Ep. 64)—if we may assume the genuineness and integrity of the writing—that a synod in Carthage has decided that children should be baptized on the second or third day after birth; Fidus waited at least until the eighth day. We do not know the precise reason for this controversy. That it is a question of the baptism of children from Christian households is not expressly said. Cyprian's argumentation that if one baptizes sinful adults, one must not hold back the children and infants corresponds to the situation of conversion baptism—in which Fidus possibly, like Tertullian, practiced a postponement of the baptism of children—but not the situation of "consecrated" parents. In any case, however, Cyprian's *argumentation* concerns the question of the *principle* of child baptism, which, if the baptism of *Christian* children was open to debate, was not uncontroversial in North Africa around the year 250 but rather was in the initial stages of becoming established. Thus if Cyprian is a witness for the practice of baptizing Christian children, this is not sufficient reason to assume the practice for the whole of Christendom around the middle of the third century.

It seems, on the contrary, that in broad areas of the church it was not until in the fourth century, after the end of the persecutions, that the baptism of *Christian* children became customary. Jeremias (1958, 102ff.) lists the following theologians born after the year 329 in a household that was already Christian, whom we know were not baptized as small children: Basil the Great, Ambrose, Chrysostom, Jerome, Rufinus, Paul of Nola, and Gregory of Nazianzus, the son of a bishop. Jeremias concludes from this that there must have been a crisis in the baptism of children in the fourth century; baptism was postponed, he says, because sins after baptism were felt to be especially serious. But if such a consideration might have occasionally played a role also with pagans inclined toward conversion, such as Emperor Constantine (cf. Jeremias 1958, 102; also Augustine *Confessions* 1.11), it would have had little meaning for Christians, especially in the age of a developed institution of penance. Actually, Jeremias (1958, 107) also concedes that the baptism of children even with the conversion of pagans was still the usual case. Aland (1961, 72) more justifiably holds Jeremias's "postponement" in the alleged "crisis in baptism" of the fourth century to be "the last epoch of early church practice" of baptizing children only after they are grown. Against this explanation, however, we must argue that this practice is attested in the first two or three centuries of Christendom with as little certainty as the baptism of the small children of Christians, which according to Jeremias is supposed to have fallen into a crisis at the beginning of the fourth century.

Actually, we may have come upon the last remnants of the early church practice of not baptizing the children of Christians at all. Then the wrongly named "postponement of baptism" of the fourth century shows that even Christians who had not previously known the baptism of their children went over to baptizing, or having themselves baptized—and at an age at which they, like pagan converts, could attend catechism instruction for adults. Only toward the end of the fourth century, after this transition period, was there a general trend toward baptizing Christian children and soon also infants. At this point, in the developing popular church more than a small role was probably played by the legal consideration that only baptism could identify Christians as such publicly. The fact that in this way the baptism of infants, but not the "believer baptism" of adults, became generally customary shows how little the practice of baptism, even after the era of persecution, was influenced by modern-style individualism and how much it was determined by corporate thinking. The supporting and shaping power of the faith given to the church and practiced in community remained determinative in the baptism of infants and was not overshadowed by the subjective decision of individual adults.

Conclusion

In view of the meager source situation, which offers us only texts that require interpretation in regard to the practice of baptism, the foregoing overview of selected important texts and developments in the practice of baptism cannot claim to expound more than a substantiated possibility in the early Christian history of the baptism of children. This picture is less familiar than the opposing pictures sketched by Jeremias and Aland. But in my view the reconstruction of the development of early Christian baptismal practice offered here does greater justice to the texts and the historical circumstances than interpretations that force a differentiated history into a false antithesis achieved on the basis of a modern point of view. Without doubt, baptism became very early the unavoidable entrance into the Christian community, but one must not regard this event in early Christendom with the presuppositions of the modern conception of personhood. The children of converts received their full share in the baptismal gift, even if they were not baptized individually. From this same point of view, it is understandable that children who were born in Christian houses to Christian parents were considered members of the Christian church, even if they had been baptized neither as infants nor as adults. Baptismal solidarity encompassed the whole church and also included children who were not even born yet: "Repent, and be baptized every one of you in the name of Jesus Christ so that your sins may be forgiven; and you will receive the gift of the Holy Spirit. For the promise is for you, *for your children* . . ." (Acts 2:38–39).

13

The Origin and Development of the Early Christian Celebratory Meal

The tradition of the Lord's Supper reveals essential aspects of early Christian theological history. If we want to uncover and reconstruct this history on the basis of the Last Supper texts, it behooves us not to begin with the "words of institution" that are handed down in 1 Cor. 11:23b–25 and Mark 14:22–24 par. These words, which are strongly shaped by Hellenistic Christianity, already stand at the end of a lengthy developmental phase and are not yet presupposed in other meal traditions such as 1 Cor. 10:16b–17 and the core of *Did.* 9.1–10.6. Even less appropriate is the *context* of the words of institution, Jesus' last meal, as the point of departure for an analysis of the meal tradition. For the narrative of Jesus' farewell repast with his disciples does not appear independently on one of the levels of tradition that precedes the Last Supper texts, but only in connection with the words of institution *as* their context. Hence the context must be interpreted on the basis of these words, rather than the words being explained on the basis of their context. In general, it is only with difficulty that one can historically reconstruct even the idea of a farewell meal that Jesus, in expectation of his imminent arrest and condemnation to death, prepares and celebrates with his disciples. The scene of a final supper in which Jesus institutes a meal to be repeated in remembrance of his imminent salvific death is entirely a cult legend, not a historical report.

The Eschatological Meal of Hope

It is helpful to note that in the various accounts of the early Christian meal celebrations there is always a clear expression of eschatological, apocalyptic expectation that is asserted alongside or in opposition to other elements of the celebration. "For underlying the Lord's Supper is the idea of the messianic meal that, in the apocalyptic view, the Messiah will celebrate with his own in the eschatological kingdom" (Werner 1959, 111). Therefore we are probably more likely to find the original significance of the early Christian celebratory meal in this expectation, since the beginning of Christian theological history is in general filled with eschatological, apocalyptic expectation (see chapter 1).

1 Corinthians 11:26

In this passage, after the traditional words of institution, we find the following explanation:

> For as often as you eat this bread and drink the cup, you proclaim the Lord's death until he comes.

This explanation was probably not formed ad hoc by Paul, for it has no connection with the Corinthian situation, which is on Paul's mind; therefore it is not taken up in the following discussion in 11:27ff. It explains, however, the repeated words, "Do this in remembrance of me" (11:24, 25); thus it presupposes this way of interpreting the words of institution and was possibly originally connected with it. In any case, even if the explanation in 11:26 originally came from Paul himself, it was probably part of the tradition that Paul had once passed on to the Corinthians (11:23). It guards against the possible misunderstanding—related to Hellenistic meals in memory of the dead—that the statement that the meal is celebrated in remembrance of Jesus means that it is to be celebrated as a memorial to something that is past or someone who has died. The remembrance accompanying the celebratory meal is, rather, the *bringing to mind* ("you proclaim") of the salvific death of Jesus, whom the church knows as its resurrected Lord ("the Lord's death") in their midst, "until he comes." This clause, "until he comes," which is superfluous for the explanation as such and yet is placed in the important final position, apparently has the purpose of maintaining the original eschatological, apocalyptic orientation of the Lord's Supper celebration, which is not expressed in the words of institution themselves.

Mark 14:25

In this passage the situation is similar, even if it is not possible to establish with any certainty the tradition history of this logion:

> Truly I tell you, I will never again drink of the fruit of the vine until that day when I drink it new in the kingdom of God.

This saying is often held to be the remnant of an old account of a farewell meal of Jesus. Such a view is suggested by the observation that such a meal, if it took place, was probably defined by apocalyptic expectation (see pp. 8ff. above). In this case, however, the original historical context of this passage would be lost, for what we now read in Mark 14:12ff. is directed toward the Passover meal, the designation of the betrayer, and the institution of the holy Eucharist, not toward a festive, apocalyptically oriented, farewell meal, at which wine was drunk. Moreover, apocalyptic imminent expectation is not evident in Mark 14:25. This farewell saying is, however, directly connected with 14:23–24, for it presupposes that *beforehand* Jesus enjoyed wine. Therefore, those who hold the words of institution to be authentic understandably retain 14:25 in its present "historical" situation. The words of institution, however, belong to an advanced stage of theological history. Also, the language of 14:25 is completely determined by the Greek translation of the Old Testament, and the expression *drink it new* does not translate at all back into Aramaic (Jeremias 1967, 174ff.); thus 14:25 was apparently originally formulated in

Greek. Here the term *new,* as in Mark 1:27; 2:21–22; 16:17, designates eschatological newness (cf. 2 Cor. 5:17) and consequently reveals an advanced stage of theological reflection. This suggests that 14:25 was not only brought into the Gospel together with the words of institution but also first formed on this occasion.

One way or the other, it is evident that Mark 14:25, like 1 Cor. 11:26 and more exclusively than that explanation, is intended to maintain and express the eschatological, apocalyptic dimension of the original meal celebration, which is no longer found in the words of institution themselves. This happens in a way that is directly connected with the celebratory meal of the church, for if Jesus will drink the wine *again* in the kingdom of God, the meal that he holds with his disciples is the earthly anticipation of the eschatological banquet.

Didache *9.1–10.7*

Especially instructive, and yet also especially controversial, is the Lord's Supper text in *Did.* 9.1–10.7. According to *Did.* 9.1 this section contains an *order* for the celebration of the Lord's Supper with the obligatory liturgical sections: 9.2 contains a prayer over the cup, 9.3 over the bread, and 9.4 an interpretive word about the bread in the form of a prayer; 9.5 forbids the admission of unbaptized people to the Lord's Supper. In 10.1–5 there is a three-part prayer of thanksgiving that assumes that the meal has already taken place. In 10.6 the liturgy ends with a closing in responsive form.

The relationship of the texts to prayer formulas of early Judaism is in places very close, without having to leave the realm of the Hellenistic synagogue and go back into the world of Semitic language; the terms *immortality* (10.2) and *spiritual food and drink* (10.3) suggest the influence of mystery piety. The words of institution and reference to a farewell meal of Jesus are completely missing, which leads some scholars to an explanation with arcane discipline and moves others to question whether the present agenda is concerned at all with the celebration of the Eucharist. Both responses are arbitrary, since the present liturgy also lacks any reference to Jesus' death and the soteriology connected with his death. In general, the theological traditions of the *Didache* do not go beyond the call to repentance in view of the coming turn of the age (cf. *Did.* 16.8), and thus one must not assume for the celebratory meal any further stage of development in theological history.

We have here, rather, a meal tradition whose foundation and origin are older than our familiar words of institution. This tradition is entirely defined by an eschatological, apocalyptic expectation that recedes in the later pieces of the liturgy but, as before, determines the character of the celebration. The church of the *Didache* knows that its members are scattered worldwide, and in this context, 9.4 interprets the bread broken and consumed in the celebratory meal with a widespread conception of the eschatological gathering of the elect (cf. *Odes Sol.* 10.5; Mark 13:27 par.; 2 Thess. 2:1; Clerici 1966):

> As this piece of bread was scattered on the mountains and was brought together into one bread, so may your church be gathered together from the ends of the earth into your kingdom.

This idea is taken up in the prayer after the meal (10.5):

> . . . and bring it together from the four winds into your kingdom, which you have prepared for it.

Accordingly, the celebration closes with a section that presumably is to be read responsively (*Did.* 10.6; cf. Lietzmann 1926, 236–37):

LITURGIST: Let grace [that is, the Lord] come and this world pass away.

CONGREGATION: Hosanna to the God of David.

LITURGIST: Let those who are holy come forward; let those who are not do penance. Marana tha.

CONGREGATION: Amen.

The words "Let those who are holy come forward; let those who are not do penance" are usually interpreted as referring to admission to the actual meal and exclusion from it. Yet that means that the whole of 10.6 must be placed before the meal activity, that is, before 10.1–5, unless this meal activity did not take place until after 10.6, both of which would be arbitrary and forced in view of the present instructive text arrangement and course of the meal. Actually, however, it is an anachronism to think at all in terms of a "coming forward" to the meal during the eucharistic celebration. And the baptized are naturally admitted without exception to the meal (cf. 9.5), as long as there has been no excommunication. Church members who are quarreling with one another are not to forgo the "coming forward" but to stay away from the meal celebration altogether (14.2). Also the unison "amen" of the gathered church does not exclude their being divided beforehand into guests and nonguests. Therefore the "coming forward" refers without question to the desired coming of grace, or the Lord. Those who are holy may approach "grace," the coming kingdom of God. Sinners, by contrast, should do timely penance, for "maranatha" ("the Lord is here") can be understood as comforting for the holy but, as in 1 Cor. 16:22, admonishing for sinners: "The Lord is near" (Phil. 4:5). Thus the responsive passage that closes the meal celebration in 10.6 is not directed toward the meal itself but uniformly toward the imminent eschaton and in this way provides a meaningful closing to the celebratory meal.

For this meal is neither a love feast nor a cultic meal that mediates salvation but, as in Mark 14:25, the anticipated eschatological banquet. The point here is not an interpretation of the "elements" or the ritual (the breaking of bread); the festal meal as such points to the eschatological culmination. The new age is often presented in the image of a festal meal or banquet in apocalyptic Judaism and correspondingly in early Christianity (Isa. 25:6; *1 Enoch* 62.14; Luke 13:28–29 par.; 14:15ff. par.; 22:29–30 par.; Mark 14:25 par.). According to Rev. 3:20 the coming Lord stands at the door of the church gathered in Laodicea and knocks, in order to have a meal with those who open the door: the earthly meal of the gathered church and the eschatological banquet are very closely connected with each other.

The beatitude of Rev. 19:9 is also to be heard in this context: "Blessed are those who are invited to the marriage supper of the Lamb."

The traditions adopted by the meal agenda of the *Didache* do not immediately reveal their time and place of origin, yet we can strongly affirm for them what is also true, as a rule, of the other traditions adopted by the *Didache*. In them we find traditions from Jewish Christian circles of the Greek-speaking synagogues in Palestine and neighboring Syria, traditions that have been resistant to the Hellenistic soteriology of Antiochene provenance (see pp. 91ff. above), and even more to Pauline Gentile Christianity, and have persisted in the original eschatological, apocalyptic expectation of the coming *Kyrios* (*Did.* 16.8). The eschatology and accordingly the custom of the meal in the churches of the apocalyptist John probably go back to this Palestinian Jewish Christianity, as has often been rightly assumed, even if Revelation betrays stronger influences from Hellenistic soteriology than does the *Didache*.

There is no need to doubt that the custom of a meal that brings the church together in anticipation of the eschatological salvation banquet goes back to the Jerusalem primitive church. The narrative of the Emmaus disciples who recognize Jesus in the breaking of the bread (Luke 24:30–31, 35), which was adopted and strongly reworked by the third evangelist, could reflect such a Jerusalem meal. In any case, such a meal corresponds completely to the apocalyptic expectation of the Parousia of the risen Jesus, who has been exalted as the *Kyrios Christos;* the participants probably became sated on the bread and also drank the festal wine when available. This meal did not have a special cult legend or "words of institution," and there is no adequate support for the view that before his death Jesus himself commissioned the disciples to regularly anticipate the eschatological banquet until the coming of the kingdom of God (Patsch 1972, 106ff.).

The idea that with its meal celebration the church continued a special table fellowship with the earthly Jesus (cf. Lietzmann 1926, 249; Nagel 1962, 9ff.), which had already been given an appropriate apocalyptic shape, cannot be excluded, but it cannot be verified by our sources. The old traditions of the sayings source do not contain a corresponding meal custom, and Jesus' table fellowship with sinners (Mark 2:13–17; cf. Luke 15:2; 19:6–7) and his meals with the Pharisees (Luke 7:36; 14:1) or with friends (Mark 14:3–9 par.; Luke 10:38–42), however one evaluates the named traditions historically, have no eschatological character and are out of the question as a model for the corresponding meal celebrations in the primitive church. Also, the assumption that the custom of the anticipatory eschatological banquet first came into being in the Easter church, when it was convinced that Jesus was the first fruits of the dead, would be a sufficient and at the same time enlightening explanation of the early meal custom.

The Meal with the Broken Bread

The observation that the eschatological significance of the Lord's Supper celebration is not found *within* the words of institution, but rather is attached to them, tells us that there is no direct path leading from the community meal held in eschatological, apocalyptic expectation to the meal custom that is attested to us by the words of institution handed down in the Hellenistic churches. Therefore the analysis of the Lord's Supper tradition must begin anew with the words of institution. Here, following the rules of form history, we must first leave the context of the words of institution unconsidered (Lohse 1964, 51). But even the words of institution themselves do not form an original unit, as the following comment shows:

> I cannot by any means consider the pairing *sōma-haima,* which occurs only in the Last Supper, to be original; rather I see in the *haima* saying an old — pre-Pauline — formation analogous to the *sōma* saying, which was probably stimulated by the farewell saying about not drinking anymore and perhaps was supposed to replace it. The *sōma* saying, taken in itself, does not refer to death; according to language usage, no one could think about it with *breaking* and without the *haima* saying no one would think about it. One would recall only the saying about breaking one's bread with the hungry (Isa. 58:7) and other sayings, as well as the term *perusa* for the Jewish blessing of the bread. The—in my view, pre-Pauline—saying, "This is my body," was probably reinterpreted by Paul. If this is the case, what it originally meant can no longer be determined; I am not convinced by any of the attempted interpretations. (Soden 1931, 29)

One can disagree with Soden about the age of the farewell saying in Mark 14:25 (see pp. 239–40 below), but he observes with justification the incongruity of the pairing of body *(sōma)* and blood *(haima)* and therefore postulates correctly an original independent bread meal with an interpretive saying that brought bread and body together. This bread meal apparently included the ritual of breaking the bread, for which there is no corresponding ritual with the cup. Also Soden convincingly asserts that the ritual of the breaking of the bread cannot have been originally related to Jesus' death.

An Independent Bread Meal

There are many other indications that an independent bread saying or bread meal must have preceded the words of institution (Heitmüller 1908, 30–31).

(1) Haenchen (1966, 479) correctly judges that in regard to the words of institution, the reader must note especially that the bread saying is found in all traditions in the short form, "This is my body," whereas "the 'wine saying' shows no such constant basic component." This state of affairs supports both the secondary origin of the cup saying and the fact that the further means of interpreting the Eucharist are based on the giving and drinking of the wine, not on the stronger tradition of the breaking and consuming of the bread.

(2) Bread is used in all cultic meals in early Christianity, while instead of wine we also find water (*Actus Vercellensis* 2; *Acts of Thomas* 121, 152; *Acts of Pionius* 3; *Acts of Paul* PH 4; Cyprian, *Ep.* 63; Clement of Alexandria *Stromata* 1.96.1; Epiph. *Haer.* 30.16.1; 42.3.3; 47.1.7; 61.1.2; cf. Harnack 1892, 117ff.; Rudolph 1961, 113ff., 380ff.), milk and honey (Tert. *Marc.* 1.14; Hipp. *Haer.* 5.8), fish, cheese (*Acts of Perpetua and Felicity* 4; Philaster *Liber de Haeresibus* 74; Epiph.

Haer. 49.2.6), and salt (Ps.-Clem. *Hom*. 11.36; 13.8; 14.1; and elsewhere); or bread is enjoyed alone (*Acts of Thomas* 26, 29, 49–50, 133, 158; *Acts of John* 106ff.; *Actus Vercellensis* 5; *Excerpta ex Theodoto* 82; Ps.-Clem. *Hom*. 14.1). Therefore Lietzmann (1926, 248) speaks of a "relative indifference regarding the second element of the Eucharist" (cf. Jeremias 1960, 46). Accordingly, the sequence bread-wine is also reversible, as attested by 1 Cor. 10:16–17 and *Did*. 9, where the wine appears first.

(3) In Mark 14:23 the saying over the cup is expressly followed by "and all of them drank from it," which Matthew turns into a command: "Drink from it, all of you" (Matt. 26:27b). In 1 Cor. 11:25 the interpretation of the cup contains a limitation, "Do this, *as often as you drink it,* in remembrance of me," whereas in Luke 22:20 this interpretation of the cup is entirely missing. There is no analogous information connected with the bread saying. The most illuminating explanation is that for a long time the Lord's Supper was not celebrated always and everywhere in both forms but only with bread, and this was increasingly felt to be inappropriate.

(4) The fact that the cup was added secondarily to the bread is quite compellingly attested by the observation that *sōma* and *haima* do not represent a conceptual pair. For as we speak of "flesh and blood," the Greeks spoke of *sarx* and *haima* (1 Cor. 15:50; Gal. 1:16; Eph. 6:12; Matt. 16:17; Heb. 2:14) and the Hebrews of *basar* and *dam* or of the Aramaic *bisra* and *dema*. The pairing of the terms *body/sōma* and *blood/haima* is singular and is attested only in the eucharistic sayings. Therefore it could have come into being only through the secondary addition of the wine to a *bread/artos–body/sōma* meal that was already fixed through an appropriate interpretation. It is no accident that in Justin (*Apol*. 1.66.1–2), Ignatius (*Rom*. 7.3; *Trall*. 8.1; *Phld*. 4.2; cf. *Smyrn*. 7.1), and the Gospel of John (6:51–56) *body/sōma* is replaced by *flesh/sarx*. Also, to the extent that this replacement was made with antidocetic intent in order to present Jesus' body unambiguously in its material nature, this process points to the unusual aspect of the pair of terms *body/sōma* and *blood/haima* found in the words of institution.

To explain this unusual pair of terms with a translation error (Jeremias 1960, 191ff.) presupposes not only a Hebrew or Aramaic original of the words of institution but also a unique, one-time translation: the first presupposition is doubtful; the second, inconceivable. Since it is a question of the false translation of the Hebrew *pair* of terms for *flesh* and *blood,* and since in Greek the equivalent of *body* and *blood* does not even exist, but only the correct *flesh* (*sarx*) and *blood* (*haima*) there can be no question of a translation error.

Following the procedure of other interpreters, Schweizer (1954) attempts to explain the discrepancy of *sōma* and *haima* in a completely different way. He questions the actual parallelism of *body/sōma* and *blood/haima* in the original words of institution. In his view, based on the tradition in 1 Cor. 11:23–25 and Luke 22:19–20, these read:

> This is my body.
> This (cup) is the (new) covenant in my blood.

In this formulation *body/sōma,* according to Schweizer, is used in the sense of "self, person," and consequently "This is my body" originally meant "This represents me," and thus the bread that the congregation consumes "is the token of the presence of Jesus himself" (1954, 582; cf. Heitmüller 1908, 35), whereas *blood* refers to Jesus' blood poured out on the cross. Now, it is very doubtful whether *body* can really be used or understood in the sense of "I myself," and the question of whether the Pauline/Lukan form of the words of institution is the original one is very controversial. Even if one accepts as given the presuppositions of Schweizer's argumentation, we must still object to his explanation on the grounds that nowhere in the tradition is *body* conceived in Schweizer's intended understanding. Thus the *misunderstanding* of the original bread saying that parallels *body/sōma* and *blood/haima* would have to be as old and original as the words of institution themselves—an impossible idea. Also the *action* of eating and drinking, which was essentially parallel from the beginning, excludes a nonparallel understanding of the *sayings* on the bread and the wine. And how is one to imagine that the *consumption* of the bread symbolizes the presence of the cultic Lord, especially a *broken* bread, which as such cannot represent the "person"? Thus the actual parallelism of *body* and *blood* was intended from the beginning. Therefore the disparity of this pair of terms can be explained only through the assumption that the double formula was preceded by a simple bread meal, whose interpretation was already established with the concept of *body/sōma*, and thus a conceptual parallelism of the double formula, as was undertaken later, was not originally possible.

(5) This observation corresponds to the fact that in a widespread and ancient tradition the *entire* action of the meal is called the "breaking of bread" (*klasis tou artou, klan arton,* and the like), and also the ritual of the breaking of bread has remained without any equivalent in the distribution and consumption of the wine (cf. 1 Cor. 10:16; Luke 24:35; Acts 2:42, 46; 20:7, 11; Ign. *Eph.* 20.2; *Did.* 9.3–4; 14.1; *Acts of John* 72, 85, 106, 109–10; *Acts of Thomas* 27, 29, 50, 121, 133; Ps.-Clem. *Hom.* 11.36; 14.1). The often expressed view that the term *breaking of bread* goes back to the Jerusalem primitive church can be supported only with Acts 2:42, 46 but cannot be proved with these passages. For in 2:42–47 we have a summary from Luke's pen, in which the pervasive Lukan viewpoints are brought to bear (cf. Schmithals 1982, 37ff.), and the term *breaking of bread* for the Christian community meal is taken by Luke from the tradition he passes on in Acts 20:7, 11, which does not come from the Jerusalem primitive church but is of deutero-Pauline origin. Nowhere else does the term *breaking of bread* appear as a designation for a whole meal. Even this expression, which is increasingly replaced above all by the term *Eucharist,* presupposes that a meal celebrated with only the breaking of bread stands at the beginning of the meal custom reflected by the words of institution, and that for this meal the breaking of bread was of fundamental importance. "The breaking of bread as the *name* of this special solemn activity is a singular, new name that is valid only for the celebration of this conventicle; it points to a singular new meaning that is present only here. . . . It means a special *ritual* moment that is so loaded with meaning that the entire celebration is given its name" (Otto 1940, 250, 252).

In the two-part Lord's Supper sayings, in which the bread saying receives its interpretation secondarily from the cup saying and "body" symbolized by the bread is consequently the body of the crucified Jesus given into death "for us," the breaking of bread has completely withdrawn into the narrative framework and become theologically meaningless. The situation is different in 1 Cor. 10:16–17, which passes on an interpretive saying about the bread that is still oriented toward the rite of bread breaking itself and for this reason cannot be understood in analogy with the cup saying. For we must agree without reservation with Soden (1931, 29) when he asserts that with the term *breaking of bread* no one thinks about the death of Jesus and no one thought of this before it was linked with the cup saying. Nor do the expansions "for you" (1 Cor. 11:24) and "given for you" refer to the breaking of bread. This is done only by the secondary reading "broken for you" in 1 Cor. 11:24, which sets up a parallel with the meaningful "poured out for you" and in this way produces a singular and rather unclear symbolism for the breaking of bread.

1 Corinthians 10:16–17

The original meaning of the breaking of bread is not hard to recognize if one notes that in 1 Cor. 10:16b the term *koinōnia* ("sharing, participation, communion") is ambivalent.

> [16a]The cup of blessing that we bless, is it not a sharing in the blood of Christ?
> [16b]The bread that we break, is it not a sharing in the body of Christ?
> [17]Because there is one bread, we who are many are one body, for we all partake of the one bread.

In connection with 1 Cor. 10:16a—and for the sake of the parallel *blood/body*— *koinōnia* in v. 16b can designate sharing or communion with the Lord Jesus, who was given into death and poured out his blood for us, only in a christological or soteriological usage. In connection with 10:17, however, *koinōnia* in v. 16b can, in ecclesiological usage, just as surely refer only to the communion of Christians among each other. Accordingly, in the first case *body/sōma* in 1 Cor. 10:16b must be understood in the sense of the crucified body of Jesus, as in 1 Cor. 11:24, 27, 29; Rom. 7:4; in the second case, however, in the sense of the church as the body of Christ, as in Rom. 12:4–5; 1 Cor. 12:27; and elsewhere. But if the bread is related to the church in this way, the ritual of the breaking of bread and the eating of the broken bread bears witness to the participation of church members in the communion of the "body of Christ": "Because there is one bread, we who are many are one body, for we all partake of the one bread."

What is the source of this ambiguity of the "sharing in the body of Christ" in 1 Cor. 10:16b? How can the passage 10:16–17 be explained in terms of form and tradition history? To answer these questions we must note the train of thought in which these sentences occur. Even the disputers of the literary unity of the First Letter to the Corinthians do not doubt that 1 Cor. 9:24–10:22 forms a self-contained context. Paul first argues *ex natura:* not everyone who begins a race also achieves victory. The desired victory prize requires the continued application of all one's powers (9:24–27). Then Paul repeats this argumentation *ex scriptura:* all members of Israel's wilderness generation began their way into the promised land under the same spiritual presuppositions, as Paul shows with the help of a baptismal and eucharistic typology. But not all of them reached the goal, for they did not remain faithful to the law with which they had begun (10:1–13). Paul fixes the meaning intended in both arguments in one sentence, "So if you think you are standing, watch out that you do not fall" (10:12), to which he adds an appropriate promise (10:13). Thus Paul apparently feels that it is necessary to warn the church against inappropriate certainty of salvation.

The concrete occasion for this warning becomes evident in the following section, 10:14–22, for the sentences that frame this passage reveal that certain circles in Corinth believe that participation in pagan cultic meals is compatible with belonging to the Christian church. Paul argues against this view by appealing to the sound judgment of his readers (10:15) in three parallel proofs that rest on an analogy between the Lord's Supper, the Jewish sacrificial meal, and the pagan cultic meal. Each of these meals puts a person in a relationship with a particular cultic lord: the Lord's Supper connects one with Christ; the Jewish sacrificial meal, with the "altar," that is, with God; and the pagan cultic meal, with demons. The key concept of the series of arguments is *sharing* (*koinōnia* or *koinōnos*). The course of the argumentation is in itself conclusive. Paul does not need to go into tangential issues, such as questions of the validity of the Jewish cult for Christians or the reality of "idols," since he imagines the desired communion in every case as a historically mediated sharing: with Gentile Christian readers in mind, he begins with the *intention* of each cult participant. From everything he has said, he draws the conclusion at the end of the passage: one cannot be in communion with the *Kyrios Christos* and with demons at the same time. Not to observe this means to try the *Kyrios* who wants to have humankind all to himself. Communion with the Lord Christ is exclusive.

The foregoing analysis of the train of thought in 1 Cor. 9:24–10:22 shows that in 10:17 we have a foreign body in this context. For in the flow of the argumentation as a whole, *koinōnia* is not used ecclesiologically but always for the description of the communion of the cult participant with the respective cult lord. "Verse 17 is like a small ecclesiological insertion" (Schnackenburg 1961, 41; cf. Neuenzeit 1960, 202), "a digression" that "works doubly inconsistently because nothing is said about one *cup*" (J. Weiss 1920, 258), and it is added only in late manuscripts. In the present substantiating context, 10:16 *in itself* fulfills the same function for the Lord's Supper as 10:18 for the Jewish cult and 10:19–20 for the pagan. And since the readers have just read 10:16a, they cannot understand the "sharing in the body of Christ" in 10:16b in any way other than soteriologically or christologically. They must be surprised by 10:17, since this sentence in no way serves Paul's desired proof that the various cultic meals put one in communion with the respective cult lord. And it is no accident that the following references to the Jewish and pagan cultic meals lack a statement analogous to 10:17. Without v. 17 the train of thought would be perfectly clear.

Yet the exclusion of 10:17 as a secondary gloss (J. Weiss, 259) is not obvious, for its insertion would be poorly motivated, and the idea expressed in 10:17
is by no means contradictory to Pauline thought. Calling the sentence a parenthetical remark by Paul is likewise difficult, for in his writings even parenthetical
remarks are usually motivated *in the context*. By contrast, the difficulties are resolved when we note that in 1 Cor. 10:16b–17 we have a set pre-Pauline formula
that is unambiguous in itself: it interprets the action of the meal in terms of the ecclesiological communion of Christians and focuses only on a bread meal with its
symbolic act of breaking bread. "In this sense the actual and only sacramental action is the breaking, distribution, and eating of the bread . . . without any allusion
to a reconciling significance of [Jesus'] death" (J. Weiss 1910, 259). In this ecclesiological tradition there is absolutely no talk of an "institution," much less of a
last meal of Jesus. The gathered church itself interprets its act: "The bread that we
break, is it not a sharing in the body of Christ?" (10:16b).

Paul incorporates the formula in v. 17 because of the word *koinōnia*. Against
the ecclesiological sense present in the formula, but in analogy to the words of
institution (11:25), he relates "body of Christ" in 10:16b to the crucified body of
Jesus and therefore interprets the "sharing in the body of Christ" as sharing with
Jesus himself based on his death, or as participation in the gift of salvation
achieved through his death. With such a meaning he could use 10:16b in the context of his argumentation, and in order to bring this meaning to light and to
strengthen and complete the argument presented in this way, he himself—in analogy to the words of institution and in a formulation parallel to the bread saying
of the formula—forms the cup saying in 10:16a, which can be understood only
in a christological, soteriological way. Whereas in this form and with such an understanding, the newly created unity of verse 10:16 directly serves Paul's argumentation, 10:17 follows out of formal necessity, for Paul is in the habit of
quoting fixed traditions in their totality, even when only a single idea in the tradition forms the actual reason for the quotation. The tension that arises in this way
between context and tradition is a well-known part of the chief criteria with
whose help one determines such traditions. Thus v. 28 in Gal. 3:26ff., v. 3b in 1
Cor. 15:3ff., v. 3b in Rom. 1:3–4, and vv. 9–11 in Phil. 2:6–11 have their function only in these traditional formulas and not in the Pauline context (see p. 52
above).

The foregoing interpretation is confirmed by a number of observations. (1)
The prior positioning of the cup now becomes understandable, for the cup saying can be connected only with 10:16b, not 10:17. (2) The puzzling and unre-
solvable ambiguity of "sharing in the body of Christ" in 10:16b is completely
explained by its joining of ecclesiological tradition and christological, soteriological interpretation. (3) In this formula we find what is compellingly postulated for other reasons as the pure bread meal that preceded the meal attested
by the words of institution, and thus in 10:16b–17 "an ancient—perhaps the
oldest—version of the Lord's Supper shines through" (J. Weiss 1910, 259). (4)
Only a bread meal without reference to Jesus' death, as found in the present formula, which relates the breaking of the one bread to the unity of the church in

the plurality of its members, could be designated in a meaningful way as the "breaking of bread"; thus we gain an explanation of this technical term, which is otherwise unexplainable as a designation for this meal, which traditionally involves both bread and wine. (5) Finally, we come across the origin of the ecclesiological sharing motif of the celebratory meal, which cannot be substantiated by the words of institution but is never completely lost in the piety and theology of the Lord's Supper.

Didache 9.1–10.6

In form, the celebration of the Eucharist in the Didache, which is handed down to us in *Did.* 9.1–10.6, is similar to the tradition in 1 Cor. 10:16b–17, in that it contains the interpretative saying about the broken bread (*Did.* 9.4) but not an accompanying equivalent for the cup, and also in that in the opening prayers the cup comes before the bread (*Did.* 9.2–3). In content, however, it is noteworthy that the handling of the bread occurs exclusively in the eschatological context of the eucharistic celebration in the *Didache*:

> As this piece of bread was scattered on the mountains and was brought together into one bread, so may your church be brought together from the ends of the earth into your kingdom. (*Did.* 9.4)

The basis for the eschatological interpretation of the bread meal is formed by the possibly older—but in any case traditional (Zech. 2:10; Mark 13:27 par.)— petitionary prayer after the meal that God may bring together the church "from the four winds into your kingdom." The interpretation itself seems to transfer the analytical concept of 1 Cor. 10:16b–17 into a synthetic image, in that it no longer presents the breaking of the bread but the origination of the bread from the grains gathered from the fields.

These observations allow the assumption that the church of the *Didache* further developed its eschatologically oriented meal celebration at the close of a general church's bread meal, without at the same time adopting its theologically advanced standpoint, especially since the *Didache* never makes reference to Jesus' death "for us." In general, the *Didache* tends to combine progressive traditions with a standpoint that is conservative in terms of theological history, as shown by the triadic baptismal formula in *Did.* 7.1 and the Matthean version of the Lord's Prayer in *Did.* 8.2. A corresponding development of the Lord's Supper liturgy might also be indicated by the peculiar fact that the bread in *Did.* 9.3 and 9.4 is emphatically called *klasma,* although the breaking of bread is virtually a contradiction of the idea of the eschatological gathering of the scattered and of the corresponding image of the gathering together of the grains into one bread. In any case, the *Didache* also attests that a pure, meaningful bread meal preceded and forms the foundation of its eucharistic celebration in both kinds.

Theological Aspects of the Bread Meal

A meal in which the communion of the guests takes place as a "sharing in the body of Christ" has to be celebrated in a church that is generally familiar with the mystical conception of the church as the body of Christ and its many members, and with the related world of ideas. This was the case in Paul's conversion theology, and thus Paul probably brought the traditional bread saying of 10:16b–17 with him from Damascus (see pp. 85ff. above). In any case, it is permissible and appropriate to illuminate in more detail the "sharing in the body of Christ," as it takes place in the celebration of the bread meal, on the basis of the corresponding sayings in Paul's letters.

Here we have two points of view:

(1) Now you are the body of Christ and individually members of it. (1 Cor. 12:27)

(2) . . . so we, who are many, are one body in Christ, and individually we are members one of another. (Rom. 12:5)

In the second of these quoted passages the meal formula in 1 Cor. 10:17 is literally adopted: "we, who are many, are one body." Thus the table fellowship reminds the participants that every individual has a special charisma (Rom. 12:6) but the out-pouring of one and the same Spirit (1 Cor. 12:4, 11), which without distinction serves the needs of the church (1 Cor. 12:7). One should strive for the greater gifts (1 Cor. 12:31), yet in the differentiation of the charismata it is a question of a difference within the unity of the Spirit, and this fact does not permit the disparagement of members with lesser gifts (1 Cor. 12:15ff.).

Beside this differentiating meaning, which is connected with the *breaking* of the bread, stands the unifying meaning produced by the bread meal with the emphasis on the *one* bread (1 Cor. 10:17):

For just as the body is *one* and has many members, and all the members of the body, though many, are *one* body, so it is with Christ. For in the one Spirit we were baptized into one body—Jews or Greeks, slaves or free . . . (1 Cor. 12:12–13)

For in Christ Jesus you are all children of God through faith. As many of you as were baptized into Christ have clothed yourselves with Christ. There is no longer Jew or Greek, there is no longer slave or free, there is no longer male and female; for all of you are one in Christ Jesus. (Gal. 3:26–28)

This unifying view of the "sharing of the body of Christ" that occurs in the meal is understandably also connected with baptism, for with entrance into the church, the natural and social differences among the baptized are eliminated. It is no accident that the phrase "no longer Jew or Greek" always stands at the top of the corresponding lists, for the equality of circumcised and uncircumcised "in Christ" means at the same time the abolition of the religious preeminence of the Jews. This universalist and law-critical tendency of the body of Christ concept corresponds to the rooting of the whole "mystical" motif complex, including the tradition of the bread meal, in Paul's Damascene conversion theology, which also includes the Christology of preexistence and incarnation, and this becomes evident in Gal. 3:26 in connection with Gal. 4:4ff. (see chapter 4 above).

The Origin of the
Bread Meal Tradition

If the ecclesiological meal celebration that stands entirely under the sign of the *breaking* of bread is rooted in the comprehensive Damascene theology, this excludes the idea that the bread meal simply developed continuously from the eschatological, apocalyptic meal custom of the primitive church. It is true that a continuity exists to the extent that the "eschatological high spirits" were maintained and in some ways strengthened in the transition from apocalyptic to pneumatic eschatology. For it is not coincidental that the thinking and traditional material of "Christ mysticism" lack an apocalyptic outlook; it is not needed by the present eschatology of the "already now" in the "sharing in the body of Christ" (1 Cor. 10:16b) and in the "children of God" of Gal. 3:26. But this very "already now" and its pneumatic basis in the context of a thoroughly ontically understood "Christ mysticism" make it necessary to assume, also for the "breaking of bread" as a meal of the gathered "body of Christ," an origin outside the Jewish Christian primitive church of Palestine.

It is notable that the language of Christ mysticism remains without a primary reference to the Christian kerygma, as is evident in the meal formula of 1 Cor. 10:16b–17, for example. Naturally, *Paul* identifies the "body of Christ" with the *Christian* church. But the term *Christ* as such is not yet Christian but Jewish. Consequently, in 1 Cor. 10:16b–17 no word about the Christian salvation event or incarnation or crucifixion is mentioned or interpreted. The term *Christ* is not primarily related to Jesus but designates the church that celebrates the meal; in this sense the formula has no "Christology." Therefore the formula in 1 Cor. 10:16b–17, or at least the religious conceptual world that underlies it, cannot have had its origin in the Christian church. This origin is to be sought, rather, in a Jewish Gnosticism in which the community itself possesses christological power (see p. 65 above). The heavenly figure of the Gnostic mythos that falls into the material world bears the designation *Christ*, and its scattered members on earth form the "body of Christ." The broken bread symbolizes the communion of the members gathered together again in the unity of the body of Christ, and the knowledge of this regained pneumatic unity means redemption. Hence in Gnostic thinking the ecclesiological and soteriological references of the bread meal come together. In the Damascene conversion theology of Paul, the language of the "Christ mysticism" was adopted with the presupposition of the Christian confession that *Jesus* is the "Christ" (see pp. 74ff. above). At this point, soteriology and ecclesiology separate, yet mystical language is still available, above all for the presentation of ecclesiological concerns. In this context the Christian church that used the language of Christ mysticism, and which Paul joined at his conversion, celebrated the breaking of bread in the presence of the exalted Lord and in the certainty of being bound to him in the unity and plurality of its members and gifts.

The Meal with Bread and Wine

Above all, the disparity of the terms *body/sōma* and *blood/haima,* used in parallel in the two-part words of institution, shows that the celebration of the meal in both kinds presupposes an independent bread meal. We do not need to look for a special religious-historical model for the expansion of the bread meal to a bread-wine meal. More or less festal or cultic meals, at which wine played a role in addition to the consumed bread, were numerous both in the realm of Judaism (1 Cor. 10:3–4; *Joseph and Aseneth* 8.5, 9; 15.5, 14; 16.16; 19.5; 1QS 6:4–6; 1QSa 2:17–21; Str-B 4/1:69–70; 4/2:621, 623–24, 627ff.) and in Hellenism (1 Cor. 10:21; Just. *Apol.* 1.66; Tert. *Haer.* 40; cf. Lietzmann 1949, 49ff.; Heitmüller 1908, 45–46; Klauck 1982, 31ff.).

The expansion of the ecclesiologically oriented bread meal to the double meal attested by the words of institution took place in a Christianity that had learned to understand Jesus' death as death "for us" or "for our sins" (cf. 1 Cor. 15:3; Rom. 3:25; 4:25). It must have been obvious that the cup that was emptied at the eschatological, apocalyptic meals of hope in anticipation of the heavenly banquet (Mark 14:25; 1 Cor. 11:26) should be interpreted in terms of the blood poured out "for us," especially if one had become familiar with the practice of giving the breaking of bread a special significance. Yet the details of when and where and how this first happened can no longer be determined with any certainty. It is conceivable, for example, that for a time the soteriologically interpreted cup appeared beside the still ecclesiologically understood breaking of bread, or that the soteriological interpretation of the cup was sufficient. There are, however, no indications of such meal customs. Our present words of institution understand the "body of Christ," which occurs symbolically in the broken bread, no longer as the church but as the body killed on the cross. In this sense, under the dominant influence of the blood poured out "for us," these words establish a parallelism of cup and bread sayings, for even the simple "This is my body" (Mark 14:22; Matt. 26:26) beside the cup saying can be understood only in parallel to the latter and related to Jesus' dead body. Here the rite of the *breaking* of bread loses its significance and recedes in favor of the blessing or prayer of thanksgiving at the beginning of the meal into the narrative context of the words of institution and into the outward course of the meal. The expansion of the interpretive saying about the bread with "for us" (1 Cor. 11:24) or "given for us" (Luke 22:19), which late manuscripts specify as "broken for us," is secondary and serves the clarification of the new soteriological significance of the meal.

The Original Form
of the Words of Institution

It is possible that one should not even ask about an original form of the words of institution of the meal of bread and wine, for such a question presupposes an "institution" of the meal in both kinds, which we do not necessarily have to assume. Yet the form and tradition of the words of institution are so uniform and constant that a kind of "establishing act" is probable. In any case, the bread saying contains the basic assertion: "This is my body." Its expansion with "(given) for you" in 1 Cor. 11:24; Luke 22:19) is clearly secondary. All the traditions also agree that the cup is primarily related to the "blood of the covenant," whereas the idea of atonement is completely lacking in 1 Cor. 11:25 and is added secondarily as an expansion of the covenant idea in Mark 14:24; Luke 22:20 ("poured out for many/you") and, further expanded, in Matt. 26:28 ("poured out for many for the forgiveness of sins"). Thus the expansion of the ecclesiologically interpreted bread meal to the soteriologically understood bread-wine meal apparently occurred first from the viewpoint of the covenant sacrifice or the covenant formation. One does not necessarily have to conclude from this that the meal celebration in two kinds came about in a church where the motif of atonement or substitution was still unfamiliar. The choice of the covenant motif, which naturally includes the forgiveness of sins (Jer. 31:31ff.), can also be explained by the fact that the idea of the covenant is closer than the idea of atonement to the ecclesiological meaning of the older bread meal, and thus the oldest form of the cup saying intentionally maintains the motif of community through its reference to the covenant. At the same time, for early Christian thinking the covenant concluded through Jesus Christ is, in any case, the new eschatological covenant, and thus the interpretation of the cup in terms of the covenantal sacrifice also persists in the continuity of the eschatological, apocalyptic meal of hope of the primitive church. Yet it is obvious that the words of institution were very soon enriched in various ways by the formulaic "for you."

Whether the Pauline-Lukan or the Markan version of the cup saying contains or comes close to the original wording is still a matter of dispute. In my view, nonetheless, most of the arguments support the Markan version as the older one (Mark 14:22; Matt. 26:26, 28):

> This is my body.
> This is my blood of the covenant.

This text formulates the bread saying and the cup saying largely in parallel, which speaks for its originality, as does the fact that the bread saying did not receive its present form—"my body" instead of "the body of Christ" (1 Cor. 10:16b)—until it was found in the context of the words of institution. Furthermore, with "blood of the covenant" it is related directly to the Old Testament texts Exod. 24:8; Zech. 9:11. One must therefore assume that these interpretive sayings are not the result of a gradual, rather unintentional development, but that they serve the establishment or "institution" of a Lord's Supper that in connection with the older meal rites was supposed to receive a form appropriate to the theological development in the church.

Consequently the Pauline-Lukan version of the cup saying is secondary, in that it, incorporating Jer. 38:31 (LXX), expressly speaks of the "new covenant" and at the same time emphatically moves this term into the foreground (1 Cor. 11:25; Luke 22:20):

> This cup is the new covenant in my blood.

"Cup" and "blood" are infelicitously separated from each other by the emphasized concept of the new covenant in this formulation, which strongly suggests its secondary character. From 2 Cor. 3:6ff. (cf. Rom. 7:6) we learn that the idea of the new covenant has great theological importance especially for Paul, for in his understanding it is no longer a matter of the nationally limited covenant of the Mosaic law but of the universal covenant of faith for all people without distinction (Käsemann 1960a, 30–31; Wegenast 1962, 99ff.). At the same time, Paul's curious assertion that he received the words of institution directly "from the Lord" shows that he did not simply pass on to the church a fixed tradition, as is doubtless the case in 1 Cor. 15:3ff., but that he modified the tradition in the spirit of the insights received "from the Lord" (Käsemann 1960a, 30), so that "the meaning that was apparent to him would stand out clearly" (Heitmüller 1908, 24). This modification can be observed most easily, however, in the emphasis on the "new covenant," which is also shown by this observation to be secondary.

If this analysis of the situation is correct, the controversial and not easily clarified question of whether the Pauline and Lukan versions of the words of institution go back to a common source, or whether Luke 22:19–20 presupposes the epistolary text of 1 Cor. 11:23–25 must be answered in terms of the latter possibility. Also supporting this solution are individual observations that must be made regarding the context of the interpretive sayings.

The Context of the
Interpretative Sayings

In the beginning the interpretative words on the lips of Jesus must have belonged in a context whose original form can no longer be determined with certainty:

> The Lord Jesus on the night when he was betrayed [handed over; delivered] took a loaf of bread, and when he had given thanks, he gave it to them and said, "This is my body."

> And he took a cup, and when he had given thanks, he gave it to them and said, "This is my blood of the covenant."

The briefer context of the cup saying in Paul and Luke ("in the same way he took the cup also . . . and said . . ."), which is inappropriate for a cultic action in which the cup saying introduces an independent meal activity, apparently rests on the literary abbreviation that appears to be appropriate in the context of a letter (1 Cor. 11:25; Luke 22:19–20 presupposes the Pauline text). Also, "after supper" is secondary, for it can refer only to the preceding bread meal, since no early Christian meal celebration is known between the (fully satisfying!—cf. Did. 10.1; Wengst 1884, 45) eating of bread and the drinking of the cup. And in view of the fact that the gathered church itself held and completed this bread meal, "after supper" is a stage direction that is inappropriate in the course of the celebratory meal—one that Paul presumably inserted because of the disorder of the Corinthian meal celebration (1 Cor. 11:20–21) in order to preserve the cultic character of the meal (cf. 1 Cor. 11:22, 34).

The explicit placing of the "institution" on the night of Jesus' betrayal [being handed over; being delivered], which is also given by the context of Mark 14:22 par., probably belongs to the original text. The establishing character of the sayings and the fact that bread and cup were interpreted from the beginning as referring to Jesus' death presuppose the situation of a farewell meal. Yet one should not understand it as historical, for the motif of betrayal [being handed over; being delivered] (after Isaiah 53) comes from the creedal tradition (Rom. 4:25; 8:32), and the darkness of the night has a symbolic meaning that is related to betrayal [being handed over; being delivered] into the power of evil (cf. Mark 14:30, 49ff.; Luke 22:53; John 13:30).

Following the interpretive saying is the falsely named "repetition command," which is found in 1 Cor. 11:24–25 with both the bread and the cup sayings, in Luke 22:19 with only the bread saying, but not in the Markan tradition at all. Actually, it *interprets* the supper event in a way that leads further: "Do this in remembrance of me [that is, of my death]." These sayings do not speak of a repetition of the meal, and there is no repetition command in the immediate cultic directions that govern the meal event. The degree to which the interpretation of the meal as a meal of remembrance is connected with ancient memorial meals for the dead (Lietzmann 1949, 58; Conzelmann 1969, 233–234; cf. Jeremias 1960, 230) must remain open here. But there is no doubt that in 1 Cor. 11:26 the act of "remembrance" in the eating of the bread and the drinking of the cup is further defined as a proclamation of the death of Jesus. The indicative "you proclaim" in 1 Cor. 11:26 corresponds to the repeated indicative "you do this in remembrance of me" in 11:24, 25 and carries it further (Lietzmann 1949, 58); the "remembrance" is achieved as a "representation" of the death of Jesus "for us." The explanation in 11:26 corresponds so well to Paul's thinking that one would like to trace it all the way back to Paul himself, and in view of the apostle's claim that he received the Lord's Supper tradition "from the Lord," it is not unlikely that in the same way Paul himself prepared the idea of 11:26 through the repetition of "do this in remembrance of me" and anchored it in traditional words (cf. Lietzmann 1926, 254–55; 1949, 58).

Other Problems

In any case, we can discern a relatively simple and essentially reconstructible tradition history of the words of institution if we follow the foregoing considerations. For the yet unmentioned deviations in Mark, Matthew, and Luke are of redactional origin and not of great importance for theological history.

Mark places the Last Supper in the context of the Jewish Passover celebration but does not pursue any of the interests related to the understanding of the Lord's Supper (Schmithals 1986, 603ff.). In the various earlier meal traditions there is no reference to the Passover meal, and the attempt undertaken especially by Jeremias (1960) to demonstrate that Jesus' last meal was actually a Passover meal has no support in the pre-Markan tradition and in the words of institution themselves. We also find in the doubling of the meal in the longer Lukan text no older tradition but rather the reflection of essentially redactional interests of the evangelist Luke (cf. Schmithals 1980, 208–9). John does not pass on the words of institution at all, yet in John 6:47ff. the evangelist shows not only that a meal with bread and wine was celebrated in his churches, but also that participation in the meal was understood as an antidocetic act of confession, as in Ignatius (Ign. *Smyrn.* 7.1 and elsewhere; cf. Just. *Apol.* 1.66). The extent to which in this connection *flesh* and *blood* were already regarded as substances and no longer designated the *event* of the body crucified "for us" and the blood shed, as in 1 Cor. 11:26, can hardly be determined.

Nevertheless, around the middle of the second century there is a clear shift in the direction of the substantial understanding and thus toward the developing idea of sacrifice. With such considerations, however, the theological history of early Christianity is already entering the realm of the early history of dogma.

All forms of the Lord's Supper are to be distinguished from the early Christian love feasts or *agape* meals, even if the celebration of the agape in later times was connected with the celebration of the Eucharist (versus, for example, Ign. *Smyrn.* 8.1–2; Tert. *Apol.* 39.14ff.). The "supper of the Lord" itself, held for the *whole* church and only for it, was not a love feast like that prepared for the poor of the church or for unbaptized catechumens (cf. Tert. *Apol.* 39). Also the agapes have their origin not in the celebration of the Eucharist but in love feasts that were customary everywhere in the Hellenistic world and also in the synagogue (cf. Str.-B. 4/2:611ff.).

Conclusion

The tradition of the Lord's Supper reflects the essential stages in early Christian theological history that are generally observable in the Pauline period. In the beginning was a customary meal of the Jewish Christian primitive church that, as the communion of the saints in *eschatological,* apocalyptic expectation, anticipates the banquet of the blessed in the perfected kingdom of God. The enjoyment of the festal wine is characteristic of this meal. The Lord's Supper liturgy in *Did.* 9–11 does not go beyond this theological context and, like the *Didache* in general and to some extent the Revelation to John, attests that a corresponding group of churches, possibly driven out of Palestine around 70, existed into the second or third Christian generation, whereas in the rest of Christendom the eschatological point of view moved away from the center of the meal celebration.

The universalist and law-free Christianity to which Paul was converted in Damascus had a bread meal celebration in which the apocalyptic expectation, under the influence of a Jewish-Gnostic enthusiasm, was radicalized into a present eschatology, and the rite of the breaking of bread as a symbolic action moved into the center of the meal event. The pointedly *ecclesiological* significance of this Damascene communion meal, the plurality and variety of the members in the unity of the body of Christ, has since then in various ways accompanied the piety of the Lord's Supper, yet in the long run it has not defined it.

A church that presumably already spoke Greek brought this bread meal back, as it were, into Jewish Christianity and combined it with the festal consumption of wine, and bread and wine were interpreted as the body of the crucified Jesus and his blood poured out "for us." This new *soteriological* meaning corresponds to the cult legend that tells of the establishment of the Lord's Supper in the circle of disciples at Jesus' farewell meal before his death. Here the death of Jesus, at first with a still detectable eschatological alignment, was interpreted as a sacrifice for the establishment of a covenant and only in a further step connected with atonement and substitutionary aspects through formulas characteristic of Antiochene Christianity.

According to the information in 1 Cor. 11:23–26, Paul also celebrated the

Lord's Supper in his own Gentile Christian churches primarily in the Antiochene manner. In the spirit of his *theologia crucis,* he expounds more clearly the relationship of the meal activity to the presentation of Jesus' death, and by putting the adopted idea of the covenantal sacrifice under the viewpoint of the *new* covenant, which he understands as God's covenant with Jews and Gentiles without distinction, he incorporates the ecclesiological motif and the universalism of his Damascene conversion theology into the Antiochene tradition in a new way.

Later dogmatic development focused the theology of the Lord's Supper one-sidedly on the soteriological aspect, especially through incorporation of the idea of sacrifice. In this way the rich aspects still found in the New Testament—namely, the soteriological ("faith"), the ecclesiological ("love"), and the eschatological ("hope") viewpoints—were lost.

14

The Conflict between Christian Church and Jewish Synagogue

If we want to understand the position of the early Christian churches with regard to the legal organization of the synagogue, we must arrange the various phenomena and conclusions in terms of two dates that form the historical framework. The first turning point is the development of independent Gentile Christian churches that were organized outside the synagogue and apart from the Jewish Christians who remained within the synagogal structure; the life and organization of these churches can be clearly observed in the letters of Paul. The second event is the *aposynagōgos* — named after an expression in the Gospel of John — that is, the exclusion of even Jewish Christian communities and their God-fearing Gentile Christian members from the synagogal organization. This exclusion occurred after the Jewish war and was connected with the reorganization of Judaism made necessary by the catastrophe of the year 70. It led to the abolishment of the coexistence of Jewish Christians and Gentile Christians and in this sense to the beginning of the early catholic church. Apart from the authentic letters of Paul, the writings of the New Testament presuppose the *aposynagōgos* and, as a rule, endeavor to overcome its consequences.

In this chapter we will seek to place the relationship of Christian church and Jewish synagogue in the New Testament period within the sketched coordinates and make it understandable within this context. The relationship of Christians and Jews, which was extremely burdened by later developments and above all by recent German history, must not guide the present inquiry. Biologically or racist motivated *anti-Semitism* is absolutely a product of the modern period. The *hostility to Jews* that was widespread in the ancient world is not much in evidence in the New Testament, since the leading Christians were themselves Jews; essentially it was able to develop only after the exclusion from the synagogue. Theologically based *anti-Judaism,* which is characteristic especially of Gentile Christianity in the New Testament period, is addressed neither against the Jews nor against Jewish tradition but against a certain understanding of the Jewish tradition, and it seeks to develop a better understanding of that tradition; this anti-Judaism did not try to overcome Judaism but to perfect it in a universalist way.

Therefore the tense relationship between Christian church and Jewish synagogue in the New Testament period must be explained and critically evaluated on the basis of its own conditions and historical presuppositions. The responsibility for the later influence of the statements in which this relationship is revealed in the New Testament must be given not to the opponents of that time but to later generations.

Gentile Christianity
before the Year 70

The origin and beginnings of Christianity outside the synagogue are only dimly visible and are disputed by scholars, since the presentation of the Acts of the Apostles can be accepted only with critical evaluation. It is certain, however, that before his conversion Paul was fighting against a Christianity that was organized outside the synagogal organization. He was converted to this Christianity (Gal. 1:13–14, 23–24; 1 Cor. 15:9), and his Damascene conversion theology shows that he fought against a law-free, universalist Christianity. Since at his conversion Paul as a *Jew* gave up the law and was at the same time called as a missionary to Gentiles, this Christianity encompassed Jews and Gentiles without distinction (see pp. 105ff. above).

There was unavoidable conflict between such a Christian community and the synagogue, which the Stephen episode in Acts describes from the Lukan viewpoint (Acts 6:1–8:1) and which Paul's references to his activity as a persecutor of Christians attest as authentic. And the violence of this conflict is sufficiently attested by the fact that Stephen and presumably also James the son of Zebedee (Acts 12:1–2) fell victim to it. The Sanhedrin and the synagogues, who claimed to represent true Judaism, could not allow the Jews to lose their influence and jurisdiction. They also did not want to permit uncircumcised Gentiles to be accepted into the covenant of Abraham and the people of God without at least becoming adherents of the synagogue in the status of God-fearers. Judging by appearances, one could say that essentially the synagogue successfully survived this first conflict with an independent Christian group. For during Paul's missionary activity of more than a decade in Syria and Cilicia (Gal. 1:21), as well as that of Barnabas (Gal. 2:1, 13; 1 Cor. 9:6; Acts 11:19–26), Paul worked again within the realm of the synagogal organization, where he was able to carry on among the numerous God-fearers the Gentile mission for which he had been commissioned. During this time, in which he was apparently not subjected to any systematic persecutions and could move about freely even in Jerusalem (Gal. 1:18ff.; 2:1ff.), he adapted himself and his theology to the large stock of Antiochene theologoumena, which were independent of his conversion theology. His practical missionary principle of becoming as a Jew to the Jews and as a Gentile to the Gentiles, in order to win both (1 Cor. 9:19–21), belongs in this phase of his activity. Consequently, there were no specifically Pauline churches in Syria and Cilicia in spite of Paul's intensive missionary activity in this geographic region. (Cf. also pp. 108ff. above.) The "Johannine" church, which according to all indications also stood in theological continuity with the Hellenistic Christianity of the circle of Stephen (Schmithals 1992, 148–49; see pp. 78–79 above and p. 331 below), lived again within the synagogue until the *aposynagōgos*.

The limitation of his Gentile mission to the boundaries of the synagogal institution was not satisfactory for Paul. At his conversion he felt called to abolish the distinction between Jews and Gentiles, between elected synagogue and rejected world, for in Christ there are neither Jews nor Greeks (Gal. 3:28). In a time that was manifestly moving toward the catastrophe of the Jewish war, and in the face of an internal crisis in polytheistic paganism, this undertaking, with which Paul could take advantage of the tendencies of the liberal synagogue, was also highly respectable from the political standpoint. Perhaps with his mission among God-fearing Gentiles in the context of the synagogue Paul had hoped to burst the bounds of the synagogue from within and spread the Christian message as universal truth. Yet his activity of more than a decade in Syria and Cilicia must have revealed such hopes as even more unrealistic, when the success of the mission among the Jews was especially disappointing (Rom. 11:1ff., 11ff.).

Therefore Paul gave up this unsatisfying missionary work and, based on his Damascene beginnings, began an independent Gentile Christian world mission and the founding of Christian churches outside the synagogal organization. To this end he first concluded at the so-called Apostolic Council (Gal. 2:1–10) agreements that had the significance of possibly avoiding a renewed conflict with the synagogue, of excluding a danger to Jewish Christians in Palestine and in the Hellenistic synagogues, and of making possible an undisturbed Gentile mission outside the synagogue. Therefore the negotiations in Jerusalem not only took place under the eyes of Jewish authorities but also included their representatives (Gal. 2:4–5). To the Jews, Paul made the concession of not attempting to carry on any Jewish mission and thereby alienating Jews in the synagogue. The presupposition of this concession and the most important point of these intra-Christian agreements was that the Jewish Christian church would proclaim the gospel to Jews within the synagogue in Paul's "virgin" mission territory (Rom. 15:20), for as always, Paul did not want to found a Gentile Christian church but to unite Jews and Gentiles in one *ekklēsia* (cf. 1 Cor. 10:32). The Jerusalem "pillars" agreed to the parallel apostolate among the circumcised (Gal. 2:9) demanded by Paul, and this task was entrusted to Peter, who had already stood out earlier as a missionary among his compatriots (Gal. 2:7–8).

It is noteworthy that Paul separated himself only organizationally from the mission among his Jewish brothers and sisters. Although he now could no longer become as a Jew to the Jews in order to win Jews (1 Cor. 9:20), he understood the mission to the Gentiles as his personal contribution to the conversion of the Jews, for he hoped that the success of his preaching among the Gentiles would make his own people "jealous" (Rom. 11:13–14). The Jew Paul cannot have forbidden Jewish Christians to join his law-free churches, but according to the information in his letters and in the Acts of the Apostles (cf., for example, Acts 18:7), he did not evangelize within the synagogues. He seems even to have circumcised the born Jew Timothy in order to avoid the synagogal reproach that he wanted to dissolve the Jewish nation as such among the Gentile peoples. He was concerned not about political emancipation but about the unity of all people in faith in Christ. When, as Paul expressly states, the Jewish Christians in Jerusalem contributed nothing to his Gentile Christian mission (Gal. 2:6–7), they were probably, in agreement with Paul, rejecting the Jewish demand that the Gentile Christian members of the Pauline churches pay the temple tax, as the God-fearing adherents of the snyagogue did. Such an act of religiously based political particularism would have diametrically contradicted Paul's intentions. Nevertheless, Paul intentionally documented the spiritual unity of the Christian community, which was organized separately out of political necessity, by obligating himself to gather from his Gentile Christian churches a collection for the Jewish Christian church in Jerusalem (Gal. 2:10). This amicable agreement was not changed by the Antiochene conflict about table fellowship between Hellenistic Jewish and Gentile Christians (Gal. 2:11ff.), which concerned the Jewish purity rules and was played out primarily between the cautious James in Jerusalem, who feared Jewish reprisals, and the liberal diaspora missionary Peter. (See also pp. 116ff. above.)

The Jerusalem agreements did not exclude local conflicts with the synagogue, especially since Paul as a Jew was still under the jurisdiction of the synagogue in whose vicinity he worked. For he directed his preaching primarily toward God-fearing Gentiles, and the fact that he "unyoked" many God-fearers from the synagogues was probably the most prominent cause of conflicts between him and the local Jewish authorities (cf. Acts 16:13–15; 18:7–8). The presentation in Acts, according to which Paul always began his mission in the synagogue and, against his intentions, was always driven anew toward the Gentiles, is naturally difficult to harmonize with the agreements of the Apostolic Council and with Paul's missionary practice and is due exclusively to the "salvation-historical" purpose of the author Luke. Yet the traditions on which Luke depends in Acts 14:1–5, 19–20; 17:1–15; 18:1–17 apparently include conflicts between Paul and synagogue leaders. Paul himself reports in 2 Cor. 11:24–25 (cf. Gal. 5:11; 6:12–13) on punishments that he had to suffer on the part of the synagogues. Yet we do not learn to what extent these punishments were imposed on him after his conversion during the early time of persecution and during his mission in Syria and Cilicia when he was active within the synagogue, and to what extent he experienced them when he was carrying on his independent mission outside the synagogue.

Yet Paul never saw himself as an apostate but always as a faithful administrator of the inheritance of his ancestors. His anti-Judaism was aimed not against the Jews (Rom. 9:1ff.) but against Jewish particularism. The faith that he proclaimed was the faith of Abraham (Romans 4; Galatians 3), and he derived the universality of the preaching of faith for Jews and Gentiles without distinction not least of all from the basic Jewish confession to *one* God of all people (Rom. 3:29–30; 10:12–13). Toward the end of his work, Paul no longer anticipated being able to make more than individual members of his people jealous in order to save them (Rom. 11:14; cf. 1 Cor. 1:19ff.), but he hoped for the eschatological salvation of the "full number" of Israelites (Rom. 11:25–27), and he contradicted those Gentile Christians who are convinced that the Jewish people have been rejected by God because of unbelief and that election has been transferred from the Jews to Gentile Christians (Rom. 11:11ff.).

Jewish Christianity
before the Year 70

We have a direct literary legacy from neither Palestinian nor Hellenistic Jewish Christianity for the period before the destruction of Jerusalem. This fact makes it difficult to determine in more precise detail the relationship of these Christian communities to official Judaism. Therefore we also cannot determine to what extent a fundamental delineation of Palestinian Jewish Christianity from the Jewish Christian communities in the Hellenistic Diaspora is at all justified in this period. Gal. 2:7–9, 12 makes it seem rather doubtful.

In any case, the church in Jerusalem and Palestine was able to live relatively unmolested in Jewish territory before the outbreak of the Jewish war. Why Agrippa I had James the son of Zebedee executed (Acts 12:1–2) we do not know, but it is possible that his execution by the consciously Jewish-oriented king was connected with the persecution of the "Hellenists," to which Stephen also fell victim. The martyrdom of James's brother John can be inferred from Mark 10:35–40 only with reservation. Yet in the year 62, according to Josephus (*Ant.* 20.9.1) and Hegesippus (in Euseb. *Hist. Eccl.* 2.1.4–5; 2.23.5ff.), James the brother of the Lord, who was apparently the leader of the Jerusalem church, was stoned at the instigation of the high priest Ananus, apparently without any serious objection from the people. From Eusebius (*Hist. Eccl.* 3.5.3) we learn that the Jerusalem church left the city before the Jewish war and settled in Pella. We learn nothing about its later fate.

There is no foundation for the occasionally encountered view that the heretical Jewish Christianity later called "Ebionitism" was a reversion to *Palestinian* Jewish Christianity; to the extent that the Ebionites honored Jesus as a prophet but did not confess him as Christ, they are rather descendants of the part of the Jesus movement that was not open to the Easter faith and to subsequent doctrinal developments, the part to which we owe the old sayings tradition (see pp. 38–39 above). With other parts of Jewish Christianity considered heretical, it is a question of a later development or classification (see p. 266 below). Paul's relationship with the Jerusalem church and its leaders is completely natural (Gal. 2:1ff., 11ff.; 1 Cor. 9:5); he gathers the collection for Jerusalem on every occasion without reservation (Rom. 15:25ff.). The view established by Ferdinand Christian Baur one hundred fifty years ago that the opposing missionaries in Paul's mission territory were Jewish Christians from Palestine is still influential today, but even in reference to the Letter to the Galatians it has no basis in the texts (Schmithals 1983). And Paul's concern that the collection gathered toward the end of his third missionary journey might not be welcomed by the Jerusalem Christians refers to the idea that "the disobedient in Judea" might take offense at this Gentile gift and put pressure on their Christian compatriots (Schmithals 1988b, 537ff.), but it betrays no tensions between Paul and the Jewish Christians of Palestine. There is no support for the idea that the life and thought of Jerusalem Christendom was essentially different from the faith that Peter as apostle "for the circumcised" proclaimed in the synagogues of the Diaspora as far as Rome (Gal. 2:7–10; 1 Cor. 9:5).

The theological thinking of this Hellenistic Jewish Christianity living within the institution of the synagogue, which with all its many strata still exhibits a relatively homogeneous basic confession, is known on the one hand from the Antiochene level of Pauline theology (see pp. 108ff. above) and on the other from the tradition that underlies the Gospel of Mark (see pp. 320ff. below). This confession is based on the (Greek) Old Testament, and even in Christology and soteriology, to say nothing of relationship to God and ethics, it does not leave the realm of what was "thinkable" in the Hellenistic synagogue. This also includes criticism of priests and the Sanhedrin and of the temple cult represented by them, which is found in the pre-Markan passion story with the report of the cleansing of the temple, especially since it probably already looks back on the destruction of the temple (Mark 13:1–2). On this narrative level the Pharisees are not yet Jesus' opponents but, like other Jewish groups, his critical dialogue partners.

Analogous to Rom. 11:11ff., Mark 7:24–30 speaks against the pride of certain Gentile Christian circles that want to replace the exclusive Jewish claim to election with a corresponding Gentile Christian one. And it reveals, along with many other traditions (Luke 7:1ff. par.; Acts 8:26ff.; 10:1ff.), that in addition to born Jews, the Jewish Christianity of the Diaspora included more than a few God-fearing Gentiles. Understandably, no anti-Jewish tendency can be discovered in the traditions of this Hellenistic Jewish Christianity. Naturally, this does not exclude individual tensions, especially since the numerous synagogues in the various regions of the Diaspora probably do not offer a uniform picture. Unfortunately, however, neither from Jewish nor from Hellenistic sources do we know anything worth mentioning about the internal relationships in the synagogues of the Diaspora. It is true that the familiar information from Suetonius (*Claudius* 25.4; cf. Acts 18:2) that Emperor Claudius (41–54) drove (the?) Jews from Rome, because they were constantly causing unrest "at the instigation of one Chrestus," focuses attention on a quarrel between Christians and Jews in at least one of the Roman synagogues, for there is widespread agreement that "Chrestus" refers to Jesus Christ. Yet we can neither shed more light on this information nor designate it as symptomatic of the existence of Jewish Christians in the synagogues, especially since the quarrel with Gentile Christians could have been brought into the synagogue.

The *Aposynagōgos*

Julius Caesar (Jos. *Ant.* 14.213ff.) and again Augustus (ibid., 16.162ff.; Philo *Legatio ad Gaium* 156ff.) had already granted members of the synagogue freedom of worship and thereby given them the privilege of not having to participate in the public cult of the goddess Roma and of Caesar, which was the obligatory act of loyalty required of the subjects of Rome. In regard to this state of affairs, Tertullian, incidentally and apparently without using an official term, calls Judaism a *religio licita* (*Apol.* 21.1). In the temple in Jerusalem there was no image of the emperor, and no sacrifice was made to the deified emperor. Instead, the Jews pledged that they would show their loyalty twice daily in the Jerusalem temple by offering sacrifices for the benefit of the emperor, and these were paid for with the temple tax from Jews in all the world and apparently also from God-fearers (Jos. *Ant.* 14.7.2; *Bell.* 2.197, 409–10; *Contra Apionem* 2.6). The termination *(Beendigung)* of this offering in the year 66 gave the signal for rebellion against Rome. The members of the synagogue, those who enjoyed that privilege, identified themselves as such through the payment of the temple tax, a half shekel (Exod. 30:13) or two drachmas (Matt. 17:24–27), which every Jew was obliged to pay from age twenty on (Philo *De Specialibus Legibus* 1.77). After the destruction of the temple, Emperor Vespasian decreed that this tax would henceforth be paid by all members of the synagogue as *fiscus iudaicus* to the temple of Jupiter Capitolinus in Rome (Jos. *Bell.* 7.218; *Dio Cassius* 66.7). The payment continued to free one from the public cult, for the privileges of the synagogue were continued. Thus it was not considered a special affront but served as proof of the loyalty of the Jews who paid it.

Before the Jewish war, very different Jewish groups and movements, including uncircumcised God-fearers, were found under the protective roof of the legal synagogal organization and enjoyed the freedom from the Roman state cult granted to the synagogue. Their common bond was the sacrificial cult in Jerusalem borne by all of them through the temple tax. When this unifying bond was loosened by the destruction of the temple and the prohibition of the sacrificial cult, under the leadership of Johanan ben Zakkai of Jamnia, Jewish circles that were hostile to zealots provided a new focus and obligatory order in the Pharisaically understood law. In the course of this worldwide reorganization of Judaism, which was apparently not completed before the beginning of the second century, the previously pluralistic synagogal organization was transformed into a one-sided Pharisaic-rabbinical community. This meant in particular that the law that in the synagogue was considered a legal entity merged with the Torah as understood by the Pharisees. Those who could not bow to the law thus understood had to leave the synagogue. Also, the confession of Jesus as the Christ was now no longer possible within the synagogue, "for the Jews had already agreed that anyone who confessed Jesus to be the Messiah would be put out of the synagogue" (John 9:22; 12:42; 16:2ff.—in these three passages we find the term *aposynagōgos*). For God-fearing Gentiles also, there was now no longer a place in the synagogue, and for this reason they are no longer found even in the rabbinical writings, which generally try to veil conditions in the synagogue before their Pharisaic reorganization. Thus the partial universalism that had developed within the liberal synagogues in regard to their numerous God-fearing adherents was abandoned; it was not a question of circumcision but of holding to the commandments of God (1 Cor. 7:19; cf. Gal. 5:6; 6:15).

The rabbinical reorganization of the synagogue was achieved under pressure and with support on the part of Rome, which was interested in orderly conditions in the synagogues and was inclined toward the Pharisees because they had proven to be a stabilizing force in the area of the Diaspora during the Jewish rebellion. Still during the siege of Jerusalem by the Romans, Johanan ben Zakkai is supposed to have received permission to undertake rabbinical education in imperial Jamnia. In particular, the separation of the synagogue from the numerous God-fearing Gentiles (Acts 13:42, 50; 16:13–14; 17:4; 18:7), as well as from the Gentile Christians living within the synagogal organization, was in the interest of Rome, as shown toward the end of the first century by the execution of Flavius Clemens, a member of the imperial family, and other persons, and also by the banishment of his wife Domitilla because of her inclination toward Judaism (*Dio Cassius* 67.14; 68.1; cf. Acts 16:20–21). The political privileges of the synagogue were to be granted only to born Jews, not to other Roman subjects; conversion to Judaism was also forbidden.

Those who had to leave the synagogue also lost the legal protection it provided. After exclusion from the synagogue, however, Jewish Christians and God-fearing Gentile Christians still could not participate in the public cult. Thus the apo-*synagōgos* immediately subjected them to state reprisals. The reorganized synagogue regarded the excluded Jewish Christians as apostates; for the pagan public, however, they were potential Jewish insurrectionists who neither took part in the cult of the emperor nor paid the *fiscus iudaicus*. Therefore, for its own protection the synagogue fought against them and denounced them to the Roman authorities, for in the public consciousness Christians were for a long time still considered a subgroup of Judaism because of their background and way of life.

The cursing of the heretics (*birkath ha-minim*)—namely, the Nazarenes—which was incorporated into the daily prayer of the Jews toward the end of the first century, forms the high point of the rabbinical reorganization of the synagogue. This significant act raises many individual questions (Maier 1982, 136ff.; Wengst 1992, 89ff.), but essentially it marks the end of the *aposynagōgos,* even if the development in the various areas of the Roman Empire probably proceeded in different ways and we learn from Jewish sources hardly anything about the corresponding processes. The widespread assumption (cf., for example, Wengst 1992, 96ff.) that the daily cursing of the *minim* was the attempt of the rabbinate to set up a united front within the synagogue, because heretics could not add their amen to such a prayer, overlooks the political background of the *aposynagōgos.* Even if this cursing is in tune with the dogmatic interests of the rabbinate, we must not underestimate the interest of the synagogue in documenting for the state its completed act of internal reorganization and above all its desire to distance itself demonstratively from the former adherents of the synagogue, in order not to endanger its own privileges.

Christians are now caught in the middle without any rights: they are oppressed and persecuted both by the synagogue—which now has once again certain powers at its disposal—and by the Roman authorities. Even one hundred years after the exclusion from the synagogue, Tertullian calls the synagogues *fontes persecutionum* (*Scorpiace* 10.10). They are the source of the public calumnies of Christians (Tert. *Ad Nationes* 1.14; *Adversus Judaeos* 13.26; *Diognetus* 5.17; Just. *Apol.* 31). This is the way that Luke, with the situation of his own time in mind, presents the Jews of the synagogue (Acts 13:50; 14:2, 5, 19; 17:5–9; 18:12–17), and he appeals to the authorities to give no credence to Jewish denunciations (Acts 23:25ff.; 24:1ff.; 25:7–8; and elsewhere). For corresponding apologetic reasons, he also takes this situation back into the trial before Pilate (Luke 23:1ff.), in which Jesus is accused by the Jews of calling for a tax boycott and making himself king. At about the same time one can observe in the Revelation to John that Christians were slandered by the synagogue "because of their revolutionary nature and for fomenting rebellion" (Bousset 1906, 209) and then persecuted (Rev. 2:9–10; 3:9). A generation after Luke and the apocalyptist, Justin likewise blames the Jews and their calumnies for the persecutions of Christians (*Dial.* 14.4–17.1; 47; 108; 110.4–5) and even reproaches them for killing Christians themselves when they have the power to do so (*Dial.* 95.4; 133.6). The zeal with which the Jews surpass even the pagans with their hatred of the Jews is described by the *Martyrdom of Polycarp* (12.2; 13.1; 17.2; 18.1; cf. *Martyrdom of Pionius* 4.8, 11; 13). The anti-Montanist quoted by Eusebius (*Hist. Eccl.* 5.16.12) asserts that no Montanist was "ever persecuted by the Jews and killed by the pagans," and here he assumes more precisely that confessors were crucified by the pagans, but Christian women were whipped and stoned in the synagogues. Even if such presentations come from the pens of the immediately affected Christians, they are still credible in principle. For it would be "downright incomprehensible if the Jewish communities in the Diaspora had not exhausted all means of distancing themselves from Christians, who under the label of 'Israel' could constitute a serious threat to the legal basis of the Jewish communities if the Roman state could no longer clearly recognize the boundaries between Jews and Christians" (Maier 1982, 135).

All the New Testament books, excepting the authentic letters of Paul but including their collection and redaction, comprise the writings of the New Testament from the period after the destruction of Jerusalem. They are all affected in varying degrees—but on the whole considerably and often even causally—by the expulsion of the Jewish Christian communities from the synagogue and by the consequences of this process. The New Testament thereby becomes the most important source for studying the *aposynagōgos,* about which the rabbinical traditions are completely silent because they want their present circumstances to be regarded as also prevailing in the older period.

In the individual writings of the New Testament the phenomenon of the *aposynagōgos* is seen from various sides with many intertwining interests and changing emphases. Anti-Jewish polemic and political apologetic vis-à-vis the state authorities are completely interrelated and interconnected. In the face of threats against the lives and property of believers, there is concern about one's own community that is directed toward preventing both apostasy into paganism and backsliding into the bosom and protection of the synagogue. The church has to separate itself both from radical Christians who in the face of persecutions repudiate the authority of the Roman state and from brothers and sisters in the faith who completely disinherit Judaism (cf. *Barnabas*) or after the expulsion from the synagogue want to free themselves from the Old Testament–Jewish native soil of Christianity.

Moreover, the Pauline, Gentile Christian churches, which, as the Neronian persecution in the year 64 shows, had always led an insecure existence, are coming more and more to the attention of Jewish Christians. The agreements of the Apostolic Council, which had previously determined the relationship of the *ekklēsiai* to the Christian communities that lived in the synagogue, became pointless with the exclusion of all Christians from the synagogue and the definitive end of the Jewish kingdom in Palestine after the end of the first rebellion; the result was closer contacts between the two communities that had previously lived in peaceful coexistence. The theological position of the early catholic church reveals that in this process the predominance lay on the side of formerly synagogal Christianity, which in numbers far surpassed the Gentile Christians, who, moreover, had to no small degree drifted off into the Gnostic heresy. The problems that then arose when certain Christian circles retained their Jewish legalistic way of life, even after exclusion from the synagogue, are revealed by Justin (*Dial.* 47). These Jewish Christian sectarians, whom the church fathers called *Ebionites, Elkesaites,* or *Nazoreans,* were by no means unified and in part were Gnostic or anti-Pauline, as the *Kerygmati Petri* show; in most cases they probably belonged to groups located above all in Syria and east of the Jordan who did not join the "catholic" church after their expulsion from the synagogue.

One must also assume that more than a few non-Christians, above all God-fearing Gentiles, joined the Christian communities after their expulsion from the synagogue. For such a process easily explains the notable fact that some pieces of early catholic literature, such as the *Shepherd of Hermas* and, less clearly, the *First Letter of Clement,* teach a non-Pharisaic Judaism that is coated with a thin Christian varnish but takes little or no notice of Hellenistic Jewish Christianity's anthropology, Christology, and soteriology, which had already taken shape in Paul's time, or of its teaching and confessional formulations. When in the *Shepherd of Hermas,* for example—which does not use the names *Jesus* and *Christ*—Christology experiences "the uncommon reduction to the status of a model and example of one person among all others," who are likewise human beings (Brox 1991, 487), we are presumably encountering not an "archaic" Jewish Christianity (ibid., 487, 490) about which we know nothing, but a phenomenon related to the exclusion from the synagogue.

The Gospel of Mark
and the Sayings Source

The reason for the *redactional* stratum of the Gospel of Mark and the sayings source (Q) is not the *aposynagōgos* but the endeavor to gain for the Christian church a group to bear a still prechristological Jesus tradition (see pp. 36ff. above, 322ff. below). Yet the secondary redactions of both writings, which are possibly from the same hand, apparently presuppose the conflict with the synagogue, without the redactor clearly revealing whether he is or was a member of intrasynagogal Christendom, or whether he observed the conflict between the synagogue and its Christian adherents from the Gentile Christian standpoint of an outsider. It is conceivable that the redactor is endeavoring, while the *aposynagōgos* is *in progress,* to gain the named bearer group and to follow the way of the Christian church outside the synagogue.

If in the basic text of the Gospel of Mark the Pharisees were still one Jewish group among others and the critical dialogue partners of Jesus, the evangelist or redactor already knows them as the authoritative representatives of Judaism and as opponents of Jesus and the church (Mark 2:18; 8:11, 15; cf. 12:37b–40). Mark's community suffers under persecutions, and the evangelist is helping them adjust to this situation by bringing an older sayings tradition up to date: one must not be ashamed of Jesus and his words (Mark 8:38), even when there is a threat of losing one's life for the gospel's sake (Mark 8:35); hangers-on and sympathizers diminish the pressure on the church (9:39–40); those who are kind to oppressed Christians are promised a heavenly reward; opponents are threatened with judgment (9:41ff.). In Mark 10:28–30 persecution because of the gospel, especially the confiscation of property, even becomes an independent theme of the evangelist. Accordingly, he introduces elements of the political apologetic into his account (15:12–14) by having Pilate determine Jesus' innocence and by making the Jews guilty of Jesus' death (cf. 12:6ff.), and in 12:35–37a he explains why the politically ambiguous designation *son of David* is not an appropriate messianic title. Perhaps the unfruitful fig tree serves the evangelist as an image of Israel (11:12–14, 20–21).

The redaction of the sayings source offers a similar picture. In expansion of an old beatitude it states that Christians are "defamed" and "excluded" (Luke 6:22) or "persecuted" (Matt. 5:11–12) by the Jews, a formulation that apparently reflects the situation of the *aposynagōgos*. The faith of the Gentile centurion in Capernaum is praised, for nowhere in Israel has Jesus found such faith (Luke 7:9 par.). Those invited first, the Jews, have definitively rejected God's invitation; Gentiles come from all directions (Luke 7:29 par.) and fill the house of God (14:15–24 par.).

The Gospel of Matthew

Matthew writes his Gospel *in the situation* of the *aposynagōgos* in order to give his newly independent community its own instruction book with rules for Christian life and piety (Matt. 28:20a); he presupposes that the baptismal instruction using the triadic confession of faith (cf. 28:19) is known and does not repeat it. He already speaks decidedly of "their" synagogues (4:23; 9:35; and elsewhere). He recommends, however, that Christians continue to pay the *fiscus iudaicus,* the former temple tax (17:24–27), although this is no longer expected of them (17:24), for "if they paid the tax, they enjoyed the generous protection that the Jewish religion was granted in the empire" (J. Weiss 1907, 348). We can doubt that this tactic for avoiding offense (17:27) was rewarded with success for very long, for it is very unlikely that it was tolerated by the synagogue. It is already completely under the influence of the Pharisees (5:20; 23:1–3, 6–7), who were able to assume their position as authorities (12:14; 22:15). They are responsible for the persecutions (5:11–12; 10:17ff.; 23:1–36) that Christians have to endure (10:22ff., 40ff.; 24:9; 25:31ff.). These persecutions occasion the evangelist's political apologetic, which is especially evident in 27:19–25 ("His blood be on us and on our children"), but it also defines 5:5, 9, 38ff.; 21:1ff.; 26:51–54. Matthew's presentation, according to which the Jews denounce the peacemaker Jesus before Pilate as a political insurrectionist and have Pilate crucify him, reflects the current situation of the Matthean communities, who in spite of their peaceful and loyal attitude are delivered by the synagogue to the oppression of the authorities. By contrast, Matthew points to the real insurrectionists, the Jews, and interprets the catastrophe of the Jewish war as divine retribution for the killing of Jesus and his messengers (22:5ff.; 23:36; 27:25).

Resistance against the injustice directed toward Christians is pointless; deprived of its rights, the impotent church is left defenseless with only the way of suffering (5:38–48), which at least will not give the opponents additional provocation and new nourishment to feed their accusations. Matthew does not even express the vague hope that the evil that is done to them will be overcome by the good that they do (cf. Rom. 12:21). Yet he impresses on Christians that they should live and suffer *publicly* (Matt. 5:13–16) and let their good deeds shine before others. In this way they bring to light the injustice that they suffer and perhaps even silence false accusations (cf. 1 Peter 2:12, 15). In any case, they will find compassionate sympathizers who praise the heavenly Father of Christians (Matt. 5:16; cf. 1 Peter 2:12); these apparently include primarily former God-fearers who likewise had to leave the synagogue. They are promised a heavenly reward if they welcome the persecuted or even refresh them with a cup of cold water (Matt. 10:40–42). These compassionate sympathizers, who without knowing it have met the Judge of the world, Christ himself, in the suffering Christians, receive the promise, ". . . just as you did it to one of the least of these who are members of my family, you did it to me" (25:40). Those who stand by the ones who suffer will see God in the last judgment, just like the latter who are persecuted for righteousness sake (5:10).

Through "false prophets" the pressure of the Pharisees on Christians reaches directly into the church (Matt. 7:15–23; 13:41–42; 24:10–12) and makes itself known as the temptation of believers to fall away from their Christian confession and return to the synagogue (13:41; 18:6–9; 24:11). By contrast, Matthew emphasizes the necessity of baptism, the confessional sign for all Christians (3:14–15; see pp. 224–25 above), and warns the church against the teachings and the behavior of the Pharisees (5:20; 16:5–12; 23:1ff.). The church should endeavor to seek its lost members (18:10–14). If necessary, the tempters and the tempted must be excluded through a disciplinary process (18:15–18; cf. 13:41–42; 22:11–14), yet with the presupposition of a constant readiness to forgive and readmit those who have been excluded (18:21–35; 16:19): "A member who has strayed from the church (through tempters) shall not be let go; rather, all means should be tried to regain that member; only if all friendly attempts have borne no fruit may one resort to excommunication" (Wellhausen 1905, 70; Schenke and Fischer 1979, 103).

The theological disagreement with the synagogue is still in progress. Matthew rejects the Jewish accusation that the Christian faith means the abolition of the Torah and prophetic proclamation. This double inheritance from those of ancient times is, rather, completely fulfilled through the Messiah Jesus; this is shown with respect to the prophetic promises by the "fulfillment quotations" formulated christologically in a way that is typical of Matthew (1:22–23; 2:5–6, 15, 17–18; etc.) and with regard to the Torah by passages such as 5:17–20; 11:28–30; 22:34–40; 23:1–4. Against the Christian confession, the synagogue fights with the gloves off. In 1:18ff. the evangelist may be defending against the Jewish accusation, also known from John 8:41, that Jesus was an illegitimate child; in 27:64ff.; 28:11ff., against the Jewish assertion that the disciples stole Jesus' body in order to feign his resurrection—accusations that were spread in the *Toledot Jeschu* literature of the early Middle Ages. Matthew answers with a list of seven "woes" and a persistent reproach of "hypocrisy" (6:2, 5, 16; 15:7; 23:13ff.): the actions of the Pharisees do not correspond to their teachings (23:1ff.); they are children of hell (23:15) and are headed toward judgment (3:7; 23:33–36).

The unavoidable *aposynagōgos,* which was brought about by political developments, led to a sharp opposition between Judaism and (Jewish) Christianity, without any anti-Jewish motifs having played a role. In Matthew the new people of God composed of Jews and Gentiles (21:43) stands over against the synagogue, which has become Pharisaical (21:45). Only this "official" Judaism, which in the time after the year 70 no longer tolerates Christians in its midst, has forfeited salvation through its rejection of the Messiah Jesus (8:11–12; 12:24, 34ff.; 21:10–22:10). According to the Gospel of Matthew, before Easter, Jesus even turns his attention exclusively to his own people (10:5, 23; 15:24, 29–31), and only through obstinacy or its own unfaith does Israel lose its share of the salvation that God still offers to all peoples through his Messiah Jesus (8:11–12; 28:18–20).

The Gospel of Luke
and the Acts of the Apostles

In contrast to the Matthean, the Lukan churches have the *aposynagōgos* definitively behind them; in this respect their situation corresponds to that of 1 Peter and *Barnabas.* For Luke the link with the synagogue is broken (Stegemann 1991, 120ff.), and because the decision for or against Judaism and Christianity has been made, in the Lukan double volume there is no longer any recruitment of community members left behind in the synagogue or any polemic against the synagogue arising from a corresponding current disagreement.

Nonetheless, the consequences of the *aposynagōgos* are unmistakable. The legal protection that the constituents of the synagogue enjoyed has been lost, and Christians, who cannot perform the imperial sacrifice, are in permanent political jeopardy. The Lukan double volume looks back on vigorous persecutions of Christians that have taken place in the recent past and have resulted on the one hand in martyrdoms and on the other in falling away from the faith (Luke 12:4–12; 17:1ff.; 21:12–19; Acts 12:1–2; 16:13–40; chap. 22–28). The Jews accuse Christians of political disloyalty and thereby cause the Roman authorities to take measures against them. These distressing experiences evoke a thorough and diverse defense of Christians, who turn the accusations made against them back on the politically rebellious Judaism of the Zealot phase (Luke 20:20–26; 23:2–15, 19, 27–31; Acts 16:13–40; chap. 22–28). For such apologetic reasons Luke also strikes from his source the term *persecution* when it could be related to the state power of Rome (Luke 6:22 par.; 8:13 par.; 18:29–30 par.), and reserves it for the hostile behavior of the Jews (Stegemann 1991, 114ff.). In this way Luke wants to make it plain that in the earlier period the Roman authorities saw through the synagogal denunciations as unjustified; they did not give the Jews a hearing and did not persecute the Christians, but instead took them into protection against the reproaches of the synagogue (Luke 23:14–15, 22; Acts 16:35ff.; 18:12ff.; 25:25; 26:30ff.; etc.). The Romans in Luke's time should also act in the same way.

At the same time Luke turns against a pre-Marcionite heresy that refers to Paul in completely removing the Christian church from its Jewish native soil and in rejecting the Old Testament. This movement, which threatened the unity of Christendom, probably had its roots in the early time of persecution, when Paul himself was destroying the Christian *ekklēsia* under commission from the synagogue (see pp. 326ff. below). According to Rom. 11:11ff. Paul is aware of the presence of radical Christians in Rome, who deny the Jews access to salvation; the pre-Markan author of Mark 7:24–30 also has in mind corresponding tendencies within Christianity. The completion of the *aposynagōgos* probably gave considerable impetus to such radical Gentile Christianity, which in the generation after Luke developed into a solemn dualism and through Marcion became an elementary threat to orthodox Christendom. Luke applies himself against this development, and by emphasizing the continuity of Old Testament, the time of Jesus, and the Christian church, he becomes the theologian of "salvation history," as well as the creator of a picture of Paul that he puts over against the anti-Jewish image of Paul of the pre-Marcionites; in a similarly great distortion of historical reality, Luke moves the great apostle to the Gentiles close to the Pharisaical thinking that had become definitive for Judaism in Luke's time.

Without question, Luke deserves credit for laying the essential ground work for the defense against Marcionism, even if we can say very little that is certain about the concrete influence of the Lukan double volume on ecclesiastical development before the formation of the canon. Yet the price that Luke was ready to pay for defense against heretics and for the maintenance of the Old Testament Jewish tradition was a high one. For in Lukan theology we have a doctrinal formation that is universalist but very strongly assimilated to the Hellenistic synagogue: sin arises through the violation of moral commandments, and Jesus is a preacher of repentance who promises the forgiveness of sins in the last judgment. Not only the *theologia crucis* of Paul but also the soteriology of Hellenistic Jewish Christianity oriented toward the death of Jesus (see pp. 91ff. above) is given up or suppressed, as is seen in an especially striking way when Luke eliminates Mark 10:45 ("a ransom for many"). Only with its acceptance into the canon of the New Testament, which also contains the original letters of Paul, is the one-sided doctrinal formation of the Lukan double volume appropriately corrected.

The Gospel of John

Wrede called the Gospel of John "a writing born out of battle and written for battle" (1903, 40), and the synagogue was the evangelist's primary opponent. Yet this evaluation is accurate only if the word *born* is restricted in a literary-critical way and the situation of the *aposynagōgos* is connected not with our present Gospel but with its basic stratum or basic text (Schmithals 1992).

The particular Jewish opponents in this oldest literary stratum are the Pharisees, who are found in a position of legal authority (John 5:9–18; 7:12–13, 32, 45; 9:13–34) that they attained only with the reorganization of the synagogue after 70 (cf. Wengst 1992, 60ff.). The synagogue is oriented toward the law as understood Pharisaically (5:9–18; 9:28–29; 19:7) and reproaches Christians for their lack of knowledge of the law (7:48–49). According to John 20:31, the dispute concerns above all the confession of Jesus as the Christ, which John supports in various ways. First, *Jesus' self-testimony* of his majesty is connected with the testimony of his miraculous works (5:36; 8:13–14, 18; 10:25) and is expanded with the "I am" sayings. Then the *testimony of the fathers* comes from the "scriptures" or "Moses" (5:37–40, 45–47; 8:18). Against the confession of Christ the synagogue argues that the true Messiah, when he comes, will remain and not go back to the Father (12:34); he will come not from Galilee but from Bethlehem as the son of David (7:52); he will remain hidden until his anointing (1:33; 7:21–24); in distinction to Jesus, he will keep the law (5:9–18; 7:21–24; 9:16); and he will not make himself like God (5:18; 19:7). In reaction to the polemic that Jesus is an illegitimate child (8:41), John calls the Jews children of the devil (8:44). The synagogue also seems to have put forth John the Baptist as its star witness against the messiahship of Jesus; for this reason the evangelist does not report Jesus' baptism by John but instead especially emphasizes the role of the Baptist as a witness to the Messiah Jesus (1:33–34).

The situation of the *aposynagōgos,* which is reflected in the foregoing phenomena, is also specifically addressed in John 9:22; 12:42; 16:2–4a: the Christian confession leads to the exclusion from the synagogue. Christians have a great fear of the privileged position of power given the synagogue by the Roman state. There are even acts of violence against Christians, which include martyrdom (16:2). In the hatred of the world, Christians are persecuted like their Lord (15:18ff.; 16:20). The gathered church closes its doors out of fear of the Jews (20:19). Nicodemus (3:1–2) and Joseph of Arimathea (19:38), influential members of the synagogue, keep their sympathies for Christians secret for fear of their fellow Jews, as do the parents of the healed blind man (9:22–23). No one can speak openly about Jesus Christ (7:13). Above all, influential members of the synagogue anxiously deny their Christian confession (7:48–52; 12:42–43).

Since all the pressure on Christians comes directly from the synagogue (5:16–18) and there is no developed political apologetic in the basic text of the Gospel of John, one should seek a place of composition in a relatively closed Jewish settlement area in the East, whether in Palestine or in such metropolises as Antioch or Alexandria, and set the time of composition not too late. The separation of Christian church and synagogue, however, is essentially complete. The basic text of the Gospel of John already speaks of Jews in opposition to Christians, even where the latter are themselves born Jews (2:6; 8:17). On the one hand, Jews are the representatives of Judaism in general with its special customs and practices (2:6; 3:1; 4:9; 19:42). On the other hand, however, they are members of the synagogue already led by the Pharisees in the time of the *aposynagōgos* (3:1; 7:32, 45–48; 8:13; 9:13–16; 12:42; 18:3), and in this sense they are the dedicated opponents of Jesus and the Christian church (1:19; 5:10–18, 45–47; 10:19; etc.).

The basic text of the Gospel of John is oriented toward Christians and takes issue with the synagogue. Thus its author carries out his dispute with the synagogue with the intention of assuring the beleaguered Christian church of its confession. When he speaks of the unity of the church, he is thinking of the joining of the

Christian communities expelled from the synagogal organization with Gentile Christianity, which had always been independently organized (10:16). The *aposynagōgos* provides the impulse for the formation of the unified early catholic church. It challenges the anxious and indecisive Jewish Christians to a *decision* for baptism (see p. 224 above) and thus for the Christian church. Those who reject Jesus will come under judgment (5:22–24; 8:21).

The author of the basic text uses the Old Testament in his theological argumentation no more than, for example, the authors of the letters of John, Ignatius, and Polycarp, and he does not discuss Jesus with the words of scripture. Only the Jewish festival pilgrims who go out to meet Jesus use a saying from Psalms (John 12:13). Jesus' authority is apparently higher than that of the Old Testament. This, however, does not dissolve the continuity with Israel. Jesus is the Messiah from Israel; salvation comes from the Jews (4:22), and only with this presupposition does Jesus say, "No one comes to the Father except through me" (14:6). In the Old Testament the Father bears witness to his Son, and this witness is held up to the Jews (1:45; 5:37–40, 45–47; 7:22–24; 8:39, 47, 51–53, 56–58). This argumentation presupposes scribal discussions about the Christian confession between the Christian church and the synagogue in which Christians use scripture recognized by the synagogue in order to substantiate and strengthen their confession. Thus, in the view of the Christian author, it is the synagogue itself that denies its heritage.

If the situation and level of argumentation in the basic text of the Gospel of John is compared with the later Letters of John and the corresponding secondary stratum of the Gospel, it is good to recognize how in the first half of the second century the dispute with the synagogue and Judaism recedes and is replaced by the internal Christian strife over orthodoxy and heresy. All the specific scripture quotations come from the later stratum of the Gospel of John, which belongs to this period. Here the guiding intention was probably to root the Christian confession in the Jewish tradition and to counter heresies that, like Marcion, rejected the Old Testament.

The Letter to the Hebrews

According to a well supported consensus of scholars, the Letter to the Hebrews is a theological treatise that was probably given a secondary epistolary conclusion. It is characteristic of this writing that its instructional discussions alternate with specific admonitions against faith fatigue and apostasy. The discussions set forth the superiority of Jesus Christ, his salvific work, and his church over the old covenant. This suggests that the author of Hebrews is addressing the Judaizing tendencies of his readers, yet this aspect does not appear in the admonitions that are inextricably connected with the instructional sections. The problems related to this ambiguity have resulted in the Letter to the Hebrews being interpreted mostly in a timeless theological fashion. Thus Grässer states that the author is a great theological thinker who "misses the length, breadth, height, and depth" of the Christian confession in order to reactivate the tired faith of Christendom at the end of the first century through a "new interpretation of the confession of the crucified and exalted Christ" (1990, viii). Yet how the complicated, typological process of weakening the Old Testament cult could help the tired faith of Christendom make a new beginning is not clear.

Actually, the Letter to the Hebrews belongs entirely in the situation of the *aposynagōgos*. Its readers were forced out of the synagogue and thereby fell under the external pressure of persecution on the part of the Roman authorities (Heb. 10:32–39; 12:1ff.). There is no question yet of martyrdom, but the harsh pressure leads to hopelessness (12:3ff., 12–13) and to falling away from the traditional confession (2:1–4; 3:1–2, 12ff.; 4:1–11; 10:25, 29; 12:28–29), whether through reversion to paganism or through a return to the safe bosom of the synagogue. Since for the author a second repentance after apostasy is out of the question (6:1ff.), in faithfulness to the baptismal confession, which is apparently present in formulaic form (2:1ff.; 3:1, 14; 4:14ff.; 10:19ff., 35ff.; 13:15), it is important to focus on good examples (11:1ff.; 12:1ff.; 13:7), to strengthen one another, and to protect each other from apostasy and error (3:13; 6:11–12; 12:15).

The tie with the synagogue has been cut; a discussion with it is no longer being held by the author of Hebrews, whose position is possibly outside the circle of the Christians addressed. The Christians who have been forced out of the synagogue hold their own assemblies (10:25) and have their own church leaders (13:7, 17), yet it is obviously difficult for them to establish their identity outside the synagogue; they are still connected with "Judaizing" (13:9–10; cf. 5:11–6:3, 11). The author, however, endeavors to convey to them insight into what is specifically Christian and to give them the courage to regard and adopt the independent Christian standpoint as the one that is in accordance with the Old Testament promise and at the same time superior to the synagogue. Jesus is the decisive word of God (1:1ff.; 9:12, 26ff.). He is far superior to the angels who conveyed the Mosaic law (1:4–2:18); his glory is also greater than the glory of Moses (3:1–6), and the eschatological "rest" promised to the Israel of the wilderness period is in truth pledged to the Christian church that holds fast to the confession of faith (3:6–4:16). With his sacrifice and as heavenly high priest, Jesus completely overshadows the Levitical high priest (2:17; 4:15; 5:1ff.; chap. 7–10; 13:10ff.; he is the mediator of the new and better covenant (8:6; 9:15; 10:16–17; 12:24). Heb. 12:18–24 contains a summary of this basic theological idea of the Letter to the Hebrews.

Nowhere is there any doubt that the *ekklēsia* is a daughter of the synagogue, and in contrast to the Lukan double volume, pre-Marcionite disputers of such a continuity never appear in the Letter to the Hebrews. But the synagogue is coming to an end (8:13; possibly a *vaticinium ex eventu* of the temple destruction), and the addressed Christians should keep in mind that Jesus also suffered outside the gates of Jerusalem—that is, the synagogue—in order to make his people holy, and they should go out to him and bear his shame (13:12ff.).

The Deutero-Pauline Letters

The Gentile Christian churches of Pauline provenance did not remain unaffected by the *aposynagōgos,* since the separate organization of Gentile Christian and Jewish Christian churches agreed upon at the Apostolic Council was now superseded, and the idea of an organizational unit that would become the "catholic" church had not yet been conceived. As the Letter to the Hebrews perhaps shows, however, Gentile Christians endeavored to use their own experiences to be helpful to Jewish Christian communities who had been forced out of the synagogue and into a situation of having no rights.

In this regard we cannot point to the pastoral epistles, but to Ephesians and to the parallel deutero-Pauline passages in Colossians. The pervasive theme of Ephesians (cf. 3:4) concerns the unity of Jewish and Gentile Christians as the one people of God (2:11–22); in particular, there is a special address to Gentile Christians (2:1–10), who are to understand their conversion as a coinheritance (3:6) of the gifts of Christ that are common to Jewish and Gentile Christians (3:1–21). Already in the opening of the letter the author invokes the unity of the church in this sense (1:22–23), and the paraeneses in 4:1–6, 25–32 exhort mutual acceptance and again support this exhortation with the unity of the body of Christ (4:7–16). The main purpose of Ephesians consists in suggesting to Gentile Christians of the Pauline churches the acceptance of their brothers and sisters in the faith who have been expelled from the synagogal organization and at the same time the task of making them familiar with the Pauline tradition. With this presupposition the admonitions against a reversion to the immorality of paganism (4:17–24; 5:1–21) also receive an immediate contextual significance: without making theological concessions to the Christians coming from the synagogue (cf. 2:15), the post-Pauline Gentile Christians also profess continued adherence to synagogal morality in accordance with their own traditional teaching (4:20–21). The adoption of the household rules, which come from the synagogal tradition, in 5:22–6:9 has this connecting function. The same situation and intention can be presupposed for the corresponding passages in Colossians, which encourage harmony and enjoin the synagogal morality of the household rules (Col. 1:9–23; 2:19; 3:15b–4:1).

The Collection and Redaction of Paul's letters

The consequences of the *aposynagōgos* apparently also occasioned the oldest collection of the Pauline letters, which is first attested by the *First Letter of Clement* (35.5–6; 47.1ff.; 49.5) and comprises seven writings: 1–2 Corinthians, Galatians, Philippians, 1–2 Thessalonians, and Romans (Schmithals 1984). This collection is intended to guarantee the influence of Pauline theology and to make the particular legacy of Paul available to "catholic" Christianity, which in the milieu of the collector and redactor is apparently composed of Pauline Gentile Christian churches and of Jewish Christians driven out of the synagogue. This purpose is served by the redactionally inserted "catholic" address in 1 Cor. 1:2b at the beginning of the collection (cf. J. Weiss 1910, 2ff.; 2 Cor. 1:1), by the gloss in Rom. 6:17 that refers to the traditional type of the Pauline teaching, and by the doxology in Rom. 16:25–27, which the redactor formulated as the closing of his collection in order to recommend the "prophetic" message of the Pauline gospel to all peoples.

In addition, the redactor is responsible above all for Rom. 13:1–7 and 1 Thess. 2:15–16. Rom. 13:1–7 lets it be known that the Christian church is under the pressure of state persecution and must adapt to it. With arguments that are completely at home in the synagogue, the editor of the letter collection admonishes his readers to strive for extreme loyalty to the Roman authorities and above all to pay their taxes on time, which is also important to Justin (*Apol.* 1.17): "Everywhere and above all, we endeavor to render taxes and imposts to your officials." The authorities will not lightly question the loyalty of good taxpayers!

In 1 Thess. 2:15–16 we find the harshest anti-Jewish text in the New Testament, which for many reasons cannot possibly have come from Paul himself:

> [14]For you, brothers and sisters, became imitators of the churches of God in Christ Jesus that are in Judea, for you suffered the same things from your own compatriots as they did from the Jews, [15]who killed both the Lord Jesus and the prophets, and drove us out; they displease God and oppose everyone [16]by hindering us from speaking to the Gentiles so that they may be saved. Thus they have constantly been filling up the measure of their sins; but God's wrath has overtaken them at last.

In v. 15 the accusations against the Jews raised by Paul in v. 14 (cf. Col. 1:22) are expanded. The Jews not only killed the prophets but also the Lord Jesus, a representation that occurs for apologetic reasons in the passion accounts of the Gospels—and the later, the more intensive—but is foreign to Paul himself. The words "and drove us out" apparently refer, if the "us" means Christians in general, directly to the expulsion from the synagogue. But if the "us" speaks only of Paul, which is not very likely, then the apologetic element would be significant, for by contrast with 2 Cor. 11:25, for example, pagan persecutions are not mentioned. Now as before—the author changes it into the present tense form—the Jews do not act in a way that pleases God, and they are hostile to all people. These are harsh anti-Jewish reproaches that would be unheard of in Paul himself but which are connected with ancient anti-Judaism, for Tacitus also says of the Jews: "Adversus omnes alios hostile odium" ("against all others, hostile hatred"—*Historiae* 5.5). When the passage says further that the Jews keep us from preaching to the Gentiles for their salvation and thereby constantly fill up the measure of their sins, it is probably referring to the continuing denunciatory behavior of the synagogue after the *aposynagōgos*. The closing assertion that God's judgment has definitively come upon them is apparently a reference to the Jewish catastrophe of the year 70, which is interpreted elsewhere in early Christian times as God's judgment on unbelieving Israel (Matt. 22:7; 27:25).

Conclusion

The anti-Jewish passage 1 Thess. 2:15–16 indicates in exemplary fashion that at the turn of the first century Christians and Jews still met only as opponents. The reason for this development, which was still not to be anticipated in Paul's time, was not least of all political. After the Jewish catastrophe and the destruction of the temple, the synagogue was forced to reorient itself under political pressure from the Romans. In the particular synagogue, guided by the rabbinate in a Pharisaic, legalistic way, there was now no longer any room for the universalist community of Christians, which proclaimed faith in the Messiah Jesus. With this the hope of early Christendom that Israel would be won to faith in the Messiah Jesus completely disappeared. Within orthodox Christendom one had increasingly not only to restrain the view that God had rejected the Jews but also to meet the challenge of heretics who wanted to free Christianity from its Jewish Old Testament roots. At the same time, the goal of overcoming the opposition between Jews and Greeks through the Christian message proved to be unattainable. Instead of this, after the beginning of the second century the church of Christians established itself as a "third race" (cf. Harnack 1924, 259ff.) beside Jews and Greeks or Gentiles, and the history of the early catholic church began.

15

The Old Testament in the New

The Holy Scripture of early Christianity was the Old Testament. In general, Palestinian Jewish Christians probably used the Hebrew Bible, but its Greek translation, the Septuagint, which was used in the synagogues scattered around the Roman Empire, soon became important for Christians as well. Later it was also translated into Syriac, Coptic, Armenian, and so forth, but these were without significance for the authors of the New Testament.

In neither the Hebrew nor the Greek version of the Old Testament was there yet in the early Christian period a fixed canon that definitively determined which writings were to be included and which excluded. The Hebrew Old Testament had grown slowly. Its oldest part was formed by the "Law" (or Torah, Pentateuch, five books of Moses); around 350 B.C. the five books of the Torah became the recognized Holy Scripture of the Jews. Later the Law was joined by the "Prophets," which, however, clearly carried less weight than the Torah. Around the year 200 B.C. the collection of prophetic writings—Isaiah, Jeremiah, Ezekiel, and twelve minor prophets—was closed, and the Holy Scripture then consisted of "the Law and the Prophets." Finally came the remaining writings, above all the book of Psalms, with varying estimations of value in comparison with the Law and the Prophets, but this process remained in flux until toward the end of the first century A.D. At that time the normative authorities of Judaism in Jamnia determined the scope of the canon of the Hebrew Old Testament, which the *Biblia Hebraica* has possessed since then, even if the order of its books and their count underwent some variation.

For early Christianity, however, this Jewish decision in Jamnia was without significance, since they had long used the Septuagint everywhere. The Greek version of the Old Testament continued the Jewish tradition that antedated the Jamnia agreement, and therefore it contained a number of writings that were not accepted into the Hebrew Bible and which today fall into the category of "Old Testament Apocrypha." Early Christendom did not undertake a canonical delimitation of the Septuagint, and therefore the manuscripts of the Septuagint always included those accepted in the Hebrew Bible but also contained additional holy writings of Judaism in varying number and selection. Thus Christians held fast to the holy writings adopted from Jewish tradition and did not deal with the question of whether one or another of these writings was correctly or incorrectly included in the Holy Scripture. It is not surprising that Christian authors in the early period of the church appealed above all to the writings that were also favored in the synagogue; Genesis, Exodus, Psalms, and the prophet Isaiah were used the most. The books of the Prophets clearly gained favor over the Law, because the Christian message could most easily be found in them.

Yet we must not assume that in the Christian churches of the early period the entire Old Testament—of whatever scope and magnitude—was always in general use everywhere. Manuscripts were costly, and one could hardly take some twenty-five rolls of Holy Scripture along on missionary journeys. Furthermore, one required only a relatively limited selection from the extensive scriptures to demonstrate the biblical basis of the Christian message, and appropriate anthologies (florilegia) were easier to handle. The described situation also adequately explains the fact that often relatively free or inexact quotations from the Old Testament are found, as well as frequent mixed quotations from several passages.

In all of this we must also keep in mind that neither Judaism nor early Christianity had a "scriptural principle" in the sense of the Reformation, and this fact is of crucial importance for the following presentation. The motto *sola scriptura,* scripture alone, is not found, especially since within its Holy Scripture, Judaism in general ascribed absolute authority only to the Law. Common gatherings served above all prayer and the clarification of the confession to the one God, along with the inclusion of the corresponding rules of the Jewish way of life. It is uncertain whether and to what extent in the early period there were regular scripture readings and interpretations in Jewish "houses of prayer" (*proseuchē*). In any case, public and private worship was related or bound to scripture only to a limited extent.

Furthermore, certain branches on the fringe of Judaism were already expressing criticism of the Torah. In Gal. 3:19–20 Paul, in connection with his attempt to devaluate the law vis-à-vis faith, argues using the idea that the law was given not by God but by angels (cf. Heb. 2:2). This view, which is found, independently of Paul, in various forms in Gnosticism, was apparently adopted by him from the Jewish circles that in the interest of a universally open Judaism wanted to abolish the barrier of the law, which closed Jews off from other peoples (cf. Schlier 1949, 109–19). It is also possible that in the Judaism of the New Testament period there was already an idea that "false pericopes" had infiltrated the law (Strecker 1958, 166–84). In any case, however, there were from time to time in Judaism, *outside* the Holy Scripture, prophets who claimed to proclaim the word of God directly. And even if these prophets did not gain easy recognition, their claim was not disputed in principle. Such Jewish prophets are frequently attested in contemporary writings (cf. for example, Acts 5:36–37; 21:38; Jos. *Bell.* 2.159; 6.300ff.; 1 Macc. 14:41; Michel 1954, 60–66); the authors of the Greek book of Baruch, of 4 Ezra, and the book of *Enoch* live completely in the traditions of the Pentateuch, but they deal very freely with the traditional material and proclaim their message, which they place on the lips of Old Testament figures, without expressly referring to the Holy Scripture. In such a sense we can also call "prophetic" the appearance of John the Baptist (Luke 7:26; 16:16) and Jesus. In like manner, Christianity was from the beginning not simply a religion of scripture, and when one asks about the importance of the Old Testament in the New Testament, one must at the same time always keep in mind that there were other authorities that were also normative for early Christianity.

Jesus

Jesus belonged to his people and therefore without doubt was familiar with their Holy Scripture. A saying attributed to him reads: "I tell you, until heaven and earth pass away, not one letter, not one stroke of a letter, will pass from the law" (Matt. 5:18; cf. Luke 16:17), and even if he did not say it himself, he would probably have agreed with it. The parable in Mark 4:29 of the growing seed refers to Joel 4:13, the parable of the mustard seed in Mark 4:32 refers to Ps. 104:12, and in general the sayings ascribed to Jesus are filled with biblical language. Yet we cannot determine in detail Jesus' relationship to his Holy Scripture and the idiosyncrasies of his usage of scripture. In the sayings source (Q), used by Matthew and Luke, when Old Testament quotations are found on the lips of Jesus (cf. Luke 3:4–6, 22; 4:1–13; 7:27; 13:35), they come from an already christologically shaped expansion of the older sayings tradition and cannot be claimed for Jesus himself. There is disagreement as to whether the antitheses of the Sermon on the Mount, which are handed down only in the Gospel of Matthew ("You have heard that it was said of those of ancient times. . . . But I say to you . . ."; Matt. 5:21–22, 27–28, 33–34), were formulated by Jesus himself. Yet these antitheses, at least in their original form, do not mean an abolition of the Torah but a radicalization that enabled prophetic unconditionality to come to expression.

The idea that Jesus proclaimed the imminent coming of the kingdom of God while referring to certain scriptural passages is not attested and is also unlikely. He appeared with this announcement as an "apocalyptically" moved prophet who was following a divine inspiration. Accordingly, a prophetic beatitude places the disciples of Jesus beside or over the old prophets and kings such as David, for "many prophets and kings desired to see what you see, but did not see it, and to hear what you hear, but did not hear it" (Luke 10:24). Above all, the saying in Luke 12:10 (cf. Mark 3:28–29; *Did.* 11.7) reveals the strength of the prophetic consciousness of mission that defined Jesus and his circle of disciples: "And everyone who speaks a word against the Son of Man will be forgiven; but whoever blasphemes against the Holy Spirit will not be forgiven." Thus the Son of Man coming to judge will even forgive an invective against his person, but not one against the prophets, who now in the Holy Spirit announce the end time and call to repentance. Naturally, the coming of the Son of Man is expected on the basis of the scriptures (Daniel, *Enoch*), and this is not a deprecation of the Holy Scripture any more than the expectation of the Spirit in the end time of the old age, which has a solid basis in the Old Testament in Joel 3. The prophetic Spirit, however, is not something that flows out of the scriptures and is bound to them, but rather he has his own authority beside the Holy Scripture. He is also the one who teaches how to interpret this scripture correctly (cf. Mark 13:14, 24–25) and thus also how to perceive the present, so that one can even say regarding those who are considered authors of holy writings: "Something greater than Solomon is here!"; "Something greater than Jonah is here!" (Luke 11:31–32).

Also connected with such apocalyptic enthusiasm is the basic confession of Christendom: God "raised Jesus our Lord from the dead" (Rom. 4:24; Gal. 1:1; 1 Cor. 6:14; and elsewhere). For apart from the question whether according to its origin it is also to be called prophetic or enthusiastic, in terms of content it means that Jesus was raised as "the first fruits of those who have died" (1 Cor. 15:20; Col. 1:18; and elsewhere). His resurrection is the beginning of the general resurrection of the dead; it marks the turning of the age. Thus it is obvious that this confession involves not a scribal statement but a prophetically uttered perception.

Early Jewish Christianity

The scope and course of the crisis into which Jesus' disciples were placed after the Easter confession, when the visible coming of the kingdom of God failed to take place, need not be further determined in the present context. It was apparently Peter who overcame this crisis by interpreting the Easter experience in a new way with his confession of the Messiah. We cannot know with which majestic title this Messiah confession was initially connected or whether it was originally based on a scriptural reference. If this was the case, then Ps. 110:1 is the only scriptural passage that seems possible: "The Lord says to my lord, 'Sit at my right hand until I make your enemies your footstool.'" Related to the Easter confession, this statement from Psalms means: God *exalted* Jesus to the position of messianic ruler "at his right hand," in order to subdue the powers hostile to God; as such, Jesus bears the majestic title *Kyrios* ("Lord"). Since Psalm 110 was already interpreted messianically in Judaism, we cannot exclude the possibility that in his Messiah confession Peter was making reference to this scriptural passage. In any case, the title *Lord* for the exalted Jesus was already firmly anchored in the worship of the Aramaic-speaking church, as shown by *Marana tha* in 1 Cor. 16:22–23 and *Did.* 10.6 (cf. Rev. 22:10–11), which, moreover, still lies completely in the realm of apocalyptic thinking and invokes the Parousia. And the idea, going back to Ps. 110:1, that God exalted Jesus so that he might conquer demonic powers is found in such a broad variety of tradition before and beside Paul (1 Cor. 15:24ff.; Eph. 1:20ff.; 1 Peter 3:21–22; Pol. *Phil.* 2.1; etc.) that it must go back to very early roots. Yet the Jewish Christian formula quoted by Paul in Rom. 1:3–4, for example, shows that the messianic majesty of Jesus can be regarded as based solely on the resurrection from the dead and the gift of the Holy Spirit, without the reference to a scriptural passage.

If the question whether the first confession of the Messiah was founded on a scriptural reference must therefore remain open, there is no question that the importance of the cross for salvation was asserted from the beginning on the basis of the servant song of Isaiah 53. The primitive church saw no problem in responding to the still controversial question Who was the servant of God in Isaiah 53? with the answer that the prophet was anticipating the suffering and death of Jesus. Isa.

53:4 tells us that the servant of God suffered for us, and in vv. 5, 6, 10, and 12 this is further defined as: for our iniquities. We read in 53:6, 12 that in his destiny of suffering the servant of God received from God "the iniquity of us all" and "poured himself out in death." Since in the corresponding early Christian formulations no specific influence of the Greek translation of Isaiah 53 can be demonstrated, we may assume that the primitive church in Palestine already interpreted the death of Jesus with the help of Isaiah 53. This view is also suggested by the general insight that from the beginning an evangelizing church could not forgo giving an explanation for the striking situation that according to God's will Jesus should have attained his glory through an agonizing death. The motif of vicarious atonement that defines Isaiah 53 was also generally familiar to contemporaries and enlightening as a salvific event.

The formula of faith quoted by Paul in 1 Cor. 15:3–5 as a tradition that was handed down to him shows that in some circumstances it became important to make the scriptural reference of the Christian confession explicit. The tradition probably had the following wording:

> Christ died / for our sins / *in accordance with the scriptures* / and was buried;
> and was raised / on the third day / *in accordance with the scriptures* / and appeared to Cephas.

The fundamental confession of Jesus' death and resurrection is the starting point of the two strictly parallel members of the foregoing formula, but not its *basic intention*. This is revealed by the repeated phrase, "in accordance with the scriptures." There is no actual *scriptural proof,* especially since the Old Testament references are not named; the formula is intended rather to show that the central Christian confession is *scriptural*. There is no doubt that the first member refers to Isaiah 53. The second member can only refer to Hos. 6:2: ". . . on the third day he will raise us up, that we may live before him." Apparently a scriptural proof was sought for the Easter confession after the fact, and with some effort this one in Hos. 6:2 was pressed into service. The Jewish Christian origin of the formula is clear, as is its intention: in the context of the synagogue it had to be demonstrated that the Christian message was covered and demanded by the authority of the Holy Scripture.

This does not, however, establish a general early Christian "scriptural principle," for otherwise the broad formulaic material of early Christendom contains no "as it is written." *The Christian confession stands on its own,* and this fact is nowhere brought into question in all the varied references to the Old Testament in the New. Early Christendom used the Old Testament, but it did not require it as the foundation of its confession. Also the typical "for us," as surely as it goes back to Isaiah 53, needs neither grounding nor assurance through this prophetic saying, and Hos. 6:2 is needed nowhere else for the Easter confession. Thus we may question whether the formulaic confession to Jesus, "who was handed over to death for our trespasses and was raised for our justification" (Rom. 4:25), is intended to make known the undoubted reference to Isaiah 53. The likewise formulaic allusion to Jesus "whom God put forward as a sacrifice of atonement by his blood" (Rom. 3:25) is no longer related linguistically to Isaiah 53, and a reference of the term *sacrifice of atonement* (*hilastērion*) to the cover of the ark of the covenant, so called in the Greek Old Testament (Ex. 25:17–22), is unlikely; the term comes rather from Hellenistic cultic language (Friedrich 1982, 60–67). Also in other contexts early Christian theology was able in many religious connections to present the salvific significance of Jesus' death and resurrection without any reference to scripture.

When in the words of institution of the Lord's Supper the cup is related to the covenantal sacrifice (Mark 14:24), Ex. 24:8 (cf. Zech. 9:11) is naturally in the background. But the motif of redemption from the power of the devil (Gal. 3:13; 1 Peter 1:18; and elsewhere) is not rooted in the Old Testament but in ancient slave law. And also the theologically very diverse idea of "dying and rising with Christ," which is familiar above all in the Pauline tradition, cannot be traced back to an Old Testament scriptural passage; rather, it uses a conceptuality offered by contemporary mystery piety to express the salvific work of Jesus Christ.

Gentile Christianity before Paul

In Damascus, Paul was converted to a law-free, universalist Christianity, which already had a preexistence Christology and which he had persecuted earlier because of the critical attitude with which this Christianity confronted Jewish particularism. He expanded and passed on many formulaic traditions of this Christianity; in none of them do we find a scriptural reference. These traditions include, for example, the statement that "in Christ" the distinction between Jews and Greeks is abolished (Gal. 3:28; 1 Cor. 12:13); this could hardly be substantiated with the Old Testament. The pre-Pauline formula, "when the fullness of time had come, God sent his Son . . . so that we might receive adoption as children," like preexistence Christology, cannot be supported at all by Old Testament scriptures, and if the wisdom mythos is supposed to have affected this idea, this connection is never established through a scriptural reference. The well-known Christ hymn in Phil. 2:6–7, 9–11 also betrays no Old Testament influence. The similarly formulaic idea of reconciliation with God ("in Christ God was reconciling the world to himself"; 2 Cor. 5:19; Rom. 5:10; Col. 1:10, 22) has nothing to do with expiation but refers rather to a political situation and language from the world of Hellenism in which it is a question of the reconciliation of opponents in war, which is often effected through an emissary (cf. 2 Cor. 5:20; Breytenbach 1989).

Judaism could recommend itself to Gentiles by referring to its great age and the uniqueness of its Holy Scriptures, and occasionally it went so far as to call Plato a student of Moses. Early Gentile Christianity apparently did not follow this procedure. Naturally, the reason in part was probably that it was not easy to find passages in the Old Testament suitable for the establishment of a movement that expanded Judaism into a universalist message of salvation. To derive freedom from the law from the Torah itself would hardly have been possible even in the boldest exegetical experiments. In these circles of a pre-Pauline Gentile Christianity, however, there was an apparently intentional and fundamental effort to avoid spreading the Christian message by referring to the Old Testament; instead of this, the focus was on the living, working Spirit, "for the letter kills, but the Spirit gives life" (2 Cor. 3:6; cf. Rom. 2:29). Those who are baptized into the "body of Christ" are made to drink of one Spirit (1 Cor. 12:13), who distributes his various gifts (Rom. 12:5–8), and in this Spirit they meet Christ himself, as the alternation between "in the Spirit" and "in Christ" indicates (Rom. 8:9–10). The importance of the prophetic Spirit and his apocalyptic message can be observed already in Jesus and in his Palestinian disciples, and wherever he expressed himself, in these circles Joel 3 probably came to mind, and the Spirit was probably understood as the promised Spirit of the last days of this age.

In pre-Pauline Gentile Christianity this early Christian experience of the Spirit was emancipated from its connection with apocalypticism, and the Spirit became a comprehensive power of revelation, which is not, as in Gnosticism, a human possession but a free gift of God (*charisma*). In the essentially pre-Pauline passage 1 Cor. 2:9–16, this "loading up" of the Spirit is still clearly recognizable. An apocryphal scripture quotation of unknown origin speaks first in the manner of apocalypticism in a notably "negative" way about the message of salvation: "What no eye has seen, nor ear heard," in order then to reach out: ". . . these things God has revealed to us through the Spirit [*pneuma*]; for the Spirit searches everything, even the depths of God. . . . Those who are spiritual [*pneumatikoi*] discern all things, and they are themselves subject to no one else's scrutiny." Whether in the pneumatically motivated Gentile Christianity that could produce such formulations there were already tendencies even to reject the Old Testament, as Marcion, for example, did later, must remain unanswered; nevertheless, the attribution of the Torah to angelic powers (Gal. 3:19) in its midst may have been usual. It is obvious, however, that the pneumatics, who by the power of the Spirit can explore everything, did not need to align themselves with the authority of the scripture, even if they did not call it into question as such. "In this sense Christians have become spiritually independent and are, so to speak, a law unto themselves in their relationship with God" (Campenhausen 1968, 35).

Paul

In Damascus Paul was converted to the Gentile Christianity that he had previously persecuted, and he knew that he was called to be the apostle to the Gentiles (Gal. 1:15–16). Afterward, however, he made contact with the Jewish Christian apostles in Jerusalem (1:18–20) and preached for more than a decade in Syria and Cilicia in the context of Hellenistic Jewish Christianity, above all to God-fearing Gentiles (1:21; 2:1). Not until the Apostolic Council did he create the prerequisites for his Gentile Christian world mission (2:1–10). Thus in his own theology he united the two theological developments of early Christianity that preceded his conversion and calling. This double basis of Pauline theology can be recognized throughout the apostle's letters. It is also to be seen in his use of the Old Testament, but this use is especially determined by the specific premises and structure of Paul's original theology.

It is evident that Paul, the educated Jew and former Pharisee, is thoroughly familiar with his (Greek) Bible. In addition to the later canonized scriptures, he also quotes apocryphal books as Holy Scripture (1 Cor. 2:9; 9:10; 2 Cor. 4:6). His language is the Jewish Greek saturated with biblicisms that was spoken in the Hellenistic synagogues of the eastern Mediterranean area, and his speech is regularly spiced with biblical expressions and literal quotations.

If Paul's language reveals itself in this way as essentially shaped in a uniformly biblical way, his *express* dealings with the Holy Scriptures in his letters — whether in the form of quotations or in the interpretation of biblical traditions — is not uniform in the same way. Naturally, for the Christian Paul the Holy Scriptures of the Jews also remained an undisputed authority. For him, along with older Christendom, there was no question that Jesus died for our sins and was raised on the third day "in accordance with the scriptures" (1 Cor. 15:1–5), and "the law and the prophets" attest "the righteousness of God through faith in Jesus Christ" (Rom. 3:21–22), the central Christian message. The corresponding inability of the law given by the angels (Gal. 3:19–20) to effect salvation is indicated by the Holy Scripture itself.

There are, however, certain concentrations in the express use of the Holy Scripture, as is already shown by the fact that in the correspondence with Thessalonica and Philippi, in Philemon, in Colossians, and in the letter of recommendation for Phoebe (Rom. 16:1–20) we find no quotations at all from the Old Testament, whereas they abound in other passages in Paul's letters. In this connection, it has been pointed out with reason that in 1 Thess. 1:9–10 Paul reports how the church members in Thessalonica, as a consequence of his preaching, have turned away from idols in order to serve the living God, and in 1 Thess. 2:14 he remarks that they were therefore oppressed by their own fellow countrymen and countrywomen. Thus we may assume that the Christians in Thessalonica were not familiar with the Old Testament, and this was already enough reason for Paul not to approach them with arguments from the Holy Scripture. At the same time, however, that would mean that in his missionary preaching Paul generally did not support his views decisively with the Old Testament, even when his Gentile hearers were more or less familiar with the Old Testament, as must have been the case with the often addressed God-fearing Gentiles. And we never read anything in the letters of Paul about a reading from scripture in a worship service (Bauer 1930, 42–47).

That this is indeed the case is confirmed when we observe in detail the way in which Paul uses the Old Testament in his argumentation when he is *in direct dialogue with the members of his church*. In such cases we must always make the formal distinction between the incidental, inconspicuous introduction of a scripture passage on the one hand (for example, Phil. 1:10; 1 Cor. 10:26; 14:25; 15:25; 2 Cor. 8:21; 9:7, 10) and express quotations on the other, because the latter are introduced with "as it is written" or a similar expression; in terms of content, however, this distinction is hardly important in most cases. When Paul expressly quotes, he generally limits himself to simple quotations of *individual* biblical sentences to support his view, but he does not interpret them and certainly does not use them for the purpose of "proof-texting." As a rule, he has already made known his view in such a way that it is clear to the reader and there can be no doubt about its validity even without the biblical quotation; occasionally he closes his argumentation in summary fashion with a Bible saying. Often the biblical quotation appears without special emphasis beside arguments from general experience and occasionally also beside a saying of Jesus (cf. 1 Cor. 9:7–14). In 1 Cor. 15:32–33 Paul quotes side by side a passage from the book of Isaiah and a familiar saying from the work of the Greek writer Menander! Thus the Old Testament quotations have a relatively incidental character, and in most cases they are also found in connection with more or less peripheral situations that are in the broadest sense paraenetic or concerned with the order of the church.

In 1 Cor. 9:8–10 the right of missionaries to support is based by Paul on a scriptural saying freely modeled on Sir. 6:19, as well as on several analogies and a reference to a saying of the Lord. In the context of his recommendation of the collection for Jerusalem, he uses Ex. 16:18 to support his statement that it is a question of a fair balance between givers and receivers (2 Cor. 8:15), and Ps. 112:9 in support of his comment that God also shares good gifts richly with the giver (2 Cor. 9:9). On his third visit in Corinth the apostle announces, with reference to a principle in Deut. 19:15, that every judgment must rest on the statement of two or three witnesses. Psalm 116:10 serves him in 2 Cor. 4:13 ("I believed, and so I spoke") in describing his apostolic service, and in Rom. 15:21 he uses a quotation from Isa. 52:15 to justify his decision not to missionize where there is already a Christian church. When in 1 Cor. 5:1–13 a disciplinary measure against one who has committed incest is demanded of the church, Paul summarizes in v. 13 with an allusion to Deut. 17:7: "Drive out the wicked person from among you." And in 1 Cor. 14:21 the various arguments with which he would like to attenuate the glossolalia in church gatherings are supported with a quotation from Isa. 28:11.

In Rom. 14:11, with the help of a mixed quotation including above all Isa. 45:23, the "strong" and the "weak" in Rome, who judge each other because of their different positions on Jewish purity laws, learn that everyone must justify his or her own behavior before God and that mutual judgment is therefore inappropriate. And especially the strong should accept the weak lovingly and, instead of puffing themselves up, be humble according to the model of Christ, as revealed in Ps. 69:9, which is related to Christ. Such love is for Paul, as also for a liberal faction in the Hellenistic synagogue, absolutely the unconditioned ethical norm, and for this reason Paul, in accordance with synagogal argumentation, presents the commandment of love more than once in biblical formulation (Rom. 12:19–20; 13:8–10; Gal. 5:14). But 1 Corinthians 13, for example, shows that he can also completely ignore this connection, for he customarily does not appeal at all to the Old Testament for the general moral norms of his paraenesis (cf., for example, Rom. 12:9–15; Gal. 5:22–23; Phil. 4:8–9). Yet in 1 Cor. 10:1–13 he battles a threatening reversion to idolatry with a detailed reference to the wilderness generation of the people of Israel as a warning example for the present generation, but he does this essentially by adopting a biblically based monitory sermon already familiar to the synagogue (cf. also 2 Cor. 11:3). And the composed quotation in 2 Cor.

6:16–18 had probably also served already in the synagogue to admonish separation from pagan impurity. In Rom. 8:36 Paul describes the sufferings that Christians meet on account of their confession with the sentence in Ps. 44:22, which was already interpreted in Judaism in terms of the martyrdom of the godly (2 Maccabees 7).

In 1 Cor. 15:35–55, in agreement with Hellenistic Judaism, Paul defends the apocalyptic expectation of the resurrection of the dead. The exegetical substantiation for the existence of an immortal spiritual resurrection body in 1 Cor. 15:45–49 with reference to Gen. 2:7 and the hymnic closing in 15:54–55 with a mixed quotation from Isa. 25:8 and Hos. 13:14 were probably already included in synagogal argumentation and do not document a specific usage of scripture by Paul (cf. also Rom. 8:19–20).

It is notable that in 1 Cor. 1:19 and 3:19–20, with three quotations (Isa. 29:14; Job 5:13; Ps. 94:11), Paul underlines his "negative" idea that the wisdom of the world is foolishness to God; for this he apparently uses a corresponding florilegium that could have already served the synagogue in its dealings with popular philosophy. In this connection he alludes in 1 Cor. 3:21 to one of his favorite Old Testament sayings, which, formed according to Jer. 9:23–24, he also cites in 2 Cor. 10:17 and quotes in 1 Cor. 1:31 as a summary of his comments: "Let the one who boasts, boast in the Lord" (cf. also Rom. 5:11; Gal. 6:14; Phil. 3:3).

This last example is unusual in that in this case Paul expresses a *fundamental* idea of his Christian message to his church while appealing directly to the Old Testament. Otherwise he always argues for the central Christian kerygma explicitly or implicitly with traditional christological formulas of faith. Also the few sayings of Jesus that Paul uses do not concern his central message (1 Cor. 7:10; 9:14; cf. 1 Thess. 4:15) and even with this presupposition are not of outstanding authority (Lindemann 1992). And the special revelations that he occasionally reports are not the content of his missionary preaching (cf. 1 Cor. 3:1–2) but concern special information mostly of an apocalyptic nature (Rom. 11:25; 1 Cor. 2:6–10a; 15:51; cf. 2 Cor. 12:1–4); by contrast, the revelation for him personally in 2 Cor. 12:9 contains nothing new but points instead to the word of grace already known to him. For this central gospel, however, he needs no express support from the Holy Scripture. When the christological and soteriological statements of faith are rooted immediately in the Old Testament text, as we have observed in the idea of the exaltation of Jesus and his atoning death, this rooting is seldom made visible. For Paul the primitive Christian "confession of faith" carries its truth in itself, as shown, for example, by Rom. 3:25; 4:23–25; 12:1; 1 Cor. 1:1; 8:6; Phil. 2:6–11; 1 Thess. 4:14; and so forth.

The picture of a rather incidental usage of scripture changes quite suddenly whenever Paul's comments reproduce his *dialogue with the synagogue,* whether it involves (and these are not always separable) the hostile Jews themselves, the God-fearing Gentiles recruited by him, the Jewish Christian adherents of the synagogue, or Judaizing tendencies in his churches. This dialogue of Paul's is found above all in Romans 1–11 and Galatians 3–4. For in the main part of his Letter to the Romans, Paul makes an attempt to convince the Gentile Christians who have come to Rome, and who as a rule belonged to the synagogal association as "God-fearers," that they now belong to a Gentile Christian church outside the synagogue; in Galatians he rejects the demand for circumcision raised in his own churches. In both cases Paul does not argue ad hoc but resorts to argumentation material—in part the same in Romans and in Galatians—that he always needed and used in his mission among God-fearing Gentiles when he wanted to lead them to his Gentile Christian churches against the resistance of the synagogue. In such discussions it was not especially a question of Christology or soteriology, which *in principle* were not contradicted by the synagogue and were even affirmed by its Jewish and Gentile Christian members. Vigorous discussions, however, were ignited by the specifically *Gentile Christian consequences,* which for Paul were connected with the message of the gospel and because of which he himself had once persecuted the church of Christ, namely, the suspension of the difference between Jews and Gentiles, the universality of the Christian faith, and the end of the law proclaimed by Paul.

In this situation and with direct and indirect dialogue partners, Paul was obliged to become "to the Jews . . . as a Jew . . . to those under the law . . . as one under the law" (1 Cor. 9:20) and to argue *with the help of* the Holy Scripture of the old covenant. He had to explain that *"through the law* I died to the law" (Gal. 2:19), that *the scripture* says that all, without distinction, are sinners (Rom. 3:9–10), and that through faith in Jesus Christ, righteousness "is attested *by the law and the prophets*" (3:21). For only in this way could he convince especially those who as God-fearing Gentiles had recognized the exclusive claim of Judaism and ventured the step into the synagogue that cut deeply into their social existence, a step that was always accompanied by recognition of the authority of the Holy Scripture or on occasion was even caused or influenced by it.

Above all in his Letter to the Romans, which Paul wrote without the direct stimulation of dialogue partners, he spreads the entire arsenal of his scripture-based and thus intra-Jewish arguments for recognition of the fact that "in Christ" the difference between Jews and Gentiles is abolished and that therefore Gentile Christianity must not be forced into the constricting legalism of the synagogue. By contrast, in the Letter to the Galatians, which deals with a concrete dialogue situation, only some of these arguments are found.

It is no accident that Paul opens his writing to Rome with the statement that God promised the gospel "beforehand through his prophets in the holy scriptures" (1:1–2). Rom. 1:17, quoting Hab. 2:4, gives the overarching theme of the letter: "The one who is righteous will live *by faith,*" to which all people are invited without distinction, not by the particularist law. In Rom. 1:18–3:20 Paul then refers to *Jewish* penitential sermons in order to explain that "all, both Jews and Greeks, are under the power of sin" (3:9), and in 3:10–19 he closes his argumentation with a long collection of Old Testament quotations. Similarly, in Gal. 3:22 he says briefly and succinctly: "But the scripture[!] has imprisoned all things under the power of sin." In Romans, after presenting the inclination of all people to sin, Paul describes in the second section, beginning with 3:21, first the nature of the righteousness of faith offered to all, using an adopted christological confession (3:21–31); then in

4:1–25 he presents detailed proof that and how this confession is also attested by Holy Scriptures. For this purpose, in addition to an important saying from Psalms (Rom. 4:7–8 = Ps. 32:1–2), he uses above all an interpretation of the figure Abraham, which is larded with biblical allusions and quotations and which has a close parallel in Gal. 3:6–18. The antithetical parallel of Adam and Christ in Rom. 5:12–21 (cf. 1 Cor. 15:21–22), again related to scripture, closes the fundamental argumentation: just as sin and death came *to all people* through Adam, so righteousness and life come *to all people* through Christ.

In the continuation of Romans, Paul deals with individual problems that arise in the dialogue with the synagogue as a result of the principle of the universality of Christianity. In Rom. 6:1–23 (cf. 3:7–8) he rejects the mean-spirited accusation that righteousness from faith through grace promotes sin; in a way that is characteristic of his use of the scripture related to his readers, he does this, understandably, not with an objective scriptural proof but with reference to baptism and its underlying Christian confession and with a personal appeal to Christians to persist in the freedom from sin that they have been granted by the righteousness that is based on grace.

Then in Rom. 7:1–16 the apostle presents the positive significance of the law that was abolished in Christ. In 3:31; 4:15; 5:13–14, 20–21; and 6:14, he had already anticipated this treatment of a theme that was especially offensive for the synagogue. In Gal. 3:19 the corresponding question is also raised: "Why then the law?"—which the apostle then answers in Gal. 3:19–4:11 in a way similar to that in Romans. It is obvious that in all these discussions the argumentation *from scripture* is and must be prominent, for the Jew or God-fearer bound to the law can be convinced only "through the law" itself (Gal. 2:19) that this, his most valuable possession between Abraham and Christ, is only a temporary measure (Rom. 5:20; Gal. 3:19). Therefore, in Rom. 7:1 Paul also begins with the statement: "I am speaking to those who know the law," and in Gal. 4:21 he questions the addressees who want to reestablish the law: "Tell me . . . will you not listen to the law?"

Finally, before Paul in Rom. 9:1–11:36 answers in detail the question already raised in 3:4—namely, what validity do the promises given Israel have, when God in Christ makes no distinction between Jews and Gentiles—he inserts in 7:17–8:39 a fundamental "teaching text" not first conceived for his letter to Rome; this text does not concern the theme of the universality of Christianity that otherwise dominates Romans 1–11, and thus, characteristically, the Old Testament does not play a role either. The first answer to the question about the promises for Israel, which is given in Rom. 9:6–29 and has a close parallel in Gal. 4:21–31, apparently was originally aimed directly at *Jewish* dialogue partners; it states that based on the scripture, it is not the bodily descendants of Abraham but those who believe as Abraham did—Jews and Gentiles—who are the "children of the promise." The second answer in Rom. 10:1–21 also argues heavily with biblical allusions, references, and quotations, when the apostle complains that the majority of the Jews close themselves off from righteousness by faith, although the scripture, in his understanding, proclaims to them this very faith in Christ. No different is the third answer in Rom. 11:1–10, which seems to come from Jewish Christian circles and states that the promises in the law and prophets are fulfilled with the multitude of Jewish Christians as the saving remnant of the otherwise stubborn Israel. This is followed in 11:11–24 by a section with which Paul, expressly addressing Gentile Christians (11:13), warns them against the view that God has chosen them *in place of* Israel. It is very characteristic of the apostle's treatment of scripture that in this section Old Testament allusions and quotations are lacking: in dialogue with those who revere the Old Testament, Paul is obliged and able to expound and defend the confession of Christendom with holy scriptures, but this confession itself also has sufficient power to convince the human heart of its truth. In his epilogue in Rom. 11:25–31 on the question of the validity of the promises given Israel, for the central assertion that "all Israel will be saved" Paul refers to a free revelatory saying, which he then reinforces with a scriptural quotation from Isa. 59:20–21 in connection with Isa. 27:9.

The argumentation in Rom. 1:17, which opens with a quotation from the book of the prophet Habakkuk and in which Paul proves for the synagogue that the distinction between Jews and Gentiles is abolished in Christ, is summarized by Paul in closing in 11:32: "For God has imprisoned all in disobedience so that he may be merciful to all." To this résumé of God's eternal plan of salvation Paul adds the magnificent, thoroughly biblical doxology in 11:33–36, which we may presume was originally followed immediately by the passage 15:8–12 (Schmithals 1988b, 519–23), in which Paul, again differentiating between Jews and Gentiles, sees the distinction abolished through Christ and celebrates the election also of the Gentiles with a chain of Old Testament quotations.

In connection with our question, special attention must be given to the much discussed third chapter of the Second Letter to the Corinthians, in which Paul refers in detail to Ex. 24:29–35. The starting point of his discussion is the accusation that foreign teachers who had been active in the Gentile Christian church at Corinth had made against Paul: that he was not at all a legitimate apostle. After rejecting individual charges, Paul defends himself especially with the fundamental statement that God validated him to be a servant of the *new* eschatological covenant (2 Cor. 3:6), which in the further course of his thoughts he distinguishes as the covenant of the Spirit, which gives life, as opposed to the covenant of Moses, which kills. In this way his argumentation gains a basic character that no longer directly reflects the situation in Corinth. This is also shown by the fact that in 2 Cor. 3:7–11 he undergirds his presentation with a traditional text, namely, the threefold *qal wachomer,* a conclusion from the smaller to the greater:

> Now if the ministry of death . . . came in glory . . .
>> how much more will the ministry of the Spirit come in glory?
> For if there was glory in the ministry of condemnation,
>> how much more does the ministry of justification abound in glory!
> For if what was set aside came through glory,
>> much more has the permanent come in glory!

Underlying this threefold text is the narrative of the (repeated) making of the covenant on Sinai (Exodus 34), in particular the motif that a heavenly glow transfigured the face of Moses when he returned to the people after meeting with God. Although in its present version Paul relates this text to his apostolic *ministry,* the wording and train of thought suggest that in the original version we may substitute for *ministry* the word *covenant,* which defines Exodus 34 (cf. 2 Cor. 3:6); in this case the text contains the fixed formulated result of an *interpretation* of Ex. 34:29–35 free of all apologetic, in which Paul demonstrates the eschatological glory of the new covenant, which towers far above even the glory of the covenant of Moses. Now he in part inserts this *interpretation* into the formulated result (2 Cor. 3:7, 10) and in part lets it follow in 3:12–18, and he does this in such a clearly evident way that the reference to the apostolic *ministry* of the new covenant is secondary to the reference to the *church* of the new covenant, whose members have been allowed to see the glory of the Lord with unveiled faces (3:18). Moreover, in his interpretation of the covering with which Moses shielded his shining face from the people (Ex. 34:33–35), Paul understood that the Israelites were not to know the transitoriness of the covenant of Moses (2 Cor. 3:7b, 13–16) and therefore even today do not know it. Here we have a vivid example of the way in which Paul seeks *by means of scripture* to convince the God-fearing Gentiles of the superiority of the Christian confession over the message of the synagogue. Also in this case there is no "proof text" that attempts to derive the Christian confession from scripture. Rather, the opposite is true: Paul begins with the confession of Christ and formulates expressly the hermeneutical principle that only in the light of this confession can one properly understand the scripture, whose authority his hearers recognize (2 Cor. 3:14–16). It is not that the Holy Scriptures of the Old Testament shed light on the confession of Christ, but rather the confession makes possible the correct understanding of scripture as witness to Christ.

This "validation" of scripture by Paul always lies behind his treatment of it, and the perusal of the sections of his letters that are essential for the Pauline usage of scripture confirms that Paul, beginning with such a validation, appeals to the Holy Scriptures, which are completely familiar to him, in very different ways and intensities, depending on the situation and the addressees. For his churches he refers, as a rule, directly to the Christian confession for the central content of the gospel, as it was already passed on to him in many kinds of rules of faith and teaching formulations. "This means, however, that Paul did not from the beginning give the young churches the Old Testament as the Christian book of sources and edification, but that he first founded his mission and teaching completely on the gospel itself and expected edification exclusively from it and from the Spirit accompanying the gospel" (Harnack 1928, 137). But when he wants to win God-fearing Christians for his churches and even missionizes among the God-fearers, both of which unavoidably stir up conflict with the synagogue itself, or when, as in Galatia, he sees his churches persuaded by Judaizing preachers and warns them against the adoption of certain observances of the Torah, he can—whenever it seems advisable—show in detailed argumentation that, and how, even the Holy Scriptures bear witness to the Christian message, if one only understands them correctly. Thus the Christian proclamation is naturally *also* scriptural in all its assertions.

If in this process Paul treats the meaning of Old Testament statements in an often quite arbitrary way when measured by modern standards of dealing with historical tradition, he stays within the bounds of what was also the usual practice, for example, in the synagogue. It is doubtful whether he, as is sometimes asserted (Koch 1986, 102–89), also changed the wording of his quotations in the direction of his intentions more than his contemporaries customarily did, yet in each case such modifications in the wording of the texts are explained by unhistorical dealing with the Holy Scripture that was necessarily subject to the prejudice of the interpreter. Thus even these incursions testify to the primacy of the confession of Christ over scriptural interpretation in matters of content and hermeneutics.

The question of the correctness of Pauline scriptural interpretation on the basis of *content* cannot be answered by a judgment on his *method*, and consequently also not with regard to the individual scriptural passages to which he refers. It can be clarified only in the context of a *comprehensive* biblical theology of the Old Testament that asks about the New Testament in the Old (Gunneweg 1993).

Hellenistic Jewish Christianity before Expulsion from the Synagogue: The Traditions of the Gospel of Mark

The Gospel of Mark is our most important and oldest witness from the Jewish Christianity of the second Christian generation. This origin of our oldest gospel writing is deduced from a wealth of individual features: Jesus often teaches in the synagogue on the sabbath (1:21–29; 3:1; 6:2); he himself and his community converse with scribes of Pharisaic and Sadducee orientation (2:6–10, 16; 7:1–15; 9:14; 11:27–33; 12:13–17, 18–27, 28–34); Jesus heals the daughter of a synagogue leader (5:21–43); the problem of healing on the sabbath is disputed (3:1–6); the lax divorce practices of the Pharisees cause offense among Jewish Christians (10:1–9); the strict Jewish purity laws of orthodox Jews are rejected by the community (15:1–16); the man healed of leprosy is sent to the priest, as the law prescribes in Leviticus 13–14 (1:44); and so forth.

A precise analysis of the Gospel of Mark must distinguish between the traditions that the evangelist adopted and his own redactional revisions of traditional material. This distinction, however, is not only disputed in particular cases; it would also be of little consequence for our topic, since the clearly recognizable redactional elements betray no interaction with the Old Testament that varies in a characteristic way from what is known in the extensive traditional material (see below). Furthermore, the redactional work of the evangelist is relatively limited, whereas the pre-Markan traditional material is very instructive in the use of the scriptures in Hellenistic Jewish Christianity. The question of whether the evangelist received the traditions he used in oral or written form, as individual pieces or already as a gospel writing, is answered differently by present-day scholars and can remain open, for all these traditions show a uniform approach to the Holy Scriptures that were common to Christians and Jews.

Generally and consistently, these traditions convey the clear impression that Jesus does not appear as a scribe but acts on his own divine authority when he calls people to repentance and bestows his salvation on those who ask, which is the case above all in the numerous miracle stories. Accordingly, at the beginning of his public ministry we read: "He taught them as one having authority and not as the scribes" (1:22, 27). Against the objection of the scribes, he sovereignly forgives the paralytic his sins (2:5–12), and their objection to his association with sinners and tax collectors is rejected with the statement that he has come to call sinners. Without the express backing of the Holy Scriptures, he suspends fasting for his disciples (2:18–19, 21–22), he heals on the sabbath (3:1–5; cf. 2:27), he speaks in parables, he heals the daughter of a Greek woman (7:24–30), and he wants taxes to be paid to the emperor. He is sovereign Lord over the demons, illnesses, and the forces of nature. And he leaves unanswered the question of the Jewish authorities about the justification for his sovereign actions (11:27–33). All of this means that the Christian church, in which these accounts are handed down, referred primarily to Jesus Christ himself or to the traditional Christian confession for their message and their faith.

Naturally, this does not mean any disrespect for the Holy Scriptures. The language of the traditions is filled with biblical expressions. Allusions to or indirect quotations of certain Bible passages, as well as biblical figures, are found in, for example, 1:11; 6:39; 9:4–5; 9:7; 12:2–5. The appearance of the wilderness preacher John is described according to Old Testament models (Ex. 23:20; Micah 3:1; etc.). The miracle stories have a strong basis in, for example, Isa. 29:18–19; 35:4–6. The narrative of the entrance into Jerusalem with the cleansing of the temple in 11:1–10, 15–17 is based above all on Mal. 3:1–4, along with Zech. 6:12–13; 9:9; 14:4, 21; Gen. 49:11; Isa. 56:7; 62:11; Jer. 7:1–15; Ps. 118:26. The passion story is continually fortified with biblical passages, as has already often been observed and investigated (Dibelius 1959, 187–88). Only in 14:27 (cf. 15:28) do we find an express quotation (Zech. 13:7). By contrast, literal allusions, as well as veiled references, are frequent, and at this point Isaiah 53 understandably plays an especially large role. In Gethsemane Jesus prays with words from Psalm 42. For the sake of our sins he is "betrayed [handed over; delivered] into the hands of sinners" and "handed . . . over to be crucified" (14:41; 15:1, 15 = Isa. 53:6, 12). Before Pilate he does not open his mouth (15:4–5 = Isa. 53:7). He is numbered among evildoers (15:6–13, 27 = Isa. 53:12). He is wounded and crushed (15:17 = Isa. 53:3, 5), despised and mocked (15:18–20, 29–32, 35 = Isa. 53:3). When he is crucified, he is offered wine to drink, mixed with myrrh (15:23 = Prov. 31:6–7). In his hour of death he prays with Ps. 22:2 (15:34). The mockers under the cross want to extend his life with a refreshing drink (15:36 = Ps. 69:22). He is given a tomb among the rich (15:42–27 = Isa. 53:9).

The narrator of all these stories is not trying to produce something like a "scriptural proof" of the holy event. The readers were probably not always aware of the biblical allusions, and in any case, the stories that develop the familiar Christian confession were not designed to gain their meaning only out of the usually vague scriptural reference. Even the schema of promise-fulfillment does not appear as such. The narrator takes it for granted that the Holy Scriptures deal with the Christ event, and that Jesus the Christ is the Messiah of Israel. Therefore he can present his narrative in the colors that the scriptures place at his disposal, without the Christian message depending on this connection for its truth.

By contrast, the scriptures receive an *argumentative* function in the discussions with the scribes in the synagogue, in which Jesus or the Jewish Christian church justifies its confession and its behavior. In the foreground of the discussion are practical questions. The freedom in regard to the sabbath commandment and the primacy of love before legalism (cf. 3:4) are justified by Jesus to the Pharisees with a reference to 1 Sam. 21:1–7, a "loving" violation of the law by David (2:25–26). In 7:1–23 Jesus accuses the scribes of hypocrisy in their dealing with the Torah and in this connection refers them expressly to Isa. 29:13 and Ex. 20:12; 21:17. Also in the dialogues on the problem of divorce (10:1–9), the way to eternal life (10:17–22), and the question of the first commandment (12:28–34), Jesus proves that he is a superior interpreter of the Holy Scriptures. And when the Sadducees, using the scripture, want to take the possibility of the resurrection *ad absurdum,* Jesus refutes them with this very scripture (12:18–27). He justifies the cleansing of the temple of sellers and buyers in 11:17 with a quotation from Isa. 56:7. Finally, in the strongly allegorizing parable of the wicked tenants (12:1–11), Christology is also placed before the Jewish authorities in the light of the Old Testament, for after the parable first speaks of the transition of the "vineyard" from the power of the Jerusalem priesthood into the hands of the Christian church, in part following literally Isa. 5:1–2, 7, Jesus then interprets the murder of the "only beloved son" by the wicked tenants—through an express reference to Ps. 118:22–23—as an allusion to his own destiny in death and exaltation. This too is naturally not a "proof text" of the truth of the Christian confession but a clear invitation to all who are convinced of the authority of the Holy Scriptures to open themselves to the Christian message, for even the scriptures witness to this message.

In the period shortly after the destruction of Jerusalem in the year 70, to which Mark 12:9 alludes ("the owner of the vineyard . . . will come and destroy the tenants and give the vineyard to others"), the Jewish Christian church probably undertook, with the traditions of the Gospel of Mark, an intentional missionary effort to promote the Christian cause in the endangered and unsettled diaspora synagogues. For this purpose the Christian confession was presented throughout in narrative form and in genres (miracle stories, exemplary stories, parables) that were familiar to the adherents of the synagogue from Jewish and in part Old Testament teaching material. From the wealth of Old Testament language and accounts, a more or less large amount flowed into each individual text, as a rule without being directly highlighted, for the Christian confession bears its truth within itself even in this environment, and it can and should be convincing by itself. Only where in view of the proximity of Jews and Jewish Christians among the readers it seems appropriate to discuss and clarify certain problems in a discussion between Jesus and the Pharisaic or Sadducee scribes or other Jewish holy men is the argument carried on with the scriptures. The corresponding disputes are in a real sense "exemplary stories" that reflect living debates and school dialogues between Jews and Jewish Christians and that at the same time are intended to enable Christians to carry on such dialogues within the synagogue. The interaction of Hellenistic Jewish Christianity with its Holy Scriptures is thus not essentially different from the way in which Paul inserts the Old Testament in his letters. Jewish Christianity needs to substantiate only its own lax understanding of the law and not the universalism of the Gentile Christian doctrine of justification, and thus the corresponding expenditure of Pauline scriptural scholarship is lacking in the Gospel of Mark. In both cases, however, the Holy Scriptures are secondary to the Christian proclamation and more clearly in evidence above all when Christian teachers must deal immediately with Jewish scribes.

Writings from the
Time of the *Aposynagōgos*

Only in recent times has the phenomenon called the *aposynagōgos* (after John 9:22 [cf. 9:34]; 12:42; and 16:2) attracted the careful attention of scholars. And both the phenomenon as such and its significance for the history of early Christianity and the understanding of the New Testament scriptures are evaluated in quite different ways.

Whereas the Gentile Christian churches that Paul founded from Syria westward toward Rome, after the Apostolic Council in Jerusalem (Gal. 2:1–10) and in observance of the understandings reached there, stood from their beginnings outside the synagogue, the Jewish Christian churches were incorporated into this institution. As far as we can know, before the Jewish war and the destruction of Jerusalem, the synagogue was not strictly organized, and it offered a home to a variety of religious currents within Judaism, including the numerous God-fearing Gentiles (Kee 1995). Its members confessed themselves to Judaism by paying the yearly double drachma for the temple in Jerusalem and were thereby also liberated from having to sacrifice to the emperor. For the sake of this privilege alone Jewish Christendom could not and would not dissolve its ties with the relatively loose association of the synagogue, and there was, moreover, no reason for them to do so. The payment of the temple tax by Jewish Christians can be clearly deduced from Matt. 17:24–27.

With the destruction of the temple in the year 70 the situation of the synagogue changed fundamentally. The temple cult, which had united the Judaism scattered around the world politically, if not spiritually, came to an end; the temple priesthood was extinguished, and the Sadducee party disappeared. Since the previous temple tax still had to be paid as *fiscus judaicus* to the temple of Jupiter on the Capitoline hill in Rome, the members of the synagogue retained the privilege of not having to participate in the sacrifice to the emperor. Internally the former association developed into a rigidly organized synagogue, as determined by the Pharisaic scribes and their understanding of the law; within the new structure the scope of the Hebrew Bible was definitively set early on, and the Torah gained absolute authority. This fundamental reorganization of the synagogue, the transition from "early Judaism" to "Judaism," seems to have been occurred at different times in different parts of the Roman Empire, but it was essentially complete after about one generation. The development was promoted by the Roman state and was in its interest, for in this way, on the one hand, the synagogues fell more definitely under state control, and on the other, their obligatory legality ended their influential openness to the world, which had been characteristic of the liberal synagogue; the circumcision of Gentiles was prohibited by Rome. In the course of the Pharisaic reorganization, God-fearing Gentiles, as well as all Jews and Jewish groups that could not or would not bow to the Pharisaic rabbinate, had to leave the synagogue; this was the *aposynagōgos* An outward sign of the successful expulsion of non-Pharisaic groups from the synagogue is the adoption of a cursing of heretics (*minim*) in the twelfth of the Eighteen Benedictions even before the end of the first century.

Consequently, the writings preserved in the New Testament that reflect the situation of the *aposynagōgos* or have it as their topic belong in all likelihood to the last decade of the first century. In this literature, therefore, it is always a question of exhorting Jewish Christians not to remain behind when their community moves out, that is, to accept the exclusion from the synagogue, although Christians thereby lose their protection against state persecutions. We may observe that on the one hand, the synagogue organized on Pharisaic principles was not happy to lose Christian constituents and sought to retain them, but on the other hand, it denounced the—in their view—apostate Christians publicly and delivered them up to persecution. The Christian authors who took quill in hand in this situation never tried to stop the development within the synagogue. They stand instead outside the synagogue and endeavor to hold Jewish Christians together, to keep them from sliding back into the synagogue in the face of persecution, and to convince them of the theological necessity of taking their own stand outside the synagogue. With this effort on both sides to attract and hold Jewish Christians, the related literature often reflects unmistakably and variously the lively and at times hate-filled discussions between Christian theologians and Jewish authorities; the fact that the theological argumentation in these discussions is frequently presented with a high degree of scholarly ability shows that at least on the Jewish side the Holy Scriptures enjoy great authority and represent the unconditional norm. In the following sections we will try to learn to what extent and in what ways Christian theologians substantiate their standpoint with the help of Holy Scriptures.

The Gospel of Matthew

The fact that the evangelist Matthew comes from a *Jewish Christian* milieu is disputed only rarely and without sufficient grounds. Yet his community already lives outside the synagogal association. The evangelist speaks of the "Jews" in third person (28:15) and of "their" synagogues (4:23; 10:17; 13:54; 23:34; and elsewhere); in 16:18 and 18:17 he already calls his own community by the name *ekklēsia,* which the Gentile Christians living outside the synagogue had chosen for their fellowship. The disagreement with the synagogue, however, has not yet come to a definitive end. Through "false prophets," the influence of the Pharisees reaches directly into the church (7:15–23; 24:10–12) and leads some to fall away and return into the synagogue (13:41; 18:6–9; 24:11), which also exerted pressure through measures of persecution (10:17–26; 23:34–36). Matthew still has to defend against Jewish assertions that Jesus was an illegitimate child (1:18ff.) and that the disciples stole Jesus' body in order to simulate his resurrection (28:11–15). Furthermore, Christians try to escape persecution by paying the temple tax (17:24–27). And the Gospel of Matthew itself has the special task of giving the community driven out of the synagogue its own church order and catechism of Christian behavior. In this connection, especially important to the evangelist is the fundamental statement that the "righteousness" of Christians who follow the radically understood commandment of love is better than that of the Pharisees (5:17–48), whose merely formal legality he calls lawlessness (*anomia*) and sharply castigates it (23:1–36; 7:15–23; 13:41).

For the evangelist the unconditional authority is Jesus himself, to whom is given all power in heaven and on earth (28:18). Matthew reinforces the corresponding information from his sources, for example, through the antitheses, in which Jesus sets over against the Torah, or its interpretation by the Pharisees, his own "But I say to you" (5:21–48). And whereas the antitheses adopted by the evangelist (5:21–22, 27–28, 33–34) only radicalize a commandment said to "those of ancient times," those formed by Matthew himself (5:31–32, 38–42, 43–48) already tend toward a critique of certain statements of the Torah. It is not, however, a question of abolishing the law and the prophets, as the reproach of the Pharisees against Christians asserts (5:17). The problem is not the authority of the Torah (5:18–19) but its proper interpretation (5:17, 20), and the evangelist makes it sufficiently clear in his redactional comments that he is familiar with his Bible (cf., for example, 5:5, 9; 11:29; 13:42; 16:27). Apparently with intention, he places the five great speeches of Jesus beside the five books of Moses, and in his intensified ethical teachings, he essentially resorts to the wealth of Old Testament material only for the commandment of love (9:13; 12:7; 19:19; cf. also 18:16). In general, Matthew's special material and his redactional comments are strikingly free of references to the Old Testament, and this confirms that while even in Jewish Christianity teaching and proclamation were connected with scripture, they were not related primarily to scripture but were based rather on the assertions of the confession.

At the same time, also in the Gospel of Matthew the picture clearly shifts as soon as the argumentation reflects the dialogue with the Jewish scribes of the synagogue. When the scribes mock Jesus on the cross, Matthew (27:43) puts words in their mouths from Ps. 22:9. In 13:10–17 he adopts from the Gospel of Mark the concealment motif with which Mark, in the context of his theory of the messianic secret, explains Jesus' parable-filled speech, but Matthew relates it especially to Israel, amplifies it into a stubbornness motif, and substantiates it with an express and detailed quotation of Isa. 6:9–10. In 21:16 Jesus contradicts the scribes, who are indignant when they hear the children praise Jesus as son of David, with an express quotation from Ps. 8:2. And when the scribes and Pharisees demand a sign from Jesus, he rejects the request with a specific reference to the Jonah story (12:40–41).

The last two examples already indicate that in Matthew's time the question of the *Messiahship of Jesus* was especially controversial, and that the confession of Jesus as the Christ of Israel brought the exclusion of Christians from the Pharisaically defined synagogue, a situation that corresponds to the express decision of "the Jews," mentioned in John 9:22, to expel from the synagogue everyone who confesses Jesus as the Christ. The demonstration that Jesus is the Messiah announced in the Holy Scripture is supported already by Jesus' family tree in Matt. 1:2–16, a scribal work, presumably by the evangelist himself, that goes back to the patriarch Abraham and identifies Jesus as the legitimate descendant of David (1:1, 6). This proof, however, especially serves Matthew's fulfillment quotations, which are so called because of the stereotypical, only slightly modified expression with which they are generally introduced: this or that happened in order to fulfill what was said by the prophets (1:23; 2:15, 17–18, 23; 4:14–16; 8:17; 12:17–21; 13:14–15, 35; 21:4–5; 26:56; 27:9). This introduction is slightly modified in 2:5–6, because here the scribes themselves quote scripture, and in 3:3, where Matthew adopts the quotation from the Gospel of Mark. With one exception, it is always an Old Testament prophetic saying that is quoted, for in 13:35 even Ps. 78:2 is considered a prophetic saying. The exception is 26:56: Mark had spoken of the fulfillment of the "scriptures" in reference to the arrest of Jesus, and Matthew narrows this down to only "the scriptures of the prophets"; apparently an appropriate passage was not readily available. There are fourteen passages in all, and in seven of them the prophet is mentioned by name, five from Isaiah and two from Jeremiah (cf. 14:17); thus the author inserts a holy number of quotations into his Gospel. In all cases the quotation reflects the idea that a report on the person or work of Jesus fulfills a statement from the Holy Scriptures, for even the payment to Judas in 27:9 has this christological reference.

It is notable that with the exception of 13:14–15, in which the disciples of Jesus ask about the reason for speaking in parables and Matthew follows a tradition from the Gospel of Mark, none of the fulfillment quotations are found on the lips of Jesus, and consequently they do not occur in disputes with the scribes and pharisees. Rather, they are an expression of scribal activity within the community, and Matthew reflects on this in 13:52: the Christian scribe, like a good master of a household, brings out of his treasure old and new, that is, the understanding of the Old Testament in the light of the New. The quotations themselves also speak against the idea that they were placed before the synagogal scribes in their present form, for sometimes they exhibit a wording already modified by Christian ideas (cf., for example, 2:6, 15), they mix various scriptural passages together, or they are not verifiable (2:23; 26:56). This confirms, on the one hand, that Matthew and his community are no longer part of the synagogal association and that consequently direct contact with Jewish teachers has been broken off. On the other hand, it shows that Matthew must continue to try to immunize the members of his community against assertions of the synagogue that Jesus was a bastard and the confession of his heavenly majesty comes from a fraudulent assertion of the disciples. He must convince them, rather, that their confession of Christ is in accord with the correct understanding of the Holy Scriptures, and that with a return to the safety of the synagogue they would be forfeiting the biblical legacy of the people of Israel. Therefore, an actual "proof through prediction" for the truth of the Christian message is not intended, for that message carries its truth within itself also for Matthew, and the subsequent scriptural reference serves apologetics, not the founding of a theological system.

The Basic Text
of the Gospel of John

There can be no doubt that the Gospel of John has some connection with the exclusion of Jewish Christians from the synagogue, for in 9:22; 12:42; and 16:2 we find the term *aposynagōgos*. In 9:22 we also learn about the formal decision of the Jews to exclude from the synagogue those who confess Jesus as the Christ; thus, as we also know from the Gospel of Matthew, the confession of Jesus as the Christ was the decisive criterion of the separation. According to 12:42–43 many Christians did not confess themselves as such, because they were afraid of exclusion from the synagogue, and in some cases their numbers included especially prominent and influential members of the synagogue, such as Nicodemus (3:1–10; 7:48–52; 19:39). Thus the influence of Jewish Christians in the synagogue before the *aposynagōgos* must have been considerable, at least in individual synagogues, and the disagreement with the Pharisees must have been accordingly great. The reason for the lack of confessional courage in many Jewish Christians is revealed in 16:1–4: outside the synagogue the confessor is threatened with bloody persecution.

Yet it is more than doubtful that the Gospel of John *as a whole* can be explained on the basis of the situation of the *aposynagōgos,* as attempted above all by Wengst (1990), for with this presupposition many characteristic statements of the Gospel of John remain unexplained. We must assume, rather, that our Gospel used as its source a *basic text* that was at pains to overcome the *aposynagōgos* and stabilize the Christian church in the new situation (cf. Schmithals 1992). In this basic text "the Jews" are members of the contemporary synagogue led by the Pharisaic rabbinate. The "high Christology" of the Gospel goes back to this basic text and is developed by its author with a clear delineation vis-à-vis the Pharisaic synagogue: "No one comes to the Father except through me" (14:6; cf. also, for example, 8:51–53, 56–58). For this author is a member of the church that has already been driven out of the synagogue, and he always speaks of "the Jews" as a foreign group that stands decidedly opposed to Christians and is already led by the Pharisees with official authority. Yet the basic text of the Gospel of John still reflects some of the harsh disputes, in which the Christian author reveals his scholarship (cf., for example, 7:21–24). In his view the *Father* bears witness to his *Son* in the law and the prophets (1:45) and through the Moses so highly cherished by the Pharisees (5:37–40, 45–47), and this witness is held up to the Jews (8:18). In 5:39 Jesus explains to the Jews: "You search the scriptures because you think that in them you have eternal life; and it is they that testify on my behalf." Yet this scriptural witness, like John the Baptist's witness to Christ, clearly stands in the shadow of the witness that Jesus bears to himself (5:36; 18:13–14, 18; 10:25; and elsewhere). The Jews contradict such a confession of Christ and make the accusation against Jesus that he was born illegitimately (8:41b), and the evangelist counters with the assertion that the father of the Jews is the devil (8:44a). Thus the battle is fought with the gloves off.

In contrast to Matthew, however, the author of the basic text does not quote any individual scripture passages that attest to the Messiahship of Jesus. *The idea* that

Moses and the prophets bear witness to Jesus as the incarnate Son of God is clearly expressed (vis-à-vis the Jews!), but the details of how the Christian side argued remain unclear. This statement agrees with the observation that in the basic text the Old Testament is, by all appearances, never quoted or used in other ways in intra-Christian argumentation; only the Jewish pilgrims who receive Jesus in Jerusalem use a saying from Psalms in John 12:13. Thus the community for whom the basic text was written stands in a theological tradition in whose environment the confession prevails on its own and requires even less substantiation and confirmation by the Holy Scriptures than was the case with Paul and with Hellenistic Jewish Christianity. This tradition is also revealed in the hymn that the author of the basic text places in the prologue of the Gospel (1:1–18). In 1:1–2, 10 he relates in free association to the biblical creation account but interprets it in a thoroughly universalist way (1:3–5), and at the end he juxtaposes the law given through Moses and the grace and truth that came through Jesus Christ (1:17) in such a way that, as in Paul, the enduring validity of the law is excluded.

We have already encountered such a tradition in the pre-Pauline Gentile Christianity that Paul at first persecuted. The preexistence Christology, the prominence of the incarnation, the universalism, the lack of a *theologia crucis,* the factual distancing from the Old Testament, and so forth all attest that the basic text is directly related theologically to this pre-Pauline Gentile Christianity. Apparently the early persecutions of the Gentile Christian *ekklēsia* carried out by the synagogue—just as in Paul, who before the Apostolic Council (Gal. 2:1–10) pursued his Gentile mission in the context of the synagogal institution—had the effect also in the rest of Gentile Christianity of connecting this mission again with the synagogal association, until the *aposynagōgos* definitively broke this connection. This Gentile Christianity of "Johannine" provenance, "liberated" by the expulsion from the synagogue, is found later in, for example, the letters of John, which likewise offer no scripture quotations, and in Ignatius; yet this distancing from the Old Testament did not generally prevail in the early catholic church. Even our present Gospel of John cites many Old Testament passages, including explicit fulfillment quotations in the manner of the Gospel of Matthew (John 12:38; 13:18; 15:25; 17:12; 19:24, 36), and 10:35 intentionally states that "the scripture cannot be annulled" (see below).

The Letter to the Hebrews

It is obvious that the writing that found acceptance in the New Testament as the Letter to the Hebrews within the *corpus Paulinum* is not a letter but a theological treatise that in various ways seeks to use the Old Testament to prove the superiority of Christianity over Judaism. Jesus is the last word of God and far superior to the words of the prophets (1:1–2); his unique sacrifice on the cross proves that the Old Testament sacrifice is inadequate (9:12–14); as the heavenly high priest, he completely overshadows the Levitical high priest (6:19–10:18; 13:10); he is above the angels who conveyed the Mosaic law (2:2); his glory is greater than that of Moses (3:1–6); he is the mediator of the new and better covenant (8:6–13). The way of salvation anticipated in the Old Testament is also that of faith in the Christian hope (10:39–11:40), and the "rest" promised to Israel is in truth the eschatological perfection promised the Christian church (3:7–4:16). In the context of this argumentation, the Old Testament, above all the book of Psalms, is quoted in detail, so that in this sense Hebrews corresponds to some passages in Romans.

The fact that the author's biblical scholarship, developed in this way, is to be understood as situation-related, and not in a timeless dogmatic way, can be derived from the concrete admonitions that alternate with scholarly comments and which warn above all against apostasy, surrendering one's confession, and leaving the Christian church (2:1–4; 3:1, 12–19; 4:1, 14–16; 5:11–6:12; 10:19–39; 12:1–13:17). The necessary connection between the scribal comments, which consistently maintain the superiority of Christianity over Judaism, and the topical warnings against apostasy is given only when the author sees his readers especially threatened, not by apostasy into paganism, but by backsliding into Judaism. Thus in the Letter to the Hebrews we find ourselves in the context of a Christian community that, in consequence of the *aposynagōgos,* has long since left the synagogue (10:32), held its own meetings (10:25), and had its own leaders (13:7, 17). After the exclusion from the synagogue it has been subject to various persecutions (10:32–36; 12:1–11; 13:3, 7), and parts of it (4:1; 10:25; 12:15–16) are no longer ready—in discipleship to Jesus, who suffered "outside the city gate"—to "go to him outside the camp and bear the abuse he endured" (13:11–13).

For the author of the Letter to the Hebrews also, the Christian confession forms the basis of proclamation, and it would be foreign to him to *substantiate* his own message with the Old Testament. This confession took shape in the realm of Hellenistic Jewish Christianity. Specifically Gentile Christian elements, as well as Pauline theologoumena, are foreign to it, even if in the meantime the church is living in a Gentile Christian way and has done away with the law (7:18–19; 9:10). The confession combines preexistence Christology with a soteriology oriented toward the salvific death of Jesus; in the face of the persecution situation, eschatology acquired an important weight and also drew to it the concept of faith (10:36–11:40). The Old Testament becomes prominent only with the separation from Judaism. It is not a part of the instruction on the basis of faith but serves the author of Hebrews as the foundation of a "mature" teaching of "perfection" (5:11–6:3). In this sense, the usage of scripture in Hebrews falls within the framework of the early Christian consensus.

The Letter to the Hebrews, however, is distinguished from the previously analyzed scriptures, in which the Old Testament gains significant weight only in the polemical and apologetic exchanges with the synagogal authorities, in that the scripture is held up and interpreted directly to the addressed Christians in order to document the far superior rank of their own confession over Judaism. This peculiarity in the treatment of the Old Testament reveals that the *aposynagōgos* is complete; the author of Hebrews is no longer in contact with the synagogue, and it no longer solicits Christians. Rather, the parts of the church who are still or again blamed for the Judaizing (13:9–10; cf. 9:10) seem to be returning or wanting to return to the protection of the synagogue, and it is this striving that the Letter to the Hebrews opposes, in order to "lift your drooping hands and strengthen your weak knees"

(12:12). With the Holy Scripture, the highest authority of the Pharisaic synagogue, he advances the view that falling away from the Christian confession means that "they are crucifying again the Son of God and are holding him up to contempt" (6:6), selling their birthright for a single meal (12:16–17), and moving from the true nature of things into the shadow of what is to come (10:1). Those who fall away to the synagogue confuse the new with the old, whose end is approaching (8:13).

The Letter to the Ephesians

In its dealings with the Old Testament, the deutero-Pauline Letter to the Ephesians moves entirely along the paths prescribed by Paul himself. The concrete reason for the letter is hard to know and therefore controversial among scholars, yet the writing obviously belongs in the situation of the *aposynagōgos*. The author no longer disagrees with the synagogue, and he uses the scripture neither for apologetics nor for polemics, but he endeavors to bring together Gentile Christians and Jewish Christians in *one* Christian church (2:11–22) and has both Christian groups in mind as readers. With its author the language of the Greek Bible no longer makes itself as noticeable as with Paul himself. But in 1:22 we find a traditional reference to Ps. 8:7 or 110:1, and the paraenesis is above all full of allusions and references to the Old Testament (2:14, 17; 4:25–26; 5:2). In addition, there are three quotations: Ps. 68:18 supports the charismatic order of the church (4:8); Gen. 2:24 is allegorized to the close communion of Christ and the church (5:31); and Deut. 5:16 supports the admonition in the household rules to be obedient to parents (6:2–3). Possibly the Gentile Christian author wants to impress the Jewish Christians with these quotations, which are entirely secondary to his comments, as well as to say that the abolishing of the law with its commandments and ordinances (2:15) does not mean denying the authority of the Old Testament.

Early Catholic Christianity

The Apostolic Council in Jerusalem (Gal. 2:1–10) agreed to an organizational separation between Jewish Christianity working in the synagogal institution and Pauline Gentile Christianity active in the world. In the early catholic church, after the expulsion from the synagogue, this separation was intentionally suspended, and thus the eventual result was the uniting of "orthodox" Jewish and Gentile Christian churches, together with the concomitant exclusion of Judaizers and, above all, Gnostic heretics. In the following analysis of scriptures, we may leave open the question of how far the process of this unification can be already presupposed; because in principle the Old Testament enjoyed high standing in both Jewish and Gentile Christianity, such high regard is also to be expected in early catholic Christianity. We can also see that early catholic Christianity generally developed more under the influence of Hellenistic Jewish Christianity than under that of Gentile Christianity, and that on the whole, consequently, the Old Testament has a growing importance, without the incidental approach to the Old Testament being given up in favor of a "theology of scripture" alongside the primacy of the church's own confession.

The Redaction of the
Gospel of Mark and the Sayings Source

In its present form, the Gospel of Mark presupposes a situation of persecution (8:34–38; 9:38–41; 10:28–31). Thus its author or the final redactor and his addressees are no longer in the synagogal association.

In Mark 1:2–3 (cf. 15:28) the evangelist was probably the first to make explicit the implicit reference of the account of the appearance of the Baptist to Mal. 3:1 and Isa. 40:3 (cf. 9:11–13). The inexact quotations of Isa. 6:9–10 and Jer. 5:21 in 4:11–12 and 8:18, which are connected with the evangelist's theory of the messianic secret, certainly go back to him; and the hair-splitting scribal interpretation of Ps. 110:1 in 12:35–37, which, however, did not come from him (cf. *Barn.* 12.10–11), was likewise inserted by him for redactional reasons. This usage of the scriptures betrays no more than the fact that the evangelist is familiar with the Old Testament and that with due cause he can make use of it. If the passion announcements formed by Mark (8:31; 9:30–32; 10:32–34) do not contain a reference to the scriptures although according to the evidence of 14:21 the evangelist is familiar with the corresponding tradition (1 Cor. 15:3–4; cf. Mark 9:12–13), this shows how little he felt compelled to buttress the central Christian message with a scriptural reference or even scriptural proof.

The same is true of the passages that are attributed to the sayings source used by Matthew and Luke in their last redaction (Schmithals 1985, 204–5), for they belong to the same level of tradition as the final redaction of the Gospel of Mark and like them possibly come from the hand of the evangelist Mark (ibid., 396–99, 403). For our purposes, two of these passages are to be noted. The inquiry of the Baptist whether Jesus is the expected Messiah (Luke 7:18–23 par.) is answered by Jesus with a reference to his miraculous deeds, which he frames with expressions from Isa. 29:18–19; 35:5–6; 42:18; 61:1, that is, with a summary that could also be used in a similar way in Jewish apocalypses to describe the marvelous glory of the messianic age. The temptation story in particular (Luke 4:1–13 par.) reveals the author's familiarity with the scriptures: Jesus, quoting scripture (Deut. 6:13, 16; 8:3), thrice rejects the unreasonable suggestions of the devil, who himself also argues with a messianic Psalm (Ps. 2:7–8) and finally even explicitly quotes Ps. 91:11–12. With the help of such scriptural scholarship the author shapes a morally successful and also theologically impressive narrative, which in regard to the importance of the Old Testament for the Christian church reveals only that it naturally continues to recognize the scriptures and relates its messianic passages to Jesus the Christ.

The Gospel of Luke
and the Acts of the Apostles

The Lukan double volume is still entirely in the tradition of Hellenistic Jewish Christianity, and the very nature of Luke's peculiar presentation of Paul in Acts shows that Paul's Gentile Christian theology did not make a notable impression on Luke's thinking. The connection with the synagogue, however, has been definitively broken, and the church has consequently met with violent persecutions;

from Acts 18:12–17, for example, we learn how the Jews distanced themselves from Christians through public denunciation and delivered them to state persecution. To a considerable measure one must read the Lukan double volume as an apologia with which the political loyalty of Christians can be demonstrated to the pagan public.

In this situation, however, Luke places great value on presenting Christianity as the true Judaism and emphasizing the unbroken connection of the Christian church with the people of God of the Old Testament. John the Baptist is the last of the prophets and at the same time the forerunner of Jesus Christ; Jesus is the *Jewish* Messiah whom all people follow; Jerusalem is his and his church's city, and the temple is the place of his and his apostles' preaching; he observes Jewish customs, and Paul also faithfully follows the laws of the Torah. The separation of Jews and Christians occurred against the will of Christendom and was caused by the malice of the Jewish leaders, who rejected their Messiah Jesus and thereby cleared the way of the Gospel to the Gentiles.

Within the framework of this presentation Luke emphatically claims the Old Testament for the Christian church. Luke 1:5–80 lets the "prehistory" of John and Jesus reflect completely the light of the Old Testament. The destiny of Jesus was already announced in the Old Testament (18:31), and the mission to the Gentiles established (Acts 13:47). Jesus preaches his inaugural sermon in Nazareth, using a text from the prophet Isaiah (Luke 4:16–21), which is fulfilled with his coming, and for the apostles and their followers the Old Testament as Christian witness becomes the comprehensive object of their sermons (Acts 2:14–36; 7:2–53; 13:16–41; etc.). No other New Testament author is so focused on the Old Testament. This does not mean that Luke needs the Old Testament as the *substantiation* of the Christian message. Rather, the familiar teaching, whose reliability Luke wants to present through his double volume, is also for him the Christian "catechism" (Luke 1:1–4). The strong appeal to the Old Testament, by contrast, serves as a "secondary" demonstration that the Christian church is legitimized by the Holy Scriptures as the true people of God and that in this sense Christianity does not represent a new message (cf. Luke 4:36 with Mark 1:17).

It is not easy to answer the question What moved Luke to make this idea and thus the Old Testament so prominent in his double volume?—especially since his interest is directed at the Old Testament as such and not at its specific contents? In recent times Luke has in various ways often been credited with a "theology of the history of salvation" that has its beginning in the Old Testament, yet historical thinking is foreign to it and to antiquity in general. Even farther from the Old Testament is any historical theology that sees salvation as an event in a historical process and that is a product of modern thinking. With his laying claim to the Old Testament, however, Luke could hardly be attempting to gain for Christianity the same tolerance that the Roman state had for Judaism, for based on the purely theological argumentation as found in the Lukan double volume, the state would hardly have drawn political conclusions, even if it was able to understand this argumentation at all. And nowhere does the author of the Gospel of Luke and Acts make a connection between his political apologetic and his intensive interaction with the

Old Testament. Nor does Luke ever reveal that he has in mind using his double volume to promote Christianity among the adherents of the synagogue; in his time the synagogue lies outside his field of vision.

Therefore, one may more probably assume that Luke is addressing tendencies *within Christendom* to disregard the Old Testament entirely. Such tendencies were already visible in Paul's time in Rom. 11:11–24 and later in Mark 7:24–30, and after the exclusion of Christians from the synagogue, they found in Apelles, Marcion, and other leaders of schools strong champions, who radically separated Christianity as a completely new message from Judaism and rejected the Old Testament as an inferior scripture. Yet we cannot know what specifically led Luke to speak in such an intensive way for the Old Testament as the Holy Scripture of Christianity, for he apparently does not see its rejection as a threat to the Christian confession as such or even to faith in God the creator. Presumably he is already confronted with a more comprehensive heretical movement, which has achieved broad recognition and from which the orthodox church can distance itself especially clearly through its confession to the Old Testament. In any case, of all the New Testament scriptures, it is above all the Lukan double work that caused the Old Testament, in and along with the New Testament, to retain its authority in the Christian church.

The Pastoral Letters and
Other New Testament Scriptures

We may mention in more or less summary fashion such scriptures as the pastoral letters, the Revelation to John, 1 and 2 Peter, Jude, and James. In their disparity they show how even before the *aposynagōgos* Hellenistic Jewish Christianity developed in different directions as it spread. For the author of the pastoral letters—by no means a student of Paul—stands in the tradition of Hellenistic Jewish Christianity and, like the Letter of James (2:14–26), speaks in the interest of the "catholic" faith against those who misuse the Pauline legacy for their own benefit. Common to these scriptures is the fact that contact with the synagogue has been lost and thus also an important reason for using the Holy Scriptures in argumentation. The occasions for the named scriptures are variable and not always discernible with certainty. Without question, however, the pastoral letters, as well as Jude, 2 Peter, and the circular letter of Revelation, deal with a rapidly spreading Christian Gnosticism. The occasion for 1 Peter and Revelation is the experience of oppression and persecution of the church by the Roman state.

The language of this scripture is, furthermore, the more or less pronounced "Jewish Greek" found in the Septuagint, and therefore it must remain an open question whether there are conscious or unconscious allusions to the Old Testament; the Revelation to John is by far the most thoroughly grounded in the linguistic and conceptual world of the Old Testament. Only in 1 Peter, however, are passages from the Old Testament expressly related to the confession of Christ; in 1 Peter 2:21–24 this is accomplished by means of a paraphrase of the original reference text in Isaiah 53, with which Christians are challenged to the discipleship of suffering; in 2:4–10 there is a similarly traditional (Mark 12:10–11; Rom. 9:32) reference to Ps. 118:22; Isa. 8:14 and 28:16, with the author comfortingly and admonishingly reminding readers of their state of salvation.

The author of the pastoral letters never tires of encouraging his readers to hold fast to the traditional teaching, which is occasionally cited formulaically but is generally presupposed as familiar. It is taken for granted that this teaching is in agreement with the Holy Scriptures: "But as for you, continue in what you have learned and firmly believed, knowing from whom you learned it, and how from childhood you have known the sacred writings that are able to instruct you for salvation through faith in Christ Jesus" (2 Tim. 3:14–15). Yet this faith is explicated not with the Old Testament but with the Christian confessions (1 Tim. 1:15; 2:5–6; 3:16; 2 Tim. 1:9–10; 2:8; Titus 3:4–8). When the author continues in 2 Tim. 3:16: "All scripture is inspired by God and is useful for teaching, for reproof, for correction, and for training in righteousness," this shows that the Old Testament finds concrete application above all in paraenesis, as the literal references and express scriptural quotations outside the pastoral letters also confirm (1 Tim. 2:12–15; 2 Tim. 2:19; Titus 2:11–12, 14; Rev. 14:5; James 2:11, 23; 1 Peter 1:16, 24–25; 3:10–12; 4:8; 5:5, 8). And thus we are also to understand in this sense the admonition to continue to "give attention to the public reading of scripture, to exhorting, to teaching" (1 Tim. 4:13; cf. *2 Clem.* 19.1; Just. *Apol.* 167.3–4). Here we also occasionally find a perceivably unbroken continuation of synagogal instruction (1 Tim. 5:18, 19; 2 Tim. 3:8; 4:14; Rev. 9:20–21; James 4:5–10). Also in doxological passages the use of biblical models is hardly distinguishable from synagogal prayer language (1 Tim. 1:17; 6:15–16; Rev. 1:7, 4:8, 11; 15:3–4), and in both cases apocalyptic eschatology employs the same scriptural passages (Rev. 1:7; 2:27; 6:16–17; 7:16–17; 19:15; 20:9; Jude 5–11; 2 Peter 3:13).

The Gospel of John and the Letters of John

Our present Gospel of John is a relatively late writing, which is attested with certainty only in the second half of the second century. Unlike the basic text (see above), the evangelist no longer finds himself in conflict with the Jews; rather, like the author of the Johannine letters, he is faced with Christian opponents (1 John 2:18–19) of Gnostic persuasion, who deny Jesus' true humanity (1 John 4:1–3); he is looking back on a great falling away to false teaching (John 6:60–62, 64–71). And unlike his source, the evangelist quotes many Old Testament passages (1:23; 2:17, 22; 6:31–33, 45; 7:38; 10:34; 12:14–16), including express fulfillment quotations in the manner of the Gospel of Matthew (12:38–41; 13:18; 15:25; 17:12; 19:24, 28, 36). In addition, he also refers a number of times to the Old Testament (1:51; 3:14; 6:49, 58; 7:42), in which he is completely at home, and in 10:35 we even read that "the scripture cannot be annulled."

It is not easy to decide whether the evangelist is simply following a "catholic" custom when he brings the Old Testament relatively forcefully into his model, or whether in such a process he is guided by a particular interest. The scriptural quotations are often used to set forth the true humanity of Jesus vis-à-vis the Docetism of the false teachers against whom the Gospel and letters speak (3:14; 6:41–51,

58; 10:33–36; 19:28–29, 36, 37), and we will recall that the Marcionites both rejected the Old Testament and also held the view that Jesus had only an apparent body. Therefore, the late attestation of the Gospel of John allows its decisive appeal to the Old Testament to be understood as a conscious antithesis to Marcionism or analogous currents and as a refutation of those teachers (cf. 5:43) whose theological program included the "annulment" of scripture (10:35; cf. Schmithals 1992, 422).

In this connection, it is strange that the Johannine letters, in contrast to the Gospel of John, at no point quote the Old Testament or even make a clear reference to it. And of all the Old Testament personalities we find only Cain as the prototype of the false teachers who are battled in the letters (1 John 3:11–12)—a sign that the author was thoroughly familiar with the Old Testament and also recognized its authority. The curious fact that he nonetheless makes no further use of the scriptures cannot be accidental: it must be intentional. It can hardly be explained by the notion of different authors, for even if the improbable view is correct that the evangelist is not identical with the author of the letters, the circumstances of composition of the Gospel and the letters are so similar in all ways, and at the same time the treatment of the Old Testament is so strikingly opposite, that one cannot trace this difference back to accidental circumstances based on the personalities of the authors. This is also true of the extremely unlikely case that the letters are older than the Gospel, and thus the author of the letters was not familiar with the use of the Old Testament by the evangelist. Thus it cannot be that the author of the letters, in contrast to the evangelist, comes from a particular Gentile Christian tradition that has long forsaken the use of the Old Testament. Nor can we say that the literary genre "letter," in distinction to the genre "gospel," could have involved renouncing the use of scripture.

The question of what intention guided the author of the letters to retain a significant relationship with the Old Testament has not yet been convincingly answered; interpreters as a rule confirm this curious state of affairs as such but do not attempt to explain it. If one assumes, however, that the Gospel of John and the Johannine letters were written also, or above all, against *Marcion,* then the *form* of the Johannine corpus—Gospel and three letters—can be easily understood as a conscious antithesis to the canon of Marcion: gospel and ten letters. With this presupposition, however, one can argue further that if Marcion, with his canon of gospel and letters, wanted to document that the Christian message contains information that is foreign to the Holy Scriptures of Judaism, the author of the Johannine corpus demonstrates, by contrast, that even the lack of Old Testament references in the *letters* by no means implies a judgment against the Old Testament, as its simultaneous usage in the *Gospel* of John shows. Since he himself is not familiar with the Pauline tradition, he probably considered the letters of the Marcionite canon, which had been shortened by the omission of Old Testament references to be authentic, yet with his own work he questions the idea of alleging that Paul rejected the Old Testament when he did not support his Gospel with the scriptures.

One can dispute the plausibility of such an attempt to explain. In any case, the

Johannine writings show that the early catholic church's position on the Old Testament stands in unbroken continuity with early Christianity: the church remains bound to the Old Testament and thus to its own heritage from the people Israel; it can be used as needed, but it is not needed to substantiate the Gospel.

The "Apostolic Fathers"

A comparison of the letters of Ignatius of Antioch with the *First Letter of Clement* is instructive, for it reveals varying interaction with the Old Testament even in the early catholic period. Here the older customs of Gentile and Jewish Christianity continue.

"Almost two generations after Paul, the Antiochene bishop Ignatius, in his letters to churches in Asia Minor and to Rome, adopts essentially the same position as the apostle toward the gospel and the Old Testament" (Harnack 1928, 138). He disagrees with the Judaizing Christians who remain bound to the Jewish law (*Magn.* 8.1), keep the sabbath (*Magn.* 9.1), and have faith in the gospel only where its assertions are confirmed by the scriptures (*Phld.* 8.2). In contrast to them, Ignatius considers the law abolished (*Magn.* 10.1–3), but he refers to the prophets as witnesses of Jesus Christ and his way of salvation (*Magn.* 8.2; 9.2; *Smyrn.* 7.3; *Phld.* 5.2; 9.2; Pol. *Phil.* 6.3), and in his discussions with these Christians he says that the message of the gospel is *also* found in the scripture (*Phld.* 8.2; cf. Pol. *Phil.* 12.1). In his letters, however, he forgoes almost entirely quoting the Old Testament or specifically referring to it. In view of the fact that elsewhere Ignatius does not hesitate vis-à-vis his Judaizing opponents to claim the Old Testament for the Christian message, his forgoing its use in his letters cannot rest on an intentional decision, especially since in *Eph.* 5.3 and *Magn.* 12 he expressly quotes the book of proverbs. Rather, he comes from a Gentile Christian tradition that could be observed already in Paul and also in the basic text of the Gospel of John, a tradition in which the Old Testament, though basically recognized, was not an object of Christian proclamation. The Old Testament was claimed vis-à-vis the Jews and Judaizers, and paraenetic instruction was taken from it (cf. Pol. *Phil.* 12.1), but the Christian message itself was developed on the basis of the confessions of faith, which Ignatius never tired of quoting (*Eph.* 7.2; 18.2; *Trall.* 9.1–2; etc.). Accordingly, Ignatius expressly subordinates the "beloved prophets" more than once to the "gospel" (*Phld.* 5.1–2; *Smyrn.* 7.2; *Phld.* 9.1–2) and explains to those who call on the scriptures of the Old Testament as the normative documents of faith: "My documents are Jesus Christ; the holy documents are his cross and his death and his resurrection and the faith aroused by him" (*Phld.* 8.2).

The author of the text *Diognetus,* who also stands in the Pauline, Gentile Christian tradition, is even more emancipated from the Old Testament than Ignatius. He never quotes it and does not use it for the presentation of the Christian message. Even where he sets Christianity apart from Judaism (1.1; 3.1–4.6), the scriptures play no role. He mockingly describes biblically based Jewish customs as a pagan would and dismisses them as superstition. He does not reflect on the proper understanding of the Old Testament. Such abstinence may be traceable in part to the fact that the author, with apologetic and missionary intent, is addressing *pagans,* who have no clear conception of the Old Testament. In the extreme way that this abstinence is visible in *Diognetus,* however, it is understandable only if the Christian tradition in which the author stands has completely renounced proving the gospel to be in accordance with scripture. If we also see something comparable in the *Shepherd of Hermas,* who is otherwise closely connected with apocalyptic Judaism and almost totally suppresses the Christian element, we are apparently observing a "scriptureless" strain of tradition that leads back even into Judaism.

From the *First Letter of Clement* we get a completely different impression in regard to the use of biblical texts. It consists in broad sections of quotations and references to the Old Testament, as well as considerations of biblical stories, and the author's own comments are full of allusions to the scripture and saturated with biblical language. As a rule, the Old Testament material, in accordance with the occasion for the letter, serves as a paradigm for the appropriate behavior of the church; Isaiah 53 is fully quoted as an example of humility worthy of emulation (*1 Clem.* 16.1–17). Although the writer also knows the letters of Paul and often uses them (47.1–4), his theology betrays that he is completely at home in a Hellenistic Jewish Christianity in which interaction with the Old Testament—in a Christian way—is accepted with a naturalness that requires no special reflection or discussion. But Clement does not derive the gospel from the Old Testament. It comes, rather, from Jesus Christ, who was sent by God and who, for his part, instructed the apostles and sent them out (42.1–3). The Old Testament plays no role in this substantiation. Thus even where it is used freely, it does not provide the foundation of the Christian message, but rather clarifies it in the realm of a church that was traditionally used to dealing with the Holy Scriptures.

One can make the corresponding observations about the *Letter of Barnabas,* whose author is interested above all in proving that the Jews have no right to appeal to the Old Testament, because in all things it was written only in reference to Christ and the "direct" understanding is a misunderstanding. There was never a covenant of God with Israel; rather, the Old Testament knows only the covenant in Jesus Christ, "for in him and to him is everything" (*Barn.* 12.7). In order to demonstrate this, the author must interpret, or be able to interpret, *all* assertions of scripture in a Christian way, which becomes possible through an extreme allegorization that shies away from no absurdity. With every reservation one could call Barnabas a "Jewish Christian Marcionite" because he sharply separates Judaism and Christianity from each other, yet—because of his being rooted in a Hellenistic Jewish Christian tradition—without rejecting the Old Testament. He does not reveal what moved him to disinherit Judaism in this way, for he has no obvious contact with the synagogue, nor does he seem to want to fight Judaizing tendencies in Christianity. Is this author, who wrote around 130 to 140, repaying in his own way the persecution of Christians brought about by the *aposynagōgos* and denunciation? It is clear, however, that the numerous "testimonies" with which he claims to prove the pervasive Christian significance of the Old Testament do not serve to validate the Christian message but only to question the Jews' right to appeal to the scriptures. Therefore he interprets the gospel into the Old Testament but does not derive it from the Old Testament. The gospel does not need the scriptures; rather, the scriptures are entirely dependent on the gospel for their correct understanding.

The other early Christian writings from the period before the formation of the New Testament canon vary in their interaction with the Old Testament within the range defined by the foregoing examples, that is, between a broad renunciation of the usage of the Holy Scriptures, on the one hand, and their intensive use, on the other, as we can observe especially clearly in Justin Martyr not long before the formation of the New Testament. Against Marcion and many Gnostics, Justin, like Luke before him, has to defend the validity of the scripture, which he vigorously interprets as a witness to Christ in his *Dialogue with the Jew Trypho,* and with which in his *Apology* he derives, over against the Gentiles, a "proof by prediction" of the truth of Christianity by demonstrating that all the details of the Christ event were precisely foretold in the scriptures. For Justin, however, it is also still true that the scripture does not standardize the gospel; rather, when scripture is quoted, referred to, or interpreted, the gospel opens up the understanding of scripture.

Conclusion

Although even in the early period of Christianity scriptural passages such as Isaiah 53 and Psalm 110 contributed importantly to the interpretation of the Christ event and to the development of the basic Christian confession, the gospel's claim of truth was, from the beginning, based not on a biblical foundation but on the Christ event itself. But because the Christian church in all its various forms understood itself as the "true Israel," it also laid its own claim to Holy Scriptures of the people Israel. In the Jewish Christian tradition the Old Testament was generally preserved as a valuable heritage; within the church it was used above all for admonition, but in the conflict with the synagogue it was also claimed as a testimony to Christ. In the Gentile Christian tradition, however, its concrete significance tended to be nil, yet the different positions on scripture did not lead to a split in the early catholic church, because their unity did not rest on a "principle of scripture" but on the common "apostolic" faith. Only when the Old Testament and faith in God the creator were *rejected* was the result separation, as the excommunication of Marcion shows.

As a *substitute* for the Holy Scriptures that he rejected, Marcion formed the Gospel of Luke and ten letters of Paul into the first New Testament. Whether and to what extent this led the early catholic church to create its own New Testament is a controversial question. In any case, however, its New Testament did not, like Marcion's, appear in place of the Old, nor was it seen as a continuation or completion of the Old. Its purpose, rather, was to standardize the "apostolic testimony to Christ" in an obligatory form for the early catholic church as a defense especially against Gnostic false teachers. Thus the New Testament took the place of the previously more or less freely formulated apostolic gospel that was handed down and taught in confessions and a variety of writings, and it appeared with the "apostolic confession of faith" *alongside* the Old Testament. Therefore the New Testament, like the confession, also took over the hermeneutic function of guiding the interpretation of the Old Testament.

It is notable that now Old and New Testament *together* form the *Holy Scriptures,* and this formal similarity of the two parts of the one *Christian Bible* led in this way to an upward revaluation of the Old Testament when it could no longer be neglected or even ignored by parts of Christendom. Yet until the threshold of the modern period the New Testament remained the hermeneutical key to the Old; the Old Testament continued to be understood and interpreted "backward," that is, based on "fulfillment" or in the light of Christian dogma. And thus a problem was raised by the question to what extent such an interpretation could make use of multiple meanings of scripture and especially of allegory. The commentaries interpreted the Old Testament in the light of the New, and "biblical theology"—this term did not arise until the seventeenth century—consisted in using Old and New Testament without distinction to provide support for the building of Christian doctrine. The "center of the scripture" lay in its second part.

Any reversal of this state of affairs becomes possible only with modern conceptual possibilities. And even where it seems justified, it cannot be based on the New Testament or on early Christendom.

16

The Importance of the Gospels in the History of Theology before the Formation of the Canon

The paramount importance of the canonical Gospels for the history of the Christian church is apparent to everyone. The cross is framed by the symbols of the four evangelists. In the liturgy the Gospel reading is given a prominent place. From the beginning Christian visual art has chosen its themes above all from the Gospels. The biblical texts of Christmas and Passion music are generally taken from the Gospels. Even in theological scholarship, Paul has at times had difficulty gaining a position equal to the Gospels, for as early as Origen (*Commentary on John* 1.6) the Gospels, and especially the Gospel of John, were placed at the head of the apostolic tradition, and other writers have followed Origen's example.

Basic Observations

Thus in the almost two-thousand-year history of church and theology, unmistakable importance has been given to the Gospel texts, which were incorporated into the New Testament in four forms, and today this still nourishes the often ill-considered judgment that the Gospels must consequently have played an important role from the beginning or from their origin. Yet even a cursory look into early Christian theological history shows that the opposite was the case. Only with the formation of the canon do the Gospels enter the broad Christian consciousness and the stage of general knowledge and use. In the first three or four generations of the Christian church, the Gospels received little attention, and their importance for the development of early Christian theology tends to be nil.

With regard to the letters of the apostle Paul, Neirynck (1986) has critically reviewed the relevant material and the more recent literature. His conclusion agrees with that of Walter (1985) and with my own judgment (Schmithals 1985, 99ff.). The Synoptic narrative material does not occur at all in Paul. For his central soteriological message he never appeals to the appropriate Jesus tradition; only for his paraenesis does he turn to a saying of Jesus, namely, in 1 Cor. 7:10–11 and 9:14. In so doing, however, he deals rather freely with the wording of the tradition and very dispassionately with its content, and he does not accord the quoted sayings any great authority (Lindemann 1992). "Elsewhere in the Pauline letters there is no certain trace of a conscious use of sayings of Jesus" (Neirynck 1986, 320).

When Strecker (1992, 166) regards this state of affairs as based on the fact "that the Synoptic narrative tradition is in no small part post-Pauline," that is only half of the truth, for the other part is likewise missing in Paul. In order to discover it in at least one case, Strecker (1992, 167) has to go back to Luther's inaccurate translation of 1 Cor. 11:23 ("in the night when he was betrayed"), although Paul did not have in mind the betrayal by Judas at all but rather was reaching back to the early Christian confessional tradition according to which God himself (*passivum divinum*) "delivered" Jesus into the darkness of human guilt and of death (cf. Isa. 53:6, 12; Rom. 4:25; 8:32; Gal. 2:20).

A careful examination shows that Paul supports his gospel completely with traditional instructional and confessional formulas, whose derivational process is also sufficiently clear on the basis of the few extant letters. At the beginning of the development of Christian doctrine stands the not yet christological confession to *God,* who raised Jesus from the dead (Gal. 1:1; Rom. 4:24; 8:11; 2 Cor. 4:14; Col. 2:12) as the "first fruits" of those who have died (1 Cor. 15:20; Col. 1:18; cf. Acts 26:23; Rev. 1:5, as well as Rom. 8:11; 1 Cor. 6:14; 2 Cor. 4:14; 1 Thess. 4:14). Thus this confession becomes audible on the level of apocalyptic thinking, and Jesus' followers, who have already received the promised Spirit of the end time, are waiting for the imminent completion of the impending turn of the age, for "if the Spirit of him who raised Jesus from the dead dwells in you, he who raised Christ from the dead will give life to your mortal bodies also" (Rom. 8:11).

This apocalyptically rooted and *theologically* refined early confession is soon used *christologically:* Jesus' resurrection means his exaltation to the right hand of God and the transference of the messianic majesty to him or his adoption as the Son of God (Rom. 1:4; 10:9; Phil. 2:9–11; Eph. 1:20; 1 Peter 1:21; 3:21–22; Heb. 1:3; Matt. 28:18–20). This is a confession that even before the conversion of Paul is connected in one branch of early Christianity with the concept of preexistence and which developed into the schema of *humbling and exaltation* (Phil. 2:6–11; Rom. 8:3; Gal. 4:4; cf. Heb. 1:1ff.).

The *christological* confession is soon expanded *soteriologically,* at first in a version preserved in 1 Thess. 1:10, ". . . and to wait for his Son from heaven . . . Jesus, who rescues us from the wrath that is coming," and in Phil. 3:20–21, "But our citizenship is in heaven, and it is from there that we are expecting a Savior, the Lord Jesus Christ. He will transform the body of our humiliation that it may be conformed to the body of his glory" (cf. Rom. 8:34; 1 Thess. 4:14), as well as in a related, likewise original form, attested by, among other texts, 1 Cor. 15:23ff. (cf. Phil. 3:21b; 1 Peter 3:21–22; Eph. 1:22ff.; Pol. *Phil.* 2.1): "He must reign until he has put all his enemies under his feet." Both forms are still rooted in apocalyptic thinking: in the imminent catastrophe of the turn of the age, the exalted Lord and Christ Jesus will appear as Savior and advocate to those who know him (Rom. 8:34).

After that, however, we find the two great soteriological designs of the *theologia incarnationis* and the *theologia crucis* or *passionis.* Incarnation soteriology was originally connected with preexistence Christology and was already taught in the law-free Christianity to which Paul was converted (Gal. 4:4; 2 Cor. 5:21; Rom.

8:3). The soteriological design oriented toward Jesus' passion and death is, by contrast, connected from the beginning with adoption Christology and belongs to Hellenistic Jewish Christianity, in whose intrasynagogal mission Paul was also active for a lengthy period until after the Apostolic Council, when he directed his efforts toward the founding of independent Gentile Christian churches outside the synagogue (1 Cor. 15:3–5; 2 Cor. 5:19; Gal. 1:4; Rom. 3:25–26a; 4:25; 8:32). The two future-oriented soteriological models—"Christmas" and "Good Friday"—which both go beyond the apocalyptic horizon and in whose context salvation is promised in the present, already stand side by side in Paul. He can combine them (Rom. 8:3; Phil. 2:8), and he develops them into his characteristic doctrine of justification (Rom. 3:25–26; 4:25; 6:1ff.; 2 Cor. 5:14, 18).

Thus it can be observed, and also shown in detail beyond what has been said, that Pauline theology, including Christology and soteriology, as well as ethics, ecclesiology, and eschatology, is consistently oriented toward the *teaching tradition* that goes back to the apocalyptic beginnings of the Easter community, was developed and handed down formulaically, and also provided the basis for reading and interpreting the Old Testament. By contrast, the material contained in the Gospels played no role worth mentioning. And this phenomenon is in no way connected with a special Pauline theology that might be explained on the basis of specific Pauline interests. For apart from the Gospels themselves, we encounter in the remaining texts of the New Testament, as well as for the most part in the apostolic fathers, the same basic situation as in Paul. We find set formulas of faith and teaching that, as a rule, are presupposed and sometimes further developed according to the situation; they form the foundation for instruction and also for the interpretation of the Old Testament. The Synoptic tradition, by contrast, does not play a role that is at all comparable. How firmly and fundamentally rooted this type of teaching was in early Christianity is still shown today by the fact that the christological article of the baptismal and faith confessions (Apostles' and Nicene creeds, etc.) move directly from Jesus' birth or incarnation to his passion, without making any reference to his life, teachings, and activity as they are found in the Gospels.

Not until a time when there were without doubt already gospel *writings* do ecclesiastical authors gradually turn their attention to the Synoptic tradition, yet in a very free and relatively detached manner (*1 Clem.* 13.2; 46.8; Ign. *Pol.* 2.2; Pol. *Phil.* 2.3; 7.2; 12.3; *Didache* and *2 Clement* more often; 2 Peter 1:16–18) and above all in reference to the paraenetic material from the tradition. Not until Justin is there also consideration of the narrative material, yet essentially only when it illustrates his basic formulaic instructional and confessional statements, using especially the prehistories and the passion and Easter accounts, whereas he is hardly interested in the miracle narratives, teaching dialogues, and disputes or the parables and illustrative stories.

I am assuming here that the named writings and writers of the second century were completely dependent not on oral but on written tradition, yet this controversial and often discussed problem is of no crucial importance for our considerations. Nevertheless, I have no reason to depart from my conviction that the form-historically postulated stage of oral tradition for the Synoptic material essentially never existed (Schmithals 1985, 298), for I know of no substantiated objections to his view. When Roloff (1990, 412; cf. Strecker 1992, 166) can raise only the following objection to my critique of Synoptic form criticism, "Curiously, Schmithals does not go into the question of the form of the pre-Johannine Jesus tradition," he presupposes what is at issue. For the view that the fourth evangelist adopted his Synoptic material not from the Synoptic Gospels but from free tradition is essentially a product of form history itself and cannot be employed to support that history, since the view that the evangelist John used the Synoptic Gospels is still in all probability correct. It is also a view on which Neirynck (1984), among others, insists with good reason, and which commends itself unconditionally, simply because the assumption is erroneous that the last of our evangelists created the literary genre "gospel" on his own, without depending on his Synoptic predecessors.

Justin is also the first writer to place importance on the fact that the Gospels are "recollections of the *apostles*," a viewpoint that would soon become normative in the formation of the canon. The two phenomena—the increasing interest in the Gospels around the middle of the second century and their evaluation as apostolic writings—belong together and are an expression of the dispute with Gnostic heretics, in which Justin was a leading participant. As "recollections of the *apostles*," the Gospels were highly suited to supporting the church's *principle of tradition* against the pneumatic immediacy of Gnostic prophecy; in this sense they appear alongside the apostolic confession and apostolic succession. Here the relatively late origin of the Gospels is further considered and the postapostolic generation is included as tradition bearer: according to Justin the Gospels were written "by the apostles and their followers" (*Dial.* 103.8); Papias traces one of the gospel writings known to him back to Mark, the student of Peter (Euseb. *Hist. Eccl.* 3.39.15); with the Gospels of Mark and Luke the New Testament contains two deuteroapostolic writings; even the Gospel of John in its original version (John 19:35), as well as 2 John 1 and 3 John 1, refer to the indirect eyewitness of the "elders" who followed the apostles. When we consider what importance for the ecclesiastical principle of tradition is ascribed by Papias and Irenaeus to the postapostolic generation of the "presbyters," the attribution (demanded in any case by the prologue of the Gospel of Luke) of individual gospel writings to the *students* of apostles involves no devaluation of these Gospels. At the same time, however, there is no question that the Gospels only gradually and for topical reasons attained the significance that was definitively substantiated by the formation of the canon and which has slowly grown in the consciousness of the church since Irenaeus. The designation preferred by Justin, *"recollections of the apostles"*—that is, "writings more of occasional content" (Bousset 1891, 15)—betrays how little the Gospels were originally considered as normative documentation of the confession, just as Papias still considered the apostolic traditions he himself was able to gather and record to be more useful than the material already recorded in the gospel writings (Euseb. *Hist. Eccl.* 3.39.4).

Thus the gospel writings moved only gradually into the position from which they were able to gain their familiar importance for later generations. They did not have this importance from the beginning and probably did not lay claim to it.

Methodological Considerations

Before we can look at the individual gospel writings and attempt to answer the questions of what their own particular claim was and what importance was actually given them originally, we must present two general and fundamental methodological considerations.

The Addressees of the Gospels

In the beginning period of historical research into the Gospels, when the problems of transmission were usually observed even more carefully than is usually the case today, the Synoptic Gospels were often regarded as private writings that were composed to aid one's own memory or for patrons (Luke 1:1–4); thus they were not an essential element in the proclamation of the gospel. In this way one can explain the apocryphal status of the early gospel tradition. Even the father of the two-source theory, Christian Hermann Weisse, thought the Gospel of Mark and the sayings source (Q) were private accounts: Mark did not want the recollections of Peter to be lost; Matthew wanted to preserve the utterances of Jesus as accurately and faithfully as possible. Later, with completely different presuppositions, Bultmann also assumes that the Gospel of John is a learned work edited from the literary legacy of its author, and Barrett is of the similar conviction that the fourth evangelist "wrote primarily to satisfy himself. His gospel had to be written: it was no concern of his whether it was also read" (1978, 135). Whether one may really make such judgments about the Gospel of John is doubtful, but there is no question that the individual Synoptic Gospels have the character of being related to a Christian community and its problems and in this sense are public and topical. None of the four canonical Gospels can be called a *private document,* and thus the noted fact that they remained hidden for a long time cannot be explained in this way. But what did the evangelists themselves want to accomplish with their literary activity?

The genre *gospel* as such does not mean that the author claims to present the Christian message, the "gospel," in a more or less comprehensive and fundamental way, especially since the authors themselves did not call their writings "gospels," for in Mark 1:1 we have the notation of a later copyist, which marks the incipit of the Gospel of Mark in a *collection* of writings and was unknown to the writers of the Gospels dependent on Mark. Papias also did not call the writings that he ascribed to Mark and Matthew "gospels." In Justin, however, this designation undoubtedly occurs as a term for a literary genre (*Apol.* 1.66.3; *Dial.* 10.2; 100.1; etc.), yet also in *Did.* 8.2; 11.3; 15.3–4 and *2 Clem.* 8.5 "gospel" probably refers to a particular, relatively freely reproduced gospel writing—apparently the Gospel of Matthew in the *Didache* and the Gospel of Luke in *2 Clement.* Thus in the first half of the second century the conviction began to prevail that the thus named writings contained the *gospel.* This conviction was apparently connected with the ascription of the gospel writings to apostles or students of apostles and thus with the early catholic church's anti-Gnostic principle of tradition: a writing that handed down the earliest events of the tradition contained the apostolic message, the gospel of Jesus Christ.

Such a conviction, however, appeared problematic already to Luther when in his *Vorrede auf das Neue Testament* [Preface to the New Testament] of 1522 he recommended that the Gospel of John as the "chief Gospel" and the letters of the apostle Paul be preferred to the first three Gospels, and critical scholarship has made such a view historically understandable. For if a gospel writing is addressed *to a Christian community itself,* which the author has in mind while writing, then, as a rule, he probably had no more intention than the author of the Letter to the Hebrews of teaching again "the basic elements of the oracles of God" (Heb. 5:12) and "laying again the foundation: repentance from dead works and faith toward God, instruction about baptisms, laying on of hands, resurrection of the dead, and eternal judgment" (6:1–2). Rather, in this case the evangelist presupposes knowledge of the faith and the recognized confession of the church, and he writes his gospel in order to give his listeners instruction in a particular situation and with reference to current problems. And in fact, none of the Gospels announces that it was written in order to recapitulate or renew Christian truth comprehensively *for the church* or to reformulate it in a certain form, say, for reading in the worship service. It is especially difficult to understand why in the face of such claims the Gospels could have remained in the literature of many Christian generations without any reaction.

The situation is different, however, if a gospel writing was intended not for the hands of church members but was directed toward *outsiders.* In this case, if the author was guided not only by apologetics but also by a missionary impulse, the writing probably contained the fundamental contents of the Christian message and was developed in a way appropriate for its particular addressees. Such a writing would doubtless have been no private writing but would have been directed toward a perhaps limited public; it would be understandable, however, that an instructional composition not intended for general church use would have only hesitatingly achieved broader validity.

With this presupposition the answer to the question about the original significance of the Gospels is a twofold principle to be gained concretely in the hermeneutical circle: a Gospel destined for the hands of church members contains as a rule no comprehensive, fundamental development of *the* gospel, but one written with non-Christians in mind presumably contains precisely this. And vice-versa: if a Gospel develops the basic truths of the Christian faith, it probably seeks its addressees outside or on the fringe of the Christian church; conversely, if it takes up specific themes in order to solve certain problems, overcome crises, ward off dangers, or clarify theological disputes, it is aimed toward a Christian church or perhaps to Christendom as a whole.

The Introduction of the
Gospel Writings into the Churches

The other methodological consideration is connected with the observation reported by Justin that in the Sunday gathering of his church, "the recollections of the apostles or the writings of the prophets are read aloud as time permits" (*Apol.* 1.67). Thus a reading from the Gospels has been added to the reading of the Old

Testament, which was customary in the synagogue. We may assume that this custom came about at the same time that the importance of the "apostolic" literature for the dispute with heretical enthusiasm was discovered, that is, around the middle of the second century, when gospel writings are found not only in Justin's writings but also in the *Didache* and *2 Clement*. In the Pauline churches the letters of the apostle Paul were probably read in a similar way as the testimony of apostolic beginnings. This is attested around 180 by the martyr Speratus from Scillium in Numidia (north Africa), who in answer to the proconsul's question What is in the cabinet? replied: "Libri et epistulae Pauli viri iusti" (books and letters of the just man Paul—whether the books included a Gospel in addition to Old Testament books is questionable).

Naturally, we cannot assume that individual churches were already using a Gospel *collection* in the period before the formation of the canon. Even if several Gospels found their way into the library of the scholar Justin, this does not mean that in worship services churches used more than the one Gospel known in their area. Marcion, naturally, canonized only one gospel writing. The view that the churches "acquired relatively quickly the newly composed 'Gospels'" and that they were "probably also sent to them unrequested" (Hengel 1984, 47–48) transplants professorial curiosity into the life of early Christian churches. The one gospel was portrayed in one gospel writing, and no church would have voluntarily taken on the problems of Gospel harmony; for this reason it is also mistaken to conclude that even in Justin's time the Gospels must have already borne the names of their respective authors, so that one could distinguish them from each other (thus Hengel 1984, 47). Indeed, Justin endeavored to grasp the Gospel literature in a unified way as "recollections of the apostles" and referred to them only in a free, harmonizing way (Köster 1990, 360ff.). "All the analogies that one might suggest for writings of such significance as the Gospels in the history of religions support the idea that *one* book was treasured highly, not several similar ones, and that in worship one read from *one* book" (Harnack 1896, 681)—if the church had already begun to use a Gospel at all. Only with the formation of the canon, in which *nolens volens* the different interests of various churches had to be considered, were the majority of the gospels that were considered apostolic made official and available to all churches, while other gospel writings were suppressed. Only now did the canonical Gospels receive names that distinguished them from each other—Marcion's gospel still did not have one (Tert. *Marc*. 4.2.3). In this context the problem of Gospel harmony, which Irenaeus had already found so difficult, arose for the first time (see p. 360 below).

The lack of response that our Gospels generally experienced until well into the second century does not allow us as a rule to determine precisely the location and extent of the areas in which they spread. Nevertheless, in light of the Synoptic hypothesis and especially the two-source theory, which Neirynck (1982; 1991) rightly defends against all recent attacks, we can gain an important insight. Matthew and Luke use their models, the Gospel of Mark and the sayings source, as *sources,* which they draw on with great freedom in their own writing, a fact on which Luke expressly reflects in the prologue to his Gospel. In my view, Mark also proceeded similarly with his model, a basic text that he adopted relatively completely yet expanded with remarkable openness (see below). If the Gospel of John also has an underlying basic text or basic gospel, as is often rightly asserted (Richter 1977; Langbrandtner 1977), and if we take the Fourth Gospel's integrity as a standard, the evangelist proceeds with his model no less arbitrarily than Mark, Matthew, and Luke do with their sources. And when he unhesitatingly lengthens Jesus' one-year activity into several years and shifts Jesus' day of death by twenty-four hours, we can see especially clearly that his Synoptic models could not have been in use in his churches as normative scriptures. For wherever a gospel writing was highly regarded and was used in worship, in instruction, or in a school program, it could no longer serve in the same place as a mere source for new literary production. One could reach a different conclusion only if the later evangelist plainly intended to suppress the work of his predecessor, which has been occasionally asserted of the author of the Gospel of John, who according to this view intended to replace the Synoptic Gospels (Windisch 1926). In the context of the Synoptic hypothesis, however, such a view has, to my knowledge, never been proposed, and the corresponding explanation regarding the Gospel of John has rightly found no response.

Thus in each case the later evangelist did not find his sources in the living teaching or school tradition of his own church, or in the liturgical material anchored in the worship service, but in the "archives" or, as was probably the usual case, in outside sources. Accordingly he introduced the tradition of the Gospels into his own churches, which had previously been satisfied with the Old Testament and with the fundamental baptismal confession and the formulas of traditional catechetical, liturgical, and paraenetic material, including Paul's letters in the case of the Pauline churches. Consequently, in contrast to the basic confessional tradition that had spread to all locations, the importance of the Gospels—whatever it might have been in each case—was originally limited to particular localities. This insight, which is a necessary result of the source criticism of the Gospels, is in complete harmony with the observation that until well into the second century the gospel tradition involved "apocryphal" literature, and thus there is no reason—as has been customary for over one hundred years—to ignore or belittle this observation or to set it aside with explanations that proceed according to the principle that what must not be cannot be. In the gospel tradition we are not dealing with fundamental material of the faith but with a *donum superadditum* (supplementary gift), with any form of which many churches were still not familiar at the beginning of the second century. The *"regula fidei* existed before there was a single book of the New Testament. . . . The scriptures of the New Testament . . . were unknown to the first Christians" (Lessing 1778, 232–33).

The Individual Gospels

Thus the two presuppositions presented in the preceding section are (1) that a Gospel does not have to contain *the gospel* and (2) that an evangelist was, as a rule, the first person to introduce the material of his writing into his church. On this basis we shall now inquire about the intention and importance of the various Gospels before their adoption into the canon.

The Basic Text of the Gospel of Mark

The critical consensus still assumes that the evangelist Mark was a collector of oral and in part perhaps also written tradition. I believe this form-historical view of the history of pre-Markan tradition to be mistaken. In truth, it is uncritical because it ignores the obvious fact that the oral tradition is not to be found where it would have to occur, and because this view refuses to recognize the obviously literary origin of the Markan narrative material. Strecker (1992, 171) objects that "if at the beginning of the Synoptic narrative tradition the Markan church had not been familiar with the oral form but only with the kerygmatic formulas, then a social identification with and a passing on of the narrative tradition would hardly have taken place," but in so doing he is attempting to use a postulate that would even be untenable if the Gospel of Mark had actually been written for the *instruction of the church,* in order to save what cannot be saved in a scholarly fashion.

By contrast, I assume that the author of the Gospel of Mark had before him a basic text that is not a collection of material but a work by an author, which can be relatively completely reconstructed and grasped theologically (Schmithals 1985, 298ff.). This basic text is apparently the first and original example of the genre "gospel"; its author is the creator of this literary form. He represents an adoption Christology that corresponds to the pre-Pauline formula in Rom. 1:3–4, yet with the previously unobserved intention of describing a messianic life of Jesus, he shifts the installation as Son of God from the resurrection to the act of Jesus' baptism by John, which he expands to an act of adoption (Mark 1:9–11). The aim and culmination of Jesus' activity are his passion and resurrection, corresponding to the pre-Markan formula in 1 Cor. 15:3–5, and the exaltation of Jesus as *Kyrios,* as in Rom. 14:9; Phil. 2:9–11; etc. (see chapter 3).

In this christological and soteriological context the narrative and instructional sections of the basic text develop a certain form of the kerygma of the Hellenistic Christianity that goes back to the missionary work of Peter (Gal. 2:9), had its early center in Antioch, was organized within the synagogal institute, and with this presupposition also devoted itself to the mission among God-fearing Gentiles (Mark 7:24–30). That form includes the message of repentance and faith in the saving good news of Jesus Christ (1:15). Since the basic text of the Gospel of Mark develops the *kerygma of the church,* its reconstruction in no way escapes "the answering of the question what preceded the written composition of the New Testament Gospels" (Strecker 1992, 166). And in response to the assertion that the Gospels are "conceived in a community-oral, not an individualistic-literary, fashion" (Strecker 1992, 169), which is demonstrable false in view of the evidence from our tradition, we can say that the basic text was conceived in a "community-literary" fashion, in that a teacher of the community transformed its kerygma into literary poetry.

The basic text of the Gospel of Mark is a thoroughly literary work that is of high quality both in detail and as a whole. It was apparently the first and only original attempt to offer the central contents of the gospel in narrative form. Its individual genres—teaching dialogues and disputes, parables, miracle stories—were already familiar to the author from the teaching material of the synagogue. These genres are transparent as vehicles for the Christian message; consequently the miracle stories have a strongly symbolic or metaphorical character. With appropriate interpretation Mark 9:26b–27 and 15:21 reveal that the central assertions of the Hellenistic baptismal confession—crucified, died, buried, and resurrected—are interpreted in a way that is found in Paul in Rom. 6:4; 2 Cor. 4:10; 5:14–15; and so forth, where the apostle likewise takes up the theological teaching concepts of Syrian-Antiochene Jewish Christianity (see pp. 99ff. above; Schmithals 1986, 421ff., 684ff.). The oldest "Antiochene" gospel writing, the basic text of the Gospel of Mark, does not try to replace these teaching and confessional formulations, which it develops narratively, but to expand them through a different kind of presentation. The author intends and achieves a comprehensive portrayal of the Christian message, but he does not connect it with any new theological conception.

There is little likelihood that the writer is presenting the familiar teaching in such a way for those who are already baptized. Even if we cannot see why an early Christian church would have had to reject a narrative version of its gospel message, it had no need for such a writing "if essential basic features and contents of the narrative tradition were not already present" (Strecker 1992, 169); the remaining Gospels actually owe their existence to an acute need on the part of the churches for which they were written. Thus in the case of the basic text of the Gospel of Mark we have a handbook for missionaries, who are given material with which they can vividly present and clarify the abstract formulations of the baptismal confession and the catechism in a form that was familiar to the intended audience: Jewish and God-fearing members of the synagogue.

The author is already looking back at the destruction of Jerusalem (Mark 12:9; 13:1–2, 30–31), in which he sees the truth of the gospel of Jesus Christ confirmed (cf. 11:15–17). The crisis of the synagogue, which was brought about by the Jewish war and was only gradually overcome by the Pharisaic restoration, opened up new opportunities for the Christian mission after 70, especially since Christians had not taken part in the rebellion. The author of the basic text, who, along with his community, is still within the synagogal association and does not plan to leave it (7:24–30), tries to take advantage of the moment.

The place where he and his community lived can no longer be determined; in his time there were Christian communities in synagogues from Antioch to Rome and presumably beyond. The basic text reveals no local color. No significance can be given to the ecclesiastical tradition that the Gospel was written in Rome by a student of Peter. More likely is a metropolis in the East, perhaps Antioch itself, but the circle of addressees is not limited to a local audience.

Whether and to what extent the writer achieved the intention of his literary activity cannot be said, but it is clear that in the course of the generation that followed the destruction of Jerusalem, the Pharisaic restoration blocked the path of the Christian mission within the synagogue. It is also clear that the ongoing communities, along with the uncircumcised God-fearers, had to leave the synagogue (see pp. 263ff. above). Therefore the basic text of the Gospel of Mark, which was lost in its original form, may never have served a church as a book for instruction and edification, but the literary influence of this first and original gospel writing cannot be easily overestimated.

The Gospel of Mark

When the evangelist Mark used the basic text for his purposes, he continued the literary genre *gospel,* but his own hand reveals that he either did not comprehend the theological conception and purpose of his model or was not interested in them as such. He used the basic text for a very limited goal; this can be inferred from his redactional reworking, which consists essentially of the various motifs of the theory of the messianic secret. These motifs include the secret of Jesus' Messiahship itself, which Jesus apparently expects to preserve through his commandment of silence; the title *Son of Man,* which is first introduced by Mark, revealing the secret to readers and letting Jesus speak in third person, as if of another person; the *esoteric* instruction of the later Jerusalem authorities, namely, the twelve and especially the trusted three: Peter, John, and James; the disciples' lack of understanding; and finally the adoption of *doublets* from the sayings tradition, which Matthew and Luke also import into their models from the sayings source.

Ever since Wrede (1901) directed the attention of theological scholars to the theory of the messianic secret in the Gospel of Mark, the meaning and purpose of this theory has been controversial. The lack of a consensus on its explanation continues today to lead some scholars to cast doubt on the messianic secret as an essential element of the Markan redaction or simply to ignore it, as is the case in an especially striking way in the commentary by Lührmann (1987). This contradicts the clear exegetical evidence and is insupportable. At the same time, I see no reason to depart from the explanation of that redactional theory given by me in connection with Wrede (Schmithals 1985, 421ff.; see pp. 44ff. above). According to this explanation, in Galilee there were followers of Jesus who had not accepted or adopted the Jerusalem confession of Jesus' resurrection or his exaltation and messianic majesty; instead they continued to believe that Jesus was a prophet who announced, but did not bring, the coming kingdom of God at the end of the old age, and who died the death of a prophet. This community of followers of the earthly Jesus handed down his prophetic-apocalyptic sayings, in which the coming Savior is God himself and the eschatological judge, the Son of Man, is not identical with Jesus. This Galilean Jesus community was probably driven from Palestine following the Jewish war, and the evangelist Mark possibly met its members in connection with the expulsion of non-Pharisaic groups from the synagogue. In any case, with his Gospel and with missionary intent Mark addresses the problem of how there could have been "unmessianic" followers of Jesus. He answers this question with the motifs of his messianic-secret theory: in Galilee Jesus kept his messianic majesty publicly secret and did not reveal it until appearing before the high council (14:61–62), because otherwise he would not have been able to work publicly, as shown by his condemnation because of his messianic claim. Therefore his messianic function and position, which even in Galilee he naturally made known to the close circle of disciples under the seal of silence, remained unknown to other followers.

The incorporation of substantial parts of the still unmessianic sayings tradition (the doublets) of these followers into his Gospel shows that Mark intended to win for the "kerygmatic" church these followers of Jesus who remained in their pre-Easter status. Moreover, if the Synoptic sayings source (Q), which takes up the unmessianic sayings material more fully in the context of a christological redaction, goes back to Mark or to his circle of churches, which I believe is probable, his intention probably met with success: the Galilean followers of Jesus addressed by him joined Mark's Christian community and in the process brought into the Easter church the sayings tradition, which now stood under the sign of the christological confession. Consequently, the Gospel of Mark and the sayings source form a consistent pair of writings, and thus it is no wonder that Matthew and Luke, independently of each other, used this double source.

The special intention that Mark was pursuing with his Gospel, however, forbids the assumption that the Gospel of Mark contains *the* gospel of the Markan community, which found its gospel rather in the traditional forms of baptismal instruction, confession of faith, and liturgical texts. This gospel was hardly expanded by the Gospel of Mark, much less suppressed or replaced, especially since the *kerygma* of his basic text was as such apparently of no interest to the evangelist Mark, or was perhaps no longer available to him.

Yet Mark's redactional hand betrays only a little about the specific character of his own theology and the teaching material of his community. In the few passages where we hear his own theological language, scholars occasionally believe they perceive the ways of speaking and thinking that are familiar to us through the letters of Paul (2:19b–20; 8:38; 9:41, 50b; 10:12, 27, 29, 45; 13:10), yet the meager indications are insufficient for classifying the Markan churches with certainty in the tradition of Pauline Gentile Christianity. The Markan churches suffer under persecutions (10:28–30; 13:9–13); the reference to judgment by governors and kings in 13:9 goes back to the evangelist himself. His church was probably organized outside the synagogue, which suggests a dating of the Gospel of Mark around 80–90 (see p. 267 above). This observation is supported by the redaction of the sayings tradition, which betrays a universalist tendency that presupposes the successful Gentile mission (Luke 13:28ff. par.; 14:15–24 par.). This christological redaction of the sayings source places special value on the majestic title *Son of God* (Luke 4:1–13 par.) and in Luke 10:22 par. contains a corresponding revelatory saying of the Johannine kind. Consequently the assumption is not erroneous that Mark's church was rooted in a theological conceptual world that was characterized by universalism and preexistence Christology, a conceptuality that also formed the common ground for Johannine and early Pauline theology. That leads to a location of the Markan church in the East, where it also could most easily have encountered the followers of the "prophet" Jesus, who lived in Galilee.

In any case, from the beginning the Gospel of Mark and the sayings source both possessed only a limited function, which is less fundamental and theological than ecclesiological and evangelistic. Therefore its *direct* importance for early theological history must be estimated as minimal. Yet the Gospel of Mark and the sayings source form the basis for the Gospels of Matthew and Luke, and the more the Gospels gain theological importance, above all through the formation of the canon, the more their traditional material also affects theological development. In the long run, and not least of all in the modern period, it became significant that the Gospel of Mark and above all the sayings source brought the unmessianic or unkerygmatic sayings tradition of the Galilean followers of Jesus into the teaching tradition of the church.

The Gospel of Matthew

Matthew makes it relatively easy to determine the importance of his writing for his readers and his time, for he himself clearly reveals the purpose of his Gospel. The commission of the resurrected One to his disciples, to which the evangelist himself is naturally also committed, is to "make disciples of all nations, baptizing them in the name of the Father and of the Son and of the Holy Spirit, and teaching them to obey everything that I have commanded you" (28:19–20a). Since in the earliest period baptism was performed "in the name of Jesus Christ" (Acts 2:38), the triadic formula, as in *Did.* 7; Just. *Apol.* 1.61.3, points to a later time for Matthew's Gospel. His church must have already had a triadic baptismal confession and given a corresponding baptismal instruction, which is presupposed in the command to baptize ("baptizing them in the name . . ."). The content cannot be precisely determined, for it is not developed at all in the Gospel of Matthew but must be inferred on the basis of a triadic confessional formulation with the help of traditional catechetical teaching material, which is discussed in the earlier period and in a specific way by the letters of Paul. The meager allusions to the corresponding baptismal proclamation that are found in the Gospel of Matthew (cf., e.g., Matt. 1:21; 18:18; 26:28; 28:18b, 20b) reveal that Matthew's community is in continuity with Antiochene Jewish Christianity with its *kyrios* Christology and a soteriology oriented toward the death of Jesus (see pp. 268–70 above).

The Gospel of Matthew itself, however, contains the *postbaptismal* instruction of the baptized community, above all in questions of ethics, church discipline and community order, polemics and apologetics, and behavior in the face of persecution. This is indicated by Jesus' second commission to his disciples, which states that they are to teach the baptized to obey everything that Jesus has commanded them, that is, the teaching material of the Gospel of Matthew itself. If one follows the two-source theory, this material rests essentially on the sources used by Matthew as models, the Gospel of Mark and the sayings source (Q), which he expanded through redactional formations (e.g., 1:18–2:23; 18:23–35; 22:11–14; 24:10–12; 25:1–13, 31–46) and supplemented with older teaching material from the postbaptismal instruction of his church (including, for example, the basic text of the antitheses in 5:21ff. and the rules for giving alms, praying, and fasting in 6:1ff., as well as the administration of discipline in 18:15–18). Matthew 1–2 comes entirely from the hand of the evangelist, who puts the confession of Jesus' virgin conception (cf. Ign. *Smyrn.* 1.1) and of his birth as son of David in Bethlehem (cf. Luke 2:1ff.), which are foreign to his models Mark and Q, into narrative form and combines them with Christian universalism (Matt. 1:2–17) and the recurring motif of fulfillment (1:23; 2:6, 15, 18, 23).

How the evangelist Matthew became familiar with his two Synoptic sources cannot be said, but his free interaction with these two models shows, in any case, that he was the first to introduce this traditional material to his church, while at the same time making use of it for his own purposes. Especially characteristic is the way in which he greatly condenses the miracle stories, which are kerygmatic in origin and not easily amenable to integration into postbaptismal instruction, and at the same time he enriches them according to the redactional tendencies of his church's teaching (e.g., 8:11–12; 9:8; 12:11–12; 15:24). It is also noteworthy that Matthew expands the passion and Easter narratives with apologetic elements (27:19, 24–25, 62–66; 28:2–4, 11–15) but does not discuss them kerygmatically, although his baptismal proclamation undoubtedly contained and developed theologically the phrase "crucified, died, buried, and resurrected." Thus in Matthew's time the Synoptic narrative material on the one hand and the triadic baptismal confession on the other, were still such clearly separated traditions in terms of tradition history and the *Sitz im Leben* of the church that the evangelist does not relate the two to each other even where suggested by the material itself.

The particular occasion for the composition of a postbaptismal instruction book can be derived from the observation that Matthew is writing under the early impression of the *aposynagōgos,* the expulsion of the (Jewish) Christian communities from the synagogues. The Pharisaic synagogue is still exerting great pressure on the members of the Matthean community to deny their Christian confession and thereby be able to continue enjoying the political privileges accorded the synagogue (cf. Matt. 7:15–23; 18:6–9). The situation of the Gospel of Matthew is no longer a time of victorious evangelization but rather one of growing external pressure that requires the band of the baptized to preserve and consolidate. The Gospel of Matthew serves this purpose, and thus its postbaptismal instruction is quite topical in its redactional and redactionally shaped parts. Polemically Matthew attacks the Pharisees' understanding of the law and offers the church Jesus' commandment of love as the fullness of the law (5:17–48; 20:20–28). In response to attacks from the synagogue, the evangelist's fulfillment quotations (cf. above all 1:18–2:23) attempt to demonstrate that Jesus is really the Messiah promised in the Old Testament. The defenseless church is encouraged to overcome the evil done to it with the good that it does (5:13–16, 38–48). Payment of the *fiscus iudaicus* (17:24–27), if it is still possible, can diminish pressure on church members. (See also pp. 268–70 above.)

There is a great deal to be said for the usual assumption that the Gospel of Matthew was composed in Syria around the year 90. It was probably written primarily for the church's leaders and teachers. But since instruction probably took place in church gatherings, the transition to use in worship was presumably smooth, although the Gospel of Matthew was doubtless not written for this liturgical purpose. Although originally limited to a local church, the Gospel of Matthew was apparently already used by Justin and the Didachist, but we cannot say at what time and to what extent broader recognition was achieved before the formation of the canon. It is hardly likely that this Gospel achieved the status of a kerygmatic or dogmatic scripture, that is, a *gospel* in the strict sense, before the canon was formed. Even though *Did.* 7.1 already presupposes that *before* baptism one was to read a treatise about the two ways that to a considerable degree is based on the ethical material of the Gospel of Matthew, which is still used freely as a source, this does not affect the character of the Gospel of Matthew as an instruction book in questions of ethics and church order. In any case, its importance for the development of early Christian theology, which was primarily bound to the *credo* formulas, remained small in the first century of its existence, and to the extent that this changed later, the misunderstanding of the Gospel of Matthew as apostolic and therefore of especially high value as *dogmatic* scripture bore doubtful fruit, and it aided and abetted many kinds of moralization of the gospel.

The Gospel of Luke

As with Matthew, Luke apparently also had the Gospel of Mark and the sayings source before him as a collection of texts that possibly already included the three stories in Luke 2, which belonged together from the beginning and were noticeably reworked by the evangelist. In contrast to the first chapter of this Gospel, which was written by Luke himself, these stories make no note of Mary's virginal conception. Like Matthew, Luke is the first to introduce Synoptic material into his church; this is shown not only by the free utilization of his sources but also by the fact that in Acts the foundation of the apostolic teaching is formed in traditional fashion by the Old Testament and the formulated kerygma (Acts 2:32–33; 3:15–16; 4:10; 5:30ff.; 10:39ff.; 16:31; etc.), as well as liturgical practice (2:38, 42ff.; etc.) and catechetical instructional material (14:15ff.; 17:24ff.), but not by the Synoptic tradition. In this sense, the Gospel and Acts still stand unrelated side by side. Also, Luke could not have devalued his models in favor of his own literary activity in the way he does in Luke 1:1–4, if they had been writings that were already known and recognized in his churches. Thus, he has come upon his sources as the "historian" he claims to be.

Like Mark and Matthew, Luke makes his models serve his own interests, without taking into consideration their original intentions. Yet the interests that he pursues with the adoption of the gospel tradition are quite different from those we observed in Matthew. He expressly announces his fundamental interest in Luke 1:4: his double volume is to give the reader the certainty of the *teaching* with which he was instructed. Thus the historical material comes as a second tradition alongside the apostolic teaching tradition, which Luke always presupposes.

It is obvious, however, that the Lukan historical work does not offer an extensive presentation of the Christian teaching and thus does not duplicate catechetical instruction. Luke develops special viewpoints. It is not a question of the Christian faith as such needing confirmation but of certain Christian teachings requiring corroboration. Thus the Lukan community is not under attack from the world but from its own midst. Yet the *unanimous* determination and interpretation of specific points in the teaching of the Lukan double volume has thus far been unsuccessful. There should be no question that the Lukan church has experienced a phase of harsh persecution. When Stegemann (1991, 268) speaks merely of an "endangerment" of Christians, this description may fit the immediate situation of the evangelist, but it must not substitute this view for the fact that in the past such endangerment has already led to martyrs and that in view of the remaining danger Luke must deal with the experience and consequences of violent persecution.

In multiple ways Luke guides his churches in mastering this situation; his "piety of the poor" is essentially a topical appeal to those church members who, in spite of persecutions, have been able to preserve their property to come to the aid of Christians who have lost all earthly possessions because of their confession (cf. Karris 1978). At the same time Luke defends Christians against the accusation of political disloyalty by showing, among other things, that in the early period Christianity was not persecuted at all by Roman authorities but rather was given protection against the attacks of the synagogue—and that should also be true to-day. Thus the Lukan church already looks back on the *aposynagōgos* and, unlike the Matthean churches, is no longer in danger of going back into the synagogue. Nevertheless, Lukan Christianity still clearly reveals its synagogal roots, for we cannot overlook the fact that Lukan church theology did not grow from Pauline, Gentile Christian roots; it represents, rather, a variant of the Hellenistic Jewish Christianity that Luke himself attributes to the apostle Paul.

How is this variant articulated in Luke's double volume, and to what extent do his two writings confirm the truth of traditional Christian teaching? Luke has of-ten been credited with a "systematic" interest, and he has been presented—in part affirmatively, in part critically—as the theologian of the history of salvation, who develops this history in three epochs: Old Testament, age of Jesus, and age of the church. It is not apparent, however, which threatened truths of the Christian mes-sage Luke is supposed to be able to ensure with such a novel scheme. Actually, these epochs were simply already present for Luke in his traditions: Old Testa-ment, Synoptic tradition, apostolic confession, and he does not address them be-cause of any systematic interest in history as such. Rather, he uses them in defense against certain heresies that are penetrating his churches and threaten the unity of the earliest Christendom, which Luke therefore strongly emphasizes (cf., for ex-ample, Acts 20:29–30). The idea that the reference here is to Gnostic dualism (thus Klein 1961) is suggested by the general time frame but not by the statements of the Lukan double volume itself, which in general does not deal with dualistic cur-rents. Rather, for the sake of the certainty of orthodox teaching, Luke stresses throughout and above all the "salvation-historical" continuity of Judaism and Christianity, as well as the rooting of the message of Jesus and the apostles in the Old Testament. Lukan Christianity appears as Judaism properly understanding it-self, and it actually stands very close to Hellenistic Judaism with its preaching of the one God, the offer of repentance and forgiveness, its moderate legalism, and the announcement of resurrection and judgment. The idea that with his incorpora-tion of Christianity into the Old Testament Jewish tradition Luke wants to con-front a "legitimation crisis" of his *own* church, which became *insecure* because of its existence *outside* the synagogue (thus Stegemann 1991, 122ff.) and wanted to assure itself of its identity as the "true Israel," is not to be found. The crisis of the synagogue was not a crisis of the Christian church, which was able instead to preserve its identity, and the separation from the synagogue is no longer on the author's mind. Actually, the *unity* of his church is threatened, and the central purpose of his double volume, the presentation of Christianity as the true Judaism, can only be directed against the attempt to make the break with Judaism more radical or total.

Against this attempt Luke emphatically expounds the function of the twelve apostles as the authoritative witnesses of the activity and message of Jesus. Moreover, Paul is not only classified with Jewish Christianity, contrary to his own self-understanding, but also structurally subordinated to the apostolic tradition of the twelve apostles; only in connection with them does he gain his authority. Thus in regard to the three epochs of salvation history and the three corresponding literary works, the Old Testament, the Gospel of Luke, and the Acts of the Apostles, we observe Luke's interest in binding these phenomena or phases to each other and in making the continuity or constancy of Old Testament message, proclamation of Jesus, apostolic preaching, and Pauline theology visible.

In other studies (Schmithals 1980; 1982) I have demonstrated this pervasive tendency of the Lukan redaction in detail and for its explanation suggested that Luke is dealing with a "pre-Marcionism" that separates Christianity from its Old Testament heritage and regards Paul as the only true apostle, who was called by Jesus after the failure of his personal disciples. Paul himself already had to attack such a radical Gentile Christianity in Rom. 11:11ff. It probably goes back to the kind of early Christianity that Paul had once fought and persecuted and to which he was converted; it contained a sharp critique of the law, to which Paul appeals in Gal. 3:19–20, even if he does not share all its views. It is easy to understand how such radical Gentile Christian ideas fell on fertile soil in the context of the *aposynagōgos* and the persecutions largely initiated by the synagogue and how Paul became an authority in such radical anti-Judaism, even though Luke's opponents had not drawn the dualistic and docetic consequences that we find later in Marcion. Against his sharply anti-Jewish and nonetheless hyper-Pauline opponents, Luke insists on the continuity of Judaism and Christianity and on the apostolic competence of the twelve. At the same time he places Paul clearly on the antiheretical front, as the pastoral letters also do in an analogous stance. In this way the "historical" presentation of his double volume communicates to the reader addressed as "friend of God" (Theophilus) the certainty that the "catholic" teaching in which he has been instructed has a solid basis in the divine history of salvation (Luke 1:1–4).

I have not encountered any substantiated objections to this redaction-historical explanation, which has been researched through the whole of Luke's double volume. In any case, it seems to me essential to acknowledge that Luke does not see the Christian message itself threatened and is not attempting to secure it through his writings; rather, he is opposing developments within Christianity itself, which he believes are wrong. With this intention, which is related to the time and place of the Lukan double volume, its significance for early Christian theological history also remains clearly limited, even if one might attribute to Luke and his specific concern a detectable influence on the corresponding theological discussion in the course of the second century, for his efforts are aimed not at a theological development but, in accordance with 1:1–4, at the *preservation* of traditional teaching. In any case, such an influence cannot be observed.

The Gospel of Luke and the Acts of the Apostles also remain largely hidden until the formation of the canon, and when the Lukan scriptures emerge, this does not happen under the circumstances emphasized by these writings themselves, as the most conspicuous appearance of the Gospel of Luke, its acceptance into the canon of Marcion, clearly shows. Many have wondered for a long time why Marcion held precisely the Judaizing Gospel of Luke to be the gospel of Jesus Christ and did not adopt, for example, the Gospel of John into his collection of scriptures. The basically correct explanation for this surprising state of affairs was given by Harnack (1924, 42), among others: the Gospel of Luke was "the only Gospel in his homeland Pontus." This situation is easily explained if the Gospel of Luke was actually written and spread in a place of disagreement with pre-Marcionite currents. At the same time it confirms that in contrast to the apostolic confessional tradition, the gospel writings contain secondary traditional material that was originally found only locally, was nonapostolic in its claim, and only slowly achieved its later importance.

The Gospel of John

Apart from the question, which of the Synoptic Gospels the fourth evangelist had before him, his completely free treatment of his sources shows how little the gospel writings were available as recognized authorities even at a relatively late time. Therefore John wants neither to suppress nor to surpass other gospels with his own; rather, he consciously wants to instruct his own church for the first time with the help of a gospel writing.

There can be no disputing the importance of the Gospel of John for the history of Christian theology and dogma. The monarchian, trinitarian, and christological quarrels, which developed in the catholic church after the formation of the canon, were related from the beginning to John's Logos Christology. From Clement and Origen until our own time, the Gospel of John as the "spiritual" Gospel has enjoyed the highest regard in many circles, and Luther greatly preferred it to the Synoptic Gospels because it is oriented more toward Jesus' words than his deeds.

It was only without effort and difficulty, however, that the Gospel of John gained entrance into the canon. The opposition of the anti-Montanist Alogi, as Epiphanius mockingly called the opponents of the *Logos* Gospel, was strenuous, and the canon itself betrays that it received the Gospel of John only on the second attempt. For although it was accepted as apostolic scripture, it received its place only after the deuteroapostolic Gospels according to Mark and Luke, where it rather unhappily had to be inserted into the Lukan double volume between the Gospel of Luke and the Acts of the Apostles, which were originally accepted into the canon as a single work (cf. also pp. 366–67 below).

Also striking is the Fourth Gospel's lack of importance before its adoption into the canon. There is no certain witness to the Gospel of John before the formation of the canon, for the first indubitable attestation, its use by the Montanists, comes at this very time. Especially in the nineteenth century an enormous amount of

330 / The Theology of the First Christians

effort was made to name outside witnesses to the Gospel of John, in order to res-
cue the apostolic authority of the Fourth Gospel, for a Gospel that left behind no
traces in the time of the formation of the canon can hardly come from the apostle
John. Yet there is seldom any question today that such efforts brought little success. Nevertheless, in 1936 the famous papyrus 52 was published, which contains
parts of John 18:31–33, 37–38 and which was soon generally dated at such an early
time that scholars were convinced that the Gospel of John was already available
in Egypt in the first half of the second century. With this one could now ignore the
lack of external witnesses, which was all the more puzzling. The early dating of
p^{52} is arbitrary, however, and with newer discoveries and investigations it has
proven untenable (Gronewald 1987).

There is in truth no manuscript evidence of the Gospel of John before the formation of the canon, and the precanonical literature still betrays no clear reflection of
the Fourth Gospel. One can say at most that Just. *Dial.* 88.7 betrays an (indirect?)
knowledge of John 1:20–23 and *Apol.* 1.61.4 of John 3:3–5, yet even in these cases
doubts remain. If Justin actually used the Gospel of John or one of its sources, it
would be remarkable that he did not trace the derived information back to a "gospel"
or to the "recollections of the apostles," as was his usual custom; thus he would have
had very little regard for his source. In this respect Justin can, in any case, be considered a witness to the early insignificance of the Gospel of John, which before the
formation of the canon did not promote the development of doctrine in any recognizable way; nor is Justin's conception of the Logos influenced by that of the Gospel
of John. Without doubt the Montanist prophets, who were the first Christian group
to refer expressly to the Gospel of John, did not take their apocalyptic views from it,
but rather appealed secondarily to its promises of the Spirit.

Regarding the circumstances of the composition and spread of the Gospel of
John, as well as the reasons for the especially striking hiddenness of this writing
that was so influential later, much can be said but little agreement reached in view
of the complex research situation. Is its author really an ingenious loner who with
the theological passion of a Jerome devotes himself to writing in his study, without thinking of any effect on others (Bultmann, Barrett)? Or is the Gospel of John
the relic of a religious conventicle, a church community thrust aside into a corner
(Käsemann). Or was it written in the far eastern part of the Roman Empire, in the
land of northeastern Jordan, during the Pharisaic reorganization of the synagogue
and the corresponding *aposynagōgos* of opposing groups, with the definite intention of motivating Christians there to remain in the community and hold fast to
their Christian confession (Wengst)? Was it written to suppress the Synoptic
Gospels (Overbeck, Windisch) but then had to settle for a modest fourth place?
Did it not appear until the middle of the second century, as asserted by Baur and
his Tübingen School? Does the Gospel of John present a more or less conscious
Gnosticism, as was asserted at the time of the formation of the canon by the Alogi,
who have many followers in the modern period? In all these cases, we can well
understand how for a long time the Fourth Gospel received little response, yet we
can hardly comprehend how under these circumstances it still found its way into
the canon.

The fact that it did would be understandable if one could regard the Gospel of John, in analogy to the letters of John, as a "catholic" gospel that was sent out into the world to battle the Gnostic heresy and that was perhaps actually written later and directed toward a worldwide Christendom. Since Wellhausen and Schwartz, however, many scholars have held that it is in general a mistake to ask such questions about the occasion, place, and time of *the* Gospel of John, because one must distinguish between basic text and revision, or because in place of the evangelist we must think of a school with many hands—a hypothesis that would make even more enigmatic the puzzle of how this writing could have remained hidden for so long.

This compilation of suggestions for solving the Johannine problem could be expanded. It suggests to scholars not to leave unconsidered the observation that the Gospel of John first came to public light with the formation of the canon, but it offers no recommendation that both explains this phenomenon historically and is capable of consensus. Yet there is no doubt, it seems to me, that in the Gospel of John we do not have a missionary text aimed at non-Christians, any more than we do in the Gospels of Matthew and Luke. Nor did its author, however, conceive a comprehensive educational text, a new presentation of the gospel, designed for a Christian church. Rather, the scholars are probably right who say that the evangelist—in a particular situation and for a particular reason within his community—intends to offer the basic, yet at the same time limited proof that Jesus the Christ is the Son of God, as the author himself explains in John 20:30–31. And since in the Gospel of John many indications suggest on the one hand that this proof was successful against Jewish quarrels with the Christian confession ("Jesus is the *Christ*") but on the other hand that like the letters of John it rejects a docetic Christology ("*Jesus is the Son of God*"), I believe that in principle the explanation is correct that includes a basic text from the time of the *aposynagōgos,* which was reworked in anti-Gnostic fashion by the author of the Johannine letters. That basic text apparently stays within the framework of a preexistence and incarnation Christology and soteriology, as presented by the hymn reworked into the prologue, whereas the antidocetic revision combines the basic text with the passion soteriology.

In both cases the Gospel of John takes up the traditional fixed christological and soteriological confession not in order to reshape it theologically or to expand it, but in order to defend it and assert it with the creative means that a gospel writing offers. The christological assertion of the Gospel of John is central, but its aim is limited and serves the defense of the established confession. Therefore the import of the Gospel of John for theological *history* is minimal before the formation of the canon, however one might determine its time of composition.

Conclusion

An inclusion of the apocryphal gospel literature in the present study would not change the picture we have achieved, especially since the apocryphal gospels as a rule presuppose the canonized Gospels and attempt either to expand them in a legendary way or to correct them in an educational way, as is the case with the wealth of Gnostic gospels. Hardly anything in the apocryphal gospel tradition can be dated with any probability in the precanonical period, and nothing that is independent of the Synoptic models. Recent attempts, such as the exaggerated one of Köster (1990), to infer a presynoptic tradition from the Coptic Gospel of Thomas or other writings in the Nag Hammadi library, from the unknown gospel of the papyrus Egerton 2, the "secret gospel of Mark," the *Diatessaron,* and so forth have no adequate basis (cf. Neirynck 1989) and can be undertaken only by ignoring the methodological insights of redaction criticism and the resulting content of redaction history. The process of the origin and development of our canonical Gospels can be discovered and traced without essential gaps by following the proven paths of source and redaction criticism, without including traditions inferred hypothetically from late texts.

Yet even if the situation were different, the results of the present study would not be changed, for nowhere is there anything of significance for theological history in the apocryphal gospel tradition that was perhaps present before the formation of the canon. But this conclusion is correctly reached by Lessing, who in 1778 stated that the *regula fidei* is "the rock on which the church of Christ was built, and not the scripture," and not only was this *regula fidei* sufficient for the first Christians, "but later Christians in the whole first four centuries held it to be entirely adequate for Christianity" (1778, 232).

Lessing traced the Synoptic Gospels back to an Aramaic protogospel, which owed its existence to a private historical interest and which anyone could therefore arbitrarily change, shorten, or expand when more exact information seemed to become available. This protogospel hypothesis did not prevail, and without doubt the early gospel literature did not actually owe its existence to a historical inquiry. Synoptic source criticism, moreover, has observed not a manifold consolidation of oral tradition but a literary process that was initiated by writers. And the Gospels consist not of personal sketches but of instructional texts that have an obligatory character for each recipient, yet their obligatory nature is related only to the assertions of the always presupposed *regulae fidei* and to the particular limited purpose of the individual evangelist's work in his time and place. None of the evangelists intended to write a gospel that was a *fundamental and comprehensive* expression of *the* gospel. Each held the "rock" of the *regula fidei* to be constant. Since his own work was supposed to lead to—or back to—this rock, it was therefore accorded not a fundamental but a transient importance. To the extent that, like the Gospel of Matthew, it expanded the confession of faith through ethics and other postbaptismal instruction, it was granted a lasting but not fundamental function.

Only the formation of the canon and the preceding ecclesiastical development with its interest in the apostolic tradition of the beginning raised the Gospels in principle to the level of importance of baptismal instruction and baptismal confession. And in fact, such status was not immediately bestowed, for Lessing was right also in this respect: "In the first four centuries the Christian religion was never proved on the basis of the scriptures of the New Testament but at most only incidentally clarified and confirmed" (1778, 233). Yet this happened through scriptures that were now recognized in all of early catholic Christendom as the normative expression of the apostolic gospel, and therefore the theological influence of the Gospels was of varying but growing importance. In the first generations of Christendom, however, the gospel writings had to forgo recognition and universal validity, nor did they in any way claim it for themselves. Therefore they are well suited to document developments within Christendom from around 70 to 170, but they themselves did not occasion or determine such developments.

Thus in the broader perspective the establishment of the Synoptic tradition — which I ascribe originally to the author of the *basic text* of the Gospel of Mark — along with the teaching and confessional formulations of instruction in the faith, had extensive consequences for Christianity. The immediate task given to these scriptures, however, was comparatively modest, and we cannot say with certainty how well it succeeded in completing this task. Hardly less consequential was the adoption into ecclesiastical tradition of the pre-Easter sayings tradition, which we can observe in the Gospel of Mark and more comprehensively in the sayings source; the concrete occasion for this apparently related process, however, seems to have been of only local importance.

The Gospel of Matthew and the basic text of the Gospel of John, each in its own place and in its own circumstances, attempt to overcome the situation created by the *aposynagōgos* (see pp. 268–70, 271ff. above). In this way they mark the ecclesiastical and — in terms of the history of theology — uncommonly important process that forced Christendom involuntarily to give up the peaceful coexistence of intrasynagogal Christian communities and Gentile Christian communions outside the synagogue, which had been practiced since the Apostolic Council, and to develop into the one common church. These writings, however, did not initiate this development, nor did they — like, say, the Letter to the Ephesians — attempt to come to terms with it theologically. Each text is directed toward its own clientele. How successful they were in keeping their individual communities from falling back into synagogal Judaism cannot be determined, even if the Didachist, for example, shows that the anthology of ethical rules in the Gospel of Matthew was gratefully adopted elsewhere.

The Lukan double volume and the Gospel of John, as read in the light of the Johannine letters and expanded antidocetically, also document important stages in early Christian history, in which the church on the one hand preserves its continuity with the Old Testament history of revelation — definitively in its dispute with Marcion — and on the other hand wards off Gnostic dualism. Whether the Lukan double volume and the Gospel of John were able to achieve their purpose in regard to these respective concerns, even in their own locations, is beyond our knowledge. These writings, however, probably did not initiate a movement in early Christian theological history. When the Gospel of John emerged into the light of history, it served the Montanist prophets — beyond any intentions of its own — in the founding of their apocalyptic prophecy.

In general, the original purposes of the Gospels are not involved in their acceptance into the canon of the church. Only such disregard of their limited purpose and their understanding as the fourfold expression of one apostolic *gospel,* which is found fundamentally in the *regulae fidei,* gave the Gospels their later importance and gained them the esteem that they soon possessed unchallenged until the time of the Reformation and beyond. Yet this also made their original understanding difficult and clouded their original significance. For the sake of their better understanding, Lessing insisted that until and even after the formation of the canon, the gospel writings stood in the shadow of the formulas of faith, and in so doing, he essentially set in motion the historical study of the Gospels. Even if his understanding of the Gospels as private compositions was mistaken, scholars would be well advised to consider Lessing's fundamental observation and not demand more of the Gospels than they themselves wanted to deliver.

17

The Historicity of Ethics
in Early Christianity

Only with reservation can the ethical reflections and admonitions of early Christian writings be treated in the context of the *history of theology*. For it is apparent that Christian baptismal, teaching, faith, and confessional formulas from the beginning through the Apostles' and Nicene Creeds contain no ethical statements. Thus ethical reflection seems to follow particular circumstances and conditions and to have no immediate relationship with dogmatic development. This observation corresponds to another: the ethical norms and concrete paraeneses of the early Christian period are, as a rule, not christologically based. Thus early Christendom knows no specific Christian ethic: "Whatever is true, whatever is honorable, whatever is just, whatever is pure, whatever is pleasing, whatever is commendable, if there is any excellence and if there is anything worthy of praise, think about these things" (Phil. 4:8).

Consequently, the moral behavior of Christians is distinguished not through unusual norms but through the best possible adherence to rules that are also valid for unbelievers as the foundation of inoffensive conduct. Faith separates Christians from non-Christians; love binds them together. Naturally, attention can be focused on the behavior of Jesus as exemplary behavior (Mark 10:45; Matt. 11:28–30; Phil. 2:5ff.; Rom. 15:2ff.; 1 Peter 2:21ff.; Heb. 12:1–3), but the thus exemplified behavior of humility, gentleness, readiness to serve, and so forth did not first come into the world through Jesus; it follows, rather, the rules of an understandable, humane morality. It is true that the early Christian paraenesis rests directly or indirectly on the relationship of indicative and imperative, on the indissoluble connection between gift of the Spirit and walking in the Spirit, between new being and new obedience, between liberation from the power of sin and sinless life. But such a connection provides the basis not for new norms but for the fulfillment of old: "How can we who died to sin go on living in it?" (Rom. 6:2; cf. Gal. 5:16–25). In this sense the "old commandment" of love is at the same time a new commandment (1 John 2:7–8). But the content of the imperative instructions is in no way derived from the indicative of the confession of faith.

Thus if one can integrate early Christian ethics into early Christian *theological* history only with reservation, then ethics must for two reasons be regarded all the closer in relation to the *history* and the historical situation of the early Christian churches. First, what is "honorable" and "commendable" depends to a certain degree on the *cultural environment*. For Palestinian Jewish Christianity the presuppositions were different from those of Christianity in the Hellenistic synagogues, and Gentile Christians outside the synagogue had to shape the morality of their lives under yet another set of circumstances. In the second place, however, we must make the important observation that the paraeneses of early Christian writings in many cases do not present in a fundamental way the obligatory rules of general morality in their particular situation; they are instead reacting to concrete historical challenges. Such challenges can result from internal Christian conflicts and lead to disputes over, for example, whether a Christian may eat meat offered to idols, dissolve a marriage with an unbeliever, have contact with a heretic, or promote the emancipation of women. With the passage of time, however, it was more and more the conflicts with the pagan public and authorities that determined the internal paraenesis of the church, for it behooved Christians to demonstrate that they were exemplary loyal citizens, even though they did not take part in the cult of the emperor.

The structure of the following analyses is determined by the changing historical situation. We will not attempt a presentation of early Christian ethics that is in any degree complete—for this see, for example, Wendland (1970), Schrage (1982), and Schulz (1987)—but rather will seek through examples to demonstrate the *historicity* of early Christian ethics.

Jesus and the
Palestinian Primitive Church

Jesus appeared as an apocalyptic prophet (see chapter 1). If this judgment is correct, we must not look for a specific ethic of Jesus, for it is no accident that individual concrete ethical paraeneses are lacking in apocalyptic literature, as we can still see in studying the Revelation to John (cf. Rössler 1960). If the end of the world is imminent, one cannot and need not orient oneself in the world with the help of reflection about appropriate ethical norms. Naturally, the Jewish apocalyptists affirm the "law of God," and they relate to this law as it is understood in their environment, but they know no casuistry and do not participate in the discussion of the correct understanding of the law. It is now wise and appropriate to the law to consider above all the fact that time is running out:

> . . . the time is near. Let the evildoer still do evil, and the filthy still be filthy, and the righteous still do right, and the holy still be holy. (Rev. 22:10–11; cf. 1 Cor. 7:29ff.)

The die is cast; this world is coming to an end. There may still be time for repentance but not for the ethical and moral shaping of the world or for a new life:

> You farmers, sow no more. . . . You women, pray no more for the blessing of children. (*2 Apoc. Bar.* 10.9, 13)

> Prepare yourselves for battle. Behave in tribulations as if you were aliens on earth. (*6 Ezra* 2.41)

> Those who now run, run in vain, and those who live with good fortune
> will immediately fall and be humbled. What is in the future is now brought
> near. (*2 Apoc. Bar.* 44.10–11)

With such instructions one can speak of an "interim ethic," but the object of this ethical teaching is the statement that in these last days all action has become pointless. The demise of the old age can no longer be avoided through better behavior. "Therefore the workers toil in vain" (*6 Ezra* 2.46). The pessimism of apocalypticism vis-à-vis the perceivable course of the world no longer permits any ethical program. Making the most of the remaining time means doing penance and renouncing this world. The fact that in the preaching of apocalyptic judgment and repentance, traditional ethical criteria for the separation of righteous and unrighteous can occasionally be mentioned in detail must not be confused with ethical paraenesis.

What such general religious-historical considerations lead us to expect is confirmed independently by the early tradition of Jesus sayings. Apart from the isolated sayings in Paul, they are evidenced first in the "doublets" (Schmithals 1985, 229ff., 396ff., 427) that the evangelist Mark adopted from the not yet christologically shaped sayings tradition and which were later also adopted by the sayings source (Q), as well as in the prototype of Mark 13, which itself comes from the same sayings tradition. These doublets and the prototype of Mark 13 are completely at home in the conceptual world of apocalypticism. Even the prohibition of divorce (Mark 10:11–12 par.), which is also found as a saying of Jesus in Paul (1 Cor. 7:10–11) and whose radicality is characteristically softened by Paul, is not intended "legally" but "for the time being" (7:20), because "the appointed time has grown short" (7:29); indeed, it is hardly an accident that Jesus himself remained single. Since the evangelist Mark had no reason to draw only apocalyptic material from the sayings tradition available to him, we must assume that without exception this old stage of the sayings tradition contained only apocalyptic material. This is especially true since the other Jesus saying quoted by Paul (1 Cor. 9:14) must have been originally connected with itinerant missionaries, who were supposed to announce the end of the old age and be supported by their listeners, so that they would lose no time in unrelated work. Also apocalyptic are other pieces of the sayings tradition not adopted by Mark, such as the original versions of Luke 6:20b–26, 29–30, as well as the saying in Matt. 5:18 par. Luke 16:17. The fact that according to this saying the Torah will remain literally in force until the imminent turn of the age—and not beyond—is not the expression of a specific ethical involvement but an indication that ethical problems will shortly take care of themselves and therefore one no longer has to make them the object of discussion.

Yet in the sayings source (Q) and in connection with its redactional christological framework some other traditions have also found acceptance, including moral instructions on everyday conduct and statements of unrestrained joy over creation, such as Luke 6:31 par.; 12:6–7, 22–34 par.; Matt. 5:45 par., which are incompatible with Jesus' apocalyptic message and must be of different origin (see p. 9 above). The hybrid "eschatological ethic" that is supposedly to be found in Jesus (Schrage 1982, 21ff.) is an artificial product of theological harmonizing without any basis in religious or tradition history. And when Schulz (1987, 32) explains in one breath that Jesus' message is "dominated by apocalyptic imminent expectation of the kingdom of God," and that Jesus "announced directly the near Creator-God who is there for the world created by him in never waning solicitude," he is combining what is mutually exclusive.

The pre-Markan narratives on fasting (Mark 2:18ff.), healing on the sabbath (2:23ff.; 3:1ff.), divorce (10:2ff.), dealing with possessions (10:17ff.), paying taxes (12:13ff.), the double commandment of love (12:28ff.), and giving alms (12:41ff.) are artful teaching texts of literary origin; without exception they owe their existence to Hellenistic Jewish Christianity (cf. Schmithals 1986). The *hostile* controversies between Jesus and the Pharisaic scribes, which are found first in redactional parts of the Gospel of Mark and then reinforced in Matthew and John, belong entirely to a later time in which the Pharisees had won controlling influence in the synagogues (see pp. 263ff. above).

On the ethics of Palestinian primitive Christianity we have no authentic information or even traditions, but there is no reason to assume that the immediate followers of Jesus behaved differently from Jesus himself and other apocalyptically motivated groups. Those who are waiting for the imminent end of the world see no reason to turn the recognized moral principles of godliness into a problem instead of continuing to follow them, unless the shortness of the remaining time suggests suspending certain actions, such as getting married and providing for the future (cf. 1 Cor. 7:1ff., 29ff.). The development of early Christology and soteriology proceeded on the eschatological, apocalyptic level, yet this did not involve a new establishment of ethics, as the corresponding formulaic material shows. "The primitive Christian churches were oriented toward the passing of this world, not toward everyday life in it; thus they were not prepared for the necessity of producing paraenetic solutions for everyday problems" (Dibelius 1959, 241). In view of this judgment, it is unhistorical to think that ethics is to be understood on the level of apocalyptic expectation "as behavior that already corresponds to that hope and anticipates it" (Wengst 1984, 60). The "wholly otherness" of the kingdom of God excluded such analogous thinking, for even the best deeds were still a part of the passing world.

We may presuppose that the Jewish Christians of Palestine also held to the usual cultic rules, yet this can hardly be inferred from late narratives such as Acts 2:46; 3:1ff.; Peter's liberal behavior attested in Gal. 2:11–12, however, excludes the idea that Jewish Christians practiced cultic observances with special strictness. The legendary report of Hegesippus on the Lord's brother James (Euseb. *Hist. Eccl.* 2.23) boasts of his great piety or "righteousness," but it reveals no rigorous legalism.

It is significant that in regard to theology the *Didache* still essentially maintained the eschatological, apocalyptic standpoint of Palestinian primitive Christianity in a later time, but for ethical instruction it turned to a Hellenistic Jewish two-ways catechism, which has no relationship to the eschatological message. Thus Christians originally possessed no ethical conception and tradition of their own, and when the passage of time and the Hellenistic environment made ethical instruction necessary, Hellenistic Christians turned back to familiar material from the synagogue.

Hellenistic Christianity

The passage of time, on the one hand, and the development of Christology and soteriology, or the "cult of Christ," on the other, caused the strength of eschatological, apocalyptic expectation to fade in early Christianity. Christians had to make a home for themselves in the world and intentionally shape their lives in the world, if not the life of the world itself. Thus we can observe that in the Hellenistic Christendom that was spreading in the *oikoumenē*—at the latest—a well-considered foundation was worked out for ethical action and for the development or intentional adoption of ethical principles.

It is noteworthy that neither the foundation nor the principles of ethics were essentially different in the various forms of Hellenistic Jewish and Gentile Christianity. This state of affairs resulted from the fact that the Christian communities did not develop a specific Christian ethic, in which their particular theological tenets were reflected, but as a rule held to the ethical views of the Hellenistic synagogue. From the beginning the Jewish Christian mission had turned its attention to God-fearing Gentiles in the Hellenistic synagogues, and the Gentile Christian churches outside the synagogue were composed primarily of former God-fearers. The liberal synagogue had found a generous principle for life in this group of members associated with it:

> Circumcision is nothing, and uncircumcision is nothing; but obeying the commandments of God is everything. (1 Cor. 7:19)

With this principle Paul is citing a synagogal rule, as also shown by the somewhat Christianized variations in Gal. 5:6 and 6:15 (cf. J. Weiss 1910, 186). The relativization of circumcision (cf. Rom. 2:12–16) integrated the God-fearing Gentiles into the synagogue and at the same time freed them of the necessity of being more observing of the cultic regulations than was required for communal life with the Jews (according to Leviticus 17–18; cf. Acts 15:29). Still obligatory for them, however, were the *moral* commandments, which are also seen in Gal. 5:6 ("faith working through love") and 6:15 ("a new creation"), and in this respect the double commandment of love. Thus Hellenistic Christianity did not teach anything new; rather, "with its demand of genuine morality, free from all particularism and all ritual, this Christianity completed the tendency of the Jewish Diaspora" (Bousset 1921, 292–93). Especially in writings from the later period (James, *Didache, 1 Clement, Hermas*), when the élan of first love was extinguished in the churches, the completed law of liberty—that is, the royal law of love of neighbor (James 1:25; 2:8)—is joined by a wealth of individual moral instructions, which are taken directly from the familiar synagogal paraenesis.

Paul

For Paul, cultic observances of all kinds, to which many of the "weak" Christians hold (Rom. 14:1ff.) on account of their former attachment to the synagogue, no longer fall in the realm of ethical difficulty. For the pure, everything is pure, but no one is to act against conscience (Rom. 14:20). Consequently, ethical consideration is required when my behavior might lead a weak brother or sister to deviate from the conviction of his or her conscience, for "'all things are lawful,' but not all things build up" (1 Cor. 10:23). The standard for behavior in such cases is love (Rom. 14:15).

Love is simply the primary ethical criterion, for faith works through love (Gal. 5:6), and thus the only thing we owe one another is love (Rom. 13:8a). Paul substantiates this fundamental insight with a teaching text that he fits into the context, but which comes from the Hellenistic synagogue (Str-B 1:357, 907; Berger 1972, 51); in it the principle that the moral law is of primary importance is summed up in the commandment of love:

> The one who loves another has fulfilled the law. The commandments, "You shall not commit adultery; You shall not murder; You shall not steal; You shall not covet"; and any other commandment are summed up in this word, "Love your neighbor as yourself." . . . therefore, love is the fulfilling of the law. (Rom. 13:8b–9, 10b)

Whoever observes the love of neighbor keeps all moral commandments.

> For the whole law is summed up in a single commandment, "You shall love your neighbor as yourself." (Gal. 5:14)

The *knowledge* of what is commanded presents no problem for Paul, even if he does not, like Matthew (7:12), expressly extend the validity of the commandment of love into the Gentile world with the help of the Golden Rule, for human beings already know what the love of one's neighbor requires. Because the believer, guided by the Holy Spirit (Gal. 5:13–6:10), also knows how to do what is commanded (Rom. 6:1–14; 8:12–17), Paul is all the more convinced that from case to case he also knows what is commanded for the sake of love, "what is the will of God—what is good and acceptable and perfect" (Rom. 12:2). Thus the Pauline ethic is entirely "unlawful."

As an orientation aid in conveying what love concretely requires in each case, Paul first offers the insight of what is just, commendable, and pure (Phil. 4:8). Then he points to his own good example: "Brothers and sisters, join in imitating me, and observe those who love according to the example you have in us. . . . Keep on doing the things that you have learned and received and heard and seen in me" (Phil. 3:17; 4:9; cf. 1 Cor. 4:16; 11:1); this also includes many topical instructions with which Paul attempts to regulate the concrete behavior of individual church members or churches as a whole (1 Corinthians 5–7; 14:13–19; 2 Cor. 5:11–15; chs. 8–9; Phil. 4:2–3; 1 Thess. 4:1–12; 2 Thess. 3:6–13; Philemon). Finally, Paul knows and teaches catalogs that are rooted in the synagogal paraenesis and describe loving behavior in exemplary fashion. The formal catalogs of virtues and vices (Gal. 5:19–23; 1 Cor. 6:9–10; Col. 3:5–8, 12–14) are thoroughly traditional, but depending on the situation, they are brought up to date by Paul in a more or less clear way. Other compilations seem to have been formulated by Paul himself:

> Let love be genuine;
> hate what is evil,
> hold fast to what is good;

love one another with mutual affection;
outdo one another in showing honor . . .
be ardent in spirit . . .
Rejoice in hope,
be patient in suffering,
persevere in prayer.
Contribute to the needs of the saints;
extend hospitality to strangers. . . .
Rejoice with those who rejoice,
weep with those who weep.
(Rom. 12:9–15,
without epistolary expansions)

The fruit of the Spirit is love, joy, peace, patience, kindness, generosity, faithfulness, gentleness, and self-control. (Gal. 5:22–23)

Love is patient;
love is kind;
love is not envious or boastful or arrogant or rude.
It does not insist on its own way;
it is not irritable or resentful;
it does not rejoice in wrongdoing,
but rejoices in the truth.
It bears all things,
believes all things,
hopes all things,
endures all things.
(1 Cor. 13:4–7)

These lists of virtues also seem to be relatively fixed teaching formulas that Paul varies in accordance with the particular occasion. They contain no specifically Christian points of view. Love always stands at the beginning of the catalog, and the individual duties and ways of behaving are self-evident as expressions of love of neighbor. They never come close to achieving legal status, but they help to find the way of love again in each new situation.

The Gospel of Mark

Whereas the evangelist Mark himself is not guided in his redaction by an interest in spreading ethical teachings, his model contains a closed ethical conception that belongs to synagogal Jewish Christianity and is in no way dependent on Paul, yet it matches completely the corresponding Pauline views. The Jewish ceremonial law is criticized through the examples of the sabbath law (Mark 2:23–27; 3:1–5) and the purity laws (7:1–16), and it is subordinated to the commandment of love of neighbor (2:27; 3:4; 7:9–13). The positive foundation of ethics is established in express agreement with the knowledgeable scribes of the synagogue: the double commandment of love provides a basis and impetus for

Christian existence (12:28–34). The one commandment of love of neighbor corresponds to the confession of one God, and since love of God and love of neighbor are indissolubly connected, the double commandment of love is the answer to the question of the greatest commandment. The pericope on the widow's offering (12:41–44), which follows immediately in the evangelist's model, gives an instructive example for the concrete enactment of love of neighbor, for which there are also known Jewish parallels (Str-B 2:46; cf. 2 Cor. 8:12). The ethical problems of the Christian household (marriage, children, possessions) were already treated by the author of the model in 10:2–22 in a theologically excessive way in the manner of household rules, and he answered the question of the relationship of Christians to state authorities in the same way (12:13–17).

The Gospel of Matthew

The evangelist Matthew defends the ethical conception of Hellenistic Christianity against the Pharisaic rabbinate, with whom he must seriously disagree when Christians are driven out of the synagogue. In terms of the Pharisaic understanding of the law, the liberal Jewish and Christian treatment of the Torah means its abolition. Against this Matthew asserts that concentration on the commandment of love, which Jesus teaches (7:12; 22:34–40), is in truth the fulfillment of the Torah, in which, consequently, not one letter is abolished (5:17–20), and thus Christians are supposed to do what the Pharisaic scribes teach but do not do themselves (23:1–2):

> You shall not murder;
> You shall not commit adultery;
> You shall not steal;
> You shall not bear false witness . . .
> You shall love your neighbor as yourself.
> (Matt. 19:18–19)

Only the comprehensive commandment of love of neighbor leads to radical obedience; Matthew makes this clear with the help of his antitheses (5:21ff.), which begin with love of neighbor (5:21–22), followed by faithfulness (5:27–28) and truthfulness (5:33–34).

Vis-à-vis the casuistic legalism of the Pharisees, which the evangelist seems to parody in 5:22–23 and which he treats in 6:1–18; 9:9–13; 12:1–8, 9–14; 15:1–20; 19:1–9; 23:1–36, he points to Hos. 6:6: "I desire mercy, not sacrifice" (Matt. 9:13; 12:7; cf. 23:23). "Mercy" is actually one of the weightier matters of the law (23:23) and the foundation of the better righteousness not achieved by the Pharisees (5:20), which Jesus as the new Moses has come to teach (2:13–21; 4:1–2; 5:1–2), as revealed in the Sermon on the Mount and, for example, in 11:28–30; 12:6, 11–12; 19:18–19; 20:20–28. Thus, at the time of the Pharisaic restoration, Matthew is pointedly asserting Hellenistic Christianity's superior ethical conception, which goes back to the Hellenistic synagogue, so that with his Gospel he may give to the churches, which must now live outside the prescribed rules of the synagogue, an already proven guideline for life and order.

Ethical Norms during Persecution

In a series of New Testament writings, the situation of persecution by the Roman state leads to characteristic ethical statements, which serve in part to make persecution bearable, in part to overcome the consequences of persecution within the church, and in part to prevent further persecutions where possible. If we look at the historical application of the individual norms, they appear as a rule to be highly appropriate and realistic. When later exalted as timeless norms, they have sometimes led believers astray and given rise to various kinds of legal confusion. Some important examples of such instructions are given below.

The Sermon on the Mount

Those who speak of the "ethic of the Sermon on the Mount" are usually thinking of the radical demands of nonviolence that are found in the Sermon on the Mount and have made this text the Magna Carta of pacifism. This section also speaks of the Sermon on the Mount in this sense, although these chapters of Matthew also contain many other ideas and at the same time the "pacifist" point of view of the Sermon on the Mount is also found elsewhere in the Gospel of Matthew. The pertinent passages are found above all in the last two "antitheses" of the Sermon on the Mount:

> You have heard that it was said, "An eye for an eye and a tooth for a tooth." But I say to you, Do not resist an evildoer. But if anyone strikes you on the right cheek, turn the other also; and if anyone wants to sue you and take your coat, give your cloak as well; and if anyone forces you to go one mile, go also the second mile. Give to everyone who begs from you, and do not refuse anyone who wants to borrow from you. (Matt. 5:38–42)
>
> You have heard that it was said, "You shall love your neighbor and hate your enemy." But I say to you, Love your enemies and pray for those who persecute you, so that you may be children of your Father in heaven . . . (Matt. 5:43–45)

The material incorporated into these antitheses comes essentially from the tradition of the sayings source (Q), which is also handed down by Luke (6:27–36). Matthew expanded it redactionally and put it in antithetical form. He has arranged it so that the fifth antithesis describes passive behavior and the sixth active. The concrete situation of the church addressed by Matthew is indicated by the words "pray for those who persecute you." Though the situation presumably varied from place to place, the churches live with persecutions and tribulations that originate from the synagogue (Matt. 5:12; 10:17ff.; 23:34): "Blessed are you when people revile you and persecute you and utter all kinds of evil against you falsely on my account" (5:11). The church is subjected defenselessly to this persecution, whether in the individual case it is undertaken by the synagogue or by the Roman authorities or by both. Christians are caught in the middle with no rights after they lose the protection of the synagogue, because they do not deny their confession and do not want to be integrated into the new Pharisaic legal order of the synagogue (see pp. 263ff. above).

In this situation the advice not to resist the evil done against one or seek one's rights but to accept humiliation and persecution, tolerate extortions without complaint, and pray for the persecutor (cf. Luke 23:34; Acts 7:60) makes immediately obvious good sense. In *Did.* 1.4, Matt. 5:42 is cited in this sense ("When someone takes what is yours, do not demand it back") and is followed by the explanation: "You cannot get it anyway!" The Christian cannot get justice; therefore resistance to injustice is pointless and only makes the situation worse. The way of suffering is the wiser and more realistic way, for at least it does not give additional provocation to opponents and new nourishment to their accusations.

Matthew does not express the related idea that through our good, we can overcome the evil done to us (thus, for example, Rom. 12:21). The idea is not excluded, but the concrete situation does not seem to permit such a hope. Nevertheless, the evangelist emphasizes to Christians that they should not hide, but like a city on a hill that cannot remain hidden, they should live and suffer publicly (Matt. 5:13–15). The intention of this recommendation is not the expectation that the behavior of Christians might become contagious and lead to missionary successes. Rather, by suffering publicly, not putting their light under a bushel, and letting their good works shine before others (5:16), Christians will bring to light the injustice they encounter and perhaps even silence the wrongful accusations of political disloyalty (cf. 1 Peter 2:12, 15). In any case, they will find compassionate sympathizers and helpers, especially among former Gentile God-fearers who likewise had to leave the synagogue, for it is said that merciful fellow human beings will "see your good works and give glory to your Father in heaven" (Matt. 5:16; cf. 1 Peter 2:12), who is thus also known as such to the sympathizers. These helpers are promised a heavenly reward if they receive the persecuted or even give them a cup of cold water (Matt. 10:40–42). Such compassionate sympathizers, who along with the suffering Christians have unknowingly also stood by the Judge of the world Christ, are also promised: "Just as you did it to one of the least of these who are members of my family, you did it to me" (25:40).

Matthew adopted the sayings from which he formed the last two antitheses of the Sermon on the Mount from the Jesus tradition, and thus even the early followers of Jesus were dependent on abandoning their own rights and meeting enemies with active love. Yet originally the salient point was not the condition of being without rights but the apocalyptic expectation of the imminent end of this world, in which the godly who were oriented toward the coming kingdom of God had to struggle constantly in order not to suffocate—especially since the imminent turn of the age would richly compensate for everything suffered: "Blessed are you who weep now, for you will laugh" (Luke 6:21).

Thus in either case it is a matter of forgoing personal rights and accepting injustice in the expectation of at least ameliorating one's own fate and in the hope of perhaps even being able to break the chain of retribution, overcome evil, and establish peace. Similar admonitions are also found elsewhere in the New Testament (Rom. 12:17–21; 1 Thess. 5:15; Phil. 2:13ff.; 1 Peter 2:21ff.), as well as in

Judaism (Prov. 20:22; 25:21–22; Isa. 53:12) and paganism. Thus we have here a general wisdom principle in which love of neighbor gains a concrete expression. For this very reason, it is not a question of appealing to the Sermon on the Mount while demanding pacifist nonviolence and the legal renunciation of rights. One's personal readiness not to resist evil can also result in evil running its course and pulling others down, so that even with good intentions love is grossly injured. Even less is the idea to fall into the arms of those who have the public duty of restraining evil, punishing wrongdoers, and rewarding those who do good (Rom. 13:3–4).

Thus what was recommended to the disfranchised Matthean churches as realistic behavior in the concrete historical situation of persecution, and was probably also apparent to them, would be grossly misunderstood as a timeless principle of ethical behavior or even a general norm for legislation.

Luke as Evangelist of the Poor

De Wette (1848, 160) observed two outstanding interests of the writer Luke, noting "how much in his writing is related to the recommendation of poverty and charity, and the rejection of wealth, on the one hand, and to the later oppressed situation of Christians, on the other." There is a necessary connection between these two redactional tendencies.

The material that Luke exhibits as evangelist of the poor is too extensive to be presented in a way that is at all complete and too well known for such a presentation to be necessary. It begins with the promise in the Magnificat of Mary that God "has filled the hungry with good things, and sent the rich away empty" (Luke 1:53) and with the preaching of John the Baptist to the crowds: "Whoever has two coats must share with anyone who has none; and whoever has food must do likewise" (Luke 3:11), and it extends into the Acts of the Apostles:

> Now the whole group of those who believed were of one heart and soul, and no one claimed private ownership of any possessions, but everything they owned was held in common. (Acts 4:32)

> They would sell their possessions and goods and distribute the proceeds to all, as any had need. (Acts 2:45)

Within the Lukan travel accounts are extensive passages composed of material from the sayings source (Q), the Lukan special material, and redactional expansions in which Jesus admonishes the wealthy not to be strongly attached to their possessions but to be prepared for generous acts of love for the poor (12:13–34; 14:12–33; 16:1–31). In addition there are peculiarly Lukan passages such as those that tell of the good Samaritan (10:29–37), the tax collector Zacchaeus who gives half his possessions to the poor (19:1–10), and the women companions of Jesus who argue about providing food from their possessions for Jesus and his disciples. Especially instructive is the fact that in numerous places Luke introduces viewpoints of his "piety of the poor" and "paraenesis for the rich" into the material adopted from Mark and the sayings source, as a Synoptic comparison reveals

(Luke 5:27ff.; 6:27–36; 11:41; 12:31, 33; etc.). This observation excludes the possibility of interpreting the Lukan "piety of the poor" as a relic of the tradition of a radical Jewish Christian church (thus Feine 1891); it must be explained instead primarily on the basis of redaction history.

This explanation has been attempted in various ways. Degenhardt (1965) limits the demand for a radical renunciation of possessions to holders of ecclesiastical office in the time of Luke, yet the demand is actually made of the disciples as representatives of the whole community (cf. Acts 2:4ff.; 4:34ff.). Conzelmann (1964, 218) holds the commonality of goods to be an ideal of the beginning period, which is not to be realized in the present but rather symbolizes the unity of the church; yet such an explanation is vitiated by the observation that Luke, above all in his Gospel, repeatedly challenges *his readers:* "Sell your possession, and give alms" (12:33). Other scholars are therefore of the view that Luke wants to see a "love communism" realized *in his time* and projects it back into the primitive church as a historical ideal with the help of the old story that Barnabas sold a field for the benefit of the Jerusalem church (Acts 4:36–37). Nowhere, however, is Luke thinking of a personal renunciation of possessions in principle but of the use of possessions in service of the members of the church who are dependent on the charity of the well-to-do; and if one can conclude from Acts 4:34–35; 5:1–11 that in the Lukan churches there was a common storehouse for food, the contribution was made voluntarily (5:4). Holtzmann (1897, 451–52) speaks of "frequently recurring fits . . . of enthusiasm for poverty and escape from the world" in Luke, yet the Lukan double volume never speaks of an ideal of poverty (cf. Conzelmann 1964, 218) but of a beneficence that presupposes wealth. One must also not spiritualize Luke's interest by pointing to the spiritual jeopardy of the rich through their possessions (thus, for example, Haenchen 1961, 192; Horn 1983, 215ff.), for if Luke can also use such jeopardy in his argumentation, for him it is still primarily not a question of saving the rich from worldly temptation but above all of benevolence and social equality, of the outward dedication of earthly goods in the service of the needy.

We find a convincing explanation of Luke's recommendations to renounce possessions, as well as the intense concern for the poor of the church that motivates him, when we place these social phenomena in the context of the situation of persecution and thus in the light of other problems that the writer Luke must overcome, as delineated by de Wette. The early persecution of Christians addressed by de Wette has already been often observed as an essential background of the Lukan double volume, even if weighted variously (see pp. 326–27 above). The justified assumption that this situation is connected with Luke's "piety of the poor" comes from the fact that Luke's paraenesis regarding poverty and possessions is directed toward Christians who are oppressed by the experience of persecution. This connection, however, is also expressly made by Luke in individual passages; cf. Luke 6:20–26; 12:22–34; 14:25–35; 18:29b–30 and the redaction-historical explanation of these passages (Schmithals 1980). At this point, however, I will only indicate two characteristic tendencies revealed by the historical background of the Lukan double volume.

Scholars have often described Luke's conspicuous apologetic tendency, which is especially evident in the trials against Jesus and Paul before Roman procurators (cf. Conzelmann 1964, 128ff.; Schütz 1969). Typically the representatives of Roman authority determine the political innocence of the one accused by the Jews (Luke 23:4, 14, 22; Acts 25:18ff.). The Acts of the Apostle ends with a strong impression of this motif: in Rome Paul preaches the message of Jesus Christ for two whole years under the eyes of the emperor *"without hindrance."* Unquestionably this tendency, which was considerably strengthened by Luke in comparison with his sources, comes from an effort to give Christians who had been denounced by the synagogue and severely persecuted by the Roman authorities an argument against the dangerous charge that Jesus himself and the apostles had already been condemned by Roman officials because of their revolutionary activities.

No less striking is the fact that Luke has stylized the passion of Jesus completely as a model martyrdom (cf. Dibelius 1959, 202ff.; Surkau 1938, 90ff.), using features that in part are already found in Jewish martyrdom accounts and which were widely adopted in the acts of Christian martyrs (Lietzmann 1936, 153ff.). In Gethsemane Jesus struggles in earnest prayer against the threatening temptation to avoid the cup of martyrdom (Luke 22:39–46). The angel of God stands by the confessor preparing himself for martyrdom (22:43–44). Without offering resistance, Jesus lets himself be arrested (22:49–51). In the high priest's house he looks at the denying Peter, who is afraid of martyrdom (22:54–62). Before Pilate, Jesus openly confesses his faith (23:1–5). A large crowd of people accompany the innocent confessor to the cross (23:27); he prays for his executioners (23:34) and as a martyr is certain of entering immediately into paradise (23:43). The crowd of spectators "beat their breasts and go home shaken by the martyr's innocent suffering" (Dibelius 1959, 204). The interrogation and death of Stephen, the first martyr among the followers of Jesus, is described by Luke in every detail according to the model of Jesus' martyrdom, and thus Stephen himself becomes in turn the model for martyrs in Luke's time.

Naturally, Luke is not writing his double volume during an active phase of persecution, but he looks back on such a phase and knows that new persecutions will come in the future. Therefore one should not only speak of an "endangerment" of the Lukan churches (Stegemann 1991, 187ff.) but also address the general situation in the time of persecution. In many ways Luke guides his churches to an appropriate endurance of persecution and even martyrdom; he teaches them to withstand the times of persecution, to give the right answers to the judges who accuse them of political insurrection, and to overcome the aftereffects of a period of distress; behavior toward apostates and contrite penitents is also treated (Luke 15).

The usual penalties for confessing Christians seem to have been the same during the entire period of persecution: first a fine and confiscation of assets, then banishment from one's homeland, and finally the death penalty. Apart from individual waves of persecution, martyrdom was not the usual punishment for the majority of confessors, who as a rule were threatened rather with the loss of possessions—as revealed, for example, by Heb. 10:32–34, which looks back on a time of persecution:

> But recall those earlier days when, after you had been enlightened, you endured a hard struggle with sufferings, sometimes being publicly exposed to abuse and persecution, and sometimes being partners with those so treated. For you had compassion for those who were in prison, and you cheerfully accepted the plundering of your possessions, knowing that you yourselves possessed something better and more lasting.

In this situation Luke's position on possessions and the renunciation of possessions is immediately understandable, and there is no longer a conflict in the fact that he underlines the dangers of wealth for believers and encourages the renunciation of possessions for the sake of the confession of Christ, yet he challenges his readers to deal responsibly and benevolently with possessions, which ˙ᵕainly presupposes having and striving for wealth. It is true, on the one hand, that those who are thrown into prison because of their confession and brought before kings and governors (Luke 21:12) must be ready to part with all earthly possessions and surrender their goods and, in extreme cases, even family and life itself (14:26). Without doubt, Luke's community had already had enough experience with apostates, whose hearts in the crucial hours were set more on earthly than on heavenly treasure (12:33–34) and who served wealth more than God (16:13); the parables of the lost (Luke 15) point to the topicality of the problem of a second repentance in the Lukan churches. In this sense, discipleship involves the readiness to give up all possessions (14:33), and in this spirit the poor, hungry, and weeping and those who are persecuted on account of their confession are called blessed (6:20–23).

On the other hand, the confessors who have lost their possessions can count on the beneficence of Christians who have not, and thus the promise to those who have lost everything in discipleship (18:28–29) that they will get back very much more in this age (18:30) is a real promise. The constant admonitions to help, to give, to feed, and the like are intended to establish and promote such solidarity. Christians of means ought not only to lend but also to give (6:27–36); the situation of those who have lost everything requires it. And as in the ideal primitive church presented by Luke, members do not claim their goods only for themselves, so also should Christians in Luke's time regard personal assets as community property, so that those who have lost their possessions will not be poor either. There is no question that such solidarity makes it easier for those who put their possessions at risk to hold to their confession, and conversely, the readiness to sell one's possessions to alleviate the needs of one's sisters and brothers does not seem such an extreme demand when one's goods were insecure anyway under the threat of the persecutor.

Thus the confessors' renunciation of possessions and the giving of goods to dispossessed confessors suggested in the Lukan double volume are concrete and appropriate modes of behavior in the situation of active persecution. They serve the maintenance of faith in the unity of the church. They do not yield timeless ethical directives. Luke neither recommends monastic poverty and a life in flight from the world to ministers or Christians in general, nor proclaims a love communism or renunciation of production, nor demands the socialization of private property. The correct kind of loving involvement with possessions, striving for possessions, and renunciation of possessions must be determined anew in each historical situation.

The Ethics of the Household Rules

In the second Christian generation the "household rules" make their entrance into the church paraenesis. This process has often been critically characterized as the adaptation of the Christian ethic to the middle class. In fact, the genre and content of the household rules were adopted from middle-class society in antiquity. From the Stoic Epictetus we learn what the model pupil must ask:

> As a pious, wisdom-loving, circumspect person, I would like to know what behavior is appropriate for me with regard to the gods, with regard to my parents, with regard to my fellow human beings, with regard to my country, and with regard to strangers. (*Diss.* 2.17.31)

This enumeration is directed toward a list of duties; the household rules contain a selection from such a list, and the New Testament household rules probably go back directly to synagogal models, such as those seen in the Jewish-Hellenistic didactic poem of Phocylides. Like the other early Christian paraeneses, they contain, as a rule, nothing specifically Christian. We find them in Col. 3:18–4:1, in Eph. 5:22–6:9, and in 1 Peter 2:13–3:7. The schema of the household rules also underlies Mark 10:1–31 (marriage, children, wealth), and passages such as *Did.* 4.9–11; *Barn.* 19.5–7; and *1 Clem.* 1.3 show how widespread this genre was in early Christendom. We should also compare 1 Tim. 2:8ff. and Titus 2:1ff. In many respects, the oldest and shortest New Testament list is also the most instructive:

> *Wives,* be subject to your husbands, as is fitting in the Lord. *Husbands,* love your wives and never treat them harshly.
> *Children,* obey your parents in everything, for this is your acceptable duty in the Lord. *Fathers,* do not provoke your children, or they may lose heart.
> *Slaves,* obey your earthly masters in everything, not only while being watched and in order to please them, but wholeheartedly, fearing the Lord. Whatever your task, put yourselves into it, as done for the Lord and not for your masters, since you know that from the Lord you will receive the inheritance as your reward; you serve the Lord Christ. For the wrongdoer will be paid back for whatever wrong has been done, and there is no partiality. *Masters,* treat your slaves justly and fairly, for you know that you also have a Master in heaven. (Col. 3:18–4:1)

In three pairs, first the various members of the household are admonished to obedience, then in each case the head of the household—as husband, father, and master of the slaves—is encouraged to deal lovingly with his housemates. Only the apparently secondary "you serve the Lord Christ" (3:24) adds a specifically Christian flavor to the present list; without this remark, one would not relate the frequently occurring "Lord" to the "Lord Christ" but to the "Lord God," and we would have before us a synagogal text.

The New Testament household rules faithfully reflect the ancient household order, in which all members of the household stood under the legal sovereignty of the father of the house. There is no hint of criticism of this order; on the contrary, it is emphatically reinforced. In responsibility to God and Christ, Christians are to live as respectable Gentiles do and keep their household in order. The first Christian generation thought no differently: Paul also encourages all Christians to remain before God in the status in which they came to faith. But what went without saying at that time had to be expressly reinforced later and developed in detail. The reason for this becomes evident when we observe that in the Christian household rules "obey" and "be subject" are especially stressed. The encouragement of the head of the household to respect the dignity of the various members of the household and to exercise his power in a moderate and humane way serves not least of all to make the uncompromisingly reinforced obedience to the master of the house easier for the members of the household to accept.

The main reason for this reinforcement is expressed in 1 Peter 2:12 (cf. Matt. 5:13–16), where the author of the household rules (1 Peter 2:13–3:7) begins with the admonition:

> Conduct yourselves honorably among the Gentiles, so that, though they malign you as evildoers, they may see your honorable deeds . . . (1 Peter 2:12)

Thus there are important *apologetic* reasons that move Christians to integrate themselves in exemplary fashion into the present social order. Christians are a conspicuous minority that now finds itself under the pressure of persecution and caught in the middle between the synagogue and the state. The accusation of asocial behavior was loud and from the standpoint of the persecutors not unsubstantiated, since Christians, though full-fledged citizens, abstained from the political cult. Thus it was all the more important for them not just to make revolutionary incursions into the social system but also to participate fully in this system in an exemplary fashion. The obedience that is fitting for Christian households, according to the household rules, and is pleasing to God is also fitting according to the standard of the world and is pleasing to all socially minded people. And since the household cult supported the head of the household, who did not have to acknowledge the public cult of the emperor within his four walls, the household order was a well-suited means, against all accusations and persecutions, for Christians to document their social loyalty and ability to integrate into society. In the name of the Lord, therefore, the household rules admonish the Christian household to be a model secular house in order to close the mouths of those who do not understand (1 Peter 2:15).

Thus in early Christendom we have, all in all, a decidedly conservative stance with regard to the present social order; there is no call for change but only for accommodation. The presupposition of this relaxed attitude regarding the existing social order, however, is the idea that "the present form of this world is passing away" (1 Cor. 7:31). From the standpoint of doing what is actually necessary, Christians moved in the social order as if they did not need it (7:28ff.). Thus conservatism with regard to the household order did not sanctify it but secularized and relativized it and kept it from becoming the law and the eternal norm. The inherent relativization of the order therefore also opened the way to its modification as soon as the appropriate time came. The principle for this modification is contained in the Christian household rules themselves, for they are characterized not only by the term *obedience* but also by the word *love*. Prudence required that in the time of persecution Christian love be realized *by example within* the prevailing household order. In other times also, love requires that one prudently endeavor to make wise modifications in the social order.

Subject to Authority

In many ages the almost unreserved admonition to be subject to authority has raised more objections than the ethics of the household rules. The "classical" texts with this admonition are found in Mark 12:13–17; 1 Peter 2:13–17; and Rom. 13:1–7. At core the statements in these texts do not go beyond what the synagogue also teaches, and the concrete historical reason for such a paraenesis was in principle the same in the synagogue and in the Christian church, even if this reason, which is clearly expressed in 1 Peter 2:13–17, has a special urgency in the church:

> For the Lord's sake accept the authority of every human institution, whether of the emperor as supreme, or of governors, as sent by him to punish those who do wrong and to praise those who do right. For it is God's will that by doing right you should silence the ignorance of the foolish. As servants of God, live as free people, yet do not use your freedom as a pretext for evil. Honor everyone. Love the family of believers. Fear God. Honor the emperor. (1 Peter 2:13–17)

This passage is traditional and could have been taken in its present form from synagogal didactic material. The first sentence concedes that earthly dominions have an order created by human beings, but one must be subject to them for God's sake, for they serve human well-being; here the formulation presupposes that the punishment of wrongdoers was harsher in antiquity than today, but that public recognitions were both more numerous and more important.

The second sentence names the reason for this admonition. If this is also based on a synagogal source, it originally related to the accusation that Jews were potential insurrectionists, which, in view of the zealot movement, the Jewish war of 66–70, and many insurrectionist movements also in the Diaspora, was not created out of thin air. This accusation is made against Christians without reason but not unexpectedly, for they refuse to make loyal sacrifices to the emperor, without having the privilege of exemption from this sacrifice that was granted to the synagogue. Therefore, among Gentiles there is talk that Christians are enemies of the general laws and ordinances and even enemies of the state, who for the sake of the kingdom of God recognize no earthly kingdom; the flames of such views about the multitudes of Christians were vigorously fanned by the synagogue (see pp. 265ff. above). In order to counter such accusations, it is important for Christians to be especially exemplary citizens, and in order to underline this reason for his admonition, the author of 1 Peter introduces the traditional didactic text with an appropriate explanation:

> Conduct yourselves honorably among the Gentiles, so that, though they malign you as evildoers, they may see your honorable deeds . . . (1 Peter 2:12)

Thus it is a logical reason, concerning the protection of Christians, that causes the author of 1 Peter to hold his readers to an especially strict observation of the prescribed civic duties. In the process they should not and do not need to deny their Christian confession: this is stated in the third sentence. For Christians the emperor is not the divine Lord. Their citizenship is in heaven (Phil. 3:20) and they are "aliens" on earth, not full citizens (1 Peter 1:2; 2:11; Heb. 11:9, 13). In this sense they are free people with respect to earthly rulers, and their exemplary obedience does not sanctify earthly dominions but secularizes them. But their freedom must not lead to "evil," to insurrection, or to the sabotaging of justice and public order. Christians honor God and love the communion of saints, but as "servants of God" they also show concern for all people and respect for the authority of the king. Jesus' advice to them is:

> Give to the emperor the things that are the emperor's, and to God the things that are God's. (Mark 12:17)

Rom. 13:1–7 is the best known of the relevant texts. It makes specific the recommended obedience of all earthly power through the statement that Christians are exemplary taxpayers:

> For the same reason you also pay taxes, for the authorities are God's servants, busy with this very thing. Pay to all what is due them—taxes to whom taxes are due . . . (Rom. 13:6–7)

The loyalty problem often flared up around the unpopular payment of direct and indirect taxes, duties, and fees (cf. Mark 12:13–17; Matt. 17:24ff.); for Christians, who did not take part in the public cult, the punctual payment of required taxes was understandably the most prominent expression of their loyalty, and also brought them the sympathy of the authorities. "Everywhere and above all, we endeavor to pay taxes and fees to your officials," writes Justin in his *Apology* to the emperor Hadrian (*Apol.* 1.17), and the descendants of Jesus' siblings, accused before the emperor Domitian because of their faith, point to the fact that with their own hands they cultivate the earth "in order to pay the taxes and earn their living" (Euseb. *Hist. Eccl.* 3.20.4). The martyr Speratus says under questioning: "Whenever I sold anything, I paid the taxes, because I acknowledge my Lord, the King of kings, and the imperial ruler over all nations" (*Acts of the Scillitan Martyrs* 6).

More striking in Rom. 13:1–7 is the fact that this text, which also comes from the synagogue, reinforces the requirement of obedience with a metaphysical substantiation of state power, which is lacking in Mark 12:13–17 and 2 Peter 2:13–17:

> Let every person be subject to the governing authorities; for there is no authority except from God, and those authorities that exist have been

instituted by God. . . . Therefore one must be subject not only because of wrath but also because of conscience. (Rom. 13:1, 5)

This theologically exorbitant demand of obedience gives Rom. 13:1–7 its particular character and provides the reason for the text's often agonizing history of influence. The statement in Mark 12:17, that one should give both God and the emperor their due, does not exclude the possibility of a conflict, and thus one might have to obey God rather than human authority (Acts 5:29). And 1 Peter 2:13–17 decidedly maintains the distinction between the kingdom of God and the state as a human institution. In Rom. 13:1–7, however, the earthly authority has become a sanctified entity. Apparently the Jewish author of this text felt it necessary to remind his readers in the Diaspora of their duty of loyalty with a strong argument and increased pressure on the conscience, in view of zealot propaganda or the war already raging in Palestine; with the pressure of persecution, the Christian tradition saw no reason to withdraw this argumentation.

Yet what was understandable and well-reasoned in such historical situations, in the view of the people concerned, causes more than just uneasiness as a timeless ethical instruction, which Rom. 13:1–7 was never intended to be. It is therefore helpful to remember that at about the same time that Rom. 13:1–7 was adopted into the collection of Paul's letters (cf. Schmithals 1988b, 456ff.), in the Revelation to John the Roman state appears no less one-sidedly as the beast out of the deep and as the great whore of Babylon, which at least places suffering under authority beside obedience to it. In a changing situation and for the sake of love, however, disobedience, contradiction, and resistance also come into the picture as possibilities in an ethical relationship with a particular state power and order.

In this sense, the New Testament paraeneses concerning one's relationship to state authority form a classical example of the historicality of ethical statements in general.

Ethical Norms in
Dealings with Heretics

Some New Testament passages reveal that dealings with Christian heretics also involve the area of ethical norms and that even in this case the concrete situation essentially determines the shape of the norms and ways of behaving. We will use two examples to show the historicity of the corresponding paraeneses.

Dualistic Enthusiasm

In early Christendom as in other realms of the Hellenistic world, there was a radical devaluation of everything earthly and bodily in favor of the pneumatic and spiritual. According to this view, which was foreign to Judaism, creation was ascribed not to God but to lower or even demonic powers. In the course of the first century the popularity of such teachings developed considerable strength, and in the second century this anticorporeal movement became a real danger to catholic Christianity in the form of dualistic Gnosticism and Marcionitism. In practice the devaluation of the body could lead both to asceticism and to libertinism, which recognized no boundaries, especially in regard to sexual matters, because the body stood outside of ethical obligations. When Paul had to deal with such currents, he confronted them above all with the usual Judeo-Christian morality, which he made obligatory with a reference to the unity of indicative and imperative, as is especially clear in 1 Corinthians 5–6.

The pneumatic, however, recognizes no difference between man and woman; their distinctive features lie entirely in the realm of the body, whereas the "spirit" is biologically neutral. Therefore radically held enthusiasm demands and practices, with religious emphasis, a dissolution of the social structures that oppose this dualistic principle. Early Christendom was decisively opposed to all emancipation movements based on such an anticorporeal position. Consequently, it is conceivable that the reinforcement of the existing order—which is also found in the ethics of the household rules and includes especially the requirement of the subordination of the wife to the husband—came about not out of an apologetic concern to present Christians in public as model fellow citizens but out of an interest in confronting dualistic-emancipatory tendencies within one's own ranks.

In any case, however, in such an actual historical context we cannot understand the striking, and to us incomprehensible, admonitions that a woman is to be quiet in church and, in distinction to the man, must wear a head covering, as demanded by the custom adopted from the synagogue:

> As in all the churches of the saints, women should be silent in the churches. For they are not permitted to speak, but should be subordinate, as the law also says. If there is anything they desire to know, let them ask their husbands at home. For it is shameful for a woman to speak in church. (1 Cor. 14:33b–35)

> Let a woman learn in silence with full submission. I permit no woman to teach or to have authority over a man; she is to keep silent. For Adam was formed first, then Eve; and Adam was not deceived, but the woman was deceived and became a transgressor. Yet she will be saved through childbearing, provided they continue in faith and love and holiness, with modesty. (1 Tim. 2:11–15)

> Judge for yourselves: is it proper for a woman to pray to God with her head unveiled? Does not nature itself teach you that if a man wears long hair, it is degrading to him, but if a woman has long hair, it is her glory? For her hair is given to her for a covering. (1 Cor. 11:13–15)

Whether the passage from 1 Cor. 14:33b–35 comes from Paul himself or was added to his letter at a later time under pressure from the aggressively evangelistic emancipation propaganda of dualistic false teachers is a controversial issue that is unimportant for our understanding of the pericope; in all the cited cases the "conservative" demands are to be understood on the basis of the defensive historical situation in which the corresponding concrete behavior was merely a foil for the fundamental question of whether one held to the confession of God as creator or not. For apart from the fact that the comprehensive reasons given for the traditional behavior must have had no great convincing power for Christians of the time, Paul is also of the opinion elsewhere that "in Christ" there is no difference between man and woman (1 Cor. 11:11–12; Gal. 3:28) and that women could also speak in worship (1 Cor. 11:5). The astonishing sentence that women may be saved through childbearing points directly to the limited, antienthusiast occasion of the present paraenesis, for in a situation of the temptation of dualism, this sentence demands a relevant, bodily confession to the God-given corporeality of human beings and to God as the creator of heaven and earth.

Thus the historicality of the quoted directives is obvious. In view of the occasion and in the context of the actual situation, they are understandable. In their time they were possibly also necessary and in any case acceptable. To make them timeless, immutable norms, however, would contradict their own intention and the fundamental principle of all ethical action: love.

Brotherly Love
in the Letters of John

It has long been observed that love of neighbor, one of the most important themes in the Johannine letters, is limited to love of one's Christian sister or brother, and this state of affairs has often been severely criticized. Even those who dispute the correctness of that observation (Schnackenburg 1963, 120–21; Schulz 1987, 526) do so because they hold such a limitation of love to be "a stuffy narrowness" (Schnackenburg 1963, 120) and inappropriate. Nevertheless, that observation is without doubt accurate:

> Whoever loves a brother or sister lives in the light, and in such a person there is no cause for stumbling. (1 John 2:10)

> We know that we have passed from death to life because we love one another. (1 John 3:14)

> Beloved, since God loved us so much, we also ought to love one another. No one has ever seen God; if we love one another, God lives in us, and his love is perfected in us. (1 John 4:11–12)

> The commandment we have from him is this: those who love God must love their brothers and sisters also. (1 John 4:21)

> But now, dear lady, I ask you, not as though I were writing you a new commandment, but one we have had from the beginning, let us love one another. (2 John 5)

Even if it is no accident that the "neighbor" is the one who is "near," it is still striking that in the Johannine letters the near non-Christian does not even come into the picture, as is the case in Paul, for example, in Gal. 6:10: "Let us work for the good of all, and especially for those of the family of faith." Do the letters of John therefore reveal the ethic of a sectarian conventicle that closes itself off against all other fellow human beings? A historical consideration of the Johannine love paraenesis does not confirm this judgment. We must note that the Johannine letters do not intend a general ethical instruction. The accusation of a lack of brotherly love is intentionally aimed against the false teachers, who are opposed in all three letters, and is related especially to the abandonment of ecclesiastical communion.

The idea that the theme of "brotherly love" must be understood strictly on the basis of the dispute with heretics comes first from the general observation that the letters carry on this dispute sentence by sentence, but it is also revealed in individual observations. When the author emphasizes that the commandment of brotherly love is not a new but an old commandment (1 John 2:7; 2 John 5–6), he is applying against the enthusiast heretics, who recognize only the "spirit" as authority, the principle of church tradition, as in 1 John 1:1–4; 2:24. He reproaches them, saying that they cannot assert that they have fellowship with God when at the same time they renounce fellowship with their sisters and brothers (1 John 2:6–7). The statement that whoever loves a brother or sister lives in the light and leads no one astray makes an important point against the false teachers, whose trademark is that they lead the orthodox community astray (1 John 2:10; cf. 2:26; 3:7; 2 John 7). And wherever "hate" is mentioned, the subject is the false teachers who assert that they are in the light and love God, but by denying brotherly love, they document that they live in darkness (1 John 2:4–11; 3:15; 4:20; cf. 3:10).

The idea that hate, or the lack of brotherly love, relates primarily to the abandonment of Christian fellowship by those who "went out from us, but they did not belong to us" (1 John 2:19), and who are trying to persuade additional members of the orthodox church to join them, can also be derived from the overall context of admonitions and accusations, which are all aimed at the retention in the fellowship of those who walk in the light and love each other (1 John 1:3; 2:10, 24–28; 3:6; 4:12–16; 2 John 9). The lack of brotherly love is the sign that one no longer belongs to the children of God (1 John 3:10, 14–15). The missing brotherly love is equivalent to false belief (1 John 4:7–10; 2 John 4–7). Only in 1 John 3:17 do we also see a benevolent aspect of brotherly love: the question "How does God's love abide in anyone who has the world's goods and sees a brother or sister in need and yet refuses help?" refers to the false teachers who assert that they love God (1 John 4:10). They have apparently wandered off into a free spiritualism and no longer bother about the bodily needs of Christians who have remained faithful. This accusation of a missing readiness to help, however, is only a side issue related to the basic dispute that the author of the letters of John is pursuing; in them he relates love and hate respectively to remaining in the right faith and leaving the brotherly fellowship.

This is the limited historical reason for the letters of John, which, like the corresponding passages of the Gospel of John, concentrate love of neighbor on love of Christian sisters and brothers. Love of outsiders, whose omission is understandable in the author's acute situation, is not thereby negated. Only when one misunderstands the statements of the Johannine letters as timeless statements of doctrine can one criticize their limitation to love of one's brothers and sisters. If, however, we recognize their particular intention, we find in John a definite application of the commandment of love and thus a further example of the historicality of ethical statements in the New Testament.

18

The Origins of the New Testament

The book—or better yet, the collection of writings—that we call "The New Testament" or "the books of the New Testament" was not present at the birth of Christianity. This collection was begun, rather, sometime in the second half of the second century by the early church itself, around one hundred fifty years after the origins and beginnings of Christianity. Naturally, the writings that were gathered into the New Testament are older than this collection itself. Their time of origin stretches over a hundred years from the letters of Paul, the oldest extant documents of early Christianity, which were written in the decade between 50 and 60, to writings such as the Second Letter of Peter and possibly also the Gospel of John, whose times of composition were well into the second century. And these writings that originated between 50 and 150 contain even older traditions that go back to the time of Christian beginnings. There are, on the one hand, recollections of Jesus' activity and, on the other, fixed formulations of testimonies of faith in Jesus as the Christ, which were already needed in the early churches for baptismal instruction and worship. In the first one hundred twenty to one hundred fifty years of its history, however, Christendom did not have the New Testament as such. In this sense the process of the origination of the New Testament does not belong to the theological history of early Christianity. But since we owe to this process the preservation of traditions without which we could not illuminate this history, it is only right that in the present connection we should also turn our attention to the origins of the New Testament.

When the historical study of the New Testament and its writings began around two hundred years ago, G. E. Lessing, who was himself engaged in this research, pointed out to opponents of the historical study of the Bible that it was not the New Testament but the early confessions of faith that were the rock on which the church was built. The writings of the New Testament, let alone their collection, were still unknown to the first Christians, and thus the study of these writings could illuminate—but not call into question—the basis of faith. With this presupposition the historical science of the New Testament quickly came on the scene two hundred years ago. In addition to introductory questions about the circumstances of origin of the individual New Testament writings and about their original wording (text criticism), a prominent role has always been played by the question of the origins of the New Testament as such, that is, the question of the process of *collecting* the individual texts (canon criticism).

On the latter question one must first ascertain that contemporaries did not pass on any direct information about the origins of the New Testament. We have communications about neither the time in which the New Testament came into being nor the place in which its writings were collected nor the motives that led to its formation nor the people or institutions that initiated or carried out their collection. We observe, on the one hand, however, that into the latter half of the second century our New Testament writings—the Gospels, the Acts of the Apostles, the letters of Paul and letters ascribed to other apostles, as well as the Revelation to John—were used *as individual* writings in different ways in different parts of Christendom. Yet they were not all in use everywhere, and they never occur as components of a collection of scripture and in this sense are never distinguished from other early Christian writings that were not accepted into the New Testament. Toward the end of the second century, on the other hand, we find everywhere the New Testament itself as a fixed collection of holy scriptures with a clear delineation that excludes other early Christian writings and includes essentially the same books that the New Testament has possessed since that time. Thus in the second half of the second century our New Testament as such came into being, but *how* it came into being is reported to us by no document and no writer of that time.

This silence is not absolutely amazing. From the time in question, say, A.D. 160–80, we have very little information at all on the church, much less on manuscripts. In those days when the church was in a struggle for survival, theologians had no interest in presenting or documenting the course of church history. And when the writing of church history began more than one hundred fifty years later, the New Testament had long since become a recognized authority. Questions were no longer asked about its origins, and the details had, in any case, probably been forgotten. The silence could also be connected with the possibility that there was absolutely nothing to report, and according to one widespread scholarly view, the collection of the New Testament scriptures actually occurred "of itself" or "by force of gravity" (Campenhausen 1968, 245).

Did the New Testament Arise "of Itself"?

It has often been pointed out in this connection that the "church father" Marcion, presumably in the decade 140–150, had already created an authoritative collection of New Testament scriptures. Marcion was a Christian who broke with the general Christian confession of faith in that he made a distinction between the God of the Old Testament and the Father of Jesus Christ, that is, between the God of the first and the God of the second article of the confession of faith, between the Creator-God and the Redeemer-God. For Marcion the God of the Old Testament is a God of justice; the Father of Jesus Christ, by contrast, is a God of mercy who frees human beings from the power of their just and judging creator. In consequence of this teaching, which was very influential at the time, Marcion rejected the Old Testament and thereby took away from his followers their familiar scripture. Thus he was obliged to replace the loss, and he did this by combining the Gospel of Luke, which he ascribed to the apostle Paul, with the ten letters of Paul as an authoritative collection, as the first Holy Scripture of the new covenant. For Marcion depended on Paul for his teaching, yet Paul's writings were later adulterated, and for this reason Marcion purged the Gospel of Luke and the ten Pauline letters of their references to the Old Testament and the Creator-God before he accepted them in his collection.

What Marcion *had to do,* because he needed a substitute for the Old Testament he had rejected, was imitated, according to many scholars, by the mainstream church without a corresponding urgency—though possibly moved in this direction by their disagreement with Marcion—in that they likewise formed the writings that were recognized by their churches as apostolic into a collection of Holy Scripture and, in contrast to Marcion, placed it *beside* the Old Testament. Other scholars, however, have observed a tendency toward such a mainstream Christian collection of scripture already in Marcion's time, and thus they hold that he only adopted this tendency and perhaps thereby accelerated the process of completing the church's New Testament. According to either conception, our New Testament forms the organic conclusion of a more or less harmonious process, but one must not ask about time and place or a particular occasion or individual originators of the process.

This widespread view, however, is hardly satisfactory. We must ask in the first place how, without a compelling reason, the scripture of a New Testament was or could be placed *beside* the scripture of the Old Testament in the Christian church, for we are dealing here in a certain sense with a problematic process in which the old and the new—stated more pointedly: the antiquated and the newly validated—are placed on the same level. In any case, the earliest church placed over against the traditional Holy Scripture of the Old Testament as the Christian New, in whose light one also read the scripture, not a second scripture but their confession of faith (*regula fidei*), and centuries after the New Testament was formed, the church still largely derives and bases the truth of its message primarily on its rule of faith. Furthermore, the individual Gospels and the writings of the apostle were already used and quoted as authorities before the formation of the New Testament, and when this happened with the words "the Lord says . . ." or "the apostle says . . .," a normative collection could hardly increase the authority of such a tradition. Thus it is hard to see how the scripture of the New Testament could come into being of itself, as it were, and without any special reason. The mainstream church was in no way obliged to imitate what Marcion had to do, and nothing in the New Testament itself reveals that it was collected in order to *suppress* the scripture of Marcion.

Above all, however, we must consider the fact that our familiar collection of New Testament writings with its clear canonical distinction is found *suddenly in the whole of worldwide Christendom* at the end of the second century. At this time our New Testament is used by the church father Irenaeus in Asia Minor, by Tertullian in Africa, and by Clement of Alexandria in Egypt, and in Rome there is an index of New Testament scriptures that comes from the same time: the so-called

Muratorian Canon. In view of the quite disparate conditions in the various ecclesiastical regions, which were in no way connected organizationally, this phenomenon would be unexplainable if the New Testament was the result of an unplanned
development. The fact that it appeared at the same time in the whole of Christendom presupposes, rather, that a formal agreement caused the new scripture to appear in the second half of the second century as a conscious creation of the
mainstream church.

We must also note that the four Gospels in particular could in no case have
found their way together through their own gravity, for it caused the churches difficulty from the beginning to have four gospel writings side by side that by no
means always agreed with each other. Without the necessity and a concrete reason, Christendom would never have saddled itself with the difficult problem of
"harmonizing" the various gospel accounts, and each church would have remained
with the one gospel writing that was familiar and in use in its worship.

We may note further that the New Testament contains three times seven or
twenty-one letters: fourteen letters of Paul to his churches and coworkers and
seven "catholic" letters addressed to all Christians. Three and seven are holy numbers, and therefore three times seven letters are appropriate for Holy Scripture. But
since not all letters were already known everywhere in worldwide Christendom,
this number did not appear everywhere by coincidence; it indicates instead a
planned development and implementation.

The New Testament as a
Collection of Apostolic Writings

Also pointing to a planned development of the New Testament, however, is the
basic observation that this collection was assembled with the presupposition that
the individual writings are of *apostolic* origin. By examining this observation we
will achieve a better answer to the question of the origins of the New Testament
than the idea that it arose "of itself." Apostolic origin does not mean that they were
all actually written by an apostle. Nor does it mean that they themselves all *make
the claim* that they were written by an apostle. It does mean, however, that they
were considered to be apostolic writings when they were adopted into the New
Testament and received corresponding titles. As a rule, the *individual* writings
originally bore no titles, but in the scriptural collection titles became necessary in
order, for example, to distinguish the four Gospels from each other. It is significant that as a title the name of the apostolic author was given—Matthew, John, Peter, and so forth—and not an indication of the content of the writing, as was the
usual custom.

The letters of the apostle Paul, to be sure, constitute a certain exception to the
rule, since they are each named for the *recipient of the letter*. They were not
adopted into the New Testament individually, however, but as a collection that is
older than the New Testament and which as a whole bore the name of the apostle,
while the individual letters were distinguished from each other by the naming of
their addressees. Moreover, in thirteen of the fourteen letters of the Pauline corpus,

the apostle Paul himself is named as the writer; since according to ancient epistolary custom, the sender opens his missive with his name, these thirteen letters *begin* with the name of Paul, and usually with the same additional identification:
"Paul, an apostle of Christ Jesus . . ." The fourteenth writing in the Pauline epistolary collection, the so-called Letter to the Hebrews, is not a letter but an instructional text or sermon, to which an epistolary closing in the manner of Paul's
letters has been added in Heb. 13:18–25. There are good reasons to assume that
this expansion was appended in the formation of the New Testament and serves to
mark this text as a work of the apostle Paul, in order to complete the fourteen letters in this epistolary collection.

Among the "catholic" letters, the two letters of Peter and the letters of James
and Jude each name their author, with the letters of Peter adding, "an apostle of
Jesus Christ." Since a corresponding addendum to the names of Jude (*Judas* in
Greek) and James is lacking, we can question whether they were written by the
apostles with these names or by other Christians. There is no doubt, however, that
these two letters were also adopted into the collection of New Testament scriptures in the conviction that their authors were the *apostles* Judas and James, who
are found in other passages in the New Testament, for example, Luke 6:15 and
Acts 1:13. With a corresponding assumption the three letters of John were also
added to the collection, although none of them mentions an addressee by name and
the fact that the author of 2 and 3 John calls himself an elder or presbyter in no
way suggests apostolic authorship. But since these three writings are undeniably
connected not only with each other but also with the Gospel of John, their ascription to the apostle John is required if one ascribes the Fourth Gospel to this apostle. This was undoubtedly the case in the gathering of the New Testament
scriptures, and it means that the three letters of John were ascribed to the *apostle*
John when the New Testament came into being, at the latest.

When the last book of the Bible, the "Apocalypse" or Revelation to John, as its
title reads, was accepted among the scriptures of the New Testament, it was also
considered a work of the *apostle* John, although the author calls himself "John,"
but not "apostle"; he does not appear as such in his writing, but rather as a prophet
from the second Christian generation. At a time when there was still no New Testament, however, Justin Martyr (*Dial.* 81.4) cites Revelation expressly as a writing of the *apostle* John. This provides even more evidence that the later New
Testament title can refer to no other John than the apostle, the brother of James
and son of Zebedee.

Since the formation of the canon, the four Gospels have appeared under the
common designation *gospel* (that is, "good news"), to which the authors' names
were added: "according to Matthew," "according to Mark," "according to Luke,"
"according to John." But whereas Matthew and John belong to the circle of the
apostles, this is not the case with Mark and Luke. The latter is a companion and
coworker of Paul (Col. 4:14; Philemon 24; 2 Tim. 4:10), and Mark, an influential
Christian of the first century (Acts 12:12; 15:37, 39), is regarded by the Christian
author Papias, writing around 150, as the companion of Peter, whose speeches he
wrote down. Thus both are *students of apostles,* and at the formation of the New

Testament the books connected with their names were not given direct apostolic status, especially since the author of the Gospel of Luke presents himself in the prologue of his book as a secondhand witness who is dependent on the tradition of apostolic eyewitnesses. If there was, nonetheless, no hesitancy in accepting into the New Testament two only indirectly apostolic writings, this shows that the criterion of apostolicity that guided the formation of the New Testament was not understood in the sense of formal authorship but in the sense of content: the scriptures of the New Testament contain the *message* of the apostles.

Finally, we must refer to the Acts of the Apostles by Luke. This writing, which together with the Gospel of Luke forms a double volume from the hand of one and the same author, bears no author's name, but in the gathering of the New Testament writings, it received the title *Acts of the Apostles.* Apparently this title also validates the apostolic principle that determined the choice of writings in the formation of the New Testament.

Apostolic Tradition
versus Pneumatic Enthusiasm

Thus it is obvious that the New Testament came into being when and because someone wanted to publish *apostolic* scriptures. In this process, however, what interest guided the collectors and editors? Who or what challenged them to make such a collection? What was their intention? What purpose did their work serve?

In answering this question we must totally disregard the modern *historical* interest in the beginnings and origins of historical events. In antiquity such interests were generally little developed, and in early Christendom totally foreign. Nor did early Christians think of buttressing their faith through historical inquiry, as has commonly been done since the end of the eighteenth century.

The answer to the question of the reason for the collection of apostolic scriptures must be sought, rather, in the current problems of the church in the second half of the second century, when this collection was initiated. This period of church history was determined *externally* by state persecutions, against which one naturally could not defend oneself through the collection of apostolic scriptures but which Christians sought to counter with *apologies,* that is, with writings in which the accusations of their persecutors were controverted and refuted. Such apologies were numerous in the second and third centuries.

Internally, however, the church at this time was in the middle of a long-term debate over a manifold heresy that entered the history of religion and the church under the name *Gnosticism.* The Gnostics were dualists who considered the body evil and the prison of the spirit, in which human beings have their true being and which gives them participation in the divine being and puts them on the same level as Christ. This divine spirit, the *pneuma,* is also what enables its bearers, the pneumatics, to perceive and proclaim the divine truth enthusiastically ("in the spirit") and *directly.* Whereas Marcion rejected the Old Testament and the message of the twelve apostles but recognized the apostle Paul as a faithful witness of the message of Jesus, for the Gnostics this tradition was suspect, and only the living, present-day witness of the divine Spirit speaking in and from them was authentic. In contrast to such pneumatics, the orthodox church referred to the unique event of the revelation through Jesus Christ and thus to the *apostolic witness* of this revelation, to the writings despised by the enthusiastic pneumatics. Thus the manifold disagreement between the mainstream church and the Gnostic heretics was focused on this one criterion and its alternative: Is the beginning and original witness of the apostles, the apostolic message, normative for Christian truth, or is this truth based on the loose, unverifiable utterances of the pneumatics?

This controversy can be observed especially well in the letters of John, which even before the formation of the New Testament dealt with the representatives of Gnostic teachings. The First Letter of John begins importantly with a reference to the incarnate Word of God, that is, to "what was from the beginning, what we have heard, what we have seen with our eyes, what we have looked at and touched with our hands." The author writes that his readers know him who was "from the beginning" (1 John 2:13–14), and he admonishes them to abide in what they have heard "from the beginning." He accuses the heretics, however, of not abiding in the traditional teaching but "going beyond" the original message (2 John 9) and thus inventing something new. Therefore his urgent admonition to his readers, written with reference to the enthusiastic pneumatics, is: "Beloved, do not believe every spirit, but test the spirits to see whether they are from God" (1 John 4:1), and the traditional apostolic message provides the criterion for such testing. That is the situation in which in the second half of the second century the original message was made binding in a collection of apostolic scripture for all Christendom in such a way that with its help Christians could turn away the proud spirits that are always producing something new.

The first ecclesiastical writer to use the New Testament extensively for this purpose was the church father Irenaeus, who came from Asia Minor and was bishop of Lyon from around the year 177. He wrote a comprehensive work against the Gnostics and not only endeavored to refute their teachings in detail with the help of apostolic message of the New Testament but also declared again and again that the original and initial apostolic tradition, which was the foundation of the faith, was taught in the mainstream church; the heretics, by contrast, had fallen away from this tradition and therefore without exception offered a teaching that was invented by them later (Iren. *Haer.* 3.1–4). Thus against the Gnostic heretics he insisted on the unique truth preserved in the apostolic tradition, and for this tradition he was the first to turn to the collected apostolic writings of the New Testament, which he quotes more than one hundred times.

Thus the reason for the collection of scriptures in the New Testament is sufficiently clear: the orthodox church wanted to confront the heretics with the apostolic tradition in a comprehensive and binding document. Such a reason for the formation of the New Testament is confirmed when we observe that at the same time the apostolic tradition was also applied in a different way. Also developing in the second half of the second century was, namely, the concept of apostolic succession, the view that in churches that the apostles founded they installed bishops, and that the oral teaching of the apostles has also been passed down reliably in an unbroken chain of successors of these bishops (Hegesippus in Euseb. *Hist. Eccl.* 4.22; Iren. *Haer.* 2.3). Moreover, at this time the mainstream church was attempting to achieve a uniform wording of the baptismal confession in the spirit of the apostolic teaching, yet this was not easy, since the various churches in the broad *oikoumenē* had always used their own form of baptismal creed. It would still be centuries before Rome would be able to implement a common form of the apostolic confession of faith.

A collection of apostolic scriptures, apostolic succession, and an apostolic confession of faith were the three norms with whose help the mainstream church established the message of Christian origins and beginnings against Gnostic enthusiasts. The collection of apostolic scriptures, the New Testament, soon became the most important and most influential of these norms, especially through the Reformation.

The Church in Rome
and the Origins of the New Testament

In what way was the New Testament formed? The fact that we know the reason for its formation and therefore understand why the New Testament is a collection of *apostolic* scriptures still tells us nothing about the *process* of collecting. It is not only the already mentioned lack of information that helps us understand why biblical scholarship has shied away from the assumption of a *conscious* formation of the New Testament, but also the fact that in the time in question, the second half of the second century, there was still no ecclesiastical organization encompassing individual churches. The churches or local church associations were sovereign and had not even joined together in regional churches, much less a worldwide organization. Thus there was still no institution that could have officially undertaken the task of forming the New Testament. But if the New Testament did not come into being "of itself" but, as we saw, as the conscious creation of the orthodox church, there must have been an agency with the authority of the universal church that acted to this end. If we ask what authority this could have been, we must answer that at that time, in which there was no overall ecclesiastical organization, this agency could have been only the Roman church and its bishop, who probably possessed not a legal but an outstanding moral authority in Christendom.

When the church father Irenaeus wants to show that the apostolic tradition is genuinely reproduced in the orthodox churches, he chooses as an example "the apostolic tradition and preaching of faith of the greatest and oldest and universally known church, which was founded and built in Rome by the two glorious apostles Peter and Paul" (Iren. *Haer.* 3.3.2). Their martyrdom in Rome had already been lifted up by other writers decades earlier to the honor of the Roman church (John 13:36; 21:18–19; *1 Clem.* 5; Ign. *Rom.* 4.3), and Irenaeus concludes that "because of its special status, every church must agree" with the Roman church. That probably means not the legal but the moral and spiritual status of the church in the capital of the *oikoumenē*. This judgment of a theologian from Asia Minor, who became a bishop in Gaul and could also act critically vis-à-vis the Roman bishop, shows that the Roman church must have already acquired recognized merit in the preservation of orthodox faith in the dispute with heretics, and the most successful efforts must have included prominently the collection of New Testament scriptures that was recognized in all churches and which Irenaeus industriously used.

A clear indication of the prominent role of the Roman church is the fact that in the formation of the New Testament, Paul's letter to the Christians in Rome is placed at the head of the Pauline letters, for we have certain information (*1 Clem.* 47.1; Tert. *Marc.* 4.5; *Haer.* 36; Muratorian Canon 50ff.) that the collection of Paul's letters originally opened with the two Corinthian letters and closed with the letter to Rome. At the end of the Letter to the Romans (16:25–27) there is still a doxology that does not belong to Romans, but which closed that older collection. The placement of Romans at the beginning of the collection lay in the interest of the Roman church and could have happened only if this church was actively involved in the formation of the New Testament. Also the well-known passage in Matt. 16:18–19 ("You are Peter, and on this rock I will build my church . . .") probably came into being itself only in connection with the formation of the New Testament and was inserted into the Gospel of Matthew. If this observation is correct, it likewise attests to the leading role of the Roman church in the formation and propagation of the New Testament.

The Formation of the New Testament

The merit of the Roman church is not to be underestimated. For it was not only a question of gathering together the writings that were apostolic, or considered apostolic, but it also and especially involved getting this collection generally recognized in the churches. Thus from the beginning the interests of the various churches and ecclesiastical provinces had to be considered. The writings gathered in the New Testament were already highly regarded in the churches—in this sense one can speak of the New Testament coming into being "of itself" and not by an authoritative decree—but in no way was each of them known and recognized in every situation. The letters of Paul were cherished in the churches that began with the missionary work of the great apostle to the Gentiles, whereas as a rule, they probably remained unknown in the remaining churches. The Revelation to John was recognized in the West but little valued in the East, whereas the eastern churches, conversely, often used the Letter to the Hebrews, which remained comparatively unknown in Western churches. Regarding the Gospels, each church naturally used only one, namely, the one that was first introduced to it. The idea of also using other gospel writings is not likely to have occurred to a church, especially since it would have let itself in for the problem of dealing with often quite different accounts of the same event.

Thus the most important task in the formation of the New Testament consisted in being careful that each church found in the new collection *its own familiar apostolic legacy* and that it was ready at the same time to recognize the corresponding traditions of other churches, which were previously foreign to it, as being of equal worth. We do not know how such an agreement was achieved under the guidance and leadership of the Roman church. Did letters go back and forth? Were there regional gatherings of bishops that were attended by Rome? Was there even a general synod in Rome already at this time? The sources provide no answers to these questions; we know only that toward the end of the second century regional synods were already able from time to time to come together. Thus they may have also played a role in the formation of the New Testament.

Though these processes remain in the dark, the result is nonetheless clear, and that is the New Testament, which by all appearances took shape in Rome between 170 and 180. It took writings recognized here and there in different degrees by different churches as documents of the apostolic message and united them into one document that was binding for *all* churches. Thus in this sense the New Testament is "a codification and legalization of the traditional," in which "the already high authority of books preserved for reading aloud was transformed into the highest" (Jülicher 1906, 467), "a compromise . . . between customs and competing traditions" (Harnack 1914, 50). This compromise also led to the side-by-side placement of four different gospel writings, each of which was in use in individual churches, although there is only one gospel and the early church had difficulties explaining the *fourfold* formation of the *one* gospel according to Matthew, Mark, Luke, and John, as well as the considerable discrepancies between them.

It would seem that at one point we could shed further light on the process that led to this result. There was in the early church, namely, a group that, for reasons that need not be discussed, was not in agreement with the adoption of the Gospel of John into the New Testament. Later, with the mockery of double meaning, these Christians were given the name *Alogi* (Epiph. *Haer.* 51.3.1), because it is illogical (*a-logos*) to reject the *Logos* Gospel—the Fourth Gospel begins, "In the beginning was the Word [*Logos*]"—and to remain without its Word (*a-logos*). With their rejection of the Gospel of John, the Alogi were not able to prevail against the majority of the churches. It is noteworthy, however, that the Gospel of John, although ascribed to an *apostle* as its author, comes fourth and last in the series of Gospels, *after* the deuteroapostolic Gospels of Mark and Luke. This familiar order, which is found already in Irenaeus (*Haer.* 3.1.1), the Muratorian Canon, and all ancient manuscripts, is later occasionally corrected. When Tertullian presents the authors of the Gospels, he first names the apostles John and Matthew, then the apostolic students Mark and Luke (*Marc.* 4.2.5). When he treats the stories of Jesus' birth and baptism, Irenaeus understandably places Luke before Mark, which has no birth story. The fourth century listing of New Testament writings in the Codex Claromontanus places the Gospel of John right after the Gospel of Matthew and thus puts the apostolic Gospels together. Occasionally Luke and John also change places in order to bring the Lukan double volume together again as such.

Always underlying these sometime insightful corrections, however, is the traditional order of the Gospels, which puts the Gospel of John in last place. Does this second-class positioning of a directly apostolic scripture mean a concession to its opponents, the Alogi? Or was the Gospel of John not added to the New Testament until after it had actually already been completed with three Gospels (a holy number!)?

Supporting this idea is the fact that it also occupies an inappropriate place in the sense that it separates Luke's Gospel and his Acts of the Apostles, which form a logically connected double volume. It would also make good sense if originally only the apostolic Gospel of Matthew and the two Gospels attributed to students of apostles, Mark and Luke, belonged to the New Testament. Then, in correspondence with the *one* apostolic gospel, only *one* apostolic gospel writing would have been accepted, and placed in its shadow would be the two other gospel writings that were intentionally attributed to students of apostles. Only through the addition of the Gospel of John did this clear plan become unclear. In any case, the peculiar order of the Gospels cannot have arisen through a growing together of writings that occurred everywhere "of itself"; it attests rather to the fact that the New Testament itself owes its existence to a planned action that produced agreement, and the formation of the New Testament was probably completed when the opponents of the Gospel of John were turned away.

In Rome, presumably, a master copy of the new collection of apostolic scriptures was produced, from which copies were then made. This was necessary because as a rule the churches previously knew and used only individual writings. Also supporting this idea are the identical order in which the books of the New Testament were arranged from the beginning, the unified titles that precede them in the collection, and the astonishingly unified text, which cut off the rank growth in the earlier manuscript tradition. There are also some passages that did not originally belong to the individual scriptures (e.g., Mark 9:12b; 1 Cor. 4:6b), one or two of which were probably even inserted in the course of the formation of the New Testament (Matt. 16:18–19; Mark 1:1; Rev. 1:1–3; John 21; and others); these changes occurred in all the manuscripts of the New Testament, which points to one original manuscript of the New Testament.

The New Testament Prevails

Naturally one must not assume that the scriptural collection of the New Testament—completed and basically accepted toward the end of the second century—immediately suppressed previous customs in all locations. The New Testament still had to become the Holy Scripture. Therefore it is no wonder that brief and relatively unimportant scriptures such as 2 and 3 John, 2 Peter, and Jude—whose earlier status was low and which were perhaps admitted into the collection only in order to reach the holy number of seven "catholic" letters—were often not highly regarded at first. Yet one should not infer from this that the seven catholic letters were still not fixed as a part of the New Testament toward the end of the second century. Above all, in the West the Letter to the Hebrews was still regarded with reserve, and in the East little value was placed on the Revelation to John. Scholarly reflection also played a role here: it was noted that although Hebrews was numbered among the letters of Paul, for reasons of content and language it could hardly have come from Paul; the author of 2 and 3 John calls himself an elder, not an apostle; and the Revelation of John must have a different author from the Gospel of John. The church fathers Origen (ca. 250) and Eusebius of Caesarea (ca. 300) list the controversial and doubtful scriptures. Always in such reflections,

368 / The Theology of the First Christians

the New Testament is presupposed as the norm, and it is in no way still in the process of formation. It is only that the decisions were not above all doubt everywhere and in every respect.

At the same time, one or another of the writings held to be apostolic or inspired by the Holy Spirit, but not admitted to the New Testament, continued to be used by some churches. These include above all the *Gospel of Peter*, the *Apocalypse of Peter*, the *Acts of Peter*, the *Acts of Paul*, the *Letter of Barnabas*, the *Didascalia Apostolorum*, and the *Shepherd of Hermas*, yet with increasing reservation and in growing separation from the Holy Scriptures of the New Testament. We learn, for example, that around the year 200 Bishop Serapion of Antioch, in response to a neighboring church's inquiry as to whether one might still read the *Gospel of Peter*, which was still familiar to the church, answered that if the church had no greater concerns, then it should feel free to read it. But when he later read the book himself, he changed his mind and forbade its use. Thus for a long time after the formation of the New Testament there was still a certain freedom in one direction or another, without calling the New Testament as such into question. The metropolitan Athanasius of Alexandria brought this freedom to an end for the church in the East when in his Easter letter in the year 367 he definitively fixed the Holy Scripture of the New Testament as the generally recognized books; the West soon followed the same procedure. Athanasius was also the first to use the term *canonical* for these scriptures; it simply means "the counted" but later received the sense of "the normative," the rule and standard of faith contained in the scriptures. Since then we speak of the canon and the canonical writings of the New Testament.

Critique of the New Testament?

The intention in the formation of the New Testament was actually to collect writings that as apostolic witnesses of Jesus Christ are to be the rule and standard of faith, together with the apostolic confession of faith and the living apostolic tradition of faith. Luther no longer accepted this oral tradition or the "apostolic succession" based on it, since it was misused and claimed exclusively by the pope in person or the papal teaching office. Luther basically depended on the scriptural sources of the New Testament, and his principle was *sola scriptura*, scripture alone. In this, however, he by no means understood the scripture of the New Testament as a "paper pope," an accusation made later. He knew that the holiness of the scripture did not lie in the letter but in the matter to which it attested. At the same time he was aware that the New Testament is not a book that fell from heaven but a collection of apostolic scripture that was made in the consensus of the general church toward the end of the second century. He also knew that this consensus did not immediately find unrestricted agreement everywhere, and therefore he himself felt called to practice a certain amount of canon criticism.

Yet Luther was moved less by historical considerations regarding the apostolic view of one or another writing than by considerations of content, for in some books of the New Testament he missed the message of the justification of sinners by grace alone and thus the "proper apostolic spirit." Therefore he writes: "What

Christ does not teach is not apostolic, even if Peter or Paul teaches it; again, what Christ preaches is apostolic, even if Judas, Annas, Pilate, and Herod preach it" (preface to the letters of James and Jude). In his preface to the New Testament he calls the Letter of James "an epistle of straw," which in his Bible he does not want included "in the number of correct main books." The Letter to the Hebrews, says Luther, is composed of wood, straw, and hay mixed with gold, silver, and precious stones, and for this reason it should not be equated with the apostolic letters. He cannot reconcile himself with the Revelation to John, which he later judged more positively. In his opinion the Letter of Jude is a superfluous writing in the New Testament. Therefore in his translation of the New Testament that appeared in 1522, he attributes to these four books an "apocryphal" status and places them at the end of the New Testament and not in the series of numbered books, which breaks off with number 23.

The German Evangelical Church did not retain this freedom of Luther's vis-à-vis the canon of the New Testament. The books criticized by Luther remained at the end of the New Testament, but they soon received their numbers, 24–27; and later Luther's critical prefaces were no longer reprinted. Not until the end of the eighteenth century did critical consciousness reawaken. In many cases historical criticism doubted the information of the early church on the apostolic composition of the writings admitted into the New Testament, and the judgment on content was now no longer based on Luther's criteria; rather, depending on theological standpoint, sometimes this, sometimes that New Testament book underwent a critical evaluation.

Serious attempts to revise the early church's decision and establish a modified collection of normative documents of the apostolic faith have, however, not been made — either through renouncing individual scriptures canonized at that time or through the addition of books not accepted into the New Testament or through a combination of the two possibilities. Nor would such attempts have any prospect of achieving their aim; because the New Testament represents the document of all Christian communions and confessions, it is unimaginable that there could be agreement on a new version of the canon of New Testament scriptures.

In spite of understandable criticism of the canon of the New Testament, however, there is no reason for such attempts. In the second half of the second century the early church assembled and brought to general recognition the documents of the New Testament with great wisdom. This is explained not last of all by the fact that they did not act arbitrarily or according to one-sided principles but sanctioned in common the scriptures that were already highly regarded in the churches and whose acceptance found general agreement. The formation of the New Testament did not bring about a new truth; rather, the churches joined together in a common defense against untruth by bringing together the various individually familiar documents of truth and making them a common possession.

We should also regard the New Testament in the same way today. For whatever distinguishes or even separates Christians from each other in the various confessions, the New Testament joins them, and when they are joined by the New Testament, they are joined in the truth.

ABBREVIATIONS

ANRW	*Aufstieg und Niedergang der römischen Welt*
BZ	*Biblische Zeitschrift*
Ep.	Epistle(s)
ET	English translation
EvT	*Evangelische Theologie*
FS	Festschrift
HTR	*Harvard Theological Review*
JBL	*Journal of Biblical Literature*
JETS	*Journal of the Evangelical Theological Society*
JTS	*Journal of Theological Studies*
KD	*Kerygma und Dogma*
KJV	King James Version
LXX	Septuagint
NovT	*Novum Testamentum*
NTS	*New Testament Studies*
RAC	*Reallexikon für Antike und Christentum*
RGG	*Die Religion in Geschichte und Gegenwart*
RHPR	*Revue d'histoire et de philosophie religieuses*
SE	*Studia Evangelica I, II, III* (=TU 73 [1959], 87 [1964], 88 [1964], etc.)
SPAW	Sitzungsberichte der preussischen Akademie der Wissenschaften
Str-B	H. Strack and P. Billerbeck, *Kommentar zum Neuen Testament*
TBl	*Theologische Blätter*
TLZ	*Theologische Literaturzeitung*
TQ	*Theologische Quartalschrift*
TRE	*Theologische Realenzyklopädie*
TRu	*Theologische Rundschau*
TU	Texte und Untersuchungen
TWNT	*Theologisches Wörterbuch zum Neuen Testament*
TZ	*Theologische Zeitschrift*
VC	*Vigiliae christianae*
VF	*Verkündigung und Forschung*
ZNW	*Zeitschrift für die neutestamentliche Wissenschaft*
ZTK	*Zeitschrift für Theologie und Kirche*

REFERENCES

Aland, K. 1961. *Die Säuglingstaufe im Neuen Testament und in der alten Kirche.*

———. 1979. "Zur Vorgeschichte der christlichen Taufe." In *Neutestamentliche Entwürfe,* 183ff.

Allison, D. C. 1987. *The End of the Ages Has Come.*

Althaus, H., ed. 1987. *Apokalyptik und Eschatologie: Sinn und Ziel der Geschichte.*

Aono, T. 1979. *Die Entwicklung des paulinischen Gerichtsgedankens bei den apostolischen Vätern.*

Baird, W. 1979. "The Problem of the Gnostic Redeemer and Bultmann's Program of Demythologizing." In *Theologia crucis—Signum Crucis,* ed. C. Andresen and G. Klein (FS E. Dinkler), 39ff.

Barnikol, E. 1956/57. *Das Fehlen der Taufe in den Quellenschriften der Apostelgeschichte und in den Urgemeinden der Hebräer und Hellenisten.* Wissenschaftliche Zeitschrift der Martin-Luther Universität Halle-Wittenberg, Gesellschafts- und sprachwissenschaftliche Reihe 6:593ff.

Barrett, C. K. 1968. *The First Epistle to the Corinthians.*

———. 1978. *The Gospel according to St John.*

Barth, G. 1970. "Erwägungen zu 1. Korinther 15,20–28." *EvT* 30:515ff.

———. 1992. *Der Tod Jesu Christi im Verständnis des Neuen Testaments.*

Bauer, W. 1930. *Der Wortgottesdienst der ältesten Christen.*

———. 1933. *Das Johannesevangelium.* 3rd ed.

———. 1934. *Rechtgläubigkeit und Ketzerei im ältesten Christentum.*

Baumgarten, J. 1975. *Paulus und die Apokalyptik.*

Baur, F. C. 1864. *Vorlesungen über die neutestamentliche Theologie.*

Becker, J. 1972. *Johannes der Täufer und Jesus von Nazareth.*

———. 1975. "Das Gottesbild Jesu und die älteste Auslegung von Ostern." In *Jesus Christus in Historie und Theologie,* ed. G. Strecker (FS H. Conzelmann), 105ff.

———. 1976. *Auferstehung der Toten im Urchristentum.*

———. 1993a. "Paul and His Churches." In idem, ed., *Christian Beginnings,* 132–210.

———. 1993b. *Paul: Apostle to the Gentiles.*

Berger, K. 1972. *Die Gesetzesauslegung Jesu.*

Betz, H. D. 1974. "Geist, Freiheit und Gesetz." *ZTK* 71:78ff.

———. 1988. *Der Galaterbrief* (ET: *Galatians* [Philadelphia: Fortress, 1979]).

Billerbeck, P. 1926. *Kommentar zum Neuen Testament aus Talmud und Midrasch 1–4.*

Blau, L. 1898. *Das altjüdische Zauberwesen.*

Bonhoeffer, A. 1911. *Epiktet und das Neue Testament.*

Bieringer, R. 1992. "Traditionsgeschichtlicher Ursprung und theologische Bedeutung der *hyper*-Aussagen im Neuen Testament." In *The Four Gospels* (FS F. Neirynck), 219ff.

Boobyer, G. H. 1954. "Mark 2:10a and the Interpretation of the Healing of the Paralytic." *HTR* 47:115ff.

Bornkamm, G. 1956. *Jesus von Nazareth* (ET: *Jesus of Nazareth* [New York: Harper, 1960]).

———. 1958. *RGG,* 3rd ed., s.v. "Evangelien, synoptische."

Bousset, W. 1891. *Die Evangelienzitate Justins des Märtyrers.*

———. 1903. *Die jüdische Apokalyptik.*

———. 1906. *Die Offenbarung Johannis,* 6th ed.

———. 1907. Preface to W. Wrede, *Paulus,* 2nd ed., 3*f.

———. 1915. *Eine jüdische Gebetssammlung im siebenten Buch der apostolischen Konstitutionen.*

———. 1921. *Kyrios Christos* (1913), 2nd ed.

———. 1926. *Die Religion des Judentums im späthellenistischen Zeitalter,* 3rd ed.

Brandenburger, E. 1962. *Adam und Christus.*

———. 1893. *Die evangelische Geschichte und der Ursprung des Christentums.*

———. 1910. *Die jüdischen Baptismen.*

Brandt, W. 1893. *Die evangelische Geschichte und der Ursprung des Christentums.*

———. 1910. *Die jüdische Baptismen.*

Braumann, G. 1961. "Markus 15,2–5 und Markus 14,55–65." *ZNW* 52:273ff.

Braun, H. 1948/49. "Exegetische Randglossen zum 1. Korintherbrief." *Theologia Viatorum* 1:26ff.

Breytenbach, C. 1989. *Versöhnung: Eine Studie zur paulinischen Soteriologie.*

Brox, N. 1991. *Der Hirt des Hermas.*

Buck, C. H., and G. Taylor. 1969. *St Paul: A Study of Development of His Thought.*

Bultmann, R. 1908. "Die neutestamentliche Forschung 1905–1907." *Monatsschrift für Pastoraltheologie* 5:124ff., 154ff.

———. 1910. *Der Stil der paulinischen Predigt und die kynisch-stoische Diatribe.*

———. 1925. *Die Erforschung der synoptischen Evangelien.*

———. 1926. *Jesus* (cited according to Siebenstern-Taschenbuch 17, 1964).

———. 1931. *Die Geschichte der synoptischen Tradition,* 2nd ed.

———. 1939. "Johannes Weiss zum Gedächtnis." *TBl* 18:242ff.

———. 1952. *Das Evangelium des Johannis* (1941), 12th ed.

———. 1953. *Theologie des Neuen Testaments* (ET: *Theology of the New Testament* [New York: Scribner, 1951–55]).

———. 1958. *Geschichte und Eschatologie.*

———. 1960. *Das Verhältnis der urchristlichen Christusbotschaft zum historischen Jesus.* Sitzungsberichte der Heidelberger Akademie der Wissenschaften 3.

———. 1964. "Ist die Apokalyptik die Mutter der christlichen Theologie?" In *Apophoreta* (FS E. Haenchen), 64ff.

———. 1965. *Theologie des Neuen Testaments,* 5th ed.

————. 1967a. "Die Bedeutung der neuerschlossenen mandäischen und mani-chäischen Quellen für das Verständnis des Johannesevangeliums." In *Exegetica*, 55ff.

————. 1967b. "Bekenntnis- und Liedfragmente im ersten Petrusbrief." In *Exegetica*, 285ff.

————. 1967c. "Die Frage nach dem messianischen Selbstbewusstsein Jesu und das Petrusbekenntnis." In *Exegetica*, 1ff.

————. 1967d. "Die Frage nach der Echtheit von Mt 16,17–19." In *Exegetica*, 255ff.

————. 1967e. "Johanneische Schriften und Gnosis." In *Exegetica*, 230ff.

Campenhausen, H. von. 1968. *Die Entstehung der christlichen Bibel.*

Clemen, C. 1914. "Der Isiskult und das Neue Testament." In FS G. Heinrici, 28ff.

————. 1924. *Religionsgeschichtliche Erklärung des Neuen Testaments* (1909), 2nd ed.

Clerici, L. 1966. *Einsammlung der Zerstreuten.*

Colpe, C. 1961. *Die religionsgeschichtliche Schule: Darstellung und Kritik ihres Bildes vom gnostischen Erlösermythos.*

Conzelmann, H. 1959. *RGG*, 3rd ed., s.v. "Heidenchristentum."

————. 1964. *Die Mitte der Zeit*, 5th ed.

————. 1969. *Der Brief an die Korinther*, 11th ed.

————. 1974a. "Gegenwart und Zukunft in der synoptischen Tradition." In *Theologie als Schriftauslegung*, 42ff.

————. 1974b. "Das Selbstbewusstsein Jesu (1963)." In ibid., 30ff.

————. 1987. *Grundriss der Theologie des Neuen Testaments* (1967), 4th ed. (ET: *An Outline of the Theology of the New Testament* [New York: Harper, 1969]).

Cullmann, O. 1950. *Urchristentum und Gottesdienst*, 2nd ed.

————. 1960. *Petrus*, 2nd ed.

————. 1975. *Der Johanneische Kreis* (ET: *The Johannine Circle* [London: SCM, 1976]).

Cumont, F. 1930. *Die Orientalischen Religionen im römischen Reich.*

Dahl, N. A. 1957. "Formgeschichtliche Beobachtungen zur Christusverkündigung in der Gemeindepredigt." In *Neutestamentliche Studien für R. Bultmann*, 3ff.

Degenhardt, H.-J. 1965. *Lukas—Evangelist der Armen.*

Deichgräber, R. 1967. *Gotteshymnus und Christushymnus in der frühen Christenheit.*

Deissmann, A. 1895. *Bibelstudien.*

Delling, G. 1961. *Die Zueignung des Heils in der Taufe.*

Dembowski, H. 1969. *Grundfragen der Christologie.*

Dibelius, M. 1953. *An die Kolosser, Epheser, an Philemon*, 3rd ed.

————. 1956. "Die Mahl-Gebete der Didache." In *Botschaft und Geschichte* 2:117–27.

————. 1959. *Die Formgeschichte des Evangeliums*, 3rd ed.

Dieterich, A. 1891. *Abraxas.*

Dinkler, E. 1967. "Petrusbekenntnis und Satanswort." In idem, *Signum crucis*, 283ff.

Dodd, C. H. 1936. *The Apostolic Preaching and Its Developments.*

Doughty, D. J. 1975. "The Presence and the Future of Salvation in Corinth." *ZNW* 66:61ff.

Ebner, M. 1991. *Leidenslisten und Apostelbrief.*

Erlemann, K. 1992. "Der Geist als *arrabon* (2 Kor 5,5) im Kontext der paulinischen Eschatologie." *ZNW* 83:202ff.

Feine, P. 1891. *Eine vorkanonische Überlieferung des Lukas in Evangelium und Apostelgeschichte.*

Fischer, K. M. 1973. "Der johanneische Christus und der gnostische Erlöser." In *Gnosis und Neues Testament,* ed. K.-W. Tröger, 245ff.

Freeborn, J. C. K. 1964. "The Eschatology of 1 Corinthians 15." *SE* 2 (TU 87), 557ff.

Fridrichsen, A. 1927. "Accomplir toute justice." *RHPR* 7:245ff.

Friedrich, G. 1982. *Die Verkündigung des Todes Jesu im Neuen Testament.*

Fuller, R. H. 1979. "Was Paul Baptized?" In *Les Actes des Apôtres,* ed. J. Kremer, 505ff.

Gnilka, J. 1968. *Der Philipperbrief.*

———. 1971. *Der Epheserbrief.*

Goppelt, L. 1978. *Der erste Petrusbrief.*

Grässer, E. 1977. *Das Problem der Parusieverzögerung in den synoptischen Evangelien und in der Apostelgeschichte* (1956, 3rd ed.

Gronewald, M. 1987. "Unbekanntes Evangelium oder Evangelienharmonie." In *Kölner Papyri* 6:136ff.

Grundmann, W. 1961/62. "Überlieferung und Eigenaussage im eschatologischen Denken des Apostels." *NTS* 8:12ff.

Gunneweg, A. H. J. 1993. *Biblische Theologie des Alten Testaments.*

Güttgemanns, E. 1966. *Der leidende Apostel und sein Herr.*

———. 1970. *Offene Fragen zur Formgeschichte des Evangeliums.*

Haenchen, E. 1961. *Die Apostelgeschichte,* 13th ed. (ET: *The Acts of the Apostles* [Oxford: Blackwell, 1971]).

———. 1966. *Der Weg Jesu.*

Hahn, F. 1963. *Christologische Hoheitstitel.*

———. 1974. "Methodologische Überlegungen zur Rückfrage nach Jesus." In *Rückfrage nach Jesus,* ed. K. Kertelge, 11ff.

Hare, S. R. A. 1970. *The Son of Man Tradition.*

Harnack, A. von. 1892. *Brot und Wasser, die eucharistischen Elemente bei Justin.* TU 7/2.

———. 1896. *Geschichte der urchristlichen Literatur bis Euseb* 2/1.

———. 1907. *Sprüche und Reden Jesu.*

———. 1910. *Entstehung und Entwicklung der Kirchenverfassung und des Kirchenrechts in den zwei ersten Jahrhunderten.*

———. 1914. *Die Entstehung des Neuen Testaments.*

———. 1924. *Die Mission und Ausbreitung des Christentums in den ersten drei Jahrhunderten,* 4th ed.

———. 1928. *Das Alte Testament in den Paulinischen Briefen und in den Paulinischen Gemeinden.* SPAW 1928, 124–41.

Haufe, G. 1966. "Das Menschensohnproblem in der gegenwärtigen wissenschaftlichen Diskussion." *EvT* 26:130ff.

Haupt, E. 1895. *Die eschatologischen Aussagen Jesu in den synoptischen Evangelien.*

Hay, L. S. 1970. "The Son of Man in Mark 2:10 and 2:28." *JBL* 89:69ff.

Heil, U. 1993. "Theologische Interpretation von 1 Kor 15,23–28." *ZNW* 84:27ff.

Heinrici, G. 1900. *Der zweite Brief an die Korinther,* 8th ed.

Heitmüller, W. 1903. *Im Namen Jesu.*

———. 1908. *RGG,* s.v. "Abendmahl im Neuen Testament."

———. 1912. "Zum Problem Paulus und Jesus." *ZNW* 13:320ff.

Hengel, M. 1969. *Judentum und Hellenismus.*

———. 1971. "Proseuche und Synagoge." In *Tradition und Glaube* (FS K. G. Kuhn), 157–84.

———. 1972. "Christologie und neutestamentliche Chronologie." In *Neues Testament und Geschichte* (FS O. Cullmann), 43ff.

———. 1975. *Der Sohn Gottes.*

———. 1984. *Die Evangelienüberschriften.*

Higgins, A. J. B. 1980. *The Son of Man in the Teaching of Jesus.*

Hilgenfeld, A. 1857. *Die jüdische Apokalyptik in ihrer geschichtlichen Entwicklung.*

———. 1884. *Die Ketzergeschichte des Urchristentums.*

Hill, C. E. 1988. "Paul's Understanding of Christ's Kingdom in 1 Corinthians 15,20–28." *NovT* 30:297ff.

Hoffmann, P. 1966. *Die Toten in Christus.*

———. 1972. *Studien zur Theologie der Logienquelle.*

———. 1973. "Mk 8,31: Zur Herkunft und markinischen Rezeption einer alten Überlieferung." In *Orientierung an Jesus* (FS Josef Schmid), 170ff.

Hofius, O. 1976. *Der Christushymnus Philliper 2,6–11.*

———. 1989. *Paulusstudien.*

Holtz, G. 1965. *Die Pastoralbriefe.*

Holtz, T. 1971. "Die Bedeutung des Apostelkonzils für Paulus." *NovT* 16:133ff.

Holtzmann, H. J. 1897. *Lehrbuch der neutestamentlichen Theologie,* vols. 1 and 2.

Holtzmann, O. 1906. *Neutestamentliche Zeitgeschichte.*

Hommel, H. 1961/62. "Das 7. Kapitel des Römerbriefs im Lichte antiker Überlieferung." *Theologia Viatorum* 8:90ff.

Horn, F. W. 1983. *Glaube und Handeln in der Theologie des Lukas.*

Horstmann, M. 1969. *Studien zur markinischen Christologie.*

Hosaka, T. 1986. "Die Christenpolitik des jüngeren Plinius." Annual of the Japanese Biblical Institute 12:87–125.

Hunzinger, C. H. 1968. "Die Hoffnung angesichts des Todes im Wandel der paulinischen Aussagen." In *Leben angesichts des Todes,* ed. B. Lohse und H. P. Schmidt (FS H. Thielicke), 69ff.

Hübner, H. 1978. *Das Gesetz bei Paulus: Ein Beitrag zum Werden der Paulinischen Theologie.*

Hyldahl, N. 1986. *Die paulinische Chronologie.*

Jeremias, J. 1958. *Die Kindertaufe in den ersten vier Jahrhunderten.*

———. 1960. *Die Abendmahlsworte Jesu,* 3rd ed.

———. 1962a. *Nochmals: Die Anfänge der Kindertaufe.*

———. 1962b. *Das Vater-Unser.*

———. 1966. "Artikelloses 'Christos': Zur Ursprache von 1 Kor 15,3b-5." *ZNW* 57:211ff.

————. 1967. *Die Abendmahlsworte Jesu,* 4th ed.

————. 1971. *Neutestamentliche Theologie* 1.

Jülicher, A. 1906. *Einleitung in das Neue Testament.*

———— and E. Fascher. 1931. *Einleitung in das Neue Testament,* 7th ed.

Jonas, H. 1954. *Gnosis und spätantiker Geist,* vol. 1: *Die mythologische Gnosis,* 2nd ed.

————. 1964. "Philosophische Meditation über Paulus Römerbrief Kapitel 7." in *Zeit und Geschichte,* ed. E. Dinkler (FS R. Bultmann), 557ff.

Jüngel, E. 1962. *Paulus und Jesus.*

Käsemann, E. 1957. *Das wandernde Gottesvolk,* 2nd ed.

————. 1960a. "Anliegen und Eigenart der paulinischen Abendmahlslehre." In *Exegetische Versuche und Besinnungen* 1:1ff.

————. 1960b. "Das Problem des historischen Jesus." In ibid., 1:187ff.

————. 1964a. "Die Anfänge christlicher Theologie." In ibid., 2:82ff.

————. 1964b. "Sackgassen im Streit um den historischen Jesus." In ibid., 2:31ff.

————. 1964c. "Zum Thema der urchristlichen Apokalyptik." In ibid., 2:105ff.

————. 1973. *An die Römer* (ET: *Commentary on Romans* [Grand Rapids: Eerdmans, 1980]).

Karris, R. J. 1978. "Poor and Rich: The Lukan Sitz im Leben." In *Perspectives on Luke-Acts,* ed. C. H. Talbert, 112ff.

Kee, H. C. 1995. "Defining the First-Century CE Synagogue: Problems and Progress." *NTS* 41:481–500.

Kertelge, K. 1973. "Die Vollmacht des Menschensohnes zur Sündenvergebung (Mk 2,10)." In *Orientierung an Jesus* (FS Josef Schmid), 205ff.

————. 1975. "Der dienende Menschensohn (Mk 10,45)." In *Jesus und der Menschensohn* (FS A. Vögtle), 225ff.

Klauck, H.-J. 1982. *Herrenmahl und hellenistischer Kult.*

Klein, G. 1961. *Die Zwölf Apostel: Ursprung und Gehalt einer Idee.*

————. 1969. "Die Verleugnung des Petrus." In idem, *Rekonstruktion und Interpretation,* 49ff.

————. 1982. *TRE* 10, s.v. "Eschatologie IV. Neues Testament."

————. 1984. *TRE* 13, s.v. "Gesetz III. Neues Testament."

————. 1986. "Werkruhm und Christusruhm im Galaterbrief und die Frage nach der Entwicklung des Paulus." In *Studien zum Text und zur Ethik des Neuen Testaments,* ed. W. Schrage (FS H. Greeven), 196ff.

Klijn, A. F., and G. J. Reinink. 1973. *Patristic Evidence for Jewish-Christian Sects.*

Klumbies, P.-G. 1992. "'Ostern' als Gottesbekenntnis und der Wandel der Christusverkündigung." *ZNW* 83:157ff.

Koch, D.-A. 1986. *Die Schrift als Zeuge des Evangeliums.*

Köster, H. 1990. *Ancient Christian Gospels: Their History and Development.*

———— and J. M. Robinson. 1971. *Entwicklungslinien durch die Welt des frühen Christentums.*

Kramer, W. 1963. *Christos Kyrios Gottessohn.*

Kreitzer, L. J. 1987. *Jesus and God in Paul's Eschatology.*

Kümmel, W. G. 1956. *Verheissung und Erfüllung,* 3rd ed.

————. 1971/72. "Das Problem der Entwicklung in der Theologie des Paulus." *NTS* 18:457f.

————. 1975a. "Ein Jahrzehnt Jesusforschung (1965–75)." *TRu* 40:289ff.

————. 1975b. "Das Verhalten Jesus gegenüber und das Verhalten des Menschensohns." In *Jesus und der Menschensohn* (FS A. Vögtle), 210ff.

————. 1984. *Jesus der Menschensohn?*

————. 1991. "Jesusforschung seit 1981." *TRu* 56:391ff.

Kuhn, K. G. 1952/53. "Jesus in Gethsemane." *EvT* 12:260ff.

Lambrecht, J. 1982. "Paul's Christological Use of Scripture." *NTS* 28:502ff.

————. 1990. "Structure and Line of Thought in 1 Cor. 15,23–28." *NovT* 32:143ff.

Lampe, P. 1992. "Acta 19 im Spiegel der ephesischen Inschriften." *BZ* 36:59ff.

Langbrandtner, W. 1977. *Weltferner Gott oder Gott der Liebe.*

Laufen, R. 1980. *Die Doppelüberlieferungen der Logienquelle und des Markusevangeliums.*

Lautenschläger, M. 1992. "Abschied vom Disputierer: Zur Bedeutung von *syzetetes* in 1 Kor 1,20." *ZNW* 83:276ff.

Leivestad, R. 1982. "Jesus—Messias—Menschensohn." *ANRW* 25.1:220ff.

Lessing, G. E. 1856. *Nöthige Antwort auf eine sehr unnöthige Frage des Herrn Hauptpastors Goeze* (1778), ed. Lachmann, 10:230ff.

Lietzmann, H. 1926. *Messe und Herrenmahl.*

————. 1933. *An die Römer,* 4th ed.

————. 1936. *Geschichte der Alten Kirche* 2.

————. 1949. *An die Korinther,* 4th ed.

————. 1962a. "Die Entstehung der christlichen Liturgie nach den ältesten Quellen." In *Kleine Schriften* 3:3–27.

————. 1962b. "Die liturgischen Angaben des Plinius." In ibid., 3:48–53.

Lindemann, A. 1987. Parusie Christi und Herrschaft Gottes. *KD* 19:87ff.

————. 1991. "Paulus und die korinthische Eschatologie: Zur These von einer 'Entwicklung' im paulinischen Denken." *NTS* 37:373ff.

————. 1992. "Die Funktion der Herrenworte in der ethischen Argumentation des Paulus im Ersten Korintherbrief." In *The Four Gospels* (FS F. Neirynck), 677–88.

Lienhard, J. T. 1983. "The Exegesis of 1 Cor 15,24–28 from Marcellus of Ancyra to Theodoret of Cyrus." *VC* 37:340ff.

Linnemann, E. 1970. *Studien zur Passionsgeschichte.*

————. 1975. "Zeitansage und Zeitvorstellung in der Verkündigung Jesu." In *Jesus Christus in Historie und Theologie,* ed. G. Strecker (FS H. Conzelmann), 237ff.

————. 1989. "Hat Jesus Naherwartung gehabt?" In *Jesus aux Origines de la Christologie,* ed. J. Dupont, 2nd ed., 103ff.

Lips, H. von. 1990. *Weisheitliche Traditionen im Neuen Testament.*

Loader, W.R.G. 1978. "Christ at the Right Hand—Ps CX 1 in the New Testament." *NTS* 24:199ff.

Lohfink, G. 1976. "Der Ursprung der christlichen Taufe." *TQ* 156:35ff.

————. 1980. *Der Ablauf der Osterereignisse und die Anfänge der Urgemeinde,* 162ff.

————. 1982a. "Das Zeitproblem und die Vollendung der Welt." In *Untersuchungen zur christlichen Eschatologie* (1975), 4th ed., 131ff.

———. 1982b. "Zur Möglichkeit christlicher Naherwartung." In ibid., 38ff.

Lohmeyer, E. 1953. *Das Evangelium des Markus,* 12th ed.

Lohse, E. 1964. *Die Geschichte des Leidens und Strebens Jesu Christi.*

———. 1968. *Die Briefe an die Kolosser und an Philemon,* 14th ed.

Lowe, J. 1941. "An Examination of Attempts to Detect Developments in St. Paul's Theology." *JTS* 42:129ff.

Lüdemann, G. 1980. *Paulus, der Heidenapostel 1.*

Lüdemann, H. 1872. *Die Anthropologie des Apostels Paulus und ihre Stellung innerhalb seiner Heilslehre.*

Lührmann, D. 1965. *Das Offenbarungsverständnis bei Paulus und in den paulinischen Gemeinden.*

———. 1972. *Die Redaktion der Logienquelle.*

———. 1987. *Das Markusevangelium.*

Luz, U. 1968. *Das Geschichtsverständnis des Paulus.*

———. 1983. "Einheit und Vielfalt neutestamentlicher Theologien." In *Die Mitte des Neuen Testaments* (FS E. Schweizer), 142ff.

Maier, J. 1982. *Jüdische Auseinandersetzung mit dem Christentum in der Antike.*

Marxsen, W. 1969. "Auslegung von 1 Thess 4,13–18." *ZTK* 66:22ff.

———. 1978. *Einleitung in das Neue Testament,* 4th ed.

Merkel, H. 1991. "Die Gottesherrschaft in der Verkündigung Jesu." In M. Hengel and A. M. Schwemer, *Königsherrschaft Gottes und himmlischer Kult,* 119ff.

Merklein, H. 1979. "Zur Entstehung der urchristlichen Aussage vom präexistenten Sohn Gottes." In *Zur Geschichte des Urchristentums,* ed. G. Dautzenberg et al., 33ff.

———. 1981. "Die Auferweckung Jesu und die Anfänge der Christologie." *ZNW* 72:1ff.

———. 1992. *Der erste Brief an die Korinther: Kapitel 1–4.*

Michaelis, W. 1954. *Einleitung in das Neue Testament,* 2nd ed.

Michel, O. 1954. "Spätjüdisches Prophetentum." In *Neutestamentliche Studien für Rudolf Bultmann,* 60–66.

Müller, M. 1984. *Der Ausdruck "Menschensohn" in den Evangelien.*

Müller, U. B. 1977. "Vision und Botschaft: Erwägungen zur prophetischen Struktur der Verkündigung Jesu." *ZTK* 74:416ff.

———. 1990. *Die Menschwerdung des Gottessohnes.*

Nagel, W. 1962. *Geschichte des christlichen Gottesdienst.*

———. 1979. *Geschichte des christlichen Gottesdienst,* 2nd ed.

Neuenzeit, P. 1960. *Das Herrenmahl.*

Neirynck, F. 1982. *Evangelica: Gospel Studies.*

———. 1984. "John and the Synoptics: The Empty Tomb Stories." *NTS* 30:161ff.

———. 1986. "Paul and the Sayings of Jesus." In *L'Apôtre Paul,* ed. A. Vanhoye, 265ff.

———. 1989. "The Apocryphal Gospels and the Gospel of Mark." In *The New Testament in Early Christianity,* ed. J.-M. Sevrin, 123ff.

———. 1991. *Evangelica II, 1982–1991: Collected Essays.*

Otto, R. 1940. *Reich Gottes und Menschensohn,* 2nd ed.

Patsch, H. 1972. *Abendmahl und historischer Jesus.*

Paulsen, H. 1980. "Einheit und Freiheit der Söhne Gottes—Gal 3,26–29." *ZNW* 71:74ff.

Penna, R. 1986. "L'Evolution de l'attitude de Paul envers les Juifs." In *L'Apôtre Paul,* ed. A. Vanhoye, 390ff.

Peterson, E. 1959. *Frühkirche, Judentum, Gnosis.*

Pfleiderer, O. 1873. *Der Paulinismus: Ein Beitrag zur Geschichte der urchristlichen Theologie.*

Pohlenz, M. 1949. "Paulus und die Stoa." *ZNW* 42:69ff.

Polag, A. 1977. *Die Christologie der Logienquelle.*

Quispel, G. 1980. "Ezekiel 1,26 in Jewish Mysticism and Gnosis." *VC* 34:1ff.

Räisänen, H. 1986. "Paul's Theological Difficulties with the Law." In idem, *Torah and Christ,* 3ff.

Reitzenstein, R. 1919. *Die hellenistischen Mysterienreligionen,* 2nd ed.

Richter, G. 1977. *Studien zum Johannesevangelium.*

Robinson, J. M. *See* Köster.

Rössler, D. 1960. *Gesetz und Geschichte.*

Roloff, J. 1990. "Neutestamentliche Einleitungswissenschaft: Tendenzen und Entwicklungen." *TRu* 55:385ff.

———. 1993. *Die Kirche im Neuen Testament.*

Rordorf, W. 1962. *Der Sonntag.*

Rudolph, K. 1961. *Die Mandäer 2.*

———, ed. 1975. *Gnosis und Gnostizismus.*

Sabatier, L. A. 1870. *L'Apôtre Paul: Esquisse d'une histoire de sa pensée.*

Salzmann, J. C. 1994. *Lehren und Ermahnen.*

Sanders, J. T. 1965. "Hymnic Elements in Ephesians 1–3." *ZNW* 56:214ff.

———. 1966. "Paul's 'Autobiographical' Statements in Galatians 1–2." *JBL* 85:335ff.

Schade, H.-H. 1981. *Apokalyptische Christologie bei Paulus.*

Schendel, E. 1971. *Herrschaft und Unterwerfung Christi: 1. Korinther 15,24–28 in Exegese und Theologie der Väter bis zum Ausgang des 4. Jahrhunderts.*

Schenk, W. 1969. "Der 1 Korintherbrief als Briefsammlung." *ZNW* 60:219ff.

———. 1984. *Die Philipperbriefe des Paulus: Ein Kommentar.*

Schenke, H.-M. 1973. "Die neutestamentliche Christologie und der gnostische Erlöser." In *Gnosis und Neues Testament,* ed. K.-W. Tröger, 205ff.

———and K. M. Fischer. 1979. *Einleitung in die Schriften des Neuen Testaments 2.*

Schenke, L. 1971. *Studien zur Passionsgeschichte des Markus.*

Schille, G. 1962. *Frühchristliche Hymnen.*

Schlier, H. 1949. *Der Brief an die Galater,* 10th ed.

———. 1958. *Der Brief an die Epheser,* 2nd ed.

———. 1962. *Der Brief an die Galater,* 12th ed.

———. 1977. *Der Römerbrief.*

Schmeller, Th. 1987. *Paulus und die Diatribe: Eine vergleichende Stiluntersuchung.*

Schmidt, K. L. 1919. *Der Rahmen der Geschichte Jesu.*

Schmithals, W. 1961. *Das kirchliche Apostelamt.*

———. 1969. *Die Gnosis in Korinth,* 3rd ed. (ET: *Gnosticism in Corinth: An Investi-*

gation of the Letters to the Corinthians, trans. John E. Steely [Nashville: Abingdon, 1971]).

———. 1973. *Die Apokalyptik: Einführung und Deutung* (ET: *The Apocalyptic Movement: Introduction and Interpretation* [Nashville: Abingdon, 1975]).

———. 1975. "Jesus und die Apokalyptik." In *Jesus Christus in Historie und Theologie,* ed. G. Strecker (FS H. Conzelmann), 59ff.

———. 1978. "Zur Herkunft der gnostischen Elemente in der Sprache des Paulus." In *Gnosis,* ed. B. Aland (FS H. Jonas), 385ff.

———. 1979. "Die Worte vom leidenden Menschensohn." In *Theologia crucis—Signum Crucis,* ed. C. Andresen and G. Klein (FS E. Dinkler), 417ff.

———. 1980. *Das Evangelium nach Lukas.*

———. 1982. *Die Apostelgeschichte des Lukas.*

———. 1983. "Judaisten in Galatien?" *ZNW* 74:27ff.

———. 1984. *Die Briefe des Paulus in ihrer ursprünglichen Form.*

———. 1985. *Einleitung in die drei ersten Evangelien.*

———. 1986. *Das Evangelium nach Markus* (1979), 2nd ed.

———. 1987. "Der Konflikt zwischen Kirche und Synagoge in neutestamentlicher Zeit." In *Altes Testament und christliche Verkündigung,* ed. M. Oeming (FS A. Gunneweg), 366ff. (see pp. 325ff.)

———. 1988a. "Echatologie und Apokalyptik." *VF* 33:64ff.

———. 1988b. *Der Römerbrief: Ein Kommentar.*

———. 1989a. "Paulus als Heidenmissionar und das Problem seiner theologischen Entwicklung." In *Jesu Rede von Gott und ihre Nachgeschichte im frühen Christentum,* ed. A. Koch et al. (FS W. Marxsen), 235ff. (see pp. 137ff.).

———. 1989b. "Paulus und die griechische Philosophie." In *Krisis der Metaphysik,* ed. G. Abel (FS W. Müller-Lauter), 34ff. (see pp. 216ff.).

———. 1991. "Apg 20,17–38 und das Problem einer 'Paulusquelle.'" In *Der Treue Gottes trauen,* ed. C. Bussmann and W. Radl (FS G. Schneider), 307ff.

———. 1992. *Johannesevangelium und Johannesbriefe: Forschungsgeschichte und Analyse.*

———. 1994. "Die Kollekten des Paulus für die Christen in Jerusalem." In *Belehrter Glaube* (FS J. Wisching), 231–52.

Schnackenburg, R. 1961. *Die Kirche im Neuen Testament* (ET: *The Church in the New Testament* [New York: Seabury, 1965]).

———. 1963. *Die Johannesbriefe,* 2nd ed. (ET: *The Johannine Epistles* [New York: Crossroad, 1992]).

Schnelle, U. 1983. *Gerechtigkeit und Christusgegenwart: Vorpaulinische und Paulinische Tauftheologie.*

———. 1986. "Der erste Thessalonicherbrief und die Entstehung der paulinischen Theologie." *NTS* 32:206ff.

———. 1989. *Wandlungen im paulinischen Denken.*

Schniewind, J. 1952. *Nachgelassene Reden und Aufsätze.*

Schottroff, L. 1970. *Der Glaubende und die feindliche Welt.*

Schrage, W. 1963. "'Ekklesia' und 'Synagoge': Zum Ursprung des urchristlichen Kirchenbegriffs." *ZTK* 60:178ff.

————. 1982. *Ethik des Neuen Testaments* [ET: *The Ethics of the New Testament* [Philadelphia: Fortress, 1988]).

————. 1991. *Der erste Brief an die Korinther (1 Kor 1,1–6,11).*

Schürer, E. 1909. *Geschichte des jüdischen Volkes im Zeitalter Jesu Christi* 3, 4th ed.

Schürmann, H. 1975. "Beobachtungen zum Menschensohn-Titel in der Redenquelle." In *Jesus und der Menschensohn* (FS A. Vögtle), 124ff.

Schulz, S. 1967. *Die Stunde der Botschaft.*

————. 1972. *Q: Die Spruchquelle der Evangelisten.*

————. 1983. "Die Anfänge der urchristlichen Verkündigung." In *Die Mitte des Neuen Testaments* (FS E. Schweizer), 254ff.

————. 1985. "Der frühe und der späte Paulus." *TZ* 41:228ff.

————. 1987 *Neutestamentliche Ethik.*

Schütz, F. 1969. *Der leidende Christus: Die angefochtene Gemeinde und das Christuskerygma der lukanischen Schriften.*

Schweitzer, A. 1901. *Das Messianitäts- und Leidensgeheimnis: Eine Skizze des Lebens Jesu.*

————. 1911. *Geschichte der Paulinischen Forschung.*

————. 1913. *Geschichte der Leben Jesu Forschung.*

————. 1967. *Reich Gottes und Christentum.*

Schweizer, E. 1954. "Das Herrenmahl im Neuen Testament." *TLZ* 79:577ff.

————. 1975. 1. "Korinther 15,20–28 als Zeugnis paulinischer Eschatologie." In *Jesus und Paulus,* ed. E. E. Ellis and E. Grässer (FS W. G. Kümmel), 301ff.

Sellin, G. 1986. *Der Streit um die Auferstehung der Toten.*

Senft, Chr. 1979. *La première épitre de Saint-Paul aux Corinthiens.*

Sjöberg, E. 1955. *Der verborgene Menschensohn.*

Soden, H. von. 1931. *Sakrament und Ethik bei Paulus.*

Sohm, R. 1909. "Wesen und Ursprung des Katholizismus." *Abhandlungen der Sächsischen Gesellschaft der Wissenschaften, Philologisch-historische Klasse* 27.3.

Stegemann, W. 1991. *Zwischen Synagoge und Obrigkeit: Zur historischen Situation der lukanischen Christen.*

Storck, G. 1980. "Eschatologie bei Paulus." Diss., Göttingen.

Stowers, S. K. 1981. *The Diatribe and Paul's Letter to the Romans.*

Strauss, D. F. 1835, 1836. *Das Leben Jesu* 1, 2.

Strecker, G. 1958. *Das Judenchristentum in den Pseudoklementinen.*

————. 1962. *Der Weg der Gerechtigkeit.*

————. 1967. "Die Leidens- und Auferstehungsvoraussagen im Markusevangelium." *ZTK* 64:16ff.

————. 1976. "Befreiung und Rechtfertigung: Zur Stellung der Rechtfertigungslehre in der Theologie des Paulus." In *Rechtfertigung,* ed. J. Friedrich et al. (FS E. Käsemann), 479ff.

————. 1992. "Schriftlichkeit oder Mündlichkeit der synoptischen Tradition." In *The Four Gospels* (FS F. Neirynk), 159ff.

Strobel, A. 1967. *Kerygma und Apokalyptik.*

Stuhlmacher, P. 1983. "Sühne oder Versöhnung?" In *Die Mitte des Neuen Testaments* (FS E. Schweizer), 291ff.

————. 1989. *Der Brief an die Römer* (ET: *Paul's Letter to the Romans* [Louisville, Ky.: Westminster John Knox, 1994]).

Suhl, A. 1975. *Paulus und Seine Briefe: Ein Beitrag zur paulinischen Chronologie.*

Surkau, H.-W. 1938. *Martyrien in jüdischer und frühchristlicher Sicht.*

Teeple, H. M. 1965. "The Origin of the Son of Man Christology." *JBL* 84:213ff.

Theobald, M. 1988. "Gottessohn und Menschensohn." *Studien zum Neuen Testament und seiner Umwelt* 13:37ff.

————. 1990. "Heilige Hochzeit: Motive des Mythos im Horizont von Eph 5,21–33." In *Metaphorik und Mythos im Neuen Testament*, ed. K. Kertelge, 220ff.

Thyen, H. 1955. *Der Stil der Jüdisch-Hellenistischen Homilie.*

Tödt, H. E. 1959. *Der Menschensohn in der synoptischen Überlieferung.*

Vielheuer, P. 1957. "Gottesreich und Menschensohn in der Verkündigung Jesu." In *Festschrift für Günther Dehn*, ed. W. Schneemelcher, 51ff.

————. 1965. *Aufsätze zum Neuen Testament.*

————. 1975. *Geschichte der urchristlichen Literatur.*

Volkmar, G. 1870. *Die Evangelien oder Marcus und die Synopsis.*

Vollenweider, S. 1988. "Ich sah den Satan wie einen Blitz vom Himmel Fallen (Lk 10,18)." *ZNW* 79:187ff.

Wallis, K. 1975. "The Problem of an Intermediate Kingdom in 1 Corinthians 15,20–28." *JETS* 18:229ff.

Walter, N. 1985. "Paulus und die urchristliche Jesustradition." *NTS* 31:498ff.

Wedderburn, A. J. M. 1973. *"En te sophia tou theou*—1 Kor 1,21." *ZNW* 64:132ff.

Wegenast, K. 1962. *Das Verständnis der Tradition bei Paulus und in den Deuteropaulinen.*

Weiss, H.-F. 1977. "Volk Gottes" und "Leib Christi." *ZTK* 102:411ff.

————. 1991. *Der Brief and die Hebräer.*

Weiss, J. 1892. *Die Predigt Jesu vom Reich Gottes,* repr. 1964.

————. 1907. *Die Schriften des Neuen Testaments,* 2nd ed.

————. 1910. *Der erste Korintherbrief,* 9th ed.

Wellhausen, J. 1905. *Einleitung in die drei ersten Evangelien.*

————. 1909. *Das Evangelium Marci,* 2nd ed.

Wendland, H.-D. 1970. *Ethik des Neuen Testaments.*

Wendland, P. 1907. *Die hellenistisch-römische Kultur.*

Wendling, E. 1908. *Die Entstehung des Marcus-Evangeliums.*

Wengst, K. 1972. *Christologische Formeln und Lieder des Urchristentums.*

————. 1984. *Schriften des Urchristentums 2.*

————. 1990 (3rd. ed.), 1992 (4th ed.). *Bedrängte Gemeinde und verherrlichter Christus: Ein Versuch über das Johannesevangelium.*

Werner, M. 1959. *Die Entstehung des christlichen Dogmas: Problemgeschichtlich dargestellt.*

de Wette, W. M. L. 1848. *Lehrbuch der historisch-kritischen Einleitung in die kanonischen Bücher des Neuen Testaments,* 5th ed.

Wetter, G. P. 1921. *Altchristliche Liturgien: Das christliche Mysterium.*

————. 1922. *Altchristliche Liturgien: Das christliche Opfer.*

Wiefel, H. 1974. "Die Hauptrichtung des Wandels im eschatologischen Denken des Paulus." *TZ* 30:65ff.

Wilcke, H.-A. 1967. *Das Problem eines messianischen Zwischenreiches bei Paulus.*

Wilckens, U. 1959. *Weisheit und Torheit: Eine exegetisch-religionsgeschichtliche Untersuchung zu 1. Kor. 1 und 2.*

———. 1961. *Die Missionsreden der Apostelgeschichte.*

———. 1982. "Zur Entwicklung des paulinischen Gesetzesverständnisses." *NTS* 28:154ff.

Windisch, H. 1924. *Der zweite Korintherbrief.*

———. 1926. *Johannes und die Synoptiker: Wollte der vierte Evangelist die älteren Evangelien ergänzen oder ersetzen?*

Winter, M. 1975. *Pneumatiker und Psychiker in Korinth.*

Winter, P. 1962. "Mk 14,53b.55–64: Ein Gebilde des Evangelisten." *ZNW* 53:260ff.

Wolff, Chr. 1982. *Der erste Brief des Paulus an die Korinther 2,* 2nd ed.

Wolter, M. 1987. "Verborgene Weisheit und Heil für die Heiden: Zur Traditionsgeschichte und Intention des Revelationsschemas." *ZTK* 84:297ff.

Wrede, W. 1901. *Das Messiasgeheimnis in den Evangelien.*

———. 1903. *Charakter und Tendenz des Johannesevangeliums.*

———. 1907. *Paulus* (1905), 2nd ed.

Yamauchi, E. 1973. *Pre-Christian Gnosticism.*

INDEX OF NEW TESTAMENT SCRIPTURE AND ANCIENT CHRISTIAN SOURCES

[One of the strengths of the present volume is the author's use of extensive references to the New Testament and other early Christian writings. The sheer number of these references, however, makes it almost impossible to index each one. Thus in the following index, references are generally grouped by chapter or passage. It is hoped that this will make it possible to find references to particular verses or passages without making the index entirely unwieldy. — Trans.]

NEW TESTAMENT SCRIPTURES

ANCIENT CHRISTIAN SOURCES

INDEX OF MODERN AUTHORS

INDEX OF SELECTED SUBJECTS